Dynasty and Destiny in Medici Art

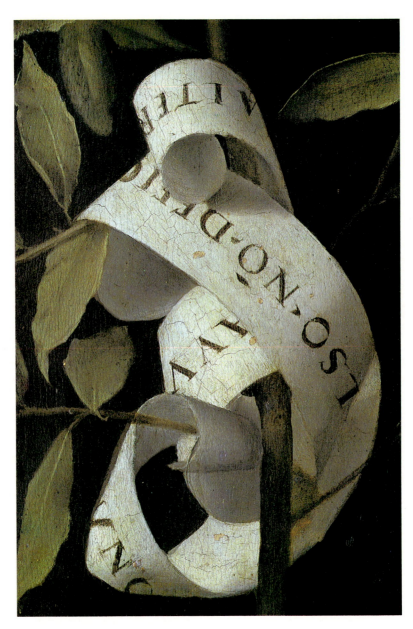

Detail from Pontormo's *Portrait of Cosimo de' Medici Pater Patriae*

DYNASTY AND DESTINY IN MEDICI ART

PONTORMO, LEO X, AND THE TWO COSIMOS

JANET COX-REARICK

PRINCETON UNIVERSITY PRESS
PRINCETON, NEW JERSEY

Copyright © 1984 by Princeton University Press
Published by Princeton University Press, 41 William Street,
Princeton, New Jersey 08540
In the United Kingdom: Princeton University Press, Guildford, Surrey

Library of Congress Cataloging in Publication Data will be
found on the last printed page of this book

ISBN 0-691-04023-0

This book has been composed in Linotron Janson

Clothbound editions of Princeton University Press books
are printed on acid-free paper, and binding materials are
chosen for strength and durability. Paperbacks, although satisfactory for
personal collections, are not usually suitable for library rebinding
Printed in the United States of America by Princeton
University Press, Princeton, New Jersey

For
H. W. H.

CONTENTS

LIST OF FIGURES

PHOTOGRAPH CREDITS

PREFACE

There is little need for an *apologia* for this study. No work known to me has dealt with Medicean imagery of dynasty and destiny as such, and the astrological theme, in particular, has not been investigated. There has been no study of cosmic imagery in Medici art at all, and indeed a prominent astrological work, the Sala dei Pontefici, has been all but ignored in the literature on the Raphael school. However, in spite of the paucity of literature bearing directly on my subject, I am nonetheless greatly indebted to the example, and in some cases the substance, of the work of others: to the pioneering studies of Saxl and Warburg on the interpretation of astrological imagery in certain Renaissance works (studies which, oddly, have had no real successors); more recently, to the fundamental interpretations of Pontormo's *Vertumnus and Pomona* by Matthias Winner and Julian Kliemann published in 1972 (Kliemann's later dissertation came to my attention only after the completion of this book; I have, however, added references to it in the notes), and to the work of other scholars who have interpreted political imagery in Medicean art, such as Candace Adelson, Eve Borsook, André Chastel, Leopold D. Ettlinger, Kurt W. Forster, Rab Hatfield, Detlef Heikamp, Paul Richelson, Nicolai Rubinstein, John Shearman, Richard C. Trexler, and Karla Langedijk (the first volume of whose monumental *Portraits of the Medici: 15th to 18th Centuries* appeared too late for citation here; I refer to the author's 1968 dissertation in Dutch on the subject). Finally, I am pleased to point out to my readers that a photographic essay with spectacular color reproductions of all the works of art in the Medici Villa at Poggio a Caiano was published shortly before the present work went to press (S. Bardazzi and E. Castellani, *La Villa Medicea di Poggio a Caiano*, Cassa di risparmi e depositi di Prato, Prato, 1982). It will be a welcome companion to this book, particularly for its wealth of illustrations of details from the portico frieze and the frescos in the Salone. The photographs in this work are by Paolo Brandinelli, who kindly provided me with the color plate of *Vertumnus and Pomona* reproduced here.

My debts in the course of the preparation of this book are great. Reversing the chronological order of events from 1976 to 1982, I should like to thank first those colleagues who took time from their own research to read the completed manuscript and who offered useful suggestions and criticism for its improvement: Kurt W. Forster, S. J. Freedberg, John Pope-Hennessy, Nicolai Rubinstein, and especially Malcolm Campbell. Additionally, John Shearman was kind enough to read Parts I and II. I have also benefited at various times from suggestions and other friendly assistance from many colleagues. Some of these are specifically indicated in the notes, but I should particularly like to single out Candace Adelson, Francis Ames-Lewis, Beverly L. Brown, Bernice F. Davidson, Charles Dempsey, Leopold D. Ettlinger, Iain Fenlon, Margaret Haines, H. W. Janson, Julian Kliemann, Susan R. McKillop, Leatrice Mendelsohn, W. R. Rearick, Thomas B. Settle, Robert B. Simon, Leo Steinberg, and Kathleen Weil-Garris. My thanks go also to students in my seminars in Medicean and Florentine art at Hunter College, C.U.N.Y., especially to several who were helpful later: Carol Burns, Anne Mezzatesta, and particularly Gabrielle Pohle.

A special kind of thanks is owed to those who assisted me in the interpretation of Renaissance astrological sources and imagery. I am indebted primarily to my former student Claudia Rousseau, who worked as a collaborator with me in 1976-1977 on an astrological reading of Pontormo's *Vertumnus and Pomona* and, although she was obliged to withdraw from the project, later contributed the material and ideas credited to her in the notes to Parts III and IV. I am also extremely grateful to Raphael Marcato, who patiently answered my questions about astrology, was kind enough to do horoscopic calculations for me, and read drafts of the relevant chapters. I am indebted as well to Michel Gauquelin, who also read those chapters, and to Neil F. Michelsen (Astro Computing Services) for the numerous computer charts which my work required.

I extend very warm thanks to Virginia Brown, who worked with me on the many Latin poems and passages from works such as astrological treatises which I quote and who generously provided all the translations not credited to others. The book quite literally could not have assumed its present form without her expert assistance. I am also grateful to Lavinia Lorch for help with the Italian translations, to be credited to her when not otherwise indicated, to Lauri Corti for assistance in typing, and to Fiorella Gioffredi-Superbi for obtaining photographs. And special thanks are due to Gino Corti, who transcribed documents in the Florentine archives and libraries for me, and to Gloria Ramakus, who typed the manuscript in exemplary fashion. Finally, I am most grateful to my former student Lynette Bosch for her dedicated research assistance since 1978.

Many libraries and institutions have provided me a friendly welcome and useful assistance, particularly the Kunsthistorisches Institut, the Biblioteca Laurenziana in Florence; the Warburg Institute, London; and especially the Harvard Center for Italian Renaissance Studies, Florence, the directors of which, Myron Gilmore and Craig Hugh Smyth, made I Tatti a congenial place of work.

Above all, I am indebted to my husband, H. W. Hitchcock, for his sharp editorial eye, helpful suggestions, and cheerful support of my work. My gratitude is expressed in the dedication to him of this book.

Florence   J. C-R.
11 June 1982

I should like to call my reader's attention to several items relating to the astrological material in this book which postdate the above preface. Patricia Fortini Brown ("*Laetentur Caeli*: The Council of Florence and the Astronomical Fresco in the Old Sacristy," *JWCI*, 44, 1981, pp. 176-80) has independently confirmed the date that I posited for the celestial cupola in San Lorenzo; the dissertation by Claudia Rousseau (cited in chap. 8, n. 37) is now completed, but not yet available; and the birthdate and time of birth of Agostino Chigi have been documented (see the forthcoming article by I. D. Rowland cited in chap. 8, n. 45). Because the latter information makes it possible to erect a horoscope for Chigi, and hence to read the Villa Farnesina ceiling more accurately, I have altered my text in chapter 8 to accord with these new data.

At this time I also express my thanks to William Hively for his editing of my manuscript, to Anna Mitchell for the diagrams in the text not credited to others, and especially to Lynette Bosch and H. W. Hitchcock for willingness to interrupt their own work to assist in reading proofs.

Florence   J.C-R.
1 August 1983

ABBREVIATIONS

Art. Bull.   *The Art Bulletin*
ASF   Archivio di Stato, Florence
ASI   *Archivio storico italiano*
BNF   Biblioteca Nazionale, Florence
Boll. d'A.   *Bollettino d'Arte*
Burl.   *The Burlington Magazine*
GBA   *Gazette des Beaux-Arts*
JWCI   *Journal of the Warburg and Courtauld Institutes*
Laur.   Biblioteca Medicea-Laurenziana, Florence
MD   *Master Drawings*
Mitt.KHIF   *Mitteilungen des Kunsthistorischen Institutes in Florenz*
Rep.KW   *Repertorium für Kunstwissenshaft*
ZK   *Zeitschrift für Kunstgeschichte*

All locations are Florence unless
otherwise indicated.

Dynasty and Destiny in Medici Art

INTRODUCTION

Quello è un corpo cosmo, che cosi è nominato dalli astrologi il mondo, che è dritto il nome del duca nostro signore . . . ; e Saturno, suo pianeta, tocca il Capricorno ascendente suo, e mediante i loro aspetti fanno luce benigna alla palla della terra, e particolarmente . . . a Firenze, oggi per Sua Eccellenza con tanta iustizia e governo retta.

That is a cosmic body, which is called the world by astrologers, and which is precisely the name of our lord, the duke; and Saturn, his planet, touches his Capricorn ascendant, and by their aspects they cast a benign light on the globe of the earth, and, in particular, Florence, which is ruled today with such justice and good government by His Excellency.

In 1577, when Giorgio Vasari wrote this exegesis of his *Saturn Castrating Heaven*, a painting in the Palazzo Vecchio in Florence, he addressed an audience which was clearly expected to understand cosmological metaphors of the rule of Grand Duke Cosimo de' Medici, who had died four years earlier. The wordplay Cosimo–Cosmos was a commonplace in the writings of ducal apologists (like Vasari himself), as was the old Medicean play on the words *palle* (the balls of their coat of arms) and the *palla* (of the earth); the comments about Saturn and Capricorn referred to salient features of Cosimo's horoscope which were ubiquitous in the art commissioned by or dedicated to him; and the notion that the *buon governo* of Florence was due to his exalted astrological destiny had been carefully fostered since his assumption of power in 1537.

In addition to cosmological symbols, from the inception of his rule Cosimo used dynastic imagery with directness and unmistakable meaning. The *apparato* for the celebration of his marriage in 1539 was devoted to dynastic propaganda—to the notion of the duke's legitimacy as ruler of Florence, his relationship to his ancestors, and his special, predestined place in Medici history (fig. 1). The decorations for the wedding banquet (according to Pierfrancesco Giambullari's description) included a pair of paintings representing "la felice tornata del Magno Cosimo [Cosimo il Vecchio] alla sua diletta patria [e] la ben fortunata natività dello Illustrissimo Duca Cosimo, come nuovo principio di più felice secolo" (the happy return of the great Cosimo [il Vecchio] to his

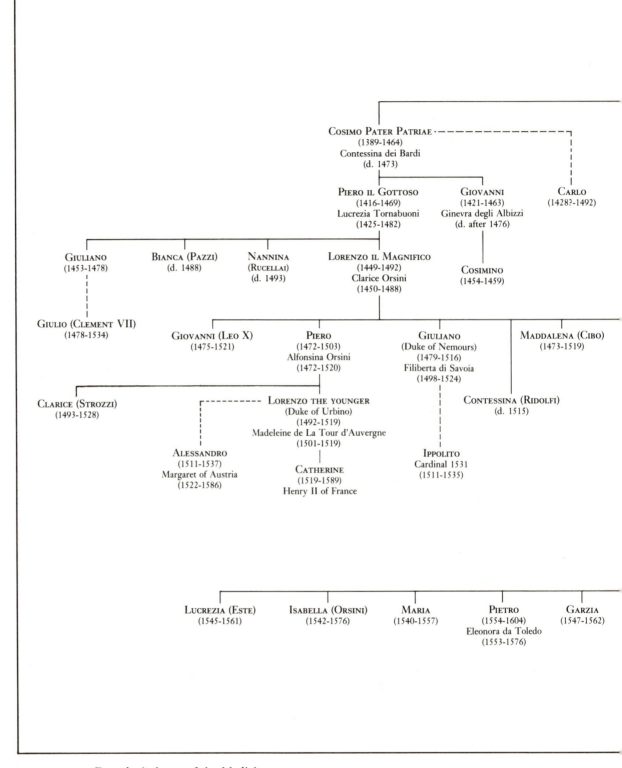

1. Genealogical tree of the Medici

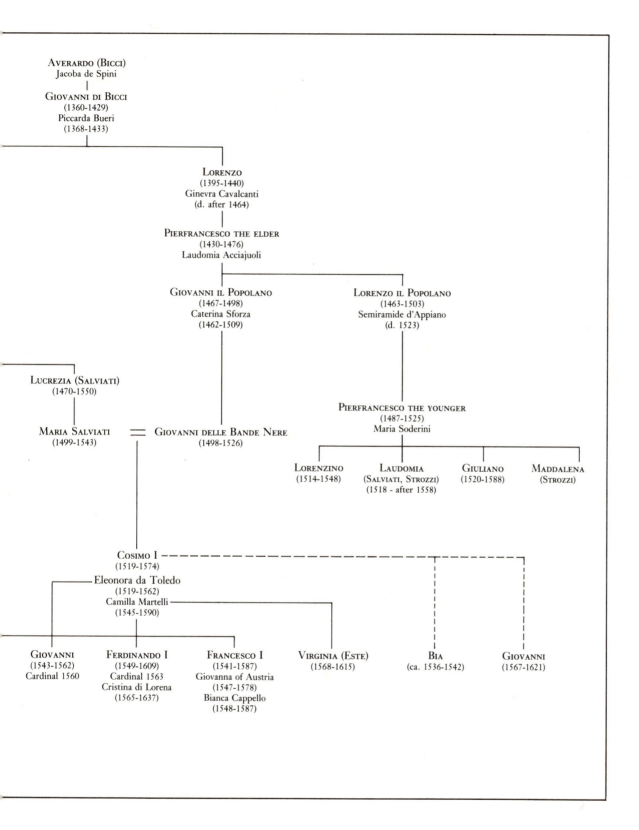

AVERARDO (BICCI)
Jacoba de Spini

GIOVANNI DI BICCI
(1360-1429)
Piccarda Bueri
(1368-1433)

LORENZO
(1395-1440)
Ginevra Cavalcanti
(d. after 1464)

PIERFRANCESCO THE ELDER
(1430-1476)
Laudomia Acciajuoli

GIOVANNI IL POPOLANO
(1467-1498)
Caterina Sforza
(1462-1509)

LORENZO IL POPOLANO
(1463-1503)
Semiramide d'Appiano
(d. 1523)

LUCREZIA (SALVIATI)
(1470-1550)

MARIA SALVIATI
(1499-1543)

GIOVANNI DELLE BANDE NERE
(1498-1526)

PIERFRANCESCO THE YOUNGER
(1487-1525)
Maria Soderini

LORENZINO
(1514-1548)

LAUDOMIA
(SALVIATI, STROZZI)
(1518 - after 1558)

GIULIANO
(1520-1588)

MADDALENA
(STROZZI)

COSIMO I
(1519-1574)
Eleonora da Toledo
(1519-1562)
Camilla Martelli
(1545-1590)

GIOVANNI
(1543-1562)
Cardinal 1560

FERDINANDO I
(1549-1609)
Cardinal 1563
Cristina di Lorena
(1565-1637)

FRANCESCO I
(1541-1587)
Giovanna of Austria
(1547-1578)
Bianca Cappello
(1548-1587)

VIRGINIA (ESTE)
(1568-1615)

BIA
(ca. 1536-1542)

GIOVANNI
(1567-1621)

beloved homeland [and] the auspicious nativity of the most Illustrious Duke Cosimo, as a new beginning of a happier century). Cosimo's birth (in 1519) was seen as fulfilling the prophecy of Cosimo il Vecchio's return from exile (in 1434), for yet another Cosimo had been sent to rule Florence; and quotations from Virgil's *Eclogue* IV under the painting of his birth further implied that Cosimo's rule marked the beginning of a new Golden Age.

The dynastic symbolism of the wedding pictures and the cosmological metaphors of Vasari's allegory are examples of the two major themes of Cosimo's art, which I shall call dynasty and destiny (and which, it seems to me, include others such as ducal *virtù*, or talent, and power). These two themes, dynasty and destiny, underlie the numerous and varied works of art produced for Cosimo over four decades by his well-schooled *équipe* of humanists and artists. In some works they manifest themselves separately (as, for example, in dynastic portraiture or astrological devices), but as often they are conflated, complementing one another in the context of the elaborate propaganda of Cosimo's *principato*.

It was not always thus in Medici Florence. The overt and personalized political imagery of Cosimo's art, which was used in support of his absolute rule, developed out of the modes of thinking and image-making of two earlier periods of Medici preeminence: first, the republican era of Cosimo il Vecchio (Pater Patriae), Piero di Cosimo (il Gottoso), and Lorenzo il Magnifico (the years between Cosimo's return from exile and the second expulsion of the Medici in 1494), and second, the decade after the Medici restoration and the expanded dominion of the family made possible by the elevation to the papacy of Giovanni, son of Lorenzo il Magnifico, as Leo X (1513-1521). During the first of these periods, imagery of Medici rule was covert, often being subsumed into the subtle conceits of Laurentian art and poetry and expressed directly only in *imprese* (devices). In the second, after the triumphal return of the Medici and their establishment of a Roman power base during Leo's papacy, cosmic and dynastic imagery began to appear in monumental art commissioned by the pope in both Rome and Florence. Medicean "metaphors of rule" (to borrow Kurt Forster's phrase) became bolder and more explicit, and the political imagery of the Medici crystallized into a well-defined repertory of symbols, devices, and *topoi*.

This book explores Medicean imagery of dynasty and destiny. It explores the images of dynastic continuity that proclaimed the family's legitimacy as rulers of Florence—although, strictly speaking, of course, one cannot refer to a Medici dynasty before the *principato* was established, with a right to male succession, by Emperor Charles V in 1532. It also explores the cosmic and astrological images that were used to demonstrate that the Medici were predestined by Divine Providence to rule. It is concerned with the origins of this imagery, but more particularly with its phases of development; for the Medicean belief in the cyclical repetition of events in their family's history, as expressed in their motto LE TEMPS REVIENT (Time Returns), their emphasis on the inevitable return of the exiled Medici to Florence, and above all their recurring dream of the recovery of the Golden Age encouraged a continual revival and reinterpretation of old imagery to suit new political needs.

But this book is not a survey, much less an attempt at a comprehensive treatment of its subject. Within the broad spectrum from Lorenzo il Magnifico to Cosimo's son Francesco, the century from about 1480 to 1580, my focus is on the central point along this chronological line—the period of Leo X. In particular, I leave to others the full exploration of Duke Cosimo's imagery of dynasty (although I have dealt at length with his lesser-known astrological imagery), for this would entail an investigation of his family portraiture as a whole (included in Karla Langedijk's major opus in progress) and of Vasari's decorative cycles in the Palazzo Vecchio, which deserve a full-scale separate treatment; also do I leave for others an in-depth investigation of the origins of Medicean imagery before Lorenzo. Concentrating on the era of Leo's patronage, then, we shall look back to the formation of Medicean imagery of dynasty and destiny in Lorenzo's time and forward to its codification under Cosimo. We shall follow Leo's revival of his father's imagery and his adaptation of it to the specific requirements of his propaganda; in turn, we shall trace the way in which Leo's imagery shaped later Medici art, as Cosimo ingeniously built on the heritage of his ancestors—as if the very act of reviving their imagery would magically restore a past idealized as a Golden Age.

Within this general theme there are yet other emphases in the present work. I have already remarked on the central figure of the Medici patron, Leo X. Another focus is the artist Jacopo da Pontormo, from whom Leo, and later Cosimo, commissioned a significant number of major works embodying the themes of dynasty and destiny. These include his contributions to festival *apparati* celebrating the Medici return of 1512, his dynastic portrait of Cosimo il Vecchio now in the Uffizi, the great fresco of *Vertumnus and Pomona* in the Medici villa at Poggio a Caiano, and (for Duke Cosimo) the lost decorations of the loggia at Villa Castello. A final emphasis is a conceit I shall call the "Two Cosimos," in which a number of the other themes of this book coalesce. It is a subtheme, moreover, that epitomizes the way in which Medici imagery constantly turned back on itself. The two Cosimos signals a cult in Medici mythology of Cosimo Pater Patriae, founder of the family's power— a cult adumbrated in Lorenzo's time, fully evident in Leo's art, and reaching its apotheosis in the art, and person, of Duke Cosimo himself.

The organization of this study reflects the three phases of Medici patronage that I have mentioned, as well as my special emphasis on the patron Leo X, the artist Pontormo, and the *topos* of the Two Cosimos. Part I deals with imagery of dynasty and rule, which was invented in the later Quattrocento and crystallized in a broad range of works, conspicuously Pontormo's *Cosimo* portrait, probably commissioned by Leo X. Part II is devoted to the dynastically oriented decoration of the villa at Poggio a Caiano. This is the only decorative complex commissioned by the Medici to span the entire period of my investigation, and it presents interesting juxtapositions of the political imagery and artistic style of three different patrons and eras— Lorenzo's building of the villa and patronage of its portico frieze in the late 1480s and early 1490s, Leo's commissioning of the frescos in the Salone (which include *Vertumnus and Pomona*) in 1520, and Grand Duke Francesco's completion of the room in the 1580s with frescos by Alessandro Allori. Parts III and IV investigate the conflation of cosmic and astrological themes with Medicean imagery of dynasty and rule, first in Leo's art (with a glance back at earlier evidence of Medici interest in such themes) and then in Cosimo's art (with an epilogue about Francesco's). A large number of individual works commissioned by the Medici that have cosmo-astrological themes (both overt and covert) are discussed in these chapters, including such major frescos as those painted for Leo in the Sala dei Pontefici by Perino del Vaga and Giovanni da Udine, Pontormo's *Vertumnus and Pomona*, and his loggia decoration for Cosimo at Villa Castello.

Each of the three periods of Medici art with which I am concerned has its own problems of documentation. As is well known, the art works of the innovative phases of Medici patronage were not directly interpreted by contemporaries, and their meanings must now be sought by indirect paths, whereas those of the period of elaboration were—as seems typical of such developments—overburdened with contemporary, or nearly contemporary, interpretation.

A vast literary apparatus exists to aid us in "reading" the imagery of dynasty and rule in the era of the *principato*: Vasari's *vite*, letters, *ricordi*, and above all the *Ragionamenti*; Vincenzo Borghini's letters and *ricordi*; Giambullari's and other accounts of festival *apparati*; and the emblem books of Paolo Giovio and his emulators. All these sources deal directly with the meanings of works such as paintings, sculptures, medals, and *imprese*, although they may fall short of telling us everything we want to know about them. For the art of Leo's time, however, there are distinctly fewer writings of this sort. The descriptions of the *apparati* of Leo's Roman festivals are of course helpful, and some of the above-cited sources also contain material on this period (and even, though to a lesser extent, on the Laurentian era), but it is unusual to find explications of specific art works. Finally, for Lorenzo's period—a time when Medici art had no avowed political function, purpose, or apologists—contemporary exegesis is practically nonexistent (I think only of the accounts of Lorenzo's *giostra*). In dealing with Leo's and even more particularly Lorenzo's art, then, I have had to depend to a great extent on comparisons from one work of art to another and on analogies with other kinds of material—for example, poetry about the Medici (which is therefore quoted liberally in the text). Some of these analogies are, perforce, speculative, and may, depending on the reader's persuasion, be taken as such. Finally, aware of the pitfalls of interpreting early Medici imagery in terms of the later, I have relied on contemporary references where possible and avoided citing later interpretation of similar images as evidence. (Indeed, there is hardly an image in Quattrocento and early Cinquecento Medici art which is not echoed later; however, except in special cases, I have not thought these references would illuminate the meaning of the imagery in the very different context of Medici art prior to the *principato*.)

There are special problems, in addition to the usual ones, in working with the interpretation (or even identification) of cosmo-astrological imagery. With some welcome exceptions, such as the Capricorn and Saturn of Duke Cosimo's horoscope or the Aries of Francesco's, few astrological images in works of Medici art are directly mentioned in contemporary sources. The reasons for this silence are paradoxical. On the one hand, such occult imagery may at times have been intended *not* to be readily accessible to any but the informed observer—especially in the Laurentian period, before astrological imagery was openly exploited for political purposes. On the other hand, allusions to celestial phenomena in the Renaissance were simply to be assumed in works of art; they were the rule rather than the remarkable exception, as is suggested by Vasari's laconic treatment of astrological imagery in works he discusses. Thus, in identifying and interpreting the astrological imagery of *imprese*, paintings, sculptures, and other works, we must resort to references to astrological matters in contemporary letters, poetry, and histories. But with rare exceptions, none of these refers to specific works of art. For example, we may learn from literary sources such as Giovanni Villani's chronicle much about the way the horoscope of the city of Florence was interpreted and how it formed an essential part of the "myth of Florence," but we ourselves must make the connections with art in which features of the horoscope are alluded to. The horoscopes themselves may also be legitimately introduced as documentation, I believe, once we have established from examples which *are* discussed in contemporary sources (such as the horoscopes of the city of Florence, Duke Cosimo, and Francesco) the way in which features of horoscopes were customarily alluded to in the art of the period. Where available, I have used charts which were published in the sixteenth century or exist in manuscript, but in the few cases where none exist I have had a chart erected by computer on the basis of a contemporary citation of the time and place of the birth or other event. I reproduce these Renaissance charts and, in all but one case, also illustrate them as recalculated by computer and diagrammed in the modern circular format. (For clarity, I have included in these diagrams only those planets known in the Renaissance.) As to the interpretation of horoscopes in the Renaissance, I have cited, sometimes in detail, the standard classical sources such as Ptolemy and Marcus Manilius, as well as manuals by sixteenth-century astrologers such as Luca Gaurico, Johannes Schöner, Giuliano Ristori, and Francesco Giuntini. However, in order to avoid overburdening the apparatus of this book, I have as often referred to "traditional astrological interpretation" or "astrological thought," a body of readily accessible lore which is, indeed, extraordinarily consistent from antiquity to the present day.

I

Imagery of Dynasty and Time in Leonine Florence (1513-1521)

The obsession with dynasty that informs the art of the Medici in the sixteenth century first became evident in works commissioned during the early years of the pontificate of the Medici pope Leo X. After an exile of eighteen years the Medici had returned to power in 1512, and the following year Cardinal Giovanni de' Medici, son of Lorenzo il Magnifico, was elevated to the papacy. In laudatory works celebrating the election of the Florentine pope, an era of renewal and a new Golden Age were declared to be at hand. Leo was styled a New Pallas, a New Jupiter, a New Hercules, and in an old wordplay on the family name the Medici pope was equated with *Christus medicus*.[1] It was confidently predicted that he would bring peace, put down dissension in the Church, and reconcile Florence and Rome. It was also believed, in a myth that was carefully fostered in Medici circles, that he would recover the glories of an era nostalgically perceived as the Golden Age of his ancestors—Lorenzo il Magnifico and Cosimo Pater Patriae, his great-grandfather.[2] Furthermore, it was fervently hoped that during Leo's papacy the future of the Medici would be secured by the birth of an heir who would ensure the power of the Medici in the new century.

The story of the gradual collapse of these hopes as Leo's papacy·neared its end belongs to a larger historical sphere. My concern here is with Pope Leo's imagery of dynasty and rule. Its initial, formative phase encompassed the six years after the Medici restoration; a second phase, significantly different in content from the first, began in 1519 and was cut short by the pope's untimely death in December 1521.

[1] Shearman, 1972, chaps. I, III.　　　　　　　[2] Chastel, 1961, pp. 11-28.

The Diamond, the Laurel, and the Yoke

TIME'S RETURN AND THE MEDICI GOLDEN AGE

The themes of dynasty and rule central to Leo's art developed out of propagandistic imagery of the first years of the Medici restoration. This imagery found visual expression primarily in festival *apparati*—ephemeral decorations proclaiming the family's return to power in Florence (and then in Rome as well, after Leo's election) to be a renewal of the Golden Age of Lorenzo il Magnifico. Two traditional Renaissance images of renewal and rebirth occur repeatedly: Time's Return and vegetative regrowth.[1] The idea of renewal was conflated with the image of the regenerating laurel—device of Lorenzo— and the basis for all such imagery was the conceit of the Return of Time in a new Medici Golden Age. In the context of a Medicean mythology that had crystallized during Lorenzo's rule late in the previous century, this imagery of Medici restoration signified a cycle of birth, life, death, and rebirth of the family. Through this imagery, then, literary and visual allusions could be made to the past, present, and future of the Medici house.

The propagandistic festivals mounted by the Medici at carnival time just preceding Leo's elevation in March 1513 didactically proclaimed the return of the Laurentian Golden Age.[2] As Jacopo Nardi was later to recall the occasion, the Medici presented "grandi e belle mascherate col trionfo del secolo d'oro, come per buono augurio della felicità de' futuri tempi" (great and beautiful masquerades with the triumph of the Golden Age, as if for good augury of the happiness of times to come).[3] The Medici sponsored two

[1] On the concept of vegetative renewal in Renaissance imagery, see Ladner, pp. 315-19.

[2] Vasari, VI, pp. 250-55. For these festivals see Shearman, 1962, pp. 478-81; F. A. Cooper, "Jacopo Pontormo and Influences from the Renaissance Theater," *Art Bull.*, 55, 1973, pp. 381-83 (who gives 6 February as the date of the *broncone*

pageant, 13 February as that of the *diamante*); and Mitchell, pp. 38-39. Their imagery is also discussed by Forster, 1966, pp. 42-44; Winner, 1972, pp. 182-83; and Kliemann, 1972, pp. 307-10.

[3] *Istoria della città di Firenze di Jacopo Nardi*, ed. L. Arbib, Florence, 1838-1841, II, p. 19.

spectacles, and the imagery of both was self-consciously retrospective. Each featured a Medici *impresa* that had been used in the previous century and was to be prominent in the art of Leo's pontificate as well. The pageant of the *diamante* (diamond ring) was presented by Giuliano, the future pope's brother and Lorenzo il Magnifico's son (later duke of Nemours), and the pageant of the *broncone* (laurel branch) was mounted by Lorenzo the younger, Pope Leo's nephew and a grandson of Il Magnifico (later duke of Urbino).

In the Renaissance, the invention of personal devices such as the *diamante* and the *broncone* had become an art governed by strict rules, such as those set forth in Paolo Giovio's *Dialogo dell'imprese*, first published in 1555.[4] An *impresa* consists of a *corpo* (image) and an *anima* (motto), which reciprocally interpret each other. Giovio's conditions for correct *imprese* require that the *anima* and *corpo* be in proper proportion to each other and that the meaning of the device be neither too obscure nor too obvious. He goes on to mention some of the attractive and desirable *corpi*: "stelle, soli, lune, fuoco, acqua, arbori verdeggianti, instrumenti meccanici, animali bizzari e uccelli fantastici" (stars, suns, moons, fire, water, verdant trees, mechanical instruments, bizarre animals, and fantastic birds). He cautions, however, that the *impresa* not represent the human form. Giovio concludes with remarks on the language of the motto, which should not be that of the owner of the device "perché il sentimento sia alquanto più coperto" (so that the feeling be somewhat more covered), and on the desirability of brevity.[5]

The Medici *impresa* of the *diamante*, with its motto SEMPER, is a simple one, but it fills Giovio's conditions perfectly: the *diamante* of the *corpo* implies hardness—Medici strength and immortality—while the Latin *anima* succinctly suggests the eternal life of the family. This *impresa* of the "diamante: SEMPER" (as I shall henceforth call it) had a number of more complex forms besides the simple ring and its motto; three (sometimes four) interlaced rings are commonly seen, and the *diamante* is often embellished with three feathers (understood to signify faith, hope, and charity), as in the illustration of the *impresa* in Giovio's work (pl. 1).[6]

The three floats of Giuliano's spectacle played on the number three—the number of the interlaced rings and of the feathers—and on themes of Time and Change reflecting

[4] Giovio, 1556, p. 6 (see also the useful annotated edition, ed. M. L. Doglio, Rome, 1978). On Renaissance *imprese* see L. Volkmann, *Bilderschriften der Renaissance*, Leipzig, 1923; M. Praz, *Studies in Seventeenth Century Imagery*, London, 1939, I, pp. 47-73; and W. S. Heckscher, "Renaissance Emblems: Observations Suggested by Some Emblem-Books in the Princeton University Library," *The Princeton University Library Chronicle*, 15, 1954, no. 2, pp. 55-68.

[5] Giovio, 1556, p. 6: "Quinta, richiede il motto che è l'anima del corpo e vuole essere communemente d'una lingua diversa dall'idioma di colui che fa l'impresa perché il sentimento sia alquanto più coperto. Vuole anco essere breve, ma non tanto

che si faccia dubbioso, di sorte che di due o tre parole quadra benissimo, eccetto se fusse in forma di verso o integro o spezzato. E per dichiarare queste condizioni diremo che la sopradetta anima e corpo s'intende per il motto e per il soggetto; e si stima che mancando o il soggetto all'anima o l'anima al soggetto, l'impresa non riesca perfetta."

[6] Giovio, 1556, pp. 26-27. The SEMPER banderole was not always present but its meaning would have been understood. For the device as interpreted in the sixteenth century, see also Vincenzo Borghini, in Bottari-Ticozzi, I, p. 226; Vasari, *Rag.*, p. 25. For the history of the device as used by Piero de' Medici from about 1450, see Ames-Lewis, pp. 126-41.

the motto SEMPER. The floats were decorated with chiaroscuri by the young Pontormo, who thus began his long career in the service of the Medici. Pontormo's paintings, now lost, portrayed the *Three Ages of Man* and the *Transformations of the Gods*.[7] Antonio Alamanni's song "Trionfo dell'Età," commenting on these paintings, uses the turn of the Wheel of Fortune as a metaphor of Medici Return:[8]

> Volan gli anni, i mesi, e l'ore;
> Questa Ruota sempre gira,
> Chi Stà lieto, e chi sospira,
> Ogni cosa al fin poi muore.
>
> Round and round go the years, the months, and the hours; this wheel turns forever; who is happy, and who sighs, everything at last then dies.

These lines echo the poetry of Lorenzo il Magnifico, especially in their preoccupation with the negative as well as the positive aspects of the theme of Time. For Lorenzo had frequently chosen images of fate, such as Fortune's Wheel, or of regeneration, such as wilting-blooming roses or dry-verdant laurel, in an awareness of the transience of each renewal.[9] Implicit in each such Laurentian conceit was its opposite—death present in life, life potential in death. In the 1513 pageant of the *diamante*, celebrating the return of the Medici after their long exile, such ambiguities were perhaps even more keenly felt than they had been in the time of Lorenzo il Magnifico.

The second Medici spectacle, that of the *broncone*, was mounted by the younger Lorenzo in a spirit of rivalry with his uncle's pageant. The history of the laurel branch as a Medici device was short compared with that of the *diamante*: it dated only from the time of Lorenzo il Magnifico. However, complex and wide-ranging associations were made with the *broncone*, and it was to become the most potent symbol of the restoration of the Medici—indeed, of the Medici dynasty itself.

The laurel was the ideal all-purpose symbol for the Medici. Its primary and most ancient association was with virtue.[10] It was also associated with the gods Jupiter and Apollo. As the attribute of the triumphant Jupiter, it was the *laurus triumphalis*;[11] as the

---

[7] Vasari, VI, pp. 251-53, where Andrea del Sarto and Andrea di Cosimo Feltrini are named as the *architetti* of the floats. Pontormo's paintings are not extant; however, Shearman, 1962, pp. 479-83, believes two chiaroscuri, *Apollo and Cupid* (Lewisburg, Pa., Bucknell University) and the *Transformation of Daphne* (Brunswick, Maine, Bowdoin Museum of Art), are fragments of the decorations (the attribution of which to Pontormo is doubted by Cox-Rearick, 1964, I, p. 100; and Forster, 1966, p. 149).

[8] Grazzini, I, p. 148.

[9] Lorenzo, *Opere*, I, p. 183:

Ogni cosa è fugace e poco dura,
tanto Fortuna al mondo è mal costante;

sola sta ferma e sempre dura Morte.

See also Lorenzo's sonnet "Amico mira ben questa figura," quoted with a device of a Wheel of Fortune in Ruscelli, p. 96.

[10] On the laurel and virtue, see H. A. Noë, "Messer Giacomo en zijn 'Laura' (een dubbelportret van Giorgione?)," *Nederlands Kunsthistorisch Jaarboek*, 11, 1960, pp. 19-29.

[11] Pliny, *Naturalis historia*, XV, XL, 133-138. This association for the laurel occurs in Renaissance *imprese* such as that of Francesco d'Avalos, which shows a laurel tree with the inscription TRIVMPHALI E STIPITE INSVRGENS ALTA PETIT (Rising from the triumphal root, it seeks the heights). See Giovio, 1556, pp. 76-77.

plant sacred to the healing god, Apollo,[12] it was given medicinal properties; thus the way was opened for puns on the name Medici (*medico* = doctor) and thereby hints of some curative powers in Medici rule. But perhaps most important for the Medici who used the device after their restoration, it symbolized continuity, return, and ultimately immortality. According to ancient tradition (as expressed, for example, by Pliny, and later reasserted by Angelo Poliziano), the laurel would never be struck by Jupiter's lightning, and thus it protected those who sought its shelter; and the evergreen tree never disintegrated but always grew with more vigor after having been cut back.[13]

Lorenzo il Magnifico had first taken the laurel as a device, for one could read in "lauro" a punning allusion to his name. Through the laurel, he could be associated with virtue, triumph, peaceful rule, and immortality—and, of course, it also made flattering allusion to his activities as a poet.

In Lorenzo's poetry and art the laurel appears as a metaphor of Medici rule in Florence and, with the addition of a motto, as a personal *impresa*. The notion of the laurel as protector of Florence was first given form by the poets of Lorenzo's circle, as, for example, by Luca Pulci in a poem written shortly after the death of Cosimo Pater Patriae in 1464:[14]

> Poi sopra al Lauro poserò il mio nido
> Mediceo, nato; impetro, o gentil prole,
> Che torni buona l'ombra ov'io mi fido,
> Diamante sempre in mezzo a Palla e 'l Sole;
> Veder l'alte eccellenze, udire il grido
> Che il Cielo e l'Universo onora e cole,
> Per la virtù di sua magnificenzia
> Florida fronda a far fiorir Fiorenzia.

Then over the laurel I will set my nest, born of the Medici. I beg, O kind-hearted children, that the shadow I trust turn fruitful—a diamond always between Pallas and the Sun: to see the high excellences, to hear the cry that the sky and universe honor and revere for the virtue of his magnificence—a florid leafage to make Florence flourish.

Later, in a sonnet "Al Oratore fiorentino," Bernardo Bellincioni describes a Fiorenza with flowers in her lap under the shade of the laurel:[15]

> Co' fiori in grembo un'altra donna bella
> Veggio, che nova Atene el mondo canta,
> Lieta posarsi e l'umbra della pianta,
> Che tanto amai in viva forma quella.

[12] Virgil, *Aeneid*, VII, 59-63; Ovid, *Metamorphoses*, 1, 452-567 (Story of Apollo and Daphne).

[13] Pliny, *Naturalis historia*, XV, xl, 134-136. For Poliziano, see chap. 2, n. 49.

[14] Luca Pulci, *Il Driadeo d'amore*, Prologue, VI, in *Poemetti Mitologici de' Secoli XIV, XV e XVI*, ed.

F. Tottaca, Livorno, 1888, p. 170. The date is based on the dedication to Lorenzo offering condolences on the death of Cosimo.

[15] Bellincioni, p. 224. See also the sonnet "Triunfo a l'ombra del mio santo alloro" (p. 35).

With flowers in her lap I see another beautiful lady, of whom the world sings as a new Athena. I see her resting happy in the shade of that plant which I so loved in its living form.

Finally, the conceit is given definitive form by Poliziano, in his *Stanze*. He addresses Lorenzo, under whose protection "Fiorenza" rests in peace:[16]

> E tu, ben nato Laur, sotto il cui velo
> Fiorenza lieta in pace si riposa,
> né teme i venti o 'l minacciar del celo
> o Giove irato in vista più crucciosa,
> accogli all'ombra del tuo santo stelo
> la voce umil, tremante e paurosa;
> o causa, o fin di tutte le mie voglie,
> che sol vivon d'odor delle tuo foglie.

> And you, well-born Laurel, under whose shelter happy Florence rests in peace, fearing neither winds nor threats of heaven, nor irate Jove in his angriest countenance: receive my humble voice, trembling and fearful, under the shade of your sacred trunk; O cause, O goal of all my desires, which draw life only from the fragrance of your leaves.

This literary conceit was translated into visual form in Niccolò Fiorentino's medal of about 1480 for Lorenzo (pl. 3).[17] A woman, with flowers in her lap and holding up the Florentine lilies, is seated under a laurel tree. She is identified as FLORENTIA, and around the medal is the inscription alluding to *lauro*-Lorenzo: TVTELA PATRIE—Protector (or Protection) of the Country.

The laurel was adopted as a personal emblem for the young Lorenzo as early as 1459: in Benozzo Gozzoli's *Procession of the Magi* in the Palazzo Medici chapel, the youthful Magus is identifiable as a Medici by the *palle* decorating the trappings of his horse, and although the image is idealized, the laurel framing his head signals that he is Lorenzo (pl. 4).[18] However, the first significant, and the most celebrated, appearance of the laurel in connection with Lorenzo was in his *giostra* of 1469, which is described in detail in a poem by Luigi Pulci and in an anonymous *ricordo*. On this festive occasion the laurel was combined with other Laurentian imagery to deliver the message that the Golden Age had returned under the Medici *lauro*. Lorenzo, his train, and their horses were dressed in his heraldic colors, violet (*pagonazzo*) and white. Dry-verdant laurel and wilt-

[16] *Le Stanze*, I, 4.

[17] Hill, no. 926. I am grateful to Nicolai Rubinstein for suggesting that this medal be associated with Bertoldo's medal commemorating the Pazzi conspiracy of 1478 and Lorenzo's triumphal return from his mission to Naples in 1480 (Hill, no. 915; Hill-Pollard, no. 252). The medal is usually dated later, as by Langedijk, p. 20 (1490).

[18] As noted by Hatfield, 1976, p. 73. (Others, such as E. H. Gombrich, "The Early Medici as Patrons of Art," in *Norm and Form*, London, 1966, p. 49; and Langedijk, p. 17, reject this identification.) There is good reason to believe that Lorenzo would have been alluded to here in the figure of Caspar, the young Magus: Lorenzo was born on Caspar's feast day (1 January) and was programmatically baptized on the feast of the Magi (6 January); see R. C. Trexler, "Lorenzo de' Medici and Savonarola, Martyrs for Florence," *Renaissance Quarterly*, 31, 1978, p. 294.

ing-blooming roses were the main devices on the banners and costumes.[19] Lorenzo's banner showed a girl making a wreath from the green leaves of a laurel tree, of which the other branches were dry. Pulci describes this image as accompanied by the French motto LE TENS [TEMPS] REVIENT:[20]

> Et nel suo vexillo si vedea
> Disopra un sole & poi l'arco baleno
> Dove a lettere d'oro si leggea
> Le tens revient: che puo interpretarsi
> Tornare il tempo e'l secol rinnuovarsi.

> And in his banner one could see a sun above, and then a rainbow where in golden letters one could read "Le tens revient": which one can understand as Time Returns and the age renews itself.

Lorenzo's laurel (the *corpo*) was thus joined by LE TEMPS REVIENT (the *anima*) and it became a proper *impresa* (as later codified by Giovio), elevated to more than a simple pun on his name. Moreover, Pulci's explanation of its meaning makes clear that the *impresa* alludes to the return of the mythical Golden Age.[21] "Il secol rinnuovarsi" is a paraphrase of Dante's famous lines in the *Purgatorio*:[22]

[19] Pulci, stanzas LXVI, LXX, mentions the wilting-blooming roses and the pages' standards "di bianco e paonazo e rose e rami." For the *ricordo* see Fanfani, pp. 535, 536, 539, which mentions "rose secche e fresche." Roses first appear as a Medici device in Fra Angelico's two altarpieces now in San Marco (pl. 39), they decorate the windows of the Palazzo Medici and the choir stalls of its chapel, and after 1469 they appear with increasing frequency because they were also a device of Lorenzo's wife, Clarice Orsini.

[20] Pulci, stanza LXIV; the description continues, LXV:

> Il campo e paonazo d'una banda
> Dall'altro e bianco e presso a uno alloro
> Colei che per exemplo il cielo ci manda
> Delle belleze dello eterno coro
> Chavea texuta meza una grillanda
> Vestita tutta a zurro ebe fior d'oro
> Et era questo alloro parte verde
> Et parte secho già suo valor perde.

Cf. also LXXI:

> Era quel verde d'alloro un broncone
> Che in tutte sue divise il dì si truova
> Et lettere di perle vi sappone
> Che dicon pure che el tempo si rinnuova.

The *ricordo* (Fanfani, pp. 535-36) describes this standard as follows: ". . . il stendardo di taffettà bianco e pagonazzo con uno sole nella sommità, e sottovi un arco baleno; e nel mezzo di detto stendardo v'era una dama ritta su un prato vestita di drappo allessandrino ricamato a fiori d'oro e d'ariento: e muovesi d'in sul campo pagonazzo uno ceppo d'alloro con più rami secchi, e nel mezzo uno ramo verde che si distendeva fino nel campo bianco; e la detta dama coglie di detto alloro e fanne una ghirlanda, seminandone tutto el campo bianco, e pel campo pagonazzo è seminato di rami d'alloro secco." There was a vogue for French mottos in the Medici jousts. The *Pallas* banner in Giuliano's *giostra* was inscribed LA SANS PAR (see G. Poggi, "La Giostra Medicea del 1475 e la 'Pallade' del Botticelli," *L'Arte*, 5, 1902, pp. 72-73). See also the *impresa* of Lorenzo's son Piero, with the motto PAR LE FUE REVERDIRA (below, n. 30); and the *impresa* of the parrot with the motto NON LE SET QUI NON L'ESSAIE (pls. 20, 27).

[21] For the background of the Golden Age myth in ancient literature, see Giamatti, pp. 11-33; H. Levin, *The Myth of the Golden Age in the Renaissance*, London, 1970, pp. 3-31; and Costa, pp. vii-xxv. On the concept in Medici Florence, see Gombrich, 1966, pp. 29-34; and Costa, pp. 39-59.

[22] *Purgatorio*, XXII, 67-72.

> . . . Secol si rinova;
> torna giustizia e primo tempo umano,
> e progenie scende da ciel nova.

> The age turns new again; justice comes back and the primal years of men, and
> a new race descends from heaven.

These lines, in turn, were based on the major poetic formulation of the cosmological
ideology of renewal in the ancient world—Virgil's prophecy in *Eclogue* IV of the return
of the Golden Age:[23]

> Ultima Cumaei venit iam carminis aetas;
> magnus ab integro saeclorum nascitur ordo.
> iam redit et Virgo, redeunt Saturnia regna;
> iam nova progenies caelo demittitur alto.
> tu modo nascenti puero, quo ferrea primum
> desinet ac toto surget gens aurea mundo,
> casta fave Lucina: tuus iam regnat Apollo.

> Now is come the last age of the song of Cumae; the great line of the centuries
> begins anew. Now the Virgin returns, the reign of Saturn returns; now a new
> generation descends from heaven on high. Only do thou, pure Lucina, smile
> on the birth of the child, under whom the iron brood shall first cease, and a
> golden race spring up throughout the world! Thine own Apollo now is king!

The importance of the conflation of Lorenzo's laurel imagery and the prophecy of the
return of the Golden Age stemming from *Eclogue* IV cannot be overstressed; it became
a Medici *topos* which was later to be the touchstone for the revival of Laurentian imagery
in the art of Leo X.

The ephemeral decorations of Lorenzo's *giostra* have not survived, but their imagery
is reflected in Florentine art of the late Quattrocento. The dry and verdant laurel tree
occurs (with a somewhat altered meaning from that of Lorenzo's banner) about 1480 in
Sperandio's medal for the poet Tito Vespasiano Strozzi, which shows him in meditation
under the tree (pl. 2).[24] The laurel and the roses with the motto LE TEMPS REVIENT occur
frequently in Laurentian manuscripts, such as on the title page of Marsilio Ficino's
translation of Plotinus (pl. 6), where the *impresa* (with a red ground, gold flowers, and
the green *broncone* with gold letters) appears twice in the vertical borders (pl. 9).[25] Laurel
was also used emblematically in Medicean paintings by Botticelli. The artist painted a
standard for the *giostra* of Giuliano de' Medici in 1475, which Vasari describes as "una
Pallade su una impresa di bronconi che buttavano fuoco" (a Pallas on a device of great

---

[23] *Eclogue* IV, 4-10. For the sources of Lorenzo's
imagery in Dante and Virgil, see Ladner, pp. 315-
17.

[24] Hill, no. 394; Chastel, 1945, p. 63. On the
motif of the dry and green tree, see Ladner, pp.

308-17.

[25] *Plotini Libri LIV, Marsilio Ficino interprete* (Laur.
MS Plut. 82, 10, f. 3r; D'Ancona, no. 1529). The
impresa also appears in other Laurentian manuscripts such as Laur. MS Plut. 35, 2 (pl. 20).

branches, which spouted forth fire).[26] And, in Botticelli's later allegory of Laurentian rule, the so-called *Pallas and the Centaur* (Uffizi), the dress of the goddess is decorated with the interlaced *diamanti* and she is crowned with the laurel symbolizing the virtue and triumph of the Medici.[27]

The most striking instance of the laurel conceit—one that anticipates how it would be used after the Medici restoration—is in Botticelli's *Adoration of the Magi*, which was probably painted for the Medici soon after the murder in 1478 of Lorenzo's brother Giuliano (pl. 5).[28] The young Lorenzo, then sole heir to the line of Cosimo Pater Patriae, stands apart from the Magi (who represent the three dead Medici—Cosimo, Piero, and Giuliano), his head surmounted by laurel which grows out of the crumbling wall of the stable. This image subtly but unmistakably asserts that the Medici *lauro*, like the tenacious laurel plant, would continue to flourish even after the recent reversal of the fortunes of the family. As in the case of Lorenzo's Fiorenza medal, this image recalls contemporary poetry. For example, in "Per la morte di Giuliano de' Medici," Bellincioni laments the dead Giuliano but then turns hopefully to Lorenzo:[29]

> Benigno popol, di te fosti pio
> Salvando al Lauro tuo fresche le foglie,
> Sotto lo qual si quieta ogni desio . . .
>   Prego el ciel che, per minor mia pena,
> Convertisca sua spoglia in verde alloro,
> E di me facci nova Filomena . . .

> O benign people, you piously looked after yourselves, keeping fresh the leaves of your Laurel under which all desire is fulfilled . . . I pray to the sky that to assuage my pain, it transforms my remains into a green laurel, and makes of me a new Philomena.

Lorenzo's laurel imagery marks the beginning of a long Medicean identification with the plant as a symbol of renewal. His son Piero used a personal *impresa* that combined symbols of his father (laurel), his uncle Giuliano (the flaming *broncone* of Botticelli's lost *Pallas*), and his mother Clarice Orsini (the Orsini roses). His *impresa* of the crossed, flaming *broncone* with roses and the motto PAR LE FUE [FEU] REVERDIRA (By fire it will flower again) thus transformed his father's *impresa* of the "broncone: LE TEMPS REVIENT" into an explicit emblem of Medicean dynastic continuity and regeneration. It appears

---

[26] Vasari III, p. 312. For this important lost work, see Lightbown, II, pp. 58-59, 165-67.

[27] For the traditional interpretation of the goddess as Pallas-Minerva, see Gombrich, 1972, "Botticelli," pp. 69-72; and R. Wittkower, "Transformations of Minerva in Renaissance Imagery," in *Allegory and the Migration of Symbols*, London, 1977, pp. 130-42. For the goddess as Camilla, see Shearman, 1975, "Collections," pp. 18-19, who reads the picture as symbolizing the Medici's "civilizing image of itself," and Camilla as an exemplar of

virtue. For a summary of opinion, see Lightbown, II, pp. 57-60.

[28] Hatfield, 1976, p. 79, identifies Lorenzo partly on the basis of the laurel but dates the work to ca. 1474. L. D. Ettlinger, "New Books on Botticelli," *Burl.*, 120, 1978, pp. 398-99, corroborates my dating and speculation as to the circumstances of the commission. For the opinion that there are no Medici portraits in the picture, see Langedijk, pp. 73-76.

[29] Bellincioni, pp. 161, 164.

in his manuscripts, such as one dated 1493, where the motto is written on a scroll wound through the branches of the flourishing laurel (pl. 7).[30] In the medallion below, Piero di Lorenzo's flaming *broncone* becomes an attribute of Fiorenza (pl. 10). Dressed in red and white, the colors of the Florentine banner of Just Government,[31] she holds up both the Medici *stemma* and Piero di Lorenzo's laurel branch. Thus, even before the exile of the Medici in 1494, their laurel had been transformed from a personal device to a symbol of Medici rule in Florence.

✻ ✻ ✻

When the Medici returned from exile in 1512, their laurel symbolism was joined with the notion of a new Golden Age in poetry lauding their return. In a poem by Giovanni Pollastrino, "Ad Jo: Card. de Medicis, de reditu Medicae Familiae in Patriam" (To Cardinal Giovanni de' Medici, on the return of the Medici family to the Fatherland), the refrain "Crescite Lauri" (O laurels grow!) is accompanied by Apollonian imagery and by a line paraphrasing *Eclogue* IV:[32]

> Iam redit Virtus: redit alma Virgo;
>
> Now Virtue returns; the kindly Virgin returns.

And, in a "Sonetto elegantissimo," one of a collection of popular verses, the imagery of the Medici restoration is set forth:[33]

> Quel glorioso excelso et verde Lauro
> sotto l'ombra del qual fiorì Fiorenza
> manchando per comun fatal sentenza,
> surgon sue piante et torna l'eta d'auro.
> Godi hor Fiorenza d'un tanto restauro:

---

[30] *Moralium Sanctissimi Gregorii Papae super Job* (Laur. MS Plut. 18, 2, f. 9r; D'Ancona, no. 1474). Other examples are Laur. MS Plut. 12, 1 (with the roses; D'Ancona, no 1392) and Laur. MS Plut. 14, 23 (with PAR LE FUE REVERDIRA; D'Ancona, no. 1460). The device was associated with Piero by Giovio, 1556, pp. 27-28. He assigned it a motto which he attributed to Poliziano, IN VIRIDI TENERAS EXVRIT FLAMMA MEDVLLAS, which suggests that the flames will burn more strongly in fresh (or young) wood; that is, the young Piero himself is identified with the *broncone*. For the sources of this condensed imagery, see Wind, p. 74, n. 74.

[31] For this device (a red cross on a white shield), see G. Dati, *Istoria di Firenze dall'anno 1380 all'anno 1405*, Florence, 1785, pp. 126-27. "Il terzo segno [della città] si è il segno del Popolo, che è una croce vermiglia nel Gonfalone bianco, e questo segno tiene in mano il Gonfaloniere della Giustizia, a signifi-

cazione, che debba mantenere giustizia a tutti, come fa Iddio."

[32] *Carmina*, VII, pp. 412-13.

[33] *Canzone*, f. 2r. Cardinal Giovanni's *stemma* illustrates f. 1r and 2v. Another, similar pamphlet also contains a poem which praises the laurel, the renewal of which will bring the return of the reign of Saturn and the Golden Age (*Sonetti*, f. 1v):

> Per la recuperta gentileza
>   Qual fiori in te quel bello e verde lauro
>   Che mitighava del mondo ogni aspreza.
> Non minor ma maggior si è il ristauro
>   Che dal tronchato laur nasce e sorge
> Vedren regnar saturno e l'età d'auro.
> El tronchon che secho era ecco hora porge
>   Allegre foglie e fiammegiante amore
>   Del qual fiorenza lieta hormai s'accorge.

For these pamphlets see Ridolfi, pp. 28-36.

per lor fortezza et lungha patienza
ritorna in te la pristina excellenza
qual sia formosa ancor dall'Indo al Mauro.
    Et che sia ver: nella fredda stagione
l'arbor tagliato ho visto in primavera
far maggior fronte et fructi el suo troncone.
Così di Allor le fronde et virtù vera
pullular veggio sceptro et tre chorone
e 'nfino al ciel salir l'ultima spera.

That glorious, sublime, and green laurel in whose shade Florence flourished; since it died because all things must die, it now puts forth its shoots and the Golden Age returns. Enjoy now, O Florence, such a great restoration, for by their courage and long patience returns to you that pristine excellence which is to remain beautiful from India to Africa. And the proof of this is that I have seen the tree cut in the cold season and in the spring putting forth more leaves and fruits. And thus I see the scepter and three crowns sprouting with the leaves of the laurel and with true virtue, reaching the last sphere of the sky.

Florence will flourish in a new Golden Age under the evergreen laurel of the Medici; winter is over and in spring the stump will sprout again; indeed, such is the laurel's *virtù* that a Medici—clearly the Cardinal Giovanni to whom the poem is dedicated—will ascend to the papacy.

The laurel is ubiquitous in Medici art of the restoration. As a *signum virtutis*, it reasserted the connection between the Medici and virtue; it suggested that the family was the protector of Florence, thus becoming a symbol of the well-being of the state itself; and it declared Medici rule in Florence to be a recovery of the Golden Age of the earlier *lauro*—Lorenzo il Magnifico.

The traditional association of the laurel with virtue was emphasized in the *impresa* of Lorenzo the younger (pl. 8). Its *corpo* is a laurel tree with two lions (symbolizing Fortezza and Clemenza);[34] its *anima*, ITA ET VIRTVS (So, too, is virtue), on a scroll around the tree, signifies that the virtue of the Medici, like the laurel, is ever green.

The Laurentian conceit of the laurel as protector, or even emblem, of the city had appeared in Il Magnifico's medal of Florentia under the laurel tree and in the miniature dedicated to Piero di Lorenzo, where Florentia holds the *broncone*. This imagery reappeared after 1512, when in poetic and visual allusions the fortune of Florence was linked to that of the Medici. In Lorenzo's *impresa* the paired lions under the laurel allude to the Marzocco, the heraldic animal of Florence, which was often depicted in pairs. Made at about the same time, a medal of Florentia struck for Giuliano on the occasion of his investiture as a Roman citizen on the Capitoline Hill in 1513 carries the message of Medici rule (pl. 11).[35] It bears the inscription RECONCILIATIS CIVIBVS MAGNIFICENTIA ET

---

[34] Giovio, 1556, p. 9.
[35] Hill, no. 881; Hill-Pollard, no. 240. The ob-

verse is inscribed IVLIANVS MEDICES L[AVRENTII] F[ILIVS] P[ATRICIVS] R[OMANVS].

PIETATE (The citizens were reconciled by splendor and piety), which alludes to the broadened base of Medici dominion after the election of Giuliano's brother as Pope Leo X earlier in the year. And its imagery forcibly restates the conceit of Lorenzo il Magnifico's medal: Florentia, who lies under the Medici laurel, also leans for support on the *palle*. A contemporary sonnet in praise of the younger Lorenzo delivers a similar message:[36]

> Sublime fronde o verdeggiante Lauro
> Sotto cui paviglione Fiorenza posa.
>
> Sublime fronds or verdant laurel,
> under whose pavilion Florence lies.

The image of the Medici laurel as protector of Florence appears in works executed not only for Medici family members but for their supporters. For example, Piero di Cosimo's *Perseus Liberating Andromeda* (pl. 12) was painted for Filippo Strozzi, a Medici partisan whose marriage to Lorenzo il Magnifico's granddaughter Clarice in 1508 had aided the Medici in their return to power.[37] In this picture allusion is made to the Medici as liberators of the city, for the chained Andromeda can be read as Florence, liberated by the Medici Perseus, who is so identified by the *broncone* placed directly below him.[38]

The laurel as symbol of the return—or, more subtly, the continuation—of the Golden Age of Lorenzo il Magnifico is a theme of Medici poetry and art of the restoration. In a poem by Medalius dedicated to the younger Lorenzo in 1516, it is declared:[39]

> Finis nulla Pilae est: Laurus et usque viret.
>
> There is no end to the *palle*: The laurel is forever verdant.

In a contemporary medal, a laurel wreath is inscribed VT LAVRVS SEMPER LAVRENTI FAMA VIREBIT (Like the laurel, Lorenzo's fame will ever be green).[40] This was the younger Lorenzo's message, for a new Laurentian age was seen to be at hand. According to Vasari, Lorenzo chose the *broncone* as his device "per mostrare che rinfrescava e risurgeva il nome dell'avolo" (to signify that he was reviving and restoring the name of his grand-

---

[36] "Scritti e canzoni in Lode di Papa Leone X°," BNF, MS Landau Finaly 183, f. 59v-60r.

[37] For the picture see S. J. Craven, "Three Dates for Piero di Cosimo," *Burl.*, 117, 1975, pp. 572-76; for the Medici and Strozzi reconciliation, see M. M. Bullard, "Marriage Politics and Family in Florence: The Strozzi-Medici Alliance of 1508," *The American Historical Review*, 84, no. 3, 1979, pp. 668-87.

[38] See Berti, 1980, pp. 27-28, and cat. 370, who identifies Perseus as a portrait of Lorenzo the younger and the youth to the far left as Giuliano. The subject of Perseus liberating Andromeda as a metaphor of Medici rule in Florence was more programmatically developed in the art of Duke

Cosimo, as in Cellini's *Liberation of Andromeda* on the base of the *Perseus* or Allori's painting in the Studiolo in the Palazzo Vecchio.

[39] "Conveniunt fateor Phoenix," in *Lauretum*, p. 19. Other poetry in this collection has similar imagery (Severus Minervius, "De titulo *Semper*," p. 14):

> Namque Deus genere e Medico tu, Laure, futurus;
> Virtutisque tuae gloria semper erit.
>
> Surely, O Lorenzo, you will be a god sprung from Medici stock; and ever shall the glory of your virtue be.

[40] Hill, no. 1109.

father); moreover, he specifies, "il broncone secco rimettente le nuove foglie" (the dry trunk putting forth new leaves) was understood to refer to both the old Lorenzo and the new.[41]

Thus, in Lorenzo's *broncone* pageant of 1513, the laurel was to be seen as the *laurus triumphalis*—symbol of a new Medici Golden Age. The floats of this pageant, which was much more elaborate than Giuliano's spectacle, were decorated by Pontormo, Baccio Bandinelli, and possibly others of their circle. Bandinelli's reliefs have not survived, but three paintings in chiaroscuro attributed to Pontormo, Andrea di Cosimo Feltrini, and Andrea del Sarto (pl. 13) contain figures with laurel branches and wreaths which suggest a connection with the pageant decorations.[42] The laurel-wreathed "statue" on the wagon pulled by *putti* (also crowned with laurel) in Pontormo's *Joseph in Egypt* of about 1518 must also reflect the mélange of art and masque that characterized these Medici spectacles to which Pontormo had earlier contributed so significantly.

The *broncone* decorations were based on a program by Nardi, the theme of which was a Cycle of Time beginning with the Golden Age of Saturn, moving through five eras of Roman history, and ending with the return of the Golden Age in Medici Florence. The first float, with paintings by Pontormo, depicted a Golden Age fantasy typical of these years. Saturn and Janus were portrayed as its rulers, the theme of Peace was paramount, and the characters were surrounded by pastoral trappings, including "staffieri in abito di pastorelli . . . , con torce fatte a guisa di bronconi secchi" (grooms in the garb of shepherd-boys . . . , with torches in the form of dry branches).[43] This last detail, of course, would have reminded the viewer of the imminent flowering of the dry branches in the new Golden Age of the younger Lorenzo. The climax of the procession showed the fulfillment of this promise. "Il carro o vero trionfo dell'età e secol d'oro" (the car, or rather, triumphal chariot, of the Age or Era of Gold) was the most elaborate of the floats, with paintings by Pontormo and reliefs by Bandinelli, including the *Cardinal Virtues* (in flattering reference to Lorenzo). But the main feature was the famous *tableau vivant* described by Vasari: a man dressed in rusty armor (identifying him with the Iron Age) lay on a great globe (*palla*) as if dead; from this recumbent figure issued "un fanciullo tutto nudo e dorato, il quale rappresentava l'Età dell'oro resurgente, e la fine di quella del ferro" (a child all naked and gilded, who represented the rebirth of the Age of Gold and the end of the Age of Iron).[44]

In this last float, then, the inception of the new Golden Age was acted out in terms of a metaphor of resurrection or rebirth, the play on the word *palla* making it clear that

[41] Vasari, VI, pp. 251, 254.

[42] On the chiaroscuri attributed to Andrea del Sarto and Feltrini (Uffizi, Gabinetto disegni e stampe 91461, 91462, 91464), see Shearman, 1962, pp. 480-81; and Freedberg, 1963, II, pp. 40-42. On those attributed to Pontormo (Rome, Montecitorio), see L. Berti, "Addenda al Pontormo del Carnevale," *Scritti di Storia dell'arte in onore di Ugo Procacci*, Milan, 1977, I, pp. 340-46.

[43] Vasari, VI, p. 252. A prototype for this use of familial vegetative insignia in *apparati* was the appearance of one hundred youths carrying staffs topped with the acorns of the Della Rovere oak in the *entrata* of Julius II into Bologna (see Paris de Grassis, *Le due spedizioni militari di Giulio II*, ed. L. Frati, Bologna, 1886, pp. 34, 89).

[44] Vasari, VI, p. 254.

Medici rule was a condition of the new Age of Gold. Time had inevitably returned. As Nardi's song accompanying the display told the audience,

> L'un Secol dopo l'altro, al Mondo viene,
> E muta il Bene in Male, e'l Male in Bene.

> One age follows the other in this world
> and changes Good to Evil and Evil to Good.

And, in the next verse, the phoenix, familiar symbol of resurrection, is introduced as the themes of Lorenzo's *trionfo* are neatly interwoven in a succinct statement of Medicean propaganda of Return:[45]

> Ed ora, essendo in fondo,
> Torna il Secol felice;
> E come la Fenice,
> Rinasce dal Broncon del vecchio Alloro,
> Così nasce dal Ferro un Secol d'Oro.

> And now, at the end, the happy Age returns and the phoenix is born from the stump of the old laurel, and thus from the Iron Age is born the Gold.

The imagery of the lost *broncone* decorations is reflected in the frontispiece to the collection of poetry honoring "il magnifico Laurentio Medici secundo," from which I have quoted (pl. 16).[46] There it is conflated with the conceit of Lorenzo as Apollo, whose reign, according to Virgilian tradition, would inaugurate the new Golden Age. Above Lorenzo-Apollo is the flourishing laurel tree sacred to the god (and the Medici); in it sits the miraculous phoenix.[47]

✳   ✳   ✳

When, not long after the Florentine celebrations of February 1513, Giovanni de' Medici was elevated to the papacy as Leo X, the traditional images of Medici renewal were reshaped to allude to Lorenzo's son, who naturally sought to enhance his own

---

[45] Grazzini, I, p. 134. A pamphlet of *canzone* of 1512 contains alternate lines about the virtues of the new Medici Golden Age (BNF, Palat. E. 6.6. 154 no. 14, f. 4): "El secol d'oro con la Pace, Iustitia e Verita e Pieta e Divinitia e Verecundia e Innocantia [*sic*]." See Ladner, pp. 318-20, on the conflation of symbolic vegetation and ornithological symbols of rebirth.

[46] N. 39, above. The frontispiece of the 1516 edition is catalogued in F. Barberi, *Il Frontispizio nel libro italiano del quattrocento e del cinquecento*, Milan, 1969, pp. 110, 125 (no. LVII). Moreni's

frontispiece, which is illustrated here, reproduces it. Its imagery illustrates the first poem in the collection (*Lauretum*, pp. 1-2; by Medalius):

> Ad citharam in medio Musarum cantat Apollo;
> Hinc Medices praestant carmine, voce, manu.

> To the music of the cithara Apollo sings in the midst of the Muses: Hence the Medici excel in song, voice, and touch.

[47] Laurel-Lorenzo-phoenix imagery occurs in several of the poems (*Lauretum*, pp. 2, 3, 9, 19), of

image through an association with Laurentian symbolism. In 1513, for example, the Roman festival of the Pasquinades was dedicated to Apollo. Its poems equated Leo with the god and, as in these lines, with *lauro*-Lorenzo and the return of the Golden Age:[48]

> Visto subito un leon virtù renascere
> et retornar de novo il secul d'auro
> de la pianta del mio amato lauro.

> A lion has seen the sudden rebirth of virtue, and once again the return of the Golden Age from the plant of my beloved laurel.

Lorenzo's dry and verdant tree was also featured in the imagery of Leo's *possesso* (the procession from St. Peter's on 11 April 1513 in which the new pope took possession of the Lateran, church of the Roman bishopric).[49] Among the paintings in the elaborate *apparato* for this splendid occasion was one showing a virtual adoration of the laurel. According to Giovanni Giacomo Penni's description,[50]

> . . . era un lauro, el quale oltra il suo piccolo seme, o frutto, producca certe palle in nelle quale in una, che nel mezo si vedea aperta, ne usciva un bambino piccolo con le mano giunte, parea che uno angelo li figurato parlassi, et a piè del verdigiante lauro si vedeva molti huomini et donne giovani et vecchi genuflexi stavano ad adorarlo.

> . . . there was a laurel, which, in addition to its little seed, or fruit, produced certain *palle*, among which in one—which one saw open in the middle—a little child came out with joined hands. It seemed that there was a painted angel speaking there and at the foot of the green laurel one saw many men and women, young and old, on their knees, adoring him.

Lorenzo's laurel, pointedly linked with Laurentian mottos of renewal and immortality, also flourished in Leo's art. In a miniature of 1515, the crossed laurel branches (conveniently forming an X which could be seen to allude to Leo X) are bound by a

---

which the following (p. 12, by Bart. Reguleus) is the most explicit:

Nascitur etruscis Lauri de funere Laurus,
   Et renovat ramos celsior ipse suos.
Hos tibi si renovat Laurus, Florentia; Laurem
   Phoenicem merito dixeris esse tuam.

From death the laurel is born for the Tuscans of Lorenzo; and loftier still it renews its own branches. If, O Florence, the laurel renews them for you, deservedly, would you say that your laurel is the phoenix.

[48] *Versi*, f. 4r. See D. Gnoli, "Storia del Pasquino," *Nuova Antologia*, 1890, ser. 3, 25, pp. 51-75.

[49] See Penni, pp. 189-231; and Sanuto, XVI, cols. 160-66, 678-690, for contemporary accounts of the decorations. See also Shearman, 1972, pp. 17-19, 48-49, 72, 85-86, 88-90 (on the connections with the imagery of Raphael's *Acts of the Apostles* tapestries); and Mitchell, pp. 117-19, for further references.

[50] Penni, p. 221. See also Sanuto, XVI, col. 686: "Et subinde una arbore cum molte pille in forma de pome, et in mezo una grande aperta per mezo in modo de la natura de una donna, et dentro un'anima, sopra il capo de la quale uno anzolo offeriva una mitra papale, e ne la fronte, a lo entrare era scripto: *Scola omnium virtutum in Ecclesia Dei rinata est.*"

scroll with the motto SEMPER (pl. 14);[51] in another manuscript by Attavante degli Atta-
vanti, both the "broncone: LE TEMPS REVIENT" of Lorenzo and the "broncone: PAR LE FUE
REVERDIRA" of Piero di Lorenzo appear in the vertical borders (pl. 15);[52] and in Monte
di Giovanni's sumptuous title page of Niccolò Valori's *Vita Laurentii Medicis*, which was
dedicated to Leo in 1518, the laurel is vividly brought to life, no longer a simple device
(pl.18).[53] Here, against a background of violet (Lorenzo's color), the *bronconi* framing the
title, the *diamante*, and the portrait medallion of Lorenzo sprout from the dead stumps,
growing to fill the entire page. Finally, Attavante's miniature of the *Monte di Scienze*
(from Tommaso Sardi's *L'Anima Pellegrina*, presented to Leo in 1513) introduces a new
variation on the laurel, suggesting its regeneration under Leo (pl. 17).[54] The borders
contain the familiar "broncone: PAR LE FUE REVERDIRA" and the *diamante*, but at the top
of the mountain is a laurel with two branches cut off (from which water flows into a
basin), and in the center is a flourishing green branch which supports a medallion of
Leo (as cardinal). The image is explicated by this verse:

> Già mai fu la dolcezza al fonte tolta
> Al tronco virdità non manca mai,
> Spogliando l'autunno salva folta.

As the spring never loses its sweetness, the trunk will never lose its green
when autumn deprives the thick forest of greenness.

Besides the regenerating laurel, another Laurentian *impresa* suggesting the idea of
Time's Return and Medici renewal was widely used by the new pope. This was a disk
with the word GLOVIS, which had appeared occasionally in Lorenzo's manuscripts, such
as one in which it is held by putti in the upper frieze (pl. 20).[55] The word GLOVIS as
such is meaningless, but, as Giovio interprets it, when read backward it delivers the
message "si volg[e]"—it turns.[56] GLOVIS can thus be understood as a cryptic version of
Lorenzo's LE TEMPS REVIENT.

GLOVIS was primarily an emblem of Time's Return and the new Medici Golden Age,

[51] *Hippocratis De morbis vulgaribus, Manente Leontio interprete* (Laur. MS Plut. 73, 12, f. 2r; D'Ancona, no. 1621).

[52] *Blondi Flavii Forliviensis Romae triumphantis libri decem* (Chantilly, Musée Condé, MS lat. 1419, f. 2r). For a companion piece to this illumination, also by Attavante, see J.J.G. Alexander and A. C. de la Mare, *The Italian Manuscripts in the Library of Major J. R. Abbey*, London, 1969, no. 59.

[53] Laur. MS Plut. 61, 3, f. 2r; D'Ancona, no. 1395.

[54] Rome, Biblioteca Corsiniana 55.K.I.; D'Ancona, no. 1572. See Langedijk, p. 28; and Kliemann, 1976, p. 52.

[55] *Lucani poetae Cordubensis Pharsaliae libri* (Laur. MS Plut. 35, 2, f. 2r; D'Ancona, no. 1615). The text is signed and dated 1485 by Antonio Sini-baldi. See also the Laurentian manuscripts *Silii Italici, Calphurnii, Hesiodi et Claudiani* (Laur. MS Plut. 37, 14; D'Ancona, no. 1616); and MS Plut. 53, 21 (n. 85, below and pl. 27). As has been noted by Kliemann, 1972, p. 321; and Winner, 1972, pp. 166-67, GLOVIS appears in Filippino Lippi's decorations of the Strozzi Chapel, S. Maria Novella (1487-1502), where it is a sign of the Strozzi partisanship of the Medici.

[56] Giovio, 1556, p. 28. Giovio associates GLOVIS with Giuliano, who also used the device—usually with the letters arranged 3-2-1 in a triangle, as in Giovio's illustration. In Leo's art, the motto is generally placed in a circle, but occasionally, as on the pavement of the Stanza della Segnatura, it is enclosed within an oblong cartouche (cf. Shearman, 1971, pl. XXXI).

but like all Medici devices it also implied their virtue. This meaning of the *impresa* is clearly spelled out in a poem of 1513 lauding the Medici return, in which G-L-O-V-I-S signifies their Glory, Fame, Honor, Victory, Justice, and Wisdom:[57]

> Contro di loro ogni forza sie strale
>   Perché virtù ogni furor raffrena
>   Et contro al cielo human poter non vale.
> Questo è quel GLOVIS che ti farà piena
>   Di gloria, laude, honore, victoria degna,
>   Iustitia e sapientia serena.

> Against them [the Medici] all strength is in vain, because their virtue restrains all furor and human will is powerless in the face of Fate. This is that GLOVIS which will fill you with Glory, Praise, Honor, worthy Victory, Justice, and serene Wisdom.

Images of time and cyclical change in Pope Leo's art complement the mottos SEMPER, LE TEMPS REVIENT, and GLOVIS. Such images appear in the borders of the *Acts of the Apostles* tapestries, designed by Raphael in 1515 for the Sistine Chapel.[58] The theme of two of the vertical borders is Time. The *Times of Day* (pl. 21) plays on the Laurentian theme of the Return of Time, with Sol-Apollo and Luna-Diana as Day and Night, surrounded by emblems of the passage of time such as the clock, the hourglass, and the Laurentian emblem of eternity—the snake biting its tail (cf. pl. 48). In the *Seasons* (pl. 22), seasonal change is a metaphor of Medici Return (as in the poem lauding the restoration which I quote above. Starting at the top of the tapestry, the seasons progress (according to the Florentine calendar with its New Year on 25 March) from spring to winter. But the sequence may also be reversed, in the same spirit as the GLOVIS-SI VOLGE motto, revealing the covert message of Medici regeneration in the ascent from the dry laurel tree of winter at the bottom of the border to the verdant laurel of spring at the top. These borders, then, establish the Laurentian theme of Time as a part of Leo's repertory of personal imagery, anticipating the monumental development of this theme in the art of the later years of his rule.

In the horizontal friezes of the tapestries, the laurel is used emblematically with other Leonine *imprese* to underscore the theme of Return. Below the *Healing of the Lame Man* (which alludes to Leo *medicus*) are the crossed branches of the medicinal laurel with the lions signifying both Leo and Florence, and to either side are scenes of Leo at Ravenna and Mantua.[59] In others of these friezes there is a heavy emphasis on the *entrata*, the public acting-out of the idea of Return; and three of the scenes depict Leo's own triumphal entries, such as one which shows him (as Cardinal Giovanni) entering Rome for the conclave of his election. All these borders, then, carry the message of the inevita-

---

[57] *Sonetti*, f. IV.
[58] White-Shearman, pp. 209-12; Langedijk, pp. 30-34; Shearman, 1972, pp. 43-44, 89.

[59] White-Shearman, pp. 199-200, 209-12; Shearman, 1972, pp. 37, 84, 89, fig. 16 (the *Healing of the Lame Man* and its border).

bility of Medici rule. Like nature's cycles of the day and the seasons, the fortunes of the Medici change and the family always returns to rule Florence.

THE CULT OF COSIMO DE' MEDICI PATER PATRIAE

In his art, Pope Leo enriched the vocabulary of Medici imagery of Return and extended its range, evoking not only the luminous era of Lorenzo il Magnifico but that of his great-grandfather Cosimo, who had consolidated Medici power after his own return from exile in 1434.

Like Lorenzo, Cosimo was the subject of laudatory works dedicated to Leo, such as Raffaello Brandolini's *De laudibus Cosmi Medices* of 1515.[60] And he was paired with Lorenzo, as in medallions on the covers of *L'Anima Pellegrina*, in which the Cosimo (pl. 19) is based on posthumous medals of the Pater Patriae (pls. 23-24).[61] The medallion of Cosimo is surrounded by the sprouting and flaming laurel and by Leo's papal emblems of the tiara, keys, and lion's head.

These images all imply that Leo will revive the Golden Age of his esteemed ancestor; unlike Lorenzo, however, Cosimo was virtually deified in Leo's art. Shortly after his elevation to the papacy, Leo staged an elaborate pageant on the Capitoline (13-14 September 1513) at which Roman citizenship was conferred on Giuliano and Lorenzo the younger. A celestial Cosimo was evoked at these festivities. According to Paolo Palliolo's description of the pageant, a personification of the Arno addressed Leo's mother Clarice about the birth of her son in Florence, "fra gli lauri di Apollo et gigli . . . onde Cosimo, patre della patria, ritornò in cielo et hora, con fervente amore et pietate di essa, incende gli suoi nepoti" (among the laurels of Apollo and the lilies, . . . whence Cosimo, father of the fatherland, returned to heaven and now, with fervent love and respect for it, inflames his own descendants).[62]

Cosimo, thus established as a deified ancestor early in Leo's rule, was introduced into his art in a politico-dynastic context. Raphael's frescos in the Stanza dell'Incendio are pairs of allegories of Leo as Leo III and Leo IV, the past popes named Leo whom the present Leo particularly revered. The *Battle of Ostia* and the *Fire in the Borgo* both contain portraits of Leo as Leo IV, and in the latter fresco Leo is alluded to a second time in the vignette of Aeneas, Anchises, and Ascanius in the left foreground (pl. 26). Referring to the flight from burning Troy in the *Aeneid* (II, 707-29), this group has rich symbolic significance. It alludes to a Leonine triumph of faith over adversity and may be seen to stand for the virtue of *pietas*, which Leo shares with Aeneas.[63] However, *pietas* refers here also to Leo's reverence toward his ancestry and to the theme of the Medici Golden

[60] Laur. MS Plut. 46, 2; D'Ancona, no. 1686.
[61] Hill, nos. 909-10; Hill-Pollard, nos. 245-46.
[62] Palliolo, p. 57.
[63] Shearman, 1971, p. 424, n. 149, points out

that Cosimo had supported the rebuilding of St. Peter's, which is depicted in the background of the fresco.

Age. For the group quotes the traditional Aeneas and Anchises from Roman coins, on which Caesar asserted his descent from Venus through her son Aeneas (pl. 25); and Augustus, in turn, used the image to make his own dynastic claims and to suggest that he, a New Aeneas, would found the Golden Age in Rome.[64]

In Raphael's group, the key to the Medicean dynastic message and the association of Aeneas with Leo is the old Anchises, who is a portrait of Cosimo Pater Patriae.[65] The association of Cosimo with Anchises draws on an established Medici conceit going back to Ugolino Verino's elegy on Cosimo's death, in which Cosimo's dying words are modeled on Anchises' prophecy of the peaceful Augustan Golden Age.[66] Against this background, then, Raphael's Leo-Aeneas not only carries the memory of his ancestor Cosimo but fulfills the prophecy of a future dominion, as he leaves the destruction of the old city to establish a new Golden Age. The child Ascanius, added by Raphael to the traditional group, must then be read as a metaphor of the future, as the Medici heir who will rule over the Golden Age established by Pope Leo. Given the fact that the fresco was painted in 1516, Ascanius can only have been intended to allude to Lorenzo the younger, the great-great-grandson of Cosimo, who had been named captain-general of the Florentine forces on 12 August 1515. This identification of Ascanius and the younger Lorenzo is also made in a contemporary poem addressed to Leo, in which the poet Reguleus asks Leo to restore the Medici and Iulus (Ascanius) to Florence:[67]

Redde, Pater, Laurum: quid gaudia nostra moraris?
Sunt mea, sunt Medica sceptra tenenda manu.
Quod tibi si Laurum, placeat concedere Iulum:
In patriam vel tu Pastor ab urbe veni.

Give back, O Father, the Laurel: why do you delay our joy? My scepter must be held by the Medici hand. But if it please you to give the Laurel, give Ascanius as well: Also you, shepherd, come from the city to your fatherland.

The Pater Patriae was also honored and the theme of Medici dynasty highlighted by Leo's programmatic revival of the feast of the Medici patron saints, the doctor-martyrs Cosmas and Damian, which had been celebrated by the family before their exile.[68] Of

[64] H. A. Grueber, *Coins of the Roman Republic in the British Museum*, London, 1910, II, p. 469. The coin is one of a series of denarii dating from 47 B.C. For the theme see Suetonius, *Divus Julius*, 6. Octavian, as *divus filius*, used this coin type from 42 B.C. (Grueber, I, p. 579).

[65] Shearman, 1971, p. 424, n. 149.

[66] "Eulogium in funere clarissimi viri Cosmi Medicis Patris Patriae a senatu populoque florentino dicti," 167-69, in U. Verini, *Flametta*, ed. L. Mencaraglia, Florence, 1940, pp. 104-10. The speech refers to *Aeneid*, VI, 756-853, from which Cosimo paraphrases Anchises' final words "parcere subiectis et debellare superbos," from lines 851-53: "remember thou, O Roman, to rule the

nations with the sway—these shall be thine arts—to crown Peace with Law, to spare the humbled, and to tame in war the proud!"

[67] "Sancte Pater, placeat patriae iam reddere Laurum," in *Lauretum*, p. 33. The scepter is the *bastone del dominio*, traditionally awarded to the captain-general. On the circumstances surrounding these events in 1515, see A. Giorgetti, "Lorenzo de' Medici capitano generale della repubblica fiorentina," *ASI*, ser. IV, 11, 1883, pp. 194-215. The plea to Leo refers to the desire of the Florentines to receive their pope, which occurred at his *entrata* on 30 November of the same year.

[68] See *Ricordanze di Bartolomeo Masi calderaio fiorentino dal 1478 al 1528*, ed. G. O. Corazzini, Flor-

the two, Saint Cosmas was of course the more important, since Cosimo, born on the saint's day, had been named after him. The celebration instituted by Leo in Rome and Florence thus came to be known as "I Cosmalia," the day as "el dì di Sº Cosimo."[69] Moreover, the conflation of Saint Cosmas and his namesake was such that the Cosmalia was understood by contemporaries as being more in honor of the Medici Cosimo than the saint. Thus, in Benedetto Lampridio's poem "In diem Cosmi Medici" celebrating the Cosmalia of 27 September 1513 in Rome, it is Cosimo de' Medici who is invoked and *his* birthday that is celebrated; and Leo, the new *pater*, is presented as the reincarnation of his ancestor:[70]

> Cosmi lux rediit sacra,
>   Quam festam populi semper habebimus;
> Haec, quando proavum Jovi
>   Nostro, & Mediceis principibus refert,
> Qui magnis Patriae Pater
>   Quaesito meritis nomine dictus est.
>   . . . magis neque
>   Dii laudant alium, nec sua patria,
> Quam Cosmum, unde suus Leo
>   Romae est, quem titulis, et nova imagine
> Testatur Capitolium
>   Patrem: . . .

The holy day of Cosimo has returned, which we shall always observe as a feast of the people, since this feast commemorates the great-grandfather of our Jupiter and the Medici princes, who was called Pater Patriae, a title sought in accordance with his great merits. . . . Neither does heaven, nor his own country, praise another more than Cosimo, whence his own Leo is at Rome, and the Capitoline proclaims him Father with honors and a new likeness.

In Florence, in the same year, there were elaborate celebrations linking Saint Cosmas, Cosimo de' Medici, and the new pope. As the chronicler Giovanni Cambi relates,[71]

   Fecie Papa Lione, che S. Choximo, et Damiano si ghuardassi, e in Firenze si

---

ence, 1906, p. 136, where it is noted that the feast of Saints Cosmas and Damian was observed in Florence (in 1513) "come se proprio fussi domenica, che pegli anni passati non s' è usato guardare." The feast of Saint Cosmas was celebrated during the lifetime of Cosimo Pater Patriae by the family (cf. the letter from Cosimo to his son Giovanni [Careggi, September, 1459] in J. Ross, *Lives of the Early Medici as Told in their Correspondence*, London, 1910, pp. 62-63). On its celebration under Lorenzo, see Chastel, 1961, pp. 227-28; and the letter from Ficino to Lorenzo, *Opera*, II, pp. 843-44 (quoted chap. 9, n. 43).

[69] Gnoli, pp. 108-24, quoting (p. 121, n. 2) a contemporary source. According to Gnoli, the saint's day was celebrated at the Vatican as a *festa di palazzo* in 1514 and 1515.

[70] *Carmina*, VI, pp. 23-24. Giovio, 1551, bk. III, p. 226, mentions this festival.

[71] Cambi, p. 31. Landucci, p. 342, adds that during the procession "si pose a' Servi [SS. Annunziata] l'immagine di Papa Lione." For other evidence of special reverence to Cosimo in Florence after Leo's elevation to the papacy, see Trexler-Lewis, pp. 122-23.

fecie una bella processione in detto dì, e andossi a hofferta la Signoria, e le Chapitudine in S. Lorenzo, dove detti Medici erano uxitati fare la festa di tali Martiri, che chominciò Choximo de' Medici.

Pope Leo ordered that the feast of Saints Cosmas and Damian be observed and that on that day there be a beautiful procession in Florence and that the Signoria and the heads of the guilds go to make their offerings at San Lorenzo, where the Medici were accustomed to celebrate the feast of those martyrs, which was begun by Cosimo de' Medici.

Saints Cosmas and Damian appeared regularly in altarpieces commissioned by the Medici until their expulsion in 1494; now, in the art of the first years of Leo's papacy, they are reintroduced. They join the Florentine patron saint, John the Baptist, in the arch of the Florentine merchants in the decorations for Leo's *possesso*.[72] They embellish a translation of a Hippocrates manuscript dedicated to Leo in 1515 (pl. 14), in which Cosmas and Damian are accompanied by the motto HINC DOLOR HINC SALVS (Here suffering, there deliverance)—alluding to Leo *medicus* as well as to the medical saints as deliverers of Florence. And, in unexecuted projects of 1517 for the facade of San Lorenzo, monumental sculptures of them were to be placed "in cima," above all the other statues.[73]

Leo's cult of the Pater Patriae is also apparent in the symbolism of his entry into Florence for the first time as pope.[74] The celebration of 30 November 1515 provided the ideal occasion for an elaborate display of Leonine propaganda especially appropriate to his native city, such as the pope's identification with Saint John the Baptist, the Florentine patron whose name he bore as Giovanni de' Medici, and with Hercules, the hero who had been adopted by the Florentines and whose *insigne leonis*, or lion skin, he bore as a pope named Leo. But the fundamental message of the *entrata* was that of triumphal return. All the Medici renewal formulae were brought out, and although there was no historical justification for it, the event was staged as a hero's return. Its symbolism ingeniously combined dynastic and papal imagery. As a papal entry, the event presented the opportunity for a Leo-Christ parallel. This theme was stated boldly on one of the triumphal arches, where the dynastic symbolism of a portrait of Leo's father Lorenzo was transformed by the inscription HIC EST FILIVS MEVS DILECTVS (This is my beloved son; Matt. 3:17).[75] Farther on, in the Piazza della Signoria, the procession passed an Arch of Justice, which was inscribed LEONI X PONT. MAX. PROPTER MERITA (To Pope Leo X because of his merits) and decorated with palms of victory alluding to Christ's entry into Jerusalem.[76] As papal entry, the event was thus to be understood as

[72] Penni, p. 214. See also Sanuto, XVI, col. 685: "A dextra Sanctus Cosma, a sinistra San Damiano."

[73] See Domenico Buoninsegni's letter (2 February 1517) to Michelangelo, quoted in C. de Tolnay, "Michel-Ange et la façade de San Lorenzo," *GBA*, 11, 1934, p. 41. The patron wanted to be sure that the saints were identifiable, for the letter continues, instructing that "queste due [santi] di sopra bisogna significarli come medici perchè furon medici."

[74] For the *apparato* in general, see Shearman, 1975, pp. 136-54; Mitchell, pp. 39-43.

[75] Shearman, 1975, p. 145, n. 28.

[76] Shearman, 1975, p. 146, n. 30.

an *adventus regis pacifici* (the coming of the King of Peace), underscoring the notion of Leo as agent of peace and reconciliation, a theme that was fundamental to his personal imagery.

In no way contradicting this Christ-symbolism was a Leo-Cosimo parallel that portrayed the *entrata* as a Medici Return. During his stay in Florence, Leo sought to associate himself with Cosimo by imitating his actions (just as he repeated the acts of past popes named Leo). For example, he slept in Cosimo's cell at San Marco on the feast of the Magi, or Epiphany—a day of great symbolic significance for the Medici.[77] And, in the presentation of a masquerade of the *Triumph of Camillus* in connection with the *entrata*, Leo was celebrated as a new Pater Patriae.[78] Return from exile was a major theme in the story of the Roman hero, Marcus Furius Camillus, who had been an exemplar of justice in Florentine republican imagery.[79] Moreover, as in a poem dedicated to Lorenzo il Magnifico, Cosimo himself had repeatedly been compared with Camillus:[80]

> . . . Te civicus error
> Jussit ab emeritis patriae discedere tectis;
> Sed Dii quam melius! vix in se vertitur annus,
> Vix Janos videre duos, quum teque, tuosque
> Indiga gens Cosmi, patrias revocavit ad aras.
> Sic etiam immeritum damnavit Roma Camillum,
> Acrisioneis illumque reduxit ab oris;

> The error of the state ordered you to withdraw from the fatherland you had served; but, how much better did heaven will it! Hardly did a year pass, hardly did they see two Januses, when the impoverished people of Cosimo recalled you and yours to the native altars. Thus also did Rome condemn the innocent Camillus and bring him back from the Argive shores.

Now, it was implied, a New Camillus, a new Pater Patriae, had come to Florence. In Nardi's song for the *entrata*, "Trionfo della Fama, e della Gloria," Camillus is called

[77] Hatfield, 1970, p. 136.

[78] Vasari, V, p. 341, in the *vita* of Granacci, who painted the scenery. Landucci, p. 345, and others recount that the play was first presented 23 June 1514 (the vigil of the feast of Saint John the Baptist), a date which already connects it with the saint's namesake, the pope. In Roscoe-Bossi, I, pp. 279-83, it is specified that the subject of the play was Camillus' victory over the Gauls and that Giuliano de' Medici and various cardinals went to Florence for the occasion.

[79] Camillus is among the six exemplars of Virtue painted by Ghirlandaio in the Sala di Gigli. He also appeared in the Trecento series of *uomini illustri* in the Palazzo Vecchio, where his epigram by Salutati emphasized the theme of exile (Han-

key, p. 364):

> Ingenio veios domui, pietate faliscos,
> Gallos virtute, quos et dictator ad urbem
> Tractus ab exilio fregi, captivaque signa
> Eripui victis, senuique camillus in armis.

> By ability I tamed the Veii, by dutifulness the Faliscans, by virtue the Gauls whom I crushed, as dictator, recalled to the city from exile, and I snatched the captured standards from the conquered and I, Camillus, grew old in arms.

[80] In Roscoe, III, p. xliii. See also the letter by Poggio Bracciolini to Cosimo in exile, cited in A. M. Brown, "The Humanist Portrait of Cosimo de' Medici, Pater Patriae," *JWCI*, 24, 1961, p. 188.

"Primo Liberator, secondo Padre," in allusion to Livy's characterization of Camillus as a New Romulus and second founder of Rome.[81] Now Leo, too, is called a "secondo Padre"—or second founder of Florence. The Florentine observer, accustomed to this genre of political allegory, would have understood that the *trionfo* of Leo-Camillus was intended to evoke both the recent re-establishment of Medici rule and Cosimo's return from exile.[82] For Nardi's song instructed the audience that, like the laurel which never loses its leaves, history and poetry are ever green:

> Perchè come l'Allor foglia non perde,
> La Storia, e Poesía sempre stà verde.

✳ ✳ ✳

Pope Leo used yet another *impresa* which connected him with the Pater Patriae and also evoked the Golden Age of his father, Lorenzo il Magnifico. The yoke with the motto N/SVAVE, or simply SVAVE (gentle), had associations with both of Leo's illustrious ancestors. The yoke was connected with Cosimo, having appeared on the two medals struck after his death in 1464.[83] These medals are inscribed PAX LIBERTASQVE PVBLICA (peace and public liberty), and they show Florentia seated over a yoke, holding the olive branch of peace and a globe—also to be read as the Medici *palla*. The yoke, however, was not Cosimo's own device; it was one of the *imprese* of Lorenzo, the presumed patron (or *destinataire*) of these medals.[84] The yoke appears in a number of Lorenzo's manuscripts: in one, a GLOVIS medallion in the upper frieze is flanked by fantastic heads supporting *palle*, with the yoke above and the motto SVAVE on a banderole (pl. 27); in another, the yoke is enclosed in the *diamante*, with the motto N/SVAVE (pl. 20).[85] This compound *impresa*—"yoke-diamante: N/SVAVE"—alludes to the benefits of Medici rule in Florence. It illustrates the phrase "anulus nectit jugum suave" (the ring joins the gentle yoke) in an ingenious manner in which each of the four words is accounted for—*anulus* (ring), *nectit* (N), *jugum* (yoke), and *suave*.[86]

[81] Grazzini, I, p. 137; Livy, *History of Rome*, V, XLIX, 7.

[82] See A. Giorgetti, "Lorenzo de' Medici, Duca d'Urbino e Jacopo d'Appiano," *ASI*, ser. IV, 8, 1881, p. 236, for a letter from Lorenzo the younger to one of his envoys stating that "in facto [the Camillus masquerade] non allude se non alla cacciata et dipoi alla revocatione della casa de Medici."

[83] There has been some confusion on the date of these medals. Following Giovio, 1556, pp. 25-26, they have been thought to have been struck to commemorate Cosimo's return from exile. The yoke was understandably associated with the theme by Giovio, who may have known the medal made for Giovanni di Costanzo in 1503 on *his* return from exile, showing a broken yoke and inscribed PATRIA RECEPTA (Hill, nos. 302-3).

[84] The yoke is connected with Lorenzo in the earliest account of Medici *imprese*, Giambullari's description of the courtyard of the Palazzo Medici as decorated for the wedding of Duke Cosimo in 1539 (p. 20): "Vedevasi nella decima [lunetta], l'antico giogo del magnifico Lorenzo, et della felicissima memoria di Leone X col N disopra puntato, et col solito suo motto, SVAVE."

[85] For the first, see Caroli Aldobrandi, *Libellus ad Laurentium Medicen Petri filium* (Laur. MS. Plut. 53, 21, f. 3v; D'Ancona, no. 1617); for the second (mentioned by Winner, 1970, p. 294, n. 66, in connection with Lorenzo), see n. 55, above. For another Laurentian manuscript with the yoke, see MS Plut. 37, 14 (n. 55).

[86] Interpreters of this compound device as later used by Leo X have followed Giovio, 1556, pp. 25-26, in explaining the N/SVAVE. However, Giovio

This "yoke: ѕᴠᴀᴠᴇ" *impresa* was revived after the Medici return to Florence in 1512. In a poem celebrating the occasion, for example, after the laurel and ɢʟᴏᴠɪѕ devices of the family are lauded, the poet praises the yoke:[87]

> Florido giglio di rosette pieno
>   Sempre a tuo vele sia prospero vento.
>   Tanto è lor grato odore dolce et ameno
> Cessan suo affani mancha ogni tormento
>   Perche'è gli à il giogo lor tanto suave
>   Che chi lo porta n'è sempre contento.

> Florid lily full of little roses, may the wind always fill your sails. Its sweet and pleasant perfume is so welcome that all troubles cease and all worries end, since its yoke is so gentle that he who wears it is always happy.

And, the connection of the yoke with Lorenzo is emphasized in a poem celebrating Leo's *possesso*, in which the various Laurentian devices are mentioned, including[88]

> el soave et dolce Iugo
> Lassato a noi dal gratioso Lauro.

> the sweet and gentle yoke
> left to us by the gracious laurel.

Throughout Leo's papacy, the device was used to stress his continuation of the rule of his Medici ancestors. Its political meaning is clear, for example, in one of the frieze borders of Raphael's tapestries, where the yoke is held up by the lions symbolic of both Leo and Florence, and the *impresa* is flanked by scenes of the Medici restoration (pl. 31).[89]

The yoke and *diamante* are ubiquitous in Leo's other Roman decorations, such as the Sala di Costantino. Caryatids shoulder yokes with rings and ѕᴠᴀᴠᴇ banderoles over Giulio Romano's portrait of *Leo X as Clement I with Moderatio and Comitas* (pl. 29), and elsewhere in the room putti carry about the Medici rings as if assembling the *impresa* itself.[90] But it was in Florence that the yoke, with its message of unity and reconciliation

---

(who did not realize that the yoke had also been Lorenzo's device) mentioned only the "yoke: ѕᴠᴀᴠᴇ" part of the *impresa* and thought it was extracted from Matthew 11:30 (*Iugum meum suave est onus meum leve*). Shearman, 1972, p. 87, who points out that the correct text is given in Moroni, 37, p. 45, translates the line "the ring unites, the yoke is easy."

[87] *Sonetti*, f. ɪᴠ.

[88] F. Cancellieri, *Storia de' solenni possessi de' sommi pontefici*, Rome, 1802, pp. 82-83. Following are the first and last stanzas of the poem:

Nel aureo tempo del famoso Lauro
  Che la Italia reggea con sue Palle
  Fioriva in Selva ogni aspro et vile Broncone

Per sua virtù vergate in carte a penna
Tal che se 'l cor non era di Adamante
Si tenea lieto al virtuoso Iugo.
Altro che Laur verde e rosse Palle
  Et Bronzon servirà mia rancha penna
  Finchè vive ad amante el dolce Iugo.

[89] Shearman, 1972, p. 85.

[90] On the *imprese* in this room and on the yoke in the Stanza della Segnatura, the Stanza d'Eliodoro, and the Stanza dell'Incendio, see M. Perry, " 'Candor Illaesvs': the 'Impresa' of Clement VII and other Medici Devices in the Vatican Stanze," *Burl.*, 119, 1977, pp. 676-86.

under gentle Medici rule, was most prominently employed. It appears on Florentine coins issued during Leo's pontificate,[91] as well as on works of art of all kinds. One of the most important of these is Bandinelli's *Orpheus* of ca. 1516-1517, which stands in the courtyard of the Palazzo Medici (pl. 30). Its message is that Leo-Orpheus is a peace-maker who ushers in a new Florentine Golden Age.[92] The base of the statue is encrusted with Medici emblems, with the "diamante: SEMPER" on the sides and the yoke (without the SVAVE) on the front and back. The image is thus one of gentle Medici rule, the graceful Leo-Orpheus himself perhaps providing the *suavitas* of the missing motto.

The compound *impresa* appears frequently in Leo's art in such a way that the parts of the device are intended to be read together even when they are widely separated. The "yoke-diamante: N/SVAVE" marks the borders of facing tapestries in Raphael's cycle; in the Sala di Costantino the yokes and *diamanti* alternate around the borders of the scenes; in the Vatican loggias the centers of alternate bays are marked with the yoke and *diamanti*; and the trappings of Leo's horses had the yoke on one side, the *diamante* on the other.[93] The *impresa* also decorates Leo's manuscripts: it appears (possibly in reference to Cosimo Pater Patriae) on the title page of *De laudibus Cosmi Medices*, dedicated to Leo on the feast of Saints Cosmas and Damian; and it is prominent in the *Medici Codex*, a collection of motets presented by Leo to his nephew Lorenzo and his wife, Madeleine de la Tour d'Auvergne, in 1518, where the "diamante: SEMPER" and the "yoke: N/SVAVE" are depicted on a page with Lorenzo's *stemma* and the crossed *bronconi* (pl. 28).[94]

The most striking and monumental Florentine appearance of the yoke *impresa* is in the Cappella del Papa, adjacent to S. Maria Novella, freshly decorated by Ridolfo Ghirlandaio, Pontormo, and Andrea di Cosimo Feltrini on the occasion of Leo's *entrata*.[95] The vault (pl. 32) is a compendium of Leonine imagery in which his *imprese* are interwoven with themes of the Passion in such a way as to suggest the Leo-Christ parallel. In four of the tondi, putti carry the instruments of the Passion, while in the other four they bear the papal arms. GLOVIS is repeated eight times. (Eight, the number of renewal, alludes to Time's Return, like GLOVIS itself, and perhaps signifies in the chapel both the Resurrection of Christ and the renewal of the Medici.) On a larger scale around the

[91] Giovio, 1556, p. 26.

[92] K. Langedijk, "Baccio Bandinelli's Orpheus: a Political Message," *Mitt.KHIF*, 20, 1976, pp. 34-52.

[93] Giovio, 1556, p. 27. See Shearman, 1972, p. 87, on the yoke in the tapestries.

[94] Laur. MS Acq. e doni 666, f. 3r. See E. E. Lowinsky, *The Medici Codex of 1518: a Choirbook of Motets dedicated to Lorenzo de' Medici, Duke of Urbino*, Chicago, 1968, III, pp. 3-16. Lowinsky identifies the manuscript as a gift from Francis I, but on the basis of Leo's personal *imprese* alone the pope is indicated as its donor. See the anonymous review in the *Times Literary Supplement*, 17 July 1969, p. 785; and L. L. Perkins, review of the *Medici Codex*,

Musical Quarterly, 55, 1969, pp. 262-65. For a conclusive summary of this viewpoint, see L. Lockwood, "Jean Mouton and Jean Michel: New Evidence on French Music and Musicians in Italy, 1505-1520," *Journal of the American Musicological Society*, 32, 1979, pp. 241-45. I am grateful to Iain Fenlon for bibliographical assistance on this matter and to Richard Sherr, who pointed out to me that the *stemma* with the arms of both the bride and groom (f. 3r) is properly considered that of Madeleine and that the work may in fact have been a gift to her.

[95] Vasari, VI, pp. 255-56; Cox-Rearick, 1964, I, p. 160; Forster, 1966, cat. 6.

central tondo of God the Father, Leo's compound *impresa* is repeated four times: the yoke supports the *diamante* with its three feathers, and a banderole with SVAVE binds the parts of the *impresa* into a single integer.

Over the entrance to the chapel in a lunette is Pontormo's fresco of *St. Veronica with the Sudarium* (pl. 33). The Passion imagery and the Medicean dynastic imagery of the *entrata* come together in this image. A saint most uncommonly represented in Florence, Veronica pointedly refers to Rome and the papacy. For the relic of the sudarium, to which physical cures were attributed, was preserved at St. Peter's. The inscription under the figure (not visible in pl. 33) spells out the message HEC EST SALV[S] V[E]STRA (This is your salvation). So placed, in Leo's private chapel, this inscription would seem to allude not only to the spiritual salvation promised by the *imago christi* but to the salvation promised by Pope Leo, savior of Florence and healer of her ills.

The *St. Veronica* is thus a fitting climax to the Leo-Christ and Roman themes of the *apparato*. And it is the most explicit example in Leo's Florentine art of the Medici pope as a new *Christus medicus*—an allusion prominent in his Roman works.[96] Since the 1512 restoration of the Medici, an old metaphor of them as healers had enjoyed wide currency. Their curative laurel was constantly evoked, as, for example, by Ariosto, who refers in the *Canzoni* to the "mediche fronde" of the "amato Lauro."[97] Popular poetry elaborated the notion:[98]

> Dulce medice et saputo
> per la nostra malattia
> che il mal nostro ha conosciuto
> et rimedia tutta via.
>
> Sweet doctor, so well aware of our sickness, you who have known our illness and are constant remedy to it.

Moreover, theater works equated the Medici return with a medical cure for Florence by way of the familiar wordplay *medico*-Medici. Eufrosino Bonini's *Comedia di Iustitia* is one of the first Florentine plays written after the restoration. According to the author, it is an allegory dedicated to the Gonfaloniere Jacopo Salviati, "nel desiderato felice ritorno de' iusti padri et invicti difensori della già afflicta patria" (on the occasion of the desired, happy return of the just fathers and unconquered defenders of the formerly afflicted fatherland).[99] Leo's emphasis on his father's laurel and his prompt revival of the cult of the medical saints were surely aimed at reinforcing this Medicean propaganda of healing. His circle at the papal court had taken up the metaphor with characteristic enthu-

[96] See Shearman, 1972, pp. 17, 50, 77-78, 80, for extensive documentation on Leo as *Christus medicus*, especially in relation to the *Acts of the Apostles* tapestries, which are contemporary in date with the Cappella del Papa. Regarding the concept in Raphael's *Transfiguration*, see K. Weil Garris Posner, *Leonardo and Central Italian Art: 1515-1550*, New York, 1974, pp. 45-47.

[97] *Canzoni*, V, 136-37, in Ariosto, p. 126.

[98] Ridolfi, p. 34.

[99] BNF, MS Magl. VII, 1211 f. 3v. See A. Magni, *La Commedia in lingua nel cinquecento: Bibliografia critica*, Florence, 1966, p. 73, cat. 9. Cf. also Machiavelli's *La Mandragola* of 1518, as discussed by Parronchi, pp. 57-69.

siasm. For example, Leo's adviser Egidio da Viterbo reminded him: "con quale spirito, con quale speranza di tutti i mortali fosse preposto egli medico a medicare i mali del mondo" (with what enthusiasm, with what expectation on the part of all mankind he was considered the greatest healer to heal the evils of the world).[100] And Zaccaria Ferreri's poem on Leo's election, *Lugdunense somnium*, conflated this metaphor with the theme of the return of the Golden Age under the new pontiff:[101]

> . . . aegra
> Curabit Medica ipse manu: convertet in aurum
> Ferrea saecla: hominum fera pectora molliet; atque
> Ambrosiam, nectarque omnem diffundet in orbem.

> He himself will cure the ills with Medicean hand: He will turn the age of iron into gold: He will soften the ferocious hearts of men: Ambrosia and nectar will he pour upon the whole world.

The decoration of the Cappella del Papa is a triumphant declaration of Leo as agent of just such a renewal. Saint Veronica identifies Leo with the healing savior, *Christus medicus*, and the figure receives the blessing of God the Father, who directs his gesture and glance from the center of the vault toward the saint.[102] The devices decorating the vault specify the way in which Leo's renewal will come about: the GLOVIS announces the themes of Medici virtue and the Return of Time, and the "yoke-diamante: SVAVE" symbolizes the eternal and gentle rule of the Medici. Here and elsewhere in Leo's Florentine art, the message is clearly stated: the Wheel of Fortune has turned and Time has returned, as Leo restores the Golden Age of his ancestors Lorenzo il Magnifico and Cosimo Pater Patriae.

---

[100] Quoted in Gnoli, p. 74.

[101] Ferreri, p. 291.

[102] J. Shearman, review of J. Cox-Rearick, *The Drawings of Pontormo, Art Bull.*, 54, 1972, p. 211, points out that a drawing after the God the Father (Louvre inv. 10241) shows that only the head and halo have been repainted and that the glance of the figure was directed at Saint Veronica.

Pontormo's *Portrait of Cosimo de' Medici Pater Patriae*

In 1519 the political situation of the Medici differed sharply from that of the years following their triumphant return to Florence in 1512. It appeared that the main branch of the family had extinguished itself, at least insofar as its legitimate members were concerned (fig. 1). When Giovanni de' Medici ascended to the papacy as Leo X in 1513, the male heirs of the family descendant from Cosimo Pater Patriae were the pope himself and his cousin Giulio (future cardinal and pope, as Clement VII). In the secular life, there were two further heirs: Leo's brother Giuliano and his nephew Lorenzo the younger. There were also two illegitimate heirs, both children: Ippolito, son of Giuliano; and Alessandro, purportedly the son of Lorenzo the younger.[1]

In the years before 1519, the prospect of dynastic continuity had seemed more promising. Leo's politico-dynastic ambitions for his family had been furthered by marital alliances of Giuliano and of Lorenzo the younger with members of the French royal family. These marriages, it was hoped, would produce the male heirs necessary for a continuation of Medici rule, but their only issue was Catherine (future queen of France), born in 1519. Moreover, Giuliano died in 1516, and his death was followed on 4 May 1519 by that of Lorenzo the younger. The Medici were thus left only a tenuous continuity with the nostalgically recalled Golden Age of Lorenzo il Magnifico and with no legitimate heir in the main line of the family.

This decline in the fortunes of the Medici is reflected in the poetry and art of the last two years of Leo's pontificate (1519-1521). The heady Golden Age celebrations held before 1519, with their promise of peace and reconciliation under the gentle yoke of

[1] While it is sometimes suggested that Alessandro was the illegitimate son of Cardinal Giulio, contemporary sources are agreed that he was Lorenzo's son. See (in addition to the miniature illustrated in pl. 44) Francesco Vettori's *Vita di Lo-renzo*, written between 1519 and 1523; and Varchi, I, p. 56, who writes of Alessandro as the "figliuolo pur naturale di Lorenzo giovane." It should also be noted that Duke Cosimo had Alessandro buried in Lorenzo's sarcophagus in the New Sacristy.

Pope Leo and their confident recall of the Laurentian era, now themselves belonged to the past. The new reality produced works of art the content of which not only implied but admitted the precariousness of Time's Return. Preeminent among these was the funerary chapel for the recently deceased Giuliano and Lorenzo (pl. 34). They were to be buried in a New Sacristy of San Lorenzo, to be built and decorated with monumental sculptures by Michelangelo as a pendant to Brunelleschi's Old Sacristy (which was, of course, also a family burial chapel). The new chapel was commissioned by Pope Leo through Cardinal Giulio, who had become regent of Florence on the death of Lorenzo the younger in 1519, and work was begun on the building in November of that year.[2] The chapel was a monument to the Medici dynasty, not merely a burial chamber for its most recently deceased members. In a mournful *finis* to that dynasty, now extinct in its main branch except for illegitimate offspring, three generations of Medici were to be entombed: Giuliano and Lorenzo on the lateral walls and the *magnifici* whose names they bore—Giuliano (father of Cardinal Giulio) and Lorenzo (father of Pope Leo)—on the main wall, the so-called *sepoltura di testa* opposite the altar (pl. 37).

The effigies of Giuliano and Lorenzo are accompanied by the *Times of Day*. On a primary level, these statues allude to the *laus perennis*—the uninterrupted prayers for intercession which were stipulated in the plans for the chapel.[3] But they also refer, of course, to the theme of Time, which had been central to Laurentian imagery and had appeared more recently in Leo's art in works such as Raphael's *Times of Day* tapestry border (pl. 21). Here, however, in the context of a funerary monument, Time is viewed as explicitly destructive. For Michelangelo's biographer Condivi, the allegories signified the consuming power of Time; and a well-known notation on one of Michelangelo's drawings for the chapel reads: "El Dì e la Nocte parlano e dicono: Noi abiano col nostro veloce corso condocto alla morte el Duca Giuliano" (Night and Day speak and say: "We with our swift course have brought Duke Giuliano to death").[4]

The Night and Day imagery refers to the deaths of the individual Medici, but given the family's situation in 1519, it must also have been intended to allude to the destruction of Medici fortunes and of any hope for the future of their dynasty. The *Times of Day* of the Sacristy are evocative reminders that Lorenzo il Magnifico's motto LE TEMPS REVIENT could mean the end as well as the renewal of Medici rule.

But the imagery of the New Sacristy also alludes to another theme, not fully realized in the execution of its decorations and hence not sensible to us today. The chapel was consecrated to the Resurrection, to which Pope Leo was particularly devoted.[5] In the

---

[2] For testimony that the commission was considered to have come from Leo, see Cambi, p. 161: "L'anno 1519 [1520 new style] del mese di marzo a l'uscita di detto anno Papa Lione fece cominciare alla chiesa di S. Lorenzo una sacrestia. . . ." For the beginning of the work, see G. Corti, "Una 'Ricordanza' di Giovan Battista Figiovanni," *Paragone*, no. 175, 1964, pp. 24-31; and A. Parronchi, "Michelangelo al tempo del lavoro di San Lorenzo in una 'ricordanza' del Figiovanni," *Paragone*, no.

175, 1964, pp. 9-24.

[3] Ettlinger, 1978, pp. 294-97.

[4] A. Condivi, *Vita di Michelangelo Buonarroti*, Florence, 1746, p. 34 ("il tempo che consuma il tutto"). For the notation on Casa Buonarroti 10A, see K. Frey, ed., *Die Dichtungen des Michelangelo Buonarroti*, Berlin, 1897, XVII; and, for the translation, Gilbert, pp. 402-4.

[5] Most important to Leo in this connection must have been the fact that his fortunes turned on Easter

chapel, this theme is signaled only by the pelican-phoenix candelabra, signifying Christ's sacrifice and resurrection, and by the doors numbering eight—the number symbolic of death and rebirth.[6] However, considering the dedication of the chapel, it is highly likely that this theme was to have been more directly and monumentally expressed above the *sepoltura di testa*, as A. E. Popp's well-known reconstruction based on Michelangelo's drawings suggests (pl. 35).[7] Below the *Resurrection* lunette, statues of the *Virgo lactans* and of Saints Cosmas and Damian would intercede for the dead of the Medici house. The Medici *topos* of Return would thus have been transformed to allude to a heavenly Resurrection of the Dead rather than the terrestrial return to power of the family in Florence.

Two other important works were commissioned by the Medici in Florence at this juncture: frescos by Andrea del Sarto, Franciabigio, and Pontormo in the Salone of the villa built at Poggio a Caiano by Lorenzo il Magnifico (pl. 36) and a portrait by Pontormo of Cosimo de' Medici Pater Patriae (color pl. 1). Like the sculptures of the New Sacristy, these paintings are concerned with themes of dynastic extinction and renewal—of Medici glorification and immortality—but they present these themes in quite different and, of course, secular terms.

All these projects have been rightly understood as reflecting the preoccupation of the Medici with a future made uncertain by the recent deaths of their two heirs and with the glorification of the Medici past as a Golden Age.[8] However, funerary apotheosis and nostalgic recall of an idealized past are not the only themes of these works. They are also concerned with the future of the Medici dynasty, for in 1519 there was reason for renewed hope: scarcely a month after Lorenzo's death a legitimate male was born who was descended from, and thus could be seen to unite, both sides of the family. The fortuitous birth of Cosimo (the future duke of Florence) may be alluded to in these dynastic works of 1519 to 1521.[9] Indeed, I propose to show that this birth is an impor-

(11 April 1512), when he was captured by the French at Ravenna. It was in commemoration of this date that his *possesso* was delayed after his elevation until 11 April 1513. For the Resurrection as the dominant theme of the chapel see E. Tietze-Conrat, "The Church Program of Michelangelo's Medici Chapel," *Art Bull.*, 36, 1954, pp. 222-24; and Ettlinger, 1978, pp. 300-301.

[6] On the candelabra see Tolnay, III, p. 165. The number of renewal, which occurs in the architecture of both baptisteries and mausolea, also alludes to the eighth house of the zodiac, ruled by Scorpio and known as the house of death and regeneration (Hopper, pp. 77, 154, 178).

[7] Popp, pp. 158-63, pl. 9. Popp's argument is accepted by Tolnay, III, pp. 49-51, 70-71, 157-58, 218-19; Panofsky, p. 203; and F. Hartt, "The Meaning of Michelangelo's Medici Chapel," *Essays in Honor of G. Swarzenski*, Chicago, 1951, pp. 150-53, among others. It will be noted that in Popp's

reconstruction the positions of Cosmas and Damian are reversed so that they look out rather than at the Virgin. I am in agreement with (most recently) T. Verellen, "Cosmas and Damian in the New Sacristy," *JWCI*, 42, 1979, pp. 274-77, that such a positioning would undermine the meaning of the *sepoltura di testa* as expressing the salvation of the Medici souls through the intervention of the Virgin and the Medici saints.

[8] The interconnected themes of these works have been noted by Winner, 1963-1964, pp. 9-11; Shearman, 1965, I, pp. 78-79; Forster, 1966, pp. 39-41; Langedijk, pp. 42-50; Winner, 1972, pp. 186-87; Kliemann, 1972, pp. 318, 324; Weil-Garris Posner, pp. 645-49; McKillop, 1974, p. 78; and Kliemann, 1976, p. 67.

[9] This possibility has been raised in relation to the laurel in Pontormo's portrait and lunette by Langedijk, pp. 49, 174; Kliemann, 1972, pp. 312, 325; and Kliemann, 1976, p. 58.

tant theme, although not always overtly expressed, in the dynastically oriented art of the Medici in the last years of Leo's pontificate; that it is the raison d'être of Pontormo's portrait; that it is a key theme in the decorations of the Poggio a Caiano Salone; and that it is alluded to in the New Sacristy.

Pontormo's portrait may have been the first of these works to be commissioned; it was the only one of them to be completed before Pope Leo's death in 1521. Since its imagery is also the least complex, the portrait may be taken as a starting point for a consideration of the themes of dynasty and rule in Medicean art of these years.

*   *   *

Pontormo's *Portrait of Cosimo de' Medici Pater Patriae* has always been recognized as an ancestor-portrait of Cosimo, great-grandfather of Leo X and great-great-grandfather of Lorenzo the younger. Likewise, it has been clear that Pontormo's lively representation of the likeness is based on the medals of Cosimo with Florentia and the yoke (pls. 23-24). Pontormo also adapted the inscription of one of these, MAGNVS COSMVS MEDICES P P P, in which a third P is added to the two standing for Cosimo's title, Pater Patriae. He reproduced this inscription (with the MAGNVS omitted) next to Cosimo's head on the high back of his throne: COSM'. MEDICES. P.P.P. The seated Cosimo is dressed in a fur-lined gown, its red color suggesting the traditional martyr's robe of a Saint Cosmas. To the left of the picture is a laurel tree, its left branch sharply cut off, its right branch flourishing. On a scroll intricately wound around the live branch is the Virgilian inscription from the *Aeneid*: VNO AVVLSO. NO[N]. DEFIC[IT] ALTER (As soon as one is torn away, another takes its place).[10]

Before considering these images in Pontormo's painting, we must re-examine the circumstances of the commissioning of the portrait, its patron, and its date. The only contemporary account which might illuminate these matters is Vasari's notice in the *vita* of Pontormo:[11]

> E dopo fece a messer Goro da Pistoia, allora segretario de' Medici, in un quadro la testa del Magnifico Cosimo vecchio de' Medici dalle ginocchia in su, che è veramente lodevole. . . . Mediante quest'opera, e particolarmente questa testa di Cosimo, fatto il Puntormo amico di messer Ottaviano, avendosi a dipingere al Poggio a Caiano la sala grande. . . . Ma mentre che si lavorava quest'opera, venendo a morte Leone, così rimase questa imperfetta.

> Afterward he executed for Messer Goro da Pistoia, then secretary to the Medici, a picture with the portrait of the Magnificent Cosimo de' Medici, the elder, from the knees upward, which is indeed worthy to be extolled. . . . [Here follows an account of the later history of the picture.] By means of this work, and particularly this head of Cosimo, Pontormo became the friend of Messer

---

[10] Adapted from Virgil, *Aeneid*, VI, 143-44: "Primo avulso non deficit alter/Aureus."   [11] Vasari, VI, p. 264.

Ottaviano; and the Great Hall at Poggio a Caiano having then to be painted.
. . . [Here follows an account of the work at the villa.] But while it was being
executed Leo was overtaken by death, and so it remained unfinished.

Vasari links the portrait with Pontormo's work in the Salone, stating that his successful
completion of the portrait brought him to the attention of Ottaviano de' Medici and that
the fresco commission followed, but was interrupted by Leo's death (1 December 1521).
However, the date of the portrait, on which the Salone commission depended, is not
specified. Nor is the picture referred to any datable external event. Vasari merely places
his notice of it after Pontormo's collaboration with Andrea del Sarto, Bacchiacca, and
Granacci on the Borgherini bridal-chamber *Story of Joseph*, which is datable 1515-1518.[12]
Vasari also places it after Pontormo's participation in a similar project for Giovanmaria
Benintendi, which may have been commissioned about 1520 but was not completed
until 1523.[13]

The first particular that Vasari gives about the Cosimo portrait is that it was painted
for Goro da Pistoia. Since Goro Gheri served as secretary to Lorenzo the younger, it
has been generally assumed that the picture was ordered by Lorenzo, whose death on
4 May 1519 would then establish a terminus for its date. A date of 1518 or early 1519
has consequently been assigned to the portrait. The usual interpretation of the meaning
of the picture follows logically: the cut-off branch of the laurel would signify the break
in Medici fortunes caused by the death of Giuliano in 1516, while the flourishing branch
and its motto would allude to Lorenzo, whose personal device was, after all, the *broncone*.[14]

The style of the *Cosimo*, with its rich, deep colors and chiaroscuro, accords perfectly
with that of Pontormo's works of 1518-1519, such as the S. Maria Visdomini *Madonna
and Saints* or the *Joseph in Egypt*. One might even see the Cosimo figure as a variant of
the St. Francis of the altarpiece or the red-robed figure with hands clasped to the left
foreground of the *Joseph*. However, there are serious objections to the association of the
portrait with the patronage of Lorenzo. First, its visual imagery does not convincingly
allude to the situation that obtained after the death of Giuliano, which left his twenty-
seven-year-old nephew as the sole legitimate heir in the branch of the family descended
from Cosimo Pater Patriae. The dramatic contrast between the dead and living sides of
the laurel and the message of the inscription around its flourishing branch point to a
more decisive event, not the mere fact of Lorenzo's survival—which would hardly have
been news in 1518 or 1519. Second, even given his descent from the Pater Patriae, the

[12] London, National Gallery. See Freedberg,
1963, II, pp. 53-56; Cox-Rearick, 1964, I, pp. 113-
22.

[13] Shearman, 1965, II, p. 259; Forster, 1966, cat.
20; McKillop, 1974, pp. 168-69. There is no firm
evidence that the Benintendi commission followed
directly on the Borgherini project, but Vasari, (V,
pp. 209-10) mentions it before Poggio a Caiano in
the *vite* of Andrea di Cosimo Feltrini and Pontormo. It is possible that, with four of the artists

deployed to the papal project in the Salone, its
execution was delayed until after Leo's death.
Franciabigio's *Bathsheba* (Dresden) is dated 1523;
Shearman dates Sarto's Pitti *St. John the Baptist* to
the same year, and Pontormo's Pitti *Adoration* may
be dated to ca. 1522 on the basis of its style.

[14] For this traditional dating and interpretation,
see Cox-Rearick, 1964, I, pp. 149-50; and Forster,
1966, pp. 134-35.

subject of the portrait is an unlikely one for Lorenzo to have commissioned. From the evidence of his art, such as the floats of the *broncone* pageant of 1513, Lorenzo's involvement with his Medici past seems to have focused on the Golden Age of his grandfather, Lorenzo il Magnifico, and on himself as agent of its revival. Cosimo de' Medici does not enter his iconography at all. We are justified, then, in asking why Lorenzo would have chosen Cosimo instead of, say, Lorenzo il Magnifico as the subject of this major commemorative portrait.

We may also question the programmatic nature of the ensemble in the light of the Lorenzo-as-patron hypothesis. For the portrait is not a mere likeness. In it, four elements have been brought together in a most calculated manner: the profile of Cosimo; the throne, inscribed with an unusual variant of his title (which, taken as an identifying label, is redundant next to the well-known profile); the laurel, device of the two Lorenzos but also understood as a general symbol of Medici revival; and the Virgilian quotation, which explicates the inevitable replacement of the old with the new, the dead with the living. If the patron was someone other than Lorenzo, his identity, and the meaning of the picture as well, must be sought in relation to this inventive synthesis.

Returning to Vasari's account, we find nothing in it, in fact, that makes the association with Lorenzo imperative. Vasari does not say that the picture was commissioned by Lorenzo or even that it was commissioned by Goro Gheri while he was Lorenzo's secretary; only that it was done for Gheri, "allora segretario de' Medici." Now, as it happened, Gheri continued to serve the Medici after Lorenzo's death. He was attached to Cardinal Giulio, who arrived in Florence on 27 May 1519 to take over the government as Leo's regent; he was involved in a power struggle with Cardinal Passerini to become Giulio's deputy on the cardinal's return to Rome; and when Giulio did leave the city in October, Gheri remained until 27 January 1520 as one of his representatives.[15] Thus, even after Lorenzo's death, Gheri could perfectly well have been involved in the arrangements for the painting at any time until his own departure from Florence.

If the *Cosimo* was not painted for Lorenzo but after his death, then the symbolism of the laurel and the Virgilian quotation—hence the whole message of the picture—must be read differently. An alternative interpretation and dating of the painting has, in fact, been put forward by John Sparrow.[16] Failing to find any precedent for the change from *primo* to *uno* in the motto taken from Virgil's line "Primo avulso non deficit alter / Aureus," he advances the date of the picture to 1537-1539, when the altered form of the inscription was used with the laurel by Duke Cosimo as a personal *impresa*. Basing his conclusion on an ambiguous statement by Giovio in the *Dialogo dell'imprese*,[17] Sparrow believes that this *impresa* was invented by Cosimo's major-domo, Pierfrancesco Riccio, and that Pontormo's picture must then be a commemorative portrait of the Pater Patriae painted for Duke Cosimo on his assumption of power.[18]

[15] Pastor, VII, p. 283. Cambi, pp. 156-57, notes of Gheri: "in fatto lui era assecutore del Chardinale [Giulio], e prima del Ducha d'Urbino." On Gheri and the Medici in these years, see Albertini, pp. 28-31; and Devonshire Jones, pp. 143-46.

[16] Sparrow, pp. 163-75.

[17] Giovio, 1556, p. 33: "Ebbe [Duca Cosimo] un altra [impresa] nel principio del suo principato dottamente trovata dal reverendo M. Pierfrancesco de Ricci suo maggior domo."

[18] Sparrow interprets Giovio's remark to mean that after Cosimo came to power Riccio invented

Since critical opinion unanimously places Pontormo's *Cosimo* before 1520 on the basis of its stylistic affinity with his other paintings of that period,[19] Sparrow's argument depends, by his own admission, on the assumption that the altered form of the Virgil text did not exist before 1537. However, such an argument does not convince, because the text had, in fact, been used earlier. The motto VNO AVVLSO NON DEFICIT ALTER occurs on Maffeo Olivieri's medal of the Veronese poet Francesco di Pier Antonio Roseti, which Sparrow himself cites and dismisses (pl. 38).[20] The reverse shows two of the most common Renaissance images of regeneration and immortality: the palm tree and the phoenix.[21] The motto, drawn from Virgil's description of Aeneas' quest for immortality, amplifies the meaning of these *corpi*, just as it does in Pontormo's portrait. However, since Roseti's activity extended at the very latest to the early 1530's and his portrait on the obverse shows a costume and hairstyle typical of the previous decade, this medal must date well before Duke Cosimo's accession.

But the changed form of the line may have been used even earlier than the Roseti medal, and in a context more directly relevant to Pontormo's portrait. Long before Pontormo wound the scroll with the quotation from Virgil around the flourishing laurel branch, the Medici appear to have hit upon the idea of symbolizing the immortality of their family by using Virgil's words with a different regenerating tree. According to a compilation of Medici devices made by Alessandro Segni in 1685 (the accurate listings of which inspire confidence in this one), Giovanni di Bicci, father of Cosimo Pater Patriae, had two *imprese*: "un diamante legato in anello d'oro . . . il pomo d'oro sul albero che lo produce" (a diamond set in a golden ring . . . the golden apple on a tree which brings it forth).[22] According to this same source, Cosimo used devices derived from these and added mottos to them: "tre diamanti legati in altrettante anella implicate insieme: SEMPER . . . il pomo d'oro che spunta dal tronco dopo lo schiantarsi dal primo: VNO AVVLSO NON DEFICIT ALTER" (three diamonds set in as many rings, interlaced to-

the *impresa*, changing Virgil's *primo* to *uno*. Of course, *trovata* can mean "found" as well as "invented." Giovio uses the word elsewhere in this sense, and he may have intended to indicate that Riccio found the *impresa* (in the Pontormo portrait) and suggested it as suitable for Duke Cosimo in 1537.

[19] Sparrow's dating has not met with acceptance, and a date of 1518-1519 has been reasserted by, among others: Langedijk, p. 49; Winner, 1970, p. 296, n. 90; Forster, 1971, p. 67, n. 4; Winner, 1972, p. 186; Kliemann, 1972, p. 312, n. 80; and McKillop, 1974, p. 84.

[20] Hill, no. 490, cites Bode's attribution of the medal to the "medallist of 1523," while Sparrow notes that the datable works of Olivieri (d. 1543-1544) belong to the 1520s. Little is known of Roseti except that he published poetry in Venice in 1532.

[21] Ladner, pp. 318-19. Tervarent, 1958, col. 296, considers the palm tree as a symbol of the poet's renown. The crossed branches below the tree are strikingly similar to the Medicean crossed *bronconi*, suggesting the possibility that the medallist was familiar with Medici imagery and may also have derived the Virgil inscription in its altered form from a Medici source.

[22] I quote from the presentation copy of Segni's treatise (ASF, *Guardaroba Mediceo* 958, f. 2), a transcription of which is given in Ames-Lewis, pp. 142-43. See also an earlier draft, Biblioteca Riccardiana, MS 1185, vol. 6, p. 4, with slightly different wording. The single ring without motto is not mentioned in the usual sources for Medici *imprese* (Giovio, Vasari, Borghini, Giambullari et al.), which do not discuss Giovanni, but it does occur in eighteenth-century compilations such as G. Allegrini, *Chronologia serie simulacrorum regiae familiae Medicae*, Florence, 1761, no. 5; or the series of commemorative medals by Antonio Selvi (Bargello 7453).

gether: SEMPER . . . the golden apple that sprouts from the trunk after the first was broken off: As soon as one is torn away, another takes its place).[23]

We recognize the first device as the "diamante: SEMPER," which appears first in connection with Cosimo and was used by succeeding generations of Medici, but the second device is less familiar. It conflates two metaphors. The *anima*, of course, refers to Virgil's regenerating golden bough and its promise of immortality, but the word *primo* in Virgil's line, signifying "first," has been changed to the more general *uno*, meaning "one." By this change away from the limiting notion of first and second, Virgil's line is transformed into a dynastic motto of never failing succession: as Cosimo succeeds his father, so others will follow him.

The *corpo* of this *impresa* did not show the laurel but the *pomo d'oro*, or orange tree. In Cosimo's time, this tree was the primary vegetative symbol of Medici regeneration, the laurel having come into use only when a Medici *lauro* made the association irresistible. The reddish, sour orange (*citrus aurantium*) that grew in Tuscany was called *mala medica*, which had a potential wordplay on the name Medici and permitted the family to make a poetic equation between the red *palle* of their *stemma* and the fruit. This conceit may have been all the more compelling because the *mala medica*, in turn, was identified with the golden fruit of the Garden of the Hesperides (*mala aurea*) and with the Golden Age.[24]

This circle of associations (*mala medica*–*mala aurea*–Medici *palle*) became a commonplace in later Medici art, but we can only speculate that such connections were made in Cosimo's time. However, the metaphor of the regenerative, medicinal *pomo d'oro* putting forth fruit alluding to the red *palle* of the Medici is completely consistent with imagery in art commissioned by Cosimo. In Uccello's London *Battle of San Romano*, probably painted in the late 1430s, oranges appear with other Medici devices such as roses and three feathers.[25] Another example is Fra Angelico's *Madonna and Saints* for the high altar of San Marco, in which Saint Cosmas, kneeling in the foreground facing the spectator, is probably a portrait of Cosimo (pl. 39).[26] Behind the Virgin and below garlands of roses is an orange grove, which may allude to the actual walled fruit garden which Cosimo had planted at San Marco. Oranges continued to be featured in Medici paintings, such as Gozzoli's *Procession of the Magi* (pl. 4); and, after Piero di Cosimo's death in 1469, they appear in an explicitly dynastic context that recalls the *pomo d'oro* device attributed to Cosimo. On the title page of a Laurentian Aristotle manuscript (pl. 41),[27] commemorative portrait medallions imitating actual medals of Lorenzo's grandfather Cosimo (pls. 23-24) and his father Piero (pl. 40) are surrounded by a profusion of the golden fruit. It is thus quite possible that Cosimo Pater Patriae used an orange-tree *impresa* with, as motto, the Virgilian line which so aptly complements the idea of

[23] ASF, *Guardaroba Mediceo* 958, f. 3.

[24] See chap. 6.

[25] G. Griffiths, "The Political Significance of Uccello's *Battle of San Romano*," *JWCI*, 41, 1978, pp. 313-16, presents evidence for a date in the late 1430s but retains the traditional mid-1550s dating.

[26] As suggested most recently by McKillop, 1980, p. 3, who points out that the two saints who face

the spectator are the name saints of the Medici brothers Lorenzo and Cosimo. See also the Bosco ai Frati altar (San Marco, Museum) of 1450-1452, where the oranges are shown in the background.

[27] *Aristotelis Logica, Ioanne Argyropylo interprete* (Laur. MS Plut. 71, 7, f. 1; D'Ancona, no. 796). See Ames-Lewis, p. 128, no. 29, for other manuscripts in which oranges appear.

the immortal tree. Indeed, such an *impresa* would have been a logical choice for Cosimo, as the first of the Medici to promulgate the notion of dynastic succession.

The laurel and the Virgilian scroll so vividly brought to life in Pontormo's portrait of Cosimo may then be an updated version of the subject's own device, the laurel, which had gained currency through its use by both Lorenzos, appropriately replacing the *pomo d'oro* as the miraculous regenerating tree which Virgil's line evokes.

We may now return to the question of the patron of the portrait. The commission for it relates to certain circumstances in the period immediately following the death of Lorenzo the younger (and before Pontormo began work at Poggio a Caiano). We recall that the Medici family was without a legitimate heir, but there were the illegitimate children Ippolito and Alessandro. In late 1519 there was talk of sending Ippolito from Rome to Florence as a symbol of continuing Medici control, but Pope Leo apparently rejected the idea, even as a temporary expedient.[28] There was no hint that Pierfrancesco the younger (ranking heir to the collateral branch of the family descended from Lorenzo di Giovanni, brother of the Pater Patriae) or his son Lorenzino were even considered to fill this role. Nor, it would appear, was Giovanni delle Bande Nere, the celebrated condottiere who was descended from Lorenzo di Giovanni through his younger son, Giovanni il Popolano.

This was the state of affairs when a son was born on 11 June 1519 to Maria Salviati de' Medici, the pope's niece and a granddaughter of Lorenzo il Magnifico. The child was not only male but legitimate; moreover, among the Medici of the younger generation who might establish a new dynasty, he alone united the two branches of the family, for his father was Giovanni delle Bande Nere. As we shall see, a brief period followed during which the new heir may have been regarded as a hope for the Medici future. However, in December 1521, Leo died. Cardinal Giulio became head of the family, and his plans for its future did not include the son of Giovanni delle Bande Nere. When Giulio became pope in 1523, Giovanni was kept occupied in battle until he was finally killed in 1526, while Ippolito and Alessandro were sent to Florence to be groomed to rule. Alessandro eventually became the first duke of Florence after the last manifestation of the Republic in 1527-1530. During these years, Cosimo was hardly regarded as a candidate for the leadership of the family. Although he frequented his cousin Alessandro's court, he passed a relatively obscure childhood at Castello di Trebbio in the Mugello with his mother, and his assumption to power in January 1537 took place only because of a succession of unforeseen events: Ippolito's death in 1535, followed by the murder of Alessandro, and the disqualification of his murderer, Lorenzino de' Medici, as a candidate for the title of second duke of Florence.

This history has obscured the fact that the birth of Leo's grandnephew in 1519 was apparently greeted by the pope as an important event for the family. Immediately after the birth Maria Salviati saw to it that her uncle the pope was informed. A letter was

[28] On the Ippolito proposal, see Albertini, pp. 28-31, 360-64. Since it was Goro Gheri himself who made this suggestion to Leo, Winner, 1972, p. 186, believes that the laurel in Pontormo's portrait alludes to Ippolito. However, nothing came of Ippolito's candidacy, and the absence of any allusion to him in the portrait's imagery makes this reading unlikely.

sent to Giovanni delle Bande Nere in Rome telling him that "Madonna Maria vostra consorte ha partorito uno bello figlio maschio" (My lady Maria your spouse gave birth to a beautiful baby boy) and requesting that Leo be asked to stand as godfather to the child "con tutto el collegio de' Cardinali" (along with all the College of Cardinals).[29] According to an account by Giovanni Batista Tedaldi, secretary to Giovanni delle Bande Nere from 1522 to 1526, the pope accepted the sponsorship of the child "per suo proprio figliuolo" (as his own son), named his cousin Cardinal Luigi de' Rossi and Malatesta Baglioni as godparents, and directed that the baptism be made known.[30]

But the most significant indicator of Leo's interest in the new Medici heir was his programmatic naming of the child Cosimo, after Cosimo Pater Patriae—who was, according to Tedaldi's account, "il più savio, il più prudente, et il più valoroso huomo che sino alhora havessi havuto la Casa de' Medici (the wisest, most prudent, and most valorous man that until then the Medici house had ever had). Considering Leo's great esteem for Cosimo's memory and the fact that no Medici had borne the name since the Pater Patriae (excepting a Cosimino, who died at age five in 1459), the choice of the name was anything but a casual one. Moreover, the other Christian names that Leo gave the child, Giuliano and Romolo, were signals of Leo's expectations for him. Giuliano, of course, was the name of Leo's recently deceased brother, a direct descendant of Cosimo Pater Patriae. Romolo was one of Leo's own given names; moreover, its allusion to Romulus, the legendary founder of Rome, suggests that the new heir was seen by Leo as an instrument in his propaganda of Florence as a New Rome.[31] Thus, the child was baptized "Cosimo giuliano et Romolo"; celebrations followed, and there were bonfires in the hills which were interpreted as signals of the pope's "allegrezza."[32]

✳   ✳   ✳

Factors other than Cosimo's legitimacy, parentage, and timely birth may have contributed to Leo's happiness. The pope was an ardent believer in the power of fate. His *impresa* GLOVIS referred not only to the Return of Time but to the turn of the Wheel of Fortune. Moreover, according to Leo's intimate Pierio Valeriano, SVPERANDA OMNIS FORTVNA (All Fortune must be overcome) was one of the mottos used with his device of the yoke.[33] Wheels of Fortune also turned in Leo's ceremonial decorations. As described by

---

[29] See Appendix I.

[30] See Appendix I.

[31] Kliemann, 1976, p. 37.

[32] For Cosimo's baptismal record, see Appendix I. For an account of these events, see Mannucci, pp. 32-33: "Impercioche dicono, che, nato il Fanciullo, per allegrezza nel Muggello i suoi luoghi (ciò è il Trebbio) fecero fuochi: il Giogo dell'Alpi, & gli altri luoghi de' Medici sù la Montagna, quegli scoprendo da lungi, & non sapendo la cagione, li fecero grandi: la Romagna Fiorentina, veduti si gran fuochi di verso Firenze, senza saper altro, fè mag-

gior fuochi: Cesena, Faenza, Ravenna, & tutta la Romagna del Papa, vedendo i Fiorentini far sì gran fuochi, pensando, che Papa Leone, il quale era Fiorentino, havesse qualche grande allegrezza hauta, gli fece grandissimi. Si che dal Muggello in sino à Lidi del Mare Adriatico si fecer fuochi per cotal nascimento. Onde all'hora gran dir se ne fece. Et mostrò la riuscita, che ciò non fosse à caso."

[33] Valeriano, 1602, p. 747. The motto is from Virgil, *Aeneid*, v, 710. In the 1625 edition, pp. 648-49, the motto is given as OGNI FORTVNA PATIENTA VINCE.

Penni, a painting on the arch of the papal mint, which was part of the decorations for Leo's *possesso*, displayed a wheel held by Fortuna with the pope at its summit.[34]

> Nel tertio [octangulo] si vedeva la ruota della Fortuna, nella summità sua il Papa, ne altri dalli canti, ma la Fortuna, che la rota tenea ferma: et eravi sospeso un breve che in nome de la fortuna tal parole risonava: IMMOBILIS CONSISTO, QUIA TE SAPIENTEM SAPIENTUM PROTECTOREM IN VERTICE SENTIO.

> In the third [octagon] one could see Fortune's Wheel and at its top, the pope. There was no one else in the other corners but Fortune, who kept the wheel fixed: and above it was hung a short saying, which in the words of Fortune read: I STAND IMMOBILE, AS I PERCEIVE YOU, A WISE PROTECTOR OF THE WISE, ON THE SUMMIT OF THE WHEEL.

Leo's concern with Fortune was centered on numerology and on the fateful days of the week or month on which key events in his life occurred.[35] For example, Friday was the day which he apparently considered to be the most "felice" and "favorevole."[36] And the eleventh was the most propitious day of the month. Leo was born on 11 December 1475; he was captured at the Battle of Ravenna on 11 April 1512 (a nadir in his fortunes but also a turning point, and coincidentally the feast of Saint Leo); and he was elevated to the papacy on 11 March 1513. Leo arranged for ceremonial occasions of his pontificate to fall on the eleventh (as if by a coincidence of fate), the most splendid of which was his Lateran *possesso*. This event was postponed until 11 April 1513, which was the first anniversary of the Battle of Ravenna, the feast day of the saint whose name he had just assumed as pope, and the date on which his revered predecessor, Leo IV, had been crowned. One of the triumphal arches of the *apparato* celebrated the mystique of the number eleven. A picture of "molti astrologi con li loro libri, e astrolabii, et sphere" (many astrologers with their books and their astrolabes and their spheres) established an astrological frame of reference for the decoration, which included octagons representing the "octo undeci notabili" of Pope Leo.[37] Verses explained these eight notable elevens, which, in an extraordinary conflation of myth and reality, included the procession then underway:

> Undecima eduxit LEONEM lux candida in ordem.
> Et patribus sacris addidit undecima,

---

[34] Penni, p. 219. Another example is a door in the Sala di Costantino decorated with a Wheel of Fortune held by two lions (see Kliemann, 1972, fig. 20). The Wheel of Fortune appears in the manuscripts of Lorenzo and Piero di Lorenzo (pl. 7).

[35] White-Shearman, p. 212; Shearman, 1972, pp. 17-18, 84-88; and Winner, 1972, pp. 168, 190, n. 50.

[36] Shearman, 1972, p. 17, n. 107, quoting an account of Leo's election, which occurred on a Fri-

day. Leo subsequently made his *entrata* into Florence on Friday, 30 November 1515.

[37] Penni, pp. 228-29. The dates on which these events occurred, indicating that adjustment was necessary to claim that all of them fell on the eleventh, are as follows: Leo's birth (11 December 1475); Leo's elevation as cardinal (March 9, 1492); Leo's escape from Florence (9-11 November 1494); Leo's liberation at Ravenna (11 June 1512); Leo's escape to Mantua (June 4-13, 1512); Leo's entrance into Florence on the return of the Medici (14 Sep-

Undecima existi patriae confinibus exul,
  Hostibus es saevis captus in undecima.
Undecima exolvit nexus et Gallica vincla,
  Nativas sedes reddidit undecima.
Undecima et votis pastorem curia solum
  Te legit, et regnum firmat in undecima.
Undecimum vates numerum celebrate quotannis.
  Carminibus cultis lux sonet undecima.

The eleventh, a shining day, brought Leo forth into the world, and to the Sacred Fathers the eleventh added him. On the eleventh you went forth an exile from the borders of the fatherland: a captive midst savage enemies, on the eleventh. On the eleventh bondage passed away as did the Gallic chains, for the eleventh gave you back your native dwelling. On the eleventh the Curia elects, with prayers, you alone the Shepherd, and strengthens the realm on the eleventh. Ye bards celebrate yearly the number eleven; with elegant songs let the eleventh day resound.

Two years after this ephemeral celebration the Leonine lucky day was made permanent in Leo's art. With the exception of his birth and the *possesso*, all of Leo's "undici" were depicted in the frieze borders to the Petrine set of Raphael's tapestries. They are among the scenes chronicling the turns of Medici fortune between their exile in 1494 and Leo's elevation in 1513, such as those showing Cardinal Giovanni returning to Florence in 1512 (pl. 31) and the homage to the new pope. The eleven vertical borders of the tapestries depict complementary themes of Time and Change, their number itself possibly commenting on Leo's good fortune. The *Times of Day* (pl. 21) and The *Seasons* (pl. 22) are joined by The *Three Fates* (pl. 42), which also echoes the theme of the turn of Fortune's Wheel and of GLOVIS. This border (and its pendant *Seasons*) may be read as commenting on one of the unfortunate turns of fate in Leo's life—the pillage of the Palazzo Medici and the flight of the Medici (1494), which are represented in the horizontal border; but it may equally well be read as alluding to the central scene of the tapestry, the *Charge to Saint Peter*, as the Fates measure the life and destiny of the New Peter—Leo himself.

The manipulation of history that made Leo's *possesso* fall on the eleventh was unnecessary in connection with the next "undici" in Leo's life. For Cosimo de' Medici was not only born on the eleventh, but the date 11 June actually coincided with one of Leo's own special days: it was the feast of Saint Barnabas, the day on which Leo had been liberated at Ravenna in 1512.[38] This coincidence can only have persuaded Leo that the birth of Cosimo was a portent of good fortune, especially since it coincided with yet other propitious events such as the vigil of Pentecost, the new moon, and the summer

---

tember 1512); Leo's election as pope (11 March 1513); and Leo's Lateran procession (11 April 1513).

[38] See Penni, p. 228, describing the *undici*: "Et el dì sancto Barnaba, apostolo del mese di Giugno, per divino ajuto di Dio più che mondana opera

aciocke quello fussi suo vicario lo libero." See Appendix I for letters of 1541, which refer to Cosimo's birth on Saturday, 11 June, the feast of Saint Barnabas.

solstice. Moreover, it occured on Saturday—the day, Benedetto Varchi tells us, on which the Florentines believed all significant events in their history to have occurred.[39]

In view of the baptism of the new Medici Cosimo, Pope Leo's revival of interest in Saints Cosmas and Damian in 1519 cannot be seen as coincidental. In September, he reinstated at the Vatican the feast of the Cosmalia, which had been allowed to lapse since 1515.[40] Shortly thereafter, the two saints began to appear in Medici art. They are the subject of a small oil painting by Bacchiacca (pl. 43),[41] which is bound with a manuscript containing a list of cardinals created by Leo and a "Genealogia Medicea" dedicated to him by Pier Cattaci (pl. 44).[42] The date of the miniature is indicated by the disk on the right side of the tree inscribed with the name of the recently born heir: CHOSIMO. Indeed, Bacchiacca's painting may have been occasioned by the baptism of Cosimo. The tree between the saints must allude to the Medici family tree and the new branch sprouting next to the more youthful, active, and prominently placed saint (Cosmas?) to the New Cosimo.

At about the same time, the Medici saints made their first appearance in monumental art after the Medici restoration of 1512. In Michelangelo's plan for the *sepoltura di testa* of the New Sacristy (pl. 35), Cosmas and Damian were to accompany two images of renewal—the *Virgo lactans* and the *Resurrection*. We may speculate, then, that the saints too were conceived in relation to this theme, and that they refer to the Medici dynasty, to its founder Cosimo Pater Patriae, and to the child Cosimo—potential agent of dynastic regeneration.

Pontormo's portrait of Cosimo Pater Patriae belongs precisely to this moment, and it seems probable that Leo himself stood behind its commission. As in the New Sacristy and the Poggio a Caiano Salone, the actual commission was given by Cardinal Giulio, and the details were handled by lesser agents like Ottaviano. In the case of the portrait (if we can believe Vasari), this agent was Goro Gheri, who was in Giulio's entourage until early 1520.

The symbolism of the portrait, which has proved difficult to correlate with any other circumstances of the later Leonine years (such as the death of Giuliano) and which is also incompatible with Lorenzo's personal imagery, is perfectly comprehensible as a commission from Leo dating from late 1519 or early 1520. The unusual combination of images in the picture was invented to commemorate a specific occasion—the naming of the newborn Cosimo after Cosimo Pater Patriae.

✳   ✳   ✳

Pontormo's *Cosimo* belongs to the tradition of portraits of *uomini illustri*, or Famous Men, of which the most prominent series was in the *studiolo* of Federico da Montefeltro

---

[39] Discussing the expulsion of the Medici in 1527, Varchi, I, p. 183, notes: "e appunto era sabato, nel qual giorno crede il vulgo fiorentino che tutte vengano così le grazie come le disgrazie a Firenze."

[40] Gnoli, p. 121, gives disruption of the hunting season by the festival as the reason for the lapse.

[41] J. Shearman, "A Manuscript Illustrated by Bacchiacca," in *Studies in Late Medieval and Renaissance Painting in Honor of Millard Meiss*, ed. I. Lavin and J. Plummer, New York, 1977, I, pp. 399-402, also attributes the miniature to Bacchiacca, dating it late 1518 to early 1519.

[42] Laur. MS Palat. 225, f. 3v-4r; D'Ancona, no. 897.

at Mantua. The half-length format, the profile, the inscription, the prominence of the hands, and the stiff drapery folds suggest that Pontormo may have taken as his model Justus van Ghent's *Portrait of Vittorino da Feltre* (ca. 1473-1474) from this series (pl. 45).[43] A series closer to hand which might also have provided a model for Pontormo was the one in the old palace of the Medici, described by Vasari as "tutti quegli uomini famosi" (all those famous men), which was painted by Lorenzo de' Bicci for Giovanni, father of Cosimo.[44]

The connection of Pontormo's portrait with the *topos* of Famous Men clearly indicates that Cosimo is portrayed here as the ideal ancestor and as an exemplar. The nature of the image is emphasized by the derivation of the likeness and inscription from the posthumous medals of the Pater Patriae (pls. 23-24). The realism and certain facial characteristics of these medals (such as the sagging muscles of the cheeks, the drooping, slightly open mouth, the downward tilt of the end of the nose, and the circles of bulging flesh around the chin) suggest that they were taken from a death mask.[45] Long before Pontormo's time they had been used as a source for portraits of Cosimo. Indeed, in Botticelli's *Portrait of a Young Man* of ca. 1470-1474, a gilded *gesso* of one of the medals is held up as an *exemplum* by the unknown sitter.[46] Later, in the *Adoration of the Magi* (pl. 5), Botticelli adjusted the image of the medal to the ideal type of the elderly first Magus.[47] In the portrait we are here considering, Pontormo has transformed the same model into an ideal-ancestor portrait, in which the sagging and furrowed face of the portrait on the medals has been smoothed and tightened, while still retaining the dignity of age. This powerfully modeled profile, together with the inscription next to it, creates an aura of the distant past. At the same time, Cosimo is brought ambiguously into the realm of the living by the sharp illumination, the clash of the vibrant reds of his gown and cap, his tensely clasped hands, and the resurgent life of the laurel tree.

The symbolism of the laurel, the Virgilian quotation, and the inscription from the medal on Cosimo's throne make this ancestor-portrait of the Pater Patriae into a complex metaphor of dynastic continuity. The laurel, symbol of Medici virtue and renewal, had expressed the idea of dynasty in Botticelli's *Adoration*, where it symbolized the living Lorenzo-*lauro*. And in the device of the "broncone: PAR LE FUE REVERDIRA," it suggested that Piero would continue his father's rule. All these traditional meanings are to be read in the laurel of the portrait, but another aspect of this symbolism is especially pertinent to its message. After 1512, the laurel imagery of the Medici had become more complex and extended than it had been before their exile, as the notion of the regenerating tree

[43] Langedijk, p. 49; and Forster, 1971, pp. 67-68.

[44] Vasari, II, p. 50.

[45] On the unmistakable characteristics of fifteenth-century portraits based on death masks, see J. Schuyler, *Florentine Busts: Sculpted Portraiture in the Fifteenth Century*, New York, 1977, pp. 115-19.

[46] See Lightbown, II, cat. B. 22, pp. 33-35, for a summary of opinions on the date of this portrait in the Uffizi. The almost effaced inscription on the medal appears to have been that of Hill, no. 910.

[47] Vasari, III, p. 315, identifies the figure as Cosimo. See Hatfield, 1976, p. 74. One of the Cosimo medals may have served as the model for Quentin Massys' *Portrait of an Old Man* (Paris, Musée Jacquemart-André), as is argued by L. Silver, "Power and pelf: a new-found *Old Man* by Massys," *Simiolus*, 9, 1977, p. 70. Silver goes on to suggest that this work, which is signed and dated 1513, was intended to represent Cosimo and that it was a tribute to the new pope, Leo X.

was conflated with the idea of weather and seasonal change. We have seen the meta-morphosis of the dry tree of winter into the verdant spring laurel in the *Seasons* tapestry border (pl. 22); likewise, in Nardi's song for the *broncone* pageant of 1513, the weather— a metaphor of the political climate in Florence—changes as the dry laurel puts forth its new leaves:[48]

> Dopo la pioggia torna il Ciel sereno:
> Godi, Fiorenza, e fatti lieta ormai.
>
> After the rain the serene sky returns:
> Be joyful, Florence, and now be happy.

However, this imagery of the laurel, with its promise of immortality and its allusion to the return of the Golden Age of the first Lorenzo, had its darker side. For if the laurel could flourish under clear skies, it could also be destroyed by stormy weather. Poliziano had employed this metaphor in his poem of 1492 on the death of Lorenzo il Magnifico. Here, the laurel, supposedly immune to lightning, has been struck by it:[49]

> laurus impetu fulminis
> illa illa iacet subito,
> laurus omnium celebris,
> Musarum choris,
> nympharum choris. . . .
>
> The laurel struck suddenly by a thunderbolt lies there; the laurel, celebrated by choirs of all the Muses, by dances of all the nymphs.

And, in Reguleus' poem of 1515, Florentia asks Pope Leo for the protection of the laurel:[50]

> Redde, precor, Laurum, rogat hoc Florentia supplex:
> Sub Lauro cives fulmina nulla timent.
>
> Give back, I beg, the laurel, suppliant Florence asks this. Under the laurel, the citizens fear no bolts of lightning.

The conceit of the threatened laurel appears again at the time of the fatal illness of the younger Lorenzo in early 1519. Like Poliziano's tree, the Lorenzo-*lauro* is threatened by the natural forces of the cosmos, by time and the elements, which become metaphors of death. In "Ne la stagion," Ariosto's elegy lamenting the illness of Lorenzo, the very life of the laurel is in danger. The poet asks, "Come gli ha tolto il suo favore il Cielo?" (How did Heaven withdraw its favor from him?)[51] The storms, ice, and snow of winter are blamed for depriving the tree of its leaves. Similar imagery occurs in a poem entitled

---

[48] Grazzini, I, p. 135.

[49] This text is stanza 3 of "Quis dabit capiti meo aquam?" (F. Arnaldi et al., eds., *Poeti latini del Quattrocento*, Milan, 1964, p. 1058). It was set in 1492 by Heinrich Isaac as a motet in tribute to Lorenzo. For the image of the immunity to light-ning, see also *Le Stanze*, I, 4.

[50] *Laurentum*, p. 32.

[51] *Capitoli*, III, 34, in Ariosto, p. 172. For the complete text, see Appendix II.

"Trionfo del Lauro" by Guglielmo Angiolini. The tree, which has been struck down by lightning and lost its leaves, has now recovered:[52]

> Notate quel che mostra il Lauro degno,
> giá di fronde spogliato,
> ora dal destro lato
> lieto raccor' ogn'uom sotto'l suo segno:
> cosí quell' alto Legno,
> ch' è dal Ciel fulminato,
> stilla benigno a quelli il dolce mele,
> che pascevano altrui d'aceto e fele.

Note what the worthy laurel shows, the laurel once without leaves, the right side of which now happily comforts all men under its sign. Thus, that high branch that has been struck down by the lightning of the sky, benignly distills for them sweet honey—while others feed upon vinegar and gall.

And at the end of the poem, Florence once more enjoys its protection:

> Godi or, Fiorenza, all'ombra del tuo Lauro
> che ti copre, e difende
> collo Scudo che splende
> di gemme oriental legate in auro.

Be happy now, O Florence, in the shade of your laurel, which covers and defends you with its shield, shining in oriental gems set in gold.

The recovery of the damaged laurel may also be the metaphor of Pontormo's portrait. In general, with the exception of Attavante's miniature of Cardinal Leo with the laurel (pl. 17), the flourishing *broncone* depicted alone symbolized the continuation of the family after death or misfortune; but now, in Pontormo's picture, the two sides of the tree are shown, and they are contrasted. Like the laurel of Angiolini's poem, the left branch is damaged. This cut-off branch would allude to the death of Lorenzo. The green branch, on the other hand, would signify the dynastic continuity of the Medici house promised by the New Cosimo. It is the *laurus triumphalis* of Medici virtue, renewal, and immortality.

The meaning of the regenerating laurel in the picture is amplified by the scroll which is wound through its flourishing branch and by the motto written on it. This combination of images is familiar from Medici manuscripts and devices (pls. 7, 8, 15, 20), in which laurel branches are embellished with scrolls on which we read (with difficulty, as in Pontormo's portrait) mottos affirming Medici regeneration: LE TEMPS REVIENT and PAR LE FUE REVERDIRA. These mottos, couched in the language of chivalry popular in Lorenzo's circle, are replaced in the Cosimo portrait by a more pointed and specific affirmation of Medicean regeneration—the Virgilian line which announces the inevitable succession of the New Cosimo.

[52] Grazzini, I, pp. 143-45.

The last image to be considered in the painting is the inscription on the back of Cosimo's throne. It reflects the ancestor-portrait convention of the "engraved" name, which is more commonly found below the likeness on a stone ledge, as in the *Vittorino da Feltre*. However, the inscription COSM'. MEDICES. P.P.P. is quite superfluous as a label identifying the famous profile of the Pater Patriae; it must have been placed next to Cosimo's head primarily to indicate the significance of the name Cosimo in the message of the picture. Moreover, its form was precisely calculated, for the inscription does not repeat any known variant of Cosimo's name and title. The Signoria bestowed the title Pater Patriae on Cosimo posthumously, in March 1465; and by 1467 his tombslab in San Lorenzo was in place in front of the high altar, with the inscription COSMVS MEDICES HIC SITVS EST DECRETO PATER PATRIAE (Cosimo de' Medici is interred here, called Father of the Fatherland by a decree).[53] The title Pater Patriae, or rather the initials P. P. that stand for it, appears on the medals that were Pontormo's source for the likeness of Cosimo. One of these is inscribed COSMVS MEDICES. DECRETO PVBLICO. P. P. (Hill, no. 910; my pl. 24); the other is inscribed MAGNVS COSMVS MEDICES P P P (Hill, no. 909; my pl. 23). The commemorative nature of these medals suggests a date for them not long after the award of the Pater Patriae title. Indeed, about 1470, derivations from them begin to appear in paintings and in manuscripts, the most important of which is the Laurentian Aristotle manuscript that I have mentioned (pl. 41).[54] Its medallion of Cosimo (accompanied by Medici *stemme* with the seven *palle* that he used) reproduces the inscription of no. 910 but combines elements from both medals in the portrait likeness. I take it that no. 910 (the inscription on which refers to the award of Cosimo's title) is the earlier of the two medals, and that no. 909 was made subsequently. The inscription on no. 909 is, in fact, quite different: there is no reference to the public decree and a third P is added to those signifying Pater Patriae. This is the inscription that was adapted by Pontormo in the *Cosimo* portrait.

There has been considerable speculation on the meaning of the letters P P P. For G. F. Hill the letters on the medal might signify *Primus* [or *Princeps*] *Pater Patriae* or, possibly, a misunderstood Latin formula like the inscription PATER PATRIAE PROCONSUL which occurs on a medal by Cristoforo da Geremia of about 1468.[55] However, *primus* does not convince without a candidate for *secundus*; *princeps* is quite at odds with the way the Medici wished their role in Florence to be understood (not to mention the conflict in meaning that the word would set up with the assertion of "public liberty" on the reverse of the medal); and there is no evidence that Cosimo was ever called proconsul.

[53] Passavant, pp. 170-71.

[54] See n. 27, above. D'Ancona, no. 796, dates the manuscript 1464-1469 and attributes it to Francesco d'Antonio del Cherico; M. L. D'Ancona, "Francesco Rosselli," *Commentari*, 16, 1965, p. 61, dates it after Piero's death because of the medallion of Piero, attributing it to Roselli. I am grateful to Francis Ames-Lewis for the opinion, based on a study of Piero's manuscripts, that this work cannot be dated before 1470 and is thus not associable with Piero's patronage at all. There is a smaller (37mm) Cosimo medal which is identical (except for the spacing of the inscription) to the medallion in this manuscript (Washington, National Gallery of Art). Hill (no. 910 bis; Hill-Pollard, no. 247) believes it to be of later date. Other derivations in manuscripts are found in Laur. MS Plut. 84, 1, f. 3 (D'Ancona, no. 797); MS Plut. 77, 24, of ca. 1490 (D'Ancona, no. 893); and Vatican MS lat. 1789.

[55] Hill, no. 910 bis and no. 755, citing a medal with a bust of Constantine.

Sparrow, on the other hand, believes that the third P in the portrait (he does not consider the medal) is "a piece of inappropriate archeologizing" meaning *posuit*.[56] There is no evidence to support this expansion, and such an inscription would surely be more appropriate on a building or other work commissioned by Cosimo than on a medal or painting commemorating the man himself.

My contention is that the P P P of the medal does represent a significant epithet and that it is probably related to the association of Cosimo with Cicero. This parallel was mooted in Cosimo's lifetime.[57] It also occurs, at the time the medals were struck, in an elegy by Naldi in which Florentia (the same personification of the city who appears on the medals) mourns Cosimo's death and compares him with Cicero as Pater Patriae.[58] It was still current at the time of Pontormo's portrait when Giovio's program for Franciabigio's *Triumph of Cicero* (pl. 72) made a parallel between the triumph of Cicero on the Capitoline and Cosimo's return from exile; and, later, in his *Dialogo dell'imprese*, Giovio asserted that the Florentia seated over the yoke on the Cosimo medals alluded to Juvenal's words "Roma patrem patriae Ciceronem libera dixit" (a free Rome called Cicero Father of the Fatherland).[59]

Not only was the imagery of the Cosimo medals understood as alluding to Cicero but the letters P P P which appear on one of them had also been associated with Cicero. For example, in the *Illustrium imagines* by the antiquarian Andrea Fulvio (dedicated to Pope Leo in 1518) a woodcut depicts a coin representing Cicero with the inscription M.TVLLIVS C. P.P.P. (pl. 46).[60] It would thus seem clear that both the title Pater Patriae, abbreviated P P, and another title, abbreviated P P P, compared Cosimo to Cicero. Two of the Ps in this second epithet must also stand for Pater Patriae, but the expansion of the third P is less certain. One suggestion, deriving from the Cosimo-Cicero parallel, is that it stands for *parens*, in allusion to the title Parens Patriae—Ancestor (or founder) of the Fatherland, which Cicero received in 62 B.C., and the associations of which in antiquity match those of Pater Patriae.[61] This later title, too, was current at the time the Cosimo medals were struck. The epithet Parens Patriae is used in reference to Cosimo in another elegy by Naldi, "Ad Perum Medicem in obitu Magni Cosmi ejus Genitoris, qui vere dum vixit optimus Parens Patriae cognominatus fuit" (To Piero de' Medici on the death of his father Cosimo the Great who during his lifetime was truly named the best Founder

---

[56] Sparrow, p. 163.

[57] For the background on the Cosimo-Cicero parallel, see Winner, 1970, pp. 270-74; and Kliemann, 1976, pp. 25-34.

[58] Naldi, *Elegiarum*, bk. III, no. 11 ("Eulogium in Cosmum Medicen patrem Patriae"), lines 369-82:

Ast ego, quae nullis astringor legibus usquam,
Libertas monitis cui data, Cosme, tuis,
Ipsa quidem tali semper dignabor honore
De te quae restant maxima facta, pater,
Temporibus priscis quali dignatus honore
Etrusca nullus civis in urbe fuit,
Denique vel qualem Ciceroni Roma togato

Libera vix uni praebuit una viro.
Namque pater patriae Tusca vocitaberis urbe,
Libera dum populis iura petita dabo.
Haec tibi, dum magnum radiis sol circuet
    orbem,
Constabunt titulis nomina iuncta tuis,
Hace tibi non fatum, non invidiosa vetustus,
Non tibi longa licet auferat ulla dies.

[59] Giovio, 1556, pp. 25-26.

[60] Fulvio, f. 9v.

[61] S. Weinstock, *Divus Julius*, Oxford, 1971, p. 202. The title was later held by Caesar and others (Weinstock, pp. 202-5).

of the Fatherland).⁶² Given the currency of the two epithets, each of which had been used in reference to Cicero and to Cosimo, it is likely that the letters P P P represent some combination of the two; and, while no entirely satisfactory expansion can be put forward, there are two reasonable possibilities: PATER PATRIAE PARENS and PATER PARENSQVE PATRIAE, the latter explicitly and the former implicitly meaning "Father and Founder (or ancestor) of the Fatherland."⁶³ Such a title would emphasize the role of the dead Cosimo as founder as well as father of Florence and would certainly be in keeping with the meaning of the medal as I have understood it.⁶⁴

The inscription COSM'. MEDICES. P.P.P. in Pontormo's portrait may have been adapted from the medal with just such a reading in mind, the allusion to the ideas of both the ancestor and the father suggesting (in the dynastic context of the painting) that Cosimo was not only founder and father of Florence but of the Medici family as well. The epithet MAGNVS which is inscribed on the medal has been dropped, possibly in order to stress the importance of the given name, Cosimo, in the message of the picture. Finally, as if to emphasize the fact that this inscription is no mere label, its letters have been arranged in an inverted triangle reminiscent of the usual 3-2-1 pattern of the *palle* or (even more striking because it consists only of letters) of the *impresa* GLOVIS, alluding to the turn of Medici fortunes. The name itself has been contracted to COSM'. MEDICES. Its letters, thus spelled, add up to eleven—Leo's lucky number and the day of the month on which the New Cosimo was born.⁶⁵

⁶² Naldi, in Roscoe, III, p. xli.

⁶³ I am grateful to Virginia Brown for advice on the expansion of this inscription. She points out that neither expansion is grammatically exact, since the "QVE" of PARENSQVE would normally be indicated by the letter Q, while in the other expansion the word PARENS is problematic, since it is unusual for *parens* to stand without some modifiers in the genitive. Thus, for example, in Mantegna's *Triumphs of Caesar*, the titles are given on two banners: one is IVLIVS CAESAR P.M. [*Pontifex Maximus*]; the other is DIVO IVLIO CAESARI D.P.P.P., which may be expanded *Dictatori perpetuo patri* [or *parenti*] *patriae*, or *Decreto publico patri* [or *parenti*] *patriae*.

⁶⁴ The Cosimo medal is not the only Medicean

medal of this period in which another letter was added to the P P signifying Pater Patriae. See the pair of commemorative medals of Cosimo's sons Giovanni and Piero which were struck after Piero's death (Hill, nos, 907-8; my pl. 40). These are inscribed PETRVS MEDICES COSMI P P F (*Patris Patriae Filius*) and IOHANNES MEDICES COSMI P P F, identifying Piero and Giovanni as sons of Cosimo Pater Patriae.

⁶⁵ An analogous inscription with a cryptic meaning is the "nomogram" in Ridolfo Ghirlandaio's portrait of *Cosimo de' Medici at Age Twelve*, in which the number of the letters indicates Cosimo's age (see chap. 10 and pl. 159).

II
Imagery of Dynasty and Time at Poggio a Caiano (1490-1582)

Pontormo's fresco of *Vertumnus and Pomona* in the Salone of the Medici villa at Poggio a Caiano (color pl. 2) is closely related in theme to his *Portrait of Cosimo de' Medici Pater Patriae* (color pl. 1), and its flourishing laurel also alludes to the dynastic continuity of the Medici made possible again after the birth of the Medici heir Cosimo in 1519. But the allusions in the fresco to dynastic themes are more profound and complex than those of the portrait. Moreover, it must be read in the context of the other decorations of Lorenzo il Magnifico's villa, which span almost a century: the frieze on the portico (ca. 1490), which its imagery pointedly recalls;[1] the frescos in the Salone by Andrea del Sarto and Franciabigio, which were also painted for Leo X; and the completion of the decoration in the early 1580s by Alessandro Allori. All these decorations elaborate on themes of Dynasty, Time, and the Medici Golden Age; and these themes are set against imagery of nature and the cosmos, which are treated as metaphors of Medici immortality.

[1] Much of the material in chapter 3 is included in my article, "Themes of Time and Rule at Poggio a Caiano: The Portico Frieze of Lorenzo il Magnifico" (see Cox-Rearick, 1982).

The Portico Frieze of Lorenzo il Magnifico

The villa at Poggio a Caiano was begun after 1485 and completed only in the late sixteenth century. Designed by Giuliano da Sangallo, it was constructed on the site of a farm which had been acquired by Lorenzo il Magnifico in 1474.[1] In his poem *Ambra* (the introduction to which is dated 5 November 1485), Poliziano praises the site of the projected villa on the river Umbro:[2]

> Quem super, aeternum staturae culmina villae
> Erigis haudquaquam muris cessura cyclopum,
> (Macte opibus, macte ingenio) mea gloria Laurens,
> Gloria musarum Laurens . . .

> Above which river, ever flowing, you, my glory, Lorenzo—Lorenzo, glory of the Muses, erect the roofs of your villa that is to be, which by no means will yield to the walls of the Cyclops. Success attend your effort, success attend your plan.

And, although a letter written by Donato Giannotti in 1533 suggests that the villa was begun in 1490,[3] considerable work must have been done earlier. An undated letter by Michele Verino (who died in May 1487) states that the walls are not yet built but the

---

[1] F. W. Kent, "Lorenzo de' Medici's Acquisition of Poggio a Caiano and an early reference to his Architectural Expertise," *JWCI*, 42, 1979, pp. 250-57. Vasari, IV, pp. 270-71, implies that there was a competition for the commission for the villa and that Giuliano won on the basis of his *modello*. On the early history of the farm, see P. Foster, "Lorenzo de' Medici's Cascina at Poggio a Caiano," *Mitt.KHIF*, 26, 1969, pp. 47-52; and Foster, I, pp. 87-107.

[2] *Ambra*, lines 596-600, in Poliziano, *Le Selve*, p. 106.

[3] Giannotti, p. 1578: "Queli che edificò il palazzo fu Lorenzo de' Medici. . . . D'èttegli principio nel 1490 a dì 12 luglio, ad ore nove." The importance of this letter was pointed out by D. R. Coffin, rev. of Foster, *Burl.*, 123, 1980, p. 350.

foundations have been laid, and the diarist Luca Landucci writes that in 1489, "Lorenzo de' Medici cominciò un palagio al Poggio a Caiano, al luogo suo, dove à ordinato tante belle cose" (Lorenzo de' Medici began a palace at Poggio a Caiano, on his estate, where he has ordered many beautiful things).[4] However, when Lorenzo died on 8 April 1492, the villa was not finished, and presumably all work on it ceased with the Medici expulsion from Florence in late 1494. There is ample contemporary evidence to attest to this state of affairs, including a letter written by Ugolino Verino after Lorenzo's death in which he states that the building was not complete.[5] Moreover, a tax report made by Lorenzo's heirs in 1495 indicates that only a third of the villa was "fornito."[6] This document is of great importance for the building history of the villa, for the third which had been finished can only have been the front section of the building. The two blocks of rooms necessary for the support of the great barrel vault of the central Salone—hence the vault itself—cannot then have been completed in Lorenzo's lifetime.[7]

Unlike the family villas at Careggi and Castello, which Lorenzo had inherited, the

[4] Landucci, pp. 58-59. For Verino's "Epistola ad Simonem Canisianum," see *Michaelis Verini Epistole*, Laur. MS Plut. 90 sup., 28, f. 39r: "Moles nondum structa, sed iacta sunt fundamenta." This letter is published in G. Targioni-Tozzetti, *Relazioni d'alcuni viaggi fatti in diverse parti della Toscana*, Florence, 1773, V, pp. 58-60. See also Cristoforo Landino's commentary on Virgil of early 1488, which refers to the villa as built. Landino, f. 46r: 'Nam et villam ita aedificavit ut excluso regio nimioque luxu et urbanos honorificentissime recipiat: et rusticanos commodissime tueatur." (For he built also his villa in such a way that, having eschewed royal and excessive splendor, he could entertain people from the city in an eminently suitable manner and gaze upon his country neighbors quite comfortably.) For the complete passage, see Kliemann, 1976, pp. 155-56.

[5] *Epigrammata* (Laur. MS Plut. 39, 40, f. 38v-39v; cited by Kliemann, 1976, pp. 152-53). For the unfinished state of the villa, see also Guicciardini, II, p. 331: "Lorenzo cominciò al Poggio a Caiano una muraglia suntuosissima e non la finí prevenuto dalla morte"; and M. Parenti, *Istorie*, BNF, MS II. IV. 169, f. 15r, who states that one of Lorenzo's last three wishes was "d'aver . . . finite le loggie allo edificio suo del Poggio." However, modern critical opinion differs as to exactly what was left incomplete. Chastel, 1961, p. 152, believes that the upper story was not finished; Winner, 1970, p. 261, that only the foundation was built; and Hersey, p. 185, suggests that the portico "may be an afterthought or a later addition."

[6] Foster, I, pp. 113-16, citing ASF, *Decima Repubblica 28 (Campione, San Giovanni, Lion D'Oro, 1498, M-Z,* f. 457v): "Pogg[i]o a Chaiano chon sue

apartenenza. Uno chasamento o vero palag[i]o il quale, sechondo il modello fatto, è fornito la 3ª parte e l'altre dua parte è fatti i fondamenti tutti e parte delle mura, chon logge e portichi atorno e ringhiera e schale fuori; e il chasamento che si chiama l'Ambra è parte rovinato e disfatto. Il detto è posto in sul Pog[i]o a chiano, popolo di S. Maria a Bonistallo, chon certe terre atorno, a primo la strada, 2° Onbrone, 3° 4° via, 5° beni de' dette redi, [in the margin to left: dassigli per suo uso]." I am grateful to Gino Corti for retranscribing this document for me.

[7] There were models for the building, however; besides Giuliano's original *modello* for his patron, there was a second model, mentioned in a letter of 5 October 1492 from Piero di Lorenzo to Ludovico Sforza, which refers to "uno modello della casa che la b[uo]na me[moria] di mio padre murava al Poggio," concluding, "Havrei voluto potere mandarli lo edificio proprio non solam[en]te questo di legno." For the text see L. H. Heydenreich, "Giuliano da Sangallo in Vigevano, ein neues Dokument," *Scritti di storia dell'arte in onore di Ugo Procacci*, Milan, 1977, II, pp. 321-22. I am indebted to Beverly Brown, whose researches confirm Foster's conclusion and who further points out that the models for the Poggio a Caiano Salone were used for the similar barrel-vaulted Salone constructed in the Villa Tovaglia in Florence ca. 1495-1500 (B. L. Brown, "Leonardo and the Tale of Three Villas: Poggio a Caiano, the Villa Tovaglia in Florence, and Poggio Reale in Mantua," *Atti del Convegno di Firenze e la Toscana dei Medici nell'Europa del Cinquecento*, Florence, 1980 (forthcoming).

villa at Poggio a Caiano was his own creation—designed, according to Vasari, "secondo il capriccio di Lorenzo" (to Lorenzo's fancy).[8] A harmonious building, set on a terrace high above the surrounding farmland and gardens, the villa is *all'antica* in the humanist tradition, perfectly fulfilling Alberti's requirements for the ideal country residence.[9]

The major external architectural feature of the villa is a neoclassical temple-front portico, which is reached by way of a double staircase from ground level.[10] This portico was elaborately decorated in Lorenzo's time (pl. 49). In the pediment a large, beribboned *stemma* with the *palle* identifies the Medici as the owners of the villa.[11] The decoration of the barrel vault of the loggia further emphasizes the ownership of the building (pl. 47). It is covered with blue and white glazed terracotta tiles arranged in a strongly articulated design of circles within squares similar to those of Sangallo's vaults in the antesacristy of Santo Spirito and the courtyard of Palazzo Scala. These circles contain Medici *imprese*: in the center are the *palle*; to the sides are the three interlaced *diamanti* with feathers and motifs inspired from the antique; and in each of the circles containing these devices are inset *bronconi*. On the east wall of the loggia is Filippino Lippi's damaged *Sacrifice of the Laocoön*. It is the only remaining part of the fresco decoration of the loggia, which was commissioned by Lorenzo, abandoned in 1494, and not taken up when work resumed at the villa after the return of the Medici in 1512.[12] This representation of Laocoön, a priest of Apollo, was perhaps planned as one of a pair, with a *Death of Laocoön* on the west wall of the loggia.[13] In any case, it may allude to the familiar identification of Lorenzo with Apollo, and it certainly gives a clear indication of his intention to decorate his villa with scenes *all'antica*.

The most important figural decoration of the portico is its frieze. This work, which was removed from the portico in 1967 and is now stored in pieces in the villa, consists of glazed terracotta tiles fitted together to form five panels, which are separated by four terms over the axes of the portico columns. There are many small lacunae where tiles have been broken, and the third term is missing. The figures are white and the background is bright blue, with the exception of the green backgrounds of the cavern in the

[8] Vasari, IV, p. 271. For Lorenzo's letter to Niccolò Michelozzi of September 1485, in which he writes "Ricorda a Giuliano da Sangallo che espedisca el modello mio," and the possibility that the model was connected with Poggio a Caiano, see M. Martelli, "I pensieri architettonici del Magnifico," *Commentari*, 17, 1966, pp. 107-11.

[9] On the character of the architecture see Hamberg, pp. 76-87; Chastel, 1961, pp. 151-56; Hersey, pp. 184-85; and Foster, I, pp. 108-67.

[10] For the facade before later additions, see Vasari's vignette of 1559 in the Sala di Cosimo in the Palazzo Vecchio, *The Arrival of Eleonora da Toledo at Poggio a Caiano* (1539). See also the lunette by Giusto Utens of 1599 (Museo Topografico) and a drawing attributed to Tribolo (Uffizi 1640A; see Marchini, pl. IIa).

[11] The 3-2-1 arrangement of the *palle* occurs in Lorenzo's time, but the curved shape of the shield and its split, curling upper edge suggest that this *stemma* dates after 1512. Cf. the *stemme* in the *Canzone pallesca* of 1512, Feltrini's drawing of 1513 for the arms of Leo X (Louvre 11159), and the *stemma* in Granacci's drawing of 1515 (Uffizi 17340orn.) for the Villa Salviati.

[12] The artist had died in 1504. The work is mentioned as unfinished by Vasari, VII, p. 4; however, the copy attributed to the Maestro di Serumido (London, Private Collection; see F. Zeri, "Eccentrici fiorentini—II: Antonio di Donnino Mazziere," *Boll. d'A.*, 47, 1962, pp. 321-22) suggests that the lower part of the composition had been completed by Lippi.

[13] Winner, 1974, pp. 83-89; and Foster, I, pp. 155-57.

first panel and the mountain in the second panel. The only other color accents are the violet and green of the panels of the temple doors in the central scene and details picked out in yellow, such as the borders of draperies, the decorations on the soldiers' costumes, the bees, fruits and flowers, and the narrow borders along the top and bottom of the work.

Traditionally ascribed to the circle of the della Robbia, the design of the frieze—its execution is due to several hands—has been attributed to Sangallo himself, to Andrea Sansovino under his direction,[14] and, most convincingly, to Lorenzo's intimate, Bertoldo di Giovanni, who died at Poggio a Caiano in December 1491.[15]

THE FRIEZE AS AN ALLEGORY OF TIME

There is general agreement that the mode *all'antica* of the frieze evokes the same ideals that inform the neoclassical architecture of the villa itself, but there has been no consensus on its meaning and the work has been characterized as enigmatic and obscure.[16] However, it has been recognized that the major theme of the frieze is Time and that its imagery is drawn from a number of ancient texts, among which the poetry of Ovid (especially the *Fasti*) and Claudian predominates.[17]

[14] For the attribution to the della Robbia and the date ca. 1490, see Welliver, 1957, p. 238; for that to Sangallo, see W. Stechow, "Zum plastichen Werk des Giuliano da Sangallo," *Italienische Studien, Paul Schubring zum 60. Geburtstag Gewidemt*, Leipzig, 1929, pp. 140-41; and, for the attribution to Sansovino and a date ca. 1485, see U. Middeldorf, "Giuliano da Sangallo and Andrea Sansovino," *Art Bull.*, 16, 1934, pp. 112-15; Chastel, 1961, pp. 155, 218, with a date ca. 1490; P. Sanpaolesi, "La Casa fiorentina di Bartolommeo Scala," *Studien zur Toskanischen Kunst: Festschrift für Ludwig Heinrich Heydenreich zum 23 März 1963*, Munich, 1964, p. 286; and A. Paolucci, in Berti, 1980, cat. 485-87.

[15] I am grateful to Sir John Pope-Hennessy for discussing his attribution with me (also cited by Foster, I, p. 472, n. 499). For Bertoldo's position in Lorenzo's household and his affinity with Lorenzo's taste, see W. von Bode, *Bertoldo und Lorenzo dei Medici: Die Kunstplastik des Lorenzo il Magnifico im Spiegel der Werke seines Liblings-kunstlers Bertoldo di Giovanni*, Freiburg, 1935, pp. 7-14. Bertoldo has been established as the author of the neoclassical stucco frieze in the house of Bartolommeo Scala (1479), which depends in letter and spirit on antiquities in Lorenzo's collection (see Chastel, 1961, p. 277; and A. Parronchi, "The Language

of Humanism and the Language of Sculpture: Bertoldo as Illustrator of the *Apologi* of Bartolommeo Scala," *JWCI*, 27, 1964, pp. 108-38). While the style of the two friezes is quite different, it is plausible that Bertoldo could also have designed the frieze for Lorenzo's villa—another neoclassical building by Sangallo.

[16] As by Seznec, p. 116, who recognized: "Apollo and Diana in their chariot, Eternity in her cavern, with souls emerging from her breast; Janus on the threshold of the temple of war. But other scenes have defied explanation, and the meaning of the composition as a whole has not been deciphered. The artist, unquestionably following a program furnished again by Politian or by some other humanist in Lorenzo's court, was evidently charged with concealing in this work some momentous secret from the wisdom of the ancients. He succeeded only too well in his task."

[17] For the most satisfactory reading, see Chastel, 1961, pp. 218-25. Chastel and Welliver, 1957, pp. 238-39, give credit to Ulrich Middeldorf for the identification of the texts. The dependence on Claudian (also a source for Poliziano's *Stanze* and Botticelli's *Primavera*) may be due to the belief, held by Poliziano, that Claudian was a Florentine (Chastel, 1961, p. 84). Petrarch had claimed Claudian as Florentine on the basis of the dedication of

The first panel is perhaps the most enigmatic (pl. 51). It is based on Claudian's account in *De Consulatu Stilichonis* of Nature in the Cavern of Eternity, the beginnings of the rule of the heavens over human destiny, and Phoebus' choice from among the Four Ages of the Golden Age for the term of the consul, Stilicho.[18] This story was adapted by Boccaccio in *Della Genealogia de gli Dei*, and it also appears in Cartari's *Imagine de i Dei*, the illustration to which is a somewhat more literal interpretation of Claudian's account than that of the frieze (pl. 50).[19]

Since the frieze panel by no means reflects Claudian's text exactly—and all its features except Nature have been variously identified—it will be useful to quote Claudian *in extenso*:

> There is a like joy in heaven . . . the Sun himself, decking his chariot with spring flowers, prepares a year worthy of thee [Stilicho].
>
> Far away, all unknown, beyond the range of mortal minds, scarce to be approached by the gods, is a cavern of immense age, hoary mother of the years, her vast breast at once the cradle and tomb of time. A serpent surrounds this cave, engulfing everything with slow but all–devouring jaws; never ceases the glint of his green scales. His mouth devours the back-bending tail as with silent movement he traces his own beginning. Before the entrance sits Nature, guardian of the threshold, of age immense yet ever lovely, around whom throng and flit spirits on every side. A venerable old man writes down immutable laws: he fixes the number of stars in each constellation and causes these to move and those to be at rest, whereby everything lives or dies by preordained laws. 'Tis he decides Mars' uncertain orbit, Jupiter's fixed course through the heaven, the swift path of the moon, and the slow march of Saturn; he limits the wanderings of Venus' bright chariot and of Mercury, Phoebus' companion.
>
> When the Sun rested upon the spacious threshold of this cavern dame Nature ran to meet him and the old man bent a hoary head before his proud rays. The adamantine door swung open of its own accord and revealed the vast interior, displaying the house and the secrets of Time. Here in their appointed places dwell the ages, their aspect marked by varying metals: there are piled those of brass; here those of iron stand stiff; there the silver ones gleam bright. In a fairer part of the cave, shy of contact with the earth, stood the group of golden years; of these Phoebus chooses the one of richest substance to be marked with the name of Stilicho. Then, bidding the rest follow behind him, he addresses them thus as they pass. "Lo! the consul is at hand

De raptu proserpinae to a certain Florentinus, a belief that was restated by Boccaccio, Villani, and Salutati (cf. the epigram formerly in the Palazzo Vecchio including him with the Florentine poets, cited by Hankey, p. 364). On the Florentines and Claudian, see A. Cameron, *Claudian: Poetry and Propaganda at the court of Honorius*, Oxford, 1970,

p. 426.

[18] *De Consulatu Stilichonis*, II, 426-57 (cited as the source for this panel by Tervarent, 1960, p. 308; and Chastel, 1961, pp. 223-24).

[19] The story was first illustrated by Cartari, 1571, p. 35, with a text translating Claudian, pp. 18-22. My illustration is taken from Cartari, 1674.

for whom we have delayed an age of nobler ore. Go ye, years long prayed for by man, bring back virtue; let genius flourish once more; may Bacchus give you joy and fruitful Ceres bless you."

Phoebus then bids Spring and Autumn, ruled by the zodiac signs of Aries and Virgo, to attend the Golden Age. The poet concludes:

> So saying he [Phoebus] entered his garden starred with fiery dew, the valley round which runs a river of flame feeding with its bounteous rays the dripping weeds whereon the horses of the sun do pasture. Here he gathers fragrant flowers wherewith he decks the heads, the golden reins, and manes of his steeds. With leaves from hence Lucifer and Aurora entwine their oozy locks. Hard by the golden year, displaying the consul's name, smiles upon his chariot, and the stars, recommencing their courses, inscribe the name of Stilicho in the annals of the sky.

It is immediately clear that the major episode which Claudian describes and Cartari illustrates is not represented here, for there is no meeting of Nature and Phoebus at the threshold of the cavern. The scene is set inside the Cavern of Eternity, so identified by the snake eating its tail, the symbol of eternity as described by Claudian. At the center of the panel is Nature giving birth to souls, who are depicted as twelve putti flying out from her. To the right of the panel, outside the cave against a blue background, is a nude youth with an astronomer's armillary sphere (on which can be clearly read the meridians and the band of the ecliptic) and a compass, which he holds up to the heavens.[20] He must refer to Claudian's description of the "immutable laws" of the stars and the planets.[21] His counterpart at the left side of the panel is an old man holding snakes, who is recessed more deeply into the cave than the other figures. He is not Claudian's "venerable old man," whose functions have been assimilated to the youth; rather, he has been understood, probably rightly, as a kind of demonic figure, possibly signifying Chaos.[22]

The first panel, then, represents *Eternity*. But implicit in the scene is the imminent birth of Time. The ages, years, seasons, and months (zodiac signs) are all mentioned by Claudian. Moreover, in Boccaccio's commentary on Claudian's account, which reads like a schema for the rest of the frieze, the units of time are explicitly laid out. He states that the numbers of the stars are divided so that we can distinguish time by sidereal motion: " . . . si come per lo circuito del sole per tutto il Cielo, habbiamo l'anno intero, et per l'istessa circonvolotione della luna, il mese, et per l'intera rivolutione dell'ottava

[20] This figure has been variously identified. Chastel, 1961, p. 224, calls him a demiurge; Wright, II, p. 237, calls him Apollo.

[21] For the astrological intention of Claudian's lines (432-40) and his allusion to the "immutable law of human destiny," see W. H. Semple, "Notes on Some Astrological Passages in Claudian," *Classical Quarterly*, 31, 1937, pp. 164-67. Both Tervarent,

1960, p. 308; and Chastel, 1961, p. 224, are of the opinion that the function of Claudian's old man has been assigned to the youth (whomever he may represent).

[22] For Chastel, 1961, p. 224, he is a demon of possible Etruscan origin; for Wright, II, p. 738, he may be the Fury of War of the Iron Age; and for Winner, 1974, p. 95, he is Laocoön.

sfera, il giorno" (from the orbit of the sun in the sky, we have the whole year, and from the circumvolution of the moon, the month, and from the revolution of the eighth sphere, the day).²³ The first panel thus establishes the theme of the rulership of the heavens over human destiny, as well as the theme of the Cycles of Time, the smaller and smaller units of which—the Age, the Year, the Season, the Month, the Day, and the Hour—are depicted in the remaining four panels of the frieze.

The second panel shows the *Birth of the Age of Jupiter* (pl. 52). It is separated from the first panel by a term (Perseus?) holding a Medusa-head and a sack over his shoulders. The scene is based on the *Fasti*.²⁴ To the left we see Saturn, his legs bound by the traditional woolen shackle, as he is described by Poliziano in *Ambra*.²⁵ He devours his children, but Rhea saves Jupiter from Saturn by substituting a stone for the child; to the right, the goat Amalthea and the bees produce the milk and honey that nourish the infant, while the noise of the Corybantes prevents the discovery of the ruse.

The third, or central panel, is introduced by a Mars-term wearing a helmet and carrying a baton. This panel is dedicated to the year and may be titled the *Birth of the Year* (pl. 53). To the left of the temple door at the center of the panel stands Janus, god of January and of all beginnings (pl. 56). He is the double-faced god of the *Fasti*, who looks both forward and backward in time as he begins the year:²⁶

> Iane biceps, anni tacite labentis origo

> Two-headed Janus, opener of the softly gliding year.

Indeed, Ovid's Janus is a cosmological god in whose hands rests the guardianship of the universe itself; and, according to Macrobius in the *Saturnalia*, Janus is to be equated with the heavens, "always in motion, wheeling in a circle and returning to itself at the point where it began."²⁷ Janus is also the god of portals. Placed over the doorway to Lorenzo's villa, he is Ovid's house-god, who looks across the frieze to east and west: ". . . and just as your human porter, seated at the threshold of the house-door, sees who goes out and in, so I, the porter of the heavenly court, behold at once both East and West."²⁸ Janus is thus the key character in establishing the theme of the Cycles of Time in the frieze, the figure around which the two sides of the composition may be seen to balance, or turn, and the figure who sets into motion the continuous, eternal Cycles of Time.

It has naturally been assumed that the temple at the doorway of which the god stands is the Janus-temple of peace, the doors of which open in time of war, and that the

²³ Boccaccio, p. 7.

²⁴ *Fasti*, IV, 195-214. See Tervarent, 1960, p. 315, n. 6, for other texts relating to this story.

²⁵ *Ambra*, lines 56-57 (*Le Selve*, pp. 74-75): "At Saturnum lanea compes / Mulcibero jubet ire parem" (But the woolen shackle compels Saturn to go at the same pace as Vulcan).

²⁶ *Fasti*, I, 65.

²⁷ *Saturnalia*, I, 9, 11. Much of the long section of the *Fasti* (I, 63-294) dedicated to Janus is cast as

a speech, in which he states his guardianship of the universe (lines 117-20): "Whate'er you see anywhere—sky, sea, clouds, earth—all things are closed and opened by my hand. The guardianship of this vast universe is in my hands alone, and none but me may rule the wheeling pole."

²⁸ *Fasti*, I, 137-40. See also II, 51: "For the month of Janus came first because the door (*janua*) comes first." The frieze is not oriented precisely to east-west, but southeast-northwest.

armed Mars who emerges from it prepares for war.[29] However, it has not been explained how such a motif could be reconciled with the theme of the Cycles of Time. Janus is, indeed, the traditional guardian of the temple of war and peace; however, in this role, he always holds the keys to its doors. There are no keys here (nor any lock on the door). Rather, the god uses both hands to count the days of the year, in the manner described by Pliny and, later, by Poliziano.[30] The Janus of the frieze, then, is to be understood as a god of the Cycles of Time, especially the year, which he opens, and the month of January, to which he lends his name.

If Janus stands for January, perhaps the puzzling presence of the god of war at the center of Lorenzo's frieze can be explained by the fact that Mars, too, was traditionally related to the cycle of the year and that, in this role, he could signify the end rather than the beginning of war. For Mars was the Roman deity after whom the first month of the old calendar was named and the god of the renewal of the year in spring.[31] This Mars, god of spring and peace, appears in the two poems on which the imagery of the frieze most closely depends. In *De Consulatu Stilichonis*, Mars *gradivus* is a god of peace;[32] and in the *Fasti* his roles as god of peace and deity of spring, whose feast is celebrated on the Kalendae Martiae, are conflated.[33] Ovid has Mars explain the nature of his feast:[34]

> Thus I inquired, and thus did Mars answer me, laying aside his helmet, though in his right hand he kept his throwing spear: "Now for the first time in the year am I, a god of war, invoked to promote the pursuits of peace, and I march into new camps, nor does it irk me to do so; upon this function also do I love to dwell, lest Minerva should fancy that such power is hers alone."

An armed Mars as Spring was a conventional type in ancient art.[35] And, in the art of

[29] For Chastel, 1961, p. 221, "la frise de Poggio représente le moment où le prête de Janus ouvre la porte fatale d'où sort Mars férocement armé." Chastel cites *Aeneid*, VII, 611-14, as the source for this scene: ". . . there are twin gates of War (so men call them), hallowed by religious awe and the terrors of fierce Mars: a hundred brazen bolts close them, and the eternal strength of iron, and Janus their guardian never quits the threshold." For Welliver, 1957, p. 240, Mars is partly in the world of war and partly in the temple of peace. Terva-rent, 1960, p. 309, titles the scene "The Temple of Janus Opens for War."

[30] Pliny, *Naturalis historia*, XXXIV, xvi, 33, describing a statue of Janus *pater*. See also Macrobius, *Saturnalia*, I, 9, 9: "an image of Janus commonly shows him expressing the number three hundred with his right hand and sixty-five with his left." For Poliziano's Janus see *Ambra*, lines 55-56 (*Le Selve*, p. 74): "Claviger in semet redeuntem computat annum / Jam dextra deus" (The key-bearing god reckons now with his right hand the year returning upon itself).

[31] For the old Roman calendar, see Ovid, *Fasti*, I, 27-44; III, 1-166; also Scullard, pp. 69-84. *Fasti*, III, 3-4: ". . . thou mayest ask, What has a poet to do with Mars? From thee the month of which I now sing doth takes its name." For Mars as god of the renewal of the year, see Scullard, pp. 84-87.

[32] *De Consulatu Stilichonis*, II, 367-70: "Thus Mars, returning victorious from the Danube or the Scythian clime, a god of peace now his shield is laid aside, enters the city wearing the consul's cloak and in a chariot drawn by white horses."

[33] Ovid, *Fasti*, III, 237-40 (Kalendae Martiae), gives the following description of the season: "Moreover, frosty winter then at last retires, and the snows perish, melted by the warm sun; the leaves, shorn by the cold, return to the trees, and moist within the tender shoot the bud doth swell; now too the rank grass, long hidden, discovers secret paths whereby to lift its head in air."

[34] *Fasti*, III, 173-76; cf. also III, 5-6.

[35] Levi, pp. 257-58, 282, 286, and 288.

the Medici in the sixteenth century, the same imagery occurs. For example, in the Sala di Opi in the Quartiere degli Elementi (Palazzo Vecchio, 1555-1557) by Vasari and his assistants, the *Triumph of Opi* (or Rhea, wife of Saturn, god of time) is surrounded by the *Seasons* and the *Months* with their accompanying zodiac signs.[36] As can be seen in Marco da Faenza's preparatory study for one of the panels, *March* is represented by Mars with his shield and the sign of Aries (pl. 58).[37] We recognize this same figure in the frieze, his action vividly evoking the bursting forth of the year in his month and in spring, the moment of the renewal of nature and the Return of Time.

If the main scene of the central panel represents the birth of the year in spring, then another feature of the panel may be explained. The *tempietto* which serves as a setting for Janus, Mars, and the priest would, of course, normally be read as the Janus-temple. If, however, the meaning of this panel is not war but the birth of the year in spring, then a work which is the probable visual source of the Mars and the temple may be significant in interpreting it. Similar miniature temples, doors ajar, occur as the central motif of Resurrection sarcophagi and appear on others as symbols of the transition from death to life.[38] One such sarcophagus (which was in Florence and may have been the sculptor's source) shows Mercury Psychopompos emerging from behind the left side of the door, just as does the Mars of the frieze (pl. 57).[39] The *tempietto*, then, may be read as the Temple of Time, and as such it announces the theme of Time's Return which is present in the remaining panels of the frieze.

To either side of the central vignette are five men in military dress. These are clearly the soldiers of Mars, god of war.[40] But here, in the context of the Cycles of Time, rather than proclaiming the military victories of the war god, they may be read as celebrating the victory of Mars as the fertilizing deity of the birth of spring.

The fourth panel depicts the *Seasons and the Months*, or the cycles of the year (pl. 54). Its theme is thus the eternal order of nature, the familiar theme that underlies the celebration of country life in antique poetry. It is analogous, for example, to the *Georgics*, in which Virgil evokes the theme of Time's Return through the labors of the farmer, which repeat the cycle of the turning year: "The farmer's toil returns, moving in a circle, as the year rolls back upon itself over its own footsteps."[41] To the left in this panel are the personifications of the seasons. They are arranged beginning with Spring (following the Mars-March imagery of the central panel), and they are characterized as in Ovid's description in the *Metamorphoses* of Apollo on his throne surrounded by the units of

[36] Vasari, *Rag.*, pp. 44-55; Allegri-Cecchi, pp. 83-90.

[37] Uffizi 15872F. See Allegri-Cecchi, p. 88. Vasari describes this Mars in the *Ragionamenti* (p. 48) as "questo soldato tutto armato di arme bianche, con la spada al fianco, e nella sinistra lo scudo, e nella destra quell'asta, che sta in atto di muoverla, con l'arco e la faretra alli omeri, questo è il mese di Marzo, il quale fu sempre appresso alli antichi il primo mese del anno."

[38] For the motif in Resurrection sarcophagi, see G. Schiller, *Ikonographie der Christlichen Kunst*, Gütersloh, 1971, III, figs. 2, 4, 11, 12. For discussion of the half-open door as a symbol of resurrection, see Haarlov, pp. 42-55.

[39] Haarlov, p. 134, cat. VI C, no. 5; Welliver, 1957, p. 239, n. 1; and Chastel, 1961, pp. 221-22, note the similarity between the two *tempietti*, but without comment as to the possible thematic significance of the temple in the frieze.

[40] Only Chastel, 1961, p. 221, even mentions these figures, who he suggests might represent the ten months of the old Roman calendar.

[41] *Georgics*, II, 401-2.

time: "To right and left stood Day and Month and Year and Century, and the Hours set at equal distances. Young Spring was there, wreathed with a floral crown; Summer, lightly clad, with garland of ripe grain; Autumn was there, stained with the trodden grape, and icy Winter with white and grizzled locks."[42] Youthful Spring-Flora, who carries flowers, is followed by a nude Summer with corn, a grape-and-cornucopia-laden Autumn, and an aged Winter. To the right of these Seasons are the labors of the fields which correspond to the twelve months of the year. In reprise of the order of the Seasons, they begin with March, who grafts trees, and end with February, who has faggots under his feet (April is missing).

The activities of the fruitful year in this agricultural panel are dependent on the themes set forth in each of the three preceding panels. The seasons and the months themselves depend on Jupiter's establishment of measured time. This theme is implicit in the second panel, for, according to ancient tradition, when the Age of Jupiter followed the Age of Saturn, Jupiter created the seasons.[43] And the regeneration of nature and its yearly cycle depend on another manifestation of universal order—the rule of the heavens, which is announced in the first panel, where the nude youth measures the heavenly bodies which have been set into their places. This interrelationship of the calendar, agriculture, and the stars is a basic premise of the antique poetry on which the imagery of the frieze depends. In the opening lines of the *Fasti*, for example, Ovid sees the passage of time as inseparable from the movements of the heavens: "The order of the calendar throughout the Latin year, its causes, and the starry signs that set beneath the earth and rise again, of these I'll sing."[44] And in farmers' calendars, such as Hesiod, *Works and Days*, or *Georgics* I, the labors of the months are determined by the rising and setting of the fixed stars.[45]

Of these ancient accounts of the agricultural year, the *Months* of the frieze seems to have the closest affinity with Columella's *De re rustica* XI. As in the Roman treatise, the labors are exclusively those of the fields and vineyard, and there is a close correspondence between the particular tasks described by Columella and those shown in the panel.[46]

[42] *Metamorphoses*, II, 25-30 (as noted by Chastel, 1961, p. 219).

[43] Ovid, *Metamorphoses*, I, 113-18. "After Saturn had been banished to the dark world of death, and the world was under the sway of Jove, the silver race came in, lower in the scale than gold, but of greater worth than yellow brass. Jove now shortened the bounds of the old-time spring, and through winter, summer, variable autumn, and brief spring completed the year in four seasons." Cf. also Aratus, *Phaenomena*, prologue, 1-18; and Virgil, *Georgics*, I, 353ff., where Jupiter is characterized as the god who set the seasons.

[44] *Fasti*, I, 1-2.

[45] See Hesiod, *Works and Days*, 383-694 (tr. H. G. Evelyn-White, London and New York, 1914), in which, for example, the beginning of the agricultural year in spring is signaled by the rising of the Pleiades (lines 383-85): "When the Pleiades,

daughters of Atlas, are rising, begin your harvest, and your plowing when they are going to set." In the opening lines of *Georgics*, I, 1-5, Virgil states the dependency of agriculture upon the stars: "What makes the crops joyous, beneath what star, Maecenas, is it well to turn the soil . . ." (see Appendix II for the entire text). On the farmer's year, see also Pliny, *Naturalis historia*, XVIII, lvii, 207ff.

[46] The labors in the frieze correspond as follows with Columella, *De re rustica*, XI, ii: March (grafting trees), 26; April (missing); May (staking vines), 44; June (threshing), 47; July (harvesting), 54; August (harrowing the soil), 60; September (vintage), 64, 67-71; October (plowing), 75; November (sowing), 85; December (olive harvest), 95; January (hoeing), 9; and February (gathering wood), 19. I have listed the figures in the order in which they appear in the frieze, whereas Columella's calendar begins in January. Cf. also bk. X, Columella's poem

Columella's work was well known to the Medici: Piero owned a manuscript of it, and in 1483 a commentary by Curio Lancellotto Pasi on Book X was dedicated to Lorenzo himself.[47] Moreover, it had served as a text for Luca della Robbia's majolica roundels of the *Labors of the Months* of ca. 1450-1456, which decorated Piero's *studiolo* in the Palazzo Medici.[48] The designer of the panel seems to have known these roundels, for a number of Luca's naturalistic figures, such as the man grafting trees, the man staking vines, and the harvester, who is *June* in the roundels (pl. 59) but represents July in the frieze, have been adapted and transformed into the more classicizing mode of the nudes in the frieze panel. The sculptor, however, has not used the zodiacal and cosmological symbols that customarily allude to the celestial order in Renaissance calendars such as Luca's. Such overt symbolism is not consonant with the mode *all'antica* of the frieze; however, the twelve months on it would have been understood as alluding to the idea of celestial order that is established in the first panel.

The *Seasons and the Months* panel also relates to another kind of order. In the Augustan poetry celebrating country life and the calendar of the year on which the imagery of the frieze depends, agriculture, and even calendar itself, is an extended metaphor of peace. The central panel of the frieze, with its Roman patron god, Mars, and its enactment of the rite of the return of the year in spring, is an image of civic order that brings peace and makes possible the prosperity of the agricultural year.

In the last panel the theme of the Cycles of Time is completed with the *Birth of the Day* (pl. 55), which is introduced by a Perseus-term like the one between the first two panels. Like the first panel it is divided into three scenes, and like the first the scenes suggest the progression from darkness to light. To the left is a scene of *Night*, drawn from Hesiod, *Theogony*.[49] In the central scene of *Dawn*, Aurora prepares Sol-Apollo and his horses for the day. The scene vividly recalls Ovid's description of the departure of Phaeton at dawn:[50]

> When Titan saw him [the morning star] setting and the world grow red, and the slender horns of the waning moon fading from sight, he bade the swift Hours to yoke his steeds. The goddesses quickly did his bidding, and led the horses from the lofty stalls, breathing forth fire and filled with ambrosial food, and they put upon them the clanking bridles.

on gardening, on October (X, 45-46): "Then let the sweet soil with the might of spades, / with iron shod, be turned . . . ; and on January (X, 91-92): "Then let him take / the shining hoe, worn by the soil, and trace / straight, narrow ridges. . . ."

[47] For Piero's *De re rustica*, see Laur. MS Plut. 53, 32; and for the commentary, see Laur. MS Plut. 52, 22. I am grateful to Virginia Brown for calling my attention to Pasi's commentary (on which, see V. Brown, "Columella, Lucius Junius Moderatus," *Catalogus Translationum et Commentariorum: Medieval and Renaissance Latin Translations and Commentaries*, Washington, 1976, III, pp. 184-

85).

[48] See Pope-Hennessy, pp. 104-12, figs. 99-110, who notes their unconventional iconography (particularly January, April, May, and December) and the correspondences with Columella's treatise. He also cites another example of the Labors with the signs of the zodiac in a Book of Hours illuminated for Lorenzo il Magnifico, now at Holkham Hall.

[49] *Theogony*, 211-13, 747-57. Chastel, 1961, p. 219, mentions the second passage.

[50] *Metamorphoses*, II, 116-21. Tervarent, 1960, p. 311, identifies the female figure as an Hour; Chastel, 1961, p. 219, calls her Aurora.

At the easternmost point of the frieze, then, the Cycle of Time is attenuated to its smallest unit of the hour—specifically the hour of dawn that begins each new day as Sol-Apollo sets out in his chariot for his daily journey across the heavens.

THE FRIEZE AND LAURENTIAN IMAGERY

The neoclassical frieze decorating Lorenzo's villa portico has fundamental affinities with Laurentian thought. The ancient poetry which inspired its imagery, together with related bucolic and pastoral works, was the focus of intensive interest in the 1480s, when an unprecdented number of translations, lectures, and commentaries were devoted to the works of Ovid and Virgil, in particular. Moreover, pastoral poetry *all'antica* had been in style in Lorenzo's literary circle since Naldi dedicated eleven Virgilian *Eclogues* to Lorenzo early in his rule.[51] Poliziano and Lorenzo himself wrote bucolic poetry modeled on Ovid and Virgil. Poliziano's *Ambra* of 1485 was followed by Lorenzo's poem of the same title, in which a creation myth was invented around the nymph Ambra, after whom his farm at Poggio a Caiano had been named.[52] Poliziano's *Rusticus* of 1483 is a poetic Labors of the Months, conceived as an introduction to the author's lectures on Hesiod and on the *Georgics*, and he also wrote a versified commentary on the *Fasti*, the very work from which the imagery of the frieze is most clearly derived.[53] These poems, like their ancient prototypes, are dedicated to praise of country life. As Poliziano declares in the *Rusticus*, paraphrasing Virgil,[54]

> O dulces pastoris opes! o quanta beatum
> Quam tenet hunc tranquilla quies! ut pectore toto
> Laetitiam totaque fovet bona gaudia mente!

> O sweet wealth of the shepherd! O how great is the tranquillity and quiet which this lucky man enjoys. How much he cherishes happiness with his whole heart and rightful joys with his whole mind.

The frieze itself may be seen as such a paraphrase—most probably one also invented by Poliziano.[55] With its evocation of ancient myths of the cosmos and of creation, its lyrical transcription of antique existence, and its idealized view of the seasons and the labors of the agricultural year, mirroring the celestial order of the heavens, the frieze is

[51] Naldi, *Bucolica*, pp. 23-58.

[52] For Lorenzo's *Ambra*, datable after 1486, see Lorenzo, *Opere*, I, pp. 291-330. For Poliziano's, see *Le Selve*, pp. 69-109. Poliziano's *Ambra* ends with a description of the site of Lorenzo's villa (see n. 2, above).

[53] *Rusticus: in poetae Hesiodi Vergiliique Giorgicon enarratione pronuntiata (1483-1484)*, in *Le Selve*, pp. 33-64. See Michele Verino's letter to Piero de'

Medici on the lost *Fasti* commentary, which was to be part of the *Sylvae* (quoted in Warburg, "Botticelli," p. 53, n. 3). See also Landino's commentary on the *Georgics* (Laur. MS Plut. 53, 37).

[54] *Rusticus*, 283-85 (in *Le Selve*, p. 49).

[55] Poliziano has often been suggested as the author of the frieze program, as by Seznec, p. 116; and Chastel, 1961, pp. 221, 225.

a georgic. It harmonizes perfectly with the ideal of rural life that Lorenzo's villa itself embodies and with Poliziano's poetic transformation of that ideal.

But the theme of the portico frieze is not limited by the *topos* of country life. Just as the underlying meaning of Medicean pastoral poetry (like that of its ancient prototypes) is political, so is that of the frieze.[56] Its theme is Medici rule, for which the regeneration of nature and the Return of Time in spring are metaphors, and its particular reference is to the rule of the owner of the villa, Lorenzo il Magnifico.

The first and last panels establish the Medicean frame of reference. In the first, the snake biting its tail—ancient symbol of the Return of Time—reads as a Medici emblem. It had long since been transformed by the family into their *impresa* of the ring with the motto SEMPER, which asserted their own eternal return, or rule. Moreover, the snake device was current at the time of the frieze in a medal of Lorenzo's cousin, Lorenzo di Pierfrancesco (pl. 48).[57] The last panel alludes to Apollo-Lorenzo. The identification of Lorenzo as the sun god, with whom he shared the device of the laurel, was a commonplace in Lorenzo's circle and occurs frequently in Laurentian poetry. For example, the story of Lauro and Ambra in *Ambra*—the very poem to which the bucolic ideal of the villa and frieze is related—is but a thinly disguised version of the tale of Apollo and Daphne.[58]

Between these framing panels—*Eternity*, with its Medicean symbol of eternal rule, and the *Birth of the Day*, with Apollo-Lorenzo as its protagonist—unfold the Cycles of Time: the *Birth of the Age of Jupiter*, the *Birth of the Year*, and the *Seasons and the Months*. These panels, too, allude to Medici rule and to Lorenzo.

The progression in the frieze from the dark Cavern of Eternity in the first panel to the radiant sunrise of the dawning day in the last has an obvious affinity with Neoplatonic concepts of the ascent of the soul from darkness to light. Indeed, the work has been interpreted by Guy de Tervarent exclusively in these terms.[59] For him, the frieze represents the life of the soul—its creation, incarnation, activities on earth, death, and ascension. Given the Medicean references in the frieze, it is probably correct to read the frieze on this level as alluding to the soul of Lorenzo—to his birth, life, death, and apotheosis as Apollo. However, the elaborate development of the theme of the Cycles of Time here suggests a further, more explicitly political reading. For the notions of the eternal cycle of death and regeneration and, especially, the idea of the Return of Time in spring, are the quintessence of Lorenzo's personal imagery.

Preeminent in Lorenzo's imagery of Time was his personal motto LE TEMPS REVIENT,

[56] The Laurentian imagery of the frieze has not been investigated; however, such a connection was intuited by Hamberg, p. 83 ("The frieze alludes to the political achievement of the Medici family in the service of peace and prosperity"); and Chastel, 1961, p. 277, discussing the frieze in the palace of Bartolommeo Scala ("Il est possible que l'on doive imaginer ici comme à Poggio a Caiano, une certaine présentation *ad hominem* . . ."). I am grateful to Claudia Rousseau and Lynette Bosch for suggestions on the political significance of the work.

[57] Hill, no. 1054. On the meaning of the medal, in which the snake rests its head on the earth, see Gombrich, 1972, "Botticelli," p. 66, n. 128; and Wind, pp. 266-67, who suggests that it illustrates Pico's proposition "Non tota descendit anima quum descendit."

[58] For this and other poetry in which Lorenzo is styled as Apollo, see Y.F.-A. Giraud, *La Fable de Daphné*, Paris, 1969, pp. 159-63.

[59] Tervarent, 1960, pp. 307-12.

which can be understood as the unwritten motto of the frieze. This motto alluded to the return of the Golden Age, which, although not depicted in the frieze, is implicit in the poem by Claudian, from which much of its imagery is drawn, and in the Apollonian subject of its final panel. And, as is suggested by the images of the regeneration of nature (the sprouting laurel, the blooming roses) which accompany it in Lorenzo's manuscripts (pls. 9, 20), this motto referred specifically to the Return of Time in spring. Indeed, long before the time of the frieze, LE TEMPS REVIENT had become the touchstone for a complex of imagery in which the coming of spring was a metaphor of the ever renewing, eternal rule of the Medici. In poetry of the late 1470s and 1480s, for example, the regeneration of nature in spring alludes to a Medici Golden Age in Florence. In the *Stanze*, recalling Ovid's Golden Age of eternal springtime, Poliziano describes such a Medici spring:[60]

> Ivi non volgon gli anni il lor quaderno,
> ma lieta Primavera mai non manca.
>
> Here the years do not turn over their calendar,
> but joyful spring is never absent.

Representations of spring in Laurentian art such as Botticelli's *Primavera* (pl. 60) must also be understood as alluding to Medici rule. The *Primavera*, destined for Lorenzo di Pierfrancesco, was probably based on a program by Poliziano from the early 1480s.[61] As has been demonstrated by Charles Dempsey, Neoplatonic interpretations of this picture should not obscure the fact that on a primary level it represents spring: the season begins with Zephyr, the west wind, is fulfilled in April (the month ruled by Venus in the rustic Roman calendar), and reaches its culmination in May (ruled by Mercury).[62] However, this *Primavera* is not a prelude to a cycle of the seasons, as has been thought, for in Medici art spring has a special, conventional meaning: it is self-contained and without sequel. Time's Return in spring is a metaphor of Medici return and rule.

Another example from Medici art, which typically elaborates and re-elaborates on its

[60] *Le Stanze*, I, 72. Cf. "ver erat aeternum" (*Metamorphoses*, I, 107).

[61] The case for Poliziano's authorship of the program, first made by Warburg, is persuasively argued by Dempsey, pp. 268-69, with reference to the affinities between the imagery of the *Primavera* and the *Rusticus*. Inventories locating the work in the townhouse of Lorenzo di Pierfrancesco in 1498 settle the matter of the younger Lorenzo as the *destinataire* of the picture, although this by no means rules out his guardian, Lorenzo il Magnifico, as its patron (see Shearman, 1975, "Collections," pp. 12-27). Since the discovery of the inventories, the date of the work need no longer be tied to the purchase by the younger Lorenzo of Villa Castello in 1477; indeed, there are indica-

tions that the picture may date after Botticelli's return from Rome in 1482. Its mature style is consonant with such a dating; it is connected in theme with the *Rusticus* of 1483; and one of its major poetic sources, Columella's *De re rustica*, X, was the subject of a commentary dedicated to Lorenzo il Magnifico in the same year (Laur. MS Plut. 52, 22).

[62] Dempsey, pp. 251-73. Some important earlier readings of the *Primavera* are those of Warburg, "Botticelli," pp. 3-35; Gombrich, 1972, "Botticelli," pp. 31-64 (see pp. 31-39 for a summary of various interpretations); Wind, pp. 113-27; and E. Panofsky, "Rinascimento dell'Antichità: The Fifteenth Century," in *Renaissance and Renascences*, New York, 1960, pp. 191-200.

topoi, may clarify this point. Bronzino's *Primavera* tapestry of 1545 shows Flora-Fiorenza with the spring zodiac signs of Aries, Taurus, and Gemini (pl. 61). Flora, carrying the *gigli* of Florence and the Medici roses, floats above a verdant springtime landscape suggestive of a Florentine Golden Age. Above, in the border, a head of Janus *bifrons* underscores the theme of the Golden Age (which he ruled with Saturn) as well as the theme of beginnings. The conceit of the Medici spring is here definitively stated: the whole ensemble is a metaphor of the Return of Time in spring and the Golden Age of Duke Cosimo de' Medici.[63]

Thus, whatever rich meanings we may find in the *Primavera*—the more subtle and complex earlier counterpart of Bronzino's tapestry—its political message is unmistakable. It is a visual elaboration of the return in spring of the Medici Golden Age, of Lorenzo's motto LE TEMPS REVIENT.[64]

All the signs of such a Medicean *primavera* are present in Botticelli's picture. The orange-grove setting is both a Medici garden (alluding to the citrus-*palle* equation) and the Garden of the Hesperides (with the golden fruits to which the *palle* were compared), itself a traditional metaphor of the Golden Age. The central figure is characterized as Medicean: she is dressed in the red, white, and green of the feathers which accompany the *diamante*; the circle cut in the foliage behind her also suggests the Medici device; and "palle" hang from the border of her cloak. But most important is the prominence of Flora in the painting. She indicates that the *Primavera* alludes not just to the Medici but to their rule in Florence, for Flora, goddess of spring, is also Fiorenza, personification of the city.

This circle of associations—Primavera-Flora-Fiorenza—was part of the myth of Florence and her special destiny. The city was thought to have been founded in March by the Romans in the time of Augustus, 25 March was considered to mark the "birth of Florence," and this day was the New Year of the Florentine calendar.[65] Thus, in Laurentian poetry and art, Flora-Fiorenza represents not only the city over which Lorenzo rules, but the mythic origins of Florence in spring at the moment of the renewal of nature. Botticelli's goddess, with flowers in her apron and laurel growing over her head, recalls Bellincioni's Fiorenza "co' fiori in grembo" under the Medici laurel. And she recalls the Fiorenza of Lorenzo's own medal (pl. 3). The motto of the medal—TVTELA PATRIE—is not, of course, present in the painting, but its message is vividly evoked by Botticelli's Flora-Fiorenza, whose birth in March marks the beginning of the Medici spring.

[63] For this work see chap. 11, "Epilogue."

[64] My association of Botticelli's pictures with Laurentian imagery of Time is to be distinguished from previous attempts to place the work in a Medici context, in which the motto is connected exclusively with Lorenzo's *giostra*, Florentine spring pageantry, and the ideal of courtly love. See G. F. Young, *The Medici*, London, 1925, I, pp. 226-28, where the work is linked with the romantic myth of Giuliano de' Medici and Simonetta Vespucci;

and P. Francastel, *La Réalité figurative*, Paris, 1965, pp. 241-89, where it is connected with the love poetry of Lorenzo il Magnifico and interpreted as an allegory of good government.

[65] See the discussion of the Roman foundation of Florence in Rubinstein, 1942, pp. 198-227; and N. Rubinstein, "Il Poliziano e la questione delle origini di Firenze," *Il Poliziano e il suo tempo, Atti del IV convegno internazionale di studi sul Rinascimento*, Florence, 1957, pp. 101-10.

The coming of spring as a metaphor of the triumph of Medici rule in Florence is also the contemporary reference of the frieze. However, the political message of the frieze, conspicuously located over the entrance to Lorenzo's villa, is far more explicit than that of the painting. It is a more didactic work, conceived in an antique mode (as Botticelli's painting is not), and its Cycles of Time conceal a message of Medici rule which adumbrates the definitive exposition of this theme in Medici art of the Cinquecento.

The central panel, the *Birth of the Year*, links the theme of the Cycles of Time with the Medicean *topos* of spring. As in the *Primavera*, the year begins in March, and the visual imagery involves a sequence of three figures and the motif of the "bursting forth" of the new season. Only the characters are different: instead of being represented by Ovid's sensuous creation myth of the metamorphosis of Chloris into Flora from the *Fasti*, the new season is announced by the gods of January and March, with Mars, deity of spring, emerging from the Temple of Time.

Like Flora, Mars had a long association with Florence, and it is through this figure—and a nexus of associations with it—that the political message of the frieze in relation to the city and the Medici is delivered. A Florentine patron deity, Mars had played an important role in the myth of the exalted origins and continued greatness of the city. Mars, tutelary god of Rome, signified the connection between Rome and Florence, founded in the month to which he gave his name. Mars was thus regarded as the first patron of the city, before Saint John the Baptist, as is expressed by Dante's Florentine citizen in the *Inferno*:[66]

> I' fui de la città che nel Batista
>
> mutò il primo padrone; ond' e' per questo
>
> sempre con l'arte sua la farà trista;
>
> e se non fosse che 'n sul passo d'Arno
>
> rimane ancor di lui alcuna vista,
>
> que' cittadin che poi la rifondarno
>
> sovra 'l cener d'Attila rimase,
>
> avrebber fatto lavorare indarno.

I was of the city that changed for the Baptist its first patron, who for this will always afflict it with his art; and were it not that at the passage of the Arno there yet remains some semblance of him, those citizens who afterward rebuilt it on the ashes left by Attila would have labored in vain.

Not only was there a statue of Mars on the Arno at the Ponte Vecchio, but the Florentine Baptistery was believed to have been an Augustan Temple of Mars and was thought by humanists such as Poliziano to be a symbol of the ancient greatness of Roman Florence.[67] Thus, in Vasari's painting, *The Foundation of Florence as a Roman Colony*, the construction of the "Temple of Mars" is prominently represented in the

---

[66] *Inferno*, XIII, 143-50. On the statue of Mars, see also *Paradiso*, XVI, 145-47. This myth is discussed by C. Bec, "Il Mito di Firenze da Dante a Ghiberti," *Lorenzo Ghiberti nel suo tempo, Atti del convegno internazionale di studi*, Florence, 1978 (Florence, 1980, pp. 3-26).

[67] Rubinstein, 1967, pp. 69-70.

middle-ground (pl. 62).[68] In the sky above is the Ram, or Aries, the zodiac sign associated with March, with Mars, and hence with the birth of Florence. In choosing Mars as the protagonist of the central panel, then, Poliziano (or whichever Laurentian humanist authored the program) thus made allusion to the Florentine New Year in spring, to the first patron of Florence, and to the birth and rebirth of the city itself. All this lore was evoked in the frieze to promote the myth of the Medici, of their eternal renewal, and particularly, of the rebirth of the city under Lorenzo.

These connections are signaled by the presence of the laurel as the attribute of Mars. Just as the figures who signify March in the *Primavera* are marked by the laurel branches above them, so the Mars-March of the frieze carries the emblem of the laurel in the crossed branches on his shield. This detail may depend on the *Fasti*, in which the laurel is sacred to Mars as the god of the renewal of the year. Laurel is the insignia of the Kalendae Martiae; it is the laurel of Apollo, which is placed at the king's door to mark the new year: "The laurel branch of the flamens, after remaining in its place the whole year, is removed (on that day), and fresh leaves are put in the place of honor; then the king's door is green with the tree of Phoebus, which is set at it."[69] The laurel, of course, is also the emblem of Lorenzo—the Florentine ruler at whose door the *Birth of the Year* is enacted—and it makes Mars into an image of Lorenzo himself.[70] His attending soldiers, most of whom turn deferentially toward him, may allude to Florentine support for his rule: the soldier next to Janus has the Medici *palle* on his breastplate and the last soldier on the right (who turns to the Spring of the next panel) has a laurel wreath on his shield.

Returning to the frieze as a whole, we may see that its sequence of scenes of the Cycles of Time balance around the central panel with Janus, who not only sets time in motion and looks to east and west but who, according to tradition, knew the past and could foresee the future.[71] The scenes to the left and right of the central panel, then, allude to the past and the future, and the association of Mars in his temple with Lorenzo and his villa suggests that the progression from the chaos implicit in the first panel to the order, peace, and prosperity of the last panels is a function of Medici rule.

The *Birth of the Age of Jupiter* introduces the theme of government, which is underscored by the Corybantes and the bees. The Corybantes, whose noise saved Jupiter from discovery, symbolized initiation and good government in Medici thought.[72] Bees

[68] Rubinstein, 1967, pp. 68-70.

[69] Ovid, *Fasti*, III, 135-44. On the laurel of Mars, see also Macrobius, *Saturnalia*, I, 12, 1. Scullard, pp. 85-87, discusses this tradition.

[70] The association of a Medici ruler with Mars as deity of spring was later made by Sereno, p. 112, describing the Capitoline festival of 1513 and Giovanni de' Medici's elevation to the papacy in March: "Nei giochi annui del tuo pontificato infatti, celebrati nel mese del marzo, proprio in quel mese che Romolo fondatore della citta a te obbedientissima consacrò al padre Marte, nel tempo in cui comincia la primavera e la terra vestita di brillianti colori sparge nel mondo onori soavissimi. . . ."

For the theme of the peaceful Mars in the art of Duke Cosimo de' Medici, see chap. 10 and, in chap. 11, "Pontormo's Decoration of the Loggia at Villa Castello."

[71] Macrobius, *Saturnalia*, I, 8, 20: "Janus is believed to have had two faces and so could see before him and behind his back—a reference, no doubt, to the foresight and shrewdness of the king, as one who not only knew the past but would also foresee the future."

[72] Chastel, 1961, p. 222. Vasari, *Rag.*, p. 45, describing the Sala di Opi, defines their relation to good (Medicean) government: "I coribanti armati sono fatti per dimostrare che a ciascuno che sia

were also an ancient symbol of rulership, government, and ordered society, one which had become a princely emblem in the Renaissance and which was even used later as an *impresa* of rulership by the Medici.[73] Bees appear as a device in a number of Lorenzo's manuscripts (pls. 20, 27). In these, the beehives are arranged in a 3-2-1 pattern which recalls the traditional arrangement of the six *palle* and of the six letters of mottos related to change in Medici fortunes, such as GLOVIS, or their benign rule, such as SVAVE (both of which also occur in these manuscripts). In the frieze the patterning of the bees is not so diagrammatic, but there are six beehives and six golden bees (the one to the upper left on the beehive has lost its color)—a symbolic vignette introducing the theme of Medici rule which is enacted in the central panel.

Following the central panel is the *Seasons and the Months*, an allegory of prosperous Medicean Florence, of the achievement of peace and order that was the accomplishment of three generations of Medici rule. The notion of agriculture as a metaphor of peace is emphasized by the double cycles of the seasons and of the months, represented by the labors. The seasons begin with Spring-Flora, whose meaning as a personifications of Florence in a Laurentian work is unmistakable (pl. 63). This figure, which is a double for Botticelli's Flora-Fiorenza, is closely based on a Roman Flora recorded in Florence by Vasari (pl. 64), which may also have served as Botticelli's model.[74] Flora has a succession of followers in Medici art, in which, as here, she signifies the return of spring and the renewal of Florence under Medici rule. These include Bronzino's goddess (pl. 61), and the series ends with the Flora-Fiorenza of Ammannati's Fountain of Juno, who takes her place in an allegory of the *buon governo* of Duke Cosimo designed for the Salone dei Cinquecento (pl. 65).[75] In this figure, imagery of the Medici spring is updated: she not only carries the usual flowers, but she wears Cosimo's insignia of the Order of the Golden Fleece, the emblem of which—the Ram—can also be read as alluding to the zodiac sign of Aries under which the city of Florence was founded.

The Labors of the Months are also peculiarly Medicean, and the choice of the particular labors seems to be related to the della Robbia roundels formerly in the Palazzo Medici. In the roundels the labors are all agricultural, rather than being the more traditional admixture of these with other activities of rural and court life. Such a choice would have been appropriate to the actual crops of Lorenzo's farm (fruit trees, grapes, wheat, olives); however, the emphasis on the growth of plants suggests that this relief is yet another instance in Medici art of vegetative regeneration as a metaphor of Medici renewal.

---

buono, si appartiene di pigliar l'arme per difesa della patria e terra sua, ed anche in tempo di letizia, sonando e cantando, fare allegrezza del buon governo della città, e rallegrarsi di tutto quello che produce essa terra."

[73] On the symbolism of bees, see W. Deonna, "L'Abeille et le roi," *Revue belge d'archèologie et d'histoire de l'art*, 25, 1956, pp. 105-31; and Tervarent, 1958, col. 1, who terms them symbols of "douceur dans le gouvernement." The *impresa* of Grand Duke Ferdinando showed a swarm of bees around the king bee, with the motto MAIESTATE TANTUM.

[74] See G. A. Mansuelli, *Galleria degli Uffizi: Le Sculture*, Rome, 1958, I, pp. 153-54 (called *Una Hora*), for this statue, the head of which is a Renaissance restoration. For the association of Botticelli's Flora with this work, see Warburg, "Botticelli," pp. 39-40.

[75] Heikamp, pp. 129-30.

In the *Birth of the Day*, the end of the frieze is joined with the beginning in one continuous cycle, as Lorenzo-Apollo ascends to immortality. Moreover, there is a hint of the Golden Age, not represented in the frieze but implicit in Claudian's text and in the presence of Apollo: arriving at the Cavern of Eternity in the west, Lorenzo-Apollo will find the Age of Gold. The frieze is also concluded with an implied parallel between the eternal cycle of day and night and the inevitable return of the Medici: just as Sol-Apollo rises from sleep each morning to make his round of the sky, so the Medici will always renew themselves—as Lorenzo's motto LE TEMPS REVIENT declares.

✳   ✳   ✳

Interpreted as a Laurentian allegory of Medici dynasty and rule, the frieze seems less of an enigma. Its imagery of the Cycles of Time is rooted in Laurentian variations on traditional Medici themes, and it finds a natural place in the art and thought of Lorenzo's later years. The frieze is linked, in particular, with certain Laurentian paintings. These paintings have rustic or pastoral imagery which refers to ancient and Laurentian pastoral poetry, and the paintings, like the poetry, have an underlying political significance. I have mentioned affinities between the imagery of the *Primavera* and that of the frieze, as well as their common point of departure from Lorenzo's theme of the Return of Time in spring and Medici rule in Florence, personified by Flora-Fiorenza. And, although it is not cast in a rustic mode, Botticelli's *Birth of Venus* is also related to the Medicean theme of the regenerative forces of nature. Venus *genetrix* personifies the same concepts of birth and renewal in spring that animate the Cycles of Time in the third and fourth panels of the frieze, and she is received by the omnipresent Flora, who stands against a Medicean orange grove.[76] But Luca Signorelli's *Realm of Pan*, painted about 1490 for Lorenzo,[77] is closest in date to the frieze, and with its enthroned protagonist it is a more obviously didactic picture about rulership (pl. 67). Signorelli's painting is a complex work which does not yield its secrets easily, but its *sacra conversazione* format and its elevated god, flanked by figures in reverential attitudes, suggest that the rustic ruler of Arcady alludes to Lorenzo himself and that the theme of the work, like that of the frieze, is Lorenzo's rule.[78]

Such an interpretation of Signorelli's pastorale is supported by the existence of a tradition in which Pan is associated with Medici rule. Lorenzo founded a cult of Pan at Villa Careggi, identifying the Florentine countryside as Arcady, his intimates as shep-

[76] Tolkowsky, p. 169. For the figure to the right as Flora, see Dempsey, pp. 267-68.

[77] The *Pan* is identifiable as the picture of "alcuni dèi ignudi" which Vasari, III, p. 689, says the artist painted for Lorenzo on a trip to Florence. For dating and references, see Chastel, 1961, p. 226.

[78] Chastel, 1945, p. 66, notes the *sacra conversazione* format, as does Brummer, 1964, pp. 57, 64-65, who calls the work a "platonic-Christian devotional picture" and identifies the youth to the

right as Lorenzo and the old man to the left as Ficino. Welliver, 1961, pp. 334-45, also relates the work to Lorenzo, identifying the old man as Cosimo Pater Patriae and the young nude to the right as Lorenzo's brother Giuliano. However, Pan himself does not seem to have been identified previously with Lorenzo except in a very general sense by Chastel, 1961, p. 232, who remarks: "si Pan représente la divinité tutélaire de Laurent—et en quelque sorte Laurent lui-même. . . ."

herds.[79] He also wrote a long *Eclogue* on Apollo and Pan, to which Signorelli's imagery may be related.[80] For Lorenzo, Pan was a universal god of nature, a cosmic deity who (as he writes in *L'Altercazione*) ruled the eternal cycle of life and death:[81]

> Pan, quale ogni pastore onora e venera,
> Il cui nome in Arcadia si celebra,
> Che impera a quel che si corrompe o genera.

> Pan, whom every shepherd honors and reveres, whose name in Arcady is celebrated, who holds sway over that which decays or generates.

The "Pan Medicus" of Laurentian thought is based on the Pan of Virgil's *Eclogue* II, who "cares for the sheep and the shepherds of the sheep," and on Servius' commentary on this Pan as a god who signified the universe, the seasons, and even the Cycles of Time.[82]

> Nam Pan deus est rusticus in naturae similitudinem formatus, unde et Pan dictus est, id est omne: habet enim cornua in radiorum solis et cornuum lunae similitudinem; rubet eius facies ad aetheris imitationem; in pectore nebridem habet stellatam ad stellarum imaginem; pars eius inferior hispida est propter arbores, virgulta, feras; caprinos pedes habet, ut ostendat terrae soliditatem; fistulam septem calamorum habet propter harmoniam caeli, in qua septem soni sunt . . . χαλαύροπα habet, id est pedum, propter annum, qui in se recurrit.

> Pan is a rustic god, formed like nature. He is called Pan, which means everything. He has horns like the rays of the sun and like the horns of the moon. His face is ruddy in imitation of air. On his breast he has a fawn skin with markings in the likeness of stars. His lower part is hairy because of the trees, shrubs, and wild beasts. He has goat's feet to demonstrate the solidity of the earth. He has a pipe of seven reeds because of the harmony of the heavens, in which there are seven tones. . . . He has a shepherd's crook because of the year that returns on itself.

Virgil's conceit alluding to political rule was taken up in Laurentian pastoral poetry, in which Pan is identified with the theme of dynastic continuity. In the *Eclogues* dedicated to Lorenzo, Naldi paraphrases Virgil's conceit of the rulership of Pan.[83] The earlier poems are about Cosimo Pater Patriae, but then in *Eclogues* IX and X Naldi tells a story of dynastic and political continuity in which successive generations of Medici are disguised as rustic characters.[84] Pan (Piero) promises the shepherds Micon and Amyntas

[79] Chastel, 1945, p. 66; and Brummer, 1964, pp. 59-60.

[80] Lorenzo, *Opere*, I, pp. 313-18; Welliver, 1961, n. 47, relates details of Signorelli's landscape with the setting of this poem.

[81] Lorenzo, *Opere*, II, p. 53 (as noted by Chastel, 1945, p. 66).

[82] Servius, III, p. 23, commentary on *Eclogue* II,

31. This passage was connected with Signorelli's picture by R. Herbig, "Alcuni dèi ignudi," *Rinascimento*, 3, 1952, p. 20. For the "cosmic Pan," see Chastel, 1961, pp. 227-232; and Brummer, 1964 pp. 55-59.

[83] Naldi, *Bucolica*, pp. 23-58.

[84] A. Hulubei, "Naldo Naldi: Etude sur la Joute de Julien et sur les Bucoliques dédiées à Laurent

(Lorenzo and Giuliano) that they will always have the benefits of the healing arts (*medicas artes*) if they follow his teaching. When he dies and becomes a star in the heavens, the rule of the pastures, or Florence, will pass to Micon-Lorenzo. Thus, in this Virgilian pastoral conceit, Naldi tells of Lorenzo, implicitly a New Pan, whose rule of an Arcadian Florence continues that of his Medici ancestors and is, in fact, a new Golden Age.

Pan Medicus also appears after the Medici restoration in 1512 in allusion to the younger Lorenzo's revival of the Golden Age of Il Magnifico.[85] Later, surely in reference to this tradition (although he had personal reasons for an identification with Pan), Duke Cosimo revived Pan Medicus. There is a tapestry after Giovanni Stradano of a *Sacrifice to Pan* in the Sala di Opi in the Palazzo Vecchio, which Vasari interprets as a metaphor of the civilizing effects of Pan's music;[86] in another tapestry, the god holds the *broncone* in the same cross-legged pose (derived from antique reliefs) as Signorelli's *Pan*.[87] And in the 1540s, as can be seen in his compositional study, Niccolò Tribolo designed an elaborate grotto for the garden of Cosimo's Villa Castello with Pan, satyrs, and Capricorn (pl. 66).[88]

Using a rustic mode analogous to Naldi's literary *pastorale*, Signorelli portrays the realm of Pan-Lorenzo as an Arcadian Florence (possibly personified by the prominently placed Venus-like nude in the foreground). Laurentian themes of harmony and peace are underscored by the music-making figures and by the nymph sleeping under the trees near the stream.[89] Indeed, the position of the nymph recalls the Medici *topos* of Fiorenza at rest under the protecting Medici laurel.

Signorelli's Pan Medicus can also be seen to embody the themes of Nature and the Cosmos that are the underlying subject of Lorenzo's portico frieze. Pan himself is characterized as Servius' cosmic god by his lunar diadem, star-studded cloak, and syrinx. Hints of the theme of the Cycles of Time may also be present: the time of day, sunset, is precisely described by the direction of the shadows and the crescent moon in the evening sky; the contrast between the dry landscape to the right and the verdant scene with the nymphs suggests the familiar theme of the Florentine *primavera*; and the con-

de Médicis," *Humanisme et Renaissance*, 3, 1936, pp. 169-96, 309-26 (connected with the *Pan* by Chastel, 1961, p. 227).

[85] See an Eclogue of 1516 by Severus Minervius, mentioned in this context by Chastel, 1961, p. 220 (*Lauretum*, p. 39):

. . . nam Lydius illis
Pan Medica de gente satus nunc ocia praestat:
Cui numen, nomenque dedit formosus Apollo.
Vnde mihi Lauri veniant ad carmina Musae.

For Lydian Pan, sprung from the healing race [Medici], now provides leisure for them [dwellers and flocks of the grove], to whom [laurel] handsome Apollo gave divinity and a name. Whence let my Lorenzos assemble at the song of the Muses.

[86] Vasari, *Rag.*, pp. 52-53; Allegri-Cecchi, p.

87.

[87] L. Berti, *Il Museo di Palazzo Davanzati a Firenze*, Florence, 1971, cat. 184, pl. 147.

[88] H. Keutner, "Niccolò Tribolo und Antonio Lorenzi. Der Askulapbrunnen im Heilkräutergarten der Villa Castello bei Florenz," *Studien sur Geschichte der Europäischen Plastik, Festschrift Theodor Müller*, Munich, 1965, p. 244, n. 29; and Monbeig-Goguel, p. 145.

[89] For the nymph in a landscape as a symbol of peace, see M. Meiss, "Sleep in Venice: Ancient Myths and Renaissance Proclivities," in *The Painter's Choice: Problems in the Interpretation of Renaissance Art*, New York, 1976, p. 219; for the similar meaning of the nymph by a stream, see O. Kurz, "Huius Nympha Loci," *JWCI*, 16, 1953, pp. 171-77.

trasting types of the shepherds around Pan-Lorenzo may also allude to themes such as the Seasons or the Ages of Man.

Pan-Lorenzo's rulership is also signaled in a way that relates to the Mars-Lorenzo of the frieze. His centrality and the deferential figures of his entourage are analogous to the arrangement of the scene of the central panel; moreover, like Mars' shield, which is decorated with laurel, Pan's crook is fashioned out of the *broncone*.[90] The crook is, of course, also the symbol of eternity which Servius describes as carried by Pan, its looped end symbolizing the year that returns upon itself. And this motif in turn has the same meaning as the emblem of the snake biting its tail in the first panel of the frieze. Held by the ruler of a Florentine Arcady, this *broncone* staff identifies Pan as Lorenzo, present embodiment of eternal Medici rule.

The frieze of Lorenzo's villa, which we have seen to be an allegory of Medici dynasty and rule related to Laurentian poetry and painting, is of crucial importance for an understanding of the frescos which were painted in the Salone of the villa by the next generation of Medici artists for Lorenzo's son Leo X. The theme of dynasty, adumbrated in the subtle Laurentian allegories, is a major focus of the Salone, where it is overtly expressed in a cycle of Roman *istorie*. The themes of Time and the Cosmos, central to these Laurentian works, are elaborated in Pontormo's fresco of *Vertumnus and Pomona*, where, in a rustic tableau which recalls the conventions of Laurentian art, the *topos* of the Medici Golden Age received its first fully elaborated presentation.

[90] For the conceit of the bishop's crozier as the Medici *broncone* (complete with sprouting laurel leaves), see the crozier with the figures of San Lorenzo, given to the church of San Lorenzo in 1520 by Leo X (*La comunità cristiana fiorentina e toscana nella dialettica religiosa del Cinquecento*, Florence, Chiesa di Santo Stefano al Ponte, 1980, cat. 36).

The Salone of Pope Leo X

THE COMMISSION AND PROGRAM

After the Medici restoration in 1512, work was resumed on Lorenzo il Magnifico's villa at Poggio a Caiano, which had been left unfinished when the family was exiled in late 1494. Between 1515 and 1519, according to documentation of extensive building activities at the villa (including delivery of a large amount of wood which would have been used as the centering for the Salone vault), the rear block of the building and the great barrel-vaulted Salone (twenty meters in length) were brought to completion (fig. 2).[1] The villa was frequented by the younger Lorenzo, who used it for diplomatic occasions and family festivities.[2] One of these was his wedding celebration on 8 September 1518, for which, according to a contemporary report, it was decorated "come d'un paradiso."[3] By this date, then, we may assume that the Salone with its stuccoed vault was essentially complete (pl. 68).

The Salone vault, based on a model by Giuliano da Sangallo,[4] repeats the design of the portico vault (pl. 47), but the entire vault is framed by narrow coffers containing the *bronconi*, and the articulating pattern of ribs and square is eliminated in favor of one of repeated circles (pl. 69).[5] Within the large circles, which "read" as the device of the

[1] Foster, I, pp. 114-15, citing documents of March 1515 to April 1519 relating to "la muraglia del Poggio a Chaiano."

[2] For Lorenzo at Poggio and his residence there during his final illness, see Pieraccini, II, pp. 249-84.

[3] B. Cerretani, "Sommario e estratto della sua storia scritta in dialogo," BNF, MS II, IV, 19, f. 5or. For further details of the wedding, see Parronchi, pp. 48-49; and Mitchell, pp. 43-46. For the proposal by Francesco Vettori that the villa be given to Lorenzo's bride as a wedding gift, see Devonshire Jones, p. 132.

[4] On the possible models by Giuliano, see chap. 3, n. 7. Vasari, IV, pp. 271, 291, wrongly attributes the execution of the vault to Giuliano himself.

[5] The module of this design is a ring the same size as the oculi of the lunettes. The rings are centered over the axes of the room (marked by the oculi and the doorways of the lateral walls), and the resulting pattern is made up of seven circles across the vault, the length of the vault requiring seven rings plus a half ring at each end. In using this design on such an immense scale, Giuliano continued the evocation of imperial architecture in

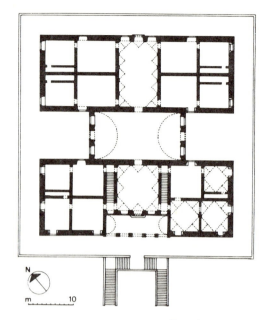

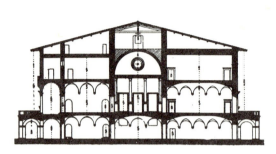

2. Poggio a Caiano, plan and elevation (after Fanelli)

diamante, two Medici emblems are repeated from the portico vault: roundels with six *palle* (the number almost always used in Leo's time) mark the center of each ring,[6] and four interlaced *diamanti* are placed against a blue background in the interstices. To these are added two Laurentian devices which were used extensively by Pope Leo: the yoke and the crossed, burning *bronconi*.[7] We have seen these devices in Leo's manuscripts. He also used them at the Vatican, where, for example, the shutters of the Stanza d'Eliodoro are decorated with the *diamanti*, the crossed, burning *bronconi* (making an "X" alluding to Leo), and the yoke (pl. 70); and the ceiling of the Sala di Costantino, which was gilded like that of the Salone, featured "le imprese del suave"—or Leo's yoke.[8]

After the death of Lorenzo the younger, Leo and Cardinal Giulio initiated the ambitious project of decorating the Salone with frescos.[9] This commission, probably dating from early 1520, brought together a team of painters—all Medici artists—who had worked

the portico of the villa, possibly intending comparison with Roman coffered vaults such as those of the Basilica of Constantine.

[6] The number of the *palle* was standardized as six in 1465, when Piero received permission from Louis XI to use the *fleur-de-lis* on a blue *palla* at the top center of the *stemma*. However, the older form with seven *palle* continued to be used by Lorenzo (the portico vault and other works), and they still appear occasionally in Leo's art.

[7] Because Vasari mentions the later gilding of the vault (below, n. 17), its stucco decorations are usually dated 1519-1521; however, the construction of a "volta a botte" is such that these embellishments cannot have been added at a later date

to its coffers.

[8] On the Vatican ceilings of 1517-1519, since destroyed, see Shearman, 1971, pp. 374-75 and n. 45.

[9] The only general account of the decoration is Kliemann, 1976, but see the studies on the contributions of the individual artists: on Pontormo, Cox-Rearick, 1964, I, pp. 38-47, 172-74; Forster, 1966, pp. 39-47, cat. 19; Winner, 1972, pp. 153-97; and Kliemann, 1972, pp. 293-328. On Sarto, Freedberg, 1963, I, pp. 54-55, cat. 48; and Shearman, 1965, I, pp. 76-89, cat. 57 (with a careful account of the circumstances of the commission). On Franciabigio, Winner, 1970, pp. 261-97; and McKillop, 1974, pp. 67-84, cat. 31.

together at SS. Annunziata: Andrea del Sarto, the Florentine *caposcuola*, who had been absent in France but was back by October 1519;[10] Franciabigio, who had designed the *apparato* for Lorenzo's wedding;[11] Andrea di Cosimo Feltrini, specialist in grotesques, who had been indispensable to the history painters on various projects;[12] and Pontormo, who had been in the service of the Medici since 1513 and recently painted the dynastic portrait of Cosimo Pater Patriae, probably for Leo himself.

Much information about the Salone comes from Vasari, who was well acquainted with the artists involved and with their Medici patrons.[13] The basic facts are these: the work was ordered by Giulio at the behest of Pope Leo;[14] the program was devised by Paolo Giovio (humanist, historian, and, later, author of the *Dialogo dell'imprese*), who was in Giulio's entourage;[15] and Ottaviano de' Medici was in charge of the supervision of the project and payments to the artists.[16] As far as the division of the work among them was concerned, Franciabigio gilded the vault with the aid of Feltrini;[17] Feltrini also did *ornamenti*;[18] and Sarto, Franciabigio, and Pontormo were each given one third of the fresco work: Pontormo was assigned the end walls and their lunettes, Franciabigio the wall opposite the entrance, and Andrea del Sarto the entrance wall.[19] With Leo's death in December 1521, all work stopped—a fact that Vasari mentions in the *vita* of each of the artists as if to emphasize Leo's personal involvement in the decoration of the Salone.[20]

Vasari's account is inconsistent regarding the date of the commission and regarding

[10] Shearman, 1965, I, pp. 3-4.

[11] Vasari, V, p. 195.

[12] Vasari, V, pp. 195, 206-209.

[13] Vasari knew Giovio as well as Giulio and Ottaviano, who later became his own patrons. Vasari discusses the Salone in the *vita* of each of the artists involved: Sarto (V, pp. 35-36), Franciabigio (V, pp. 195-96), Feltrini (V, p. 209), and Pontormo (VI, pp. 264-65); however, since he came to Florence only in 1524 (VII, p. 651), he was not on the scene at the time the work was in progress.

[14] Vasari, V, p. 35 (see also V, p. 195): "Dovendo Giulio cardinale de' Medici, per commessione di papa Leone, far lavorare di stucco e di pittura la volta della sala grande del Poggio a Caiano."

[15] Vasari, V, p. 195. On Giovio, see Zimmermann, pp. 404-26. Shearman, 1965, I, p. 78, points out that the cardinal and Giovio were both in Florence in the summer of 1520. In July Giovio wrote a letter from Florence to Benedetto Giovio (Giovio, *Lettere*, I, p. 86, no. 3).

[16] Vasari, V, pp. 35, 195; VI, p. 264. Ottaviano (1482-1546), a distant cousin of Leo X and Cardinal Giulio, was descended from a minor branch of the family orginating before 1400. For Ottaviano's career as administrator and artistic consultant to the Medici, see Wright, II, pp. 368-79.

[17] Vasari, V, p. 195, in the life of Franciabigio:

". . . la quale servitù [work on the *apparato* for the wedding of Lorenzo the younger] fu cagione ch'egli ebbe l'opera della volta della sala del Poggio a Caiano a mettersi d'oro, in compagnia d'Andrea di Cosimo. . . ." Vasari's only other reference to the vault contradicts this assertion and is, I believe, misleading. In the life of Sarto (V, p. 35), he states that Cardinal Giulio "far lavorare di stucco e di pittura la volta della sala grande del Poggio a Caiano." Certainly the papal arms may have been added at this time, but there is no reason to believe that any other stucco work was done by Franciabigio and Feltrini. Both had worked on papal arms on the occasion of Leo's elevation to the papacy—Feltrini at SS. Annunziata (Vasari, V, p. 207) and Franciabigio at San Pancrazio (Shearman, 1965, I, p. 18, n. 1); however, neither was a stucco specialist.

[18] Vasari, V, p. 209: "Andò col Francia al Poggio, e gli ornamenti di quelle storie condusse di terretta. . . ."

[19] Vasari, VI, p. 264 (on Pontormo): "gli furono date a dipignere le due teste, dove sono gli occhi che danno lume (cioè le finestre) dalla volta infino al pavimento." Vasari is not explicit regarding Sarto and Franciabigio, but it is a reasonable assumption that they were each assigned an entire lateral wall.

[20] Vasari, V, pp. 36, 196; VI, p. 265.

Franciabigio's role in the project. He relates that Franciabigio's work on Lorenzo's wedding *apparato* led to a commission to gild the vault; and, indeed (although Vasari does not so state), the artist may have been involved in the decorations which turned the Salone into such a "paradise" for the occasion. Vasari continues: "e poi cominciò, per concorrenza di Andrea del Sarto a di Jacopo da Puntormo, una facciata di detta . . ." (And afterward, in competition with Andrea del Sarto and Jacopo da Pontormo, he began, on a wall in that hall . . .).[21] Vasari says in the life of Sarto that Franciabigio was "dato carico di tutta l'opera" (given the responsibility for the whole work), suggesting an original commission to him, which would date between Lorenzo's wedding and his death; however, further on, both here and in the life of Franciabigio, Vasari states that it was Giulio who carried out the pope's wish to have the Salone decorated.[22] Now the cardinal did not come to Florence until 27 May 1519, and Sarto may not have returned from France until as late as October—a combination of circumstances which suggests the following sequence of events. Franciabigio was commissioned to gild the vault after Lorenzo's wedding and may have continued the work to the extent of designing the layout of the room.[23] However, the project was delayed and the frescos were not begun. Lorenzo fell ill in November 1518 and it soon became clear that he was suffering from a mortal illness.[24] After his death in May 1519, Giulio's arrival in Florence, and Sarto's return from France, the decoration was freshly projected on orders to Giulio from Pope Leo—probably in early 1520.[25] At this time, as John Shearman has suggested, the team of artists went to Rome to discuss the project with their patron.[26]

Such a chronology would be consistent with the fact that a year and a half later, when Leo died, neither Sarto nor Franciabigio had finished even half of their part of the decoration: Sarto had painted only the *Tribute to Caesar* (pl. 71) and Franciabigio had painted only the *Triumph of Cicero* (pl. 72). Regarding the date of Pontormo's entrance into the project, it should be recalled that he was employed to work in the Salone after his successful completion of the portrait of Cosimo Pater Patriae, which may have been commissioned as late as January 1520. Moreover, Vasari attributes Pontormo's participation in the Salone project to his friendship with Ottaviano,[27] who was in charge

---

[21] Vasari, V, p. 195.

[22] Vasari, V, pp. 35, 195.

[23] The fact that Franciabigio was assigned the wall opposite the main entrance, which might have been considered the more important of the lateral walls, supports the contention of Freedberg, 1963, II, p. 104, n. 2; and McKillop, 1974, pp. 79-81, that the overall design of the project was due to Franciabigio. Shearman, 1965, I, pp. 82-83, leans toward Sarto as its author.

[24] For a day-by-day account of Lorenzo's long illness based on contemporary diaries, see Pieraccini, II, pp. 269-79.

[25] The work is placed in 1520 by the chronicler Francesco Baldovinetti, whose last entry for 1520 is ". . . emassimo papa ljone fornjscje lamuragla delpoggio acchajano." See C. von Fabriczy, ed.,

"Mitteilungen über neue Forschungen" (Aus dem Gedenkbuch Francesco Baldovinettis), *Rep.KW*, 28, 1905, p. 544.

[26] Shearman, 1965, I, pp. 86-88. Vasari, V, p. 55, implies that Sarto went to Rome after Raphael's death at Easter (which fell on 8 April in 1520). Shearman and McKillop, 1974, pp. 82-83, point out instances of Roman influence in the frescos, the most compelling being that of Raphael's Stanze on Sarto's *Caesar*, which is not present in his *modello* (Louvre 1684; see Shearman, 1965, II, pl. 75c), presumably made before his Roman experience.

[27] Vasari, VI, p. 264: "Mediante quest' opera, e particolarmente questa testa di Cosimo, fatto il Puntormo amico di messer Ottaviano, avendosi a dipignere al Poggio a Caiano la sala grande. . . ."

of the day-to-day proceedings of the work, rather than Giulio, who commissioned the decoration. It is even possible that Pontormo was brought into the project after Sarto and Franciabigio, subsequently going to Rome (as the others had done earlier) and only then executing the drawings showing the influence of the Sistine ceiling and Raphael's Stanze that we take to be his earliest studies for the lunette (pls. 75-76).[28] Such a late date for the beginning of Pontormo's work would then explain the apparent dependence of these studies on drawings by Michelangelo for the New Sacristy, which must date early in 1521 (pls. 73-74).[29] As Kathleen Weil-Garris Posner has shown, certain of Pontormo's ideas for the lunette—a central roundel with plaques, garlands, and putti; reclining river-god types—are closely related to the decorative transposition of Sistine ceiling imagery that occurs in Michelangelo's drawings.[30] An entry in 1521 into the project is also feasible in view of the fact that Pontormo completed scarcely a quarter of his share, finishing only the lunette of *Vertumnus and Pomona* before the Salone decoration was abandoned late in the year.

In 1531, after the siege of Florence and the final restoration of the Medici, the same family members who had been responsible for the work in 1520-1521 took up the project again. According to Vasari (by then himself in the service of the Medici), Giulio (Pope Clement VII) ordered Ottaviano to have Pontormo continue the decoration of the room, and scaffolding was erected, but Pontormo did not progress beyond the cartoons, which represented "un Ercole che fa scoppiare Anteo . . . una Venere e Adone . . . una storia d'ignudi che giuocano al calcio" (a Hercules who is crushing Antaeus . . . a Venus and Adonis . . . a scene of nude figures playing football).[31] Not only did nothing come of this campaign but, surprisingly, after his assumption of power in 1537 Duke Cosimo did not proceed with the decoration of the room, limiting his patronage of the villa to tapestries of hunting scenes after cartoons by Stradano.[32]

The Salone was completed in the later sixteenth century. In 1578-1582 Alessandro Allori finished the decoration for Grand Duke Francesco de' Medici, following a program by Vincenzo Borghini.[33] As can be seen in his compositional scheme for the work (pl. 77),[34] Allori enlarged Sarto's and Franciabigio's frescoes, removing the painted col-

[28] Uffizi 454F and 6660Fv; see Cox-Rearick, 1964, I, cat. 131 and 133. For Roman influences in the drawings for the lunette and the question of Pontormo's trip (or trips) to Rome, see Cox-Rearick, 1964, I, pp. 38-44, 172-90.

[29] Paris, Louvre 837 and 838; see P. Joannides, "Michelangelo's Medici Chapel: Some New Suggestions," *Burl.*, 114, 1972, pp. 541-46.

[30] Weil-Garris Posner, pp. 646-48, cites Uffizi 6660Fv and 454F, to which should be added 455F (Cox-Rearick, 1964, I, cat. 132, fig. 124), in which the three men on the lower wall resemble the river gods in Louvre 838. However, I still have doubts about the connection between 455F and either of the Salone lunettes, at least insofar as the final definition of the subjects as *Vertumnus and Pomona* and *Hercules and Fortuna* is concerned.

[31] Vasari, VI, pp. 275-76. See also Vasari, V, p. 196, where Duke Alessandro de' Medici is cited as responsible for the commission. No drawings by Pontormo have been identified with the first two subjects (however, cf. Uffizi 6570Fr; Cox-Rearick, 1964, I, cat. 327); but a large compositional drawing (Uffizi 13861F) and several figure studies relating to it (Uffizi 6505F, 6616Fr, 6616Fv, 6738F), shows a scene of nudes playing ball which may be connected with the *calcio* players (Cox-Rearick, 1964, I, cat. 307-11).

[32] Vasari, VII, p. 618; and G. G. Bertelà, in Barocchi, cat. 125-32.

[33] See Allori, p. 29; and Allori's letter to Borghini of 25 July 1578, in V. Borghini, pp. 126-27.

[34] Lecchini Giovannoni, cat. 37.

umn two thirds of the way across each wall to make single, undivided scenes extending to the corners of the room.[35]

Since, in effect, Allori "completed" Sarto's and Franciabigio's frescos by extending them, it has been assumed that they were left unfinished. However, there is no evidence that the narrow picture fields that orginally existed to the right of the painted columns were to have been part of the *Cicero* and *Caesar* scenes. On the contrary, both artists carried their work to exactly the same point on their respective walls (surely an amazing coincidence if they were constrained to stop their work at Leo's death). Moreover, Sarto's *modello* for his fresco shows a composition of exactly the same format as the one he painted.[36] We may also be aided in determining the original design of these walls by considering a dependent fresco scheme such as Francesco Salviati's Sala delle Udienze of 1543-1544 (pl. 78).[37] The long east wall of the Sala, with its *sopraporta* and its two *istorie*, is framed by narrow, vertical panels with allegorical figures, which are similar in proportions to the end panels of the Salone walls as they are drawn in Allori's compositional plan. Perhaps, then, Giovio's program also called for allegorical figures in these corner spaces.

Allori also completed the three walls of the Salone that had already been begun and painted the entire northwest wall.[38] As a pendant to Franciabigio's *Cicero* on the northeast wall, he painted *Scipio Africanus Meeting Hasdrubal at the Court of Syphax* (pl. 79).[39] As a pendant to Sarto's *Caesar* on the southwest wall, he painted *Titus Flaminius at the Council of the Achaeans* (pl. 80).[40] Between the *Cicero* and *Scipio* scenes Allori painted a *sopraporta* of *Magnanimitas, Magnificentia, and Liberalitas* (the first and last are labeled), with an inscription commemorating the original patron of the room, Leo X (pl. 81); opposite, between the *Caesar* and *Titus* frescos, Allori painted *Fortitudo, Prudentia, and Vigilantia* (the first and last are labeled) and an inscription commemorating his patron, Grand Duke Francesco, whose arms are placed above the group (pl. 68).[41] Turning to the end walls, on the southeast wall under Pontormo's lunette he painted the *Virtues*—inscribed PIETAS, VIRTVS, and IVSTIZIA (pl. 37); on the northwest wall are the *Rewards of Virtue*, inscribed FAMA, GLORIA, and HONOR (pl. 68).[42] In the lunette above he painted

[35] Allori, pp. 28-29, mentions his revisions in a *ricordo* of 18 September 1582: "Nella storia di Francia ne ho rifatto il terzo, e lavato e rinetto e rifatto l'aria e rifatto [?] più che li duoi terzi. . . ." And, regarding Sarto's fresco: "la quale storia è stata lavata e rinetta e finita da me." It is inscribed: ANNO D.N̄I M.D. XXI ANDREAS / SARTIVS PINGEBAT / ET A.D. MDLXXXII. ALEXANDER / ALLORIVS SEQVE-BATVR.

[36] See above, n. 26.

[37] The dependence of the Sala delle Udienze on the Salone in other aspects of its design is remarked by Shearman, 1965, I, pp. 80-83.

[38] For Allori's work in the Salone, see Allori, pp. 9-11 (1579), 18 (1581), and 28-29 (1582); the letter of 25 July 1578, mentioned above, n. 33; and payments to Allori of 17 February 1578 and 28 February 1581, published in V. Borghini, p.

126. Allori's additions and their documentation are noted by Shearman, 1965, I, pp. 78-81; and McKillop, 1974, pp. 71-73.

[39] Allori, p. 9, mentions this fresco in a *ricordo* of 30 June 1579. He signed and dated the fresco twice: 1578 on the base of the column in the background, and 1582 on the bench to the far right.

[40] Allori, p. 29, mentions this fresco in a *ricordo* of 18 September 1582. The work is signed on the scroll held by the dog to the lower right, ALEXANDER ALLORIVS PINGEBAT.

[41] Allori, pp. 28-29, mentions the *sopraporte* in the *ricordo* of 18 September 1582.

[42] "La Fama, la Gloria, et l'Honore" are mentioned in Allori's letter of 25 July 1578 (in V. Borghini, p. 127); all the personifications are cited in his *ricordi* as completed by 18 September

Hercules and Fortuna in the Garden of the Hesperides (pl. 68).[43] These extensive additions brought the decoration that had been begun some sixty years earlier to completion. And, in fact, they dominate the Salone, which, despite Allori's attempts to harmonize his work with the High Renaissance style of Leo's artists, has a pronounced flavor of the late Maniera.

✳   ✳   ✳

This account of almost a century of work on the Salone decorations invites speculation as to the nature of, and possible interrelation between, three programs for its decoration. The first, and the one which is of primary interest here, was Giovio's partly executed scheme, for which no written evidence has survived. It may have been based on a now unrecoverable plan for the room (by a Laurentian humanist such as Poliziano), which he recast in accord with the special demands of Leonine propaganda. The second would have been Pope Clement's abortive attempt to complete the room with the introduction of mythological subjects. The third and last must have been a reworking of Giovio's scheme by Francesco's iconographer, Vincenzo Borghini, in which the myth of the Medici was reinterpreted in the light of the grand-ducal view of Medici history and destiny.

Lacking documentary evidence, we cannot determine with certainty the scheme of the Salone as it was projected in 1520 by Giovio and the three artists, but some suggestions may be made. These are based on the frescos painted in the two campaigns of work in the room and on preparatory studies for the work, in particular Allori's drawing for the completion of the decoration. This drawing is a valuable document, for its differs significantly from what Allori painted and it contains his notes on the subjects, and the meanings as he understood them, of his three major frescos. In addition to this visual and written evidence there are late sixteenth-century notices of the work in the *vite* of Vasari, in Raffaello Borghini's *Il Riposo* (1584), and in the *ricordi* and letters of Allori himself.

The only general statement about the theme of which Salone occurs in Vasari's *vita* of Franciabigio, in which he relates that Pope Leo had the room decorated in memory of his father Lorenzo, who had wanted it painted with scenes from antiquity.[44]

> . . . la quale opera aveva fatto cominciare la liberalità di Papa Leone per memoria di Lorenzo suo padre, che tale edifizio aveva fatto fabbricare e di ornamenti e di storie antiche a suo proposito fatto dipignere. . . .

This work had been undertaken by the liberality of Pope Leo, in memory of his father Lorenzo, who had caused the edifice to be built, and had ordained

1582 (Allori, p. 29). They are also mentioned by R. Borghini, p. 627.

[43] See Allori's letter of 25 July 1578 (in V. Borghini, p. 127), in which he tells Borghini that Grand Duke Francesco has requested that he insert the date in the disk below the oculus (which was, in fact, left blank). The lunette is mentioned in the *ricordi* (Allori, p. 29) as completed by 18 September 1582: ". . . è figurato i pomi degli orti Esperidi guardati dalle Ninfe, da Ercole e dalla Fortuna." R. Borghini, p. 627, describes it as "i pomi hesperidi guardati dalle Ninfe, da Ercole, e dalla buona Fortuna."

[44] Vasari, V, p. 195.

that it should be painted with scenes from ancient history and other ornaments according to his pleasure.

We do not know what subjects Lorenzo had in mind or whether any of them were retained by Giovio; however, Giovio's program for the room may be deduced from the evidence at hand. The placement in the Salone of the scenes painted by Leo's artists, and later by Allori, may be followed in reference to Allori's drawing and to a diagrammatic reconstruction of Giovio's scheme (fig. 3).[45]

Considering first the end walls (and leaving for later discussion the lunettes by Pontormo and Allori in the upper zone), we should note that Vasari makes no mention of what Pontormo planned to paint below the lunettes. The *Virtues* and the *Rewards of Virtue* are indicated (and labeled) in the six square fields above the windows in Allori's compositional drawing, but the two groups are reversed.

Franciabigio's fresco on the northeast wall is described by Vasari as representing ". . . quando Cicerone dai cittadini romani è portato per gloria sua" (the scene of Cicero being carried in triumph by the citizens of Rome).[46] Borghini later interpreted the work as an allegory of the return from exile of Cosimo Pater Patriae (1434):[47]

> . . . il Franciabigio vi lasciò non finita l'historia quando Cicerone dopo l'esiglio, essendo portato in Campidoglio fu chiamato Padre della Patria; e questa historia allude al ritorno di Cosimo Medici il vecchio in Firenze.

> Franciabigio left unfinished the story of when Cicero, after his exile, was carried to the Capitol and called Pater Patriae; and that story alludes to the return of Cosimo il Vecchio to Florence.

Allori's *Scipio* fresco is mentioned in his *ricordi* as "la storia della cena di Siface con Scipione e Asdrubale" (the story of the dinner of Syphax with Scipio and Hasdrubal).[48] This scene appears in his compositional scheme, but it is placed on the opposite wall. Below it, Allori gives an interpretation of the subject as an allegory of Lorenzo de' Medici's trip to Naples (1480):

> Quando Scipione sendo proco'solo in Spagna si trasferì in Africa e si mise in mano di Siface Re di Numidia, dove ordinò e conchiuse con lui lega. Alludendo all'andata del Mag.co Lore.zo a napoli a Re Ferrando.

> The story of when Scipio as Proconsul in Spain moved to Africa and put himself in the hands of Syphax, King of Numidia, where he ordered and concluded an alliance with him; alluding to Lorenzo il Magnifico's trip to Naples to King Ferrando.[49]

[45] The background design of this reconstruction is after Shearman, 1965, I, p. 81, fig. III.

[46] Vasari, V, p. 195. In the Anonimo Magliabecchiano, ed. C. Frey, *Il Codice Magliabecchiano*, Berlin, 1892, p. 117, the fresco is called a triumph of Caesar ("l'istoria di Cesare, che è portato . . .").

[47] R. Borghini, p. 626.

[48] Allori, p. 9.

[49] R. Borghini, p. 627, gives a similar interpretation: ". . . la cena di Siface Re de' Numidi fatta da lui à Scipione dopo che egli hebbe rotto Asdrubale in Ispagna; volendo con questa historia dimostrare la gita del magnifico Lorenzo al Re di Napoli, da cui fu in vece del mal talento, che haveva verso di lui grandemente honorato."

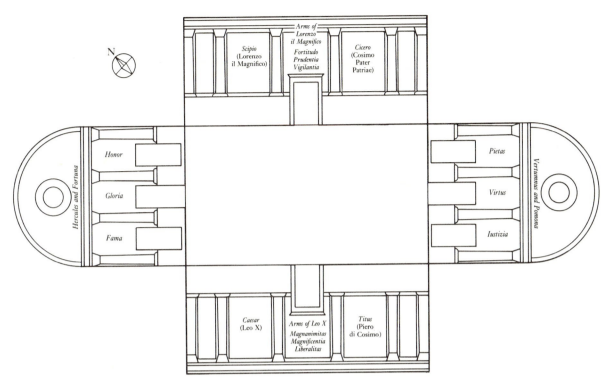

3. Original scheme of the decorations of the Salone, Poggio a Caiano

Next to the *Scipio* in Allori's drawing, and opposite the doorway over which he eventually painted it, is the *sopraporta* of *Magnanimitas, Magnificentia, and Liberalitas.* In the sketch, the first two personifications are reversed.

Andrea del Sarto's fresco on the southwest wall is described by Vasari as "una storia, dentrovi quando a Cesare sono presentati i tributi di tutti gli animali" (a scene representing Caesar being presented with tribute of all kinds of animals.[50] In his *ricordi,* Allori calls the fresco "una mezza storia sulla quale è uno imperatore presentato da diversi e varii presenti" (a half story in which there is an emperor receiving various gifts).[51] Borghini later interpreted the fresco more specifically as an allegory of the gift of exotic animals to Lorenzo il Magnifico (1487):[52]

> Andrea vi cominciò una historia, dove si vede Cesare in Egitto presentato da molti popoli con vari doni, volendo, chi trovò questa inventione, significare quando il magnifico Lorenzo Medici il vecchio fu di varii, e stranieri animali presentato. . . .
>
> Andrea began a story where one sees Caesar in Egypt being presented with various gifts from many nations; and he who invented this subject wished to signify that time when Lorenzo il Magnifico was presented with various exotic animals.

[50] Vasari, V, p. 35. While Vasari does not so state, it is clear from his *Tribute to Lorenzo il Magnifico* (Palazzo Vecchio), which is modeled on this fresco, that he believed it alluded to Lorenzo.

[51] Allori, p. 28.

[52] R. Borghini, p. 626.

Allori's *Titus* fresco, the pendant to Andrea's *Caesar* on the southwest wall, appears in his compositional study, where it is placed on the northeast wall. Below it, Allori gives an interpretation of the scene as an allegory of Lorenzo's diplomacy at the Diet of Cremona (1482):

> Quando Q. Flaminio si transferì nel co'siglio degl'Achei per consultare la guerra contro il Re Antioco, che disegnava co' gra'de esercito passare in Grecia. Alludendo quando nella dieta di Cremona, aspirando i vinitiani d'impadronirsi di tutta Italia, alla quale dieta sendovi transferito il Mag.co Lore.zo interroppe ogni loro diseg.no.

> The story of when Q. Flaminius moved to the Council of the Achaeans in order to advise concerning the war against King Antiochus, who was planning to cross over into Greece with a large army; alluding to the time when the Venetians, in the Diet of Cremona, were aspiring to take over all of Italy; and when Lorenzo il Magnifico went there he broke off all their plans.[53]

Next to the *Titus* fresco in Allori's drawing—and opposite the doorway over which he eventually painted it—are the allegories *Fortitudo, Prudentia, and Vigilantia.* In the sketch, Fortitudo and Vigilantia are reversed.

It is clear from this summary that our knowledge of the program of the Salone is based on identifications of its subjects and interpretations of their meaning dating from the later sixteenth century. And even these are incomplete: Vasari's hint about the Laurentian origin of the program does not indicate what the subjects of the "storie antiche" might have been; he gives the subjects of the *istorie* which were painted in 1521, but an interpretation of them as allegories of Cosimo and Lorenzo is made only in 1584 by Borghini; Allori gives the Roman subjects of his *istorie* and interprets them as allegories of Lorenzo; and Allori labels the twelve personifications of virtue and its rewards but does not suggest to whom they might refer.

Not only do all these interpretations postdate Giovio's program by many years, but the extent to which Vincenzo Borghini and Allori followed Giovio's original scheme is far from clear. Allori's frescos suggest a general intention to harmonious coexistence with the earlier work.[54] However, the alternative positions of the end wall personifications, the *sopraporte,* and the *istorie* in his planning drawing indicate that Allori was not following the earlier program to the letter—and, perhaps, that he imperfectly understood its meaning. In considering Allori's additions, then, we must make a distinction

[53] R. Borghini, p. 627, gives a similar interpretation: ". . . l'historia di Tito quinto Flaminio, che orando nel consiglio degli Achei contro l'Ambasciadore degli Etoli, e del Re Antioco, dissuade la lega, che con gli Achei cercavano di fare detti Ambasciadori; applicata questa historia alla dieta di Cremona, in cui il Magnifico Lorenzo disturbò i disegni de' Vinitiani, che aspiravano à farsi padroni di tutta Italia."

[54] R. Borghini, p. 626, notes that Allori used

some of Sarto's ideas in his completion of the *Caesar*: ". . . questa historia da Andrea lasciata imperfetta è stata finita da Alessandro, parte seguitando le figure d'Andrea, e parte di sua invenzione." (It should be noted that Borghini does not state that the "figure d' Andrea" were motifs which Sarto intended for this fresco.) For Allori's general adherence to Giovio's program, see Shearman, 1965, I, p. 81; and McKillop, 1974, p. 73.

between the Roman subjects of the frescos and a possible reading of them as Medici allegories. Allori may indeed have followed Giovio's indications as to the Roman exemplars to be depicted—Scipio and Titus—but he seems not to have understood how these scenes were intended to relate to the *Cicero* and *Caesar* scenes already painted in the Salone or to whom they were intended to refer.

THE *ISTORIE* AND *SOPRAPORTE*

The broad outlines of the program of the Salone, as Giovio conceived it and as Borghini completed it, are traditional. The combination of Famous Men, Virtues, and imagery of apotheosis, conveying a message of Medici power, virtue, and immortality, links the Salone to the tradition of Renaissance public rooms in which didactic frescos represent *uomini illustri* and Virtues, accompanied by appropriate *imprese*.[55] Such pictorial cycles of great men of action and fame first appeared in the wake of Petrarch's *De viris illustribus vitae*. In these, historical Roman exemplars, together with other *illustri*, were portrayed with the Virtues they exemplified, often with explanatory *tituli*, or captions.[56] A condensed version of this formula, in which the Virtues were not personified, occurred in the context of civic humanism in the art of the Florentine Republic. In the late Trecento, twenty-two portraits of Famous Men with Latin epigrams by Coluccio Salutati decorated a room (no longer extant) in the Palazzo della Signoria.[57] And, in 1482, Domenico Ghirlandaio's Roman heroes Scipio, Caesar, and Camillus in the Sala dei Gigli suggest that the civic virtue of the Florentines was to be equated with that of their Roman republican counterparts. These decorations and others reflect the preoccupation of the Florentine humanists with their Roman heritage, with the myth of the Roman foundation of Florence, and especially with the notion of Florence as a New Rome.[58]

The Famous Men theme reappeared after the Medici restoration of 1512, as the family began to shape this *topos* to fit the special requirements of their propaganda. Roman exemplars were used in public pageants to dramatize the themes of Medici Return, the legitimacy of the dynasty, and Medici virtue. Nardi's program for the *broncone* pageant of 1513 called for an elaborate allegory of Medici government based on Roman models. As described by Vasari, the first float carried the gods of the Golden Age (Saturn and Janus), which was followed by *trionfi* of Roman kings and emperors representing differ-

[55] Langedijk, pp. 44-46; and McKillop, 1974, p. 68.

[56] Mommsen, pp. 95-116; and Rubinstein, 1958, pp. 179-207. Perugino's frescos in Perugia, Collegio del Cambio (1507), are late examples of this tradition. The Cardinal Virtues are each allotted three Roman exemplars, with *tituli* explaining the connection between them.

[57] Hankey, pp. 363-65 (the Camillus epigram is quoted in chap. 1, n. 79).

[58] Rubinstein, 1942, p. 225 (on Leonardo Bruni).

See also chap. 1, n. 80 (on Cosimo and Camillus), and chap. 3, n. 67 (on the Roman foundation of Florence). Programs featuring Roman exemplars also appeared in a domestic context, as in Castagno's cycle from Villa Carducci (M. Horster, "Castagnos Florentiner Fresken 1450-1457," *Wallraf Richartz Jahrbuch*, 17, 1955, pp. 79-99) or the lost cycle for Giovanni di Bicci de' Medici (Vasari, II, p. 50). For earlier, non-Florentine, examples in a private context, see Horster, p. 82, n. 1; and Rubinstein, 1958, p. 194.

ent effects of *buon governo:* Numa Pompilius (religion), Titus Manlius Torquatus (*virtù* and prosperity), Julius Caesar (victory), Augustus (poetry), and Trajan (law); the last float, representing the return of the Golden Age, implicitly linked the Medici not only to the Golden Age of Saturn and Janus but to its alleged revival in ancient Rome.[59] In 1515 the *Triumph of Camillus* was enacted in Florence not only in reference to the theme of Medici Return but to the idea of Roma *rinata*, the rebirth of Rome in Florence under the Medici; and, in the *entrata* of Pope Leo which followed, with its reproductions of Roman arches, columns, and obelisks, the theme of Florence as a New Rome under Leo was stated in most forceful terms.[60]

In Rome, as well, these themes were enacted at the great pageants attending Leo's ascendancy to the papacy—the event which marked the Romanization of Florence in fact as well as fantasy. The arch of the Genoese merchants in the Lateran *possesso* was dedicated to Leo as peacemaker, with representations of the *illustri* Numa Pompilius (characterized as Roman king of peace), Antoninus Pius, Mutius Scevola, Fabius Manlius, and Scipio Africanus.[61] But the most elaborate development of the theme of the unity of Rome and Florence was in the decorations of the theater on the Capitoline, which was built for the ceremonies celebrating the conferral of Roman citizenship on Giuliano and Lorenzo the younger in 1513.[62] There, representations of Roman *illustri* demonstrated the unity of the Romans and Etruscans, the ancient glory of Florence as a Roman colony, the reconciliation of the two cities under Leo, and, according to Marcantonio Altieri's description of the festivities, "Roma rinata."[63] The temple-front entrance facade (fig. 4) and the walls of the theater (fig. 5) were designed like proscenia with fluted, gilded columns framing monumental paintings *all'antica*, which were in chiaroscuro, imitating reliefs.[64] The facade paintings depicted scenes alluding to the foundation of Rome (*Saturn Greeted by Janus on His Arrival in Latium*), the foundation of the Capitoline (*The Surrender of the Tarpeian Rock to the Sabines*), and the foundation of the Temple of Jupiter Optimus Maximus, which had stood on the hill in antiquity (*Romulus Bringing Spoils to Jupiter* and the *Dedication of the Temple of Jupiter*).[65] The *imprese* above the paintings echoed the theme of the unity of Florence and Rome: the Tiber and the Roman She-Wolf with Romulus and Remus were on one side, the Arno and the Florentine Marzocco (with a *palla*) were on the other. Inside the theater, an assortment of Roman

[59] Vasari, VI, pp. 252-55.

[60] Vasari, V, p. 24; Shearman, 1975, pp. 149-50.

[61] Penni, pp. 224-26.

[62] See the descriptions by Altieri, pp. 6-8; Palliolo, pp. 25-35; and Sereno, pp. 114-16. The *apparato* is discussed by Gnoli, pp. 83-107; Cruciani, pp. xiii-xcvi; and Mitchell, pp. 119-24.

[63] Altieri, p. 6.

[64] Sereno, p. 116: "Così si vede il teatro ornato con quindici quadri, a cui vanno aggiunti i quattro che sono all'esterno. Tutto è costruito imitando l'oro e l'argento, con splendore celeste." Palliolo, pp. 27, 33, describes the chiaroscuri and emphasizes the style *all'antica* of the ensemble: "Le figure tutte

. . . sonno di grandezza sopra naturale, . . . né sonno con molto varietate di colori adornate, ma in tal forma composte che al tutto assimigliano a quelle che in viva pietra intagliate se vedeno. . . . Le figure tutte sopradette sonno armate et ornate secondo la usanza antiqua de' Romani, in modo tale che in ogni parte assimigliano alle imagini et simulacri quali in archi triomphali et altri luoghi vedemo egregiamente sculpite."

[65] Altieri, p. 7; Palliolo, pp. 26-27; and Sereni, pp. 114-15. The *Tarpeian Rock* was by Peruzzi, who also did the scenery for the comedy that was performed at the celebration (Vasari, IV, pp. 595-96; see Frommel, cat. 36; and Bruschi, p. 216, n. 23).

4. Reconstruction of the facade of the Capitoline theater (after Cruciani)

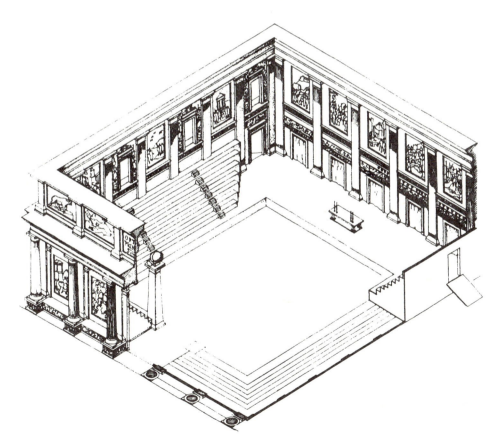

5. Reconstruction of the interior of the Capitoline theater (after Cruciani)

exemplars (such as Aeneas, Romulus, Scipio, and Augustus) were depicted in scenes illustrating the friendship of the Romans and Etruscans. As was customary in Famous Men schemes, the friezes above the scenes were filled with appropriate *imprese*—in this case, the Medici *palle*, yokes, *diamanti*, and lions.

The site of the festival, its date, and its decorations suggestively linked the Medici with the sacred traditions of ancient Rome—indeed, with her very destiny. The day chosen for the festival was the date on which the first Temple of Jupiter had been dedicated.[66] This connection was emphasized by the painting of the dedication on the facade of the theater, by the unusual square plan of the theater, and by its hexastyle facade, modeled after the ancient temple. Moreover, the festival was joined with an out-of-season celebration of the Palilia, or the birthday of Rome. As Altieri relates,[67]

> Poi, con magnifica et honorata compagnia, dargli un sontuoso e splendido pranzo, con grata dimostratione di publica letitia, applicando tal solennità alli Natali di Roma et intitolarla le PALILIE, per esser, se dir si puote, rinata Roma, cioè liberata da Sua Santità d'affanno e di miseria, e dato principio e modo di più felice vita con grandissima speranza di megliore conditione.

> Then with magnificent and honorable company, they gave him a sumptuous and splendid meal, with a welcome demonstration of public happiness, applying such solemnities to the birthday of Rome and calling it the PALILIE, since, in a manner of speaking, Rome was reborn, that is, freed by His Holiness from troubles and woes and given the beginning and the means for a happier life along with the hope of a better condition.

A Medici pageant on the Capitoline on 13 September would thus have been understood as celebrating the rebirth of the city under Pope Leo (implicitly a New Jupiter). Indeed, in his life of the pope Giovio declared that with this festival the Golden Age seemed truly to have returned to Rome.[68]

In these Capitoline decorations, dramatic scenes in which the Roman *illustri* were the protagonists thus substituted for the static mode of the earlier portraits of exemplars in Florence. However, there is no indication in this or in the other Medici *apparati* of 1512-1515 that the exemplars were to be read as alluding to specific Medici personalities. Beginning about 1514, on the other hand, a new narrative mode was exploited by Leo for personal propaganda, following the model of Pope Julius II. In the Stanza dell'Incendio, scenes representing the deeds of past popes named Leo (such as the *Fire in the Borgo*, which refers to Leo IV) transparently alluded to the virtuous deeds of Leo, suggesting that they fulfilled the prophecy of the earlier events. And, in the Sala di Costantino,

[66] Scullard, pp. 186-87. Palliolo, p. 27, describes the theater, which had six columns like the first three Jupiter temples. See Scullard, p. 187, for a reconstruction of the Jupiter temple facade. Bruschi, pp. 199-203, gives several reasons why a rectangular plan was chosen for the theater, to which may be added its reference to the Jupiter temple.

[67] Altieri, p. 6. For the Palilia (21 April), see Scullard, pp. 103-5; and Gnoli, pp. 89-90.
[68] Giovio, 1551, bk. III, p. 173: ". . . furono fatti . . . giuochi scenici, essendo fabricato un theatro . . . con si notabile e ricco apparato di tutte le cose, che l'antica felicita dell'età dell'oro parve essere ritornata con la liberalità del Papa."

which is contemporaneous with the Salone, this typological formula was enriched to include eight papal portraits accompanied by Virtues and other personifications. One of these groups is *Leo X as Clement I with Moderatio and Comitas*, in which the portrait of Leo conflates the living pope with his ancient exemplar (pl. 29).

The Salone at Poggio a Caiano is the Florentine counterpart of these Roman works. Its *istorie* featuring Roman exemplars and depicting events which prophesy the civic virtue and rule of the Medici recall the Capitoline theater decorations, and the *illustri* alluding to specific Medici figures elaborate in secular terms the imagery of the Stanze. Moreover, the scheme of fictive architecture articulating the walls of the room is distinctly Romanizing. It echos the hexastyle villa portico designed by Sangallo for Lorenzo il Magnifico,[69] but it is updated through reference to the Roman theater, the design of which (for Lorenzo's son Leo) has also been attributed to Sangallo.[70]

The cycle *all'antica* invented by Giovio for the Salone is the first such decoration in Florence. Here, following the precepts of Alberti, who recommended that the decoration of villas, particularly the "buildings of princes," should contain paintings of the "memorable actions of great men,"[71] Giovio projected a cycle of ancient events and allegorical figures alluding to the Medici in which their theme of Time's Return was expanded to embrace the idea of the cyclical repetition of history, as the Medici, fulfilling the greatness of the antique exemplars, are rewarded for their *virtù*.

Giovio's training as a humanist, historian, and Medici courtier fitted him well for the task of devising the program for the Salone decorations. Having come into the service of Leo X in Rome in 1513, Giovio had been at the papal court during the years of the great Leonine festivals and the decorative projects at the Vatican and would thus have been well versed in the themes and images of Medicean propaganda. He was also keenly interested in literary portraits of *uomini illustri* imitative of the biographies of Plutarch and Suetonius; and in 1521 he was already making plans to set up his famous museum on Lake Como, in which portraits of famous men and *elogia*, or brief biographies, were to be combined in a *templum virtutis* of the great exemplars of the past and present.[72] As a result of these leanings, Giovio's program for the Salone was one in which "art and history, image and letter, were inseparably linked."[73] However, unlike earlier *uomini illustri* cycles, and unlike Giovio's own later historical programs such as that for Vasari's frescos in the Palazzo della Cancelleria (pl. 90), the literary apparatus of the Salone

[69] In the Salone the intercolumniations are irregular because the designer was constrained to follow the intervals dictated by the spacing of the rings on the ceiling: one picture field is centered over the doorway under the central soffit ring, and the side fields are each subdivided by a column aligned with the center of the first complete ring at the end of each wall. Winner, 1970, p. 262, suggests that the articulation of these walls reflects Sangallo's own plans for their design.

[70] Bruschi, pp. 204-13, presents a convincing argument for the attribution of the theater's design (its architect was Pietro Rosselli) to Giuliano.

[71] Leone Battista Alberti, *Ten Books on Architec-*ture, IX, iv (tr. J. Leoni, London, 1755, repr. London, 1965, p. 192): "And as the subjects of both poetry and painting are various, some expressing the memorable actions of great men; others representing the manners of private persons; others describing the life of rustics: the former, as the most majestic, should be applied to public works, and the buildings of princes."

[72] Langedijk, p. 47; and Zimmerman, p. 409. For a letter of 28 August 1521 referring to the portraits of literary *illustri* in his collection, see Giovio, *Lettere*, I, p. 92, no. 8.

[73] Zimmerman, p. 409.

scheme is largely unexpressed. There are no *tituli* or inscriptions to identify either the subjects of the Roman *istorie* or their Medicean references.

✷   ✷   ✷

Franciabigio's *Triumph of Cicero* shows Cicero returned from exile and carried in triumph to the Capitoline, where he was named Pater Patriae in 62 B.C.[74] Since the allusion to the return from exile of Cosimo Pater Patriae is clear, this fresco may be discussed first as indicative of the complex layering of meaning and reference that characterizes Giovio's program. Cicero, who had been prominent in all earlier Famous Men cycles in Florence, was the humanist's paradigm of civic virtue.[75] The allegory of Cosimo as Cicero in Franciabigio's fresco depends on the traditional association made between Cosimo and Cicero, in particular, on the parallel that was drawn between the patterns of exile and return that characterized their careers, the association of both with the rebirth of the state, and the fact that both received the title Pater Patriae.[76] These similarities became the basis for a picture of Cosimo's status in Florence that was idealized; for Cosimo's return from exile in 1434, unlike Cicero's, could not be characterized as a triumph, and, unlike Cicero, Cosimo did not receive the title Pater Patriae on his return—or, for that matter, at any time during his life.

The manipulation of Medici history represented by the allegory of Cosimo as Cicero coincides exactly with the early Cinquecento view of the events of 1434, including that of Giovio, author of the program for the fresco. For it was Giovio who associated the medal of Cosimo, Florentia, and the yoke with a Ciceronian return from exile; and, in his *elogium* on Cosimo, Giovio connected the conferral of the Pater Patriae title with the return to Florence:[77]

> . . . secundissimisque fere omnium suffragiis decretum emanavit, quo exhilarata civitas redeuntem summis gratulationibus excepit; tanto quidem plebis et populi studio, ut non secus ac olim Cicero revocante Senatu Romano, Cosmus a Florentia libera Pater Patriae fit appellatus.

> And with the approving votes of almost everyone there came forth a decree, wherewith the citizens, rejoicing, received him in his return with citizens, rejoicing, received him in his return with great thanksgiving indeed with such enthusiasm on the part of the people that just as Cicero long ago—when the Roman Senate called him back—Cosimo was proclaimed by a free Florence Pater Patriae.

[74] *Plutarch's Lives* (Cicero, XXIII, 3, and XXXIII, 5).

[75] Cicero was included in both the *illustri* cycles in the Palazzo della Signoria. He appeared in the Trecento cycle, with an epigram by Salutati (quoted in Hankey, p. 365) and, as the only nonmilitary exemplar, among Ghirlandaio's six *illustri* in the Sala dei Gigli. For Cicero in Florentine thought, see H. Baron, "Cicero and the Roman Civic Spirit in the Middle Ages and the Early Renaissance," *Bulletin of the John Rylands Library*, 22, 1938, pp. 88-97; and Baron, pp. 121-25, 127-29, 145-51.

[76] For the background of the Cosimo-Cicero parallel, see the valuable study on this fresco by Winner, 1970; also Kliemann, 1976, pp. 25-34.

[77] Giovio, 1557, p. 133 (cited by Winner, 1970, n. 28).

Machiavelli, too, makes such assertions. In the *Istorie fiorentine*, commissioned by the Medici in the same year as the Salone decoration, he declares Florentine history to have properly begun with Cosimo's return and implies that the Pater Patriae title was accorded at that time.[78] The same conflation occurs in Franciabigio's fresco: the historical event of Cosimo's return is conjoined with the theme of the triumphal *entrata* and with the accolade Pater Patriae, both of which were central to the myth that Medici rule was established by Cosimo in 1434 on a note of unequivocal triumph.

Besides its primary allusion to the foundation of the state through the establishment of Medici rule in Florence, the *Cicero* introduces a number of the salient themes of the Salone decoration. It epitomizes, of course, the theme of Medici Return, which played such an important role in Leo's personal imagery. Thus, as the Camillus masque and the Florentine *entrata* alluded to the recent restoration of the Medici as well as to its prototype in 1434, so the reference to Cosimo's return as Pater Patriae in the *Cicero* is reinforced by allusions to other high points in Medici history. One of these is to Lorenzo il Magnifico, to whom, we recall, Vasari says Pope Leo dedicated the Salone decoration. Lorenzo also made a "return"—from his mission to Naples in 1480 on behalf of Italian peace—and he was also called Pater Patriae.[79] As will be shown, this association sets a pattern for the *istorie* of a secondary allusion in each to Leo's father, the builder of the villa in which these scenes are painted. Another reference is to an event in contemporary Medici history. There are a number of portrait-like heads in the crowd, prominent among which is Cicero himself (pl. 83). As can be seen in comparison with the profile *all'antica* on Giuliano's medal with Virtù and Fortuna-Occasio (pl. 84), Cicero is a portrait of Giuliano, who had been the first of the Medici to enter Florence on the return of the family in 1512.[80] Figures in the group welcoming Cicero, which recalls the crowd witnessing the liberation of Andromeda (Florence) in Piero di Cosimo's picture (pl. 12), may also be portraits of Florentines who played important roles in the events of 1512.[81]

The *Cicero* also highlights the related themes of Rome-Florence reconciliation and the Roman citizenship of the Medici, which were the primary messages of the Capitoline ceremony and *apparato* of 1513. This Roman theme is established by the elaborate setting, which is a fantastic reconstruction of the ancient Capitoline with the Temple of Jupiter in the background.[82] (When Allori enlarged the fresco, he further emphasized its Capitoline locale by completing the temple and adding an obelisk, a Tiber, and a

[78] See Machiavelli, I, p. 7; II, p. 234: "E rade volte occorse che uno cittadino, tornando trionfante d'una vittoria, fusse ricevuto dalla sua patria con tanto concorso di popolo e con tanta dimostrazione di benivolenzia, con quanta fu ricevuto egli tornando dallo esilio. E da ciascuno voluntariamente fu salutato benefattore del popolo e padre della patria."

[79] McKillop, 1974, pp. 72-73. See also Kliemann, 1976, p. 31, for other instances of Lorenzo's being called Pater Patriae.

[80] Winner, 1970, pp. 275-76; and Kliemann, 1976, p. 33. For the medal see Hill, no. 465 bis.

[81] Vasari's painting of the 1512 Medici return in the Sala di Leo X in the Palazzo Vecchio shows just such a group of citizens greeting Cardinal Giovanni and his entourage—among them, a portrait of the Gonfaloniere Giovambatista Ridolfi (Vasari, *Rag.*, p. 134).

[82] Winner, 1970, pp. 275-76, 285-86. For literature and Renaissance reconstructions of the temple, see F. Saxl, "The Capitol during the Renaissance: A Symbol of the Imperial Idea," in *Lectures*, London, 1957, I, pp. 200-214; and T. Buddenseig, "Zum Statuenprogramm im Kapitolsplan Pauls III," *ZK*, 32, 1969, pp. 177-228.

statue of Mars.)[83] The portrait of Giuliano as Cicero, who was the only one of the honored Medici actually to have been present at the ceremony, also alludes to the 1513 event. Moreover, Giuliano can be read as symbolizing the family in general, for in the proclamation read at the ceremony the "privilegi della Civiltà di Rome" were granted not only to Giuliano and Lorenzo but to "tutta la casa de' Medici."[84] Thus, this first fresco of the Salone *istorie* is an allegory not only of the foundation of Medici power in Florence but of Medici dominion in Rome as well.

Bearing in mind that the *Cicero* is an allegory of the beginnings of Medici rule, with secondary references to Lorenzo il Magnifico, the Medici restoration, and their Roman citizenship, we may now consider the other three *istorie*. As we have seen, Allori and Borghini related these frescos to events from the 1480s in the life of Lorenzo. Interpreters of the Salone have generally accepted this reading of the program, although with some uncertainty about an unbalanced scheme in which one *istoria* alludes to Cosimo and three to Lorenzo.[85] I would contend, however, that while there are allusions to Lorenzo in all the frescos, he is not the primary subject of the decoration. The presence of the allegory of Cosimo in the series indicates a different kind of scheme entirely. This fresco stands for the establishment of Medici rule and for the establishment of the ruling branch of the family descended from Cosimo. The other three *istorie* are allegories of Cosimo's descendants—his son Piero, his grandson Lorenzo, and his great-grandson Leo X—in which the political and dynastic continuity of the Medici are presented as mutually reinforcing aspects of power and rule. The series not only pays homage to Lorenzo; it is a comprehensive view of the Medici past, an allegory of the Golden Age of the Medici in republican Florence which precisely reflects the Medicean interpretation of their "history" in 1521.

The pendant to the *Cicero* on the northeast wall of the Salone is Allori's *Scipio Meeting Hasdrubal at the Court of Syphax*, which is the only one of the three frescos which Allori and Borghini connect with Lorenzo actually to relate to him. It alludes both to the circumstances and to the purpose of Lorenzo's most celebrated act of civic virtue—his daring and dangerous trip to Naples to meet with King Ferrando on behalf of Italian peace.[86] Allori's scene shows Scipio, who risked danger in foreign lands to negotiate

[83] All these additions are relevant to the Capitoline setting, but the Mars (which actually stood on the hill) may also refer to the theme of Mars as patron of Florence (as on the portico frieze), as well as to Allori's patron Francesco de' Medici, in whose horoscope Mars played an important role (see chap. 11, "Epilogue").

[84] Altieri, p. 3. See also Palliolo, p. 24: "Ma parse essere conveniente dedicare a Leone, ottimo Principe, il teatro nel Campidoglio, et ivi gratamente raccogliere per suoi patritii el Magnifico Juliano, Laurentio et sua posteritate (come fecero) con le cerimonie et spettacoli che a' suoi luoghi diremo."

[85] Shearman, 1965, I, pp. 78-79, 85, accepts the association of the 1521 frescos with Cosimo and Lorenzo but does not attempt to interpret Allori's scenes. Winner, 1970, p. 265, notes that such an unbalanced arrangement might not reflect Giovio's original intention but suggests no alternate program. McKillop, 1974, pp. 72-73, rationalizes the scheme by connecting all the scenes with Lorenzo, believing that the *Cicero* alludes to Lorenzo because he was called Pater Patriae when he returned in triumph after his trip to Naples. Kliemann, 1976, p. 13, accepts Borghini's reading of three of the scenes as Laurentian but (p. 73) suggests that originally Cosimo and Lorenzo might each have been given one entire wall.

[86] There are accounts of Lorenzo's trip from the time of the Salone, such as that of Machiavelli, II, pp. 192-96, who states that Lorenzo "avendo esposto la propria vita per rendere alla patria sua la pace."

peace in 206 B.C. and persuaded his adversaries, with his eloquence, to adhere to the Roman cause.[87] The African seaport in the background also relates to Lorenzo's destination, the harbor of Naples.

Scipio was a natural choice as prototype of the great Lorenzo. Regarded as a model of the complete man and an examplar of republican virtue, Scipio had been prominent in Florentine commemorations of Famous Men—from Petrarch's lengthy *vita* to the cycles in the Palazzo della Signoria.[88] His inclusion in Giovio's allegory of the Golden Age of the Medici was as inevitable as that of Cicero. So, too, was his being paired with Cicero in complementary scenes, for the divinely inspired Scipio was Cicero's own exemplar of virtue and had been paired with him in earlier groups of *illustri* in republican Florence, such as Ghirlandaio's Roman heroes in the Sala dei Gigli.

The two *istorie* on the northeast wall, then, celebrate Leo's most illustrious Medici ancestors, Cosimo Pater Patriae and Lorenzo il Magnifico, with secondary references to contemporary Medici history in the *Cicero*. Giovio must also have intended a contemporary reference in the *Scipio*, most probably an allusion to Leo's own act of diplomacy in his meeting with King Francis I at Bologna in 1515.[89] However, since this fresco was not painted during the Leonine campaign of work in the Salone, there are no portraits (like those in the *Cicero*) to indicate such an additional level of reference. Instead, Allori's *Scipio* is a portrait of *his* patron, Grand Duke Francesco.[90] It is an image of rulership somewhat more blatant than the allegories belonging to the Leonine campaign of decoration, in which Allori's Scipio-Francesco sits Christ-like at the banquet table in a way that evokes the traditional composition of the Last Supper.

In the *Scipio* (and in the *Titus* as well) Allori echoed the compositions of the 1521 frescos: the setting of the *Scipio* closely reflects that of the *Caesar* across the room. In Allori's compositional drawing there is a dividing column like those which originally articulated the 1521 frescos. Allori omitted this column when he painted the *Scipio*, but the columns of the loggia maintain the same intervals, the loggia reflects in mirror-image the diagonally placed palace of the *Caesar*, and, like Caesar directly across from him, Scipio is seated at the base of the pivoted structure. The statues of the gods from whom Scipio drew inspiration repeat the motif of the statues of the gods in the *Caesar* fresco, the Hercules and Juno statues to the left also being characterized as the virtues Fortitude and Prudence.[91] These statues allude to divine protection of the Medici and to the theme of Medici virtue which is carried out elsewhere in the room.

[87] The main source for the scene is Livy, *History of Rome*, XXVIII, XVIII, 1-12, where Scipio's eloquence is particularly noted. See a description of the Salone from 1698 in which it is claimed that there was an inscription from Livy, XXVIII, relating to the fresco (ASF, *Manoscritti* 211, f. 7v; quoted in Kliemann, p. 166). Petrarch, I, pp. 483-87, paraphrases Livy's account of the meeting, and in the *Africa* (tr. F. Marretti, Venice, 1570, bk. III) he describes the Numidian palace. See also, on the danger of the trip, *Appian's Roman History*, VI, 6, 30 (tr. H. White, Cambridge, 1913, I, p. 185): "So much danger did Scipio incur both going

and returning. . . ."

[88] On Scipio in Renaissance art, see Chastel, 1961, pp. 251-52. Scipio appears, with an epigram about the meeting with Hasdrubal by Salutati, in the Trecento cycle (Hankey, p. 364).

[89] McKillop, 1974, p. 77. This meeting is allegorized in Raphael's *Coronation of Charlemagne* in the Stanza dell'Incendio (1517).

[90] For portraits of Francesco, see Berti, 1967, figs. 22, 24-30.

[91] Petrarch, I, pp. 483-87, mentions the statues of gods in the palace. On Scipio's divine inspiration, see H. P. L'Orange, *Apotheosis in Ancient Por-*

The frescos on the southwest wall of the Salone signal the achievements of two further Medici in the guise of Titus Flaminius and Caesar. To the left of the doorway is Allori's *Titus Flaminius at the Council of the Achaeans*, which depicts the oration in 196 B.C. in which Titus persuaded the Greek states to join Rome. The representatives of the Achaean league carry a banner so inscribed, and the man at Titus' feet who records the agreement writes words from Livy's account praising Titus' diplomacy in dealing with his opponents.[92] Titus, who is an unusual exemplar not appearing in other *uomini illustri* cycles in Florence,[93] may have been selected because this episode in his career lent itself perfectly to an allegory of Piero, whose presence in the Salone scheme completes the dynastic sequence from Cosimo, his father, to Lorenzo, his son. The oration to the Achaeans neatly allegorizes the one act of Piero's brief rule that had lasting significance for Medici destiny: Piero resolved the financial and political crisis following the death of his father, which involved a conspiracy against him in 1466.[94] Like the exemplar Titus, his means was diplomacy, and in a speech he eloquently persuaded his Florentine opponents to join the Medici. As in the *Scipio*, the setting of this fresco underscores this double reference to the Roman hero and the Medici leader. In Allori's compositional drawing and in his large *modello* for the scene,[95] the council meets in a colonnaded palace hall, but in the fresco the meeting place has been shifted to the banks of the Grecian river where Titus' meeting took place, a river which could also be read as the Arno.

Across from the *Cicero* commemorating Cosimo's establishment of Medici rule, then, is an allegory of the consolidation of that rule by his son, Piero. As in the other *istorie*, the Giovian program for this fresco must have included an allusion to Lorenzo and a secondary reference to contemporary Medici events. The Laurentian reference is to his diplomacy at the Diet of Cremona—the event which Allori and Borghini took for the primary level of meaning in the scene. The most obvious contemporary analogue (and an event which is in fact celebrated elsewhere in Leo's art) is the Lateran Council of

traiture, Oslo, 1947, pp. 49-53. We cannot know what gods were included in Giovio's program for the *Scipio* as an allegory of Lorenzo; however, Juno, Venus, and Mercury (whose caduceus appears on Scipio's coins as a symbol of divine inspiration) all have Medicean associations. Moreover, Apollo's placement directly over the figure of Scipio would have been appropriately Laurentian. The addition of Hercules to the group is, of course, an allusion to one of the favorite Medici exemplars (see chap. 6).

[92] The inscription reads as follows: QVNTIJ LEG[A] (Livy, *History of Rome*, XXXV, XXXVII, 4); ACHEOS E[N] PROBE SCIRE [AETOLO]RVM OMNEM FER[OCIAM] [I]N VERBIS NO[N] FACTIS ESSE E[T] [I]N CONCILIIS MAG[IS] CONCIO (Livy, XXXV, XLIX, 2). (Quinctius and the commissioners . . . for the Achaeans knew well that all the fierceness of the Aetolians consisted in words and not in actions, and was seen in councils and assemblies more than

in battle.) Kliemann, p. 166, publishes a description of this fresco dating from 1698, in which it is claimed that it was accompanied by an inscription from Livy, XXXV (apparently not this inscription, which is in the scene itself).

[93] As far as I have been able to determine, Titus appears only in very expanded cycles such as Petrarch's *De viris illustribus vitae* (I, pp. 315-423) and the *Sala Virorum Illustrium* in Padua (Mommsen, p. 103). However, as pointed out by Kliemann, 1976, p. 143, n. 353, Ludovico Alamanni cites Titus as an exemplar of neutrality in a letter of 1516.

[94] N. Rubinstein, *The Government of Florence Under the Medici (1434-1494)*, Oxford, 1966, pp. 159-66.

[95] Warsaw, University Library, Royal Collection T. 174, 141/III. See Z. Wazbinski, "Artisti e pubblico nella Firenze del cinquecento: a proposito del topos 'cane abbaiante,'" *Paragone*, no. 327, 1977, p. 5.

1513-1516, through which Leo dealt with issues of church reform and sought to reaffirm papal supremacy.[96] However, since this fresco was not painted in 1521 but in 1582, when reference to the Council would have had little meaning, there are no allusions to Leo in the scene. Instead, as in the *Scipio*, Allori portrayed his own patron, Francesco, as Titus. In contrast to his first idea for the fresco on the compositional plan, which shows a seated orator (possibly reflecting Sarto's idea for the scene), Allori's Titus is posed in imitation of an imperial *adlocutio*—a motif typical of Medici art of the *principato* (as, for example, in Vasari's *Duke Cosimo with the Prisoners of Montemurlo* in the Palazzo Vecchio).

Sarto's *Tribute to Caesar* to the right of the entrance door of the Salone brings the history of the Medici up to date. It pays homage to Leo X as a ruler receiving tribute in the form of gifts of animals. This tribute is immediately identifiable as the Medicean frame of reference of the scene: it alludes to the gift of exotic animals made to Leo in 1514 by the king of Portugal in tribute to the supremacy of his rule.[97] Since a similar gift had been made to Lorenzo il Magnifico in 1487, the event itself was a Medici *topos*.[98] It is treated as such here, for Sarto includes animals and other gifts from both tributes. To the left and in the background are the lion, the sheep, the green vase, and the "giraffa molto grande e molto bella e piacevole" that are mentioned in the accounts of the gift to Lorenzo.[99] Like the gift itself, the famous giraffe was a *topos*—instantly identifiable with Lorenzo (and it may not be coincidence that the man at the base of the statue who leads the eye back to the giraffe is dressed in livery of violet and white, Lorenzo's heraldic colors). The animals in the left foreground—the monkeys, parrot, civet cat, and chameleon—all refer to Leo's own zoo, which was so famous that its contents were described by Vasari, and which was surely accessible to Sarto on his trip to Rome made shortly before this fresco was painted.[100] One of these animals from Leo's zoo, the parrot, which is conspicuously perched on top of the cage of birds, may have additional Leonine significance. According to Vasari, Leo's brother Giuliano (who shared the GLOVIS motto with him) had an *impresa* of a parrot on a sheaf of millet with the motto GLOVIS, which referred to the virtues of Leo's pontificate.[101]

[96] Pastor, VII, pp. 54-59. The Council is allegorized in Raphael's *Oath of Leo III*, Stanza dell'Incendio.

[97] Pastor, VII, pp. 74-77; Roscoe-Bossi, V/VI, pp. 7-12. See Winner, 1964, pp. 71-109, on the famous elephant, Hanno, which was part of the gift.

[98] The gift is detailed by Landucci, pp. 52-53. See Shearman, 1965, I, p. 85; and Kliemann, 1976, pp. 15-17, Appendices 14-20, for other references. Shearman, 1965, I, p. 85; Winner, 1970, p. 266; McKillop, 1974, p. 77; and Kliemann, 1976, pp. 15-21 (in the most detailed discussion of the matter), believe that the gift to Lorenzo is the subject of the fresco and the gift to Leo a secondary reference, while I would argue for the reverse. Allori picked up the idea of alluding to the two animal gifts in the *Scipio*, where Lorenzo's animals, the

primary subject of the fresco, are in the foreground and Leo's elephant is in the background. Moreover, one of Allori's additions to the *Caesar* carries out the theme of gifts from exotic lands, for the boy with the turkey alludes to Duke Cosimo's importation of animals from the New World. On this subject see D. Heikamp, *Mexico and the Medici*, Florence, 1972, p. 11.

[99] Landucci, p. 52. See Kliemann, 1976, pp. 19-20, on the giraffe and its representation in pictures by other artists.

[100] Vasari, IV, p. 362: "tutti quegli animali che papa Leone aveva, il camaleonte, i zibetti, le scimie, i papagalli, i lioni, i liofanti, ed altri animali più stranieri." For Leo's animals see Kliemann, 1976, pp. 17-19.

[101] Vasari, *Rag.*, p. 120.

On the steps below the emperor are other figures which indicate a Leonine reading of this scene. The dwarf has been identified as a servant of Leo's nephew, Ippolito, who was attached to his court.[102] And, next to the dwarf, barking at the intruding *exotica*, is an ordinary dog. This animal may be Medicean, a joke on the dog which had once been part of the family *stemma*.[103] That the dog was intended to be read in this sense is indicated by Allori's adoption of the motif in the *Titus*, where a dog advances down the foreground steps with a *cartello* in his mouth carrying a message to the opponents of the Medici: "si latrabitis, latrabo" (if you bark, I too will bark). This motif reminds the observer that, like the *Titus*, the *Caesar* scene is an allegory of Medicean political power.

The emperor who receives the animal tribute (pl. 86) may have been intended to be a portrait (albeit very idealized) of Leo himself, which can be compared with the youthful pope on his *Liberalitas* medal (pl. 85).[104] However, the issue of likeness is not crucial, for the figures around the ruler encourage such a reading. In two later Medici allegories of rulership, the identity of the ruler, who is not a portrait likeness, is implicit in the portraits of the members of his entourage which surround him. In Bronzino's *Crossing of the Red Sea* of 1541 (pl. 88), a reading of Moses as Cosimo is made clear by the portraits of his major-domo Pierfrancesco Riccio as Aaron (the black-bearded man to the left of Moses) and his general Alessandro Vitelli (seated in front of Moses).[105] And, in the *Triumph of Camillus* in the Sala delle Udienze (many features of which derive from the Salone decoration), Salviati has included himself as the dark-haired man looking over his shoulder in front of Camillus-Cosimo (pl. 89).[106] Likewise, in Sarto's fresco, there is at least one such portrait in the emperor's entourage: next to him Sarto has portrayed himself, his hand placed to his breast as if in homage to his patron.[107]

The Medicean references in Sarto's fresco seem clear, but neither the Roman episode represented nor the emperor receiving the tribute can be identified with certainty. Vasari, who usually specifies "Giulio Cesare" when he means Julius Caesar, calls the emperor simply "Cesare," and we cannot exclude the possibility that he meant Augustus Caesar.[108] Borghini elaborated on the place but not the protagonist, titling the scene "Cesare in Egitto," and it has since been assumed that the fresco depicts a tribute to Julius Caesar in Egypt.[109] However, while the scene has a number of elements sugges-

[102] Shearman, 1965, I, p. 246.

[103] P. Litta, *Famiglie celebri italiane*, Milan-Turin, 1819-1885, IV, p. 64 (the cover of Foligno de' Medici's chronicle of the Medici of 1373, showing the dog with the *palle*). Cf. also Segni's list of Medici devices (Laur. MS Ashb. 660, f. 2), where the dog is mentioned as part of the device of Averardo de' Medici; and the terracotta doorframe of the Medici bank, Milan (Castello Sforzesco), attributed to Michelozzo (1462-1468), which has two heraldic dogs.

[104] Hill-Pollard, no. 379.

[105] For Riccio, see Salviati's portrait of 1550 in Prato, Palazzo Communale (*Prato e i Medici nell '500: Società e Cultura artistica*, Prato, 1980, cat. 5, figs. 11-12). For Vitelli, see Vasari's *Election of Cosimo*

as Duke and *Duke Cosimo with the Prisoners of Montemurlo* in the Sala di Cosimo, Palazzo Vecchio (Vasari, *Rag.* p. 190).

[106] Identified by Cheney, I, p. 171.

[107] Identified by Shearman, 1965, I, p. 246.

[108] Kliemann, 1976, p. 22, makes this point, noting another example in which a scene described by Vasari as representing "Cesare" included a tribute related to a generalized imperial theme. See Vasari, IV, p. 596, describing Peruzzi's facade for Francesco Buzio (c. 1520): "e nella facciata figurò le storie di Cesare quando gli sono presentati i tributi da tutto il mondo; e sopra vi dipinse i dodici imperadori."

[109] The work has been variously titled *Tribute to Caesar* (Freedberg, 1963, I, p. 54), *Tribute Presented*

tive of a foreign land such as Egypt—the high mountain in the distance, the female cult statue on the socle next to the palace stairs, and perhaps even the circular temple[110]— there is no event in the life of Julius Caesar involving a tribute of animals in Egypt, and no detail in the fresco points to this identification of the scene. Moreover, if the scene alludes to Leo (even on a secondary level), then the identification of the emperor as Julius, who was the namesake and exemplar of Leo's predecessor, Julius II, is practically to be excluded.[111]

It is possible that the emperor was not meant to be read as an historical figure at all but alludes only to the idea of empire, and that the scene is a *topos*.[112] However, I believe he can probably be identified as Augustus. First—but not crucial to the argument, for the Medicean level of reference to the living ruler is the primary message of the fresco— there *is* an animal-tribute episode in the life of Augustus (who received a rhinoceros, a snake, a tiger, and a white elephant) that at least provides an historical point of reference for the scene.[113] Moreover, an Augustan reading of the emperor and his entourage is suggested by the dependence of Caesar-Leo on the Aurelian *Liberalitas Augusti* relief from the Arch of Constantine (pl. 87), which had already served Renaissance artists as a model for portraits of papal receptions.[114] But most compelling is the fact that Leo identified his papacy with the notion of a new Augustan Golden Age of peace (particularly in contrast to that of Julius II).[115] Thus, as this fresco alludes to expanded Medici dominion in Rome through Leo's papacy, so it alludes not only to the idea of a Medici Golden Age in Florence but also to the *topos* of an Augustan Golden Age in Rome.

Support for the hypothesis that the *Caesar* refers to the new Augustan Age of Pope Leo X can be found in a later scene of tribute to a pope, Vasari's *Tribute to Paul III* of 1546 (pl. 90).[116] Like the Salone, the decorations of the Sala dei Cento Giorni are based on a program by Giovio; moreover, its scheme recalls the original plan of the Salone walls as I have read it, with architectural *quadrature*, fluted columns, and *istorie* flanked by narrow panels with allegorical figures.[117] The scene of the pope receiving tribute

---

to *Julius Caesar in Egypt* (Shearman, 1965, I, p. 78), *Tribute of Animals to Caesar* (McKillop, 1974, p. 70), etc.

[110] Shearman, 1965, I, p. 88, notes that Sarto's temple recalls the circular building in Raphael's tapestries the *Sacrifice at Lystra* and *Saint Paul Preaching in Athens*. The statue, the attribute of which is difficult to make out, assumed greater importance in the original format of the fresco, in which it occupied the center of the composition (see Shearman, 1965, I, pl. 75a; also Sarto's *modello*, pl. 75c).

[111] I am indebted to John Shearman for advice on this point. See, for example, Julius' medal inscribed IVLIVS CAESAR PONT. II (R. Weiss, "The Medals of Pope Julius II, 1503-1513," *JWCI*, 28, 1965, pp. 163-82). See also Partridge-Starn, pp. 52-55.

[112] As suggested by Kliemann, 1976, pp. 22-23.

[113] Suetonius, *Divus Augustus*, 43; and Dio Cassius, *Roman History*, 54.9 (on Augustus' receipt of these animals, some of which were from the potentates of India, and his exhibition of them in Rome).

[114] Partridge-Starn, pp. 10, 54.

[115] For Leo as Augustus *pacator orbis* after Julius as Caesar, see Shearman, 1972, p. 15 (with other examples).

[116] See Vasari, VII, p. 680; Bottari-Ticozzi, V, pp. 150-53 (Anton Francesco Doni's letter describing the Sala and quoting the inscriptions); and E. Steinmann, "Freskenzyklen der Spätrenaissance in Rom," *Monatschefte für Kunstwissenshaft*, 3, 1910, pp. 45-58.

[117] Noted by Shearman, 1965, I, p. 83 (except for the speculation about the narrow panels, which is mine).

from the ambassadors depends on Sarto's tribute scene in several respects, such as the setting with its steps and symbolic statue, the off-center seated pontiff, and the portraits, which include the self-portrait of the artist as a member of the papal entourage.[118] However, the most telling connection is Vasari's inclusion of the Medicean *topos* of the animal tribute—complete with Lorenzo's giraffe, Leo's parrot and elephant.[119] In contrast to Sarto's *Caesar*, the literary element which explicates the meaning of his complex scene is present in Vasari's work: at the center of the fresco just below the steps (not shown in pl. 90) is the inscription AVREVM SAECVLVM CONDIT QVI RECTO AEQVABILIQVE ORDINE CVNTA DISPENSAT (He founds the Golden Age who administers all things with right and equable order); and above, accompanying a bust of Alexander, is the inscription SVPRA GARAMANTAS ET INDOS PROTVLIT IMPERIVM. Both these inscriptions are derived from the following passage in the *Aeneid*, which alludes to Augustus' revival of the Golden Age of Saturn and to his empire:[120]

> Augustus Caesar, Divi genus, aurea condet
> saecula qui rursus Latio regnata per arva
> Saturno quondam, super et Garamantas et Indos
> proferet imperium. . . .

> Augustus Caesar, son of a god, who shall again set up the Golden Age amid the fields where Saturn once reigned, and shall spread his empire past Garamant and Indian.

If Sarto's fresco, with its animal tribute, was also planned by Giovio to make an allusion to the Golden Age of Augustus, it would be a fitting conclusion to the cycle of Medici *istorie* in the Salone. For here, in contrast to the "republican" *istorie* lauding the deeds of Leo's ancestors, is an "imperial" work which alludes to the newly enlarged dominion and world view of the Medici during his papacy. Moreover, as we shall see, the theme of Leo's Golden Age is most compatible with the meaning of the parts of the Salone decoration still to be discussed. The *Hercules* lunette (in its hypothetical original program) presents Leo's Golden Age in a different, mythological, guise; and Pontormo's *Vertumnus and Pomona* (this time with an explanatory Virgilian inscription) depicts an idyllic scene of gods, which recalls Virgil's "Golden Age amid the fields where Saturn once reigned."

The Salone *istorie* are complemented by Allori's *sopraporte* of Virtues. These must have been part of the original scheme and may even have been begun before work

---

[118] The figure who echoes the pose of the *Mercury* (as Industria!) has the features of Vasari. Cf. the self-portrait to the far right in *Paul III Rewards Merit* (noted by Steinmann, p. 58), the self-portrait in the Uffizi, the woodcut in the *vite*, etc. Moreover, the whole figure is a self-quotation from Vasari's likeness of himself as a younger man in the Camaldoli *Deposition* of 1537.

[119] Noted by Winner, 1964, p. 106; and Kliemann, 1976, p. 23 (but not in connection with a reinterpretation of the meaning of the *Caesar*).

[120] *Aeneid*, VI, 794; noted by Kliemann, 1976, p. 23.

stopped in 1521. Visual evidence for this is found in the two *sopraporte* of Virtues (which are painted in chiaroscuro) in Salviati's Sala delle Udienze of the 1540s (pl. 78), which, as I have noted, depends on the Salone in other respects. Furthermore, in 1533, Giannotti recorded three frescos on the lateral walls of the Salone:[121]

> Nelle due faccie maggiori vi sono tre pitture che non sono finite; una ve ne ha di mano di Andrea del Sarto, che era molto buono maestro, et morì l'anno dinanze all'assedio, l'altre non sono di maestri da curarsi di intendere nomi loro.

> In the two major facades there are three unfinished paintings; one of them is by the hand of Andrea del Sarto, who was a very good master and died the year before the siege; the others are by masters whose names one need not bother to remember.

Besides the *istorie* by Sarto and Franciabigio (which Giannotti must have assumed were unfinished because they did not fill the entire wall space), then, there was a third unfinished fresco. Apparently, it was not by Sarto and it is unlikely to have been Franciabigio's second *istoria* (which is not contiguous with the *Cicero*), but it could well have been the northeast wall *sopraporta* by Franciabigio and Feltrini.[122]

Allori's compositional drawing for the Salone also suggests that at least one of the *sopraporte* existed when he began work—and that these groups were placed as they would logically have been in a room decorated by Leo X in honor of Lorenzo il Magnifico. The group of *Magnanimitas, Magnificentia, and Liberalitas*, which honors Leo, is on the southwest wall adjacent to the *Caesar* fresco, which alludes to him, while the group of *Fortitudo, Prudentia, and Vigilantia*, which must have been conceived as honoring Lorenzo, is on the northeast wall. Now, in the late 1570s, with the new patronage of the Salone, it must have been thought desirable to reverse these groups in order to celebrate Grand Duke Francesco by placing the *sopraporta* honoring him over the entrance to the room. Consequently, at the expense of their connection with the subjects of the *istorie*, Allori reversed the *sopraporte*, thereby destroying the coherence of the original scheme. The *Fortitudo, Prudentia, and Vigilantia* originally planned for the northeast doorway was painted over the entrance doorway with an inscription identifying Allori's patron, Francesco; the *Magnanimitas, Magnificentia, and Liberalitas* group originally planned for the southwest doorway was painted on the other wall, with an inscription commemorating Leo: LEO DECIMVS PONTIFEX MAX AVLAM HANC ILLVSTRARE ET ORNARE COEPISSET (Pope Leo X began to embellish and decorate this room).

In the original scheme, as it can be inferred from Allori's drawing and from the Medicean subjects of the *istorie*, the Virtues commented pointedly on the personalities celebrated in the adjacent frescos. In the center of the Leonine *sopraporta* was Magnificentia, who alludes to papal glory—and, surely, only to Leo. (However, apparently already thinking of relating these virtues to Francesco, Allori reversed Magnanimitas

[121] Giannotti, p. 1576.
[122] Shearman, 1965, I, pp. 81-83, suggests that Vasari's attribution to Feltrini of "ornamenti . . . di terretta" may have referred to work on the *sopraporte*, as well as a *basamento*.

and Magnificentia in his drawing, portraying the latter holding the grand-ducal crown.) Liberalitas adjoined the *Caesar* fresco. Liberality was a conspicuous feature of Leo's personal imagery, as in his medal inscribed LIBERALITAS PONTIFICA (pl. 85).[123] Moreover, this Leonine virtue was celebrated in Giovanni da Udine's *Giuochi di putti*, one of a series of tapestry designs for the Sala di Costantino, which is known from the engraving by the Master of the Die (pl. 82).[124] There, in a three-figure arrangement with garlands of fruit not unlike those of the *sopraporta*, a putto symbolizing Leo as Apollo plays with the same symbols of rule that are carried by the Magnificentia, and the other putti hold up basins of coins signifying Leo's liberality. The third figure of the Leonine *sopraporta*, Magnanimitas, could be seen to allude to Leo, since magnanimity was the classical virtue of the lion, from whom Leo took his papal name. On the other hand, the virtue also complements the *Titus* (to which it would have been adjacent), for that fresco is an allegory of Piero, whose magnanimity toward his enemies is the virtue singled out for praise in sixteenth-century accounts of his successful resolution of the conspiracy against the Medici.[125]

The group of *Fortitudo, Prudentia, and Vigilantia*, actually painted over the door on the southwest wall, relates more closely to the *Cicero* and *Scipio* of the northeast wall. Prudentia, in the center, could allude to the prudence of both Leo's great forebears, and Fortitudo would have been adjacent to the scene of Scipio-Lorenzo on his dangerous mission. Moreover, in view of the Ciceronian character of these two *istorie* (which show Cicero and his exemplar, Scipio), Prudentia and Fortitudo would have been appropriate between them, for they were the very virtues that Cicero considered fundamental to a just ruler.[126] They are also the virtues personified as Juno and Hercules in the *Scipio* fresco. Vigilantia, to the right of this *sopraporta* and next to the *Triumph of Cicero*, would have commented on Cicero-Cosimo's return from a watchful exile.[127] Indeed, the three virtues of the *sopraporta* were the very ones chosen by Vasari in the early 1560s to accompany his *Exile of Cosimo il Vecchio* in the Sala di Cosimo il Vecchio in the Palazzo Vecchio. In the compositional study for the ceiling (pl. 92), Prudentia is on the left of the *Exile* panel; on the right (as Vasari explains) is Fortitudo, who holds "uno scudo

[123] Among many examples: Liberalitas was featured in Leo's *possesso* (Penni, p. 212); the statue of him by Domenico Aimo that was installed after his death in the Palazzo dei Conservatori on the Capitoline (now S. Maria in Aracoeli) was inscribed OPTIMI LIBERALISSIMIQVE PONTIFICIS MEMORIALE S.P.Q.R. (Giovio, 1551, bk. III, p. 173). Liberalitas continued to be the chief virtue associated with Leo in later Medici art: see the 1539 wedding *apparato* of Duke Cosimo, in which Pier Francesco Foschi's *Entrata of Leo X into Florence* was accompanied by the device of an upright basin signifying Liberalitas (Giambullari, p. 26); Vasari's praise of Leo's "Liberalità e virtù" in *Rag.*, pp. 159, 164; and the pairing of Leo and Liberalità in the program of the Villa Castello garden (chap. 11, n. 13).

[124] Bartsch, XV, 208, 32. For the history of these tapestries and the drawings for them, see P. Poun-

cey and J. Gere, *Italian Drawings in the Department of Prints and Drawings in the British Museum: Raphael and His Circle*, London, 1962, I, pp. 87-89. Four of the series are now in Budapest, Musée des arts décoratifs, and were in the exhibition, *Tapisseries anciennes des XVIe, XVIIe et XVIIIe Siècles provenant du Musée des arts décoratifs de Budapest*, Lausanne, Musée des arts décoratifs, 1969, nos. 8-11. (I am grateful to Candace Adelson for this information.)

[125] Guicciardini, p. 6, states that Piero had more clemency than either Cosimo or Lorenzo.

[126] Baron, p. 73.

[127] Vigilantia and Fortitudo are reversed in the compositional plan, but in Allori's *modello* for this *sopraporta* at Windsor Castle 6018 (Popham-Wilde, cat. 59, pl. 40) they appear as Allori painted them and as they were probably placed in Giovio's scheme.

drentovi una grue, la quale si fa per la Vigilanza" (a shield in which is a crane, which stands for Vigilance).[128] The derivative iconography of Vasari's work, as much as any other factor, suggests that Giannotti may have been right about a third incomplete fresco on one of the lateral walls of the Salone, and that before work was stopped at Leo's death in late 1521 Franciabigio and Feltrini had begun the *sopraporta* on the northeast wall, which would have complemented the allegories of Cosimo Pater Patriae and Lorenzo il Magnifico.

✳   ✳   ✳

The *istorie* of the Salone, then, glorify four generations of Medici as *uomini illustri*, as the rulers of Florence whose acts of civic virtue bring them Roman citizenship and place them on the same level of heroism as Cicero, Titus, Scipio, and Augustus. The series may be read thematically—two scenes of Medici diplomacy (Titus-Piero and Scipio-Lorenzo) are balanced by two scenes of tribute (Cicero-Cosimo and Augustus-Leo), in which a parallel is made between Pope Leo and his revered ancestor, Cosimo Pater Patriae. It may be read dynastically—two pairs of Medici fathers and sons face each other across the room. But, most important, it may be read historically as an account from a Medicean perspective of the Medici and Florence. The establishment of Medici rule by Cosimo Pater Patriae is followed by deeds on behalf of republican Florence by the contemporaries Piero and Lorenzo (represented by the contemporaries Titus and Scipio), and the series concludes with the expansion of Medici rule to Rome by Leo X in the guise of Augustus. A subtheme in all the scenes (except, of course, the *Scipio*) is the life and accomplishments of the great Lorenzo, honored by Leo's dedication of the room to him.

It is evident that my reading of the Salone differs fundamentally from the "Laurentian" interpretation of the *istorie* current since the late sixteenth century. This interpretation was formulated by the propagandists of the *principato*—Vasari, Allori, and Borghini—and it reflects a view of early Medici history quite different from that of Leo's time.

In this later view of the Medici past, which crystallized after Duke Cosimo's assumption of power in 1537, the necessity of establishing dynastic continuity as a basis for Medicean claim to rule was not as urgent as in Leo's time, and Medici history became more selective. This point of view is reflected in the *apparato* for Cosimo's wedding in 1539, where, in paintings now lost, three scenes from Cosimo's life were paralleled with scenes from the Medici past: the return from exile of Cosimo Pater Patriae, Lorenzo il Magnifico's trip to Naples, and Leo's *entrata* into Florence (fig. 19).[129] While the allegorical mode of the Salone has been abandoned in favor of direct historical narrative, it is clear that the first two scenes correspond with the *istorie* on the northeast wall of the Salone, where Cosimo and Lorenzo are alluded to in the figures of Cicero and Scipio, and that the papal *entrata*, which has become the quintessential Leonine event in the eyes of the Florentines, corresponds with the southwest wall *istoria* of Leo-Augustus. There is no equivalent to the Titus-Piero scene.

[128] Vasari, *Rag.*, p. 90.   [129] Giambullari, pp. 25-29.

This selective view of Medici history was elaborated in the Quartiere (apartments) in the Palazzo Vecchio (1562-1565), the decorations of which by Vasari and his assistants are the subject of the *Ragionamenti*—Vasari's lengthy exegesis in the form of a dialogue with Prince Francesco. Toward the beginning of the work, Vasari succinctly states the late sixteenth-century point of view of a Medici past dominated by Cosimo Pater Patriae, Lorenzo il Magnifico, and Leo:[130]

> L'altra [monte], dove Iano e Saturno dormono, è l'età d'oro, stata in diversi tempi in Toscana nel governo di Cosimo e Lorenzo Vecchio, ma quella dove la quiete e la libertà facevano ombra alla città di Fiorenza e a tutta Italia fu il pontificato di Lione X.

> The other [hill], where Janus and Saturn sleep, is the Golden Age, which was in Tuscany at various times under the government of Cosimo and Lorenzo the elder, but the time when calm and liberty shaded Florence and all of Italy was the pontificate of Leo X.

The sequence of rooms in the Quartiere of Leo X follows this formulation, with Cosimo, Lorenzo, and Leo each being given a room decorated with scenes from their lives. The episodes chosen are familiar. In the Cosimo room, for example, the centerpiece of the ceiling is the *Return from Exile*, the relationship of which to the whole scheme can be seen in Vasari's preparatory study (pl. 92).[131] Following the iconography established in Franciabigio's *Cicero*, the return is a triumphal *entrata* in which Cosimo (modeled on Pontormo's portrait) is greeted by the welcoming Florentines with a standard inscribed PATRIE PATER SALVE.[132] The centerpiece of the ceiling in the Sala di Lorenzo is a *Tribute to Lorenzo*, in which the pose of Lorenzo and the animal-tribute *topos* are derived from Sarto's *Caesar*, which Vasari seems to have read as an allegory of Lorenzo.[133] The subjects of the other political scenes in this room—*Lorenzo at the Court of Naples* and *Lorenzo at the Diet of Cremona*—are those which were associated with the *Scipio* and *Titus* of the Salone in the later sixteenth century. In the Leonine room, the major scene is Leo's Florentine *entrata*, as it had been in Cosimo's wedding decorations.

Thus, three of the Medici *illustri* who were the subjects of the Salone *istorie* were prominent in Medici art of the *principato*—first in the wedding *apparato*, then in Vasari's cycle—but the fourth, Piero, does not appear. In the *Ragionamenti*, Vasari has Francesco ask for an explanation of this omission. Vasari replies:[134]

> Ma io passo tutto con silenzio di storia, parendomi che e' non bisognasse far altro che il ritratto suo nella camera di suo padre.

[130] Vasari, *Rag.*, pp. 40-41.

[131] Paris, Louvre 2176; see Monbeig-Goguel, 1972, cat. 209.

[132] Vasari, *Rag.*, p. 94, describes this scene, perpetuating the Medici version of Cosimo's return that was first given visual form in Franciabigio's *Cicero* in the Salone: ". . . l'altre gente, che vi sono attorno, è il populo; vedete che v'è corso a vederlo entrare le donne con i putti, che hanno portato con loro gli olivi, le grillande ed i fiori per fiorir le strade; e communemente da' suoi cittadini e dal populo, con quel motto attorno a quell'aste sotto, è chiamato Padre della Patria."

[133] For Vasari's description of his work, see *Rag.*, pp. 106-10. Shearman, 1965, II, p. 246, notes the derivation of the figure of Lorenzo from Sarto's.

[134] Vasari, *Rag.*, p. 104. Vasari goes on to say that he does not want to depict "cose odiose" in

But I pass over all with the silence of history, since it seems to me that he [Vasari] need not do anything but his [Piero's] portrait in his father's room.

And, even when Francesco relates the story of the unsuccessful conspiracy against Piero and his diplomatic resolution of the crisis of 1466, Vasari remains negative:

> Vostra Eccellenza in breve ha detto i gesti suoi, senza che io li dipinga, e mi hanno confermato nella mia medesima openione di non far di lui altra storia.

> Your Excellency has briefly told of his deeds, without my having to paint them, and they have confirmed my opinion not to paint another story of him.

From the point of view of Duke Cosimo's iconographers, then, Piero's brief rule was regarded as an insignificant interlude. It is thus not surprising that Allori read the *Titus* fresco as an allegory of Lorenzo il Magnifico, the great Medici hero of the late Quattrocento; nor that he reversed the *Scipio* and *Titus* scenes in his compositional plan for the Salone, for they must have seemed to him to be interchangeable Laurentian allegories.

Giovio took a closer (and thus less selective) view of Medici history than Vasari, Borghini, or Allori. In 1520, Piero de' Medici could not be so easily passed over—and he was, after all, Leo's grandfather. He was a generational link, and without him the message of dynastic continuity in the Salone decoration would have had a lesser impact. Giovio's program is dominated by dynastic concerns, by the idea of unbroken succession from Cosimo Pater Patriae to the present—propaganda that would have been urgently appropriate after the death in 1519 of the younger Lorenzo, the last heir to the line of the family established by Cosimo.

Laudatory writing about the Medici from the Leonine years clearly indicates that this notion of continuity was of signal importance in the way they wished their history to be understood. The family was welcomed back from exile by a sonnet, "Cosimo: Piero: Laur fu tanto amato" (Cosimo: Piero: a laurel [Lorenzo] was so loved).[135] Likewise, Ferreri's poem on Leo's election praises the Medici stock—from Cosimo to Piero to Lorenzo to Leo:[136]

> Quanta fuit Cosmae, et genito prudentia Petro:
> Quantus erat Petri soboles Laurentius alma,
> Pontificisque parens, et gloria gentis Etruscae;
> Qui nedum patriae pater, ast et totius orbis
> Et pater, et princeps, et dux erat, atque magister . . .

> How great was the prudence of Cosimo and his son Piero;
> How great was Lorenzo, dear son of Piero,
> Father of the pope and glory of the Etruscan people,
> Who is not only Pater Patriae but also father
> And prince and leader and teacher of the whole world.

---

his decorations, only "esempli e gesti grandi." The portrait to which Vasari refers is below the *Exile of Cosimo* in the Sala di Cosimo il Vecchio.

[135] *Canzone*, f. 2r.
[136] Ferreri, p. 287.

The histories of the period also present a sympathetic picture of Piero. In Machiavelli's *Istorie fiorentine* he is included among the Medici rulers and his virtue is praised; moreover, Piero's oration to the Florentines, the very event that is allegorized in the *Titus*, was selected for extensive commentary, including accounts of the speech itself.[137]

The careful underscoring of Medicean dynastic continuity in the Golden Age of republican Florence that we have seen in Giovio's program for the Salone is also characteristic of the few other Medici commissions in Florence dating from the last years of Leo's papacy. Adhering to the requirements and limitations of a very different kind of commission, the program of the New Sacristy in San Lorenzo makes a similar claim to rule based on dynastic continuity (pls. 34, 37). There were to be four tombs (a fifth, for Cardinal Giulio, was dropped early in the planning), with those of Giuliano and Lorenzo the younger balancing those of their Quattrocento forebears, the Magnifici. Moreover, the new burial chamber was conceived as a pendant to the Old Sacristy, which contains the tombs of other Medici forebears (including Piero), and the two sacristies were placed in a diagrammatic relationship to Verrocchio's slab marking the tomb of Cosimo Pater Patriae, located between them in front of the high altar of the church.

Other works celebrating the Medici dynasty in support of their claim to rule might have been forthcoming but for the death of Leo, which prevented the completion of the Salone and interrupted work on the New Sacristy. For example, there is some evidence that Pontormo's portrait of Cosimo Pater Patriae was the first of a dynastic portrait series, which would have commemorated the Medici in the tradition of *uomini illustri* portrait cycles.[138] Piero, who might not seem a likely candidate for a portrait in 1520 except as part of a series, is the subject of several studies by Pontormo, one of which shows him in a pose and format that are similar to those of the *Cosimo* (pl. 91).[139] Such a portrait series, if realized, would have been a private counterpart to the monumental dynastic statement of the Salone *istorie*.

[137] In the dedication to the *Istorie fiorentine*, p. 4, Machiavelli includes Piero in his recitation of the successive heads of the family and their virtue: ". . . la bontà di Giovanni, la sapienza di Cosimo, la umanità di Piero, e la magnificenza e prudenzia di Lorenzo." For the events of 1466, see Machiavelli, I, pp. 131-47; and N. Valori, *La vita del magnifico Lorenzo de' Medici il Vecchio scritta da Niccolò Valori patrizio fiorentino*, Florence, 1568, n.p. See also R. Hatfield, "Machiavelli on the Regime of Piero de' Medici," *Studies on Machiavelli*, ed. M. P. Gilmore, Florence, 1972, pp. 325-26, and Appendix 3, on Machiavelli's account of Piero's speech and its source in the account by Fra Giovanni di Carlo, a Medici apologist. Even earlier, in Lorenzo's own time, Piero's actions on this occasion were thought to be the distinguishing feature of his rule. See Poliziano, *Le Stanze*, II, 3 (following lines about Cosimo):

E quanto Petro al paterno valore
n'aggiunse pregio, a con qual maraviglia
dal corpo di sua patria rimosse abbia
le scelerate man, la crudel rabbia?

[138] Such a series would have anticipated Bronzino's series of the Medici of the 1550's, executed for Duke Cosimo (Gallerie; see Baccheschi, figs. 134-57). For Vasari's *Lorenzo il Magnifico*, apparently painted as a pendant to the *Cosimo*, see chap. 10, and pl. 157.

[139] Rome, Gabinetto Nazionale delle Stampe F. C. 137r; see Cox-Rearick, 1964, I, cat. 85. For other studies see cat. 86-89. In these drawings Piero is shown holding a letter. There is a portrait the same size as the *Cosimo* in which Piero (dressed in red robes) holds a letter (see Cox-Rearick, 1964, II, fig. 84). Langedijk, p. 137, n. 141, suggests that these drawings were for a portrait of Cosimo's brother Lorenzo.

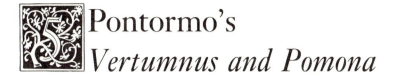

Pontormo's
Vertumnus and Pomona

In the Salone at Poggio a Caiano (pl. 68) the themes of Romano-Florentine unity and papal dominion, which are prominent in the Roman decorations of Pope Leo X, are joined with the familiar themes of Medici art in Florence—Cycles of Time and the regeneration of nature as metaphors of Medici dynasty and eternal rule. As we have seen, the decoration of the Salone evokes a Golden Age of Medici rule in republican Florence of the Quattrocento and its renewal during Leo's pontificate. The dynastic continuity of the Medici, on which the present regime based its claim to rule, is didactically reviewed in Roman *istorie* celebrating four generations of Medici (pls. 71-72, 80-81). The theme of Medici virtue is taken up in the *sopraporte*, as well as in the frescos of the end walls (both painted later by Allori). Finally, themes of Medici apotheosis and of the celestial order which guides Medici destiny are elaborated in Pontormo's *Vertumnus and Pomona* (color pl. 2) and Allori's *Hercules and Fortuna in the Garden of the Hesperides* (pl. 118). The complex decoration of the Salone is thus the climactic realization in Medici art of the myth of dynasty, destiny, and immortality that was adumbrated in the poetic metaphor of the Cycles of Time on the portico frieze of the villa.

THE LUNETTE AND MEDICI *IMPRESE*

Pontormo's and Allori's lunette frescos comprise the upper zone of the decoration of the Salone. Separated from the walls below by a cornice and by dark borders, and framed by the curve of the great vault, they are more closely related visually to its profusion of Medici *imprese* than to the *istorie* on the lateral walls. And, in view of the traditional metaphor of ceiling decorations as the heavens, they should be read as part of the celestial zone of the vault and their decoration interpreted as alluding to celestial themes. High above the *istorie* celebrating the civic virtue of past and present Medici rulers, these frescos refer to the future—to Medici apotheosis and immortality.[1] Allori's *Hercules and Fortuna* celebrates the apotheosis of Leo X, patron of the Salone (as will be discussed in chapter 6); Pontormo's *Vertumnus and Pomona* also celebrates Leo's rule, but, additionally, it is a monumental reprise of the theme of his *Cosimo* portrait: dynastic continuity, hence Medici immortality, is promised by the birth in 1519 of a New Cosimo.

The theme of immortality is already implicitly present in the *imprese* of the vault (pl. 69). Their function is to symbolize the eternal glory of the Medici, whose virtuous deeds are depicted in the earthly zone below. Two of these *imprese*—the *broncone* (also present in the narrow coffers around the lunettes) and the *diamante*—specifically express the notion of immortality. Surrounded by such symbols, and in such a location, the Medici *stemma* itself may also be understood as signifying Medicean immortality. The metaphor of the *palle* as celestial bodies had long been current in Medici imagery. In Fra Angelico's *Madonna and Saints* at San Marco (pl. 39), the stars bordering a carpet decorated with zodiac signs also read as the *palle* appropriate to a picture in which Cosimo de' Medici is portrayed as Saint Cosmas. The *palle* were also equated with the planets, as in these lines from poems by Madalius and Severus Minervius dedicated to the Medici in 1516:[2]

> Sex habet errantum rutilos Sol aureus orbes;
> Sex Medicum hinc rutilis aurea scuta Pilis.

The golden sun has six gold-red wandering orbs; hence the golden shields with the six red-golden Medici *palle*.

> Septem sunt superum Deum,
> Quae coelo rutilant, fulgida lumina:
> Et sex sunt Medicae Pilae,
> Princeps, signa tibi, quas puto sidera.

There are seven shining lights of the gods on high, which glitter in the heavens; and six are the Medici *palle*, O Prince, your signs, which I take for stars.

These *palle*-planets or *palle*-stars were understood as symbols of Medici immortality. In his poem on Leo's election, Ferreri declares that their spherical form symbolizes immortal glory:[3]

> . . . quid signant sex poma rubentia, et aurum?
> Aurum sidereos (ait) effigiando nitores
> Fert illustre genus veluti coelestis origo.
> Sexque pilae, quod eis sit sphaerica forma, figurans
> Immortale decus. . . .

[1] McKillop, 1974, p. 74, relates the imagery of immortality to the Florentine literary tradition which "established the notion that great deeds for the fatherland were to be rewarded by a place in the heavens," citing a letter by Petrarch in which he reformulates this Ciceronian precept (Petrarch, *Familiarum rerum*, ed. V. Rossi, Florence, 1933, I, p. 130).

[2] *Lauretum*, pp. 1 and 8. See also an ode by Severus Minervius in the same collection (p. 24) in which Apollo speaks of the *palle* as "Sex Pilae tecum rutilant, ut orbes / Sex modo mecum" (With you six *palle* glitter like gold, as six orbs in rhythm with me).

[3] Ferreri, pp. 286-87.

What do the six blushing apples and the gold signify? The gold, he says, by representing the starry luster, as their celestial origin, denotes the illustrious race. And the six *palle*, because they have a spherical form, portraying immortal glory.

And, Ferreri continues, the number of the *palle* also signifies immortality:[4]

> . . . Stat parte sui perfectus in omni
> Hic numerus: quoniam ex tribus, atque duobus, et uno
> Constat, et aeternum quid, et indelebile monstrat.

> This number is perfect in each of its parts; because it consists of three, and two, and one and shows an eternal and indestructible quality.

The emblematic composition of Pontormo's lunette seems to have been contrived to emphasize correspondences with the *imprese* of the vault. The *broncone* is, of course, present in the laurel which arches over the scene. The *palle* are not represented in the fresco, but the GLOVIS disk below the oculus (pl. 93) echoes the size, shape, and six elements of the *palle* roundels on the vault. Indeed, Pontormo seems at first to have planned to show the *palle* here: in his preliminary sketch of the tablets and figures around the oculus (pl. 76), the tablet above the window resembles the GLOVIS tablets of the Cappella del Papa (pl. 32); the roundel below the window may then have been intended to display the *palle*.[5]

Pontormo's idea of placing a Medici device below the oculus may have been inspired by a similar arrangement in the Old Sacristy (pl. 94).[6] In 1521, at the very moment when interest must have been focused on Michelangelo's design for the New Sacristy, itself derivative from Brunelleschi's (pls. 34, 37), the earlier one would have been a natural model. The design of lunettes with oculi above tripartite walls articulated by fluted Corinthian columns, niches, and doorways already recalls elements of the Old Sacristy design; Pontormo's GLOVIS disk below the oculus, echoing the *stemme* below the roundels in Brunelleschi's pendentives, simply emphasizes the allusion to the earlier Medici room.

Also striking is the way in which the oculus of the lunette, which is about the same size as the large rings of the vault, "reads" as a Medici *diamante*. This equation is even more obvious in Pontormo's preliminary sketch, where the oculus is taken as a starting point for an arrangement of tablets and figures around it. Moreover, if we see it as the

---

[4] Ferreri, p. 287. Six was one of the perfect numbers of numerological tradition, a number that was also associated with gestation and growth (see Macrobius, *Somnium Scipionis*, pp. 102-3). The emphasis on the number six in Medicean devices, mottos, and names (six *palle*; six letters in GLOVIS, SEMPER, and N / SVAVE; six letters in Medici and Cosimo) suggests that there may have been a numerological basis for some of these. In this connection it may be significant that the return from exile of Cosimo Pater Patriae occurred on 6 Octo-

ber and that the Medici closely identified with the feast of the Magi (Epiphany) celebrated on 6 January.

[5] See also Pontormo's compositional study, which may have been connected with the genesis of the lunettes, in which the *palle* are placed below the oculus (chap. 4, n. 30). In Medici art such roundels with devices were often interchangeable, as in a Laurentian manuscript where the *palle* are in one roundel and, in an identical one, GLOVIS (pl. 20).

[6] Winner, 1972, p. 197, n. 82.

diamante, the oculus also reads as a frame. This conceit had occurred in Medici art before, in small-scale works such as a late fifteenth-century mirror with *Venus and Mars* in a *diamante* frame (pl. 95).[7] Pontormo monumentalizes the idea, and in a play on levels of reality the "picture" framed by the window is sky, like the background of the fresco itself. At night this sky would be filled with the real stars of the heavens, with which the observer may equate the *palle*-stars of the golden vault.

Finally, if the *broncone*, GLOVIS, and the *diamante* are implicitly present in the design of the lunette, perhaps Leo's yoke is also there. It might be symbolized by the double walls, which Pontormo has almost diagrammatically emphasized and against which the oculus, or the *diamante* of Leo's compound *impresa*, seems to be suspended.

The connections between the fresco and the *imprese* of the vault suggest that its design was thought out in relation to other Medicean works of art in which *imprese* predominate. For example, the idea of a sequence of roundels in Pontormo's preliminary sketch is developed and joined with the motif of the *broncone* in a compositional study (pl. 75). The design of the latter drawing recalls the title page for Valori's *vita* of Lorenzo—a work, like the Salone, dedicated by Leo in memory of his father (pl. 18).[8] Other precedents are the shutters of the Stanza d'Eliodoro, where the crossed, flaming *bronconi*, the *diamanti*, and the yoke are combined (pl. 70); or the lower frieze of a Medicean manuscript of about 1500 (pl. 96).[9] In this work a number of *imprese* are joined in a manner which Pontormo's design recalls: within a "diamante" medallion, a shield with the *palle* is affixed to a laurel tree. Its trunk is cut off but at the top new branches sprout from each side. At the base of the tree is a scroll with PAR LE FUE REVERDIRA, and at the top a yoke is tied to the tree with a scroll inscribed with the motto N/SVAVE. Suspended from either end of the yoke are two pendants with six jewels, which echo the six *palle*.

These correspondences between elements in the lunette and nonfigurative Medici art, together with the emblematic features and inscriptions in the design, suggest that it might be read on one level as a giant Medici *impresa*, with *corpi*, or images, and *anime*, or words—so conceived as to complement and contrast with the *istorie* below. Bearing in mind such a possibility, we may now turn to the *corpi* and *anime* of the fresco, to its dramatis personae and its inscriptions.

THE DRAMATIS PERSONAE AND INSCRIPTIONS

Pontormo's fresco has been taken to tell Ovid's story of Vertumnus and Pomona from

[7] London, Victoria and Albert Museum (attributed to the style of Antonio del Pollaiuolo and dated ca. 1465 by Pope-Hennessy, I, cat. 129). See also the terracotta medallion attributed to Luca della Robbia in which the *diamante* frames the lion head of Leo X (A. Marquand, *Della Robbia Heraldry*, Princeton, 1919, p. 234, fig. 217).

[8] Langedijk, p. 44.

[9] Laur. Plut. MS 63, 33, f. 45r; D'Ancona, no.

1618 (as Giovanni Boccardino). There is no indication in this manuscript of who its Medici recipient might have been; however, devices in the left vertical frieze (with the flaming *broncone*) and the initial (with the two Wheels of Fortune and the lute with broken string) are similar to those in manuscripts made for Piero di Lorenzo, such as Laur. MS Plut. 18, 2, of 1493 (pls. 7, 10).

the *Metamorphoses* ever since Vasari's brief description of Pontormo's work in the Salone named the agricultural gods as the protagonists of the fresco:[10]

> . . . gli furono date a dipignere le due teste, dove sono gli occhi che danno lume (cioè le finestre) dalla volta infino al pavimento. . . . Onde avendo a fare un Vertunno con i suoi agricultori, fece un villano che siede con un pennato in mano, tanto bello e ben fatto, che è cosa rarissima; come anco sono certi putti che vi sono, oltre ogni credenza vivi e naturali. Dall'altra banda facendo Pomona e Diana con altre dee, le avviluppò di panni forse troppo pienamente: nondimeno, tutta l'opera è bella e molta lodata.

> There were given to him to paint the two ends where the round openings are that give light—that is, the windows—from the vaulting down to the floor. . . . Thus, having to execute a Vertumnus with his husbandmen, he painted a peasant seated with a vine-pruner in his hand, which is so beautiful and so well done that it is a very rare thing, even as certain children that are there are lifelike and natural beyond all belief. On the other side he painted Pomona and Diana, with other goddesses, enveloping them perhaps too abundantly with draperies. However, the work as a whole is beautiful and much extolled.

The tale of Vertumnus and Pomona is a pastorale with erotic overtones in which Vertumnus assumes various picturesque disguises in order to enter the walled garden of Pomona and win her love. In the absence of conflicting testimony, the fresco has been understood to portray these ancient Italian gods, and its subject has been deemed appropriate to the decoration of a villa built on the site of Lorenzo il Magnifico's farm.[11]

On a primary level of interpretation, Vertumnus and Pomona are indeed the subjects of the fresco. They are to be identified as the figures who sit on the lower wall, framing the scene.[12] This scene is set in Pomona's walled garden, as described by Ovid: ". . . she shut herself up within her orchard and so guarded herself against all approach of man." Pomona is clearly the owner of the garden in the fresco (pl. 97). Placed at the extreme margin of the composition, she invites us into her domain, leaning forward and making eye contact with us. This intimacy is reinforced by her three companions, all of whom—in contrast to the men on the other side of the lunette—look out at the spectator. Pomona also accords perfectly with Ovid's description of her as a goddess of fruit trees (*poma*), which she cares for with the pruning-hook (*falce*): "She cared nothing for woods and rivers, but only for the fields and branches laden with delicious fruits. She carried no javelin in her hand, but the curved pruning-hook with which she repressed the too luxuriant growth and cut back the branches spreading out on every side."

[10] Vasari, VI, p. 265. For the text from *Metamorphoses*, XIV, 623-97, see Appendix II.

[11] For this traditional interpretation, see Cox-Rearick, 1964, I, pp. 172-74. See also Shearman, 1965, I, p. 79, who sees the lunette as "an evocation of the joys of *villeggiatura*, and in particular, of Lorenzo's *poggio*"; and Forster, 1966, pp. 41-47, and p. 136, cat. 19, who relates the scene closely to Ovid's text. Among the earlier critics, only Chastel, 1961, p. 156, doubted that Vertumnus and Pomona was the sole subject of the lunette, suggesting that it might be a variation on the themes of the Seasons and the Ages.

[12] Kliemann, 1972, pp. 300-303. Winner, 1972, p. 165, identifies the gods as the couple flanking the garland.

The instrument in the fresco is partly effaced, but the traditional Roman pruning-hook is shown in Pontormo's preparatory study for the goddess (pl. 98).[13] Pomona's partner to the left of the lunette is Vertumnus (pl. 99). He is identifiable as Ovid's god, who disguised himself as an old reaper with a basket: "Oh, how often in the garb of a rough reaper did he bring her a basket of barley-ears! And he was the perfect image of a reaper, too."

Further excursion into interpretation of the lunette as the story of Vertumnus and Pomona encounters difficulties. The rustic couple is accompanied by companions not mentioned by Ovid; and if Vasari is correct, one of these is Diana, a goddess who finds no place in Ovid's tale.[14] Moreover, Borghini, who wrote about the lunette in 1584, just after Allori finished the decorations of the Salone, did not seem to know that Pontormo's fresco represented Vertumnus and Pomona. Rather, he describes it as a pastorale of indefinite subject: "Il Puntormo vi dipinse intorno a un' occhio alcune Ninfe, e Pastori (Pontormo painted around an oculus some nymphs and shepherds).[15]

Borghini's failure to recognize the subject of the work as Vertumnus and Pomona is understandable, for Pontormo followed neither of the usual ways of representing the story. One of these was the *trionfo*, in which the old Vertumnus and the young Pomona ride in a chariot drawn by satyrs, as in the woodcut from Francesco Colonna's *Hypnerotomachia Poliphili* of 1499 (pl. 100). The other was a narrative scene, usually representing the comic-erotic episode of Vertumnus, disguised as an old woman, in Pomona's garden.[16] But Pontormo's fresco tells no story at all. His casually dressed *villani* are arranged emblematically in a shallow, schematic setting identifiable as a garden only by the laurel above the oculus and the formal garland below it. Moreover, Pontormo's peasants do not behave like actors in an Ovidian pastorale. They are isolated from one another—and, with one exception, noninteracting—and a number of them stare insistently out at the spectator.

This atypical presentation of the Vertumnus and Pomona story, together with the emblematic character of the composition, the symbolic laurel, and the inscriptions, suggest that the often-noted stylistic novelties of the fresco[17] reflect not only an intensive phase of individualistic experimentation on the part of Pontormo, but complex and hitherto unexplained levels of symbolism in the work. And, in fact, in recent years, the traditional one-dimensional reading of the content of the fresco has been questioned as insufficient, and additional meanings have been read in the work. Ovid's Vertumnus and Pomona have been allowed to remain in Pomona's garden (although not without disagreement as to which of the pair are the rustic gods); the inscriptions have been read

[13] Uffizi 6673Fv; see Cox-Rearick, 1964, I, cat. 148. Kliemann, 1972, p. 301, cites Cartari's description of Pomona's pruning-hook in support of his identification of the figure. See Cartari, 1571, p. 234: "una piccola falce da tagliare gli rami superflui de gli alberi fruttiferi." A pruning-hook identical to the one in Pontormo's study appears in Perino del Vaga's *Vertumnus and Pomona* (London, British Museum, Sloane 5226-96).

[14] Vasari, VI, p. 265: "Dall'altra banda facendo Pomona e Diana con altre dee. . . ."

[15] R. Borghini, p. 626.

[16] As, for example, in Francesco Melzi's painting of ca. 1510 (Berlin) or Rosso's drawing of 1532-1533 for the Pavillon de Pomone at Fontainebleau (Louvre R. F. 559); or depicting a later moment in the story, Perino del Vaga's drawing of ca. 1527 for the *Loves of the Gods* (above, n. 13).

[17] As by Freedberg, 1961, I, pp. 558-66; and, in relation to the preparatory studies, by Cox-Rearick, 1964, I, pp. 38-46.

(with varying results); other literary sources for the imagery of the fresco have been identified; the remaining characters have been named (although, again, without any consensus of opinion); and it has been suggested that the fresco conveys a politico-dynastic message related to that of the *istorie* of the lateral walls of the Salone.[18]

✳   ✳   ✳

We may now, in the light of the traditional Ovidian interpretation of Pontormo's work, turn our attention to its inscriptions and then to the other characters who repose in Pomona's garden.

The first inscription to be noted is Pontormo's signature to the lower left, under Vertumnus: I[ACOBVS] F[LORENTINVS] P[INXIT].[19] This inscription, of course, is not related to the content of the fresco, but four other inscriptions are crucial to an interpretation of its meaning. These are related to one another, a connection that is visually expressed by their arrangement in an inverted equilateral triangle around the oculus, its lower vertex marked by the GLOVIS disk, its other vertices marked by the standards carried by the putti. These inscriptions are all, to some degree, enigmatic, and none of them (except possibly GLOVIS) has a demonstrable connection with the story of Vertumnus and Pomona. But they are the primary indicators of two additional levels of meaning in the fresco: a mythological-literary level and a political, or Medicean, level. The inscriptions on the tablet above the oculus and on the two standards lead the observer to Virgil's *Georgics*; GLOVIS is, of course, Medicean, but as we recall, it is rooted in a Virgilian idea; and all these inscriptions lead to a reading of the lunette as representing the Cycles of Time—or the Seasons—and, ultimately, the new Golden Age of the Medici.

The inscription that dominates the fresco from its central position in the tablet above the oculus—STVDIV[M] QVIBVS ARVA TVERI—is the titular inscription of *Vertumnus and Pomona*. The phrase is taken from the proem to the *Georgics*.[20] In this passage Virgil invokes the gods of agriculture and then Augustus to bring peace to the land and, implicitly, a return of the Golden Age of Saturn. In Virgil's text, the antecedent to "Studium quibus arva tueri" is "dique deaeque omnes," which would have been supplied by the literate observer. The tablet inscription thus means "O gods and goddesses all, whose love guards our fields." It tells us that Vertumnus and Pomona's companions are Virgil's "dique deaeque omnes"—that they are also gods.

The first two gods invoked by Virgil, Liber and Ceres, have been interpreted by Virgil commentators, beginning with Servius, as the Sun and Moon:[21]

[18] Winner's interpretation, briefly stated in 1963-1964, pp. 9-11, is expanded in his article (1972, pp. 153-97) and touched on in his study of the *Cicero* fresco (1970, pp. 261-307). McKillop's reading (1970, pp. 1-10) is summarized in her pages on the *Cicero* (1974, pp. 74-76). Kliemann's substantial study (1972, pp. 293-328) agrees with some of Winner's conclusion and contains important additional material. This study was republished in 1976, pp. 40-72, as part of the author's dissertation.

[19] Kliemann, 1972, p. 296, n. 5. I can offer no interpretation of the letter D painted next to the band at the left edge of the fresco.

[20] Identified by Winner, 1963-1964, pp. 9-10. See Appendix II for the text. Pontormo's work is included (with a summary of the Winner-Kliemann interpretation) in the exhibition catalogue, *Virgilio nell'arte e nella cultura europea*, Biblioteca Nazionale Centrale, Rome, 1981, pp. 91-92.

[21] Servius, III, pp. 130-31. See also Macrobius, *Saturnalia*, I, 16: "Virgil points to both the moon and the sun as the guides of the year." Kliemann,

VOS O CLARISSIMA MVNDI LVMINA LIBER ET ALMA CERES. Stoici dicunt non esse nisi unum deum, et unam eandemque esse potestatem, quae pro ratione officiorum nostrorum variis nominibus appellatur: unde eundem Solem, eundem Liberum, eundem Apollinem vocant; item Lunam eandem Dianam, eandem Cererem, eandem Iunonem, eandem Proserpinam dicunt. Secundum quos pro Sole et Luna Liberum et Cererem invocavit. . . . QVAE DVCITIS ANNVM. Quorum cursu tempora computantur; nam per lunam mensis, per solem annus ostenditur.

O YE MOST RADIANT LIGHTS OF THE FIRMAMENT, LIBER AND BOUNTEOUS CERES. The Stoics say there is only one god and his power is one and the same, which by reason of our offices is called by various names. Whence they call the same god the Sun, Liber, Apollo. They call the Moon, Diana, Ceres, Juno, Proserpina. According to the Stoics, he evoked Liber and Ceres in place of the Sun and Moon. . . . YOU WHO LEAD THE YEAR. By whose course the seasons are reckoned. For by means of the Moon, the month is shown; by means of the Sun, the year is shown.

In Renaissance illustrations of the introduction to the *Georgics*, the Sun, as Sol-Apollo, and the Moon, as Luna-Diana, are invariably depicted in the sky above a scene of agricultural workers in the fields. For example, in a late fifteenth-century French manuscript illumination (pl. 101), the deities preside from the heavens;[22] and in the woodcut frontispiece to Sebastian Brant's 1502 edition of the *Georgics*, Liber and Ceres (or Sol-Apollo and Luna-Diana) are represented to the upper right by the faces of the Sun and Moon (pl. 102). Brant's edition could well have been known to Giovio and Pontormo, having been copied in many Venetian editions dating from 1507 to 1520.[23]

1972, pp. 313-16, who connects the fresco with this passage, notes the traditional equations Liber = Bacchus = Apollo = Sol and Ceres = Diana = Luna, as well as Landino's commentary of 1488 on *Georgics* I, 21-23 (Landino, f. 58v): "*Dii deaque*: Legerat poeta apud M. Varronem duodecim illum in suo de re agraria libro invocasse deos, quos duces agricolarum appellat. . . . Sunt autem sex mares, totidemque feminae. Quorum primi sunt iuppiter et tellus, qui omnes fructus agriculture celo et terra continent. Quapropter magni parentes dicuntur: Juppiter pater et tellus mater. Secundo in loco posuit solem et lunam, quorm tempora observantur, cum quaedam serantur et condantur in tempore. Tertio in loco invocat liberum et cererem, qui horum fructus maxime necessarii sint ad victum. Ab his enim cibus et potus venit e fundo. Verum hos quatuor ipse duobus nominibus solis et lunae invocat." (*Gods and goddesses*. The poet had read in Marcus Varro that he [Varro] had invoked twelve gods in his book *On Agriculture*, and he calls these

gods the "patrons of the farmers." . . . Six are masculine and six are feminine. The first are Jupiter and Tellus who contain all the fruits of farming on heaven and earth. For this reason they are called "universal parents": Father Jupiter and Mother Earth. Then he placed the sun and the moon whose courses are observed when certain things are sown and stored at the right time. Thirdly, he invokes Liber and Ceres whose fruits are especially necessary for nourishment. With their help come food and drink from the farm. However, he invokes these four with the names of the sun and moon).

[22] Edinburgh, University Library MS D. b. VI, 8, f. 19r; see C. R. Borland, *A Descriptive Catalogue of the Western Medieval Manuscripts in Edinburgh University Library*, Edinburgh, 1916, pp. 281-83, cat. 195.

[23] On Brant's Virgil, *Opera* (Strassburg, 1502), of which pl. 102 reproduces f. 34r, and the Venetian editions of 1507, 1510, 1514, 1515, 1520, etc.,

Since the gods of the Virgilian text quoted in the titular inscription of the lunette are usually shown in the sky, it seems reasonable to identify the gods who are silhouetted *against* the sky in Pontormo's fresco as Liber and Ceres, or Sol-Apollo and Luna-Diana.[24] (I shall henceforth call them by these names, although it should be recalled that their other identities, particularly Luna-Diana as Ceres, remain important.) These gods, each placed at the apex of a figural triangle, thus dominate the male and female sides of the fresco—a division which is, of course, entirely consistent with Ovid's story of Vertumnus seeking entrance into Pomona's female domain. The nude Sol-Apollo reaches up toward his sacred laurel (pl. 103). Luna-Diana is identifiable with Virgil's Ceres, goddess of the harvest, by her attributes—the wreath of cornstalks and poppies in her blond hair, and her white shawl (pl. 104).[25] Moreover, this rustic, seated figure with her puffy draperies is clearly based on the typical Renaissance Ceres; and she seems particularly close to a northern type of the goddess, of the sort depicted in an engraving of *Summer* by Virgil Solis (pl. 105).[26] Pontormo's penchant for northern prints at the time of his work at Poggio a Caiano is well documented, and a northern source might account not only for the type of the rustic harvest goddess but for the Germanic flavor of the costumes of all three goddesses.[27]

The inscriptions on the *vexilla* held by the putti relate to the theme of the gods in the heavens that is implied in the Virgil inscription of the central tablet. On the banner to the right are the letters IVP P (pl. 106). As has been noted by Matthias Winner and Julian Kliemann, Cristoforo Landino's commentary on the lines in *Georgics* I from which the central inscription was taken names Jupiter and Tellus as the two major gods.[28] The banner thus refers to Jupiter, and its letters may be expanded to IVPPITER PATER. By placing the invocation to Jupiter in a separate banner, Pontormo sets him apart from the agricultural gods of the central tablet, perhaps following the first mention of Jupiter in the *Georgics*, where he is called *pater ipse colendi* (the great father).[29]

The inscription on the standard to the left completes the allusion to Jupiter's sovereignty (pl. 107). It is a single word, which has been read by Winner as V.INA (LVCINA or

see T. K. Rabb, "Sebastian Brant and the First Illustrated Edition of Virgil," *The Princeton University Library Chronicle*, 21, 1960, pp. 187-99. See also G. Mambelli, *Gli Annali delle edizioni virgiliane*, Florence, 1954, p. 54, no. 131 (1515 edition), and p. 56, no. 138 (1519 edition). Some of the woodcuts from the 1519 edition are discussed and illustrated by Prince d'Essling, *Les Livres à Figures vénitiens de la fin du XVᵉ siècle et du commencement du XVIᵉ*, Florence-Paris, 1907, Pt. I, vol. i, pp. 65-75.

[24] Winner, 1972, pp. 161-64; also McKillop, 1970, p. 4; and Kliemann, 1972, pp. 314-16 (all citing the Brant frontispiece).

[25] Winner, 1972, p. 162; and Kliemann, 1972, p. 297, cite some of these attributes of Ceres. Cf. Virgil, *Georgics*, I, 962 ("flava Ceres"); *Georgics*, I,

212; Ovid, *Fasti*, IV, 615-20; V, 355-58. In Renaissance painting, Ceres is typically shown as blond (cf. pl. 132).

[26] Bartsch, IX, 261, 134. The engraving is later than Pontormo's fresco, but the Ceres is a traditional type.

[27] Is it significant that Vasari, VI, p. 265, criticized the draperies of the goddesses (". . . le avviluppò [Pontormo] di panni forse troppo pienamente: nondimeno tutta l'opera è bella e molto lodata") in a tone similar to that reserved for his negative remarks about the Dürer-inspired Passion Series frescos (Vasari, VI, pp. 266-67).

[28] Winner, 1972, p. 160; Kliemann, 1972, pp. 324-25. For the passage see n. 21 above.

[29] *Georgics*, I, 121. See also I, 353ff. (*ipse pater statuit*).

LVMINA) and by Kliemann as VTINAM . . . (would that!).[30] Kliemann is more nearly correct, but the fragmentary last letter is not an M but a T. (If the first stroke were that of an M, it would be a thin line, as in the M in the inscription on the throne in Pontormo's portrait of Cosimo Pater Patriae.) Thus, the word is not VTINAM but VTINAT. This verb of wish should be read with Jupiter as its subject, the two inscriptions belong together, and they read IVPPITER PATER VTINAT (Jupiter the Father wishes it).[31] This inscription, then, comments on the line from the *Georgics* in the central tablet, adding that it is the wish of the great Jupiter that the Golden Age return.

Balancing the tablet above the oculus is the GLOVIS roundel. Since GLOVIS descends from Lorenzo's Golden Age motto, LE TEMPS REVIENT, and ultimately from Virgil's prophecy of the return of the Golden Age in *Eclogue* IV, it echoes the inscription evoking the Golden Age from the *Georgics*.[32] With its suggestion of turning, GLOVIS also affirms the relation of Virgil's celestial deities, Sol-Apollo and Luna-Diana, to the general theme of the Cycles of Time: as the Sun and Moon, they are Day and Night; and, as we have seen, they are Virgil's "most radiant lights of the firmament, that guide through heaven the gliding year." They rule the heavenly cycles of the year, the solar cycle belonging to Sol-Apollo and the lunar cycle to Luna-Diana.

If the gods on the wall above rule the cycles of the heavens, then the four gods below, which include Vertumnus and Pomona, may be interpreted as ruling the cycles of the earth, or the seasons. As agricultural gods and as symbols of the regeneration of nature, Vertumnus and Pomona were traditionally connected with the theme of the Four Seasons. In Ovid's story, for example, Vertumnus changes according to the seasons, becoming the old, white-haired woman who enters Pomona's garden in winter; and the story itself is an allegory of the changing seasons. Likewise, in the *Hypnerotomachia Poliphili*, these gods are deities of Time, and Polifilo sees them as accompanied by personifications of the seasons.[33] Pontormo also developed the theme of the Seasons associated with Vertumnus and Pomona. In the fresco, however, instead of being accompanied by the Seasons—or being connected with them, as in the *Metamorphoses*—Vertumnus and Pomona actually personify Winter and Spring.

The key to this reading is Kliemann's interpretation of Pomona as *terra mater*, goddess of the earth, and Vertumnus as Janus *coelum*, god of the heavens, god of turning, of change, and of the beginning of the year in his month of January.[34] Thus, Vertumnus-Janus, depicted by Pontormo as an old man (cf. the old woman in Ovid's story), is Winter; and Pomona, dressed in the green of that season, is Spring.[35]

The remaining seasons, summer and autumn, are often associated with Ceres and

[30] Winner, 1972, p. 160; Kliemann, 1972, pp. 324-25.

[31] For the unusual verb *utino*, which does not occur before in the Renaissance, see R. E. Lathan, *Revised Medieval Latin Word-List*, London, 1965, p. 502. I am grateful to Virginia Brown for clarifying this inscription for me.

[32] Winner, 1963-1964, p. 10; Winner, 1972, pp. 166-70; and Langedijk, 1968, p. 44.

[33] *The Dream of Poliphilus: Facsimiles of 168 Wood-cuts in the "Hypnerotomachia Poliphili,"* Venice, 1499, ed. J. W. Appell, London, 1889, no. 66.

[34] Kliemann, 1972, pp. 300-303; also his expanded discussion in 1976, pp. 41-46, Appendices 31-46, with citations from Annio da Viterbo's commentary on Ovid, *Fasti*, I, 120, and other texts and commentaries.

[35] See Kliemann, 1972, p. 317; and 1976, pp. 59-63, Appendices 32-33, for Pomona as Spring.

Bacchus, gods of the summer and autumn harvests; however, in Pontormo's fresco, these gods are assimilated into the Luna-Diana and Sol-Apollo characters on the upper wall. Their function as seasonal deities is taken over by the couple on either side of the garland: Summer, with a red drapery linking her to the goddess above her, reclines next to Pomona (pl. 108); Autumn, reclining next to Winter and wearing a sowing bag appropriate to his season (as does Autumn on the portico frieze; pl. 54), is linked to the god above him by his glance and his violet costume (pl. 109).[36]

The seasonal cycle represented by these four figures is echoed in the garland held by the putti seated on the wall above Summer and Autumn.[37] While most of its fruits are citrus (the Medici fruit symbolizing immortality), berries are on the autumn-winter side and the roses of spring and summer bloom on the extreme right side. The GLOVIS disk, which announces the theme of Time, is placed at the center of the garland, where it aptly comments on the eternal turning of the seasonal cycle of the earth.

As in the case of the *istorie* and *sopraporte* in the Salone, which inspired later Medici artists, Pontormo's figures became models for the subject of the Seasons. In Vasari's decorations in the Palazzo Vecchio, the imagery of which is so frequently derivative, the Seasons in the Sala di Opi[38] depend on Pontormo's. The theme of the room is Time, presided over by a *Triumph of Opi*. Around her are the *Seasons* and below, in a frieze, are the *Months* with their zodiac signs such as March with Aries (pl. 58). Like Pontormo's, Vasari's *Seasons* are accompanied by garlands of seasonal fruits and flowers; they are reclining like three of Pontormo's personifications; Summer is seen from behind like Pontormo's Summer; and Winter is an old man whom Vasari identifies as Vertumnus (pl. 111).[39]

THE GODS OF THE MEDICI GOLDEN AGE

The theme of the Golden Age in Pontormo's fresco, which is signaled by its inscriptions, and the theme of the Cycles of Time, which is present in the Sun, Moon, and Four Seasons, express ideas more specific than a nostalgic evocation of a past Golden Age and its hoped-for return. As we have seen, such imagery had topical significance for the Medici during Leo's papacy, and, like the *istorie* below, the fresco alludes to contemporary Medici events and personalities. It has been so interpreted, for example, by Kurt Forster, who read the work as an allegory of Medici power in which Virgil's gods and their fruitful land symbolize the Golden Age of Leo X.[40] However, Winner and Kliemann propose that its political message was still more explicit, that it hinged

---

[36] Kliemann, 1972, p. 317.

[37] Kliemann, 1972, p. 318.

[38] See chap. 3, n. 36.

[39] Vasari, *Rag.*, p. 47: ". . . e quest'altro, che segue in quest'altro quadro, vecchio e grinzuto, col capo coperto, che sta rannicchiato con le ginocchia, che ha il fuoco appresso, abbrividato di freddo,

tutto tremante, è fatto per il Verno, cioè Vertunno, che anche a esso non manca li suoi festoni, sì come gli altri, pieni di foglie secche, suvvi pastinache, carote, cipolle, agli, radici, rape e maceroni."

[40] Forster, 1966, pp. 39-47. See also Winner, 1963-1964, p. 11; and McKillop, 1970, p. 10.

on the threat to the dynasty presented by the illness (and eventual death) of Lorenzo the younger in 1519. According to their reading, the choice of the gods Vertumnus and Pomona, as well as the laurel, was inspired by the imagery of a contemporary poem which uses the metaphor of the dying laurel to allude to Lorenzo's illness.[41] The poem is Ariosto's "Ne le stagion," which was written between his visit to the sick Lorenzo in late February 1519 and Lorenzo's death on 4 May.[42] In this elegy, the language of which recalls both the *Georgics* and Laurentian poetry, the poet calls on Phoebus, Bacchus, Vertumnus, and Pomona, as well as other rustic gods, to come to the aid of the dying *lauro*-Lorenzo:[43]

> Febo, rettor de li superni segni,
> aiuta 'l sacro Lauro, onde corona
> più volte avesti nei tessali regni;
>   concedi, Bacco, Vertunno e Pomona,
> satiri, fauni, driade e napee,
> che nuova fronde il Lauro mio ripona;
>   soccorran tutti i dèi, tutte le dèe
> che de li arbori han cura, l'arbor mio;
> però che gli è fatal: se viver dee,
>   vivo io; se dee morir, seco moro io.

Phoebus, master of the supernal stars, aid the sacred Laurel, whose crown you often wore in the Thessalian kingdoms; grant, O Bacchus, Vertumnus, and Pomona, satyrs, fauns, driads, and dell-nymphs, that my Laurel put forth new leaves; may all the gods, all the goddesses who take care of trees, aid my tree; because it is destined: if it must live, I live; if it must die, with it I die.

Winner and Kliemann interpret the fresco as alluding to the very situation that inspired the poem: Lorenzo's fatal illness and the Medicean hopes for the restoration of their power. The lines "soccorran tutti i dèi, tutte le dèe / che de li arbori han cura" are a paraphrase of the lines from the *Georgics* from which the quotation in the tablet is taken (with *arva* changed to *arbori*). The invocation to the gods should thus be read as referring not only to the restoration of peace and the Golden Age but to the restoration of the health of the *lauro*-Lorenzo. Moreover, Kliemann interprets the left side of the lunette as expressing the theme of the bad fortunes of the Medici, with its putti grimacing in distress and the inscription on the standard (which he reads as VTINAM) being a plea to Ariosto's gods for the life of the laurel.

The imagery of Pontormo's fresco does indeed allude to that of Ariosto's poem; how-

---

[41] Winner, 1972, pp. 171-77; Kliemann, 1972, pp. 304-6.

[42] Kliemann, 1972, p. 304.

[43] For the entire poem, see Appendix II. My interpretation of Ariosto's lines differs in a significant detail from that of Winner and Kliemann. Kliemann, pp. 306, 315, does not mention Phoebus but identifies Pontormo's Sol-Apollo with

Ariosto's Bacchus. Winner, 1972, p. 177, connects Ariosto's Phoebus with Virgil's "most radiant lights of the firmament" and Ariosto's Bacchus with Virgil's Liber; however, Virgil's Liber *is* one of the "radiant lights," and it is with Liber (or Sol-Apollo in the lunette) that Ariosto's Phoebus should be connected.

ever, I would interpret the connection somewhat differently. In the fresco—as opposed to the poem, which was written when Lorenzo's life was still in balance—the plea to the gods has already been answered. The wish of Jupiter, stated in the inscription IVPPITER PATER VTINAT, has been fulfilled; Fortune's Wheel has turned, and the Medici laurel grows again from the dead stumps. The Golden Age of Lorenzo il Magnifico, signaled by GLOVIS (with its promise of Time's Return) and by the quotation from the *Georgics*, which evokes the peaceful Age of Saturn, has been recovered under his son, Leo X.

*   *   *

Pontormo's rustic gods inhabit an idyllic garden like the one Ariosto describes in the opening lines of his elegy. Ariosto's garden is a metaphor of the Florentine Golden Age before the laurel was threatened:

> . . . una piagga amena,
>   che di bianco, d'azur, vermiglio e d'auro
> fioriva sempre . . .

>   . . . a pleasant plain which, of white and blue, bright red, and gold, was always blooming . . .

This very imagery evokes poetry from the time of Lorenzo il Magnifico, such as Poliziano's description in the *Stanze* of the Garden of Venus:[44]

> ovunque vola veste la campagna
> di rose, gigli, violette e fiori;
> l'erba di sue belleze ha maraviglia:
> bianca, cilestra, pallida e vermiglia.

> Wherever he [Zephyr] flies he clothes the countryside in roses, lilies, violets, and other flowers; the grass marvels at its own beauties: white, blue, pale, and red.

The colors of the Golden Age garden that Ariosto nostalgically recalls are the red, blue, and gold of the Medici *stemma* and the red and white of the city of Florence. These are the very colors of the decorations on the vault which frames Pontormo's lunette.[45] Within the fresco, as well, we find ourselves in Medicean, even Laurentian, domain. The pale yellow walls of Pomona's garden, which repeat the color of the walls of the villa, evoke the sunlit outdoors of Lorenzo's farm; Lorenzo's sacred laurel shades the rustics, and the ends of the garland are heavy with the Medici citrus (*mala medica*) and roses.

Each of the six gods seated on the walls of Pomona's garden plays a specific role in

[44] *Le Stanze*, I, 77. Ariosto, p. 124, uses similar imagery in a poem written on the death in 1516 of Filiberta di Savoia, wife of Giuliano de' Medici ("Anima eletta," *Canzoni*, V, 69): "Ma velenosi serpi / per le verde, vermiglie e bianche e azzure / campagne. . . ."

[45] Kliemann, 1972, p. 311, n. 75.

this tableau of the Medici Golden Age. They are arranged in pairs, of which the first is the rustic Vertumnus-Janus and Pomona, who frame the scene visually and conceptually at each level of its meaning. They are the protagonists of Ovid's story, but they are also actors in a pastorale of the Medici Golden Age, for Vertumnus and Pomona are among the gods invoked by Ariosto to restore the life of the Medici laurel. Vertumnus, as Winter, and Pomona, as Spring, are also central to the imagery of the Cycles of Time. Moreover, as Janus, Vertumnus is specifically identified with January and the beginning of the year. In his role as house-god and as ruler of the year, Janus was a key figure on Lorenzo's portico frieze (pl. 56). Now, the idealized Janus *bifrons* of the frieze has been brought inside the villa to appear in rustic disguise as Ovid's old Vertumnus.

Leaving for later discussion the role of Vertumnus-Janus in the tableau of the Golden Age, we may consider his partner, Pomona. As Spring, Pomona presides over a springtime garden of sprouting laurel and blooming roses. As we have seen in connection with the *Birth of the Year* and the *Seasons and the Months* on the frieze (pls. 53-54) and in Botticelli's *Primavera* (pl. 60), springtime imagery in Medici art has a conventional meaning: it alludes to Time's Return and the return of the Golden Age. Like the gardens of Laurentian art—those of the *Primavera* and the *Stanze*—the garden of the fresco alludes to the Medici Golden Age.[46] And Pomona, as Spring, recalls her earlier Laurentian counterparts. She plays the same role in the lunette as Flora plays in the *Primavera*: like Botticelli's goddess, Pomona (who is also placed to the right of the painting) signals the entrance to the garden of the Medici Golden Age and the renewal of the Florentine year in spring. There are also hints in this figure's costume and pose of the old theme of Medici rule in Florence. Her turban with its large knot has been ingeniously shaped to resemble the *diamante* with its pointed stone, and her pose recalls that of Florentia on Giuliano de' Medici's medal (pl. 11). Like Florentia, Pomona lies under the protection of the laurel, ready with her pruning-hook to care for the regenerating Medici tree.

As a personification of Spring in a Golden Age garden Pomona is connected with the quotation from the *Georgics* and the Jupiter inscription at the top of the lunette. For Virgil closely associates the Golden Age with spring. In *Georgics* II, for example, he pictures the renewal of spring, which is immediately joined to "ver illud erat"—the springtime that was, or the Golden Age.[47] And Jupiter, for Virgil, is the *pater omnipotens* to whose nurturing power he attributes the coming of spring.[48]

The second pair reclining on the lower wall have been identified as Autumn and Summer. But if the other couples—Vertumnus and Pomona, Sol-Apollo and Luna-Diana—are gods, are not these figures also to be identified as gods? Returning to the literary sources of the fresco, we find that the only couple besides Liber and Ceres that Virgil invokes is Pan and Minerva, who cannot be the figures in the lunette. And

[46] For gardens as a metaphor of the Golden Age, see Giamatti, p. 37ff.

[47] *Georgics*, II, 324-45, especially 336-38: "Even such days [of the earth's renewal in spring], I could suppose, shone at the first dawn of the infant world; even such was the course they held. Springtime that was; the great world was keeping spring. . . ."

[48] *Georgics*, II, 323-27: "Spring it is that aids the woods and the forest leafage; in spring the soil swells and calls for the life-giving seed. Then Heaven, the Father almighty, comes down in fruitful showers into the lap of his joyous spouse, and his might, with her mighty frame commingling, nurtures all growths."

Ariosto invokes no other couple among the inhabitants of his springtime garden. However, he does name two more goddesses—Venus and Diana:

> Vener, lasciando i templi citerei
> e li altari e le vittime e li odori
> di Gnido e di Amatunte e de' Sabei,
>   sovente con le Grazie in lieti cori
> vi danzò intorno; e per li rami in tanto
> salian scherzando i pargoletti Amori.
>   Spesso Diana con le ninfe a canto
> l'arbuscel suavissimo prepose
> alle selve d'Eurota e d'Erimanto.
>   E queste ed altre dèe sotto l'ombrose
> frondi, mentre in piacer stavano e in festa,
> benediron tra lor chi il ramo pose.

Venus, leaving the Cytherean temples, the altars, victims, and perfumes of Gnidus, of Amathus, and the Sabeans, often danced around it [the laurel] with the Graces in joyful choruses; and in the meantime, little cupids playfully climbed in the branches. Often Diana with her nymphs preferred this sweetest little tree to the bosks of Eurota and Erimantus. And these and other goddesses under the leafy shade, while they were enjoying and celebrating, blessed among themselves he who planted the branch.

Ariosto's Venus, Diana, and the little cupids climbing in the branches of the laurel are all present in the fresco. Diana is the same figure as Virgil's Ceres, or Luna—the goddess on the upper wall who must, in turn, be the figure Vasari thought was Diana. Below her is Summer, whom I would associate with Ariosto's Venus. In the rustic context of the fresco, with its *villani* sitting on the garden wall under the shade of the laurel, this Venus is an agricultural deity like her companions. In a characterization perfectly in keeping with the conceit of rustic disguise, she is Venus *hortorum*, ancient Roman goddess of gardens.[49] As patroness of gardens, she complements Pomona, who cares for the Medici laurel. And, like Pomona, she alludes to the Golden Age of Medici Florence. For Pontormo's figure is the same goddess who played a leading role in the myth of the Medici Golden Age in the time of Lorenzo il Magnifico. The "regno di Venere" (rule of Venus) is elaborately detailed in the *Stanze* and in other poetry from Lorenzo's circle.[50] And it is Venus who is the subject of Botticelli's Medicean mythologies: the *Primavera*, where Venus *hortorum* rules over a garden that alludes to Medici Florence; and the *Birth of Venus*, where the goddess comes to the shores of Tuscany

[49] On sources for Venus *hortorum*, see Dempsey's discussion (pp. 257, 260-62) of the Venus of the *Primavera*. Varro, *De lingua latina*, VI, 20, mentions the dedication of the summer Vinalia to Venus; Varro, *De re rustica*, I, 1, 6, lists Venus among the twelve patrons of agriculture; Pliny, *Naturalis historia*, XIX, XIX, 51, places gardens under the guardianship of Venus; and Columella, *De re rustica*, X, 194-214, connects Venus *hortorum* with her month of April.

[50] See Poliziano, *Le Stanze*, I, 69-125, and other texts quoted in Warburg, "Botticelli," pp. 29-46; and Gombrich, 1972, "Botticelli," p. 206, n. 30.

(Porto Venere, according to the legend). Like Botticelli's Venus, who arrives in a shower of the roses sacred to her (and also a Laurentian device), Pontormo's Venus is accompanied by the roses of the garland.[51] Next to the GLOVIS and the blooming roses, Medici laurel sprouting behind her, this Venus *hortorum* vividly recalls such Laurentian imagery, updated to allude to the recovery of the Golden Age by Lorenzo's son, Leo X.

We shall not find Venus' partner in Ariosto's elegy, for the poet mentions no further gods; nor does Autumn correspond with any of the other deities invoked by Virgil. However, given the theme of the Golden Age in the fresco, this figure can only be Saturn, ruler of the Golden Age—of Virgil's *Saturnia regna*.[52] Pontormo's youthful Saturn is not based on Chronos, the familiar aged personification of Time, but on Saturnus, the rustic Roman agricultural god, whose joyful feast corresponded with the season of sowing and was enacted as a symbolic return of the Golden Age.[53] Saturnus was typically shown wearing leggings symbolizing the germination of the seeds planted in late autumn.[54] Pontormo's Autumn, with his sowing bag and leggings, represents this Golden Age deity. Like Apollo, Diana, and Venus, Saturn appears here in his rustic form so that he may inhabit the pastoral tableau of Vertumnus, Pomona, and Virgil's agricultural gods.

A source for Pontormo's Saturn as sower may have been Brant's illustrated edition of the *Georgics*, the frontispiece of which I have cited as a source for the imagery of agricultural gods ruled by the Sun and Moon in the heavens (pl. 102). Another woodcut in the book is an elaborate representation of Saturn as agricultural god of the Golden Age (pl. 110).[55] The cosmos diagram in the center refers to Saturn as god of time; above, he is sower and reaper; below, he arrives in Latium; and to the right are the Italian farmers whom he taught the art of agriculture.[56]

Saturn's presence in the fresco is consonant not only with the theme of the *Saturnia regna*, to which the Medicean *topos* of Time's Return refers, but with the tablet quotation from the *Georgics*: "[dique deaeque omnes,] studium quibus arva tueri." For the peaceful country life of the *Georgics* is described by Virgil as a survival of the Golden Age of Saturn, and the farmers who lived that life are characterized as Saturn's last descendants, with whom Justice lived until the end of the Golden Age. These themes, to which Pontormo's Golden Age tableau alludes, are set forth in the conclusion of *Georgics* II:[57] "O happy husbandmen! too happy, should they come to know their blessings! . . .   Yet

[51] See, among many texts favored by Medici iconographers, Columella, *De re rustica*, where Venus is characterized as a garden deity and connected with flowers, especially roses (X, 286-87): "Lo, now Dione's daughter with her flowers / the garden decks, the rose begins to bloom. . . ."

[52] See *Eclogue* IV, 4-10 (quoted in chap. 1, "Time's Return and the Medici Golden Age"). On Saturn's rule of Italy, see *Aeneid*, VI, 791-95; VIII, 314-29; and *Georgics*, II, 136-76. On the myth of the Golden Age, see chap. 1, n. 21. McKillop, 1970, pp. 5-6; and 1974, p. 75, suggested that this figure be identified as Saturn.

[53] On Saturn's traditions in art and literature,

see Klibansky et al., pp. 127-214; and A. Chastel, "Le Mythe de Saturne dans la Renaissance italienne," *Phoebus*, 1, 1946, pp. 125-34. On the Saturnalia (17-21 December), see G. Vaccari, *Le Feste di Roma antica*, Turin, 1927, pp. 197-99.

[54] Varro, *De Lingua latina*, V, 64, called Saturn *ab satu*. On his leg wrappings, see Macrobius, *Saturnalia*, I, 8, 5.

[55] Virgil, *Opera*, f. 68v. McKillop, 1970, p. 6, noted this source for Pontormo's figure.

[56] See Macrobius, *Saturnalia*, I, 7, 21, 25, on Saturn's introduction of agriculture into Latium and his veneration as a founder of a better life.

[57] For the complete passage, see Appendix II.

theirs is repose without care, and a life that knows no fraud, but is rich in treasures manifold. . . . Among them, as she quitted the earth, Justice planted her latest steps." And, in the very last lines, the theme of Saturn's peaceful rule of Italy is recalled yet again: "Such a life the old Sabines once lived, such Remus and his brother. . . . Nay, before the Cretan king [Jupiter] held scepter, and before a godless race banqueted on slaughtered bullocks, such was the life golden Saturn lived on earth. . . ."

Like Venus, Saturn had played a role in Laurentian imagery. In the imagination of Florentine poets, the peaceful agricultural Saturn of ancient poetic tradition accompanied the Medicean Golden Age so that, like the theme of the Medici *primavera*, the *Saturnia regna* became a *topos*.[58] Cosimo was seen to have revived Saturn's age, as was Piero,[59] but more than any other, Lorenzo was identified with the *Saturnia regna*. For example, in Luigi Pulci's *Morgante*, which is modeled on *Eclogue* IV, the Golden Age of Saturn is recovered by Lorenzo-Apollo, under whose sacred laurel,[60]

> tornano i tempi felici che furno
> quando e' regnòe quel buon signor Saturno

> The happy times return
> when that good lord Saturn reigned.

Not only was the Lorenzo-Saturn equation a commonplace, but Saturn occupied a special place in the imagery of Lorenzo's Neoplatonist circle.[61] He was an exalted figure in whom the ideals of the intellectual life and the rural were fused. Ruler of contemplation, he was also the patron of farmers, who were traditionally known as the "children of Saturn." At Villa Careggi, which was the seat of the Platonic Academy and the focus of Lorenzo's idealization of country life, imagery of Arcady, of Pan, and of Saturn was fostered by Lorenzo. On the feast of Saints Cosmas and Damian in 1480, a kind of Medicean Saturnalia was held at the villa for the peasants (Virgil's descendants of Saturn!). The notion of Saturn as ruler of the Golden Age was conflated with the familiar Laurentian themes of rustic or pastoral life (Pan), and all these beneficent gods of the countryside were evoked to celebrate the festival of the Medici saints.[62]

Such imagery was never given pictorial expression in Lorenzo's time, but it is vividly recalled in Pontormo's fresco, where Saturn (dressed in the violet and white of Lorenzo himself) finds a natural place among Virgil's gods and goddesses in a tableau of the new Medici Golden Age. He is near the GLOVIS roundel, which echoes Virgil's prophecy of

[58] Gombrich, 1966, pp. 29-34; and Costa, pp. 31-55. Saturn also appears as a youthful, agricultural god in non-Medicean art of the late Quattrocento (see the *Florentine Picture Chronicle*, ed. S. Colvin, London, 1898, pl. 30).

[59] On Cosimo, see "Eulogium in Cosmum Medicen patrem patriae," lines 343-50, in Naldi, *Elegiarum*, bk. III, no. 11, pp. 82-91; on Piero, see Naldi, *Bucolica*, pp. 137-38.

[60] L. Pulci, *Morgante*, ed. F. Agena, Milan, 1955, p. 1113. Lorenzo is also associated with the return

of the Golden Age by Luigi Pulci in the *Giostra*, stanza XXVII: "Ne per tornar Saturno e el mondo d'auro / Che non sara mai piu si gentil Lauro."

[61] Klibansky et al., pp. 241-74; Chastel, 1961, pp. 227-29. Ficino's *De triplici vita* glorifies Saturn as patron of the Platonic Academy, and Lorenzo styled himself as head of a circle of "Saturnines."

[62] Chastel, 1961, pp. 228-29. See Ficino's letter to Lorenzo in *Opera*, I, pp. 843-44 (quoted in chap. 9, n. 43).

the return of the Age of Saturn, and his partner is Venus, a patroness of Lorenzo's Golden Age; but, above all, Pontormo's youth is identifiable as the ruler of the Golden Age by the company he keeps.

Next to Saturn is Janus, co-ruler of his Golden Age. This traditional couple had appeared in Medici imagery both before and after the 1512 restoration. In Poliziano's *Ambra* (the subject of which is the villa at Poggio a Caiano), Saturn, as god of sowing, is paired with Janus, god of the year:[63]

> Claviger in semet redeuntem computat annum
> Jam dextra deus. At Saturnum lanea compes
> Mulcibero jubet ire parem . . .

> The keybearing god reckons now with his right hand the year returning upon itself. But the woolen shackle compels Saturn to go at the same pace as Vulcan.

In 1513, these same gods presided over the recovery of the Golden Age in Rome at Pope Leo's festival on the Capitoline, where a painting on the facade of the theater depicted *Saturn Greeted by Janus on His Arrival in Latium* (fig. 4). The gods were accompanied by Medici devices, including a lion (alluding to Leo) with a *palla* and a snake biting its tail.[64] And, in Florence, earlier in the same year, Pontormo himself had painted Saturn and Janus together. A float in the *broncone* pageant, which equated Medici return with the recovery of the Golden Age, is described by Vasari as including Saturn and Janus as its rulers:[65]

> Il primo [carro], tirato da un par di buoi vestiti d'erba, rappresentava l'età di Saturno e di Iano, chiamata dell'oro; ed aveva in cima del carro Saturno con la falce et Iano con le due teste e con la chiave del tempio della Pace in mano.

> The first [float], drawn by a pair of oxen decked with herbage, represented the Age of Saturn and Janus, called the Age of Gold; and on the summit of the car were Janus with the two heads and with the key of the Temple of Peace in his hands.

The pastoral mode of the *broncone* pageant is most interesting in relation to *Vertumnus and Pomona*. Saturn and Janus were attended by figures in rustic garb, by pairs of nude shepherds and their grooms carrying *bronconi*.[66] The combination of the Golden Age gods and the pastoral imagery suggests that this pageant may have served as a prototype for Pontormo's pastoral fresco of the Medici Golden Age. The pairs of nude shepherds, for example, may have inspired Pontormo's original idea for the putti at the top of the

[63] *Ambra*, lines 55-57, in *Le Selve*, pp. 74-75
[64] *Palliolo*, p. 26: "Imperoché nel primo, cominciando da man destra se vede il vecchio Saturno con la falce in spalla che tocca la mano a Jano, quale porta duo volti, l'uno denante l'altro a dietro, et sedendo sopra un sasso apresso l'uscio e fenestra d'una casa, tiene in la sinistra una chiave;

el destro piede posa in terra, el sinistro sopra uno serpente el quale se stesso divora. Sopra questi Dei, fra le predette due gran cornigi, sta un grandissimo leone che 'l destro piede denante sopra la palla tien fermo."
[65] Vasari, VI, pp. 252-53.
[66] Vasari, VI, p. 252.

oculus, who were first conceived as pairs of youths, as Pontormo's study for the figures to the right of the oculus shows (pl. 112).[67]

Saturn is also closely connected with Sol-Apollo, toward whom he looks, and Apollo's violet drapery repeats the color of his jacket. This link between Saturn and Apollo is important in delineating the theme of the Medici Golden Age in the fresco, for it was during the reign of Apollo that Virgil's *Saturnia regna* would ensue. As we have seen, this imagery from *Eclogue* IV was an established part of the Medicean myth of *their* Golden Age. Moreover, the Saturn-Apollo imagery in the lunette seems to be connected with the Laurentian *topos* of country life, which so many aspects of Pontormo's fresco recall. Lorenzo's festival of Saints Cosmas and Damian at Villa Careggi was conceived as taking place under the joint patronage of Saturn and Apollo.[68] So, here, Virgil's exalted pair are transformed by their rustic guise as *villani* resting under the protection of the laurel into the countrified patrons of the celebration of the Medici Golden Age at Lorenzo's villa.

Sol-Apollo's counterpart on the right side of the lunette also plays a role in this tableau of the Medici Golden Age. As "alma Ceres," partner to Virgil's Liber, the goddess is central to the theme of agriculture, which is Virgil's—and Pontormo's—metaphor of the peaceful Golden Age. For according to the very same poetic tradition in which Janus and Saturn introduced agriculture in the Golden Age, it was Ceres who restored agriculture to the world after the Golden Age had ended. In *Georgics* I, Ceres is characterized as "the first to teach men to turn the earth with iron"; and, for Ovid, her introduction of agriculture was synonymous with the establishment of laws, or government: "Ceres was the first to turn the glebe with the hooked plowshare; she first gave corn and kindly sustenance to the world; she first gave laws."[69]

The Ceres of Virgil and Ovid figured in Laurentian imagery. She appears in Naldi's eclogue on the death of Piero, which is a prototype for Ariosto's neo-Laurentian "Ne la stagion." Naldi evokes the recovery of the Golden Age under the new Medici shepherd Pan-Lorenzo: the trees regenerate, while blond Ceres and Liber (Apollo) enjoy their abundant crops.[70] Ceres in Pontormo's fresco, who is paired with Liber (Apollo), echoes this tradition, playing her accustomed role as harbinger of a new Golden Age.

As Apollo's partner, the goddess has further reverberations in relation to the theme of the Virgilian Golden Age. While such a reading cannot be proven, she may be a mythic character whose presence is mandatory in the *topos* of the Golden Age. This character is Astraea, personification of Justice, who is celebrated by Virgil and Ovid as the last of the gods to leave the earth at the end of the Golden Age and the first to

---

[67] Cambridge, Fogg Art Museum 1932.342r; see Cox-Rearick, 1964, I, cat. 151. For other studies of the putti as youths, see Uffizi 6660Fr (cat. 150); Louvre 2903r-2903v (cat. 154-55). See also Uffizi 6660Fv, where Pontormo studied the paired putti of the Sistine ceiling (pl. 76).

[68] See Ficino's letter to Lorenzo, in *Opera*, I, pp. 843-44 (quoted in chap. 9, n. 43).

[69] *Georgics*, I, 147-48; and *Metamorphoses*, V, 341-

45.

[70] *Eclogue* X, 65-70 (in Naldi, *Bucolica*, p. 54):

hinc decus arboribus veniet frondesque vire-
  bunt
quae nunc arescunt. pratis color inde redibit
laetior, et virides nascentur collibus herbae.
flava Ceres alto spectabit vertice fruges,
quas olim maerore gravi confecta reliquit.

return with its recovery. In *Georgics* II this figure is Iustitia, who left Saturn's descendants, the farmers, last.[71] She is Ovid's "maiden Astraea, last of the immortals, [who] abandoned the blood-soaked earth" when the Iron Age began.[72] And, in *Eclogue* IV, she is the Virgin whose coming heralds the return of the Golden Age of Saturn during the rule of Apollo: "iam redit et Virgo, redeunt Saturnia regna."

Virgil's Virgin-Iustitia entered the mainstream of Renaissance thought with Dante, who equated her with Astraea and whose famous lines "secol si rinova; torna giustizia e primo tempo umano, e progenie scende da ciel nova" echo Virgil's renewal formulation.[73] These lines were the basis for the Laurentian mottos about the return of the Golden Age—LE TEMPS REVIENT, which is implicit in the imagery of Pontormo's fresco, and GLOVIS, which is actually inscribed in it.

Imagery of Astraea and the Golden Age was a commonplace, and two examples will suffice to show how she was evoked in political imagery close in time to Pontormo's fresco. Astraea appears in *Orlando Furioso*, which was written in 1516, only shortly before Ariosto's "Ne la stagion." Embedded in this work is an oblique prophecy of the empire of Charles V, in which Astraea plays her customary role. The future emperor is identified as the successor to the Roman emperors, a ruler who will bring Astraea-Giustizia and the other Virtues back to earth:[74]

> Astraea veggio per lui riposta in seggio,
> anzi di morta ritornata viva. . . .

> I see Astraea placed by him on her throne,
> from the dead returned alive.

Astraea was also featured in Medici art of the restoration, which insistently emphasized the theme of Return which she embodies. In the Capitoline festival of 1513, she leads the Cardinal Virtues as Giustizia, who will bring immortality to the Medici. According to Aurelio Sereno's description,[75]

> La prima di queste sorelle [Astraea] così parlò al Medici: "Ti consegno la spada e sarai duce alle nostre quadrighe, e di essa tu solo sei degno, con essa toccherai gli astri, per essa il tuo nome vivrà in eterno."

> The first of these sisters [Astraea] spoke thus to the Medici: "I deliver to you the sword and you will lead our quadriga; you alone are worthy of this sword; with it you will touch the stars, by it your name will live in eternity."

There is, then, the possibility that Pontormo's goddess is also to be understood as

---

[71] *Georgics*, II, 473-74 (see Appendix II).

[72] *Metamorphoses*, I, 149-50.

[73] *Purgatorio*, XXII, 67-72. See *De Monarchia*, I, xi (tr. G. Vinay, Florence, 1950, p. 55): where Dante explains that Virgil's "Vergine erà l'appellativo della giustizia detta anche Astraea. . . ."

[74] *Orlando Furioso*, XV, xxv-xxvi. This reference is indicated by F. A. Yates, "Charles V and the Idea of Empire," in *Astraea: the Imperial Theme in the Sixteenth Century*, London, 1975, p. 23. For the Astraea myth in the Renaissance, see F. A. Yates, "Queen Elizabeth as Astraea," *JWCI*, 10, 1947, pp. 27-37. In Elizabeth's personal imagery, Astraea-Giustizia was conflated with the Moon goddess, just as she had been earlier in Pontormo's fresco.

[75] Sereno, pp. 117-18.

Astraea-Giustizia, who joins Apollo in heralding the return of the *Saturnia regna*. In the fresco she takes her place among the Golden Age deities who, like her, are in rustic disguise as the farmers over whom she once ruled and over whom she will rule again in the new Golden Age of the Medici.

As Astraea-Giustizia, this goddess would also allude to the theme of Medicean Justice. Her red and white costume combines the traditional colors of justice, as they appear, for example, in the Florentine heraldic banner of Just Government.[76] She also recalls a more emblematic Fiorenza-Giustizia of a Medici miniature—a seated, frontal figure, dressed in red and white, who holds the *broncone* (pl. 10). Like this figure, Pontormo's goddess is shown with the *broncone*, but in keeping with the conceit of rustic guise it is not a formal *impresa* which she holds but simply a branch of the regenerating laurel tree.

THE LAUREL, THE BIRTH OF COSIMO, AND LEO-APOLLO

The reciprocal relationship between the gods and the Medici laurel is a major conceit in Pontormo's lunette. The laurel shades and protects the gods of the Medici Golden Age in their garden; the gods, in turn, actively relate to it: Pomona lies ready to prune the tree, and the gods on the upper wall reach up into its branches.

Given the use of the laurel as a Medici symbol from the time of Lorenzo il Magnifico, one of its meanings in the fresco is certainly Medici rule and the familiar idea of a Medici Golden Age symbolized by the rebirth of nature in spring.[77] As we recall, this conceit was crystallized in Poliziano's *Stanze* and in Lorenzo's medal of Florentia under the laurel (pl. 3); and, after restoration, Giuliano's medal of Florentia under the laurel and supported by the *palle* conveyed the same message and conflated it with the idea of the reconciliation of Rome and Florence (pl. 11). Poetry lauding the Medici return took up the same theme: Angiolini's "Trionfo del Lauro" repeats the familiar refrain, "Godi or, Fiorenza, all'ombra del tuo Lauro"; and Ariosto's "Ne la stagion" provides an immediate point of departure for the imagery of the laurel:

> E queste et altre dèe sotto l'ombrose
>   frondi, mentre in piacer stavano e in festa,
>   benediron tra lor chi il ramo pose.

The laurel arching over the figures is a monumental visualization of this imagery, and the goddesses, in particular, make pointed reference to the idea of a personification of Florence under the protection of the Medici tree.

But what beyond the general notion of the Medici Golden Age might the laurel signify in this fresco? Given the uncertain future of the family after the death in 1519 of Lorenzo the younger, the flourishing laurel under which the gods rest so contentedly

[76] See chap. 1, n. 31.
[77] The theme of the laurel in the lunette has been extensively discussed. See Winner, 1963-1964, pp. 9-11; Winner, 1972, pp. 177-83; Forster, 1966, pp. 43-47; and Kliemann, 1972, pp. 303-4, 325-27.

must have been intended to symbolize as much a future as a present Golden Age. The laurel here, in fact, had been seen to allude to hopes for the renewal of the Medici after the death of Lorenzo, and to the Medici heir—either the child Ippolito or the newborn Cosimo.[78]

It should be evident that the laurel alludes not to Ippolito but to the New Cosimo, the legitimate heir born of the union of the two branches of the family soon after Lorenzo's death, whom Leo X himself had named after Cosimo Pater Patriae. The event was commemorated, as we have seen, in Pontormo's dynastic portrait of the old Cosimo, with its *impresa* of the "laurel: VNO AVVLSO NON DEFICIT ALTER," which refers to the replacement of the dead *lauro*-Lorenzo with the new heir. *Vertumnus and Pomona*, an immediately subsequent work by the same artist for the same patron, incorporates this theme within the larger dynastic cycle of the Salone. The laurel, ever green and self-regenerating, flourishes anew after having been cut back and puts forth its green branches—among them the new sprout, Cosimo—over the springtime garden of Medici Florence. But, in contrast to the portrait, this theme is not explicated by an inscription. The message of the laurel, like that of other elements in the fresco, is masked by Pontormo's deceptive pastorale. In this nondidactic work, nothing is explained: the quote from the *Georgics* does not tell us whose "love guards our fields," the other inscriptions tease with hidden meanings, and the dramatis personae, as if taking their cue from the *Metamorphoses*, shift identities. Likewise, the laurel alluding to Medici death and rebirth is poised between the worlds of reality and symbol: just as the rustics seated under it strike their unrhetorical poses, so its branches grow naturally against the blue sky.

The fundamental idea of the laurel as a metaphor of death and rebirth is already clearly expressed in Pontormo's compositional study for the fresco (pl. 75). In this drawing, the heavy trunk of the tree twists around the oculus and crosses above it in a manner that recalls the title page of Valori's *Vita Laurentii Medicis* (pl. 18). In the miniature, the laurel flourishes profusely in commemoration of Lorenzo's fame and virtue, but in the drawing the growth of the tree has been adjusted to accord with the metaphor of the changing seasons in "Ne la stagion." For Ariosto blames winter for depriving the tree of its leaves:

> Lassa! onde uscì la boreal tempesta?
> onde la bruma? onde il rigor e il gelo?
> onde la neve, a' danni miei sì presta?
>   Come gli ha tolto il suo favore il Cielo?
> Langue il mio Lauro, e de la bella spoglia
> nudo gli resta e senza onor il stelo.

Oh woe! whence came this northern tempest? whence the fog? whence the cold and frost? whence the snow so quick to work against me? How did Heaven withdraw its favor from him? My Laurel languishes, and of its beautiful remains the stem alone is left, naked and without honor.

[78] Winner, 1972, pp. 186-87, mentions Ippolito, while Kliemann, 1972, pp. 312 and 325, suggests Cosimo.

On the right side of the drawing the branches are bare, leaves are fluttering to the ground, while on the left side new leaves have begun to sprout. This imagery is a variant on the Medici image of the dry and verdant laurel, first seen in the banner of Lorenzo il Magnifico's *giostra* and then in works of the Medici restoration such as Angiolini's "Trionfo del Lauro," Raphael's *Seasons* tapestry border (pl. 22), and Pontormo's *Cosimo* portrait. In this drawing, as in the *Cosimo*, the contrast between the dead and living branches (alluding to the death of Lorenzo and the birth of Cosimo) is unmistakably stated. However, in the fresco, the difference between the two sides is more subtle. The imagery of dry versus verdant—death and life—is modified, and only hints such as the exposed laurel stump and the laurel sprigs that fall at the feet of Vertumnus-Janus remain to remind us of the threat to the Medici tree. For the new life of the tree has begun, and the laurel arches over the whole scene: Ariosto's plea to Apollo, Vertumnus, and Pomona has been answered and once again the garden of Florence is protected "sotto l'ombrose frondi."

Pontormo also made a change in the relation between the figures and the laurel after his compositional drawing. In the drawing all the gods care for the tree, as they hold on to its branches in gestures which recall the standard motif in "Golden Age" pictures of figures reaching up into fruitful trees. And, even after some aspects of the design were changed and the putti took their places around the oculus, Pontormo's studies still show them grasping the laurel branches.[79] In the fresco, however, this motif is reserved for the two Virgilian figures—Luna-Diana, who holds a branch of the laurel much as the traditional Ceres holds her harvest emblem, and Sol-Apollo, who reaches up toward his sacred tree.

Sol-Apollo is the figure most actively connected with the laurel. His action, which is emphasized by the diagonal swath of violet drapery that he holds in his hand, is, strictly speaking, the only movement in the fresco. As such, it must have some significance, and we may ask if Sol-Apollo is merely reaching for the laurel or if he is preparing to prune the tree and thus to take an active part in its regeneration. The question must remain moot, but there is some evidence to suggest that the god's role as tender of the laurel was once more explicitly defined. In his description of the fresco, Vasari mentions "un villano che siede con un pennato in mano, tanto bello e ben fatto, che è cosa rarissima."[80] The nude Sol-Apollo is surely the only one of the three gods whom Vasari would have praised in such terms. Moreover, since Vertumnus and Saturn already hold their own attributes, Sol-Apollo is the only one of the gods who *could* have held a pruning-knife—presumably in his right hand, which rests on the wall, and which, on close inspection, does appear to have been tampered with. Now Allori writes in his *ricordi* that he cleaned Pontormo's fresco and repainted the sky.[81] Perhaps at that time he removed the *pennato* (and partly effaced Pomona's pruning-hook) in an attempt to make the scene less overtly rustic and more in keeping with the formal garden that he painted in the *Hercules* lunette.

---

[79] Uffizi, 6511Fr, 6661F, 6646F, and 6512F (Cox-Rearick, 1964, I, cat. 152-53, 157-58).

[80] Vasari, VI, p. 265 (see chap. 4, "The Salone of Pope Leo X," for the entire passage).

[81] Allori, p. 29: ". . . il quale [la lunetta] ho rinetto e lavato e rifatto l'aria."

If Sol-Apollo did originally hold a knife, then the two tree deities—Pomona, goddess of fruit trees (*poma*), and Apollo, patron of the *lauro*—would have held the two most common Roman pruning instruments, the *falx vinitoria* (or *pennato*) and the *falx arboria* (or hook).[82] We lack further evidence about the appearance of the fresco before Allori's time; however, these same instruments are emblematically paired in the context of imagery alluding to the decline of Medici fortunes after the death of Leo X in Franciabigio's *Portrait of a Medici Steward* of 1523 (pl. 114).[83] In this portrait, the instruments hang on the wall as poignant reminders of the once verdant Medici tree, in contrast to Pontormo's scene of the regenerating laurel, where the pruning-hook and presumably the knife were in active use.

Pontormo's Sol-Apollo reaches up into the branches of the laurel to work the miracle of renewed life. As if in response, laurel seems to sprout around his very body. It frames him, distantly echoing the idea of the laurel around the child Lorenzo in the chapel of the Palazzo Medici (pl. 4). As agent of the laurel's renewal, Sol-Apollo is the key figure in the fresco. In him the theme of the regenerating Medici laurel is conflated with the idea of the recovery of the Golden Age of the first *lauro*, Lorenzo il Magnifico.

This important character plays a key role in the contemporary frame of reference of the fresco, for Pontormo's rustic Apollo may have been intended to allude to Pope Leo.[84] Aside from repeating the old conceit of Lorenzo as Apollo, seen on the portico frieze (pl. 55), such an identification of a Medici ruler with an explicitly rustic god is very much in the tradition of the Laurentian imagery which Pontormo's fresco recalls in so many respects. In the pastorales by Poliziano and Naldi, Lorenzo and other Medici are disguised as shepherds and rustic gods, whose adventures are metaphors of the vicissitudes of Medici rule. Signorelli's *Realm of Pan* (pl. 67) belongs to this tradition; and, indeed, its rustic Pan-Lorenzo, who presides over an Arcadian scene with other rustic characters around and below him, might be seen as a prototype for the Sol-Apollo of the lunette.

Leo, who also had personal reasons relating to his horoscope which encouraged an association with Sol-Apollo (see chapter 8), continued his father's identification with Apollo, according him an important place in his imagery. In Gambello's medal of 1513-1514, Apollo is accompanied by Leo's attributes of the lion with his paw on a Medici *palla* (pl. 116).[85] Later, in Giovanni da Udine's tapestry design for the Sala di Costantino, the same idea is elaborated (pl. 82). In an allegory of Leo as immortal ruler of the world, the crowned putto with scepter and key, his foot resting on the *palla-mondo*, personifies Leo as ruler and pope, receiving the golden tribute signifying his liberality.

---

[82] K. D. White, *Agricultural Implements of the Roman World*, Cambridge, Mass., 1967, pp. 86-88, 93-96.

[83] McKillop, 1974, pp. 83-84, 107-8, identifies the work as the portrait of "un lavoratore e fattore di Pier Francesco de' Medici al palazzo di San Girolamo da Fiesole . . ." mentioned by Vasari (V, pp. 197-98). She dates the picture ca. 1520-1521, but John Shearman has pointed out to me that the

following inscription can be read on the left side of the ledger: "MDxxiij" and, on the right page, ". . . florē . . . / ogi adi 20 . . . / . . . S. girolamo."

[84] Sol-Apollo has been seen to allude to the Golden Age of Sol-Leo, with reference to the zodiac sign of Leo, by McKillop, 1970, p. 6; and Winner, 1972, pp. 174 and 186.

[85] Hill, no. 451.

Above, on the fruitful garlands of Leonine prosperity, are the miraculous birds of rulership and immortality, the eagle and the phoenix; and in the center is Apollo's symbol, the sun.

If Sol-Apollo is understood to allude to Leo himself, then the theme of the regenerating laurel in the lunette comes more sharply into focus. Metaphorically, the laurel for which Sol-Apollo cares is Lorenzo, Leo's father, whose memory he tends (we recall Vasari's report that the Salone decoration was dedicated to Lorenzo). But the tree is also the once-dying Medici laurel, and it represents the new life which has come to the family during Leo's rule. Thus, Sol-Apollo is the Phoebus on whom Ariosto called to cure the sick trees; and he is Apollo *medicus*, the healer. This felicitous notion, which is related to the metaphors of illness and cure elsewhere in Leo's imagery (and, of course, to the idea of the medicinal laurel tree itself), was current in Medici poetry of the time. For example, in this ode by Severus Minervius of 1515, Apollo addresses the Medici:[86]

> Dextera ut vires medicas habebam;
>   Sic tuam prolem Medicam vocavi;
>   Quae feret regnis Italis salutem,
>   Praesidiumque.

> Just as I had healing powers in my right hand, so I have called your progeny Medici, and they shall bring well-being and protection to the Italian realms.

And, in the *Versi posti a Pasquillo*, dedicated to the new pope in 1513, there are frequent references to Leo as Apollo *medico* and to the related ideas of the restoration of peace and the Golden Age.[87] The title page gives visual expression to these ideas (pl. 117). It shows Apollo-Leo, who, like Bandinelli's Orpheus-Leo, is based on the Apollo Belvedere. He is surrounded by Medici emblems: his viol has six pegs (like *palle*), his flutes are crossed like the *bronconi*, and behind him, like the Apollo of Pontormo's fresco, is the flourishing laurel. Pontormo has transformed this literary tradition of Leo (and Lorenzo before him) as Apollo *medicus* into an image of bucolic actuality, as his rustic god restores the Medici tree.

Sol-Apollo may be read on yet another level as alluding to Leo. As has been frequently observed, Pontormo posed his figure in a way that recalls the *Jonah* of the Sistine ceiling. As a paraphrase of the *Jonah* (a figure who is also accompanied by a miraculous tree), Sol-Apollo alludes to the interpretation of *Jonah* as a type of Saint Peter, hence of the pope himself. This connection would have been more obvious in 1520 than it is today: as can be seen in a copy of the figure made before the section below it was destroyed to make way for the *Last Judgment*, beneath the feet of the prophet was the papal *stemma* of Julius II (pl. 115).[88] As a paraphrase of the *Jonah*, Sol-Apollo may also have been understood to allude to the conventional notion of Jonah as a type of the

[86] *Lauretum*, p. 24.

[87] *Versi*, f. 1r. See also the indirect reference to Leo as Apollo *medicus* on the arch of Agostino Chigi in the Lateran *possesso*. The inscription referred to Leo as peacemaker and healer, and the statues rep-

resented Apollo and Mercury, patrons of medicine (Penni, p. 210).

[88] Windsor Castle 10368; see Popham-Wilde, cat. 465.

resurrected Christ, a nuance which meshes with Apollo's role in the fresco as agent of the renewed life of the Medici laurel.

Precisely framed within the triangle of Sol-Apollo, Vertumnus-Janus, and Saturn—the three gods of the Golden Age—is a tawny (golden?) dog (pl. 99). This animal appears quite naturally among the rustics, its significance masked by the pastoral masquerade; and since dogs were traditionally associated with both Saturn and Vertumnus, its presence might be left unremarked.[89] However, this dog is Medicean, and probably alludes to the old Medici *stemma* of Averardo, which featured a dog.[90] The motif occurs elsewhere in the Salone: in two of the *istorie* dogs advance down the steps in front of their Medici owners, and there are two dogs, emblematically placed, in Allori's study for the *Hercules* lunette (pl. 77). As a companion to the gods of the Golden Age, Pontormo's dog is also such a Medici protector.

But the dog is so purposefully placed below Sol-Apollo and so exactly framed by his feet that it is tempting to read it as a specifically Leonine emblem. The connection with Leo has been suppressed in the fresco, but in Pontormo's preparatory study for the dog a ball lies between his feet (pl. 113).[91] This ball (*palla*) not only puns on the Medici *palle*, but it suggests that the animal may be a rustic substitute for the ubiquitous Leonine motif of the lion with the *palla*.[92] Indeed, in Leo's art, this motif is often associated with Saturn, Janus, and Apollo—the very deities whom the dog accompanies in Pontormo's fresco. In Leo's Apollo medal, a lion with the *palla* stands at the feet of the god; and the painting on the facade of the Capitoline theater of *Saturn Greeted by Janus on His Arrival in Latium* was surmounted by the lion with a *palla* (fig. 4).[93]

The golden dog under Sol-Apollo thus completes Pontormo's tableau of the new Medici Golden Age, emphasizing the rulership of Leo, patron of the Salone.[94] Spring, the season of the Golden Age (and of the birth of the Medici heir, Cosimo) has arrived as laurel sprouts from the dead stumps of the tree around the Medici gods. Luna-Diana holds a newly verdant branch and Pomona lies ready to care for the most recent sprout of the Medici tree. All the goddesses look contentedly out of their garden, and the putto attending them smiles as he holds the garland of blooming Medici roses. The putti above the oculus wave their *vexilla*, which declare Jupiter's wish that the life of the Medici laurel be renewed and their Golden Age return.

[89] For the dog and Saturn, see Valeriano, p. 66; and Klibansky et al., p. 322 and n. 127. For Vertumnus, often portrayed with a dog in ancient statuary, see Cartari, 1571, p. 135.

[90] See chap. 4, n. 103.

[91] Stockholm, National Museum 931 / 1863r; see Cox-Rearick, 1971, cat. 142a.

[92] This emblem (which carries its own recollection of the Florentine Marzocco) is used emblematically in Leo's art, as on the doors of the Stanze, the Raphael tapestry borders, coins, etc. In the eighteenth century, when medals were made by Selvi commemorating the Medici, Averardo de' Medici's device was represented as a dog with its paw on a *palla* (Bargello; Hill, no. 284).

[93] Palliolo, p. 26 (quoted above, n. 64). See also Gambello's plaquette of a lion with a *palla* (Armand, III, p. 45).

[94] In this connection it may be significant that the dog is the only character in the lunette that is not one of a pair. As such, it is the eleventh figure in the composition and hence a possible allusion to Leo's lucky number.

Allori's Completion of the Salone

HERCULES AND FORTUNA IN THE GARDEN OF THE HESPERIDES

Across the great vault of the Poggio a Caiano Salone opposite Pontormo's *Vertumnus and Pomona* (color pl. 2), which celebrates the Golden Age of Leo X, is Allori's *Hercules and Fortuna in the Garden of the Hesperides* (pls. 68, 118). In his *ricordi*, Allori attributes its *invenzione* to Vincenzo Borghini.[1] It has thus been assumed that the Herculean subject was selected by the grand-ducal iconographer and that it refers exclusively to Francesco de' Medici, who, like his father, Duke Cosimo, used Hercules in his art to enhance his image as a virtuous and powerful ruler.[2] However, as in the case of Allori's *istorie* on the lateral walls of the room, the second lunette may have been part of a coherent scheme originating with Giovio's program for the Salone.[3] Such a scheme, it must be admitted, is less easily deduced from the evidence than that of the lateral walls, for the *istorie* painted in 1521 (especially the *Cicero*, with its reference to Cosimo Pater Patriae) suggest that Giovio planned an historical cycle alluding to the Medici, while Pontormo's fresco is not only enigmatic in itself, but its Ovidian subject brings no natural pendant to mind.

In spite of the paucity of evidence, Allori's *Hercules and Fortuna* probably does reflect the Leonine program for the second lunette, at least in its essentials. The subjects of the cartoons Pontormo made for the end walls of the Salone in 1531 have connections, albeit indirect ones, with the Garden of the Hesperides subject. The cartoon of the

[1] Allori, p. 29: ". . . et poi tutto il resto [of the Salone decoration] è stato difinito da me comandatomi per sua gratia dal Ser^mo Gran Duca Francesca, dove ho fatto dirimpetto all'arco di Iacopo da Puntormo tutto con gran (certa) inventione del Rev.^do Priore delli Innocenti di Firence Don Vincentio Borghini, Dio l'habbi in gloria, dove come ho detta nell'arco di contro al detto di m.° Iacopo è figurato i pomi degli orti Esperidi guardati dalle Ninfe, da Ercole a dalla Fortuna. . . ."

[2] For some aspects of Cosimo's Hercules imagery, see Forster, 1971, pp. 72-82. Francesco's Hercules pictures include Allori's *Hercules and the Muses* (Uffizi) and *Hercules Slaying the Dragon in the Garden of the Hesperides* (Studiolo, Palazzo Vecchio).

[3] Langedijk, p. 45; and Kliemann, 1976, p. 86, are also of the opinion that Allori followed Giovio's program for the lunette.

nudes playing ball may allude to the *palla-palle* wordplay and thus to the conceit of the *palle* as the apples of the Hesperides, which, as we shall see, is prominent in Allori's fresco.[4] And the subjects of the other two cartoons, *Hercules and Antaeus* and *Venus and Adonis*, are both related to the story of Hercules' eleventh labor.[5] Moreover, there is a drawing by Pontormo of a Fortuna who stands with her foot on a globe (*palla*) holding a swath of drapery over her head in a gesture like that of Sol-Apollo in *Vertumnus and Pomona* (pl. 119).[6] This drawing of a subject which occurs nowhere else in Pontormo's art is datable 1520-1521 on the basis of its style, and it may be tentatively connected with the plans for the second lunette. But most important, both the choice of the labor of the Garden of the Hesperides and the way the myth is allegorized suggest that *Vertumnus and Pomona* and *Hercules and Fortuna* were planned as a pair. The story that Allori's fresco tells belongs to a different literary tradition from Pontormo's Ovidian tale, but the two myths have enough in common to have provided the basis for a pair of complementary, and perhaps piquantly contrasting, Leonine allegories. On a narrative level, both tell of a hero who enters a walled garden, which, in Allori's fresco, is guarded by a dragon. Allori's scene takes as its starting point the well-known, if seldom represented, eleventh labor of Hercules, in the course of which the hero kills the dragon and procures the golden apples from the garden. On a symbolic level, both stories are ultimately concerned with immortality: Pontormo's through the eternal regeneration of nature, symbolized by the agricultural gods, the Seasons, and the new growth of the laurel; Allori's through the symbolism of the labor itself, traditionally interpreted as a metaphor of the conquest of death.

Allori made an obvious attempt to harmonize his fresco with Pontormo's, just as he emulated the mode of the earlier *istorie* in his *Titus* and *Scipio* scenes on the lateral walls of the Salone (pls. 79-80). Like Pontormo's fresco, Allori's is symbolic in character, not so much telling a story as presenting its characters emblematically against a schematic background. The Garden of the Hesperides, with its double walls, is copied from Pontormo's (although this Maniera garden is formal compared with the rustic simplicity of Pomona's retreat), as are the frames around the oculus and the tablets above and below it. The symmetrical disposition of the ten figures echoes Pontormo's pairs of gods and putti, as does the addition of an eleventh figure, which is also an animal. And, like Pontormo's fresco, *Hercules and Fortuna* has no trace of narrative action, for Allori does not depict the labor itself but its aftermath. The fresco presents a symbolic scene in which Hercules and the nymphs coexist peacefully in the Hesperidian garden.[7] The

[4] Kliemann, 1976, p. 84. For the cartoons see chap. 4, n. 31.

[5] Since Hercules killed the giant, Antaeus, while searching for the garden, this story might even be considered to be part of the Hesperides myth; *Venus and Adonis*, on the other hand, is connected with the labor of the golden apples through the tradition that the tree bearing the *mala aurea* sacred to Venus was the metamorphosis of the body of Adonis. For a summary of sources and versions of the eleventh labor, see R. Y. Hathorn, *Greek*

Mythology, Beirut, 1977, pp. 330-32. For the metamorphosis of Adonis, see Pontano, p. 29; and for the association of Venus with the Garden of the Hesperides and the *mala aurea*, see text below.

[6] Rome, Gabinetto Nazionale della Stampe F. C. 121r; see Cox-Rearick, 1964, I, cat. 107.

[7] For the Roman relief from Villa Albani which is a prototype for Allori's unusual handling of the subject, see E. Panofsky, *Hercules am Scheidewege*, Leipzig, 1930, pp. 127-28, pl. XLV. For a rare depiction of the actual labor in Renaissance art,

nymphs hold up the fruits, which, the story relates, were ultimately returned to them, while Hercules, wearing his lion skin and leaning on his club, sits in triumph over the slain dragon. Seated on the left side of the garden, he is the heroic counterpart of Pontormo's trio of rustic gods. Finally, as in Pontormo's fresco, the garden and its vegetation are treated emblematically. The citrus trees are the counterpart of Pontormo's laurel, and the six oversized citrons which the nymphs and putti ostentatiously display allude to the Medici *palle*. As Allori notes in an inscription under this scene in his preparatory study for the Salone (pl. 77), "I pomi d'oro guardati da Ercole e da le Ninfe chiamati da molto mala medica" (The golden apples guarded by Hercules and the nymphs, called by many medicinal [Medici] apples).

This inscription indicates that the *pomi d'oro* are the "subject" of the fresco (in the same sense that the laurel is the subject of Pontormo's), but Allori emphasizes the symbolic character of the scene far more emphatically than does Pontormo. He interpolates elements into it which are extraneous to the story and transform it into an allegory of the victory of Virtù over Fortuna. The first of these is the portrait of Francesco de' Medici *en Hercule*. The fresco is thus an example of a popular *topos* of late Renaissance princely iconography in which the ruler is a New Hercules, who will follow the hero's virtuous path to the reward of immortality. The second of these is the group of Fortuna-Occasio (characterized by her wheel and forelock) and the Vices. Fortuna herself has become a Virtue: she is Buona Fortuna, standing victorious over the Vices, her wheel held firm, and holding aloft the grand-ducal crown and scepter—the earthly rewards of the virtuous hero. In the tablet above the window, the inscription VIRTVTEM FORTVNA SEQVETVR (Fortune will follow Virtue) explicates the scene as an allegory of the victory of Francesco, the New Hercules, over the vicissitudes of fortune.

The style of Allori's fresco, with the conventional attitudinizing of its dramatis personae, depends on the formal vocabulary of the Maniera, and in some respects so does its style of ideas. The blatantly obvious presentation of Francesco as a New Hercules, complete with the trappings of his rule, has no real parallel in Leonine art. Nor does the literal spelling-out of Fortuna's triumph over the Vices, which depends on the Bronzinesque conventions of the late Maniera art of Francesco's court.[8] However, underlying these superficial aspects of Allori's fresco is an allegory perfectly compatible with what we know of Giovio's program for the Salone. The lunette tells of the reward of immortality that comes to the ruler who follows the *exemplum virtutis*. As an allegory of Leo X, it would have neatly completed the cycle of *uomini illustri* in the lower zone of the

---

see Annibale Fontana's medal for Francesco Ferdinando d'Avalos (Hill-Pollard, no. 442). This representation of Hercules plucking the apples from the tree is drawn from the same Roman relief that was copied by Pirro Ligorio (Brummer, 1970, fig. 205). The more usual reference to the labor in depictions of Hercules is the three apples signifying his virtue, which he holds as an attribute in works such as the Capitoline Museum bronze and the Farnese marble (Naples), as well as in various de-

rivative Renaissance statues.

[8] For example, Bronzino's *Allegory of Happiness* of ca. 1565 (Uffizi) is filled with personifications like those in this group, including Fortuna-Occasio herself. Allori's *modello* for the fresco at Windsor Castle 0139 (Popham-Wilde, cat. 58) is even more closely dependent on Bronzino's picture than the fresco (cf. especially the fallen Vice near Hercules).

Salone, comparing Leo, patron of the room, with Hercules, the prototypical hero and one of the greatest exemplars of them all.

These correspondences might all be dismissed as the product of Vincenzo Borghini's ingenuity in devising themes which would complement those already painted in the Salone and of Allori's zealous imitation of features of Pontormo's lunette. However, each element in the *Hercules* allegory is presented in terms of imagery that already existed in Medici art of Leo's time. The themes of Hercules as a Medici hero and the triumph of Virtù over Fortuna, the Garden of the Hesperides as a metaphor of the Medici Golden Age, and the conceit of the *mala aurea–mala medica* all occur in Leo's imagery. Furthermore, the way these themes are conflated in the *Hercules* (even given Allori's Maniera translation of the subject) is entirely characteristic of that imagery.

As is well known, by the mid-Quattrocento the Medici had appropriated Hercules, *exemplum virtutis* and symbol of the freedom of the city of Florence, into their art.[9] From 1459, when Antonio del Pollaiuolo painted three *Labors of Hercules* for the Palazzo Medici,[10] to 1492, when Michelangelo made a colossal marble *Hercules* in memory of Lorenzo il Magnifico,[11] Hercules *florentinus* can rightly be said to have been transformed into the Medici Hercules. Lorenzo, in particular, associated himself with the hero. Pollaiuolo's pictures hung in his room in the Palazzo Medici, he commissioned a number of works representing Hercules, and he encouraged literary comparisons between himself and his exemplar.[12] Moreover, it was probably Lorenzo who, in an astute political gesture, adopted the ancient Hercules seal of the city and had it mounted in an elaborate setting with his devices of the *diamante* and feathers, the crossed *bronconi*, and the yoke (pl. 121).[13]

Several of these Medicean works representing Hercules—in particular, the Pollaiuolo canvases of the *Labors* and the Michelangelo statue—were uncommonly large in scale. Moreover, they were prominently displayed in public and semipublic locations, where

---

[9] Ettlinger, 1972, pp. 119-41.

[10] L. D. Ettlinger, *Antonio and Piero Pollaiuolo*, London, 1978, pp. 26-27, cat. 44. My dating of these important lost works to 1459 (and Piero de' Medici's patronage) is based on Antonio's letter of 1494 declaring that he painted them thirty-four years before and on the fact that the Medici hosted a major *festa* to celebrate the visit of Pope Pius II in April-May 1459. The Medici palace was elaborately decorated for the occasion (C. Volpi, *Le Feste di Firenze del 1459*, Pistoia, 1902, p. 213; and R. Hatfield, "Some Unknown Descriptions of the Medici Palace in 1459," *Art Bull.*, 52, 1970, pp. 232-49); and, while they are not mentioned, large canvases of such programmatic subject matter would have perfectly suited the requirements of such an *apparato*. I thank Lynette Bosch for suggestions regarding this hypothesis.

[11] Ettlinger, 1972, pp. 137-39; A. Parronchi, *Opere giovanili di Michelangelo*, Florence, 1968, II, pp. 36-43. Michelangelo's lost *Hercules*, with his club resting on the ground, imitated the pose *all'antica* of the Quattrocento Florentine Hercules seal (see Parronchi, fig. 14e) rather than the type with the club on his shoulder that appears in later versions of the seal (pl. 121) and in Bandinelli's *Hercules* for the *entrata* of Leo X (pl. 122).

[12] See Ettlinger, 1972, pp. 128-35, who mentions Pollaiuolo's two *Hercules* panels in the Uffizi and his three bronzes of the subject, and pp. 136-37 for Landino's writings on Hercules.

[13] This work is considered by Ettlinger, 1972, p. 141, and others to have been made for Duke Cosimo in 1537. The inscription around the seal is his; however, as U. Middledorf, "Überraschungen im Palazzo Pitti," *Pantheon*, 32, 1974, p. 22, suggests, the handle dates from the time of Lorenzo. I would add that the base of the seal (on which Duke Cosimo's *stemma* is superimposed) is also Laurentian because it bears devices such as the yoke, which were used by Lorenzo but not by Cosimo.

they were still to be seen after the Medici restoration in 1512.[14] The conceit of the Medici *Hercules*, then, would have been a commonplace in Leo's Florence—and hardly a surprising choice for one of the lunettes in a room which Leo had decorated in memory of Lorenzo.

Leo, in fact, continued his father's association with Hercules, thus enhancing the notion that Lorenzo's Golden Age had returned with his rule. Indeed, his papal name virtually invited the parallel. Much was made of the possibilities of the imagery that a pope named Leo could share with Hercules, whose primary attribute was the lion skin of his first labor. Leo's advisor, Egidio da Viterbo, even declared that Hercules was a type of Leo, since he was first Tuscan hero to wear the *insigne leonis*, or lion skin.[15] The parallel was featured in the decorations of Leo's 1515 Florentine *entrata*, in which an arch with leonine imagery was inscribed LEONI. X. LABORVM VICTORI (Leo X, Victor over the Labors).[16] The procession bearing Leo around the city passed Bandinelli's colossal imitation-bronze *Hercules*, which can be seen in the Loggia dei Lanzi (his head turned to look at Michelangelo's *David*) in a detail from Vasari's painting of the *entrata* (pl. 122).[17] Bandinelli's work honors Leo but also refers back to Lorenzo, for it challenges Michelangelo's colossal *Hercules* honoring Lorenzo and in pose it is a giant version of the Hercules seal.

The second theme of Allori's fresco, the triumph of Virtù over Fortuna-Occasio, hardly needs to be justified as a feature of an early Cinquecento program such as Giovio's scheme for the Salone. It was a literary *topos* beloved of Florentine writers, from Alberti to Machiavelli, whose elaboration on the subject in *Il Principe* (dedicated to Lorenzo the younger) was written only a few years before the Salone decoration was undertaken; and, in contemporaneous representations of the theme, as here, Hercules often personifies Virtù.[18] But most to the point is the major role played in Leo's own imagery by the concepts of fate and fortune. We need only recall his belief in the powers

[14] Pollaiuolo's canvases (six *braccia* square) were in the Palazzo Vecchio, Sala dei Dugento, in 1510 (F. Albertini, *Memoriale di molte statue et picture*, Florence, 1510, n.p.), and there is no reason to believe that they were moved after the Medici return. Michelangelo's *Hercules* was in the Palazzo Strozzi, presumably in the courtyard, until it was sold to Francis I by Giambattista della Palla in 1530.

[15] Quoted by Shearman, 1972, p. 89.

[16] Shearman, 1975, p. 145, n. 29. No mention is made of Fortuna in the description of the arch, but it may be significant that three of the virtues attributed to Leo-Hercules—Sicurtà, Constantia, and Fermezza—are the opposites of the characteristics usually associated with Fortuna, and that its theme may thus have been the triumph of Leo's Herculean *virtù* over Fortuna. A Leo-Hercules comparison is also implicit in the inscription on a *tempietto* in Piazza Sta. Trinita, which declared that Florence was under the protection of "due Leoni"

(D. Moreni, *De ingressu summi Pont. Leonis X. Florentiam descriptio Paridis de Grassis*, Florence, 1793, pp. 9-11).

[17] Shearman, 1975, pp. 149-50 and n. 41. The location of Bandinelli's *Hercules* near Michelangelo's *David* is, of course, highly symbolic. It also relates to Michelangelo's own project for a *Hercules* pendant to his *David*, designs which Vasari, VI, p. 148, says Michelangelo showed to Leo X and Cardinal Giulio.

[18] Machiavelli, *Il Principe*, chap. 25 (ed. S. Bertelli, Milan, 1968, pp. 98-101). For this theme and the voluminous literature on it, see E. Panofsky, "Good Government or Fortune," *GBA*, 68, 1966, pp. 305-26, especially nn. 3, 5, and 10; and F. Kiefer, "The Conflation of Fortuna and Occasio in Renaissance thought and iconography," *Journal of Medieval and Renaissance Studies*, 9, 1979, pp. 1-27. For examples of Hercules as Virtù in this imagery, see Marcantonio's engraving of *Herculean Virtue chastising vicious Fortune* and Giovanni

of fate and his GLOVIS *impresa*, the very device (suggesting the turn of Fortune's Wheel) that is represented in Pontormo's lunette. There were also images of fate and fortune in Leo's art, such as the picture of Leo's Wisdom stopping Fortuna from turning her wheel in his Lateran *possesso* or the *Three Fates* tapestry border (pl. 42).[19]

The theme of Virtù and Fortuna presented in *Hercules and Fortuna* is underscored by the inscription VIRTVTEM FORTVNA SEQVETVR. This motto existed in Medici imagery before Allori's lunette. In Duke Francesco's wedding *apparato* of 1565, it accompanied a statue of *Virtù and Fortuna*,[20] and it was used (anachronistically) by Vasari as the motto for his *Return from Exile of Cosimo il Vecchio* (pl. 92). Moreover, the motto is a variant on one that had been used by both Leo and his brother Giuliano. Giuliano's medal, with its Ciceronian inscription DVCE VIRTVTE COMITE FORTVNA (With Virtue as leader, Fortune as companion), shows the reconciliation of Virtù and Fortuna-Occasio (pl. 84).[21] An arch in Leo's Lateran *apparato* was inscribed with a similar sentiment;[22] and another related motto, SVPERANDA OMNIS FORTVNA, was used by Leo with his device of the yoke.[23] The motto above the oculus in Allori's fresco, then, may have been adopted by Borghini from Giovio's original program for the lunette. Unlike Pontormo's fresco, however, there is no balancing motto in the roundel below the window; it might also have been filled with GLOVIS, alluding to the turn in fortune of the Medici brought about by the *virtù* of Leo-Hercules, but it remains tantalizingly empty.[24]

The themes in Allori's fresco of the Medici Hercules and the triumph of Virtù over Fortuna had already come together in Leo's art in the borders of Raphael's tapestries, the imagery of which is a rich compendium of Leonine themes. The *Hercules* border is, of course, an allegory of Hercules-Leo (pl. 120). It shows Hercules holding the celestial globe; above is Fame, the hero's constant companion, and above Fame is Leo's papal *stemma*.[25] The message is clear: through feats of Herculean *virtù*, Leo, like his exemplar, triumphs over Fortuna and achieves fame and immortality.[26] Fortuna is not actually

---

Francesco Caroto's medal *Hercules chastizing Vice* of ca. 1518, cited by Wittkower, pp. 103-5, figs. 150 and 152.

[19] See chap. 2; and, for more examples, Kliemann, 1972, pp. 322-24.

[20] Cini, p. 567.

[21] Hill, no. 456 bis. The motto derives from "Omnia summa consecutus es virtute duce, comite fortuna" (*Familiares* X, 3, 2). Fortuna-Occasio derives from the Fortuna *redux* of Roman coins, with her rudder and cornucopia. For the theme see Wittkower, pp. 101-3.

[22] LEONE X PONT. MAX. VIRTVTE DVCE, COMITE FORTVNA, SALVA EST ROMA (Penni, p. 223). See also the related inscription VIRTVTIS ALVMNO, FORTVNAE DOMINATORI (Penni, p. 206).

[23] See chap. 2, n. 33. This motto and similar sixteenth-century emblems dealing with the theme are discussed by R. Wittkower, "Patience and Chance: the Story of a Political Emblem," in *Al-legory and the Migration of Symbols*, London, 1977, p. 112.

[24] In his letter to Borghini of 25 July 1578 (V. Borghini, p. 127), Allori writes that Francesco has requested that he insert the date in the disk. The year 1578 did have special significance for Francesco: on 5 June, only a month before Allori's letter, he had married Bianca Cappello in a secret ceremony, an event which was not made public until a year later (Berti, 1967, pp. 302-3). It might be noted that the disk appears to have been repainted and may once have borne this date or some other inscription.

[25] See the Mantuan set of tapestries for the scene of Hercules and the Centaur at the bottom of the tapestry, which is lacking in the Vatican set (Shearman, 1972, fig. 28; my pl. 144).

[26] Shearman, 1972, p. 89, interprets the theme of the series as a "triumph of Virtù over Occasio."

personified in the borders, but the concept is represented by the *Times of Day* (pl 21), the *Seasons* (pl. 22), and the *Three Fates* (pl. 42), all of which comment on the turns of fortune in Leo's life portrayed in the horizontal friezes (pl. 31). Moreover, alluding to Leo himself, the *Hercules* serves as a kind of introduction to the series, since it is placed to the left of the first tapestry on the left wall of the chapel—*Saint Paul Preaching in Athens* (which, incidentally, contains a portrait of Leo among the auditors).

If my contention that the *Hercules and Fortuna* reflects Giovio's plan for the second lunette is correct, then it may be seen in the context of Leo's art as a monumental elaboration on the program of the tapestry borders. The particular Herculean labor chosen for the fresco was compatible with the theme of Medici apotheosis in the Salone (which will be discussed in chapter 8), and it may also have seemed particularly suitable as an allegory of Pope Leo. Given his predilection for numerology, Hercules' eleventh labor might have had special significance for the pope, whose lucky number was eleven; and, given his obsession with himself as a reincarnation of his Leonine predecessors, the feat of the killing of the dragon might have evoked a personal response. For this feat recalls a miracle attributed to Leo's favorite papal exemplar, Leo IV, who killed a dragon that was terrorizing Rome and built walls around the Vatican, which then came to be known as the *città leonina*.[27] In 1518, not long before the decoration of the Salone, Leo actually imitated an act of Leo IV connected with the miracle of the dragon: according to a contemporary account, he invoked divine aid against the menace of the Turk by carrying the sacred icon of the *Sancta sanctorum* through the streets of Rome, just as the earlier Leo had done to rid Rome of the dragon.[28]

Hercules and Fortuna in the Garden of the Hesperides as a subject for the second lunette also had broader implications, permitting the conflation of several congenial themes which expand on the celebration of Medici virtue and its rewards in the Salone decoration. The first is the symbolism of the garden itself. There was a well-established tradition in political iconography for the Garden of the Hesperides as a metaphor of the ruler's domain. The garden lent itself to identification with actual places, and in this sense its imagery coincided with the traditional political *topos* of the return of the Golden Age. For example, in the imagery of French royal *entrées*, such as those of Charles VIII and Francis I, the king is Hercules; the garden, France or a conquered territory.[29] And

[27] Moroni, 38, p. 24. The other two miracles of Leo IV are commemorated in the Stanza dell'Incendio in the *Battle of Ostia* and the *Fire in the Borgo*.

[28] P.G.V. Giannini, *Notizie istoriche . . .* , Rome, 1798, p. 7 (pointed out in a different connection by Shearman, 1972, p. 18, n. 21): "Così S. Leone Papa IV vedendo che un Drago divoratore presso la Chiesa di S. Lucia in Selci . . . , col suo fiato pestilenziale uccideva chi gli si avvicinava, per la Festa della B. Vergine Assunta in Cielo ordinò una solenne Processione, andò egli col Clero seguendo l'Immagine del SSmo Salvatore dal Laterano sino alla Chiesa di S. Adriano, e di là al luogo, ove era il Drago, ed essendosi accostato il S. Pontefice alla

caverna, pregò con viva fiducia, e con molte lagrime il SSmo Salvatore, acciò lo mettesse in fuga, o lo facesse perire; indi recitando l'Orazione sopra il Popolo, proseguì la Processione sino alla Basilica di S. Maria Maggiore, e da quell'ora in poi non apparve il fiero Dragone, la qual Processione in memoria di ciò, ogn'anno nelle notte della gran Festa della stessa B. Vergine Assunta in Cielo con molta solennità si continuò sino all'anno 1566 . . . Leone Papa X. l'anno 1518. il dì 14 di Marzo la portò processionalmente per implorare il divino aiuto contro la potenza del Turco."

[29] M.-R. Jung, *Hercule dans la Littérature française du XVIᵉ siècle: de Hercule courtois à Hercule baroque*, Geneva, 1966, pp. 37-39. In royal *entrées*, this theme

in Florentine poetry, the garden is defined as Florence, defended by her hero, Hercules.[30] In Allori's fresco, as in an actual Medicean garden at Villa Castello, with Tribolo's and Ammannati's *Fountain of Hercules and Antaeus* (pl. 170), the Garden of the Hesperides is guarded by Hercules (we recall that Allori used the word *guardata* in referring to the work). Hercules is the counterpart of the gods who guard the laurel in Pontormo's fresco, but he protects another Medici emblem—the *palle*, which are symbolized by the apples of the Hesperides.

The last of the elements in Allori's lunette that figured in Leo's imagery is the fruit itself, for Hercules' eleventh labor would have no general Medicean significance comparable to that of Pontormo's Golden Age tableau were it not for the nexus of associations around the *mala aurea*. Hercules' spoil was understood in Leo's time as symbolic of the hero's virtue.[31] Thus, the golden apples underscore the theme of Medici virtue in the Salone and are the counterpart of the laurel, which is the emblem of virtue in Pontormo's fresco. The golden apples were also connected with the *saecula aurea*: the fruits were consecrated to Venus, and the garden in which they grow was identified with the Golden Age.[32] Thus, the Golden Age garden inhabited by Pontormo's gods (including Venus herself and Pomona, whose name puns on the *pomo d'oro*) is complemented by another Golden Age garden opposite it. Finally, the *mala aurea* symbolize immortality, since they had long been identified with the medicinal citrus fruit, called *mala medica*.[33] It is this pun on the Medici fruit, or the *palle*, to which Allori refers in the explanatory caption on his drawing for the lunette: "I pomi d'oro . . . chiamati da molto mala medica."

The circle of associations *mala aurea–mala medica–palle* was, of course, not invented by Vincenzo Borghini and Allori, but, as we have seen, it had been current since the time of Cosimo Pater Patriae, who apparently had an *impresa* showing a regenerating tree of

---

was often signaled by the episode with Atlas (cf. Raphael's tapestry border) or Hercules' choice between Virtue and Vice. In the entry of Charles VIII into Vienna in 1490, Charles puts the "garden of France" in order and liberates the Hesperides; in the 1515 entry of Francis I into Lyon, Hercules-Francis rules the garden of the duchy of Milan.

[30] See, for example, the *canzone* by Francesco Sacchietti, *Il Libro delle Rime*, ed. A. Chiari, Bari, 1936, CXCIV, 37-48 (p. 211).

[31] The bronze Hercules of the Capitoline (which, incidentally, was installed there by Leo in 1521) carries three apples, which were understood to signify chastity, temperance, and prudence by Valeriano, 1625, p. 717; and Giraldi, pp. 30-34 (writing in Rome in 1513). For Vasari, *Rag.*, p. 81, the *mala aurea* stand for the virtue of the prince.

[32] The connection of the Garden of the Hesperides with Venus is due to Servius, I, pp. 552-53, commentary on *Aeneid*, IV, 484-85: "*Hesperidum templi costos*. Hesperides, Atlantis filiae nymphe,

secundum fabulam hortum habuerunt, in quo erant mala aurea Veneri consecrata." (The Hesperides, nymphs and daughters of Atlas, had, according to report, a garden in which there were golden apples sacred to Venus. . . .) "*Sacros ramos. Vel Veneri, vel Iunoni dedicatos.*" (Sacred branches. Dedicated to Venus, or to Juno.) The *mala aurea* as the fruits of Venus and the imagery of the Venusian garden is elaborately developed in Pontano's poem on citriculture, *De hortis hesperidum*, pp. 28-31. See also A. Alciati, *Emblemata . . .*, Padua, 1621, pp. 870-72 (*Mala Medica*). For other sources of this tradition, see Wind, p. 80; and, with reference to the Garden of the Hesperides as the *sito de Venere*, see Brummer, 1970, pp. 232-33.

[33] For the *mala aurea*, or fruit of the Medes, as a medicinal citrus, see Athenaeus, *Deipnosophistae*, III, 83-84. See also Servius, III, p. 231, on *Georgics*, II, 127 (which connects Virgil's fruit of the Medes with citrus); Pontano and Alciati, cited above, n. 32.

"golden apples."³⁴ The symbolic citrus also occur in the Quattrocento in a number of Medici paintings until, in Laurentian art and poetry, they recover their primary association as the fruits of Venus. The Venusian gardens of the *Stanze* and of Botticelli's mythologies (pl. 60) all contain *pomi d'oro*.³⁵ Therefore, just as the Venusian gardens themselves are to be understood as both Hesperidian and Medicean, so their fruits symbolize both the *mala aurea* and the Medici *palle*.

Citrus fruits alluding to the *palle* and the *mala aurea* also occur in Leo's imagery, where, as earlier, they signify virtue and immortality. Ferreri's description of the *palle* as "six blushing apples portraying immortal glory" sums up the conceit.³⁶ And it is not coincidental that the most prominent fruits in the garland in Pontormo's fresco are citrus, which underscore the idea of Medici immortality and of Apollo *medicus*, the healer.

If the *Hercules* fresco was indeed an allegory of Leo in Giovio's program, then its fruits may also have some kind of personal reference to him, perhaps to his citrus garden in the Vatican Belvedere. This garden was interpreted by contemporaries, like Baldassar Castiglione, as a Garden of the Hesperides:³⁷

> Hic ubi odoratum surgens densa nemus umbra
> Hesperidum dites truncos nos invidet hortis.

> Here where the fragrant grove, rising in the dense shadow, does not envy the abundant tree-trunks in the Gardens of the Hesperides.

Moreover, it would seem that the statue of *Commodus* (or *Hercules*), which was placed near the entrance to the garden, was understood as guarding its precious golden fruit.³⁸

The imagery of Hercules in the Garden of the Hesperides implicit in Leo's Belvedere garden was later adopted in the gardens of Roman villas to allude to the virtue and immortality of their princely owners. The garden of the Villa d'Este at Tivoli was dedicated to the Hesperidian Hercules as an *exemplum virtutis*.³⁹ The garden at Villa

³⁴ See chap. 2. The citrus-*palle* connection was first argued by S. Tolkowsky, "The *Palle* of the Medici: a Florentine Riddle," *Hadar*, 4, 1931, pp. 91-92; and Tolkowsky, pp. 167-70. For this subject see also S. R. McKillop, "The Apples of the Hesperides as a Medici Symbol," paper read at the College Art Association, San Francisco, 1972; and see Kliemann, 1976, pp. 83-84, Appendix 42 (Laurentius Vitellius, "Arborea," dedicated to Piero di Cosimo), and Appendix 43 (Giovanni Pollastrino, "De Fluentia Nympha conversa in Laurum," a poem dedicated to Cardinal Giovanni in which Florence transforms herself into a laurel whose fruits are in competition with the apples of the Hesperides).

³⁵ Poliziano, *Le Stanze*, I, 94: "Raggia davanti all'uscio una gran pianta, / che fronde ha di smeraldo e pomi d'oro: oro: / e pomi ch'arrestar fenno Atalanta. . . ."

³⁶ Ferreri, p. 286 (see chap. 5, "The Lunette and

Medici *Imprese*," for the passage).

³⁷ *Delle Lettere del Conte Baldessar Castiglione*, ed. P. A. Serassi, Padua, 1771, II, p. 294 (poem on the so-called *Cleopatra* in the Belvedere). Brummer, 1970, pp. 234-38, discusses the Hesperidian imagery of this poem. There was precedent in Medicean poetry for the interpretation of Medici gardens as Hesperidian. See, for example, Alessandro Bracesi's "Descriptio horti Laurentii Medicis": Non fuit hortorum celebris tam gloria quondam Hesperidam . . ." (in Roscoe, IV, p. lxxvi).

³⁸ See Brummer, 1970, pp. 234-37. The garden also displayed a statue of *Hercules and Antaeus*. This subject, thematically related to the Hesperides myth, was later projected for the Salone itself, as well as for the garden of Villa Castello (see chap. 11, "Pontormo's Decoration of the Loggia at Villa Castello").

³⁹ D. R. Coffin, *The Villa d'Este at Tivoli*, Princeton, 1960, pp. 78-92. The garden contained three

Carpi had a nymphaeum which contained statues of shepherds, nymphs, and putti; next to the entrance was a statue of Hercules holding the golden apples of the Hesperides, and over it was the inscription AT SECVRA QVIES ET NESCIA FALLERE VITA.[40] The subject of this line from *Georgics* II is the farmers, and its context is the life of the Golden Age.[41] Thus, in this nymphaeum, the Virgilian notion of the farmers' "repose without care" is linked to the theme of Hercules in the Garden of the Hesperides.

It is tempting to speculate that the imagery of the lunettes in the Poggio a Caiano Salone was developed out of similar ideas, for these same two themes are juxtaposed. Only, in the Salone, instead of coexisting in a single composition, they are divided between the two frescos. Both are set in gardens of the Medici Golden Age: in Pontormo's, Apollo (Leo) tends the renascent *lauro*, which evokes the laurel of Lorenzo il Magnifico's gardens; in Allori's, Hercules (Francesco, but originally Leo) guards the sacred *mala medica*, in a translation of the *tableau vivant* of Hercules in the citrus grove of the Belvedere. Both scenes, moreover, tell of the immortality of the Medici, whose past and present deeds of civic virtue are celebrated in the *istorie* below: in *Hercules and Fortuna*, immortality comes to the Medici hero as a reward of his Herculean *virtù*; in *Vertumnus and Pomona*, it comes through the future of the dynasty made possible by the new sprout of the Medici tree.

VIRTUE AND ITS REWARDS

Completing the decoration of the end walls of the Salone are Allori's personifications of the *Virtues* and the *Rewards of Virtue*. Below *Vertumnus and Pomona* are *Pietas, Virtus, and Iustizia* (pl. 36); and below *Hercules and Fortuna* are *Fama, Gloria, and Honor* (pl. 68). These figures comment on the themes of Fortune and Virtue presented in the lunettes, and they complement the theme of virtue and its rewards that is set forth in the *istorie*, in which two scenes of civic virtue (*Titus, Scipio*) are juxtaposed with two scenes of tribute (*Cicero, Caesar*).

The four personifications adjacent to the lateral walls of the room are placed so that they relate thematically, with greater and lesser precision, to the *istorie*. Pietas is next to the *Triumph of Cicero* (pl. 72), the scene which tells of the devotion to the fatherland displayed by Cosimo Pater Patriae as well as by his exemplar. Iustizia is next to *Titus*

---

statues of Hercules as well as a Fountain of the Dragon alluding to the Garden of the Hesperides.

[40] For the Villa Carpi nymphaeum, see E. MacDougall, "Ars Hortulorum: Sixteenth Century Garden Iconography and Literary Theory in Italy," in *The Italian Garden*, ed. D. R. Coffin, Washington, 1972, pp. 53-55. The details are from the description by U. Aldovrandi, *Delle Statue di Roma*, in L. Mauro, *Le Antichità della città di Roma*, Rome, 1558, pp. 298-99. Above the entrance was

a sleeping shepherd; inside the grotto to the right was "uno Hercole giovane ignudo co'frutti de gli Hesperidi in mano; e sta poggiato ad un tronco con la spoglia del Leone, e con vaga attezza si tiene la gamba sinistra sopra la destra." There followed statues of the faun, a sleeping nymph, and putti. For engravings of the sleeping shepherd and the nymph, see MacDougall, figs. 11-12.

[41] *Georgics*, II, 467. For the entire passage, see Appendix II.

Flaminius at the Council of the Achaeans (pl. 80), in allusion to the justice displayed by Piero de' Medici in dealing with the enemies of the family. Honor is next to *Scipio Africanus Meeting Hasdrubal at the Court of Syphax* (pl. 79), referring to the rewards that came to Lorenzo il Magnifico as a result of his trip to Naples in the cause of peace. Finally, Fama is next to the *Tribute to Caesar* (pl. 71), referring, of course, to the fame of Leo X, present head of the Medici house.

The *Virtues* and *Rewards of Virtue* are also carefully coordinated with the subjects of the lunettes. As we have seen in a poem celebrating the return of the Medici in 1512, GLOVIS alludes not only to the turn of Fortune and the Return of Time, but to Medici virtue.[42] It spells out the first letters of *Gloria, Laude, Onore, Victoria, Iustizia,* and *Sapientia*. This acronym was used to link the *Virtues* and the *Rewards of Virtue* with the GLOVIS motto and hence to the lunettes above them. The personifications are arranged so that Fama, *GL*oria, and *O*nore are under *Hercules*, while Pieta*S*, *V*irtus, and *I*ustizia are under *Vertumnus and Pomona*. The change in sequence under Pontormo's lunette and two substitutions of personifications were made in order to make more pointed the connection between these figures and the content of the lunettes while still retaining the association with G-L-O-V-I-S. Thus, under the figure planned to represent Hercules-Leo, Fama—accompanying Hercules as in the tapestry border (pl. 120)—replaces the less forceful and Herculean Laude. Next to Caesar-Leo in the *Tribute to Caesar* and beneath Leo as the immortal Hercules, Fama trumpets his eternal glory. Under *Vertumnus and Pomona*, Virtus replaces Victoria, thus embodying the theme of virtue signified by the laurel, while still representing the *v* of the GLOVIS motto. To the left, substituting for Sapientia, is Pietas, requiring that the last rather than the first letter of the word represent a letter in GLOVIS.[43] Pietas alludes to Cosimo Pater Patriae in the adjacent *Cicero*, but it is also appropriately placed below Apollo-Leo, who tends the laurel of his revered father Lorenzo. To the right, under Pontormo's Luna-Diana, who I have suggested also represents Justice, is Iustizia. Alone among the Virtues, she turns to look up toward the lunette, her costume of red and white—the colors of justice—echoing the dress of her earlier rustic counterpart in *Vertumnus and Pomona*. Finally, there may be a cryptic message in the *Virtues* which links them to the IVP P inscription in the lunette, to Jupiter, and hence to the theme of Rulership which is so important in the Salone: if read from the right (backward, like the SI VOLGE read in GLOVIS), the first letters of Iustizia, Virtus, and Pietas spell IVP.

[42] See chap. 1, "Time's Return and the Medici Golden Age."

[43] Vasari also makes a substitution like this later, when he interprets GLOVIS as meaning *Gloria, Laus, Onor, Virtus, Iustizia,* and *Salus* (*Rag.*, p. 120).

III

Cosmic and Dynastic Imagery in the Art of Leo X (1513-1521)

Cosmic themes in Pontormo's *Vertumnus and Pomona* in the Salone at Poggio a Caiano (color pl. 2) complement the other themes of the *istorie* and of the lunettes which have been discussed in Part II. As we have seen, the *istorie* allude to the past and present glory of the Medici, to their *virtù* and its rewards (pls. 71-72, 79-80); the lunette frescos allude to the future, to the return of the Golden Age, and to Medici immortality. These themes are given an added dimension in both lunettes—assuming the *Hercules* (pl. 118) to have been planned by Giovio—by cosmic and astrological imagery appropriate to their location in the upper zone of the room, high above the depiction of the deeds of the Medici on earth. This imagery complements the themes of Nature and the Cycles of Time which are expressed, particularly in Pontormo's neo-Laurentian work, in the garden settings, the symbolic Medici laurel and citrus, the personifications of the Seasons, and the GLOVIS motto. For the earthly Cycles of Time were understood in the Renaissance as reflections of the celestial order, and imagery of the cosmos and the stars might equally be used as metaphors of Medici Return, destiny, and immortality.

Before discussing this cosmic and astrological imagery, which may not be readily accessible to the observer unaccustomed to reading occult references in Renaissance art, it will be helpful to investigate the background out of which it emerged: first, astrological beliefs in Florence and their reflections in Medici art and thought; then, as the contemporary frame of reference for the imagery of the Salone lunettes, astrological imagery in other art commissioned by Leo X.

 # The Medici and Astrology

In Renaissance Florence, as elsewhere, astrology was part of humanist learning, and astrological concepts enjoyed wide currency.[1] Indeed, astrological beliefs were so deeply ingrained in Renaissance thinking as to be hardly identifiable as a system of thought, much less a science with fixed guidelines; they were rather a wide-ranging set of assumptions. The seven planets (which, in Renaissance parlance, include the sun and moon), the twelve signs of the zodiac, and even the fixed stars had conventional meanings which could serve as guides to action in life, or, in literature and art, as symbols of the human condition.

In the Renaissance, the configurations of the celestial bodies in the heavens were seen as the determinants of the course of history and of life itself. Events, even historical epochs, were typically viewed and rationalized in terms of celestial phenomena.[2] Planetary conjunctions were understood as especially significant in this respect, as, for example, the conjunction of Jupiter and Saturn in the sign of Scorpio on 25 November 1484, which occasioned the famous prophecies of the reform of Christianity by Landino and others.[3] Moreover, as had been true throughout history, astrology was used in

[1] On Renaissance astrology see J. Burkhardt, *The Civilization of the Renaissance in Italy*, New York, 1975, II, iv, pp. 484-93; Thorndike, V-VI; D. C. Allen, pp. 3-100; Garin, chaps. III-IV, especially pp. 63-92. For Florence, in particular, see R. Davidsohn, *Firenze ai tempi di Dante*, Florence, 1929, pp. 184-91; and Soldati, chaps. II-IV. There is also much pertinent material in Zambelli, passim.

[2] See Villani, bk. VI, 27, 92; VIII, 48; IX, 65; X, 113, 157; and XI, 1, 20, 33, 68, 100, 114, etc. See also N. Rubinstein, "Some Ideas on Municipal Progress and Decline in the Italy of the Communes," *Fritz Saxl (1890-1948): a Volume of Memorial Essays from his Friends in England*, ed. D. J. Gordon, London, 1957, pp. 165-83.

[3] *Commento di Christophoro Landino fiorentino sopra la Commedia di Dante Alighieri poeta fiorentino*, Florence, 1481, f. IXv (commentary on *Inferno*, I, 105). This prophecy is discussed in the context of Florentine thought of the late Quattrocento by Chastel, 1961, pp. 344-46. For the theme of astrological prophecy and *renovatio* in the period, see also Vasoli, pp. 130-240; and D. Weinstein, *Savonarola and Florence: Prophecy and Patriotism in the Renaissance*, Princeton, 1970, pp. 84-94.

attempts to influence the course of events. In Florence, for example, the Signoria habitually followed astrologers' advice as to the auspicious moment for the conferral of the *bastone* of command on the captain-general of the Republic.[4] Astrologers were also consulted as to the best time for the laying of the foundation stones of major buildings. Important examples in Florence are the Palazzo Strozzi (begun 6 August 1489) and the Fortezza da Basso (begun 15 July 1534 on the advice of Giuliano Ristori, who was astrological adviser to both Duke Alessandro and Duke Cosimo de' Medici).[5] And, as we discover from Giannotti's letter describing it, some important part of the building of the villa at Poggio a Caiano was begun "nel 1490 a dì 12 luglio, ad ore nove" (12 July 1490 at 9 hours) on the recommendation of Ficino, who was Lorenzo's astrologer.[6]

It is not surprising to find that belief in the power of the stars influenced Florentine cultural life as well as its practical affairs. From Dante and Boccaccio, whose preoccupation with astrology is well-known,[7] to the circle of Lorenzo il Magnifico, and later the courts of Leo X and Duke Cosimo, literature and the visual arts in Florence (and, in Leo's case, in Rome) contain much astrological imagery. Ficino and others of Lorenzo's time filled their writings with arcane references to horoscopy, and astrological images were frequent in popular poetry. For example, Lorenzo himself wrote a carnival song on the influence of the planets:

> Sette pianeti siam, che l'alte sede
> lasciam per far del cielo in terra fede.
> Da noi son tutti i beni e tutti i mali . . .

We are seven planets who leave our high seat to bring to earth belief in the heavens. From us comes all good and all evil.

And Luigi Pulci set the stage for his account of Lorenzo's *giostra* with a declaration of the influence of the stars over the affairs of men:[8]

[4] On the *cerimonia del bastone* at the time of Lorenzo il Magnifico, see E. Casanova, "L'Astrologia e la consegna del bastone al Capitano generale della Repubblica fiorentina," *ASI*, ser. IV, 11, 1891, pp. 3-13. For the ceremony of conferral to Lorenzo the younger in 1515, see Trexler-Lewis, pp. 100-103.

[5] J. R. Hale, "The End of Florentine Liberty: The Fortezza da Basso," *Florentine Studies*, ed. N. Rubinstein, London, 1968, pp. 518-19, reproduces (fig. 13) the horoscope for the foundation time of the Arx Florentina (ASF, *Carte Strozziane*, ser. 1, 129, f. 196r). The chart is also included in Gaurico, bk. I, f. 9r, where it is attributed to Ristori.

[6] Giannotti, p. 1578: "Queli che edificò il palazzo fu Lorenzo de' Medici. . . . D'èttegli principio nel 1490 a dì 12 luglio, ad ore nove. M. Marsilio Ficino gli dette il tempo nel quale lo doveva principare, benchè l'araldo di palazzo di quel tempo,

che era astrologo, non approvava tal punto, et affermava che tale edificio, fondatosi in quel tempo che fu fondato, sarebbe disfatto, ma poi con maggiore magnificentia riedificato." The time is cited here according to Renaissance reckoning, in which the hours of the day were counted from sunset. Calculations give 4:44 a.m. as the hour chosen by Ficino for the beginning of the work (not, in fact, the actual foundation of the building; see chap. 3). It is notable that the date selected by the astrologer (12 July) was in Cancer, the zodiac sign traditionally associated with the home.

[7] For a detailed study of Boccaccio and astrology, as well as bibliography on Dante and astrology, see J. Levarie Smarr, "Boccaccio and the Stars: Astrology in the 'Teseida,'" *Traditio*, 35, 1979, pp. 303-32.

[8] For Lorenzo's poem see *Opere*, II, p. 251; for the *giostra* poem see Pulci, stanza III.

Io dico con coloro che sono discreti
Che le cose del mondo son guidate
Dal corso delle stelle e de pianeti
Ne per tanto pero son distinate
Quantunche questi effecti sieno secreti
Et cio che fanno e di necessitate
Ogni nostro concepto ogni nostro opra
Ispira e viene dalla virtu disopra.

I say with those people who are wise that the things of this world are guided by the course of the stars and the planets. Not, however, because they are predestined, though these effects are secret, and what they do is of necessity. All our ideas and every action of ours is inspired by and comes from the power above.

Given this ambiance, and given the degree to which astrological ideas were taken for granted, the virtual silence on the part of contemporary commentators about astrological and hermetic meanings in works of art is understandable. Vasari, for example, ignores or comments only laconically on astrological symbolism, even when it is overt. For example, he makes no remarks on the astrological features of such decorations as Francesco Cossa's cycle of the months in the Palazzo Schifanoia, Ferrara (pl. 132); or Raphael's *God the Father and the Celestial Universe* in the cupola of the Chigi Chapel, S. Maria del Popolo (pl. 123); or Peruzzi's ceiling of the Sala di Galatea in the Villa Farnesina (pl. 149). Concerning some other astrological decorations, such as Perino del Vaga's ceiling in the Sala dei Pontefici (pl. 145); Giulio Romano's ceiling of the Sala dei Venti in the Palazzo del Te, Mantua; or Pontormo's loggia for Duke Cosimo de' Medici at Villa Castello (fig. 20), Vasari names some of the planets and the zodiac signs depicted but makes no attempt to interpret their significance. Clearly, for Vasari and others, allusions to celestial phenomena and the occult were among the expected features of the art of their time; they were the rule, rather than the remarkable exception. However, for us to follow suit and to underestimate the relevance of these beliefs to the interpretation of certain Renaissance works, out of ignorance or skepticism as to their objective validity, would be to leave an important dimension of their meaning unexplored.

Before turning to the astrological content of Medici art, we must first consider the fundamental notions of the cosmos and the zodiac in the Renaissance. The astrological lore that was part of the medieval heritage of Renaissance Florence was overlaid in the Quattrocento with a veneer of ancient hermetic and astrological knowledge, which was revived along with other manifestations of the culture of antiquity. These concepts were inseparable from religious beliefs: faith in the power of the stars was reconciled with Christianity through the notion that the heavenly bodies were created by God to exercise his divine powers—as, for example, by Ficino, who states that the blessings of the zodiac come to man through the love of God.[9] The Ptolemaic *imago mundi* having long been assimilated into Christian theology, images of the cosmos and the zodiac occurred

[9] *De amore*, V, 13.

frequently in sacred art.[10] A glance at two such images will serve to identify some of the astrological conventions that the Renaissance observer would have understood—a language of pictorial symbols (and later of mythological associations) which allude to the cosmos, the zodiac, the stars, and the planets.

A woodcut from the *Nuremberg Chronicle* (1493) shows a characteristic Renaissance view of the cosmos (pl. 124). The diagram shows the earth at the center of the universe, surrounded by the planetary spheres. These are occupied by the symbols for the luminaries (a blazing sun and a crescent moon) and by stars, which stand for the five planets known in the Renaissance (Mercury, Venus, Mars, Jupiter, and Saturn). Beyond the planetary spheres is the zodiac band with the ancient pictorial symbols for the twelve signs, which roughly correspond with the months of the year. They read counterclockwise from the right: the Ram for Aries (March), the Bull for Taurus (April), the Twins for Gemini (May), the Crab for Cancer (June), the Lion for Leo (July), the Maiden for Virgo (August), the Scales for Libra (September), the Scorpion for Scorpio (October), the Archer for Sagittarius (November), the Goat for Capricorn (December), the Water Bearer for Aquarius (January), and the Fish for Pisces (February).[11] In the empyrean is an enthroned Christ with a host of saints, which vividly evokes the notion of God's sovereignty over all.

Raphael's cupola in the Chigi Chapel of 1512-1516 is a more monumental cosmos image—and it is a work created in Leonine Rome.[12] God the Father is at the center of a celestial wheel (different from the zodiac) in which the planets and the stars are depicted. The planets are not represented by symbols (as in the *Nuremberg Chronicle*), but, in the mode of High Renaissance art, they are personified as the gods with whom they had been associated since antiquity. Thus, Sol-Apollo and Luna-Diana stand for the sun and moon, and the planets are represented by the gods whose names they bear. Each deity is accompanied by an arc (suggesting a segment of the zodiac band) on which is depicted the zodiac signs which the planet is thought to rule. According to the ancient system of planetary rulerships, based on the concept of the *magno anno* (the great year), the universe was believed to have taken a certain configuration at the time of creation, to which it would return at the end of time, when the heavenly bodies would resume their original places.[13] Thus, the sun and moon rule the signs in which they were located

---

[10] See Chastel, 1961, pp. 207-17, on Renaissance views of the cosmos. In order to avoid overburdening the apparatus of chaps. 7-9, and 11, I have not cited modern astrological manuals regarding basic astrological concepts and terminology. However, the reader may consult the fundamental work, A. Bouché-Leclercq, *L'Astrologie Grecque*, Paris, 1899, repr. 1963; as well as the excellent introduction by C. P. Goold to Manilius, *Astronomica*, pp. xvii-cxxii.

[11] The signs of the zodiac are thirty-degree arcs of the circle of the orbit of the earth around the sun, measured from the vernal equinox, when the sun crosses the celestial equator. Today, 0° Aries occurs on 21 March; in the early sixteenth century, however, due to the precession of the equinoxes (which results in the desynchronization of the zodiac signs and the constellations bearing the same names), the beginning of the astrological year was earlier. The vernal equinox and 0° Aries fell on 11 March, with a consequent shift back for the beginning of each of the zodiac signs. Thus, the equation of Aries with March, Taurus with April, etc., was even more precise in the Renaissance than it is today.

[12] Saxl, pp. 53-57; Seznec, pp. 80-83; and J. Shearman, "The Chigi Chapel in S. Maria del Popolo," *JWCI*, 24, 1961, pp. 140-42.

[13] See chap. 8, nn. 60-61.

at the beginning of time—Leo and Cancer, respectively—and each planet rules two signs, the first diurnally, the second nocturnally, as follows: Mercury rules Virgo and Gemini (the signs adjacent to Leo and Cancer); Venus rules Libra and Taurus (the next two signs on either side of the wheel); Mars rules Scorpio and Aries; Jupiter rules Sagittarius and Pisces; and Saturn rules Capricorn and Aquarius, the two adjacent signs opposite Leo and Cancer. These rulerships are illustrated in countless astrological manuscripts, as, for example, the lavishly illuminated *De Sphaera* of the 1470s, where Jupiter, with his two signs, Sagittarius and Pisces, is depicted against a diagram of the cosmos (pl. 126).[14] In Chigi's chapel the seven planets with their zodiac signs and the angel with the globe displaying the fixed stars are depicted in the celestial wheel, the eight sections of which may allude to the familiar association of the number eight with death and resurrection. In the center of the wheel, God the Father receives the soul of Agostino Chigi into the heavens, presiding over a universe as it was believed to have been at the time of creation and as it would be again with the Return of Time. In this funerary chapel, then, the planets, the stars, and the zodiac signs are thus related to the Christian cycle of creation, death, and resurrection.

The planetary rulerships which are depicted in the Chigi Chapel are shown in a diagram of the archetypal zodiac, along with other zodiacal features to which I shall be referring (fig. 6). Starting at the point equivalent to 9:00 and reading counterclockwise, we find the twelve signs of the zodiac, each of which is ruled by a planet. In this chart the signs and planets are represented by conventional glyphs, as well as by name, and each of the signs is further associated with one of the four elements—indicated in the outer circle. Thus, to take an example, Aries (♈) is the first sign of the zodiac, its planetary ruler is Mars (♂), and its element is fire.

The planetary rulerships are often alluded to in Renaissance works of art in a more covert fashion than in the Chigi Chapel. For example, they are fundamental to an understanding of a body of astrological lore associated with the origins and destiny of Florence itself. As I have mentioned in connection with the *Birth of the Year* panel of the Poggio a Caiano frieze (pl. 53) and Vasari's painting of the *Foundation of Florence* (pl. 62), a vital part of the myth of Florence was the identification of the city with the sign of Aries (corresponding roughly with the month of March) and with Mars, planetary ruler of Aries. These connections were made because the city was believed to have been founded by Augustus at a time when the sun was in Aries and when Aries was in the ascendant (that is, rising on the eastern horizon) with the planets Mars and Mercury in favorable aspect (or relation) to the ascendant.[15] Thus, from ancient times, Aries was assigned the geographical rulership of Florence, just as the sign of Leo was identified with Rome, and Libra with Italy itself.[16]

[14] Modena, Biblioteca Estense, MS Est. lat. 209, α.X.2.14, f. 5v. See Ludovici, pp. 30-32.

[15] See the discussion and references in Rubinstein, 1967, p. 71, especially Filippo Villani, *De origine civitatis Florentiae* (Laur. MS Ashb. 942, f. 10v), who states that Caesar founded Florence "saliente arietis singno super lineam circularem nostri orizzontis quo . . . tunc Mars atque Mercurius be-

nignissimis aliorum siderum aspectibus pariter ferebantur"; and Cino Rinuccini, *Risponsiva alla Invettiva di Messer Antonio Lusco* (in C. Salutati, *Invectiva in Antonium Luschum*, ed. D. Moreni, Florence, 1826, pp. 206-7), who claims the city was founded with the "ascendente l'Ariete sei gradi sotto il dominio di Marte."

[16] These rulerships are constantly repeated in

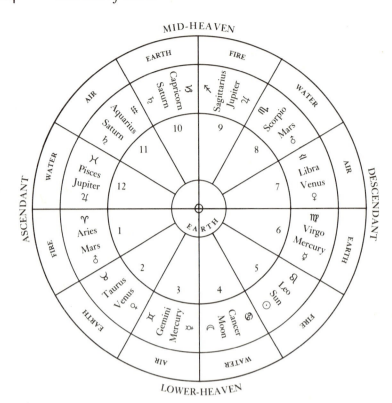

6. Archetypal zodiac (showing zodiac signs, Renaissance planetary rulerships, houses of the zodiac, and the elements corresponding to the signs)

With their penchant for seeing a predestined repetition of events in their history, the Florentines embellished the legend of the birth of the city under Aries, placing the refoundation of the city by Charlemagne under the same sun and ascendant sign, with Mars in favorable aspect to it.[17] A horoscope of this second "Florentiae Natalis," or rebirth of Florence (dated 5 April 802), is included in the collection of horoscopes published in 1552 by Luca Gaurico (fig. 7).[18] On the eastern horizon, rising at the moment of the rebirth of the city, is Aries, indicated by the conventional glyph (♈). As we shall see presently, this eastern angle, or ascendant, was considered the most important angle of a horoscope. Moreover, in this horoscope of the rebirth of Florence, the ascendant in

---

Renaissance treatises on astrology. See, for example, Vatican, Pal. MS lat. 1368, f. 50v: "Aries-Florentia; Leo-Roma; Libra-Italia." See also L. Gaurico, *Praedictiones super omnibus futuris luminarum deliquiis figurae coelestes Venetiarum Bononiae, et Florentiae* . . . , Rome, 1539, n.p.: "Aries-Florentia . . . Leo-Roma . . . Libra-Italiae pars." I owe these references to Claudia Rousseau.

[17] On the refounding of the city under Aries and Mars, see Villani, bk. III, 1: "E dissesi ancora per gli antichi, che' e' Romani per consiglio de' savi astrolagi, al cominciamento che rifondaron Firenze, presono l'ascendente di tre gradi del segno dell' ariete, essendo il sole nel grado del sua esal-

tazione, e la pianeta di Mercurio congiunta a grado col sole, e la pianeta Marti in buono aspetto dell' ascendente." Villani then continues to describe the results for Florence of her foundation under "Mars in Aries," noting particularly that the city was "sempre in grandi mutazioni" and (in allusion to Mars' association with war) that the Florentines were always fighting among themselves (see also IV, 7).

[18] Gaurico, bk. I, f. 8v. For the horoscopes of the foundation of Rome under Libra, then under the sign of Leo, see f. 4v-5r. For a circular computer diagram of the Florentine horoscope, see Cox-Rearick, 1982, fig. 20.

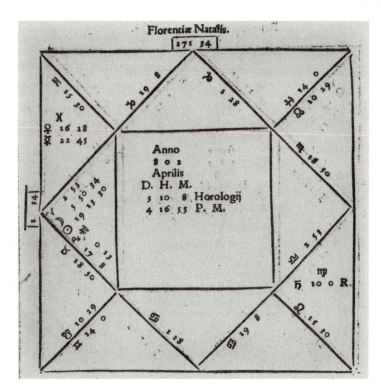

7. Horoscope of the rebirth
of Florence, 5 April 802
(after Gaurico)

Aries is marked by the presence of no fewer than four powerful planets: Mars (♂; ruler of Aries), the sun (☉), the moon (☽), and Jupiter (♃).

This celestial configuration was never forgotten. The destiny of Florence was seen as inextricably linked with Aries and Mars. Hence, whenever the Ram, symbolizing Aries, or the god Mars appear in Florentine art, particularly when they appear together, we can be virtually certain that allusion is being made to the special astrological destiny of the city.

✳   ✳   ✳

Cosmic and astrological imagery is found from the beginnings of Florentine monumental art. Cycles of the zodiac signs and personifications of the planets are included in the late medieval decorations in the Spanish Chapel (S. Maria Novella) and on the Campanile. A border including zodiac signs frames the fresco of *St. Anne and the Expulsion of the Duke of Athens from Florence* (now in the Palazzo Vecchio); Leo, the sign corresponding to the date of this important event for the freedom of Florence (26 July 1343), appears at the top of the band. In the Duomo, Domenico Michelino's lunette of *Dante and Florence* (1465) has a cosmological setting (pl. 127).[19] In this work, the planetary spheres with the planets (represented by their traditional glyphs; cf. fig. 6) and the sphere of the fixed stars are shown as varicolored bands arching over the poet and his

[19] R. Altrocchi, "Michelino's Dante," *Speculum*,   on other Renaissance representations of the spheres.
6, 1931, pp. 15-59. See Chastel, 1961, pp. 211-14,

city. Like the zodiac signs in the archivolts of medieval cathedral portals, these spheres symbolize the heavens and the higher spiritual world. Zodiac wheels of Arabic inspiration were inlaid in the pavements of Florentine churches, where, like the mosaic zodiac-calendars of antiquity, they were understood to reflect the celestial order above. The marble zodiac in San Miniato (1207) has been shown to have an elaborate occult significance related to its orientation to the sign of Taurus.[20] The zodiac wheel of the Baptistery is similarly related to the sign of Cancer, in which the summer solstice occurs, for it incorporates a central solar disk which had once been located under the lantern, where it was illuminated by the sun at the solstice (pl. 125).[21] Like some other zodiacal images, this wheel has an inscription pointing up the idea of the turning of the heavens: the palindromic phrase EN GIRO TORTE SOL CICLOS ET ROTOR IGNE suggests that the zodiac of the pavement is a reflection of the zodiac of the heavens, and the palindrome itself evokes its eternal motion.

In Florence in the mid-Quattrocento, a different kind of astrological representation began to occur: now the zodiac signs are not depicted as in the archetypal zodiac wheels or *sphaera* I have cited but as they appear in the sky at a given moment, surrounded by the extrazodiacal constellations.[22] Moreover, the planets are shown as occupying specific, rather than random or archetypal, locations against this starry background. The zodiac and the planets are thus shown in motion, or in relation to time and space, in representations which are pictorial horoscopes (*horus* = hour). These portray the appearance of the heavens at a precise time and from a particular place—as if, for example, the planets shown above the horizon in Gaurico's horoscope of the rebirth of Florence were to be depicted by an artist against the array of celestial bodies visible in the sky from Florence on 5 April 802.

Pictorial horoscopes of this kind were made to commemorate events. However, they had a purpose beyond the merely commemorative: they could suggest that the events alluded to by the positions of the stars and planets were astrologically predestined. The first example of this new genre is, in fact, Medicean. The celebrated painted cupola over the altar in the Old Sacristy of San Lorenzo shows the stars as they appeared during the month of July in Florence in the early fifteenth century (pls. 94, 128). This work has been interpreted as commemorating the date 9 July 1422 (the supposed day of the consecration of the high altar of San Lorenzo) or the date 6 July 1439, a highly significant day on which the union of the Greek and Western churches was proclaimed

[20] F. Gettings, *The Occult in Art*, New York, 1979, pp. 28-29, 42-47.

[21] Villani, bk. I, 60: "E troviamo per antiche ricordanze che la figura del sole intagliata nello smalto, che dice: *En giro torte sol ciclos, et rotor igne*: fu fatta per astronomia: e quando il sole entra nel segno del Cancro, in sul mezzo giorno, in quello luogo luce per lo aperto di sopra ov'e il capannuccio." This zodiac wheel is placed so that the symbol for Cancer is at the mid-heaven. On the history of this work, see L. Ximenes, *Del Vecchio e Nuovo Gnomone fiorentino*, Florence, 1757, pp. XVI-

XX; and G. B. Befani, *Memorie storiche dell'antichissima Basilica di San Giovanni di Firenze*, Florence, 1884, pp. 36-38. Later, Brunelleschi's astronomical adviser, Paolo Toscanelli, installed a gnomon in the Duomo, where light entering a hole in the lantern strikes a marker on the pavement just outside the North Sacristy at noon on the summer solstice.

[22] On the types and evolution of astrological representations, see Saxl, pp. 12-20; and Seznec, pp. 33-37.

at the closing session of the Council of Florence.[23] Astronomical calculations show that the positions of the planets on the zodiac band in the fresco are indeed those of 6 July 1439;[24] and since Cosimo de' Medici, as Gonfaloniere, had acted as host to Pope Eugenius IV and the Council and had lent financial support to it, there would have been sufficient pretext for the commemoration of the event, with the implication of Cosimo's part in it, in the sacristy of the Medici church.[25]

The sacristy cupola seems to be the only astrological representation actually commissioned by Cosimo, but his study of the subject with Paolo Toscanelli is attested by his biographer Vespasiano da Bisticci.[26] Moreover, in Fra Angelico's *Adoration of the Magi*, a painting close in date both to the Council and to the cupola, Cosimo is suggestively connected with astrological imagery. The fresco is in Cosimo's own cell at San Marco and it apparently commemorates the consecration of the church in 1443 to Saints Mark, Cosmas, and Damian.[27] Saint Cosmas is, of course, Cosimo's name saint, since he was born on 27 September 1389, the feast day of the Medici saints.[28] Thus, it is not sur-

[23] A. Warburg, in "Berichte über die Sitzungen des Instituts," March-May, 1911, *Mitt. KHIF*, 2, 1912-1917, p. 36; and idem, "Eine astronomische Himmeldarstellung in der alten Sakristei von S. Lorenzo in Florenz," in *Gesammelte Schriften*, Leipzig, 1932, I, pp. 162-72, 366-67, proposes the 1422 date; but in the appendix, p. 367, to his posthumously republished article, the 1439 date of the Council is suggested. Beer, 1967, pp. 187-88, favored the 1422 date, although admitting that the 1439 date was possible. For a summary of opinion and yet other dates, see E. Battisti, *Filippo Brunelleschi*, Milan, 1976, pp. 354-57.

[24] This conclusion is based on an analysis of horoscopes for the two dates. These rule out 9 July 1422 and confirm the 6 July 1439 date, the chart for which (calculated at 12:00 noon) shows the sun at 21° Cancer 52' and the moon at 48° Taurus 26'. In the fresco these points in Cancer and Taurus are indicated by the conventional symbols for the sun and moon. (The crescent is the symbol for the moon and does not, as has been assumed, indicate a new moon. That phase of the moon, in any case, is incompatible with its position in Taurus in relation to the sun in Cancer.) Given the condition of the painting, it is difficult to tell whether a dot in Taurus to the right of the moon and another in Leo are vestiges of the symbols for Saturn and Venus; however, these dots do correspond to the location of Saturn and Venus on 6 July 1439 at 3° Taurus 51' and 15° Leo 05', respectively. The remaining planetary positions for this date are Mercury at 18° Leo 23', Mars at 8° Taurus 13', and Jupiter (which would have been below the horizon and thus not visible) at 22° Capricorn 09'. In connection with the 1539 date, it

should be noted that a July sky is also shown in a similar painting in the *scarsella* of the Pazzi Chapel, which may commemorate the same event (see the appendix to Saxl mentioned in n. 23 above; and Dezzi Bardeschi, fig. 15).

[25] On Cosimo and the Council, see S. Ammirato, *Istorie fiorentine*, Florence, 1647, II, 5, p. 30: "Cosimo avendo dato ordine a tutte quelle cose che a tanto apparecchio erano necessarie, a 22 di gennaio ricevette il Pontefice coi soliti honori accompagnato da tre Cardinali, e da molti Prelati nella Città." See also V. P. Chiaroni, *Lo Scisma Greco e il Concilio di Firenze*, Florence, 1938, pp. 63, 69; J. Gill, *The Council of Florence*, Cambridge, 1959, pp. 175, 189, 299-300; and, on the financing of the Council, R. De Roover, *The Rise and Decline of the Medici Bank 1397-1494*, New York, 1966, p. 207.

[26] Vespasiano da Bisticci, *Le Vite . . .*, ed. A. Greco, Florence, 1976, II, p. 193: ". . . se di filosofia quello medesimo, se erano astrologi egli n'aveva uno universal giudicio, per essere sempre praticato con maestro Pagolo et con altri astrologi, in quale cosa vi dava fede, et usavala in alcuna sua cosa."

[27] This fresco is variously dated between 1439 and 1444; but in view of the date of the consecration and the fact that Pope Eugenius IV stayed in this cell for the occasion, the 1443 date seems the most likely (as is pointed out by Hatfield, 1970, p. 136).

[28] For Cosimo's horoscope see Cardano, no. XLIX, who places his birth at sunset on 27 September 1389, with the sun at 12° Libra, the ascendant at 12° Aries, and the mid-heaven at 12° Capricorn. This chart is erected according to the

prising to find that Cosimo is portrayed in this fresco at the exact center of the composition (pl. 129).[29] This portrait may be the first instance of a member of the family being portrayed in a representation of the important Medici theme of the Magi; however, unlike later Medicean pictures of the Magi like Gozzoli's (pl. 4) or Botticelli's (pl. 5) where there are no cosmic references, Cosimo is portrayed as an astrologer holding an armillary sphere.

The Old Sacristy is the first major Medicean decoration in which the family used art in the service of politics. The imagery of dynasty in its *imprese* and tombs and the imagery of Medici apotheosis in the allusion to Cosimo's father Giovanni in Donatello's reliefs of Saint John the Evangelist are complemented by the astrological cupola painting, which suggests that the family's power and influence are linked to epochal events, themselves prefigured in the stars. As such, this ensemble is a significant early example of the Medicean belief in their own special destiny and an important precedent for the conflation of dynastic imagery, Medici *imprese*, and cosmic symbolism that was to occur later in the decorations at Poggio a Caiano.

Astrological references in Medici art display a greater subtlety and complexity in the later Quattrocento. The sacristy cupola, however novel and seminal, is a simple sky map, populated by the pictorial symbols for the constellations and the glyphs for the luminaries that had been in use throughout the Middle Ages. On the other hand, the astrological imagery of the Laurentian years, and that after the Medici restoration of 1512, is characterized by an elaborate mélange of astrological lore and classical mythology. This new mode depended on certain developments of the mid- to late Quattrocento: the full-scale revival of ancient astrological and hermetic texts; the vogue for the occult, which encouraged the expression of astrological concepts in a pictorial language of metaphor and cryptic allusion; and the reintegration of the gods who personify the planets and constellations with the formal vocabulary of ancient art.[30]

The unprecedented popularity of astrology and horoscopy in the humanist circle of Lorenzo il Magnifico was due especially to the activities of Ficino, who translated hermetic texts and practiced an astrology based on ancient sources, some newly discovered or translated.[31] The fundamental, unassailable source for the calculation and interpretation of horoscopes was Ptolemy's *Tetrabiblos*, but later handbooks, such as the *Mathesis*

equal-house system of domification used by Cardano (see chap. 9, nn. 25-26).

[29] I owe the suggestion that the central figure is a portrait of Cosimo to Francis Ames-Lewis. It should be compared with the presumed portrait of Cosimo as Saint Cosmas in Fra Angelico's San Marco *Madonna and Saints* of the same date (pl. 39).

[30] On the recovery of antique texts, see F. Saxl, "The Revival of Late Antique Astrology," in *Lectures*, London, 1957, I, pp. 73-84. On the occult see Wind, pp. 1-61; and Dezzi Bardeschi, pp. 33-67.

[31] Much of Ficino's oeuvre is concerned with

hermeticism and astrology, on which see Thorndike, IV, pp. 562-73; F. A. Yates, *Giordano Bruno and the Hermetic Tradition*, London, 1964, pp. 20-83; Chastel, 1975, pp. 163-67; and Garin, pp. 72-86. For some of the ancient texts in the Medici collections, see A. M. Bandini, *Catalogus Codicum Manuscriptorum Bibliothecae Mediceae Laurentianae*, supp., Leipzig, 1961, II, pp. 10-72. For a listing of astrological texts known in the Renaissance, see J. Parr, *Tamburlaine's Malady and other Essays on Astrology in Elizabethan Drama*, University of Alabama Press, 1953; repr. Westport, Conn., 1971, pp. 112-50.

by Firmicus Maternus, were also important. Also significant for astrological imagery in art, in particular, was the rich tradition of ancient astrological poetry by Aratus, who identified the myths associated with some of the constellations in his *Phaenomena*; by the Hellenistic poet Eratosthenes, whose *Catasterismi* completed this process; by the Augustan poet Marcus Manilius, and the mythographer Hyginus. The works of these and other authors, which were available in manuscript in the Medici collections, reflect the mythologizing of the stars and planets that took place in antiquity—the development that, as Panofsky so aptly put it, "transformed the firmament into a rendezvous of mythological figures."[32]

Drawing on such sources, Ficino and others recovered ancient astrological traditions. An important instance of this revival was the adoption by Renaissance iconographers of the system of zodiacal guardianships developed by Manilius, in which the possibilities of astrological imagery were expanded to include the traditional pairs of Olympian gods as guardians of the zodiac signs.[33] According to this system, which is not to be confused with the ancient planetary rulerships of the archetypal zodiac, pairs of gods were associated with the opposing zodiac signs. Pallas and Vulcan were assigned to Aries and Libra respectively (an association which explains the popularity in Florence of Pallas, ruler of the Florentine sign of Aries). The other pairs were Venus and Mars (Taurus and Scorpio); Apollo and Diana (Gemini and Sagittarius); Mercury and Vesta (Cancer and Capricorn); Jupiter and Juno (Leo and Aquarius); and Ceres and Neptune (Virgo and Pisces). This system of guardianships is important for the understanding of certain details in Medicean programs, but it was most popular in northern Italy, where it provided the basis for the major astrological cycles by Cossa in the Palazzo Schifanoia and by Giulio Romano in the Palazzo del Te.[34] In Cossa's cycle of the months, for example, August (Virgo) is represented by a *Triumph of Ceres* (pl. 132), the Manilian ruler of Virgo, rather than by Mercury, the planetary ruler of the sign.

There are no monumental astrological cycles analogous to that of the Palazzo Schifanoia in Medici art of the later Quattrocento. However, the new mode *all'antica* of representing the constellations as gods makes its appearance in richly illustrated astrological manuscripts such as the *Medici Aratus*, where, in a depiction of the constellation Hercules (pl. 130), a Pollaiuoloesque nude slaying the dragon of the Hesperides scarcely resembles medieval representations of the constellation, in which figures of Arabic extraction, often fully clothed, brandish swords and scythes.[35]

Later, cosmic and astrological allusions begin to appear in monumental art, especially in Laurentian works such as Botticelli's *Venus and Mars* and *Primavera*, Signorelli's *Realm of Pan*, and the frieze at Poggio a Caiano.[36] However, these works are quite unlike the overtly astrological mythologies of the courts of northern Italy like Ferrara and Mantua,

[32] Panofsky-Saxl, p. 232.

[33] See Ficino, *De amore*, V, 13, drawing on Manilius, *Astronomica*, 2, 433-47.

[34] For Cossa's cycle see Warburg, "Schifanoia," pp. 247-72; for the Sala dei Venti, see Gombrich, 1972, pp. 109-19.

[35] *Arati De Signis celestibus* (Laur. MS Plut. 89 sup.

43, f. 11r; D'Ancona, no. 914). For the medieval Hercules representations, see Panofsky-Saxl, figs. 15-17, 21A, and 21B.

[36] The balance of this chapter was published in my article "Themes of Time and Rule at Poggio a Caiano: The Portico Frieze of Lorenzo il Magnifico" (Cox-Rearick, 1982).

for their astrological symbolism is muted and their occult content is not announced by a readily identifiable apparatus of celestial symbols. Rather, it is hinted by an aura of hidden symbolism and by veiled references which we penetrate only with difficulty—and, in each case, incompletely.

Botticelli's *Venus and Mars* carries an astrological message which would probably have been understood by contemporaries, even though the picture has no astrological signs or symbols (pl. 131).[37] Like the mirror of *Venus and Mars* (pl. 95), Botticelli's picture is a conventional marriage image, based on the astrological tradition of the power of Venus, planet of love, over Mars, planet of war. This very notion is elaborated by Ficino in precise astrological terminology in *De amore*, where he points out that Venus masters Mars when the two planets are, astrologically speaking, in aspect.[38] Indeed, the positioning of Botticelli's gods opposite one another is such that it might well have been intended to bring to mind the trine (120°), which is considered the most harmonious of the zodiacal aspects. The "aspect" of the reclining figures, together with the dominance of the alert Venus over the spent and sleeping Mars, suggests that the picture is indeed a delicate parody on the theme of harmony through love.[39]

The astrological theme of the *Primavera* (pl. 60), which is also signaled by a figure who stands for the planetary Venus, is based on the fundamental notion of the complementary nature of the celestial and earthly Cycles of Time: the signs of the zodiac and the months of the year. This idea animates the Villa Schifanoia cycle, in which the progression of the months on the earthly level is accompanied by the zodiac signs above and, finally, by the triumphal scenes of the Olympian rulers of the signs. This idea is also present in Botticelli's picture, but, instead of occupying different strata, the heavenly and earthly levels are conflated. We have already seen that the painting reflects the sequence of the rustic Roman calendar, with the months of April and May being represented by their rulers, Venus and Mercury. But these figures are also astrological:

[37] Although *Venus and Mars* has been connected with Medici patronage, the association is by no means certain. The work appears in none of the early inventories of the Medici collections; moreover, as Gombrich, 1972, "Botticelli," p. 68, suggests, the wasps above the head of Mars may be a punning allusion to the Vespucci family (*vespa* = wasp) and to their *stemma*, which shows the wasp.

[38] As noted by Gombrich, 1972, "Botticelli," pp. 66-69, who cites this passage from Ficino, *De amore*, V, 13: "Mars is outstanding in strength among the planets, because he makes men stronger, but Venus masters him. . . . Venus, when in conjunction with Mars, in opposition to him, or in reception, or watching him from sextile or trine aspect, as we say, often checks his malignance . . . she seems to master and appease Mars, but Mars never masters Venus. . . ." (For the planetary aspects referred to by Ficino, see below, n. 44.) Comparison with a more overt depiction of the same theme supports an astrological reading of Botticelli's pic-

ture. Rosso's famous presentation drawing of *Venus and Mars* (Paris, Louvre 1575) is an allegory of the marriage of Francis I and Eleanor of Austria, in which Francis-Mars is "defeated" by the love of Eleanor-Venus, whose small assistants carry away Mars' armor and weapons (just as do the *satyrini* in Botticelli's picture). This meaning is clearly signaled by the two zodiac signs above the figures: "rising" at the top center of the composition above Mars are the scales of Libra, diurnal house of Venus, and sign of love and concord; "descending" to the right, almost hidden by the putti and roses, is the scorpion, for Scorpio, diurnal house of the warlike Mars. For this work, executed in 1530, see J. Cox-Rearick, *La Collection de François Ier*, Paris, Musée du Louvre, 1972, pp. 36-37, no. 42.

[39] For the comic and erotic character of Botticelli's picture, see P. Barolsky, *Infinite Jest: Wit and Humor in Italian Renaissance Art*, Columbia, Mo., 1978, pp. 37-44.

Venus and Mercury are the planetary rulers of Taurus (April) and Gemini (May), and these zodiac signs are implicit in the picture.

The clue to this occult meaning of the *Primavera* lies in an anomaly of the composition, which reads from right to left like the counterclockwise movement of the zodiac signs in the heavens (fig. 6).[40] This is a compositional device that was used later by Bronzino in his *Primavera* tapestry of 1545 (pl. 61), which represents the Medici Spring and the return of the Golden Age under Duke Cosimo's rule. Flora-Fiorenza presides over the three spring signs of the zodiac—Aries, Taurus, and Gemini—which move "backward" from the lower right to the upper left, just as Botticelli's three groups of figures progress from right to left. The theme of these works is identical: the return of the Medici to rule in Florence is as inevitable as the return of spring to Flora's city, and both events are seen as earthly reflections of the eternal turning of the zodiac signs in the heavens.

If the symbolism of the planets in Botticelli's *Primavera* had been carried out consistently, Mars—planetary ruler of Aries—would appear to the right of Venus and Mercury. He does not, but his presence is, in fact, suggested there by a series of allusions to the *Fasti*: Zephyr, the west wind, or the "first breath of spring," is brought by the sign of Aries and the month of March; the laurel associated by Ovid with Mars as god of spring is present over this group (and nowhere else in the picture), and Flora is linked by Ovid with Mars, whose very birth she brought about.[41] Instead of Mars, Botticelli depicted Flora, the patroness of the Florentine spring—a figure who perhaps conveys even more forcibly the message of Time's Return in spring as a metaphor of the ever renewing rule of the Medici in her city.

The astrological allusions in the works of art thus far discussed have related to very general ideas: the notion of the eternal return of the zodiac cycle, particularly its beginning in spring (the *Primavera*), and the idea that the planets affect human destiny (*Venus and Mars*). However, there are many Renaissance paintings which refer specifically to the natal horoscopes of individuals or to other important dates in their lives, much as the cupola fresco of the Old Sacristy pictures the positions of the planets in the sky to commemorate the events of 6 July 1439. I have discussed one such horoscope, that of the rebirth of Florence (fig. 7), which may be taken as an example to show the features of the horoscope considered important in the Renaissance. This horoscope (or chart, as it may be called) should be read in comparison with the archetypal zodiac (fig. 6); however, it is drawn according to Renaissance practice in a square (hence the term "angle" for the cardinal points of the chart), rather than the circle used today, in which each triangular segment of the Renaissance diagram is rendered as a pie-shaped slice of the celestial wheel. It is a diagram of the heavens in which the positions of the zodiac

[40] Dempsey, pp. 254, 266-67, n. 64, notes that in an "eccentric reversal" the picture moves from right to left and that there is an analogy between

this direction and the sequence of the zodiac signs.
[41] For the laurel of Mars, see *Fasti*, III, 135-44. For the birth of Mars, see *Fasti*, V, 223-60.

signs and the celestial bodies are determined by the place (Florence) and time (5 April 802, at 4:16 a.m.). In this or any horoscope, a frame of reference is established by the two most significant angles of the chart. The first of these is the ascendant, which is marked by the sign and degree of the zodiac rising in the east. In this case, the ascendant is 2° Aries 53', indicated by the glyph for Aries (♈) at the left edge of the chart. The second important point is the medium coeli, or mid-heaven. It is the culminating angle of the horoscope, located approximately ninety degrees above the ascendant at the top of the chart.[42] In this case, the mid-heaven is 1° Capricorn 28' (♑). The plane of the ascendant-descendant forms the east-west axis of the horoscope coordinate system, and the plane of the lower-heaven and mid-heaven forms its north-south axis. The quadrants formed by these angles are trisected to form the twelve houses of the horoscope, which are counted counterclockwise from the ascendant.[43] The cusps (imaginary lines forming the boundaries of the houses) and the planets are located against this zodiacal background by sign and degree. The astrologer notes these locations and also considers the relative positions of the planets and house cusps to one another in degrees of zodiacal longitude. These angular distances are called the aspects of the horoscope.[44]

To the Renaissance astrologer, following antique practice, the first consideration in interpreting a horoscope (be it that of a person, a city, or a building) would have been the signs marking the ascendant and the mid-heaven, which were considered the two points of greatest power in the chart.[45] The sign on the ascendant was thought to signify the individual's life as a whole, and the planet ruling the sign on the ascendant was considered the most important lord, or ruler, of the entire horoscope.[46] In the horoscope for the rebirth of Florence, for example, the ascendant is Aries and the "lord of the chart" is Mars, ruler of Aries, which, because it was "in domicile" (in the first house, ruled by Aries in the archetypal zodiac) would have been considered especially power-

[42] Technically, the mid-heaven is the upper point of intersection of an imaginary circle passing through the observer's zenith and the center of the earth with the plane of the ecliptic.

[43] In the archetypal zodiac (fig. 6), the first house corresponds with Aries, the second with Taurus, etc. (As it happens, the horoscope of the rebirth of Florence has Aries in the ascendant, and thus its house and sign positions correspond approximately with those of the archetypal chart.) As the earth turns on its axis the houses progress through the zodiac at the rate of approximately one sign every two hours. The luminaries and planets spend from two and one-half days (moon) to two and one-half years (Saturn) in each sign. By noting the contacts between the advancing houses and the planets, which also move counterclockwise, the astrologer makes predictions about the individual's future.

[44] The major aspects are described in these terms: geometric figures inscribed within the zodiac circle indicate trine, quartile, and sextile aspects, while

diameters of the circle indicate opposition. A conjunction occurs when two or more planets are in the same degree of the zodiac or within orb (an arc of 6° to 10°). In general, aspects are considered effective within orb, depending on the planet and aspect in question.

[45] Ancient authorities stress the importance of these points: see Ptolemy, *Tetrabiblos*, III, 3; Manilius, *Astronomica*, 2, 788-840; and Maternus, *Mathesis*, II, XIX. For the primacy of the ascendant and the mid-heaven in the Renaissance, see astrological manuals such as J. Schöner, *Opusculum Astrologicum* . . . , Nuremberg, 1539, canons XXXIX and XLI; Schöner, bk. II, pp. 113-14; and Giuntini, 1573, f. 13v-14r.

[46] On the ruler of the chart, see Maternus, *Mathesis*, IV, XIX, who explains the various ways of determining this planet in antique practice. In the Renaissance, the ruler of the ascendant sign seems to have been preferred as the lord of the chart (see Schöner, bk. III, chap. 6; Giuntini, 1573, f. 13v-14r).

ful. The other planets in the first house—the sun, moon, and Jupiter—would also have been considered particularly influential in the interpretation of this chart. The sign on the mid-heaven (in this case, Capricorn) was thought to signify the individual's career, public life, and honors, while the planet ruling that sign (in this case, Saturn) was termed the "lord of the mid-heaven."

Because of this emphasis on the ascendant, the sign occupying that position in the horoscope was considered by ancient and Renaissance astrologers to be the individual's personal zodiac sign rather than, as today, the sign in which the sun was located at his birth. (In some cases, as in the horoscope of the rebirth of Florence and others we shall be considering, the "sun sign" and the ascendant are the same.) Thus, in antiquity and in the Renaissance, when a ruler wished to enhance his image by allusion to his "stars," the ascendant sign was often chosen as a personal device. The most conspicuous example in antiquity is Augustus, who adopted his ascendant Capricorn, although he was born on 23 September, when the sun was in Libra.[47] Thus, Capricorn appears with the Augustan emblems of Fortuna and Imperium—the tiller, the globe, and the cornucopia—on Augustan coins (pl. 134); and, in the *Gemma Augustea*, it is placed as a celestial emblem next to the head of Augustus as the Olympian Jupiter (pl. 133).[48] In the Renaissance this Augustan practice was followed by popes and princes alike. For example, Clement VII used his ascendant sign of Leo, rather than Gemini, the sign the sun occupied at his birth.[49] This preference is seen in the woodcut frontispiece to Sigismondo Fanti's *Triompho di Fortuna*, dedicated to Clement in 1526 (pl. 136).[50] This elaborate astrological allegory, based on a drawing by Peruzzi, shows the pope between Virtus and Voluptas; he is seated on a celestial globe being carried by Atlas and turned by Bona Fortuna so that the zodiac signs appear in counterclockwise sequence from the lower right and the sign of Leo is located at the summit just under the seated pope. Later, Paul III adopted his ascendant Aquarius as an *impresa*. The sign appears on his

[47] For Augustus' birth when the sun was in Libra, see Suetonius, *Lives*, II, V, 1; and Manilius, *Astronomica*, 4, 547-53. For Augustus' adoption of Capricorn as his sign, see Suetonius, II, XCIV, 12: "Tantam mox fiduciam fati Augustus habuit, ut thema suum vulgaverit nummumque argenteum nota sideris Capricorni, quo natus est, percusserit." (From that time on Augustus had such faith in his destiny, that he made his horoscope public and issued a silver coin stamped with the constellation Capricorn, under which he was born.) See also Manilius, *Astronomica*, 2, 507-10: "Capricorn on the other hand turns his gaze upon himself (what greater sign can he ever marvel at, since it was he that shone propitiously upon Augustus' birth?)." Suetonius (II, XCIV, 5) also relates a story about Augustus' birth that would seem to confirm the reason for Augustus' choice of the Capricorn for his emblem of fortune: "Publius Nigidius Figulus the astrologer, hearing *at what hour* the child had been delivered, cried out: 'The ruler of the world

is now born' " (italics mine). The positions of the sun (in Libra) and the planets in the zodiac signs would obtain at any hour of the day on which Augustus was born, but it is the ascendant, which changes approximately every two hours, that establishes the relationship between the signs and the houses of the chart, making it possible for an astrologer to erect a horoscope. For a discussion of Augustus and the symbolism of Capricorn (in which, however, the astrological significance of the Capricorn ascendant is not interpreted correctly), see Dwyer, pp. 59-67.

[48] Dwyer, pp. 65-66.

[49] Gaurico, bk. II, f. 20r-20v, publishes a horoscope for Clement (born 26 May 1478) with the ascendant at 29° Leo; and Giuntini, 1581, I, p. 120, gives the ascendant as 17° Leo.

[50] See R. Eisler, "The Frontispiece to Sigismondo Fanti's *Triompho di Fortuna*," *JWCI*, 10, 1947, pp. 155-59; and on Peruzzi's drawing for it see Frommel, cat. 100, pl. LXXVa.

papal medals, as well as in Perino del Vaga's zodiacal lunette in the Vatican logge, where a large Water Bearer dominates the composition (pl. 137).[51] Among secular rulers, Isabella d'Este, whose interest in astrology is well known, adopted her ascendant Sagittarius—ruler of the ninth house, associated with wisdom—as a personal device. It appears with a star and a winged Astrology (based on Mantegna's tarot-card figure) on her medal of 1498 by Gian Cristoforo Romano (pl. 135).[52] Finally, as will be shown in chapter 11, both Duke Cosimo de' Medici and his son Francesco made extensive use of their ascendant signs of Capricorn and Aries in their propaganda of rule.

Long before Cosimo and Francesco made Capricorn and Aries synonymous with the notion of a Medici rule predestined in the stars, family members had used horoscopic imagery in their art. However, prior to the overt astrological images of Pope Leo's art, such allusions in Medici art were covert. The use of astrology as propaganda of absolute rule belongs to the Cinquecento—to Leo's papacy and, later, to the Medici *principato*. In the republican Florence of Cosimo Pater Patriae and Piero di Cosimo, on the other hand, the Old Sacristy cupola was the only overtly astrological work commissioned by the Medici; and in Lorenzo's time only a few covert allusions to features of his natal horoscope give evidence of the preoccupation with astrology in his circle.

No correct horoscope for Lorenzo was published in the Renaissance.[53] However, the hour of his birth necessary for the erection of a chart is given by Scipione Ammirato: "Nacque Lorenzo in calende di Gennaio, dell' an. 1449 alle 15 hore" (Lorenzo was born on the calends of January in 1449 at 15 hours).[54] Translating this time into modern clock time beginning at midnight (rather than time as it was reckoned in Renaissance Florence, when the hours were counted from sunset), we arrive at a birthtime of 7:30 a.m. In the horoscope based on this time for Florence (fig. 8), the sun (☉) and the ascendant are both in Capricorn (♑), making this sign of extreme importance for Lorenzo. Saturn, ruler of Capricorn, would then be the lord of the ascendant. The mid-heaven of the chart is marked by Scorpio (♏); Mars, ruler of that sign, would then be the lord of the mid-heaven.

While there is no corroborating evidence for Lorenzo's time of birth, and what follows must remain speculative, there are, in fact, several instances of imagery relating to Mars and Capricorn in Lorenzo's art. The first of these is the helmet for his *giostra* of 1469. The object does not survive, but it is described by Pulci:[55]

[51] B. F. Davidson, "Pope Paul III's Additions to Raphael's Logge: His *Imprese* in the Logge," *Art Bull.*, 61, 1979, pp. 398-401. For the horoscope of Paul III (born 28 February 1468), in which the ascendant is at 24° Aquarius 48′, see Gaurico, bk. II, f. 21r.

[52] For Isabella and astrology, see Lehmann, pp. 138-39; for the medal, which is inscribed BENE MERENTIVM ERGO, see Hill, no. 221. I am grateful to Peter Porçal, who has found documentation on Isabella's birthtime, for confirming that Sagittarius is the ascendant in her chart. For the tarot card, see Hind, IV, pl. 348 (series C29).

[53] The horoscope in Giuntini, 1581, I, p. 159, is based on an erroneous birthdate of 6 August 1448. All sources are in agreement as to the January 1 date of Lorenzo's birth; for his baptism on 6 January, see chap. 1, n. 18.

[54] S. Ammirato, *Opusculi*, Florence, 1642 ("Ritratti d'huomini illustri di Casa Medici," p. 33). I owe this reference to Claudia Rousseau. Ammirato goes on to note that his citation of the year and day is based on the reckoning of the church year from 1 January (". . . percio'che noi computiamo l'anno secondo l'uso della Chiesa dal primo Gennaio").

[55] Pulci, stanza XXXI.

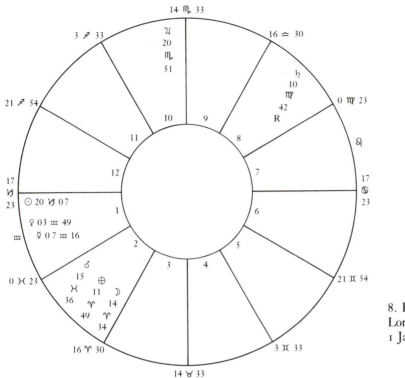

8. Horoscope of
Lorenzo il Magnifico,
1 January 1449, 7:30 a.m.

L'Aquila rossa insu l'elmetto un Marte
Sopra sua stella fè d'argento e d'oro.

He made a Mars on top of the helmet and a red eagle above his star in silver
and gold.

Moreover, a Florentine engraving which has been dated about 1470 shows a helmet
which matches Pulci's description rather closely (pl. 138).[56] The imagery is clearly astrological, and the design of the helmet must have related to Lorenzo's own horoscope.
In particular, the Capricorn head at the back of the helmet refers to the sun and ascendant sign of his chart, and the combination of Mars and the eagle at the top may
allude to an important conjunction in it. Mars (as ruler of Scorpio) is lord of the mid-
heaven, and Jupiter, whose traditional symbol is the eagle, is conjunct to the mid-heaven
at 20° Scorpio 51'. This planet, the so-called greater benefic, would have been seen to
exert a powerful and positive influence at the culmination of Lorenzo's chart.

A more monumental work which alludes to a feature of Lorenzo's horoscope is Signorelli's *Realm of Pan* (pl. 67), one of the most important mythological pictures commissioned by Lorenzo. As I have noted, this painting remains to be fully interpreted, but
it is surely an occult work in which themes of the Cosmos, Time, and Nature allude to
Lorenzo's destiny. Pan, with his lunar diadem and starry cloak, is characterized as

[56] Hind, I, pt. I, p. 47, no. A.I.55.

Servius' cosmic god; this depiction, the ancient association of the god with the zodiac,[57] and his specific connection with Capricorn, suggest that Pan was intended to refer to the Capricorn ascendant and sun of Lorenzo's horoscope.[58] For according to mythographers such as Hyginius, Pan was put into the heavens by Jupiter and became the constellation of Capricorn.[59] Moreover, the legend of Pan's transformation into a celestial sea-goat had been embellished with rulership associations,[60] which are compatible with the notion of the benign rule of Pan Medicus (Lorenzo) in Florence. Indeed, in later Medici art (to which we occasionally must have recourse in order to interpret their earlier, more covert, symbolism), Pan and Capricorn were programmatically juxtaposed in allusion to the Capricorn ascendant of Duke Cosimo's horoscope. In Tribolo's design for a Grotto of Pan (pl. 66), a statue of the god is seated on crossed *broncone* in a niche above a large relief panel of Capricorn. However, in the more subtle treatment of the theme for Lorenzo, the zodiacal animal is not depicted; rather, Pan Medicus *is* Capricorn, the allusion to the immortality of the god in the heavens being indicated by the stars on his cloak, which are arranged in a recognizable approximation of the triangular constellation—almost as a label identifying the cosmic god with the astrological destiny of Lorenzo himself.

We may now return once more to the portico frieze at Poggio a Caiano (pl. 49), which I have discussed as an allegory of Laurentian rule. While it should be clear that its visual language precludes the use of zodiac signs or the like, its cosmic frame of reference is announced in the first panel, where the nude youth measures the heavens with his armillary sphere and compass, and in the last panel Apollo-Lorenzo ascends to the heavens. Within this context, Janus, god of January and of beginnings, may allude to Lorenzo's birthday on 1 January,[61] and the scene of Sol-Apollo at dawn with which the frieze concludes surely alludes to the rising sun of Lorenzo's own horoscope. But more important is Mars, who occupies the very center of the frieze over the doorway to Lorenzo's villa. I have identified him as the god of the Medici *primavera*, as the personification of Lorenzo's motto LE TEMPS REVIENT—the theme which animates the entire frieze—and as alluding to Lorenzo as ruler of Florence. But Mars may make further allusion to the theme of the Medici and Florence in the frieze. As I have shown, Mars was the original patron of Florence by virtue of his rulership of Aries, sign of the birth and rebirth of the city. Thus, Mars refers to the *topos* of the astrological destiny of

[57] Chastel, 1961, pp. 230-31, emphasizes the cosmic character of Signorelli's figure, connecting Pan as a god of time with an ancient gem in which the god is encircled by the signs of the zodiac (his fig. 3). For Servius, see chap. 3, "The Frieze and Laurentian Imagery."

[58] It is tempting to read other horoscopic allusions in the figures around Pan (Venus?). However, the moon in the sky behind the god, in combination with the rays of the sun coming from the right, establish the time of day as sunset, a time which enhances the atmosphere of Saturnian melancholy in the painting but which is hardly compatible with the sunrise time of Lorenzo's birth.

[59] See Hyginus, *Fabulae*, 196; and *Poetica Astronomica*, II, 28, for the story of the gods who changed themselves into animals (which subsequently became constellations) in order to escape from the monster Typhon.

[60] For example, the account of the Typhonomachy by the Augustan astrologer Publius Nigidius Figulus, in which Pan's defeat of Typhon is presented as saving the world from tyranny (discussed by Dwyer, pp. 66-67).

[61] McKillop, 1974, p. 76, noted the allusion made by Janus to Lorenzo's birthday.

Florence. Moreover, Mars also rules Scorpio, sign of the mid-heaven of Lorenzo's own horoscope; so the planet would have been seen to govern Lorenzo's career and public life—or his rulership. Thus, Mars suggests a predestined connection between Lorenzo and his city: placed at the exact midpoint of the frieze (like the mid-heaven of a horoscope), he symbolizes both Lorenzo's own destiny as ruler of Florence and the rebirth of the city itself under his auspicious stars.

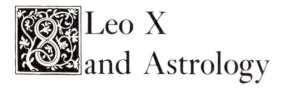

Leo X and Astrology

LIBRA, LEO, SOL-APOLLO, AND HERCULES

When Lorenzo il Magnifico's son, Cardinal Giovanni de' Medici, was still a youth, Ficino predicted on the basis of his horoscope that he would become pope.[1] Later, in 1513, when Giovanni was elevated to the papacy as Leo X, astrology became a major influence in the affairs of his court. We have already seen evidence of Leo's belief in fortune and the magic of numbers: he chose as his *impresa* Lorenzo's GLOVIS, with its allusion to the turn of the Wheel of Fortune, and he was obsessed with the power of the number eleven, which marked the date of his birth and of his elevation to the papacy. Leo was also a believer in the influence of the stars, and his entourage, like that of other Renaissance princes, included astrologers such as Valeriano who drew up horoscopes, made prognostications based on them, and presumably served as advisers to the papal iconographers.[2]

Leo's natal horoscope is known from a number of sixteenth-century publications, among them Francesco Giuntini's *Speculum astrologiae* of 1581 (fig. 9).[3] Giuntini's chart may also be erected in the more familiar circular format (fig. 10).[4] It will be noted that in the center of the chart, Giuntini gives the time of Leo's birth in astronomical time

[1] Giovio, 1551, bk. III, p. 152: "Dicevasi anchora che Marsilio Ficino, il quale era stato astrologo di grande autorità, per sua felice et real natività, essendo egli fanciullo, ne posto in ordini sacri, gli haveva promesso il papato." See D. C. Allen, p. 51, on a similar prediction by Gaurico in 1493.

[2] See Roscoe-Bossi, V, pp. 279-83, for the pontifical letter creating a professorship at the Sapienza for "Magister Valerianus . . . in Astrologia." On Cardinal Giovanni's friendship with Valeriano from 1509, see Roscoe-Bossi, X, pp. 76-77. For general remarks on Leo and astrology, see Thorndike, V, pp. 252-53. For an elaborate prognosti-

cation relating to the year 1515 for Leo, see Iacobus Cracoviensis, *Natalis coeli constitutio Leonis X*, Lucca, Bibl. Statale MS 1473 (noted by Thorndike, V, p. 253; and Zambelli, no. 3.4.1., p. 378).

[3] Giuntini, 1581, I, p. 120.

[4] This chart is based on Giuntini's ascendant of 20° Sagittarius 40', which gives a birthtime of fourteen minutes later than that reached by translating the astronomical time of Giuntini's citation into conventional time. This insignificant difference may be the result of Giuntini's rectification of the chart.

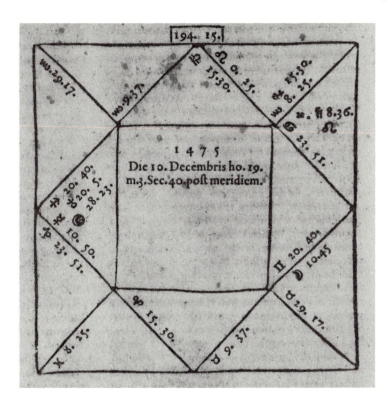

9. Horoscope of Leo X,
10 [*sic*] December 1475
(after Giuntini, 1581)

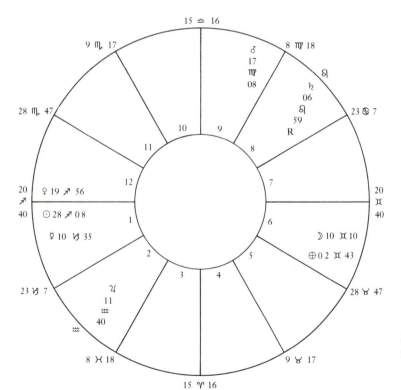

10. Horoscope of Leo X,
11 December 1475, 7:17 a.m.

(which begins at noon) as "Die 10. Decembris ho. 19. m. 3. Sec. 40. post meridiem," which is translatable into conventional time as 11 December at 7:03 a.m.[5] Turning to the details of the horoscope: Sagittarius (♐) is the ascendant, the sun (☉) and Venus (♀) are rising in conjunction in the first house near the ascendant, and the mid-heaven is marked by Libra (♎). As ruler of Sagittarius, Jupiter is lord of the ascendant and of the chart. According to the complex traditions of astrological interpretation developed in antiquity and elaborated in the Renaissance, all these positions, especially the features of the eastern angle of the horoscope, would have been viewed as most auspicious.[6] And, as we shall see, these salient features of Leo's natal horoscope were the basis for the astrological imagery in his art.

But even before such images occurred in his own art, Leo was associated with astrological imagery in laudatory works connected with his elevation to the papacy. Ferreri's poem on Leo's election, resorting to astrological predestination, suggests that the event was "written in the stars." In this, he was following a papal tradition that had been exemplified most recently in the art of Leo's predecessor, Julius II. The day of Julius' election (31 October 1503) is symbolized in the Stanza della Segnatura, where the positions of the constellations in Raphael's *Astronomy with the Celestial Globe* are those of the autumn sky (pl. 140).[7] Ferreri's poem opens with a visionary, astrological setting, which is the poetic equivalent of Raphael's globe:[8]

> Alta Dionaei repetebant aequora pisces
> Frontibus occiduis, ariesque Ammonius ardor

[5] Giuntini's time of birth for Leo is approximated in the other extant charts, such as two published by Gaurico, bk. II, f. 18r-18v., in which the time is given according to Florentine reckoning (from sunset) as 14:35 and 14:37, which are equal to 6:55 and 6:57 a.m., modern clock time. It should be noted that all the published charts are inconsistent with Leo's baptismal record. See Archivio dell'Opera del Duomo, *Libri dei battezzati in Firenze, 1473-1481*, f. 35r: "Lunedì addì 11 di dicembre 1475. Giovanni Damasco et Romolo di Lorenzo di Piero de' Medici, popolo di Santo Lorenzo, nacque addì 11 hore 13—battezzato addì 11." If this time was reckoned from sunset, it equals 5:20 a.m., or one hour forty minutes earlier than the time given in Giuntini's chart. Two explanations may be offered to explain this inconsistency. The first is that the time was rectified by astrologers in order to give the Medici child the auspicious birth at sunrise which is recorded in all the extant charts and which is stated elsewhere by Giuntini, 1581, II, p. 1166: "Dies 11 [December] Leo Pontifex maximus X Florentinus Medices, natus anno 1475 in ortu Solis." The second possibility (which I owe to Claudia Rousseau) is that the birthtime is cited in sidereal time, reflecting the presence at the Medici birth of astrologers, who translated the hour of the child's birth (19 h., 3., 40 s.) into sidereal time ("hore 13").

[6] This is not the place to discuss interpretations which may or may not have been made by Leo's astrologers. However, the sun rising in conjunction with Venus (which, at 1° from the ascendant, would have been regarded as in the first house) at the eastern angle of the chart in the fire sign of Sagittarius would have been regarded as one of the most positive features of the chart, as would the placement of Jupiter, benefic planet of good fortune, in the second house, traditionally related to money.

[7] Rash-Fabbri, pp. 98-100. Later popes also celebrated their elevations in terms of astrological imagery. See Lechner, pp. 101-8, for Andrea Sacchi's *Divina Sapienza* (Palazzo Barberini), commissioned by Urban VIII to celebrate his elevation on 6 August 1623.

[8] Ferreri, p. 271. In the presentation copy of Ferreri's poem (BNF, Banco rari 158, f. 2v), the lines quoted are marked in the marginal index "Martius mensis." This volume is dated, at the end of the poem, "XV cal: Aprilis M.D. XIII." However, as Shearman, 1972, p. 1, n. 2, has

Signiferae princeps, primusque auriga coronae
Limen Apollineis referans ingressibus amplo
Aurigerum vellus procul ostentabat olympo;
Pleiadum coetus vicinos ibat in ortus:
Omneque sub verno nemus instaurabat honore.
Dormio. Me variis tunc ardua somnia versant
Subter imaginibus. . . .

Venusian fish were falling back upon the high seas with westerly rolls; and Aries the Jupiterian, glowing prince of the zodiac and first charioteer crossing again the crown's starting point with Apollonian steps, was exhibiting from afar the Golden Fleece to mighty Olympus. The group of the Pleiades was rising nearby and renewing every grove with springtime honor. I sleep. The deep dreams come hovering over me in the shape of varied images. . . .

Ferreri's imagery is very exact (more so than Raphael's): in a few lines he describes not only the day but the hour of Leo's election on 11 March at about 8:00 a.m.[9] The first line refers to Pisces as the Fish of Dione—or Venus, the planet which in astrological tradition is "exalted" in Pisces.[10] The poet then evokes Jupiter and the sun as in Aries (the Golden Fleece, or the Ram), and finally the rising of the Pleiades. Referring to a horoscope erected for Leo's election time (fig. 11), we find that Pisces (♓) has risen and that an extraordinary group of planets have just risen in Aries (♈) and are rising in Taurus (♉), the sign on the ascendant: the sun (☉) is in the first degree of Aries; Jupiter (♃) is also in Aries; Venus (♀), Mars (♂), and the moon (☽) are in conjunction in Taurus.

Ferreri, of course, selected the more auspicious features of Leo's election horoscope, emphasizing the planets, signs, and stars that were rising in the eastern sky on that morning. The sun and the benefic Jupiter were in Aries, which is not only the first sign of the zodiacal year, the sign of the vernal equinox, and the sign of the sun's exaltation but the sign of the birth of Florence and the Florentine New Year—surely good omens for a Medici pope. In addition to this array, the star cluster of the Pleiades, an ancient

---

pointed out, the poem can hardly have been completed within a week of Leo's elevation. It was published at Lyon, 10 September 1513 ("decimo Cal: sete[n]bres MD.XIII").

[9] For an account of Leo's election, see Pastor, VII, pp. 25-26. Contemporary reports of the event give the hour reckoned from sunset. See Penni, p. 192: "La matina sequente, ed hore XIV [8:00 a.m., or 14 hours after the preceding sunset at approximately 6:00 p.m.] rotta la finestra del conclava, quale era murata. . . ." The news reached Florence the same evening, "a ora due" [8:00 p.m.], according to Landucci, p. 336. See also Sanuto, XVI, p. 35, for the letter written by the Dieci in Florence, dated "11 Martii, hora quarta [10:00

p.m.], sending the news to Venice.

[10] Each planet is thought to be exalted (and its influence benign) in a particular zodiac sign and thought to be "in detriment" (with unfortunate influence) in the opposite sign, as follows: sun (Aries-Libra), moon (Taurus-Scorpio), Mercury (Aquarius-Leo), Venus (Pisces-Virgo), Mars (Capricorn-Cancer), Jupiter (Cancer-Capricorn), and Saturn (Libra-Aries). The association of Pisces with Venus is based on the myth that Venus and Cupid, fleeing the monster Typhon, changed themselves into the fishes that became the constellation (Hyginius, *Poetica Astronomica*, II, 30). Venus and Cupid stand for Pisces on the horoscope ceiling of Agostino Chigi (Saxl, p. 27; my fig. 13).

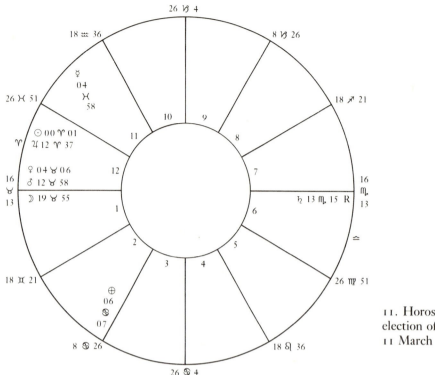

11. Horoscope of the
election of Leo X, Rome,
11 March 1513, 8:00 a.m.

celestial metaphor for spring, was rising at 22° Taurus. The poet then evokes the renewal of spring on earth, joining the venerable Medicean metaphor of Time's Return in spring with the imagery of the heavens to celebrate the advent of the new Medici pope.

The theme of Leo's exalted astrological destiny, adumbrated in Ferreri's poem, was celebrated in Leo's personal imagery and art. Three features of the pope's natal horoscope were incorporated into his imagery to embellish the notion of an astrologically predetermined papacy: the mid-heaven in Libra, the rising sun in the ascendant Sagittarius, and Jupiter, lord of the ascendant. Leaving Jupiter for discussion in connection with Leo's horoscopic ceiling in the Sala dei Pontefici, we may consider the Libran and solar imagery in Leo's art.

The sign of Libra at the mid-heaven in the horoscope of a ruler would have been regarded as auspicious, for Libra's illustrious astrological tradition specifically related it to rulership, which is the province of the tenth house.[11] As the sign of the autumnal equinox, Libra divides the zodiac into halves, balanced in equilibrium. Libra thus came to be associated with other polarities (day-night, male-female) and with the harmonious balance of opposites. As the sign of the seventh house of the zodiac (thought to influence partnership and union), Libra is ruled by Venus, planet of love and peace, and the sign was believed to bring reconciliation and concord. Finally, Libra is symbolized by the balance, or scales, which was read as a symbol of justice.[12]

[11] Soldati, pp. 283-84. On the traditions of Libra, see R. H. Allen, pp. 269-72.

[12] On Libra and justice, see, for example, Manilius, *Astronomica*, 4, 547-51: "When Autumn's

The association of Libra with balance, harmony, reconciliation, and justice led to its becoming an emblem of rule in ancient Rome. It was linked with the very destiny of Italy, for according to the tradition in which the signs of the zodiac were connected with places (Aries-Florence, Leo-Rome, etc.), Libra was assigned to Italy.[13] Moreover, it had imperial associations. Libra was the sun sign of Augustus, the peacemaker, whose apotheosis Virgil described in the *Georgics* as the celestial sign itself: ". . . or whether thou [Augustus] add thyself as a new star to the lingering months, where, between the Virgin and the grasping claws, a space is opening (lo! for thee even now the blazing Scorpion draws in his arms, and has left more than a due share of the heaven!)."[14] These lines are illustrated in the frontispiece to the Brant edition of the *Georgics*, in which the signs of Virgo and Scorpio flank a crown signifying Augustus-Libra in the sky (pl. 102).

Not only was Libra thus ideally suited to be a symbol of Leo's rule of justice and peace, but the sign had been identified since antiquity with the yoke—which was, of course, the *corpo* of Leo's *impresa*. Identified as such by Ptolemy and called "the celestial yoke" by Latin writers, Libra was seen to yoke the halves of the zodiac, to yoke night and day, and (as zodiacal ruler of Italy) to yoke Italian territories.[15] All this lore was current in the Renaissance, the last notion, in particular, being used by the Medici in the mid-sixteenth century as an image of political dominion. A woodcut of 1567 (which also appears in various other books printed by Torrentino) shows the ducal *stemma* and the traditional figure of Justice with her sword and scales (pl. 139).[16] The scales signify Libra, zodiacal ruler of Italy, and they function like a yoke, binding together Florence and Rome—symbolized by the Ram (Aries) and the Lion (Leo).

We cannot be certain that figures of Justice in Leo's art were more than personifications of a ruler's virtue, but two examples suggest that they were also intended to signify his Libran mid-heaven. Penni describes a painting of "la dea della Iustitia, con la bilancia in mano, senza spada" (the goddess Justice, with the scales, but without sword), in the arch of the papal mint in Leo's Lateran *possesso*.[17] In the context of a decoration which featured a Wheel of Fortune with Leo at the summit, pictures of Leonine events occurring on his lucky day, and a picture of astrologers, this Justice without the sword must have read as a Libran image. A medal struck after Leo's death is even more explicit (pl. 141).[18] Leo's rule is characterized by Peace, Justice, and Abundance, who, in addition to their traditional attributes, display Medici devices. Peace burns arms and holds the *diamante* with its three feathers signifying virtue; Abundance holds a cornucopia and a

Claws [Scorpio] begin to rise, blessed is he that is born under the equilibrium of the Balance. As judge he will set up scales weighted with life and death; he will impose the weight of his authority upon the world and make laws."

[13] Manilius, *Astronomica*, 4, 773-77: "Italy belongs to the Balance, her rightful sign: beneath it Rome and her sovereignty of the world were founded, Rome, which controls the issue of events, exalting and depressing nations placed in the scales: beneath this sign was born the emperor."

[14] *Georgics*, I, 32-35.

[15] Ptolemy, *Tetrabiblos*, I, 19, 2; IV, 4, 183, refers to Libra as the yoke (*zugon*). Manilius, *Astronomica*, 1, 610-12; 3, 443-47, calls Libra *jugum* and characterizes it as the "sign which forces day and darkness to shoulder the same yoke."

[16] De Ruberti, dedication page. See also Pausanias, *Veteri Graeciae descriptio*, Florence: Torrentino, 1551, f. 1r.

[17] Penni, p. 229.

[18] Hill, no. 886. It is inscribed MEMORIE OPTIM PON.

palla; and Justice holds the scales and, instead of the sword, Leo's Libran yoke of just and peaceful rule.[19] The inscription FIAT PAX IN VIRTVTE TVA (May there be peace in your virtue) alludes to the theme of the rewards of virtue that is familiar in other Leonine art.

The rising sun in the ascendant Sagittarius in Leo's horoscope may have encouraged his being associated with solar imagery—with Sol-Apollo and with the sign of Leo, zodiacal house of the sun. In fact, much Apollonian imagery in Leo's art has astrological overtones. In Gambello's medal, for example, Apollo-Leo holds up a blazing sun (pl. 116). Alluding to Apollo as an *exemplum virtutis*, he speaks the words of the inscription VIRTVTE TVA LVX MEA IN TE (Your light lies in virtue, my light in you). In Giovanni da Udine's tapestry design for the Sala di Costantino, the symbols for the sun and the sign of Leo are conflated in a device over Apollo-Leo's head (pl. 82). Moreover, the notion of Leo as "sun" pope was acted out in an explicitly celestial setting in the Capitoline pageant of 1513, the imagery of which was seminal for Leo's propaganda. There, the pope's Roman mother, Clarice Orsini, was personified in a tableau of the unity of Florence and Rome. This theme was symbolized by the usual river gods, the Tiber and the Arno, but also by Leo's yoke, which united Romulus and Remus with the constellation of Ursa Major ("la celeste Orsa"). In her speech, Clarice styled herself Latona, mother of a New Apollo:[20]

> Io son hora dicesa dal stellante cielo, da quella parte più sublime dove l'Orsa sostene il polo. . . . La mia Roma a Leone solo, el quale in questo ventre portai et come un'altra Latona, producendo un nuovo sole al mondo, ho discacciate le tenebre.

> I have just now come down from the starry sky, from that more sublime region where the Bear upholds the [North] Pole. . . . My Rome is Leo's alone, whom I bore in this womb; and as another Latona, bringing a new light into the world, I set the darkness to flight.

The image of the celestial Orsa is, of course, a pun on the name Orsini. The conceit also occurs in a poem of 1515 by Antonius Nerlius lauding the ancestry of Lorenzo the younger:[21]

> Laurus ut Vrsina est merito de prole creatus:
>   De Medica est merito sic quoque gente satus.
> Altera coelesti nomen deducit ab Vrsa,
>   Altera phoebea nomen ab arte trahit.

> As the Laurel [Lorenzo] was justly created from Ursine stock, so he is also deservedly begotten from the Medici. One derives its name from the celestial Bear, the other takes its name from the Phoeban art [of healing].

The rising sun in Sagittarius in Leo's horoscope may also have influenced his choice

---

[19] The Justice is a variant on the usual figure with sword and scales, which appears, for example, on medals made for Julius II (Rash-Fabbri, p. 113, fig. 8).

[20] Palliolo, p. 56.

[21] *Lauretum*, p. 5.

of a papal name.[22] There were, of course, a number of other felicitous associations that would have made the name appealing: the lion's connection with Florence, as the Marzocco; the lion's association with Rome, as its zodiacal ruler, and with the Vatican, known as the *città leonina*; and the lion's identification with virtue, especially magnanimity. However, the sign of Leo is the house of the pope's rising sun, and no other zodiac sign had a greater mystique of power associated with it.[23] Moreover, when Leo's intimate, Zanobi Acciaioli, celebrated his papacy in a poem of 1513, he made a round of puns on Leo, the sun, the house of the sun, and wisdom (alluding to the ninth house, ruled by Sagittarius, sign of the sun in Leo's chart), which leaves no doubt that the name had astrological associations for Leo's circle:[24]

> Sol, LEO noster, domus anne Solis?
>   Ipse Sol idem, domus atque Solis;
> Quem sub arcano Sophia nitentem
>   Pectore gestat.

> Are you the Sun, our Leo, or the house of the Sun? Yourself the very Sun, and also the house of the Sun, which, as it shines, Wisdom carries secretly within her breast.

The heraldic lion alluding to the papal name is ubiquitous in Leo's art (cf. pls. 30-31); however, the celestial lion also made several appearances in the year of Leo's elevation. Gambello's medal shows Apollo-Leo holding up the sun directly over a lion (pl. 116); and in the Lateran *possesso* there was a painting on the arch of Agostino Chigi (himself a devotee of astrology) showing Virtue placing the sign of Leo into its place in the zodiac band between Cancer and Virgo. As Penni describes it,[25]

> Quella che era virtù era in loco più elevato che queste altre, et havea un leone che lo porgea nel zodiaco alla vergine, e lei infra se el cancro lo metteva,

[22] Langedijk, p. 133, n. 49, suggests that Leo's choice of the name was due to his having been born under the sign of Leo. This is incorrect; moreover, this sign is insignificant in Leo's horoscope and is, in fact, an intercepted sign (one not marking a house cusp).

[23] On the "Sole in Leone" and hermetic tradition in Florence, see Dezzi Bardeschi, pp. 52-57. For an example close to the Medici, see Ficino's discussion of Aries, sign of the sun's exaltation, and Leo, its house, in *De sole*, tr. A. Fallico and H. Shapiro, *Renaissance Philosophy* I, *The Italian Philosophers*, New York, 1967, p. 121. Ficino characterizes Aries as the "prince of constellations," and "the constellation which is the house of the Sun, that is, Leo, is the heart of the constellations and controls the heart of all living things." For the traditions of Leo, see R. H. Allen, pp. 252-55.

[24] In Roscoe-Bossi, X, pp. 253-56. In the poet's marginal notes to his manuscript of this poem (Bib. Marucelliana, Misc. greca-latina italica MS A. 82,

f. 237r-239r) the following comment is appended to these lines: "Interrogationis occasio data est mihi quia astrologi dicunt Leonem esse domum Solis." (The opportunity for my question has been given to me because the astrologers tell me Leo is the house of the Sun.) The title of the poem alludes to the Leo-Apollo equation, as well as to Leo's favorite papal exemplar, Leo IV: ODE ZENOBII ACCIAIOLI, QUA LEO X LUMINARE MAIUS ECCLESIAE, SOLI SEU APOLLINI COMPARATUR, INVITATURQUE AD COLLIS QUIRINALIS ORNATUM: EXEMPLO LEONIS ILLIUS QUI PARTEM URBIS TRANSTYBERINAM DICI A SE LEONINAM VOLUIT (The ode of Zenobi Acciaioli, in which Leo X, a great luminary of the church, is compared to the Sun, or Apollo, and is summoned to adorn the Quirinal Hill after the example of that Leo who wished the trans-Tiber part of the city to be called Leonina after himself). On Acciaioli (1461-1519) and Leo, whose librarian he later became, see Roscoe-Bossi, IV, pp. 208-12.

[25] In Roscoe-Bossi, V, pp. 211-12.

vedevasi in questa zona gemini, el cancro, la vergine, et parte della libra, et questo leone portò dalla virtù alla vergine.

The figure of Virtue was in a higher position than the other figures, and she had a lion which she was handing to Virgo in the zodiac. And Virgo was placing it between herself and Cancer. And one could see in this zone Gemini, Cancer, Virgo, and part of Libra, and this lion offered by Virtue to Virgo.

The celestial lion, house of Leo's rising sun, is thus associated with the theme of his virtue, as in his medal. The conceit makes a bold parallel with Virgil's famous apotheosis of Augustus (quoted above), in which Augustus is lifted into the heavens as the newly created sign of Libra, literally becoming the sign in which the sun was located at his birth.

Later, the lion appears in Giulio Romano's *Leo X as Clement I with Moderatio and Comitas* (pl. 29), again in connection with papal virtue. Leo is seated under a *baldacchino* decorated with seven zodiac signs. These were not chosen at random, but are the signs beginning with the ascendant Taurus and reading to the descendant Scorpio in the horoscope of his election (fig. 11). The center sign of these seven is Leo, and it is placed directly over the pope's head. Just as Augustus is identified with his ascendant Capricorn next to his head in the *Gemma Augustea* (pl. 133), so Leo is associated here with the celestial lion, which stands for the auspicious rising sun of his horoscope.

Hercules is also presented in Leo's art in an astrological context. Raphael's tapestry border of *Hercules Holding the Celestial Globe with Fame* is a complex allegory of the triumph of Leonine *virtù* and the achievement of immortality (pl. 120). But its imagery is also astrological: not only does it feature the celestial globe, but in the original version of the work (preserved in the set of tapestries at Mantua), the feat of Hercules killing the centaur was represented below (pl. 144).[26] This scene alludes to Leo's ascendant, for according to the legend Sagittarius was the centaur Chiron, who was placed in the heavens by Jupiter.[27]

In astrological tradition, Sagittarius symbolizes wisdom, the province of the ninth house of the zodiac, which Sagittarius rules, and this theme is elaborated in the central scene of the tapestry. Holding the globe of Atlas, who sits below him, is the cosmic Hercules-Sol, an identification depending on the ancient equation between Hercules' twelve labors and the twelve signs of the zodiac through which the sun appears to travel each year.[28] This subject was represented in later Medici art, as in Vincenzo de' Rossi's design for *The Labors of Hercules-Sol* (pl. 143), a fountain in which the twelve labors refer to Duke Cosimo as Hercules-Sol.[29] In the tapestry, in contrast, the centaur stands for the entire cycle, highlighting Leo's special sign of Sagittarius.

[26] See chap. 6, n. 26.

[27] Hyginus, *Poetica Astronomica*, II, 38.

[28] For the globe as an emblem of Hercules' Divine Wisdom and its signs as his twelve labors, see Servius, I, p. 208; II, p. 62, commenting on *Aeneid* I, 745; VI, 395. For Renaissance opinion, see Cartari, 1581, pp. 291-92: "Macrobio nel primo di Sa-

turnali ma come ho già detto più volte di ch'egli intende per tutti gli altri Dei, così vuole intendere di Hercole ch'ei fa il Sole, e che i gloriosi suoi fatti, che sono dodici i più celebrati siano i dodici segni del Zodiaco che superate dal Sole perche scorre per quelli in tutto l'anno."

[29] H. Utz, "The *Labors of Hercules* and Other

The globe carried by Hercules-Sol is the celestial globe, which symbolizes the hero's knowledge of the heavens and is generally taken as an emblem of Divine Wisdom. Because of the association of Sagittarius with wisdom, the globe in depictions of this subject often features the sign of Sagittarius, as in Pietro da Cortona's ceiling fresco of 1642 in the Sala di Apollo, Palazzo Pitti.[30] However, the images on the globe could also be manipulated so that it featured a zodiac sign particularly meaningful to the patron of the work. In the drawing for Cosimo's fountain, for example, the sign prominent on the globe is Capricorn, which was the ascendant in his horoscope. Here, the sign of Leo at the center of the globe alludes to the house of Pope Leo's Sagittarian sun and thus to Leo himself.

The globe is fashioned into a celestial metaphor of Pope Leo's elevation and dominion (pl. 142). Its sign of Leo suggests that just as the celestial lion rules the heavens, so Leo-Hercules rules the earth, which is placed beneath his feet. The image is thus a visual pun playing on the name Leo: *Leo* is the name carried by the pope, the *insigne leonis* is worn by Hercules as an emblem of virtue, and the *signum leonis* is the zodiac sign. The latter two are, of course, the same, since the legendary origin of the constellation is the Nemean lion of Hercules' first labor. But this is not all: the stars on the globe are arranged so that they approximate the night sky at the time of Leo's election in March 1513. Toward midnight the constellations of Gemini, Cancer, Leo, and Virgo would have been visible above the horizon. The northern polar constellation Ursa Major lies above Leo, Boötes is above Virgo, and the group of Hydra, Crater, and Canis Major extends along the southern horizon. Hercules' celestial globe is thus a visual counterpart of Ferreri's election poem, which opened with an evocation of the stars at the moment of Leo's elevation. It also takes up the Julian conceit of the globe in the Stanza della Segnatura, suggesting that the papacy was predestined in Leo's stars. However, the notion of celestial predestination is carried one step further in Leo's tapestry. The presence of Ursa Major presented an opportunity to symbolize Leo's "fated" connection with Rome and the papacy through his mother, Clarice Orsini. As we have seen in the imagery of the Capitoline festival, the wordplay Ursa-Orsa-Orsini was an established feature of Leo's celestial imagery. To complete the polar metaphor, Argo Navis, the celestial ship and the southernmost constellation known in the Renaissance, balances the Bear. The polar constellations would thus read as a complementary pair: Ursa, who gave birth to the New Hercules; and Argo, perhaps to be understood as the Ship of the Church, which Leo-Hercules literally holds in his hand.

Hercules is also featured at Poggio a Caiano in Allori's *Hercules and Fortuna in the Garden of the Hesperides* (pl. 118). Since this fresco was painted so long after the Leonine campaign of work in the Salone and its connection with Giovio's program cannot be documented, its astrological significance in relation to Leo can be discussed only hypothetically. However, I have argued that its program is based on the original plan for the

Works by Vincenzo de' Rossi," *Art Bull.*, 53, 1971, pp. 347-61.

[30] M. Campbell, *Pietro da Cortona at the Pitti Pal-ace: A Study of the Planetary Rooms and Related Projects*, Princeton, 1977, pp. 111-12, fig. 60.

lunette as an allegory of Leo, and some suggestions as to its astrological content may be made.

The cosmic symbolism of *Hercules in the Garden of the Hesperides* lies, quite simply, in the subject itself, which is an astrological theme and was so interpreted in the Renaissance. Just as the Nemean lion and the crab that Hercules killed during his fight with the hydra were catasterized as the constellations of Leo and Cancer,[31] so Hercules himself became a constellation. And, as we have seen in the illustration from the *Medici Aratus* (pl. 130), this constellation was understood as representing Hercules killing the dragon of the Garden of the Hesperides.[32]

The garden itself also had cosmic associations. The name Hesperides refers to sunset and to Hesper (Venus), the evening star, and in ancient poetic tradition Hesperides was a metaphor for the west.[33] Moreover, according to Salutati, the garden was beyond the planets in the stars, its miraculous tree was cosmic, and the *mala aurea* were heavenly bodies.[34] This myth was taken up in Leo's time by Giraldi (in the *Hercules vita*) and by Valeriano, for whom the golden apples are stars, the nymphs are the Daughters of the Night, and Hercules is Hercules-Sol, or the Sun.[35]

Given the association of imagery in Allori's *Hercules* with Leonine imagery; given the location of the lunette at the western end of the Salone, which would coincide with the mythical location of the Garden of the Hesperides; and given the cosmic interpretations of the eleventh labor current in Leo's own circle, it is reasonable to suppose that the fresco was initially planned not only as an allegory of Leo's Herculean virtue but as an apotheosis of Leo-Hercules, who achieves immortality in the heavens for his virtuous deeds on earth. Below the hero—and corresponding to the figure above him in the *Hercules* tapestry border—is Fame, who proclaims his immortal glory.

THE SALA DEI PONTEFICI

Astrological ideas find expression in Pope Leo's monumental art in Pontormo's lunette in the Salone at Poggio a Caiano (to be discussed in detail in chapter 9) and in the ceiling of the Sala dei Pontefici (pls. 145-146), decorated by Giovanni da Udine and Perino del

[31] Hyginus, *Poetica Astronomica*, II, 23-24. These labors stand for the signs of Cancer and Leo in Chigi's astrological ceiling (Saxl, pp. 23-24; my fig. 13).

[32] Hyginus, *Poetica Astronomica*, II, 3, 6. For the history and pictorial traditions of the constellation, see Panofsky-Saxl, pp. 230-40; F. Saxl, "Illuminated Science Manuscripts," in *Lectures*, London, 1957, pp. 96-110; and R. H. Allen, pp. 236-46. The association of the constellation with the labor is elaborated by Salutati, bk. III, xxv, 22 (ed., II, pp. 314-15), in which Hercules kills the dragon and receives the reward of immortality in the heavens.

[33] Ovid, *Fasti*, I, 137-40.

[34] Salutati, bk. III, xxv, 1-11 (ed., II, pp. 308-11).

[35] Giraldi, p. 32; and Valeriano, 1625, p. 717, which is based on Macrobius, *Saturnalia*, I, 20, 6-10: ". . . quelli, che dell'Astrologia si compiacquero, per le mele d'oro vogliono significarsi le stelle; massimamente appo d'Esiodo, dove l'Esperidi sono figliuole della notte, e Hercole dicono esser il Sole, al partire di cui quella pretiosa messe sparsamente nasca, e si offerisca a gl' occhi de' mortali."

Vaga and datable to late 1520-1521.[36] In contrast to the Salone, the Vatican Sala, which is the culminating and largest room of the Appartamento Borgia, is a state room, and its decoration is more decisively a ruler's propaganda. The astrological imagery dominating the room was conceived as a metaphor of papal supremacy and power; it is imagery of cosmic predestination enhancing the idea of the return of the Golden Age during the papacy of Leo X.[37]

The meaning of Leo's Roman Sala (like that of his Florentine Salone) depends on an interplay between terrestrial and celestial spheres and on the implicit assumption that the heavens influence temporal events. Thus, the astrological imagery of its vault must be understood against the background of imagery of papal history in the zone below it. Referring to a diagram of the decoration of the Sala (fig. 12), we see that between the pendentives of its vaults are ten lunettes. These were to contain scenes from the history of the papacy, which would have completed the historical component of the program; however, only the *tituli* (inscriptions) above them naming the papal subjects of the projected *istorie* were executed. The ten popes, arranged chronologically, include Leo's favorite exemplars, Leo III and Leo IV, and all the popes seem to have been chosen for their relevance to the events and goals of Leo's own papacy: relations with France (Stephen II, Hadrian I, Leo III); the seat of the papacy at Rome (Sergius II, Leo IV); the crusades (Urban II); and the suppression of heresy and healing of schisms, including the reconciliation of Rome and Florence (Boniface IX, Gregory XI, Martin V). To this group is added Nicholas III Orsini, who calls attention to the theme of Leo's Orsini ancestry, which we have already encountered in his imagery. The ten papal *tituli* are painted on the same level as the celestial imagery of the pendentives. This juxtaposition of the historical church with the eternal stars suggests that, having played a role in maintaining or restoring papal power on earth, each of Leo's predecessors has been rewarded with immortality in the heavens.

The papal inscriptions (and the *istorie* that were to accompany them) serve as a setting for imagery glorifying the present pope. For it is Leo X, the eleventh pope in the Sala—in allusion to his lucky number—who is the main subject of the decoration. Imagery alluding to his papacy is present in the oculus at the center of the ceiling (pl. 147), where Perino's Victories carry his censer and tiara, and Fame trumpets his glory.[38] Leo's personal imagery is also present below, in the company of his predecessors. Each corner of the room is marked by a stucco panel in which his *stemma* is accompanied by Pallas-Minerva (pl. 148). The goddess conventionally stands for Divine Wisdom and peace,

[36] See Freedberg, 1961, I, pp. 566-69, 606 (dated "1521, mainly"); M. V. Brugnoli, "Gli affreschi di Perino del Vaga nella Cappella Pucci," *Boll. d'A.*, 47, 1962, pp. 343, 350 (on the giving of the commission only after September 1520); and B. Davidson, "Early Drawings by Perino del Vaga, Part One," *MD*, 1, 1963, p. 10 (on Giovanni da Udine's responsibility for the general plan of the room only and its execution by Perino).

[37] I am indebted to Claudia Rousseau for making available to me material on the Sala, especially the interpretation of the panels *Gemini*, *Canis Major*, *Cygnus*, *Aquila*, and *Lyra*. For full discussion of this complex work, I refer the reader to her dissertation, "Astrological Iconography in Medici Art and Decoration," Columbia University, in progress.

[38] Vasari, V, p. 596: "Nel mezzo della volta è un tondo con quattro figure finte per Vittorie, che tengono il regno del papa e le chiavi. . . ." The keys that Vasari mentions are not present, and the fourth figure carries a psaltery.

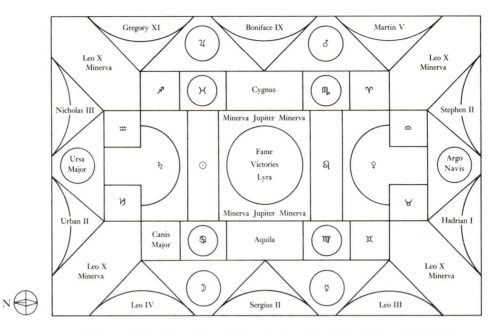

12. Scheme of the decorations of the ceiling of the Sala dei Pontefici, Vatican

but she also alludes to Leo's city of Florence. The origin of the association was astro-logical: as Mars was the planetary guardian of the Florentine sign of Aries, so, according to the Manilian system, was Pallas-Minerva its Olympian guardian.[39] Thus, the city was thought to be under the rulership of the two gods and was characterized—by Poliziano, for example—as "la città di Marte e di Minerva."[40] The Medici had adopted Pallas (the wordplay Pallas-*palla* could connect her with their *stemma*) in the time of Lorenzo il Magnifico, and in his imagery Leo himself was often associated with the goddess.[41] Here in the Sala, surmounted by Leo's Medicean and papal devices, Pallas-Minerva identifies the pope as the ruler who brings her city into peaceful concord with Rome. Moreover, she assumes a celestial aspect in keeping with the imagery of the room: Perino portrays the goddess as if descended from the heavens with Leo's tiara and keys, in an image that is reminiscent of a poem predicting his papacy.[42]

> Dalla più alta stella
>> Discende a celebrar la tua letizia,
>> Glorïosa Fiorenza,
>> La dea Minerva agl'ingegni propizia . . .

[39] Manilius, *Astronomica*, 2, 439; 4, 135; and Ficino, *De amore*, V, 13. In the Palazzo Schifanoia cycle, based on the Manilian guardianships, March is represented by a *Triumph of Pallas*.

[40] "In morte del Magnifico Lorenzo de' Medici," *Le Stanze*, p. 385.

[41] For example, in the Lateran *possesso* Leo was hailed as a New Pallas in an inscription on Agostino Chigi's arch (Penni, p. 210), which equated him with the peaceful and wise Pallas in comparison with Venus (the libertine Alexander VI) and Mars (the warlike Julius II); and Ferreri's poem on Leo's election characterizes him as a seeker after Wisdom-Pallas (p. 282).

[42] Grazzini, I, p. 139 (as by Agnolo Divizio da Bibbiena). The poem has also been attributed to Poliziano (*Le Stanze*, p. 381).

Verrà tempo novello
Che arai le tre corone e le due chiave.

From the highest stars, O glorious Florence, the goddess Minerva, propitious to men of talent, descends to celebrate your joy. . . . A new age will come when you have the three crowns and the two keys.

The rest of the decoration of the Sala elucidates Leo's astrological destiny through a selective presentation of features of his horoscope and of extrazodiacal constellations which were auspiciously located at the time of his birth. Some of the major images are described by Vasari in the *vita* of Perino:[43]

> Onde quella volta fu dipinta da Giovan da Udine e da Perino; ed in compagnia feciono e gli stucchi e tutti quegli ornamenti e grottesche ed animali che vi si veggono, oltra le belle e varie invenzioni che da essi furono fatte nello sparti-mento, avendo diviso quella in certi tondi ed ovati, per *sette pianeti del cielo* tirati dai loro animali; come *Giove* dall'aquile, *Venere* dalle columbe, *la Luna* dalle femmine, *Marte* dai lupi, *Mercurio* da'galli, *il Sole* da'cavalli, e *Saturno* de'serpenti: oltre *i dodici segni del Zodiaco*, ed *alcune figure delle quarantotto imagini del cielo*; come *l'Orsa maggiore*, *la Canicola*, e molte altre, che per la lunghezza loro le taceremo senza raccontarle per ordine, potendosi l'opera vedere: le quali tutte figure sono per la maggior parte di mano di Perino.

> And that vaulting was painted by Giovanni da Udine and Perino. They exe-cuted together the stucco-work and all those ornaments, grotesques, and ani-mals that are to be seen there, in addition to the varied and beautiful inven-tions that were depicted by them in the compartments of the ceiling, which they had divided into certain circles and ovals to contain the seven planets of heaven drawn by their appropriate animals, such as Jupiter drawn by eagles, Venus by doves, the Moon by women, Mars by wolves, Mercury by cocks, the Sun by horses, and Saturn by serpents; besides the twelve signs of the zodiac and some figures from the forty-eight constellations of heaven, such as the Great Bear, the Dog Star, and many others, which by reason of their number we must pass over in silence, without recounting them all in their order, since anyone may see the work, the figures of which are almost all by the hand of Perino.

The astrological imagery of the Sala (only partially accounted for by Vasari, who assumes the observer will understand it) begins in the pendentives between the papal *tituli* with panels of the four planetary deities *Mars*, *Jupiter*, *Mercury*, and *Luna-Diana* (on the lateral walls), and the polar constellations *Ursa Major* and *Argo Navis* (on the end walls). Above the gods are the zodiac signs ruled by each planet. (Above Luna-Diana, which rules only one sign, the constellation of Canis Major, Vasari's "la Canicola," substitutes for the second sign.) The three remaining planets, together with the signs

[43] Vasari, V, pp. 595-96 (italics mine).

they rule, have been elevated into positions of great prominence at the ends and in the center of the vault, where they are painted on a larger scale than the planets below. At each end, riding frontally in their chariots and surmounted by canopies and decorative figures, are *Saturn* (with *Capricorn* and *Aquarius*) and *Venus* (with *Taurus* and *Libra*); in the center, on either side of the central apotheosis of Pope Leo, are *Sol-Apollo* and *Leo*. The other two sides of the central panel above the lateral walls are occupied by large, oblong panels (not mentioned by Vasari) with the constellations *Cygnus* and *Aquila*.

The immediate prototype for the astrological program of the Sala is Peruzzi's horoscope ceiling of 1511 in the Villa Farnesina (pl. 149). It was painted for Agostino Chigi, whose interest in occult and cosmic themes is also attested in the decoration of his arch for Pope Leo's Lateran *possesso*[44] and in the celestial cupola of his funerary chapel. The ceiling of the Sala di Galatea in Chigi's villa is the first monumental work of the Renaissance in which the fame of a living individual was audaciously declared to have been predestined in the stars. It established the model adapted several years later to the purposes of Pope Leo's propaganda of *his* astrological destiny. In both decorations, the celestial images are arranged in interlocking, geometric picture fields—many of them triangular—around a central oblong. This pattern, these triangles, and particularly the central square of Leo's ceiling are reminiscent of the horoscope as it was often drawn in the Renaissance (cf. figs. 7, 9). Also, in both ceilings the immortal glory brought by the stars to the fortunate subject is trumpeted by Fame at the summit of the decoration. However, considered in detail, the two schemes present a number of differences. As was indicated many years ago by Saxl, the mythological scenes on the ceiling allude to the positions of the planets at Chigi's birth in relation to the zodiacal and extrazodiacal constellations; however, thanks to the recent discovery of Chigi's birthtime (29 November 1466 at 21½ hours), a natal horoscope may be erected for him, and it becomes clear that the ceiling is a pictorial horoscope, with the angles aligned approximately with the orientation of the room (fig. 13; based on Saxl, but with the correct planetary positions and angles of the chart added).[45] As can be seen in this diagram, there are only ten spandrels in which to place the twelve zodiac signs. Exercising artistic license (as the iconographers of the Sala dei Pontefici and Pontormo's lunette at Poggio a Caiano would later do), the ideator of the scheme eliminated Aries and Libra (which have no planets

[44] Penni, pp. 211-12.

[45] For previous interpretations of the ceiling, see Saxl, passim (with an appendix by A. Beer, pp. 61-67); Saxl, "The Villa Farnesina," in *Lectures*, London, 1957, I, pp. 189-99; Seznec, pp. 76-83; and Beer, pp. 189-99. Saxl and Beer determined a birthdate of 1 December 1466 from the positions of the planets in the zodiac signs on the ceiling; however, the date is wrong and, consequently, Mars was placed in Libra and Jupiter in Aries, and it was concluded that the planets were represented in the zodiacal constellations (not signs) in which they were located at Chigi's birth. With the recent finding of Chigi's actual birthdate and time (see I. D. Rowland, "The Birthdate of Agostino

Chigi: Documentary Proof," *JWCI*, forthcoming, in which the time is given as "a di 29 di detto mese [novembre] a ore 21½"), it is possible to calculate the time of birth in modern clock time by determining the time of sunset and counting ahead 21½ hours, arriving at a birthtime of 3:08 p.m. From this time Chigi's horoscope can be erected, which has the positions shown in fig. 13. I am grateful to Ingrid Rowland for providing me with a copy of her article (the main point of which was discussed by her in a talk at the College Art Association, Philadelphia, February 1983) and to Kathleen Weil-Garris, who is preparing a major study on Chigi's ceiling and chapel, for discussing her interpretations of these works with me.

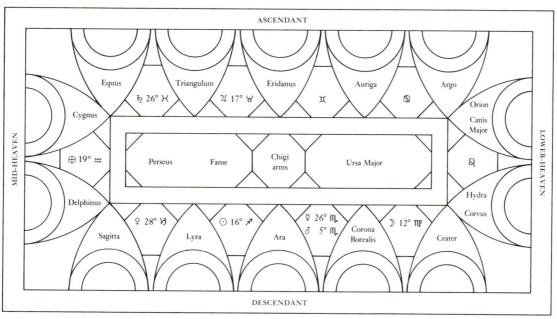

13. Scheme of the decorations of the ceiling of the Sala di Galatea, Rome, Villa Farnesina

in Chigi's horoscope) so that the "mid-heaven in Aquarius" (represented by *Jupiter and Ganymede*) and the "lower-heaven in Leo" (*Hercules and the Nemean Lion*) could be placed on the long axis of the room (but the Ram and the Scales are depicted within the Taurus and Scorpio panels to indicate these important equinox points). Thus, on entering, the observer looks up at Chigi's *stemma* (since replaced) and, beyond it, to his Aquarian mid-heaven—the culmination of his horoscope.[46] The ascendant (Taurus) and the descendant (Scorpio) then fall opposite one another on the short axis of the room, the cycle beginning with the ascendant, which is in conjunction with "Jupiter in Taurus" (*Jupiter with Europa and the Bull*), and continuing counterclockwise around the room with the remaining signs and planetary positions: Gemini (*Leda and the Swan*); Cancer (*Hercules and the Hydra*); "lower-heaven in Leo," as noted above; "Moon in Virgo" (*Luna-Diana and Erigone*); "Mercury and Mars in Scorpio," represented by the two gods; "Sun in Sagittarius" (*Sol-Apollo and the Centaur*); "Venus in Capricorn" (Venus *Anadyomene with Capricorn*); "Pars Fortunae in Aquarius" (*Jupiter and Ganymede*, the planet Jupiter being the ruler of the Pars Fortunae); and "Saturn in Pisces" (*Saturn with Venus and Cupid*, Venus and Cupid standing for Pisces, as in Ferreri's poem quoted above, but the fish are also shown in the panel).

Peruzzi's zodiacal scheme is complemented by figures in the triangular sections be-

[46] The chart calculated from a birthtime of 3:08 p.m. gives the mid-heaven at 28° Capricorn 13′, or less than 2° from Aquarius. Lacking a chart erected at the time, we cannot know which slightly different time and/or calculations Chigi's astrologer may have used; however, it is clear in comparing my chart with the placement of the signs and planets on the ceiling that Aquarius was taken as the mid-heaven, possibly as a result of a minor rectification of less than 2° or as a result of birthtime of seven minutes later (which does, in fact, result in a mid-heaven at 0° Aquarius and an ascendant at 23° Taurus 7′).

tween the zodiac signs and in the center of the vault representing extrazodiacal constellations. These are known as the *paranatellonta*, constellations which rise to the north and south of the ecliptic (the sun's apparent path around the earth).[47] In Renaissance astrological practice, these "stelle fisse," as they were called, served as additional indicators of an individual's destiny, especially when they were in conjunction with the ascendant or mid-heaven angles of the chart. Giulio Romano's Sala dei Venti is an elaborate program based on this admixture of zodiacal and extrazodiacal constellations; and, in astrological paintings which relate to specific horoscopes like Chigi's and Pope Leo's ceilings, the inclusion of key *paranatellonta* is the rule rather than the exception.[48] For example, in Mantegna's *Parnassus*, the date of Isabella d'Este's marriage (12 February 1490) is commemorated by the personifications of Venus, Mars, and Mercury (which were all in Aquarius) and by the extrazodiacal constellation Pegasus, the westernmost bright star of which was also in that sign.[49] In Chigi's scheme the *paranatellonta* relating to each zodiac sign are depicted adjacent to the signs, as indicated in figure 13.[50] But the constellations which have been elevated to the center of the vault on either side of Chigi's *stemma* have special significance. In the panel aligned to the north is *Ursa Major* (represented by the wagon, its antique name), the northern polar constellation which never sets and, in astrological tradition, is associated with constancy and immortality. In the other panel is Fame accompanied by Perseus and Medusa and other figures. Perseus has been associated by Saxl with *virtù celeste* and may certainly be seen as an exemplum;[51] however, the constellation is also one of the *paranatellonta* of Taurus, the ascendant in Chigi's chart, as well as being in mythological tradition the son of Jupiter (conjunct the ascendant in the horoscope), who transformed the hero into the constellation.

In contrast to Peruzzi's scheme, which is easily readable once its principle of organization is understood, the astrological imagery of Leo's Sala at first seems arbitrary. The zodiac signs do not progress in their normal order, no planetary positions are pictured, and five extrazodiacal constellations are depicted in locations where one would expect to find planetary deities or zodiac signs. Moreover, Saturn, Venus and the sun, together with the sign of Leo, have been elevated into the center of the ceiling. This imagery does refer to Leo's horoscope, but, unlike Chigi's ceiling, the scheme of the Sala is not a straightforward representation of Leo's astrological destiny; rather, certain features of his horoscope have been given prominence, and certain extrazodiacal features have been added, to emphasize the themes of papal dominion and the return of the Golden Age during Leo's rule. This message, although clear in certain obvious respects (such as the

[47] The doctrine of the *paranatellonta* is drawn from Manilius, *Astronomica*, 5; and Maternus, *Mathesis*, VIII.

[48] For the Sala dei Venti, see Gombrich, 1972, pp. 108-18. See also another sixteenth-century cycle, Titian's *poesie* for Philip II, in which the astrological destiny of the prince is delineated partly in reference to extrazodiacal constellations (Tanner, pp. 159-66); and Urban VIII's *Divina Sapienza*, which includes personifications of the con-

stellations as they appeared on the day of his elevation to the papacy (Lechner, pp. 97-108).

[49] Lehmann, p. 174. As noted by E. Schröter, *Die Iconographie des Thema Parnassus vor Raffael*, Hildesheim, 1977, p. 283, the date of the wedding was 12 February, but the difference of one day would not alter Lehmann's conclusions, based on 11 February.

[50] Saxl, pp. 22-30.

[51] Saxl, pp. 30-32.

giant celestial lion), is disguised; it is veiled by the oblique allusions and intricate conceits characteristic of Medicean astrological art of the early sixteenth century.

The key to the choice of celestial images in the Sala is the emphasis on the planets and constellations (both zodiacal and extrazodiacal) which mark the angles of Leo's chart, especially the all-important ascendant and mid-heaven. For example, this principle seems to have dictated the arrangement of the zodiac signs above the planetary deities. The signs ruled by the four planets represented on the lateral walls have been placed so that the corners of the room are occupied by *Aries, Gemini, Sagittarius*, and the extrazodiacal constellation *Canis Major*. With reference to Leo's chart, it becomes clear that these panels represent the angles of his horoscope. Three of them are immediately identifiable: *Aries* is the lower-heaven, *Sagittarius* is the ascendant, and *Gemini* is the descendant, the last two being opposite one another, like the ascendant and descendant of the chart. Furthermore, Sagittarius and Gemini have been portrayed in such a way that they signal the positions of the sun and the moon in these two signs. The Centaur, in the northeastern corner of the room, is sharply lit from the front, as though from the rising sun; the Twins, in the southwestern corner, are portrayed in an unusual fashion as an androgyne, and the female part of the figure holds a red rose, which is a common hermetic and alchemical symbol for the moon.[52] The fourth panel, *Canis Major*, is on the western side of the room along with *Gemini*; it also stands for the descendant, but the allusion is indirect. The constellation of Canis Major is parallel to Cancer, with which it is paired here; but at the time of Leo's birth its largest star, Sirius, was near the western horizon and therefore closely related to the descendant in Leo's horoscope.

It will be noted that the mid-heaven, the culminating angle of the chart which is associated with rulership, is not included in this zone of the ceiling. Rather, the sign of Libra which marks Leo's mid-heaven is indicated by Saturn and Venus, the two planets connected with Libra in astrological tradition. *Venus*, elevated at one end of the vault with its signs, is, of course, planetary ruler of Libra; *Saturn*, at the other end of the vault, is considered exalted with beneficial influence when in Libra.

The central area of the vault above *Venus* and *Saturn* panels is entirely devoted to imagery related to the conjunction of the ascendant and the "sun in Sagittarius" in Leo's horoscope. Flanking the central panel are the panels of *Sol-Apollo*, who rides his chariot from east to west (in relation to the orientation of the room), and *Leo*, house of the sun and, of course, an allusion to Leo's name. Within the central square are a number of ingenious references to Leo's ascendant sign. (Sagittarius itself is depicted below, as one of the signs ruled by Jupiter.) Two deities who are connected with Sagittarius in astrological tradition are depicted in the stucco friezes on the east and west sides of the square. These are Pallas-Minerva (also featured in the corners of the room), who, like Sagittarius, is associated with wisdom; and Jupiter, who is planetary ruler of Sagittarius and thus lord of the ascendant in Leo's chart. Jupiter, moreover, is related to the sign of Leo, depicted in the adjacent panel. According to the Manilian system of zodiacal

[52] T. Burckhart, *Alchemy: Science of the Cosmos, Science of the Soul*, tr. W. Stoddart, Baltimore, 1971, pp. 149-50. For a manuscript of ca. 1550 which illustrates the association of the red rose with the moon, see E. Ploss, H. Roosen et al., *Alchimia, Ideologie und Technologie*, Munich, 1970, pl. on p. 203. I owe these references to Claudia Rousseau.

guardianships so widely adopted in the Renaissance, Jupiter was the guardian of Leo, and it was believed that through Leo Jupiter gave the arts of rulership to mankind.[53]

The large panels of *Cygnus* and *Aquila* complement the imagery of the central square of the vault. Although neither the Swan nor the Eagle seem at first to have any connection with the now-familiar images of Leo's horoscope, they are, in fact, related to Jupiter, lord of the ascendant, and to the sign of Sagittarius itself. According to mythological-astrological tradition, Jupiter assumed the guises of a swan and an eagle in the stories of Leda and Ganymede, these birds ultimately becoming the constellations Cygnus and Aquila.[54] Moreover, these Jupiterian constellations are among the *paranatellonta* of Sagittarius and were, in actuality, rising with the sun and Sagittarius on the morning of 11 December 1475 when Leo was born. With them was the constellation Lyra, which is symbolized in the center of the oculus in the psaltery carried by one of the Victories.[55] These three constellations, known as the summer triangle, are thus represented on the vault in the same geometrical relationship as they had in the eastern sky at Leo's birth, with the triangle—Lyra at its apex, and Aquila at 20-22° Sagittarius—pointing toward the horizon. They reinforce the imagery of the *Sol-Apollo* and *Leo* panels, as well as the Jupiter and Minerva figures, to make the center of the vault into a monumental affirmation of the power of Leo's rising sun.

All this imagery of the vault carries the message of Leo's predestined papacy. For example, the *paranatellonta* of Sagittarius are cited by later astrologers as important indicators of Leo's astrological destiny. Giuntini mentions Aquila at 22° Sagittarius and Spica coinciding with Leo's mid-heaven as influencing Leo's attainment of the papacy.[56] But, more generally, the imagery alludes to notions of renewal which are related to traditional Medicean themes, now recast to suggest that the return of the Golden Age is attributable to the fortunate stars of Leo X.

Ever since his elevation to the papacy, Leo's commentators and apologists had presented their subject as an agent of political and ecclesiastical renewal.[57] The myth of the imminence of a Leonine Golden Age was fostered especially by Egidio da Viterbo, who

[53] Ficino, *De amore*, V, 13: "Jupiter, through Leo, makes a man most fit for governing of Men and Gods, that is, fit to manage well both divine affairs and human."

[54] On Cygnus see Manilius, *Astronomica*, 1, 337-41; and Hyginus, *Poetica Astronomica*, II, 8. On Aquila, which was charged with keeping Jupiter's thunderbolts, see Manilius, *Astronomica*, 1, 342-45; 5, 436-500; and Hyginus, *Poetica Astronomica*, II, 16. For a summary of the traditions of Cygnus and Aquila, see R. H. Allen, pp. 55-59, 192-95.

[55] For the traditions of Lyra, see R. H. Allen, pp. 280-84.

[56] Giuntini, 1573, f. 239r: "Sed Alexander sextus et Leo decimus fere habent eandem constellationem, quia uterque habuit Aquilam volantem in horoscopo in 22 parte Sagittarii, et in medio coeli Spicam, unde ad ponticatum venerunt." (But [Pope] Alexander VI and Leo X have almost the same

constellation because each had the flying Eagle in his ascendant in the 22nd degree of Sagittarius and Spica in the mid-heaven, whence they came to the papacy). As Giuntini indicates, Alexander VI also had Sagittarius in the ascendant and hence Jupiter as lord of the horoscope. Indeed, in the Sala delle Sibille in the Appartamento Borgia, he is represented on the ceiling as a "child of Jupiter." I thank Kathleen Weil-Garris for calling my attention to this image.

[57] For the epithets and prophecies of Leo's early rule, see Shearman, 1972, pp. 1, 14-21, 75-76, 86-87. On Leo as Pater Angelicus and the context of such prophecies, see Vasoli, pp. 217-22, 231-33. The most striking single example of this kind of propaganda is Ferreri's *Lugdunense somnium* . . . , written on the occasion of Leo's election, from which I have quoted extensively.

transferred this *topos* from Julius II, for whose papacy he had entertained similar hopes.[58] Egidio's formulae of cosmological renewal involved the mystique of numbers as indicators of the workings of Divine Providence. The number of greatest significance was ten. It was the number of divine emanations, of perfection, and the most sacred number which Leo himself assumed in taking the papal name.[59] (And, not coincidentally, it was the number of the house cusp in a horoscope which signified the culmination of an individual's destiny at the mid-heaven.) According to the tenfold division of time which Egidio derived from the mysteries of the Cabala, the present age, that of Leo, was the tenth: it was an age of regeneration and peace which would be achieved by the charismatic figure of the pope, "the first pontiff of the tenth age," and it was related to the concept of the *magno anno*, according to which time would begin again and the stars would all return to their original places in the heavens.[60]

The decoration of Leo's horoscope ceiling is redolent of such notions. High above the popes of previous ages is the apotheosis of the first pope of the tenth age, whose very name combines the zodiac sign of Leo with the sacred number ten. In the flanking panels Sol-Apollo has returned to his original house in the sign of Leo. These images, in turn, are accompanied by the other planetary deities and their respective houses, with their sequence and placement alluding to Leo's own chart. Particularly emphasized by their location at either end of the vault are the deities who stand for Leo's mid-heaven—the tenth cusp, signifying his public life. Saturn and Venus symbolize peace and reconciliation through their sign of Libra, geographical ruler of Italy. Moreover, Saturn, with Apollo, is the god of Virgil's prophecy of the Golden Age in *Eclogue* IV, which was traditionally interpreted as alluding to the cosmological renewal of the *magno anno*.[61]

The idea that Leo, a New Apollo, was destined by his stars to rule a new Golden Age in Italy is amplified by the panels of *Argo Navis* and *Ursa Major*, which anchor the sequence of images on the vault at either end. These constellations emphasize the theme of Leo's dominion, since they delineate the poles of the celestial globe, which are suggested by the bosses at the centers of the panels. Indeed, this imagery could be seen as a monumental expansion of the conceit of the celestial globe held by Hercules in Raphael's tapestry border. There, the constellations allude to Leo's fated connection with Rome through his Orsini mother, from whom he descends, and the Ship of the Church, which he guides. The same message was surely intended here—and the Orsini reference is even hinted in the placement of the inscription celebrating the Orsini pope, Nicholas III, to the right of *Ursa Major*.[62] The placement of these polar constellations at the ends

[58] O'Malley, pp. 110-17; J. W. O'Malley, "Fulfillment of the Christian Golden Age under Pope Julius II: Text of a Discourse of Giles of Viterbo, 1507," *Traditio*, 25, 1969, pp. 265-338; and H. Pfeiffer, "Die Predigt des Egidio da Viterbo über das goldene Zeitalter und die Stanza della Segnatura," *Festschrift Luitpold Dussler*, Berlin, 1972, pp. 237-54.

[59] O'Malley, pp. 93, 112. On the tradition of the number ten, see Aristotle, *Metaphysica*, I, V,

3-4; Hopper, pp. ix-x, 10-11, 34-38, 61-63, 85; and S. K. Heninger, *Touches of Sweet Harmony: Pythagorean Cosmology and Renaissance Poetics*, Berkeley, 1974, pp. 84-89.

[60] O'Malley, pp. 102-9. On the *magno anno*, see G. B. Ladner, *The Idea of Reform: Its Impact on Christian Thought and Action in the Age of the Fathers*, Cambridge, Mass., 1959, pp. 10-12.

[61] Servius, III, pp. 44-45.

[62] The juxtaposition of the Orsini pope and Ursa

of the vault which alludes to Leo's astrological destiny is thus an ingeniously conceived metaphor of the rule of Leo, the sun pope, who illumines the very ends of the world from the church in Rome. Laudatory writing throughout Leo's rule had referred to him in such terms. Egidio used similar metaphors to express the idea of Leo's papacy at Rome, with spheres of influence radiating from that center;[63] and Ferreri anticipates the visual elaboration of the theme in the Sala in his comparison of the newly elected Leo to Apollo:[64]

> Vidisti, o fili, nova tu miracula coeli?
> Vidisti ne novum foedus, nova saecla, novumque
> Imperium, et Titana novum, qui illuminat orbem?

> Have you seen, O my son, the new miracles of heaven? Have you seen the new covenant, the new age, the new empire, and the new Titan who illumines the world?

Major is not the only instance of a connection between the papal inscriptions and the astrological imagery of the Sala. Martin V is next to Mars and under Aries, the sign ruling Florence. Martin was conspicuously associated with Florence, having reconciled Florence and Rome (as Leo hoped to do), making an *entrata* into Florence and otherwise favoring the city (see Pastor, I, pp. 212-14; Moroni, 41, pp. 175-78).

[63] See, for example, Egidio on the papal city as the predestined center of the world, with spheres of power radiating out from it (cited in O'Malley, p. 125). The whole question of Egidio's influence upon and possible participation in the decorative programs at the Vatican under Julius II and Leo X merits further investigation, especially in the light of the apparent connections with his thinking in the programs of the Sala dei Pontefici, the Stanza della Segnatura (see the articles cited in n. 58 above), and the Sistine ceiling (recently suggested by Dotson, pp. 223-56, 405-29).

[64] Ferreri, pp. 292-93.

Astrological Imagery in *Vertumnus and Pomona*

The Salone at Poggio a Caiano (pls. 36, 68) is in many ways the Florentine counterpart of the Sala dei Pontefici (pl. 145). Both decorations are based on programs dating from 1520 to 1521, both were initiated at the behest of Pope Leo, and both allude to the return of the Golden Age under Medici rule. However, the Vatican Sala is a state room and its decoration emphasizes papal supremacy, while the Salone, in the more private setting of Lorenzo's country villa, is devoted to dynastic themes appropriate to a Medici decoration in Florence. Likewise, the two decorations both contain astrological imagery, but it is different in mode. The entire vault of Leo's Sala (we recall that the *istorie* were planned but not executed) is given over to astrological symbolism in which planets, zodiac signs, and constellations announce the exalted astrological destiny of the pope. On the other hand, in the Salone, astrological imagery is restricted to the lunettes: *Vertumnus and Pomona* (color pl. 2) and, if my association of the second lunette with Giovio's program is tenable, *Hercules and Fortuna* (pl. 118). Moreover, the readily identifiable symbolism of the Sala, or of Chigi's astrological ceiling (pl. 149), is not present. Rather, the mode of the astrological imagery is oblique, with suggestion, indirection, and disguise setting it apart from the Roman works. Instead of referring to the current Roman style (as the Salone *istorie* do), the imagery of *Vertumnus and Pomona* is reminiscent of the poetic, allusive style of Laurentian mythologies like the *Primavera* (pl. 60) and the *Realm of Pan* (pl. 67), in which astrological allusions are covert.

The subject of *Vertumnus and Pomona* itself has no astral component (unlike *Hercules and Fortuna in the Garden of the Hesperides*); nor, as in Leo's Roman Sala, are zodiac signs and planets designated by conventional signs. Rather, the identity of the gods as planets and the location of their garden in the heavens are hidden by the conceit of rustic disguise which is fundamental to the conception of Pontormo's fresco at each level of its meaning. We have seen that the sprouting laurel is a metaphor of Medici renewal through the birth of the new heir, Cosimo. The fragmentary and enigmatic inscriptions (including the reversed letters of GLOVIS–SI VOLGE) also suggest the possibility of hidden meanings. And the pastoral theme signals the notion of disguise, which is the characteristic device of the literary pastorale. Indeed, the ostensible subject of the fresco is the story of the disguises assumed by Vertumnus to gain entrance to Pomona's garden. This idea of disguise is present in all three of the poetic sources of the lunette: Ovid's story is the quintessential rustic tale, in which the disguises of Vertumnus are metaphors for the eternal cycles of change in nature; Virgil's plea for peace in the *Georgics* is dressed in bucolic imagery, as is Ariosto's appeal to the gods in "Ne la stagion" on behalf of the stricken laurel-Lorenzo. Even Pontormo himself—the painter whose vibrant images of the nature gods evoke all these literary sources—uses the conceit in an invention which expresses *in nuce* the spirit of the fresco: in an Ovidian metamorphosis, Vertumnus is wittily presented as a self-portrait in which Pontormo transforms himself into an old man, projecting his likeness into his own future (pl. 99).[1] Below him, almost like a label, are the initials which stand for his signature IACOBVS FLORENTINVS PINXIT.

THE PLANETS AND THE ZODIAC

The conceit of rustic disguise is also skillfully manipulated to conceal—but ultimately to reveal—the astrological message of the fresco: it veils an evocation of the stars as portents of Medici renewal, which is predestined, as it were, in the heavens.

A number of clues indicate that a cosmic scheme of some kind underlies Pontormo's pastoral scene. The first of these is the tablet quotation from *Georgics* I, a poem in which the farmer's year is explicitly described in astrological images, and the opening premise of which is that the heavens rule the activities of men: "What makes the crops joyous, beneath what star, Maecenas, is it well to turn the soil. . . ."[2] The perceptive viewer, recognizing the quotation from the conclusion to this very passage, would readily associate the fresco with celestial phenomena.

Such an association is reinforced by the blue sky above the walls of Pomona's garden, which suggests that, like Hercules' garden, it is set in the heavens. Moreover, unusual bands framing the sky indicate that it is intended to evoke the cosmos as well. The painted frame has seven bands, there is a dark band edging the fresco, and within the sky, another band (there are also seven bands around the GLOVIS disk). All these recall the seven planetary spheres of the cosmos, as they were depicted in Renaissance illustrations (cf. pls. 110, 124, 126) and paintings such as *Dante and Florence* (pl. 127), where the spheres are also shown as bands bordering the blue sky of a monumental lunette.

[1] The placement of the self-portrait is characteristic of Pontormo, who often depicted himself as a participant in sacred works: he is Saint James in the Visdomini altar (1518), a bystander in the Pitti *Adoration of the Magi* (1522), the man carrying the end of the cross in the Certosa *Way to Golgotha* (1523), a bystander in the S. Felicita *Entombment* (1526-1528), Saint Benedict in the Louvre St. Anne altar (1528-1529), etc.

[2] For the text, see Appendix II. A long section of the poem itself (lines 204-350) is a farmer's calendar, which instructs the farmer to carry out his tasks in accord with the rising and setting of the fixed stars.

The dramatis personae of the fresco also suggest celestial phenomena. As we have seen in Renaissance illustrations to the proem of the *Georgics* (pls. 101, 102), from which the tablet quotation is taken, the celestial nature of Virgil's "gods and goddesses all" was understood. Moreover, the notion of the luminaries' acting through the agency of love was a familiar Neoplatonic conceit, which was elaborated in writings of the circle of Lorenzo il Magnifico.[3] However, rather than placing Sol-Apollo and Luna-Diana *in* the sky, Pontormo has posed them on the upper wall *against* the sky. He has also subtly indicated that they are to be read as personifications of sun and moon. The preparatory studies for Vertumnus, who sits below Sol-Apollo, show the god as if illuminated by the light of the sun. In three of these he shades his eyes as if against its rays, and, in the most finished of the series, light falls on him as if radiating from Sol-Apollo above (pl. 150).[4] In a study for Luna-Diana, Pontormo indicates the crescent that she usually wears on her brow (pl. 151).[5] However, the lunar identity of the figure is only hinted in the fresco by the circular shape of her white shawl and, possibly, by the unusual roundness of her white-capped head.

The identity of Sol-Apollo and Luna-Diana as celestial bodies reinforces the themes of dynasty and the Cycles of Time in the lunette. In astrological thinking, the sun and the moon stand for the idea of the Father and the Mother, a symbolism which is congruous with the themes of familial continuity and birth in the lunette, and which is reinforced by the division of the scene into male and female sides. These figures also, of course, rule the yearly cycle of the sun and the monthly cycle of the moon. Hence, Sol-Apollo is the only one of the gods in the fresco to reach up into the band bordering the sky, which we may take to symbolize the sphere of the zodiac, through which the sun appears to makes its yearly journey.

The progression of the seasons of the earth, represented by the four gods on the wall below Sol-Apollo and Luna-Diana, echoes the heavenly cycles above. The nonplanetary gods Vertumnus-Janus (Winter) and Pomona (Spring) are the gods of heaven and earth, who frame the celestial scene (just as they frame the fresco as the story of Vertumnus and Pomona). However, the other two Seasons, who double as the agricultural gods Saturnus and Venus *hortorum*, are the planetary deities Saturn and Venus. This second male-female pair of the heavens also stands for the idea of the Father and the Mother in traditional astrological interpretation, and thus the Saturn and Venus of the lunette may be seen to underscore its theme of dynastic continuity.[6]

[3] Ficino, *De amore*, V, 13.

[4] Uffizi 6599Fr (Cox-Rearick, 1964, I, cat. 137). See also Uffizi 6685Fv (cat. 134), Uffizi 6515Fr (cat. 135), Uffizi 6685Fr (cat. 136), and the faint sketch on Uffizi 6742Fv (cat. 29). McKillop, 1970, pp. 4-5, remarked on this modeling.

[5] Uffizi 6531F (Cox-Rearick, 1964, I, cat. 149). Michelangelo's *Night* in the New Sacristy wears such a diadem.

[6] Ptolemy, *Tetrabiblos*, III, 4. Although Vertumnus and Pomona are not celestial bodies, the triangle of male figures on one side of the fresco and the triangle of female figures on the other suggest the canonical Ptolemaic triangles—the northeast (masculine, ruled diurnally by Saturn) and the southwest (feminine, ruled diurnally by Venus). See Ptolemy, *Tetrabiblos*, I, 18. These two groups may also correspond with the related Ptolemaic notion of planetary sects, or families, the sun and Saturn representing the Father and belonging to the masculine, diurnal sect; Venus and the moon representing the Mother and belonging to the female, nocturnal sect (Ptolemy, *Tetrabiblos*, I, 17).

The planetary nature of Sol-Apollo, Luna-Diana, Saturn, and Venus is also indicated in other ways. They are positioned along a diagrammatically precise arc, which begins and ends in the sky with Sol-Apollo and Luna-Diana and which echoes the lower curve of the oculus and the garland. Along this arc, these four figures are joined by color: violet is shared by Sol-Apollo and Saturn, red by Luna-Diana and Venus, while outside the arc on which the planets are disposed Vertumnus and Pomona are dressed in earthy green and ocher. But perhaps most singular is the way Pontormo has decisively isolated each of the figures from his companions. Except for the male-female separation, which might have been suggested by the Vertumnus and Pomona story, there is nothing in Giovio's and Pontormo's literary sources to indicate such a radical mode of composition. This diagrammatic arrangement of isolated figures is all the more striking in relation to Pontormo's compositional study (pl. 75), where the gods are arranged into two groups of three, but are giant and cramped in their space. In the airy outdoors of the fresco, however, the ratio of the figures to the space is reversed.[7] The delicate forms of the gods, fixed in their triangular arrangement, are carefully isolated from one another, as if to hint that they be read as celestial bodies.[8]

All these elements suggest a cosmic reference of some kind; however, the Seasons in particular indicate that this pastoral tableau alludes to the zodiac and that its planetary deities are to be read in a zodiacal context. Earthly and celestial cycles of time were viewed as harmoniously complementary in the Renaissance, as in antiquity. Moreover, the themes of the Seasons and the Zodiac had long been linked in art, often appearing in a context of funerary apotheosis (implications of which are certainly present in the lunette).[9] In sarcophagi of the *Four Seasons* type, for example, the frieze of the Seasons is interrupted by the zodiac wheel (pl. 152).[10] Pontormo's "frieze" of the Seasons is similarly punctuated by the oculus. I have read this window as alluding to the Wheel of Fortune, the turn of which brings the renewal of Medici rule; and the fact that the Wheel of Fortune and the zodiac were virtually interchangeable in Renaissance thought suggests that the oculus may also carry such a meaning here.[11]

The arrangement of the Seasons beginning with Spring and ending with Winter on either side of the oculus encourages such a reading. This sequence is normal for Florentine art, as, for example, in the portico frieze of the villa itself (pl. 54). However, the

[7] This development can be followed in Pontormo's studies for the individual gods, such as a study for Pomona in which the leg of Luna-Diana touches her, while in the fresco the figures are decisively separated (Uffizi 6515Fv; Cox-Rearick, 1964, I, cat. 147). For discussion of similar lines of development in drawings for other figures, which involved a shift in the spacing of the walls, see Cox-Rearick, 1964, I, pp. 177-90.

[8] The two figural triangles may have been intended to evoke the well-known Ptolemaic concept of the harmonious trine aspect between planets separated by 120° in a horoscope. In view of the theme of love expressed in the quotation from *Georgics* I in the tablet, it is possible that the "trines"

of figures carry a message of the harmonious coexistence of the planets in the heavens.

[9] On these traditions in ancient art, see Webster, passim; and Levi, pp. 251-91.

[10] G.M.F. Hanfmann, *The Seasons Sarcophagus in Dumbarton Oaks*, Cambridge, Mass., 1951, I, pp. 3-72. For the *Seasons* sarcophagus in Pisa, Campo Santo, see II, no. 464, fig. 37.

[11] On Fortuna and the zodiac, see A. Doren, "Fortuna im Mittelalter und in der Renaissance," *Vorträge der Bibliothek Warburg*, I, 1922-1923, pp. 71-144; and H. R. Patch, *The Goddess Fortuna in Mediaeval Literature*, Cambridge, Mass., 1927, pp. 76-80.

placement of Spring on the right and the consequent right-to-left sequence in the lunette indicates its zodiacal frame of reference. This right-to-left (or reversed) movement of the Seasons from Spring echoes that of the zodiac in the heavens, in which the signs move counterclockwise from Aries, which corresponds to the vernal equinox and the month of March (fig. 6).

In art, from the illustrated calendars of antiquity to Renaissance cycles, the Seasons and the Months had always been keyed to the counterclockwise movement of the zodiac signs, even when the signs themselves were not pictured.[12] In the cycle at Palazzo Schifanoia, for example, the zodiac band is projected as a horizontal frieze, and the months, beginning with March on the east wall, follow it in a counterclockwise progression around the room. Moreover, in an individual scene such as August, the three decans of the corresponding zodiac sign (Virgo) and, above it, the triumph of the ruling goddess (Ceres) all move from right to left (pl. 132). Likewise, in Chigi's horoscope ceiling in the Sala di Galatea, the signs move to the left around the room (fig. 13).

This convention is also found in Medici art from the late Quattrocento, although it becomes explicit only later in works of the *principato*. Two of these, both linked closely in theme to Pontormo's lunette, show a zodiacally related reversal of the Seasons. In Bronzino's *Primavera* tapestry, the theme of Time's Return in spring is expressed not only by the presence of Flora-Fiorenza but by three zodiac signs of her season (Aries, Taurus, and Gemini), which move diagonally from the lower right to the upper left of the composition (pl. 61).[13] In Francesco Poppi's *Golden Age* of 1567 (based on a design by Vasari), the Seasons are shown in the heavens, beginning with Spring to the right and progressing to Winter on the left (pl. 154). The connection between these Seasons and the zodiac is indicated not only by their reversed order but by the inscription held by the putto, which alludes to the Golden Age and to the "now most beautiful year," presumably the year which begins in Aries (sign of the birth of Florence and of Francesco de' Medici), pictured as the Ram in the sky.[14]

These works, coming from a time when astrological as well as other traditional Medici themes were explicitly spelled out in their art, aid in clarifying the meaning of earlier Medici paintings, in which such zodiacal themes are only implicit. Botticelli's *Primavera* (pl. 60), for example, tells of Medici renewal in a Golden Age of eternal springtime, signaled by the implicitly present zodiac signs of the renewing year. And Pontormo's fresco, the imagery of which is actually closer to Botticelli's subtle painting than to the more overtly propagandistic Medici art of the later Cinquecento, elaborates on the same

[12] For example, see the mosaic calendar from Carthage (British Museum), in which the Months and the Seasons begin at the lower right of a zodiac-like wheel and move counterclockwise. For this calendar and others, see Webster, figs. 18 and 20; Levi, p. 279, no. 69, and the diagram on p. 281. In these calendars, personifications of the Sun and Moon often accompanied those of the Seasons and Months.

[13] See chap. 11, "Epilogue." In Bacchiacca's *Seasons* of 1552-1553 (Uffizi 524, 526-27), another tap-estry series executed for Cosimo, the zodiac signs and the seasons move from right to left (see M. Viale Ferrero, *Arazzi italiani del Cinquecento*, Milan, 1961, illus. on pp. 72-73).

[14] Vincenzo Borghini's *invenzione* for this work is quoted in Scoti-Bertinelli, p. 205. For Vasari's drawing for this painting, based on Borghini's program and inscribed in the sky O BEGL'ANNI DELL'ORO / NUNC FORMOSISSIMVS ANNVS (O beautiful years of gold; now most beautiful year), see Paris, Louvre 2170 (Monbeig-Goguel, cat. 224).

theme. However, while the *Primavera* shows only the season of spring, the Seasons in *Vertumnus and Pomona* encompass the entire yearly cycle.

The important Medici theme of the Cycles of Time is also emphasized in the lunette by repetition. As in the portico frieze panel with its two yearly cycles, the Seasons and the Months, the cycle of the year is repeated in the lunette by the seasonal garland, the spring and summer end of which is held by the putto above Venus, the autumn and winter end by the putto above Saturn. And, since these seasonally related putti sit at the lower "corners" of the oculus and since there are two more putti in similar positions above the window, it is possible that the four figures are to be read as secondary personifications of the Seasons, echoing the horizontal frieze of the Seasons on a vertical plane above. These putti-Seasons would then move counterclockwise (beginning with Spring at the lower right) around the oculus, which evokes the turning of the zodiac wheel in the heavens.[15]

Seen in relation to the cycles of the Seasons and to the oculus above it, the GLOVIS disk takes on additional significance. Not only does it signal the theme of Time's Return and—centered on the seasonal garland and flanked by the Seasons—refer to the seasonal cycle (which is, of course, a metaphor of Time's Return), but it may also provide a clue to a zodiacal reading of the lunette. Like the solar disk in the Baptistery with its palindrome inscription (pl. 125), GLOVIS reads backward, and it spells SI VOLG[E]—it turns. GLOVIS may then be a covert instruction to the observer that the fresco be read not only in relation to the turning of the year, the season, the month, and the day on earth, but to the complementary turning of the zodiac in the heavens.

MEDICI HOROSCOPES AND THE MEDICI GOLDEN AGE

Pontormo's *Vertumnus and Pomona* contains a veiled message of Medicean astrological destiny, which reinforces several of the themes of the fresco. In a general sense, it heightens the theme of Fortune. This theme, actually personified in the *Hercules and Fortuna* lunette, is present here in the symbolism of the cycles of nature and the cosmos. More specifically, it enhances the theme of Pope Leo, patron of the Salone, who is alluded to in the figure of Sol-Apollo, and the theme of Cosimo, the newborn Medici heir, who is alluded to in the newly sprouting laurel. Astrological imagery, drawn from the horoscopes of these two Medici, proclaims the Virgilian notion of Leo, the New Apollo who heralds the return of the Golden Age, and Cosimo, a New Saturn, born during his rule.

As is the case with Apollo imagery elsewhere in Leo's art, Pontormo's Sol-Apollo, who rises above the other figures on the eastern side of the lunette, refers to the auspi-

[15] These figures recall the traditional seasonal personifications at the corners of ancient calendars. See above, n. 12; also the mosaic calendar from Antioch, showing March to June with Spring (Levi, fig. 2). In this calendar the Seasons are represented as female busts; in others, they are seated figures; and in medieval calendars of this type, they are often putti-like angels (cf. Webster, fig. 82).

ciously placed rising sun of Leo's horoscope. Other allusions to his horoscope are to the same features of his chart which were selected for emphasis by his iconographers in the Sala dei Pontefici (fig. 12). In the Sala, the *signs* of Leo's sun and moon are placed opposite each other, as they are in the horoscope; in the lunette, the personifications of the sun and moon, Sol-Apollo and Luna-Diana, sit on opposite sides of the oculus. In the Sala, the Libran planets, Saturn and Venus, occupy the ends of the vault in allusion to Leo's auspicious "mid-heaven in Libra"; in the lunette, Saturn and Venus are the planetary deities on the lower wall. Moreover, the Libran theme is underscored by the actual setting of Pontormo's scene. I have suggested that the design of the garden walls and the oculus might allude to Leo's *impresa* of the yoke and *diamante*. However, the design even more precisely resembles the glyph for Libra—the celestial yoke (≏).

The motif of the walls intersecting the oculus was clearly the initial organizing principle of Pontormo's design (cf. pls. 75-76); however, in the fresco, the upper wall has been lowered, the oculus projected higher against the sky, and the horizontals of the walls more clearly marked. The separation of the walls can be followed in Pontormo's studies for the individual gods, as in a drawing showing Pomona and Luna-Diana closer together than they are in the fresco; the poses of Saturn and of Pomona, both of whose legs initially hung down over the wall, were also changed as the composition developed, so that their legs no longer obstruct the horizontal of the wall.[16] In the fresco, the walls are widely separated, the deities isolated from one another, and the depth of the lower parapet reduced so that both walls read as if on the same plane as the oculus. This flattening, which emphasizes the analogy with the Libra glyph, is visually confirmed by the spatial situation of the garland with the GLOVIS disk: the putti who hold it are seated on the upper wall, but the disk hangs in front of the lower wall. Finally, the reference to the Libra glyph is made unmistakable in the outermost band of the painted frame of the oculus, which is slightly pinched-in at the two points where it intersects the upper wall (a feature, incidentally, not copied by Allori).

The astrologically predestined rulership of Leo-Apollo, the sun pope, under Libra, the sign of justice and peace, is the primary cosmic theme of Giovio's and Pontormo's program. But there is a second message as well, one which is more hidden and complex, perhaps even occult in the sense that its meaning may not have been intended to be readily intelligible except to the informed observer. Further astrological imagery, based on the horoscope of the newborn Cosimo, delineates this other message of the fresco: that the dynastic continuity and immortality of the Medici made possible by the birth of the New Cosimo in the rule of Leo was predestined in the stars.

Like Leo's horoscope, the horoscope of Cosimo is known from a number of sixteenth-century sources, both published and unpublished. For purposes of comparison with the lunette—for which a simplified chart must have been used, in any event—these are

[16] Uffizi 6515Fv (see above, n.7); Cambridge, Fogg Art Museum 1932.342v (cat. 139); and Uffizi 6514Fv (cat. 146).

virtually interchangeable. However, the horoscope in Giuntini's *Speculum astrologiae* of 1581 (fig. 14) is the closest to one that can be erected on the basis of Cosimo's recorded hour of birth.[17] Therefore, I shall use the data of Giuntini's chart here, but shall also refer to the rectified chart by Giuliano Ristori, on which he based a long prognostication written for Cosimo just a few months after he became duke of Florence in 1537 (fig. 15).[18]

Giuntini's chart is accompanied by a brief commentary, in which he notes that the horoscope has been rectified by a certain Petrus de Sylva Hispanus according to the rules of Ptolemy.[19] He indicates that Cosimo's birth, which was preceded by a new moon, took place under the sign of Gemini (♊), which is ruled by Mercury (☿); that the ascendant [*horoscopus*], which is the indicator of the life of the individual, is located in Capricorn at 24° ♑ 16'; and that Mercury is located in Cancer (♋). The other features of the chart are as follows: Scorpio (♏) marks the mid-heaven; Saturn (♄) is rising in conjunction with the ascendant—only four degrees from it; Venus (♀) is in conjunction with Mercury in the seventh house in Cancer;[20] Mars (♂) is in Leo (♌), which is an intercepted sign (one not represented on a house cusp); Jupiter (♃) is in Libra in the eighth house; and the moon (☽) is in Sagittarius (♐) in the eleventh house. Not indicated in Giuntini's chart, but present in Ristori's (where it is located in the seventh house), is an important point in the horoscope known as the Pars Fortunae (the Part of Fortune ⊕), which relates to prosperity.[21]

Considering the way in which Pontormo's imagery of dynastic regeneration and the return of the Golden Age links the destinies of the Medici pope and the Medici child (quite apart from any astrological symbolism), we must first recognize certain correlations between the two Medici horoscopes which would have been noted by astrologers of the time. The charts are related as if by reflection: Leo's birthday was 11 December, with the sun at 28° Sagittarius 08' south declination, close to the winter solstice; Cosimo's birthday was 11 June, with the sun at 29° Gemini 03' north declination, on the very eve of the summer solstice. Furthermore, because the ascendants of the two hor-

---

[17] Giuntini, 1581, I, p. 127. For Cosimo's time of birth and horoscope, see Appendix I.

[18] See chap. 11, n. 43.

[19] Giuntini, 1581, I, p. 127 (*Cosmi Medicis Nativitatis*): "Petrus de Sylva Hispanus vir scientificus, rectificavit nativitatem Cosmi Medicis magni Ducis Hetruriae, secundum regulam Ptolemaei ad instar Mercurij. Nam novilunium praecessit nativitatem in 15. gradibus & 24. minutis Geminorum: cuius loci fuit gubernator Mercurius: quoniam ipse habebat domicilium & triangularitatem: quia nativitas erat nocturna: posuit ergo in horoscopo 24. grad. & 16. minuta Capricorni, sicut fuit Mercurius in Cancro. Quod autem bene regulasset hanc nativitatem, demonstravit horoscopus, semper vitae significator, ut dicit Ptolemaeus, qui per directionem venit ad terminos Martis, & ad quadratum Saturni, & ad trigonum Martis in signis paucarum

ascensionum in anno. 55. currente suae aetatis. Anno domini 1574. Quare ipso anno vitam complevit. Et sic relinquitur, regulam Ptolemaei esse veram."

[20] Like Saturn, which is close to the cusp of the first house, Venus is so close to the cusp of the seventh house (ruled by Venus) that astrologers, like Ristori, placed it there.

[21] Ptolemy, *Tetrabiblos*, III, 10, explains that the Pars Fortunae is located in respect to the moon as the ascendant is located in respect to the sun (see also Manilius, *Astronomica*, 3, 96-159). This formula places the Pars Fortunae of Cosimo's chart at 10° Cancer 37' in the sixth house, but Ristori, f. 156v and 157v, calculates it in the seventh house in conjunction with Venus and Mercury, where he considers it to be auspiciously placed.

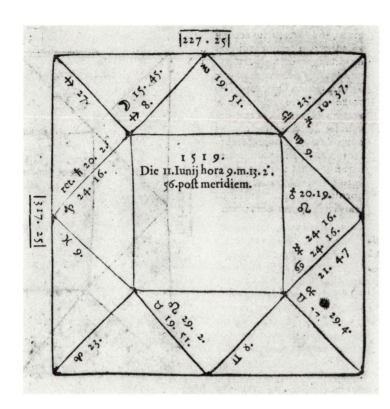

14. Horoscope of
Duke Cosimo de' Medici,
11 June 1519
(after Giuntini, 1581)

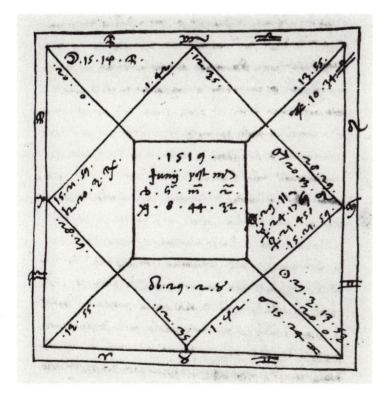

15. Horoscope of
Duke Cosimo de' Medici,
11 June 1519,
by Giuliano Ristori
(Laur. MS 89
sup., 34, f. 135r)

oscopes are located in adjoining signs, the relationship between the signs and the houses is such that all the signs in Leo's chart are one house ahead of those in Cosimo's chart: that is, Leo's ascendant is in Sagittarius, Cosimo's in Capricorn; Leo's mid-heaven is in Libra, Cosimo's in Scorpio; etc. The mirror-image relationship of the charts and the sequential relationship of the signs reading from the ascendant might have been seen to indicate a predestined connection between the two individuals and, indeed, the possibility that this new Medici child, born on Leo's lucky day of the eleventh, would continue the Medici dynasty.

Astrological imagery in the fresco suggests just such notions of connection and continuity, echoing its dynastic themes on a cosmic level. A literal conflation of the two charts was, of course, not attempted; however, their relationship is suggested by the correlation of Leo's "sun in Sagittarius" and mid-heaven in Libra" with some of the most auspicious features of Cosimo's horoscope.

Before discussing this imagery, I should like to suggest the way in which the lunette could lend itself as a "setting" for a zodiacal scheme and how Cosimo's horoscope could be used as the basis for such a design. A horoscope, by definition, depicts the zodiac circle (360°); however, a lunette (180°) is an ideal format for the illustration of Cosimo's particular chart, for all his planets except the sun are above the horizon, or within a semicircle of 180°. It would thus be possible to indicate in the lunette the location of Cosimo's occupied houses from the seventh through the twelfth houses and any of his planetary positions except the sun. The inclusion of these houses and planetary positions accords well with the traditional astrological interpretation of "elevated" planets. Ptolemy, for example, considered planets above the horizon in a horoscope to have greater potency than those below, especially if they were located at the angles (as are three of the planets in Cosimo's chart).[22] Moreover, the impossibility of representing the sun of Cosimo's horoscope in such a scheme would apparently not have been regarded as an obstacle, for Ristori indicates that the placement of the sun was very unfavorable;[23] and indeed, Cosimo's "sun in Gemini" was never alluded to later in his own art.

Not only is the lunette thus ideally suited to the representation of the most positive houses and planets of Cosimo's horoscope, but it was already marked off into thirty-degree segments like those of a chart by the *palle* roundels which are placed around its

[22] On this important point, see Ptolemy, *Tetrabiblos*, III, 10: "In the first place we must consider those places [houses] prorogative in which by all means the planet must be that is to receive the lordship of the prorogation; namely, the twelfth part of the zodiac surrounding the horoscope [ascendant], from 5° above the actual horizon up to the 25° that remains, which is rising in succession to the horizon; the part sectile dexter to these thirty degrees, called the House of the Good Daemon; the part in quartile, the mid-heaven; the part in trine, called the House of the God; as the part opposite, the Occident. Among these there are to be preferred, with reference to power of domina-

tion, first those [degrees] which are in the mid-heaven, then those in the orient, then those in the sign succedent to the mid-heaven, then those in the occident, then those in the sign rising before mid-heaven; for the whole region below the earth must, as is reasonable, be disregarded when domination of suich importance is concerned, except only those parts which in the ascendant sign itself are coming into the light."

[23] See Ristori, f. 151r: "la vile et mala qualità del luogo ove si truova il Sole." See also f. 168r: "Et finalmente essendo molto deboli le forze del Sole, per il suo cader nel VIª [casa]," and f. 169v: "la tanto vile positura del Sole in questa natività."

edge. The cusps of the houses of the chart could thus correspond with these already-existing markers, and the whole lunette could be seen to represent the 180° of the horoscope above the horizon, with its base reading as the horizon, or the ascendant-descendant axis of the chart. At the center of the baseline is the GLOVIS disk, which may be read in this context as the earth. Cosmological diagrams show the earth at the center of the planetary spheres and the wheel of the zodiac (pl. 124), and in horoscope diagrams the earth is conceptually the center point of the horizon-line dividing the elevated houses from those below the horizon (fig. 6). GLOVIS, then, reads symbolically as the very point from which we view the heavens, the constellations, and the stars.[24]

Vertumnus and Pomona is, of course, a complex work of art, not an illustration of a horoscope. In order to indicate certain aspects of Cosimo's horoscope within the context of its poetic imagery, some license had to be taken. The thirty-degree divisions around the edge of the lunette suggest that a simplified horoscope using the ancient equal-house system of domification, the so-called Modus Equalis method of Ptolemy, may have been used. According to this system of erecting a chart, all the houses are exactly thirty degrees (rather than varying as in other methods), and all the cusp signs repeat the degree of the ascendant sign.[25] This system was in general use in the sixteenth century, as can be seen, for example, in Gerolamo Cardano's horoscope for Charles V, where the ascendant is rounded off to Capricorn 18° and the house cusps are all placed at eighteen degrees of the subsequent signs (fig. 16).[26] Using Giuntini's planetary positions, but with the ascendant rounded off so that it coincides with the position of Saturn at 20° Capricorn, we may erect a similar horoscope for Cosimo (fig. 17).[27]

The house cusps and zodiac signs of this horoscope—the planets will be placed later—can be projected over the design of the lunette (fig. 18). We count from the ascendant at the lower left twenty degrees to 0° Capricorn, to the cusp of the twelfth house at 20° Sagittarius, which corresponds to the *palle* roundel with which Sol-Apollo's arm is aligned. We then continue to the cusp of the eleventh house at 20° Scorpio (the mid-heaven of Cosimo's chart), which corresponds to the roundel with which the putto's standard is aligned. The cusp of the tenth house is at the zenith of the chart (counting 90° from the

[24] There are other clues that the GLOVIS disk signifies the earth. It is, of course, round like the globe; moreover, it is visually equatable with the *palle* roundels of the vault, and the *palle* had long been associated with the earth in Medici imagery through the wordplay *palla-mondo*. GLOVIS may also be a pun on GLOBVS (as in a Medici manuscript of Leonardo Dati's astrological poem *La Sfera*, f. 39).

[25] In the equal-house system of domification, the houses were determined by ancient astrologers either by dividing the ecliptic into twelve equal divisions (or arcs) of 30° of space (the equal-house method) or by the unequal trisection of the arc between the ascendant and the mid-heaven (see O. Neugebauer and H. G. Van Hoesen, *Greek Horoscopes*, Philadelphia, 1959, pp. 7-8).

[26] Cardano, no. VII. On the equal-house system in the sixteenth century, see Gaurico, f. 65v, where its use is attributed to the fifteenth-century astrologer Paris de Cesere, and to his contemporaries, Cardano and Schöner.

[27] I am grateful to Claudia Rousseau for demonstrating to me the way certain features of the lunette accord with such a simplified version of Cosimo's chart. It will be noted that the only issue in making these correspondences is the minor rectification (3°) which must be made in the ascendant in order to place both Saturn (at 20° Capricorn 25′) and Venus (at 21° Cancer 47′) on the horizon. This rectification results in an ascendant degree which corresponds with 9:17 p.m., but for clarity I have retained Giuntini's planetary positions based on 9:13 p.m. in fig. 17.

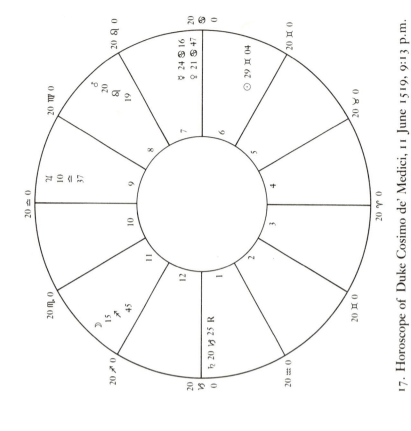

17. Horoscope of Duke Cosimo de' Medici, 11 June 1519, 9:13 p.m. (equal-house)

16. Horoscope of Charles V, 24 February 1500 (after Cardano)

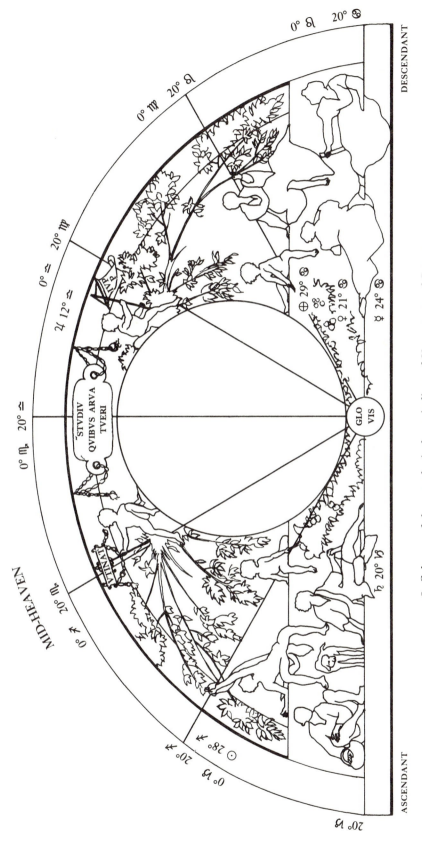

STVDIV
QVIBVS ARVA
TVERI

VLTINAT

GLO
VIS

MID-HEAVEN

DESCENDANT

ASCENDANT

0° ♑

20° ♋

♋ 20°

0° ♏

20° ♏

0° ♎

20° ♎

♉ 12°

0° ♏

20° ♎

0° ♐

20° ♏

⊕ 29°

☌ 21°

♄ 24° ♋

♄ 20° ♑

☉ 28°

0° ♑

20° ♐

20° ♑

18. Scheme of the astrological symbolism of *Vertumnus and Pomona*

ascendant), and it corresponds to the central roundel. To the right of the tablet, the cusps of the ninth house (Virgo) and the eighth house (Leo) correspond to the next two roundels, 0° Leo corresponding to a point 10° above the horizon; finally, the descendant at 20° Cancer marks the horizon itself.

✳ ✳ ✳

Turning now to the figures in the fresco in relation to this schematic projection of Cosimo's chart, we find that there are geometric correlations between five of the six figures nearest the oculus, or "zodiac wheel," and the following features of the horoscope: "ascendant and Saturn in Capricorn," "descendant, Venus, Mercury, and the Pars Fortunae in Cancer," "Jupiter in Libra," and the "mid-heaven in Scorpio." Of the elevated planets, only the "moon in Sagittarius" and "Mars in Leo" are not represented.

The most striking correlation is between the Venus and Saturn of the fresco and the aspect of opposition at the angles between "Saturn in Capricorn" and "Venus in Cancer" in Cosimo's horoscope. Indeed, in the fresco, this aspect is reproduced exactly: if the wall on which these figures recline is understood as the horizon-line of the horoscope, the planets lie along the horizon-line just as they do in the chart. Their mirror-image positions (echoed by their attending putti) also suggest opposition, and Venus not only reverses Saturn's pose but turns away while he turns toward the observer. Moreover, Saturn's upward-turning movement and Venus' lowered pose suggest that Saturn is rising and Venus is setting, just as the planets do in Cosimo's horoscope.

Pontormo's Saturn, the agricultural god in this pastoral tableau, carries the message of the return of his peaceful Golden Age under the Medici. Read as the "Saturn in Capricorn" of Cosimo's horoscope, however, the youthful sower has additional meaning: he connects Cosimo, a New Saturn, with the myth of the Medicean Golden Age.

I do not suggest that in 1520 the infant Cosimo de' Medici was thought of as a New Saturn (although later he certainly was), only that the astrological destiny of the child as revealed in his horoscope would have been seen as unequivocally Saturnian. His horoscope is dominated by the planet: rising in the ascendant Capricorn and ruler of the sign, Saturn is in domicile and is the lord of the ascendant, as is attested by Ristori and Gaurico.[28] Saturn is also well aspected, being in opposition to Venus and Mercury

---

[28] Ristori, f. 135v., begins his analysis of Cosimo's chart with a discussion of its most important planets, Mercury, Saturn, and Jupiter. Ristori considers Saturn a powerful planet because of its favorable aspects (especially the opposition to Mercury), and he notes that, according to Maternus, Saturn would be considered the principal lord of the chart. See f. 140r on Saturn as lord of the ascendant in its house; f. 152v on "Saturno . . . ben situato"; f. 155v on "il signore dell ascendente fortunato . . ."; f. 168r on "le felicità Vostre da stelle per natura maligne, come da Marte et da Saturno . . ."; and f. 168v on Saturn in Capricorn, which ultimately brings "le attioni grandissime et felicissimi accrescimenti di prosperità." In his commentary on the chart, Gaurico, bk. II, f. 16r, notes Mars, Mercury, and Saturn as its lords: "Quid autem interea portendant Mars in occiduo cardine platice supputatus, et Stilbon [Mercury] ibidem partiliter, Saturnus horoscopi Ecodespotes, et Luna in cacodemone, alii diiudicent." (What the meaning is of the appearance of Mars on the western horizon [*sic*] and Mercury almost in the same place and Saturn as Lords of the horoscope, and the Moon in Sagittarius, let others judge.)

at the angles, the opposition of Saturn to Venus in this position being considered by Ptolemy to be "a prediction of continuous happiness."[29] These aspects were an important consideration, for Saturn is known as the greater malefic and thought to bring misfortune if badly placed. Finally, Saturn has the additional advantage of enjoying "familiarity" with Jupiter, the greater benefic.[30]

The dual characteristics attributed in the Rennaisance to Saturn as a planet were the same as those associated with Saturn as a god.[31] Saturn was often conceived as Time the Destroyer and pictured as an old man ruling his unhappy children. But the planet was also thought of as a positive force which ruled geometry and agriculture, particularly the season of sowing associated with its late autumn domicile of Capricorn. In the Sala dei Pontefici, it is a benign old Saturn, patron of time (the snakes) and agriculture (the scythe and sheaf of wheat), who rides his chariot (pl. 146), and the same figure appears as "Saturn in Pisces" in Chigi's horoscope ceiling (fig. 13). The Saturn of Pontormo's fresco is also a beneficent figure: he is portrayed in accord with the conceit of rustic guise as a sower, ready to sow the now-assured harvest of Medicean dynastic continuity.

Capricorn had further positive associations which may have led to Cosimo's Capricorn ascendant being signaled in the fresco. More than any other other zodiac sign, Capricorn had an exalted tradition. It is, of course, the sign of the birth of Christ (and it occurs in Renaissance art in this context).[32] It is also the sign of the rebirth of the sun after the winter solstice. As the sign of the return of light as the days lengthen, Capricorn was traditionally paired with Cancer, sign of the summer solstice and the beginning of the return to darkness. Thus, according to Macrobius' well-known formulation, Cancer and Capricorn are the zodiacal doors through which the soul passes on its way to earth—the *porta hominem*—and on its way to immortality—the *porta deorum*.[33] As the "gate of

[29] On the importance of the planets at the angles, see Ptolemy (quoted above, n. 23). Ptolemy, III, 4, also calls attention to the importance of Saturn and Venus as standing for the Father and Mother. See also Ristori, f. 140r, 149r, 149v, and 153r, on the Saturn in opposition to Venus and Mercury as a positive aspect of the chart.

[30] The term "familiarity" connotes a harmonious relationship between two planets, as when one is located in the domicile of another or—as in the case of Saturn and Jupiter in Cosimo's chart—one (Jupiter) is in the sign of exaltation (Libra) of the other. Ristori (f. 150v, 160r-160v) discusses this positive relationship between Saturn and Jupiter in Cosimo's chart.

[31] See chap. 5, n. 61. The Neoplatonist's Saturn was the benevolent ruler of contemplation and agriculture, who is shown as a scholar carrying a sheaf of wheat in Dati's *La Sfera*, f. 3r. On Saturn as responsible for agriculture and as the "Dio dei lavoratori," see Villani, bk. X, 118, who notes the influence of the planet over the season of sowing

(at the time of the sign of Capricorn). Discussions of horoscopes in the circle of Lorenzo il Magnifico deemed Saturn's influence positive. See, for example, the mention of the beneficent Saturn in the ascendant Aquarius (its domicile) in Ficino's horoscope ("Lettres sur la connaissance de soi et sur astrologie," ed. and tr. A. Chastel, *La Table Ronde*, Paris, 1945, no. 2, p. 204).

[32] See, for example, J. L. Ward, "Hidden Symbolism in Jan van Eyck's Annunciations," *Art Bull.*, 57, 1975, pp. 196-205.

[33] *Somnium Scipionis*, I, 12 1ff. For this tradition see Deonna, pp. 64-66; and Dwyer, p. 60. This tradition is exemplified in Renaissance astrological art in Agostino di Duccio's zodiacal reliefs in the Tempio Malatestiano, Rimini (see pl. 178). As C. Mitchell has pointed out ("The Imagery of the Tempio Malatestiano," *Studi romagnoli*, 2, 1952, pp. 77-90), the sign of Cancer is shown over the city of Rimini as the gate through which Sigismondo (born 19 June) descended to the world to rule. See also Naldi, "Ad Cosmum Medicean de eius lau-

the gods," Capricorn thus came to be associated with rebirth, resurrection, and immortality.

Capricorn was also considered fortunate as an individual's zodiac sign. In ancient astrological tradition Capricorn was regarded as a royal sign and, when prominent in a chart, credited with the creation of kings.[34] Moreover, as I have noted, it was the ascendant in the horoscope of Augustus and regarded by Suetonius as one of the omens "from which it was possible to anticipate and perceive his future greatness and uninterrupted good fortune."[35] In Augustus' personal imagery, the Capricorn was a device associated with symbols of Imperium and Fortuna, such as the globe, tiller, and cornucopia which appear in Augustan art (pls. 133-134).

It was primarily because of the Augustan association that Capricorn came to be connected with immortality, Imperium, and Fortuna in Renaissance thought. Valeriano, for example, relates Capricorn to the souls of the dead and propitious fate, noting that it is found on the medals of Augustus, "augurando (come dicono gl'astronomi) somma felicita a queli che sono nati di lui" (prophesying, as the astronomers say, highest happiness to those born under it).[36] Thus, when the future Charles V was born on 24 February 1500 with Capricorn in the ascendant (fig. 16), the sign was considered to augur his future greatness.[37] Charles later used it as a sign of his imperium, as, for example, on a triumphal arch in his entry into Milan in 1541, where "suo Marte amato assiso in Capricorno" (his beloved Mars seated in Capricorn)[38] conflated his Capricorn ascendant and Mars, lord of his mid-heaven in Scorpio.

Capricorn also had compelling Florentine connections, which in turn were linked with the tradition of the Augustan Capricorn. Augustus was widely regarded as the true founder of Florence.[39] In Vasari's *Foundation of Florence as a Roman Colony* (pl. 62), for example, he appears as one of the triumvirs with a Capricorn decorating his helmet. Moreover, as we have seen, the sign marks the mid-heaven of the horoscope of the rebirth of the city in 802 (fig. 7), and it was the sun sign and ascendant in the horoscope of Lorenzo il Magnifico (fig. 8).

Astrologers looking for auspicious signs in the horoscope of the newborn Medici heir

dibus," lines 145-52, in *Elegiarum*, bk. III, no. 4, pp. 70-75, where the poet describes the birth of Cosimo Pater Patriae as a descent through the sign of Cancer (not, in this case, his birth sign; see chap. 7, n. 28):

Hinc iter ingrediens Medices ubi sidera
 Cosmus
Splendida deseruit, superorum quilibet illum
Ad cancri portam fuerat comitatus euntem,
Nam licet ulterius nulli prodire deorum.

Hence when Cosimo de' Medici, beginning his journey, left the shining stars, one of the gods accompanied him on his way as far as the gate of Cancer, for none of the gods were permitted to go any farther.

[34] See, for example, Maternus, *Mathesis*, VIII, 28, 1: "Whoever has the ascendant in the first degree of Capricorn will be a king or emperor." On Capricorn's rulership associations, see Deonna, pp. 64-66.

[35] Suetonius, *Lives*, II, XCIV, 12 (quoted in chap. 7, n. 47).

[36] Valeriano, 1625, p. 122.

[37] Cardano, no. VII. For other horoscopes of Charles V, see Gaurico, bk. II, f. 38v; and Giuntini, 1581, I, p. 204.

[38] G. Albicante, *Trattato del Intrar in Milano di Carlo V*, Milan, 1541, n. p. (cited in Tanner, pp. 155-56).

[39] Rubinstein, 1967, pp. 64-73. See also chap. 3, n. 65.

could hardly have failed to notice its Capricorn ascendant. Not only did it have the associations mentioned above, but Charles V, whose chart with its ascendant at 18° Capricorn is so similar to Cosimo's, had been elected Holy Roman Emperor on 3 July 1519, less than a month after Cosimo's birth.

Later commentators certainly made much of this auspicious feature of Cosimo's horoscope. Writing in 1537, when Cosimo had just become duke, Ristori connects his astrological destiny with that of Florence, noting that Cosimo was predestined to become ruler of the city "perché l'ascendente della genitura è il mezo cielo della città" (the ascendant of the horoscope is the mid-heaven of the city).[40] Later, after Duke Cosimo elaborated the conceit of himself as a New Augustus, no reference to his horoscope or account of his life was without mention of the connection between his Capricorn ascendant and his rulership. In 1573, for example, Giuntini compared this aspect of his powerful horoscope with that of Charles V, noting that they both also had the mid-heaven in Scorpio, and going on to remark:[41]

> Et plura essent examinanda, quae cum pauci advertissent nescierunt cognoscere, et ipse (ut vident omnes) auget imperium suum: fugavit hostes suos, et vicit inimicos, et sunt expectanda maiora.

> And more things could have been observed which had been noticed by a few, but not understood; and this same [Cosimo], as everyone sees, increases his imperium: he put his enemies to flight and conquered his adversaries, and of him even greater things are expected.

And, in 1572, Cosimo's biographer, Mario Matasilani, states that Cosimo remembered,[42]

> che da Don Basilio metematico gl'era stata pronosticata una richissima heredità, e gl'haveva detto che nello ascendente della sua genitura era quella me-

[40] Ristori, f. 168r-168v.

[41] Giuntini, 1573, bk. V, f. 238v: "Verum ad haec accedunt, quod habet doriforiam Lunae, et stellam lucidam Coronae in culmine coeli, et duo simulacra: Equum alatum in horoscopo et Coronam septemtrionalem.

"Hanc similem constellationem habet Dux magnus Ethruriae invictus: Erat enim Cosma vir privatus, nobilis genere. Habuit enim haec duo simulacra et coniunctionem illam scilicet gradus illius coniunctionis in culmine coeli, habet et Coronam septemtrionalem et pegasum: ultra quod Mars dominus medii coeli est cum Basilisco in 21. grad. Leonis in sua conditione, et dominus ascendentis in ascendente, in suo domo."

(But to this it must be added that the horoscope has a doryphora of the moon and the shining star of the Crown at the zenith, and two constellations: the Winged Horse in the ascendant and the Northern Crown.)

(The Grand Duke of Etruria, the unvanquished, has this similar configuration. For Cosimo was of course only a private citizen, of noble stock. He had indeed these two constellations and that conjunction, namely the degrees of that conjunction at the zenith, and he also has the Northern Crown and Pegasus. In addition to this, Mars, the lord of the mid-heaven, is with the Basilisk at 21° Leo, in his position, and the lord of the ascendant is in the ascendant in his own house.)

I thank Claudia Rousseau for indicating this passage to me. For further on Giuntini's comparison of the two horoscopes, see n. 49 below and chap. 11, "Capricorn and the Crown of Ariadne."

[42] Matasilani, p. 31. See also Mannucci, p. 42: ". . . egli [Cosimo] haveva la futura grandezza mostrata pel Capricorno, ch'egli haveva nell'ascendente con felicissimo aspetto guardato da' Pianeti, come haveva avuto gia Augusto, e novellamente Carlo Quinto."

desima felice stella del Capricorno illuminato da mirabil' aspetto de' pianeti insieme d'accordo, come già era avvenuto ad Augusto.

that it had been predicted by the mathematician Basilio that he would have a very rich inheritance and he had been told that in the ascendant of his horoscope there was that same felicitous constellation of Capricorn, illuminated by the marvelous aspect of planets harmoniously joined, as had already occurred in the horoscope of Augustus.

Returning to the fresco, we can see that the theme of the Medici Golden Age is signaled by Cosimo's "Saturn in Capricorn" and that this figure is juxtaposed on the "ascendant," or eastern, side of the lunette with Pope Leo's "sun in Sagittarius," which is symbolized by Sol-Apollo seated on the wall above Saturn. This sequence of a "rising" Sol-Apollo followed by a "rising" Saturn hints at a connection between the destinies of two generations of Medici. It also revives and personalizes an old Laurentian conceit in which the notion of a Medici Golden Age was connected with Saturn, Apollo, and the Medici patron saints. I have mentioned that Pontormo's Apollo and Saturn in their bucolic setting recall the same two gods as joint patrons of the feast of Saints Cosmas and Damian held at Villa Careggi in Lorenzo's time. In his letter to Lorenzo describing the event, Ficino evokes a kind of sunrise Saturnalia—a Golden Age festival celebrated by the descendants of Cosimo Pater Patriae, who is identified with Jupiter.[43] These rites are cosmic, Ficino contends, for just as Saturn and the sun are joined in the heavens, so the rites of Apollo, patron of Lorenzo's Academy, and Saturn, patron of the farmers, will be joined at Careggi. Pontormo's fresco, with its *villani* and its planetary deities Sol-Apollo and Saturn, suggests just such a Medicean festival, recalling Laurentian imagery but celebrating also the new Medici Golden Age of Leo X.

Sol-Apollo and Saturn as planetary deities alluding to specific Medici horoscopes also relate to the theme of the Virgilian Golden Age, which is established in the tablet quotation from the *Georgics*. For, if Sol-Apollo alludes to Leo and Saturn to the newborn Cosimo, then the Golden Age theme already implicit in the quotation becomes relevant to the rule of Leo, to the birth of the Medici heir, and to the family's hopes for their immortality. This hint of the dawn of a new Golden Age during the reign of Leo-

[43] Ficino, *Opera*, I, pp. 843-44. The (abridged) text reads as follows: "Cum hodie Oriente Sole, summa uetusti montis fastigia peterem, montis, inquam, Vecchij, quem Marsilio suo colendum Cosmus ipse mandauit. Atque in hac huius sylua passim oberrans Caregiana palatia contemplarer, repente uenit in mentem, festum Cosmi Damianique diem iam illuxisse, quod animis ab ipso Cosmo eiusque filiis et nepotibus celebratum. Hic equidem non potui non dolere dum inde nullos usquam perspicerem ciues ad Cosmica (ut fieri solet) solennia confluentes. Cum subitò Iouius ille Cosmus cui Iuppiter iam conciliata Iunone ciuile imperium sine fine dedit, ab excelsa quercu propitius nobis aspirans, eiusmo di moerentes oraculis consolatur. Sacra, inquit, hodie, Marsili, mea Laurentius quidem urbana pius instaurat, tu uerò rustica mox, si mihi parueris, eadem hoc in luco nobis instaurabis. . . . Hodie Saturnus in coelo Phoebusque iunguntur. Hoc est Marsili uoluntas nostra sicut in coelo fit hodie, ita fieri et in terra, ut Apollinea nunc utrobique Saturnijs coniungantur. . . . Vera haec ferme (ut narro) sunt magnanime Laurenti. . . . Ita demum Apollineum, id est, philosophicum Saturnijs hominibus, id est, senioribus agricolis tuis paraui conuiuium, neque id quidem absque delphica lyra. Atque solennia Cosmica qualiacumque pro tempore, pro loco, pro facultate, potuimus in Phoebea Saturnij montis academiola libenter feliciterque celebrauimus. . . ."

Apollo in Pontormo's fresco thus brings the cycle of Medici history in the Salone to a close with a dream of future dominion.

Other planetary positions of Cosimo's horoscope besides the important "Saturn in Capricorn" in opposition to "Venus in Cancer" are also alluded to in the fresco. Mata-silani, quoted above, mentions the "marvelous aspect" of Capricorn to a harmonious planetary conjunction. He refers to the conjunction of Mercury and Venus (only three degrees apart) in Cancer. As I have mentioned, the opposition of Mercury and Venus in Cancer to Saturn in Capricorn at the ascendant-descendant angles of the chart is a positive aspect of Cosimo's horoscope; likewise, the Mercury-Venus conjunction itself was traditionally regarded as an exalted one.

It is clear that Mercury is not represented with Venus in the fresco; however, I believe that the presence of this planet is hinted (in Pontormo's characteristically covert manner). Unlike the other planets, which are designated as either masculine or feminine, Mercury is considered a "common" planet which might shift its sex according to the sex of the planet it attends.[44] Thus, when it is associated with the moon or with Venus (as here), Mercury was often represented as an hermaphrodite (Hermes-Aphrodite) to in-dicate its masculine-feminine nature.[45] Pontormo's "Venus in Cancer" may thus be taken to represent both planets: feminized by its proximity to Venus, Mercury is subsumed into the figure and is implicitly present at this point in the lunette. Indeed, the unusual view of the goddess from the rear, which recalls the traditional hermaphrodite pose of ancient sculpture, may even have been intended as a clue to this reading.

The Pars Fortunae, which is close to the Venus-Mercury conjunction in Ristori's horoscope for Cosimo (fig. 15), may also be indicated in the fresco. Ristori considers it auspiciously located; and, indeed, Ptolemy states that when the planet attending the sun (Venus, in this case) is in agreement with the Pars Fortunae, the subject of the horoscope will inherit the patrimony intact.[46] Medici patrimony would certainly have been significant in relation to the themes of the Salone and the lunette, and the putto who sits on the wall above Venus may signal this feature of Cosimo's chart. Smiling happily as he holds up the flowering garland and sitting directly under the banner of Jupiter (planetary ruler of the Pars Fortunae and hence associated with fortune), the putto may well allude to Cosimo's Pars Fortunae and to Medicean *fortuna* in general.

Another positive position in Cosimo's chart is that of Jupiter, benefic father and giver of the arts of rulership, which is auspiciously placed in Libra, sign of peace and justice. Jupiter is also well aspected, being sextile to the moon and maintaining familiarity with Saturn by its location in Libra, the sign of Saturn's exaltation.[47] Cosimo's "Jupiter in

[44] Ptolemy, *Tetrabiblos*, I, 17.

[45] Boccaccio, f. 51v, refers to Mercury as femi-nine when accompanying Venus or the moon. This tradition is reflected in Medici art: Cini, p. 170, describes a hermaphrodite Mercury in the "carro di Mercurio" in the 1565 wedding *apparato* of Francesco de' Medici. See also Pontormo's draw-ing of a hermaphrodite Mercury for the loggia of Villa Castello (pl. 173).

[46] Ptolemy, *Tetrabiblos*, III, 4. For Ristori's

opinion, see n. 21 above. It is probable, in view of the association of the Pars Fortunae with pros-perity, that the astrologer Basilio's prediction of Cosimo's "richissima heredita" was based on his interpretation of this position in the chart.

[47] On Jupiter's familiarity with Saturn, see above, n. 30. On Jupiter's importance in Cosimo's chart, see Ristori's opinion, cited in n. 28. See also Ri-stori, f. 146v, on the good placement of the benef-ics, Jupiter and Venus: "Onde in questa genitura

Libra" is indicated in the fresco by the banner inscribed ɪᴠᴘ ᴘ carried by the putto to the right above the oculus, which coincides with the beginning of the sign of Libra in the zodiacal scheme of the lunette. The putto holds this banner up into the wide band around the edge of the lunette, which I have taken as alluding to the zodiac band; moreover, it is distinguished in type from the standard held by the putto to the left of the oculus and it approximates the shape of the conventional glyph for the planet Jupiter (♃).

The sign of Libra in which Jupiter is located in Cosimo's horoscope (and which marks the mid-heaven of Leo's chart) is, as I have noted, suggested by the design of the walls in the fresco in conjunction with the oculus: together, they resemble the distinctive glyph for Libra (♎). This sign is also implicit in the tablet with its quotation from the *Georgics*, which is located at the very top of the fresco partly within the "zodiac band." For in the proem from which the phrase ꜱᴛᴠᴅɪᴠᴍ ǫᴠɪʙᴠꜱ ᴀʀᴠᴀ ᴛᴠᴇʀɪ is quoted, Augustus himself is apotheosized as the sign of Libra in which the sun was located at his birth. And, in the Brant woodcut illustrating the proem, the scales of Libra are actually depicted in the sky between Virgo and Scorpio (pl. 102).

A final position in Cosimo's chart that is alluded to in the lunette is the "mid-heaven in Scorpio." This position was often remarked upon by commentators on Cosimo's horoscope in the sixteenth century. He shared this mid-heaven with Charles V, just as their Capricorn ascendants were close together; but, more significant, 20° Scorpio was the degree of the famous conjunction of Saturn and Jupiter in Scorpio in 1484, which occasioned prophecies of the reform of Christianity.[48] Giuntini notes this coincidence and declares that when the mid-heaven is found at 20° Scorpio, the subjects of such horoscopes shall be "distinguished and exalted and kings."[49]

This important point in Cosimo's horoscope is indicated in the design of the fresco by the standard inscribed ᴠᴛɪɴᴀᴛ, which coincides with 20° Scorpio in the zodiacal scheme of the lunette and is wholly within the "zodiac band" of the sky. As is the case with the Jupiter banner, Pontormo provides a visual clue to the presence of Scorpio here in the tassels attached to the standard, which are arranged so as to resemble the glyph for Scorpio (♏). If we bear in mind that in astrological tradition the sign of Scorpio (ruler of the eighth house of the zodiac) is understood to symbolize death and rebirth,[50] a central theme of the fresco, we may now see that this putto with his standard alludes to Cosimo's birth as a triumph of life over death and is yet another indicator in the fresco of the theme of the return of the Golden Age during the rule of Leo X.

The remaining figure to be considered is Sol-Apollo's partner, Luna-Diana. She does

---

trovandosi Giove nella VIII house [casa] et Venere nella VII [casa] stelle benigne."

[48] On which see chap. 7, n. 3.

[49] Giuntini, 1573, bk. V, f. 238v: ". . . ipse habebat 20. partem Scorpionis in culmine, quae quidem pars fuit locus coniunctionis Saturni et Iovis anno 1484. Nam dicunt Iudaei quod in cuiuscunque nativitate fuerint gradus harum coniunctionum in horoscopo vel culmine, erunt sublimati ex exaltati, et Reges . . ." (He had 20° Scorpio at

the mid-heaven, and this degree was the place of the conjunction of Saturn and Jupiter in the year 1484. For the Jews say that whenever the degree of this conjunction is present in the ascendant or the mid-heaven on the occasion of someone's birth, they will be distinguished and exalted and Kings).

[50] On the traditions of Scorpio in the Renaissance, see L. Aurigemma, *Il Segno zodiacale dello Scorpione nelle Tradizioni occidentali dall'antichità greco-latina al Rinascimento*, Turin, 1976, pp. 137-87.

not represent a planetary position; however, just as Sol-Apollo's location under the cusp of Sagittarius in the zodiacal scheme of the lunette is a clue that he is to be identified with Pope Leo's sun, so the position of Luna-Diana under the cusp of Virgo gives a clue to her meaning. As I have discussed in chapter 5, Luna-Diana as Ceres and as Astraea-Giustizia (the related deities of renewal) is an important indicator of the theme of the Golden Age in the fresco. Traditional associations of Ceres and Astraea with Virgo only make the message stronger. Virgo, the last sign of summer, was identified with Ceres, goddess of the harvest. Aratus, for example, refers to Virgo as "the Maiden, who in her hands bears the gleaming ear of corn"—the latter alluding to Spica, the brightest star in the constellation, which was seen as Ceres' grain.[51] Manilius assigns Ceres to the guardianship of Virgo, and the goddess appears in this role in the Manilian astrological cycle at Palazzo Schifanoia.[52] There, August is represented by a *Triumph of Ceres* and a representation of Virgo in which the goddess and the personification of the zodiac sign are the same type (pl. 132). Moreover, Renaissance personifications of Virgo invariably depict her as identical to Ceres—a rustic, seated girl, her head wreathed in grain, holding up her harvest emblem. A *Virgo* from a late fifteenth-century astrological treatise shows this type (pl. 153),[53] a figure which may be compared with the Ceres in Solis's engraving of *Summer* (pl. 105). Pontormo's Luna-Diana corresponds to this familiar Virgo type, even to her blond hair and her red and white costume, which are Virgo's colors.[54]

Virgo was associated with Ceres because of its season, but in the legend that was elaborated in antiquity the sign of Virgo was also identified with the mythical figure of Astraea: according to Aratus, after the Virgin Justice left the earth at the end of the Golden Age, she *became* the constellation of Virgo.[55] Virgo, long connected with justice through its proximity to the scales of Libra, itself became an exemplar of justice, as is detailed by Manilius and others.[56] The conflation of Astraea with Virgo and the identification of Virgo with justice continued to be asserted in the Renaissance (as for example, by Ficino),[57] and it can be assumed that these associations were a commonplace in Medici circles of Pontormo's time.

Luna-Diana under the cusp of Virgo thus plays an important role in delineating the

[51] Aratus, *Phaenomena*, 96-97. See also Hyginus, *Poetica Astronomica*, II, 25. On the traditions of Virgo, see R. H. Allen, pp. 460-66.

[52] Manilius, *Astronomica*, 2, 442 ("spicifera est Virgo Cereris"). For the Palazzo Schifanoia see Warburg, "Schifanoia," pp. 258-65.

[53] Leopold of Austria, *De Astrorum scientia*, Augsburg, 1489, p. 4.

[54] See, for example, the red-gowned Virgo in *De Sphaera* (Ludovici, pl. VII).

[55] Aratus, *Phaenomena*, 96-136. See also the references in n. 51 above. The association between the Virgin Justice and the sixth sign of the zodiac may be covertly indicated by Virgil in *Eclogue* IV, in which the Virgin's return is described in the sixth line of the poem.

[56] See Manilius, *Astronomica*, 4, 542-46: "At her rising Erigone [Virgo], who reigned with justice over a bygone age and fled when it fell into sinful ways, bestows high eminence by bestowing supreme power; she will produce a man to direct the laws of the state and the sacred code, one who will tend with reverence the hallowed temples of the gods."

[57] See a number of references in Ficino's writings. For example, Ficino adds to Dante's reference to Astraea: "Chiamavasi la Vergine la Giustizia, la quale chiamavano ancora Astraea, cioè stellante" (P. Fraticelli, ed., *Opere minori di Dante Alighieri, De Monarchia*, tr. M. Ficino, Florence, 1834-1839, III, p. 29).

message of Time's Return and the return of the Golden Age. She closes a circle of associations, for Virgil's Virgin Justice, Dante's Giustizia, Astraea, Ceres, and Virgo are all to be understood as the same symbolic figure of renewal. In the fresco, this mythical cosmic deity has descended to earth in the rustic disguise of Pontormo's agricultural goddess, who has returned the farmers—Virgil's descendants of the Golden Age of Saturn—to the care of their peaceful garden in the new Golden Age of Medici Florence.

Beneath the pastoral disguise of Ovid's tale of the agricultural gods, Pontormo has thus created a tableau of the Medici Golden Age. It is signaled by the quotation from the *Georgics*, by GLOVIS, and by the Golden Age deities—Apollo, Janus, Saturn, Venus, and Astraea. And, beneath this meaning of the fresco, there is still another level, for these characters are the gods who rule the cycles of nature and the cosmos, of heaven and earth (Vertumnus-Janus and Pomona)—and four of them (Sol-Apollo, Luna-Diana, Saturn, and Venus) are planetary deities. Sol-Apollo, Luna-Diana, and the Libran planets (Saturn and Venus) refer to Pope Leo's rulership. In addition, because of their placement in Capricorn and Cancer, which is a clue to the horoscopic scheme of the lunette, the latter two planets refer to the horoscope of the newborn Medici heir, in which these positions, as well as those of "Jupiter in Libra" and the "mid-heaven in Scorpio" occur. All this cosmic imagery suggests that the astrological destinies of Leo, the New Apollo, and Cosimo, the New Saturn, are linked, and that the return of the Golden Age of the Medici is indeed predestined in the stars.

VERTUMNUS AND POMONA, LAURENTIAN ART, AND THE NEW SACRISTY

Returning once again to Pontormo's *Vertumnus and Pomona* in the context of a Salone conceived for Lorenzo il Magnifico and decorated by Leo X, we may consider the way in which its imagery is related to both Laurentian and Leonine art.

Pontormo's fresco stands alone among the works of art commissioned by Leo in its elaboration of Laurentian themes, particularly those relating to Nature, Time, and the Cosmos. Some of these themes had, of course, been programmatically revived on the occasion of the first Medici pageants after their restoration in 1512. But the *diamante* and *broncone* decorations were temporary festival *apparati* which, although they were surely vivid in the minds of the Florentines, were not permanent reminders of Medicean dynasty and destiny. And some of the individual motifs in the lunette had been adumbrated in works such as Raphael's tapestry borders of the *Times of Day* (pl. 21) and the *Seasons* (pl. 22), in which there are echoes of Lorenzo's mottos of Time—LE TEMPS REVIENT and GLOVIS—and Day and Night are personified as Sol-Apollo and Luna-Diana. But these borders are small-scale works, emblematic in character, and their function is to comment on the narratives of the tapestries, whereas in the Salone the same themes are elaborately developed in a monumental lunette in which the Medici who are the subjects of the *istorie* of the lateral walls below are identified with the celestial Cycles of Time and the planets of the heavens.

Pontormo's Ovidian pastorale, which masks themes of Time and the Cosmos, is in many respects profoundly retrospective, even neo-Laurentian in character. Giovio and Pontormo reached back to themes, conventions, and images of Laurentian art to convey messages of Medicean dominion and dynasty in a work which is nonnarrative, symbolic, and poetic in mode. As such, *Vertumnus and Pomona* contrasts strongly with the other sections of the Salone that were painted in 1520 and 1521. The subjects of Sarto's and Franciabigio's *istorie* were based on Roman history, while the themes of the lunette were drawn from the very Augustan poets, Virgil and Ovid, who had been favored by Naldi, Poliziano, and Lorenzo himself. Moreover, Ariosto's "Ne la stagion," the contemporary poem on which the imagery of the gods and the *lauro* was drawn, is itself neo-Laurentian in form and content. Thus, in contrast to the Romanizing, narrative style *all'antica* of the *istorie*, which is that of Leo's art in Rome, *Vertumnus and Pomona* is a highly self-conscious evocation of a past Laurentian art. This lyrical, nostalgic quality perfectly expresses the Medicean longing for the recovery of an idealized past, and the heightened and focused realism of Pontormo's *villani* and putti poignantly contrasts with the ephemeral fantasy of this Golden Age dream.

More than any other work of Leo's patronage, then, Pontormo's fresco recalls the subtle poetry of Laurentian art, in which themes of Nature, Time, and the Gods convey a veiled message of Medicean dominion which would not belie the myth of a republican Florence. The gods posing as rustics, the theme of the changing seasons, and the laurel-garden setting of the fresco all recall the humanist allegories of Botticelli and Signorelli (pl. 67), in which rustic gods in country settings act out Medicean eclogues such as those by Naldi and Poliziano. And the theme of the Cycles of Time, in particular, is reminiscent of the Months (and zodiac signs) in the *Primavera* (pl. 60) and the units of time on the portico frieze of the villa itself (pl. 49). Pontormo takes up this Laurentian imagery; however, rather than reading in a simple linear fashion as in the *Primavera* or the frieze, the yearly cycles of the heavens and the earth—the zodiac and the seasons—are conflated in his more complex, multileveled work.

Pontormo not only continues the general theme of the units of time of the frieze, but he emphasizes the theme of Dawn in a way that suggests the possibility that a Laurentian plan for the decoration of the lunette may have been available to him.[58] The succession of the Ages, the Year, the Seasons, the Months, the Day, and the Hour on the frieze concludes at its eastern end with Dawn as Apollo-Lorenzo ascends in his chariot into the sky (pl. 55). Inside the Salone at its southeastern end in *Vertumnus and Pomona*, the day that dawned on the frieze begins anew. Perhaps Lorenzo's own horoscope, with its rising sun, was once to be alluded to in this lunette; but, when the Salone was decorated for Leo, whose horoscope also featured a rising sun, the solar symbolism was transferred to him. On the ascendant side of the lunette is Janus, a figure borrowed

---

[58] Such a possibility is suggested by Chastel, 1961, p. 156: "On peut se demander si la lunette . . . n'est pas le vestige de l'ancien programme inauguré par les motifs de la frise extérieure et in- terrompu en 1492: on comprend mal cette évocation champêtre dans l'ensemble pompeux conçu pour Léon X."

from the cast of characters of the frieze and a god, we recall, to whom was attributed knowledge of the past and the future. Janus, one of whose epithets in antiquity was *Matutinus pater* (god of daybreak), signals the presence of the rising sun of Pope Leo's horoscope above him, and the figure next to Janus is the "rising" Saturn of the horoscope of Cosimo, the new Medici heir. This theme of sunrise, a metaphor of rebirth, thus suggests that Time has indeed returned for the Medici, just as Lorenzo's mottos LE TEMPS REVIENT and GLOVIS promised it would. Lorenzo's son Leo has recovered the Golden Age, and the immortality of the Medici is assured by the recent birth of the new heir.

The cycle of the day initiated in the frieze and continued in the sunrise of Pontormo's lunette would have concluded in the *Hercules* fresco at the southwestern end of the Salone. As painted later by Allori, it is of course an allegory of Grand Duke Francesco as Hercules, victorious over the forces of fate and fortune (pl. 118); however, if my hypothesis that its program dates from the Leonine campaign of work is tenable, then Sol-Apollo's journey through the heavens to the west would terminate in Hercules' Garden of the Hesperides—the western, astral garden which is yet another metaphor of the Golden Age. The sun sets and the cycle of the Salone decoration ends with the apotheosis of Leo as the immortal Hercules.

Pontormo's fresco also revives Laurentian imagery of Time in another sense. The notion of the dynastic and political continuity of the Medici through time is of course the unifying theme of the Salone decoration. It is the connecting link between the disparate scenes from Roman history on the lateral walls and, in turn, between these *istorie* and Pontormo's fresco. In the *Cicero* and *Caesar*, homage is paid to the founder of the Medici dynasty and Medicean political power, Cosimo Pater Patriae, and to Leo X, the present ruler of an expanded Medici dominion that includes Rome; in the *Titus* and *Scipio*, the virtuous deeds on behalf of the Florentine Republic of Piero di Cosimo and Lorenzo il Magnifico are celebrated. Pontormo also hints at this theme of successive generations of Medici rule, but rather than equating the Medici with historical Roman exemplars, he alludes to them by way of the rustic gods of Augustan and Laurentian (and neo-Laurentian) poetry. The trio of gods to the left of the lunette may be Pontormo's reworking of the *topos* of Medici generations. This theme was elaborated in Lorenzo's time in poems such as Naldi's *Eclogues*, in which the succession of Medici from Cosimo to Piero to Lorenzo was alluded to by the conceit of Medici figures as Pan and other rustics. The notion of equating Medici rule with units of time was taken up by Medici iconographers after the restoration of the family in 1512, specifically in the *diamante* pageant presented by Lorenzo's son Giuliano. The major theme of this spectacle, it will be recalled, was Time and the Medici. Alamanni's song "Trionfo dell'Età," which contains the line "volgan' gli anni, le mesi, le ore," is Laurentian in spirit, paraphrasing Poliziano's *Stanze* (I, 72). Indeed, it is a reprise of the theme of the portico frieze, in which the units of time progress from the large to the small, from the Ages down to the very hour of dawn. Moreover, the floats of the pageant were decorated in a similar spirit with scenes from Ovid's *Metamorphoses*, thus reviving a favorite Laurentian theme of transformation. And, as if to establish the link between all this imagery and Medici Return with perfect clarity, these scenes were inscribed ERIMVS SVMVS, FVMIVS—alluding to the past, present, and future of the Medici House.[59]

Naldi's conceit of the Medici as rustics, as well as the idea of combining their "history" with scenes from the *Metamorphoses*, seems to be reflected in the trio of gods on the left side of the lunette. These gods, who include Ovid's Vertumnus in disguise as an old man, may represent a kind of Medicean "Three Ages." The youthful Saturn would allude to the future (and to Cosimo), Sol-Apollo would allude to the present (and Leo), and the old Vertumnus-Janus would allude to the past, to beginnings, and perhaps even to Cosimo Pater Patriae, founder of the branch of the family which had only recently come to an end with the death of Lorenzo the younger.

This reading is compatible with the subjects of the frescos to the left below and directly below Vertumnus-Janus. On the lateral wall is the *Cicero*, which refers to the Pater Patriae (just as the *Caesar* diagonally opposite refers to Leo, who would have been allegorized as Hercules in the left corner of the northwestern lunette). Below is Pietas (Fama is beneath Hercules), which signals the theme of reverence toward ancestors that we have seen elsewhere in Leo's art in quite a different form—in Raphael's quotation of the Aeneas-Anchises group, in which the latter is portrayed with the features of Cosimo Pater Patriae (pl. 26). Finally, the two dead laurel sprigs that I have taken to allude to the recent deaths of the last two heirs of Cosimo's line of the family have fallen at the feet of the old Vertumnus, while, in contrast, new laurel sprouts around Sol-Apollo and Saturn. Thus, on the side of the fresco with the "Medici" gods, there is an echo (in rustic, or natural, guise) of the *impresa* of the dead and living laurel that had been given such memorable form by Pontormo in his portrait of Cosimo Pater Patriae.

There are hints of the same neo-Laurentian themes and images of dynasty and renewal that occur in Pontormo's *Vertumnus and Pomona* in the New Sacristy, the program of which is exactly contemporary with that of the Salone (although, of course, it underwent considerable modification after Leo's death). The schemes of the walls, particularly the *sepoltura di testa* (pl. 37) and the end walls of the Salone (pl. 36), are remarkably analogous.[60] In both, the wall is articulated into three bays by a Sangallesque Corinthian order and each is surmounted by a lunette; in both, the triumph of the Medici over death is asserted in regeneration imagery appropriate to the function of the room. In the sacred context of the Sacristy, the *sepoltura di testa* seems to have been planned to symbolize the apotheosis and renewal of the Medici. The central section of the wall is designed as a triumphal arch, which would have framed not only the Madonna and the Medici saints but the tombs of the *magnifici* as well. This motif, perhaps echoing Michelangelo's initial design for all four tombs as a free-standing *arcus quadrifons*,[61] emphasizes the theme of the triumph of the Medici over death. Within this arch are the *Virgo lactans* and the *Saints Cosmas and Damian* (in allusion to Cosimo, founder of the family,

59 Vasari, VI, p. 251.
60 Weil-Garris Posner, p. 747.

61 See Tolnay, III, pp. 204-5, figs. 83-88.

as well as to his newborn namesake); and above it, in the projected lunette of the *Resurrection*, Christ rises above the Medici saints and the great ancestors of the *capitani* who are depicted on the lateral walls of the room.

This wall, as projected at the time of the Salone decoration, is clearly the sacred counterpart of Pontormo's fresco as I have understood it. There, triumph over death is expressed in the image of the regenerating laurel, alluding in particular to the birth of the New Cosimo. The plant is brought to life by Sol-Apollo. This figure's complex symbolism alludes to the same theme of resurrection that was to be prominent in the Sacristy. For we recall that Apollo is a paraphrase of the *Jonah* of the Sistine ceiling, and, besides being a type of the resurrected Christ,[62] the prophet himself is imbued with solar symbolism.

The imagery of the lateral walls of the Sacristy, with the tomb here identified as that of Lorenzo the younger (pl. 34)[63] and the tomb of Giuliano, also has much in common with the imagery of the Salone, especially as originally planned by Michelangelo. The lateral walls of both the Salone and the Sacristy are dedicated to the theme of the unity of Florence and Rome and to the idea of a *Roma rinata* under the Medici pope. Michelangelo's *capitani* are dressed *all'antica* as if for their investiture as Roman citizens in 1513; and Roman exemplars with whom the Medici are identified are depicted in the *istorie* in the Salone. The decoration of these walls also commemorates the role played by the Medici in the Florentine Republic: in the Salone, Lorenzo and Piero act on behalf of peace and reconciliation in the guise of Scipio and Titus (if my conclusion that these were the original subjects of the room is correct); in the Sacristy, the younger Lorenzo's role as captain-general of the Republic is symbolized by the *bastone del dominio* (baton of rule) that he holds.[64] But the most important point of similarity between the imagery of Michelangelo's tombs and that of the Salone is the revival of the Laurentian theme of Time and the Medici in Pontormo's lunette and in the allegories of the *Times of Day* (pl. 34). Michelangelo's figures, which—significantly—were at one stage planned as the Seasons,[65] recline in mirror-image, just as Pontormo's Summer and Autumn are placed in mirror-image on either side of the GLOVIS motto. The theme, whether the four Seasons of the fresco or the four Times of Day in the Sacristy, is the same: the eternal return and immortality of the Medici echo and reflect the order and cycles of nature and the cosmos.[66] But Time is viewed somewhat differently in the two works: in the Sacristy,

---

[62] The Medici may later have associated the theme of the Resurrection with the *Jonah*. For the possibility that the initial commission to Michelangelo for the fresco below the *Jonah* in the Sistine Chapel was for a *Resurrection* rather than a *Last Judgment*, see Tolnay, V, pp. 10-20. It is notable that in the context of the ceiling Jonah symbolizes the fulfillment of Zacharias' prophecy of Christ as the Branch (6:12), which is rendered in the Vulgate as Oriens (rising sun), the common term for the ascendant of a horoscope. For the connection between this prophecy of Zacharias, the prophet depicted at the entrance to the chapel, and Jonah as a type of Christ, located over the altar, see

F. Hartt, "Lignum Vitae in Medio Paradisi: The Stanza d'Eliodoro and the Sistine Ceiling," *Art Bull.*, 32, 1950, p. 199. See also Dotson, pp. 416-18, with reference to Egidio da Viterbo's commentary on Zacharias and on Christ as the sun.

[63] For the identification of this tomb as Lorenzo's see chap. 10.

[64] For the republican theme in the Sacristy, see Trexler-Lewis, pp. 117, 159-60.

[65] Panofsky, pp. 201-6.

[66] See the interesting suggestion by Gilbert, pp. 402-3, on a possible connection between Michelangelo's imagery of Time and Dante's conception in the *Convivio* of "life as being an arc that rises

although hope for the future is still present, Time has temporarily defeated the Medici. As Michelangelo's notes on an architectural drawing for the chapel read,[67]

> El Dì e la Nocte parlano e dicono: "Noi abiano col nostro veloce corso condocto alla morte el Duca Giuliano; è ben giusto che e' ne facci vendecta come fa. E la vendecta è questa: che avendo noi morto lui, lui così morto à tolta la luce a noi e cogli ochi chiusi à serrato e' nostri, che non risplendon più sopra la terra. Che arrebbe di noi, dunche facto, mentre vivea?"

> Night and Day speak and say: "We with our swift course have brought Duke Giuliano to death. It is just that he, the Duke, takes revenge as he does for this, and the revenge is this, that, as we have killed him, he, dead, has taken the light from us, and with his closed eyes has locked ours shut, which no longer shine on earth. What then would he have done with us while alive?"

In the Salone, on the other hand, Time plays a more positive role: the paintings depict the broad sweep of Medici history from the early Quattrocento to the present, and they emphasize the alliance of Time with the Medici from the return from exile of Cosimo Pater Patriae to the potential new beginning signaled by the birth of his namesake. In the lunettes, in particular, the earthly and heavenly Cycles of Time join with Fortuna and Medici Virtù to ensure the glorious future of the Medici house.

Not only are both the Salone and the Sacristy decorations concerned with the themes of Time's Return and the renewal of the Medici, but it is clear from Michelangelo's drawing for the tomb with Day and Night (here identified as Lorenzo's, pl. 73) that he planned to introduce into the chapel imagery of nature and the cosmos that is closely related to that of Pontormo's lunette.[68] Michelangelo conceived this monument as populated with allegories of cosmic deities: Day and Night are personified as the Sun and Moon, the same luminaries who sit on the upper wall in Pontormo's fresco. Day's head is surrounded with a radiating corona like that of Dawn in the portico frieze at Poggio a Caiano (pl. 55), and Night wears the traditional lunar crescent.[69] The effigy of Lorenzo himself is an Apollo-like nude in the Medici tradition of the Apollo alluding to Lorenzo il Magnifico on the portico frieze (pl. 55). The river gods—in mirror-image like Pontormo's Saturnus and Venus *hortorum*—are nature gods accompanied by putti and *bronconi*, as are Pontormo's agricultural deities.[70] Finally, above the river gods in niches on either

---

and then falls and has four segments, the four ages of man, the four seasons, the four times of day." On Dante and the Medici concepts of Time's Return (out of which the imagery of Pontormo's lunette was generated) see chap. 1, "Time's Return and the Medici Golden Age."

[67] See chap. 2, n. 4.

[68] While the nature of the relationship between the two programs remains to be elucidated, see Weil-Garris Posner, pp. 645-49; and my chap. 4, "The Commission and Program," for the suggestion that Michelangelo's drawings for the tombs

(my pls. 73-74) may have been germane to Pontormo's conception of *Vertumnus and Pomona*.

[69] C. de Tolnay, "Nouvelles remarques sur la Chapelle Médicis," *GBA*, 73, 1969, pp. 70-71.

[70] In this connection it is worth noting that the coffers of the dome of the Sacristy were once painted by Giovanni da Udine with nature imagery described by Vasari, VI, pp. 560-61, as "fogliami, rosoni, ed altri ornamenti di stucco e d'oro . . . alcuni fogliami, uccelli, maschere, e figure. . . ."

side of the effigy are allegorical figures. These correspond with a mourning Earth and a joyous Heaven described by Vasari as to be executed by Tribolo:[71]

> . . . volle Michelangelo che il Tribolo facesse due statue nude . . . l'una figurata per la Terra coronata di cipresso, che dolente ed a capo chino piangesse con le braccia aperte la perdita del duca Giuliano; e l'altra per lo Cielo, che con le braccia elevate, tutto ridente e festoso, mostrasse esser allegro dell'ornamento e splendore che gli recava l'anima e lo spirito di quel signore.

> Michelangelo wished Tribolo to make two nude statues . . . , one was to be a figure of Earth crowned with cypress, weeping with bowed head and with the arms outstretched, and lamenting the death of Duke Giuliano, and the other a figure of Heaven with the arms uplifted, all smiling and joyful, and showing her gladness at the adornment and splendor that the soul and spirit of that lord conferred upon her.

These figures are also mentioned in Michelangelo's notes about the tomb, quoted above, in which the words "el cielo . . . e la terra" are written over the lines quoting the speech of Night and Day in the same relation to the passage as are the allegories to the Times of Day in the drawing. The tomb, then, if executed according to this drawing, would have included several of the same allegorical figures as appear in Pontormo's lunette: an Apollo-like protagonist, reclining mirror-image allegories of Time, and framing figures of Heaven and Earth corresponding to Pontormo's framing figures of Janus, ruler of the heavens, and Pomona, goddess of the earth.

It is possible that Michelangelo's plan for the Sacristy had further cosmological dimensions related to the cosmic and astrological ideas which are reflected in Pontormo's fresco. For example, Varchi's interpretation of the Sacristy decoration as analogous to Dante's vision of the cosmos in the *Paradiso* suggests that the allegories of the *Times of Day* represent the terrestrial world as a mirror of the celestial universe.[72] According to Varchi, the allegories are based on Dante's description of the moment of the vernal equinox, when dark and light are equally divided—a moment which he equates with his ascent to Paradise, with Christ's resurrection, and with the creation of the world.[73] Moreover, unlike the Salone paintings, it is possible that the cosmic imagery of the Sacristy sculptures also included the symbolism of light itself, possibly that of the sun at the equinoctial point which Dante describes.[74]

Since none of the three walls of the Sacristy was executed as planned, the close relationship between the program of the Sacristy and that of the Salone is not apparent

[71] Vasari, VI, p. 65.

[72] L. Mendelsohn, "Benedetto Varchi's 'Due Lezzioni': Paragoni and Cinquecento Art Theory," diss., New York University, 1978; Ann Arbor, 1979, pp. 313-22.

[73] B. Varchi, *Due lezioni di M. Benedetto Varchi* . . . , Florence, 1549, p. 117.

[74] The cosmic iconography of the vernal equinox in the chapel is being investigated by Leatrice Mendelsohn, whose preliminary findings were presented in a paper at the College Art Association, San Francisco, February 1981: "Propaganda in Paradise: Michelangelo's New Sacristy Revisited." I am grateful to the author for a copy of the text of this paper. For another approach to light symbolism in the chapel, related to the symbolism of the Magi, see Trexler-Lewis, pp. 124-38.

today. There are no mottos such as the GLOVIS to guide the viewer to the presence of cosmic imagery in the chapel. Moreover, Laurentian imagery of nature and the cosmos which traditionally accompanies the Laurentian theme of Time embodied in the *Times of Day*, and which links the imagery of the tombs to *Vertumnus and Pomona*, does not appear; and the New Sacristy is quite without the neo-Laurentian cast of Pontormo's painting.

We can only imagine that after Leo's death in late 1521, following which the New Sacristy decoration assumed its final form, the last hope of recovering Lorenzo's Golden Age was felt to be lost and that the poetic conceits of Time, Nature, and the Cosmos which express the theme of the Medici Golden Age in Pontormo's fresco were no longer appropriate to the new political reality. Under the next Medici pope, Clement VII, the New Sacristy was only partially completed and no further work was done in the Poggio a Caiano Salone. The focus of Medici interest shifted to Rome; Alessandro—the son of Lorenzo the younger—was groomed to rule Florence; and Pope Leo's hope, the New Cosimo, was all but forgotten.

IV

Cosmic and Dynastic Imagery in the
Art of Duke Cosimo de' Medici (1537-1574)

The cosmic and dynastic imagery in Medici art during the papacy of Leo X was seminal for the art of the *principato* of Duke Cosimo de' Medici (1537-1574). Just as Leo had sought to demonstrate Medicean dynastic continuity and destiny by reviving imagery associated with his father Lorenzo il Magnifico, so in his own early art Duke Cosimo looked to the past. Lacking an inheritance of imagery from his father, Giovanni delle Bande Nere, Cosimo turned to the rich heritage of the art of Leo, the major Medicean art patron in the republican Florence of the early Cinquecento. Leo was also the last (if tenuous) link with the Golden Age of Lorenzo il Magnifico, as well as the ancestor who had named the New Cosimo after Cosimo Pater Patriae.

Cosimo's iconographers revived and developed many of the themes of Leonine art, especially those which had been prominent in the decorations at Poggio a Caiano. From the very beginnings of Cosimo's patronage in 1537 until about 1555, there were echoes in his art of the familiar Leonine themes of Medici Return, dynastic continuity, the Golden Age, and astrological destiny. Leonine (ultimately Laurentian) conceits resurfaced: the regenerating laurel, Florence under the protection of the laurel, the Medici Hercules, the Medici *illustri* and their virtues, cycles of nature, time, and the cosmos as metaphors of dynasty. These and other themes of earlier Medici art, thus revived, were transformed to suit the purposes of the new regime.

The
Two Cosimos

Pontormo's *Portrait of Cosimo de' Medici Pater Patriae* (color pl. 1) which equates the newly sprouting laurel with the birth in 1519 of a New Cosimo—the future Duke Cosimo—was of seminal importance for subsequent Medici art. The influence of its imagery is evident in contemporary portraiture, and the work was an important touchstone for the revival of the ancestor-portrait in paintings executed in 1534 during the short rule of Duke Alessandro de' Medici (1531-1537). But, most significant, the imagery of the portrait was adopted to allude to the New Cosimo himself—both before and after 1537, when he became second duke of Florence.

Not long after the death of Leo X in late 1521, Pontormo's image of the cut-off laurel was adapted by Franciabigio in his *Portrait of a Medici Steward*, dated 1523 (pl. 114). The picture was painted for a member of the collateral branch of the Medici, Pierfrancesco the younger, whose son, Lorenzino, was at that time a potential heir to Medici rule. Its somber mood and symbolism reflect the decline in Medici fortunes in the interregnum after Pope Leo died and before Cardinal Giulio became Pope Clement VII in late 1523. Below the steward, suspended in front of the ledge, like the GLOVIS disk in Pontormo's *Vertumnus and Pomona* (color pl. 2), is the Medici *stemma*; next to it, hanging over the steward's arm, are the keys to the Medici House, which are in his charge. These also refer to the papal keys so recently held by Leo, which it was hoped would come to Giulio. To the right are two laurel sprigs that have fallen from the Medici tree. They are a metaphor of death recalling the cut-off laurel in Pontormo's *Cosimo* portrait; but, more explicitly, the conceit seems to have been borrowed from *Vertumnus and Pomona*, where two laurel sprigs, which may symbolize the deaths of Giuliano and Lorenzo, fall at the feet of the old Vertumnus (pl. 99). Moreover, the pruning implements hanging on the wall next to the steward are the same ones which Pontormo portrayed in the hands of Pomona (the pruning-hook) and Sol-Apollo (who probably held a pruning-knife, now effaced). These symbolic implements, associated with the care of the once verdant Medici laurel, now hang above its fallen branches—spotlighted but unused. In view of the date of the picture, this symbolism probably alludes to the cumulative misfortune that had befallen the Medici: the death of Leo, suggested by the papal keys, as well as the earlier deaths of Giuliano and Lorenzo.[1]

Pontormo's portrait of Cosimo Pater Patriae remained in Medici possession in Florence, entering the collection of Ottaviano and, according to his protégé Vasari, passing on Ottaviano's death (in 1546) to his son Alessandro.[2] Besides Pontormo's picture, Ottaviano's notable collection of portraits of Medici *illustri* included three portraits by Raphael, dating from Leo's pontificate, and two by Pontormo, dating from about 1526. Of these, Pontormo's *Cosimo*, his *Alessandro de' Medici*, and his *Ippolito de' Medici* remained in the collection of Ottaviano's heirs, together with Raphael's *Giuliano de' Medici* and *Leo X with Cardinals Giulio de' Medici and Luigi de' Rossi*, while Raphael's *Lorenzo de' Medici* entered the ducal collection after Cosimo's assumption of power in 1537.[3] In 1534, however, all these portraits belonged to Ottaviano. They were joined in his collection by two allegorical portraits painted by Vasari himself. One of these alludes to imagery in Pontormo's *Cosimo*; the other was conceived as its pendant.

Vasari's *Duke Alessandro de' Medici* (pl. 155) was painted in the first half of 1534 for the duke, who later gave the picture to Ottaviano.[4] In this portrait, Vasari made a complex set of references to other Medici portraits in order to aggrandize and legitimize the duke. Alessandro's profile pose and the burning helmet to the left of his stool allude to Francesco del Prato's medal of 1534 of the duke as peacemaker, which is inscribed FVNDATOR QVIETIS.[5] In this medal, as in the portrait, Alessandro is presented as the peace-giving Mars, a theme which is signaled by the glyph for Mars (♂) below the

[1] McKillop, 1974, p. 84, considers the picture to be a *memento mori* alluding to Giuliano and Lorenzo. John Shearman has suggested to me that the sitter was Pierfrancesco himself and that the upstanding laurel branch might symbolize Pierfrancesco's own hopes for the future of the collateral branch of the family.

[2] Vasari, VI, p. 264. Besides being a patron and collector, Ottaviano was in charge of various papal commissions (such as the decorations at Poggio a Caiano; see chap. 4, n. 16) and functioned as a liaison between the Medici and their artists. Vasari, who worked under Ottaviano's patronage from the early 1530s, thought of himself as Ottaviano's "fanciullo e creatura," painted works for him, and copied others in his collection, such as Raphael's *Leo X with the Cardinals* (cf. Vasari, V, pp. 41-42; VI, pp. 68-69; VI, p. 574; VII, pp. 655, 657, 659, 660, 672, 694).

[3] See Vasari, VI, p. 273, on Pontormo's *Alessandro* (Lucca) and *Ippolito* (lost), commissioned by Ottaviano. Vasari, IV, p. 352, records the *Giuliano* and *Lorenzo* portraits (both lost) in the collection of the heirs of Ottaviano; however, as he notes in a *ricordo*, the *Giuliano* was "in casa Ottaviano"

while the *Lorenzo* was in Duke Cosimo's *guardaroba* (*Lo Zibaldone di Giorgio Vasari*, ed. A. Del Vita, Rome, 1938, pp. 260-61). The early history of the *Lorenzo* is confirmed by the 1553 palace inventory, which lists a portrait of Lorenzo "vestito alla franzese" (Conti, p. 102). The source of Vasari's apparent error in the *vita* may be the copy of the *Lorenzo* that Vasari, III, p. 437, records as having been made for Ottaviano by Aristotile da Sangallo. On the problem of the *Lorenzo* portrait, see K. Oberhuber, "Raphael and the State Portrait—II: The portrait of Lorenzo de' Medici," *Burl.*, 113, 1971, pp. 436-43; and J. H. Beck, "Raphael and Medici 'State Portraits,'" *ZK*, 38, 1975, pp. 127-44.

[4] The commission is noted in Vasari's *ricordo* of 8 January (Vasari–Del Vita, p. 21), and Vasari's letter of 18 August refers to the completed picture (Vasari-Frey, I, pp. 27-29). On the gift of the portrait to Ottaviano, see Vasari, VII, pp. 657-58.

[5] Vasari, V, p. 384; and Hill-Pollard, no. 217. The connections between the portrait and the medal are discussed by Langedijk, p. 52; and Forster, 1971, pp. 69-70. Vasari-Frey, I, p. 28, notes that Alessandro holds the *bastone del dominio*.

figure of Peace burning arms. The laurel tree growing to the left quotes the laurel of Pontormo's *Cosimo* portrait, while the pose of the armored figure and the baton he carries vividly recall Michelangelo's so-called *Giuliano de' Medici*, which had been installed in the New Sacristy before the artist's departure from Florence in September 1534 (pl. 156).[6]

These allusions have been noted, but their meaning has not been explained. Taken together, the laurel tree and the quotation from Michelangelo's statue deliver the most important message of the picture. The laurel had last been used as a personal *impresa* in 1512 to 1519 by Lorenzo the younger (pl. 8). It was not adopted as such by Alessandro after he became duke in 1532; nonetheless, it is conspicuous in this state portrait. Vasari's exegesis on the picture explains the laurel as a metaphor of Medici Return:[7]

> Quel tronco secco di lauro che manda fuori quella vermena diritta e fresca di fronde è la casa de' Medici, già spenta, che per la persona del duca Alessandro deve crescer di prole infinitamente.

> That dry laurel branch which puts forth that erect and fresh leafy twig is the Medici house, once extinguished, which must grow with infinite progeny in the person of Duke Alessandro.

This explanation is hardly appropriate to Alessandro's situation in 1534, except in the most general sense, and it may be suggested that an understood but unstated meaning was attached to the laurel in the portrait. For in Medici imagery the tree was not only an image of regeneration, it was a symbol of dynastic and political continuity. It had been used by Lorenzo the younger to suggest his legitimate descent from his grandfather Lorenzo il Magnifico, and it had appeared in Pontormo's *Cosimo* portrait as a visual metaphor of the end of Cosimo's line with the death of Lorenzo in 1519 and the beginning of a new Medici line in the person of the newborn Cosimo. Now, in 1534, it was introduced into Vasari's state portrait (not coincidentally, a profile portrait like the *Cosimo*) in support of the illegitimate Alessandro's claim that he was the son of Lorenzo and thus, as the remaining descendant of the main branch of the family, the legitimate ruler of Florence.

The claim of legitimacy made by the laurel quoted from Pontormo's portrait is reinforced by the quotation of Alessandro's pose from Michelangelo's New Sacristy statue, known as Giuliano, but more probably to be identified as Lorenzo. As has been persuasively argued by Richard Trexler, the depiction of the two Medici in the New Sacristy must have observed the "decorum of sovereignty."[8] Lorenzo carries his symbol and attribute as the Florentine captain-general—the *bastone del dominio*, which could not have been used as an attribute for Giuliano, who was papal captain-general. The official

[6] Vasari, VI, pp. 633-34, on the installation of the *capitani* in their niches, and VII, p. 656, on Vasari's visit to the New Sacristy shortly before Michelangelo's departure, when the statues were still "in terra." Vasari's account of this visit is followed immediately by notices of his first two works for Alessandro, one of which is the portrait of the duke.

[7] Vasari-Frey, I, pp. 27-29.

[8] Trexler-Lewis, pp. 109-17 and pp. 141-60 (an appendix on the history of the identification of the statues). I am grateful to Richard Trexler for allowing me to read the relevant sections of this article before its publication.

Roman status of Giuliano, on the other hand, is indicated by the *mappa*, ancient symbol of Roman consuls, held in his hand.[9] In addition, there are elements in Michelangelo's drawing for the tomb with Night and Day which indicate that it was for Lorenzo's, not Giuliano's, tomb (pl. 73). The bases of the caryatids holding the shells are decorated with crossed *bronconi*, Lorenzo's device (although, to be sure, it was also used by Leo), and the river gods with their laurel wreaths and putti are strikingly reminiscent of the decorations for Lorenzo's *broncone* pageant of 1513 (pl. 13). Moreover, the statue, which is receiving a crown from two winged figures, is conceived as an Apollo-like nude, the very god from whom Lorenzo took the attribute of the laurel and with whom, like Lorenzo il Magnifico before him, he was compared in panegyric.

The other portrait of 1534 that was influenced by Pontormo's *Cosimo* is Vasari's commemorative portrait of Lorenzo il Magnifico (pl. 157). The work was proposed by Vasari to Duke Alessandro but painted for Ottaviano instead.[10] Apparently conceived as a companion piece to the *Cosimo* already in Ottaviano's collection, Vasari's *Lorenzo* is obviously inspired by it; the ancestor-portrait idea is the same, the composition of the seated figure is in mirror-image to Pontormo's, and the two pictures are almost identical in size.[11] There is no laurel in this portrait, but Vasari takes up the theme of virtue signified by the laurel in Pontormo's picture by surrounding Lorenzo with four inscriptions referring to his virtue. The major one, on the plinth to the left, reads SICVT MAIORES MIHI ITA ET EGO POSTERIS MEA VIRTVTE PRELVXI (Just as my ancestors did for me, so also have I illumined the way for my descendants by my virtue).[12] This inscription links the subjects of the two portraits, for the most prominent of Lorenzo's ancestors was, of course, Cosimo Pater Patriae.

Not only did Pontormo's *Cosimo* thus influence Vasari's exercises in allegorical portraiture for his Medici patrons, but its dynastic imagery was taken up in two portraits of the young Cosimo himself, painted in the decade before he became duke of Florence. Both declare Cosimo's legitimacy as a Medici heir: one, by Pontormo, presents him as heir to both branches of the family; the other, by Ridolfo Ghirlandaio, acknowledges the conceit of the New Cosimo that is the message of Pontormo's portrait of Cosimo Pater Patriae. Pontormo's *Maria Salviati with Her Son Cosimo* (pl. 158), which belongs to

[9] Trexler-Lewis, p. 115.

[10] Vasari's letter proposing the work to Alessandro is undated (Vasari-Frey, I, pp. 17-18), but his *ricordo* of 17 August 1534 refers to the picture (Vasari–Del Vita, p. 22): "Ottaviano me fece fare . . . magnifico Lorenzo de' Medici." Vasari also refers to the portrait in the letter of 18 August 1534, cited above, n. 4. In the *Vite*, VII, p. 658, Vasari locates the *Lorenzo* in the collection of Ottaviano's heirs.

[11] The dimensions of Pontormo's *Cosimo* are 86 × 65 cm; of Vasari's *Lorenzo*, 90 × 72 cm. The dependence of Vasari's picture on Pontormo's and the likelihood that it was painted as a pendant to the Pontormo have been frequently argued (Cox-Rearick, 1964, I, p. 153; Forster, 1966, p. 135;

Langedijk, p. 49; Winner, 1970, p. 296; Forster, 1971, pp. 67-69). Sparrow, pp. 173-74, on the other hand, believes the pictures were executed in reverse order, the *Cosimo* having been painted in 1537-1539 for Duke Cosimo (or for Ottaviano) as a pendant to Vasari's picture of 1534.

[12] The other inscriptions are VIRTVTVM OMNIVM VAS (vessel of all virtues), which is on the vase of flowers and alludes to it as an emblem of virtue; PREMIVM VIRTVTIS (reward of virtue), which is on the mask; and VITIA VIRTVTI SVBIACENT (vices are subject to virtue), which is on the plinth to the right. In a still later posthumous portrait by Luigi Fiamingo (from Poggio a Caiano, inv. 106), Lorenzo is posed against a view of Florence with a laurel tree adapted from Pontormo's *Cosimo*.

the period of the last Medici exile (1527-1530), shows Maria wearing a widow's veil in mourning for Giovanni delle Bande Nere, who had died in late 1526.[13] Although these were years when the future of the family as rulers of Florence must have seemed doubtful indeed, the composition of this dynastic painting is ingeniously conceived to read like a chart of Cosimo's double Medici ancestry. Cosimo, who holds his mother's right hand, is presented as her heir and, through her, as a descendant of the main branch of the Medici. (Maria was a granddaughter of Lorenzo il Magnifico.) But Cosimo is also shown as the heir to the collateral branch, that of his father, Giovanni, whom we may understand to be the subject of the medal that Maria holds in her left hand.

The other Cosimo portrait is Ghirlandaio's *Cosimo de' Medici at Age Twelve* (pl. 159), painted in 1531 just before Cosimo's cousin Alessandro became first duke of Florence.[14] As in the case of Vasari's *Alessandro*, the meaning of this portrait reveals itself only if it is seen in relation to earlier Medici portraits. To the upper right is an unusual cartouche of the type that often carries the *palle* in the art of Leo X (cf. pls. 30, 148). However, instead of the *palle*, it contains a "nomogram" of the letters of Cosimo's name, intertwined in a way reminiscent of the interlaced *diamanti*. Aside from identifying the child as a Medici Cosimo, the nomogram carries a secret message, for COSIMO MEDICO reduces the letters of the name to twelve, which was Cosimo's age in 1531.[15] The altered spelling of the name Medici to Medico also alludes to the familiar wordplay on the curative powers of the Medici, which had been so frequent in Leonine art. Moreover, the placement of the abbreviated name to the upper right suggests a deliberate recall of Pontormo's portrait of Cosimo Pater Patriae, in which the number of letters in the name COSM MEDICES—eleven—also makes a veiled reference to the day of the New Cosimo's birth on 11 June 1519. If this inscription does indeed comment on the earlier one, then it seems likely that the medal that Cosimo holds (in imitation of his mother in the double portrait) may also refer to him as the New Cosimo. The likeness on the medal is effaced, but in view of the other imagery in the picture it can only have been one of the small replicas of the Cosimo Pater Patriae medals which were made.[16] The message of the picture is thus clear: this is the son of Maria Salviati and Giovanni delle Bande Nere, a son who bears the honored name Cosimo, and he, rather than the illegitimate Alessandro, is the rightful heir to Medici rule in Florence.

✳   ✳   ✳

When Cosimo de' Medici did become duke after Alessandro's murder, six years after Ghirlandaio's portrait was painted, the symbolism of Pontormo's portrait of his ancestor

[13] See Cox-Rearick, 1964, I, pp. 300-301; K. W. Forster, "Probleme um Pontormos Porträtmalerei (II)," *Pantheon*, 23, 1965, p. 223 (as by Bronzino); H. Keutner, "Zu Einigen Bildnissen des Frühen Florentiner Manierismus," *Mitt.KHIF*, 8, 1959, pp. 146-47 (as by Pontormo, but dated 1537); and F. Zeri, *Italian Paintings in the Walters Art Gallery*, Baltimore, 1976, II, cat. 211 (as by Pontormo, but dated 1537).

[14] The work is listed in the 1553 inventory of Cosimo's *guardaroba* as "uno quadro del ritratto del Duca Cosimo d'età di XII anni" (Conti, p. 86), where Vasari, VI, p. 545, also locates it.

[15] Forster, 1971, p. 72.

[16] Langedijk, p. 59. On the replicas of the Cosimo medals, see Clapp, p. 148.

and namesake was taken up by the image-makers of the new regime. The flourishing laurel and the Virgilian motto of the Pontormo portrait symbolized the new circumstances perfectly, for once again a Medici had emerged to revive the dynasty after an untimely death. Indeed, even before Cosimo was declared to be Alessandro's successor, Virgil's line (in its unaltered form) was quoted by Cardinal Cibo in a speech recommending Cosimo to the Quarantotto as the new ruler of the city.[17] And, after his election, the new duke revived whole *imprese* of the portrait. It first appears on a medal by Domenico di Polo which shows the eighteen-year-old, beardless Cosimo as he looked in late 1537-1538 (pl. 162).[18] On the reverse is the flourishing laurel tree, one branch of which is broken, and the inscription VNO AVVLSO (on a scroll around the tree) NON DEFICIT ALTER (encircling the image). The *impresa* then appears in the decorations of the first courtyard of the Palazzo Medici on the occasion of Cosimo's marriage to Eleonora da Toledo in June 1539. The description of the *impresa* by Giambullari, the author of the program, makes it clear that its message was the same as that of the medal:[19]

> Nella quarta [lunetta] era un Lauro troncato, con la sua cima talmente rivolta alla terra che ben pareva del tutto perduto, ma un rigoglioso Pollone in su'l vecchio ceppo germugliando, interamente lo ristorava: come in una altra medaglia di sua Eccellentia si vede, e diceva il motto, VNO AVVLSO.

> In the fourth [lunette] was a broken laurel tree, its summit so bent toward the earth that it seemed entirely lost, but an exuberant new shoot was coming out of the old stump, completely renewing the tree, as is seen on another medal of His Excellency, and there was the motto VNO AVVLSO.

Some years later, in 1555, the precise nature of this message was spelled out by Giovio in his *Dialogo dell'imprese*. Recounting Cosimo's personal *imprese*, he writes:[20]

> Hebbe un altra [impresa] nel principio del suo principato dottamente trovata dal Reverendo M. Pierfrancesco de Ricci suo maggior duomo, e fu quel che dice Vergilio nell'Eneida del Ramo d'oro col motto VNO AVVLSO NON DEFICIT ALTER, figurando un ramo suelto dell'albero, in luogo del quale ne succede subito un'altro; volendo intendere che se bene era stata levata la vita al Duca Alessandro, non mancava un'altro ramo d'oro nella medesima stirpe.

[17] Varchi, III, p. 276, recounts Cibo's speech.

[18] Supino, no. 257. Regarding the date of this and other medals showing the beardless Cosimo and inscribed COSMVS MEDICES REIP [VBLICAE] FLOREN[TINAE] DVX II, it should be recalled that the official *privilegio* from Charles V allowing Cosimo to use the title Duca di Firenze was delivered only on 30 September 1537 and that Cosimo proclaimed his new status and began to use the title Duca in an edict of 16 October (L. Cantini, *Vita di Cosimo de' Medici Primo Gran Duca di Toscana*, Florence, 1805, pp. 73-74, and doc. IV, pp. 507-

13).

[19] Giambullari, pp. 19-20. Giambullari's precise account is cast in the form of a letter dated 12 August 1539 to Giovanni Bandini, Florentine ambassador to Charles V, which was intended as ducal propaganda meant for the emperor's eyes. "Una medaglia" refers back to Giambullari's description (p. 19) of the *impresa* of the first lunette, the subject of which was identical to Cosimo's medal inscribed SALVS PVBLICA (see chap. 11, n. 69).

[20] Giovio, 1556, p. 33.

He had another *impresa* at the beginning of his *principato*—learnedly found [or invented] by his major-domo, the reverend Pierfrancesco Riccio—and it was the saying of Virgil about the golden bough in the *Aeneid*, with the motto "As soon as one is torn away, another takes its place." The image was a branch torn from the tree and another immediately sprouting in its place. It signified that even if Duke Alessandro had died, there would not fail to be another "golden bough" in the same family.

Thus, probably on the suggestion of Riccio, who was Cosimo's artistic adviser in the first years of the *principato* and who, of course, would have been familiar with Ottaviano's collection of Medici portraits, Duke Cosimo adopted the "laurel tree: VNO AVVLSO" as his own *impresa*.[21] Invented twenty years earlier to signal his baptism as the New Cosimo, it could now be understood to allude to the inevitability of his accession to power on the death of Alessandro.

Thus established as a ducal *impresa*, the regenerating tree, its motto unnecessary, was introduced into Cosimo's art to reinforce the message of his predestined rule. It appears, for example, with Camillus-Cosimo in Salviati's *Triumph of Camillus* of 1543 (pl. 89). Here, like Cosimo Pater Patriae on his return from exile in 1434 and like Leo X in his 1515 Florentine *entrata*, Duke Cosimo is compared to Camillus returning from exile to re-establish his power. As in Pontormo's *Cosimo* portrait and in the ducal *impresa* derived from it, the notion of Medicean Return and regeneration through the agency of Duke Cosimo is symbolized by the flourishing right side of a laurel tree with damaged branches on the left—an image which vividly recalls the "lauro . . . da Ciel fulminato" of earlier Medici poetry.

Shortly thereafter, the *broncone* was included in Cosimo's first official state portrait by Bronzino (pl. 161).[22] It shows him as a military commander, as Alessandro had been

[21] The "laurel tree: VNO AVVLSO" *impresa* was not used in Cosimo's later art. The laurel tree with broken branch and VNO AVVLSO is illustrated in the *impresa* handbook by Ruscelli, p. 114; but, generally, the broken and flourishing laurel tree, which no longer had any significance, was replaced by the palm tree, symbol of immortality. The *impresa* thus came to signify Medici immortality through the fecundity of Cosimo and Eleonora. It appears in this form in Giovio, *Dialogo*, Lyon, 1559, p. 52; and in G. Simeoni, *Le Sententiose Imprese . . .*, Lyon, 1562, p. 76, where it is accompanied by an explanatory verse:

Alla pianta, c'ha più d'un ramo verde,
S'un ne vien tronco, un'altro ne succede,
Cosi in van s'affatica ogn'un, che crede
Che per un ramo un vecchio arbor si perde.

See the discussion of this and similar regenerating tree *imprese* by Ladner, pp. 304-6; see also Sparrow, pp. 170-71.

[22] Mentioned by Vasari, VII, p. 597; see also Forster, 1971, pp. 74-75. In the Kassel version (here reproduced) of this much replicated work Cosimo wears the insignia of the Order of the Golden Fleece, which he received 29 July 1545. However, in an earlier version of the picture (sold Christie's, 26 November 1971, lot 47; now in a private collection), which also includes the *broncone*, he is shown without the decoration. On this version, see the article by R. B. Simon, "Bronzino's Portrait of Cosimo I de' Medici in Armor" (forthcoming; *Burl.*), in which the painting is identified as the prototype of the state portrait painted in 1544 for Paolo Giovio, who inscribed it COSMVS / MEDICES DVX / FLOR on the tree stump. Simon makes the interesting suggestion that the inclusion of the *broncone* was due to Giovio, who had authored the program at Poggio a Caiano in which it figured so prominently. For an engraving of this

presented a decade earlier. As in the *Alessandro*, the theme of the Pax Medicea is emphasized by the portrayal of Cosimo as a peaceful Mars, indicated by the helmet which he has removed and placed atop the tree stump.[23] Also as in the *Alessandro*, the theme of peaceful rule is linked with the dynastic symbol of the *broncone*, as the laurel growing beside him asserts the idea of the regeneration of the Medici in his person. However, in Bronzino's picture, unlike Vasari's, the three-quarter format of the figure and the placement of the *broncone* in close juxtaposition to the duke make an unmistakable allusion to Pontormo's portrait of Cosimo Pater Patriae.

In the only important later occurrence of the image of the dead and regenerating laurel in Cosimo's art, the tree alludes not only to Cosimo himself but to the future of the dynasty—by then assured by the births of his many children. This work is a *portiera* (doorhanging) designed by Bronzino for the Palazzo Vecchio in 1549 (pl. 163). Bearing the arms of Cosimo and Eleonora and inscribed FVNDATA ENIM ERAT SVPER PETRAM (For it had been founded on a rock), it is an allegory of the foundation of a new branch of the Medici dynasty by Cosimo, represented by Apollo and his sprouting laurel, and Eleonora, represented by Pallas-Minerva and her olive tree. The winds of Good Fortune blow from the vertical borders, and the branches of the trees signifying Medici virtue, dynasty, and peace intertwine through the ducal coronet, which surmounts the *diamante*—the familiar *impresa* signifying Medici immortality.

Pontormo's portrait of Cosimo Pater Patriae itself also figured in the duke's propaganda. He used it didactically in a context that suggests an awareness of its having been connected with his own naming after Cosimo. This context was the duke's marriage, which was the first opportunity after his assumption of power for a large-scale display of his as yet incompletely crystallized personal imagery. Many of the themes that would appear again and again in works of art commissioned by him were given their first visual expression in its elaborate *apparato*. Two themes, in particular, were preeminent in these early years before 1543, when Cosimo's power in Florence was consolidated by the return to him by Charles V of the fortresses of the city. One was the notion of his legitimate right to succeed Alessandro and the other was the myth that he had always been destined to do so. Useful in demonstrating these propositions were two related assertions. The first was the idea of Cosimo's legitimacy as a Medici ruler, due to his descent from both branches of the family. This theme, which had been announced years earlier in Pontormo's portrait of Cosimo with his mother, was to be the animating theme in a number of major decorations commissioned early in Cosimo's rule, such as Bandi-

portrait in Giovio's collection, which features a very prominent *broncone*, see Giovio, 1577, p. 390. I am grateful to Robert Simon for allowing me to read his article prior to its publication.

[23] Cf. the reading of the helmet on the ground as a symbol of peace in Vasari-Frey, I, p. 28. For contemporary interpretations of Giovio's *Cosimo*

portrait as representing the peaceful Mars, see two poems printed with Giovio's *elogium* on Cosimo (1554, pp. 436-38). In that by Paolo Giovio the younger he is compared with Mars *gradivus*, as, implicitly, Lorenzo il Magnifico had been in the Poggio a Caiano frieze (see chap. 3, nn. 32-34).

nelli's *Udienza* in the Salone dei Cinquecento in the old Palazzo della Signoria (or Palazzo Vecchio, which I shall call, simply, the Palazzo). Here, in statues *all'antica*, Giovanni delle Bande Nere joins the *illustri* of the main branch of the family descended from Cosimo Pater Patriae, in an assertion of Cosimo's double legitimacy.[24] Later, too, in Vasari's apartments in the Palazzo, Cosimo's ancestors are celebrated in a cycle in which the notion of Medici *illustri* adumbrated in the Poggio a Caiano Salone is expanded and updated.[25] In the Salone, Cosimo Pater Patriae, Piero di Cosimo, Lorenzo il Magnifico, and Leo X (in the guise of Roman exemplars) represent the four generations of Medici which had ruled from 1434 to 1520; in the apartments, the focus is less on the glory of the family in general and more on the ancestry of Cosimo himself; his descent on the one hand from Giovanni delle Bande Nere and, on the other, from Cosimo Pater Patriae through Lorenzo il Magnifico. The papal rooms dedicated to Leo and Clement aside, the very layout of this suite—with the Sala di Duca Cosimo flanked by the room of his father on one side and those of Cosimo Pater Patriae and Lorenzo on the other—is a diagram of the duke's double legitimacy.

The second assertion which was useful in demonstrating the idea of Cosimo's legitimacy and destiny as ruler of Florence was the notion I shall call the conceit of the "Two Cosimos." The duke took every opportunity to capitalize on the fact that Leo X had named him after the Pater Patriae and on his identity as the second Medici Cosimo. Thus, shortly after his assumption of power, an *impresa* was invented which may have been intended to make explicit his double descent and to suggest that a parallel be drawn between himself and the first Cosimo. This *impresa*, showing two crossed anchors with the motto DVABVS (by means of two), first appears on Domenico di Polo's medal of late 1537-1538 (pl. 160).[26]

The "two anchors: DVABVS" was the key *impresa* in the decorations of the second courtyard of the Palazzo Medici, where Cosimo's wedding banquet took place on 6 July 1539. According to Vasari, its decoration was "un suntuosissimo apparato pieno di storie; cioè, da una parte di Romani e Greci, e dall'altre di cose state fatte da uomini illustri di detta casa Medici" (a most sumptuous decoration all full of stories; on one side of the Greeks and Romans, and on the other sides of deeds done by the illustrious men of that Medici house).[27] The main themes of this decoration were the new duke's relationship to his Medici *antenati* (ancestors), his blood legitimacy, and his special, predes-

[24] Adelson, in Barocchi, cat. 100.

[25] Allegri-Cecchi, pp. 32-39. Heikamp, pp. 122-23, notes the dynastic theme.

[26] Supino, no. 258. Unlike the "laurel tree: VNO AVVLSO," the "two anchors: DVABVS" became one of Cosimo's permanent *imprese*. However, its meaning was misinterpreted by Ludovico Domenichi (in Giovio, *Dialogo . . .* , Lyon, 1574, p. 230), who guessed that it alluded to the dual security given to Cosimo by Charles V and the Florentine fortresses. As Minor-Mitchell, p. 136, have noted, the fortresses were not restituted to Cosimo until 1543, or four years after the wedding. Their suggestion that the anchors signified Cosimo and

Charles V may be valid in relation to the use of the *impresa* in 1539; however, this cannot be its major meaning, for the *impresa* was used by Cosimo long after this concern of his early years ceased to have significance.

[27] Vasari, VI, p. 87. To what part of the decoration Vasari's "storie . . . di Romani e Greci" refers is unclear. The decoration was designed by Tribolo and Aristotile da Sangallo. A model reconstructing the courtyard decorations (but without the portraits in the south loggia which I discuss) was exhibited in *La Scena del Principe, Firenze e la Toscana dei Medici nell' Europa del Cinquecento*, Palazzo Medici-Riccardi, Florence, 1980, cat. 1.35.

tined place in Medici history. This message was delineated in six pairs of large chiaroscuri, displayed along the east and west walls of the courtyard, in which events from Cosimo's life were paralleled with events from the history of the Medici (fig. 19).[28] Giambullari describes the first pair as representing "la felice tornata del Magno Cosimo alla sua diletta patria" (the happy return of the Great Cosimo to his beloved homeland); and, opposite this painting, "la ben fortunata Natività dello Illustrissimo Duca Cosimo, come nuovo principio di piu felice secolo" (the auspicious nativity of the Most Illustrious Duke Cosimo, as a new beginning of a happier century).[29] Duke Cosimo's birth was thus equated with Cosimo il Vecchio's return from exile, and, in quotations from *Eclogue IV* that accompanied the scene, the advent of his birth was connected with the coming of a new Golden Age.[30] Above the scene of the duke's birth was the *giglio* of Florence, and above the scene of the return from exile was the *stemma* of Duke Cosimo. Moreover, the roundels accompanying the scenes link the two events: above the *Return from Exile* were two doves on a golden branch with a line from the *Aeneid* alluding to the *imprese* of the "laurel tree: VNO AVVLSO" of Pontormo's portrait of Cosimo Pater Patriae; above the *Birth of Cosimo* was the old Medici symbol of rebirth, the phoenix.[31] The theme of the Two Cosimos, with its conflation of old and new, of Florence and the Medici, was thus forcibly stated in this first pair of scenes with their accompanying imagery. This idea was reinforced throughout the series: each of the remaining pictures had its own insignia, according to Giambullari, but all were embellished with the device of "le due Ancore, nuova impresa di sua Eccellentia" (the two anchors, new *impresa* of his Excellency).[32]

Following an old Medici tradition in their wedding *apparati*, Cosimo displayed portraits of his ancestors in the loggia of this courtyard. This custom, initiated at the wedding of Lorenzo il Magnifico and Clarice Orsini in 1469, had been continued at that of Lorenzo the younger and Madeleine de la Tour d'Auvergne on 8 September 1518. Freshly painted, Raphael's *Leo X with Cardinals Giulio de' Medici and Luigi de' Rossi* (pl. 165) was displayed, according to Alfonsina Orsini's account, "sopra alla tavola, dove mangiava la Duchessa et li altri signori, in mezo, che veramente rallegrava ogni cosa" (above the table where the duchess and the other lords ate, in the center, where it truly gladdened everything).[33] Later, in 1533, a diarist recorded that portraits of the following

[28] Vasari, VI, pp. 442-46, lists the subjects and most names of the artists who painted these pictures; Giambullari, pp. 22-30, describes the decorations in detail, but without the artists' names. Forster, 1971, pp. 91-93; and Kliemann, 1976, pp. 74-77, discuss the ensemble as a prototype for Vasari's decoration of the Palazzo Vecchio apartments.

[29] Giambullari, pp. 25-27. Vasari, VI, p. 443, attributes the scene of Cosimo's return to Bacchiacca, whose drawing for it (Stockholm, National Museum 139/1863) was identified by Winner, 1970, p. 280, fig. 17.

[30] Giambullari, p. 27: MAGNVS AB INTEGRO SAECLORVM NASCITVR ORDO / IAM NOVA PROGENIES / RE-

DEVNT SATVRNIA REGNA.

[31] Minor-Mitchell, pp. 130, 133.

[32] Giambullari, p. 24. It is notable that Giambullari makes a point of mentioning the novelty of this *impresa*, while he does not so characterize the "laurel tree: VNO AVVLSO" device, which was drawn from earlier Medici imagery.

[33] Alfonsina Orsini's letter of 8 September 1518 to Pope Leo's secretary was obviously intended to flatter the pope by mentioning the display of his portrait at his nephew's marriage to Madeleine, a political match that had been made by Leo himself. For the text of the letter, see Parronchi, pp. 52-53.

STAGE

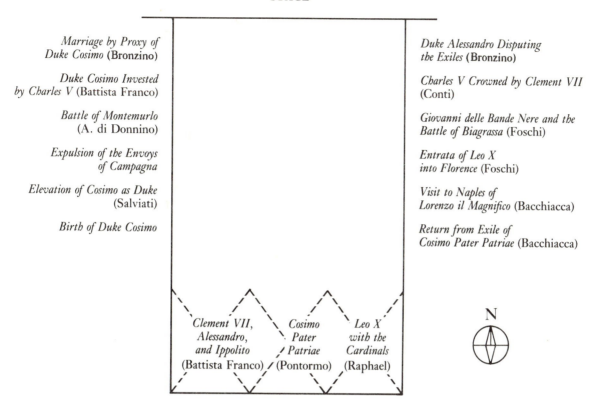

Marriage by Proxy of
Duke Cosimo (**Bronzino**)

Duke Cosimo Invested
by Charles V (**Battista Franco**)

Battle of Montemurlo
(**A. di Donnino**)

Expulsion of the Envoys
of Campagna

Elevation of Cosimo as Duke
(**Salviati**)

Birth of Duke Cosimo

Duke Alessandro Disputing
the Exiles (**Bronzino**)

Charles V Crowned by Clement VII
(**Conti**)

Giovanni delle Bande Nere and the
Battle of Biagrassa (**Foschi**)

Entrata of Leo X
into Florence (**Foschi**)

Visit to Naples of
Lorenzo il Magnifico (**Bacchiacca**)

Return from Exile of
Cosimo Pater Patriae (**Bacchiacca**)

Clement VII,
Alessandro,
and Ippolito
(**Battista Franco**)

Cosimo
Pater
Patriae
(**Pontormo**)

Leo X
with the
Cardinals
(**Raphael**)

N

19. Scheme of the decorations of the second courtyard of the Palazzo Medici for
the wedding of Duke Cosimo de' Medici and Eleonora da Toledo

Medici *illustri* were hung in the same place for the wedding festivities of Duke Alessandro: "il Papa [Clement VII], el Mag. Giuliano, el Mag. li Lorenzo giovane, Cosimo vechio, el Cardinale Ipolito, el Duca nostro, Lorenzo e Giuliano vecchi, e così tutta la casa parata" (the Pope, the Magnificent Giuliano, the Magnificent Lorenzo the younger, Cosimo il Vecchio, Cardinal Ippolito, our Duke, Lorenzo and Giuliano the Elder, and thus the whole house was arrayed).[34]

Like Alessandro, but more selectively, Cosimo drew on the resources of his and Ottaviano's collections for portraits of his *antenati* which could be used to demonstrate his legitimacy, the inevitability of his rule, and the idea of himself as a reincarnation of Cosimo Pater Patriae. These were displayed under the three arches of the south loggia of the courtyard opposite the stage where the entertainment took place. Giambullari describes this decoration in detail:[35]

> Et pero me ne ritorno alla opposita loggia, parata di Rasi chermisi à frangie d'Oro, dal posare della volta fino à terra: Questa nella Lunetta del mezo, ha-

[34] Jacopo di ser Guido d'Anghiani, "Diario dal 1437 al 1533 (Dialogo sulle nozze del Duca Alessandro," BNF, MS Nuovi Acquisti 982, f. 169r. I am grateful to Margaret Haines for the transcrip-

tion quoted. Some of these portraits must be those which I have mentioned (above, n. 3) as in the collection of Ottaviano.

[35] Giambullari, p. 30.

veva un' naturalissimo ritratto del Magno Cosimo vecchio, addornato con gruppi et compassi di festoncini, che lo accompagnavano à duoi gran' tondi, con la nuova Ducale impresa delle Ancore intraversate, con il loro motto, DVABVS. Et nella testa di Levante il ritratto di Leon. X. con li duoi Reverendissimi Cardinali, Iulio de Medici et Luigi de Rossi, d'intorno alla sedia, cosi naturalmente figurati, che vivi parevano à chi li conobbe. Il che anche interveniva de ritratti nel' altro quadro, cioe Clemente VII, co'l Reverendissimo Ipolito, et Illustrissimo Alessandro de' Medici, posto nella faccia, o voglian' dir' testa di Ponente.

Therefore I go back to the opposite loggia, hung with gold-fringed crimson satin from the bottom of the vault to the floor. In this loggia's middle lunette was a very natural portrait of the Great Cosimo il Vecchio, adorned with clusters and arcs of little festoons that accompanied it in two big roundels. There was also the new ducal *impresa* of entwined anchors and their motto, DVABVS. And on the eastern side the portrait of Leo X, with the two most Reverend Cardinals Giulio de' Medici and Luigi de' Rossi around the seat, so naturally figured that they seemed alive to people who knew them. The same was true for the portraits in the other painting, that is, Clement VII, with the Most Reverend Ippolito and the Most Illustrious Alessandro de' Medici, placed on the western side.

This description gives the subjects of the portraits: in the center was Cosimo il Vecchio; on the east side of the loggia were Leo X with the Cardinals Giulio de' Medici and Luigi de' Rossi; and on the west side were Clement VII with Cardinal Ippolito de' Medici and Alessandro de' Medici. Since the primary purpose of this description was to convey to Charles V the propaganda message of the *apparato*, Giambullari gives no artists' names in connection with these portraits of Medici *illustri*. On the other hand, Vasari, whose later account of the *apparato* is more concerned with the decorations as art, identifies the painters of the scenes from Medici history, but he does not mention either the south loggia or the portraits which Giambullari tells us were displayed there. This omission may be explained by the fact that these portraits were not part of the ephemeral décor created especially for the occasion by Cosimo's artists but were pictures borrowed from the Medici collections. Two of them had been painted for Leo X in 1518 to 1520; the third was a pastiche, created in 1539 to round out and bring up to date the display of Cosimo's illustrious Medici ancestors.

As has been recognized,[36] the portrait of *Leo X with the Cardinals* was Raphael's famous picture, which had first been displayed in the Palazzo Medici courtyard in 1518 at the wedding celebration of Lorenzo the younger. This portrait belonged to Cosimo, who had obtained it from Ottaviano de' Medici after he became duke.[37] In displaying this

---

[36] Kaufmann, p. 53.

[37] Vasari's letter concerning his copy of the work refers to Cosimo as its owner (Vasari-Frey, I, pp. 92-93). Elsewhere Vasari, V, p. 43, states that the

picture had belonged to Duke Alessandro, who gave it to Ottaviano, from whom Cosimo acquired it. On the early history of the picture in Florence, see V. Golzio, *Raffaello nei Documenti*, Vatican, 1936,

picture, Cosimo paid homage to his great-uncle and early benefactor, who had marked him for fame and power by baptizing him after Cosimo Pater Patriae. (Coincidentally, one of Cosimo's godparents, Cardinal de' Rossi, is also in the portrait.)

The second papal portrait may be identified as Battista Franco's *Clement VII with Ippolito and Alessandro de' Medici*. The work is lost, but it is known from Vasari's description[38] to have been painted by Battista in Cosimo's *guardaroba* (storage room) after originals by Sebastiano del Piombo,[39] Titian,[40] and Pontormo,[41] and it was inventoried in Cosimo's collection in 1553.[42] Battista, who had been in the duke's employ since 1537, was an important contributor to the wedding *apparato*, for which he painted battle scenes on the triumphal arch that transformed the Porta al Prato, and he contributed the painting *Duke Cosimo Invested by Charles V* to the second courtyard ensemble.[43] The triple portrait must have been made as the ideological pendant to Raphael's picture, the likenesses changed to depict the only comparable "sitters"—the second Medici pope and the two Medici cousins, one of whom was the duke from whom Cosimo claimed succession. Considering that it hung as a pendant to *Leo X with the Cardinals*, Battista's triple portrait must have been about the same size as Raphael's picture, and it probably reflected the design of its authoritative prototype as well.[44] Indeed, such a dependence is suggested in Vasari's *Supper of St. Gregory*, a derivative work which was painted the year after

pp. 151-54, 262, 264; Freedberg, 1963, II, pp. 131-33; Shearman, 1965, II, pp. 265-66.

[38] See Vasari, VI, pp. 574-75: After the death of Alessandro, "Battista fu messo al servizio del duca Cosimo ed a lavorare in guardaroba: dove dipinse in un quadro grande, ritraendogli da uno di Fra Bastiano e da uno di Tiziano, Papa Clemente et il cardinale Ippolito, e da un del Pontormo il duca Alessandro."

[39] No portrait of Clement is listed in the 1553 inventory of Cosimo's collection. Vasari, V, p. 581, does note, however, that a Sebastiano portrait of Clement was sent to Florence in 1532 at Michelangelo's request to serve as a model for portraits of the pope, after which Michelangelo gave it to Ottaviano de' Medici (cf. L. Dussler, *Sebastiano del Piombo*, Basel, 1942, pp. 69-70, n. 58, with other documentation). Vasari, V, p. 581; VI, pp. 204-5, lists portraits by Bugiardini based on it: one with Clement seated and Fra Niccolò della Magna standing, the other with Clement seated and Baccio Valori kneeling, both now lost. On the problem of the Sebastiano *Clement* which went to Florence and derivations from it, see M. Hirst, *Sebastiano del Piombo*, Oxford, 1981, pp. 110-12.

[40] Titian's "Ippolito all'ungaresca" of 1533 (now Pitti) was in Cosimo's *guardaroba* (Vasari, VII, p. 441; Conti, p. 102) and could have been Battista's model, but as in Bronzino's miniature (Uffizi) and Vasari's tondo (Palazzo Vecchio, Sala di Leo X),

his costume would have been changed to a cardinal's robes. A Titian portrait of *Ippolito in Armor* was also in Cosimo's collection and could equally well have been the model (Vasari, VII, p. 441; Conti, p. 139).

[41] Pontormo's *Alessandro* (now in Philadelphia) was not in Florence in 1539 (Clapp, pp. 170-71) and could not have served as Battista's model, but the miniature he made in connection with it was in Cosimo's *guardaroba* (Vasari, VI, p. 278) and may have been the model.

[42] The picture is listed without author in the 1553 inventory (Conti, p. 86): "Uno quadro di pittura grande con ornamento di noce intagliato drentrovi papa Clemente, Ipolito et Alessandro."

[43] Vasari, VI, pp. 575-77.

[44] Vasari refers to Raphael's picture as "di buona grandezza" (it is 1.54 × 1.19 m). Vasari and the 1553 inventory (above, nn. 38, 42) call Battista's picture "grande." Such derivations from Raphael's picture were by no means novel, for a number of replicas with the sitters changed to suit the patron's needs had been made in Florence in the mid-1530s. Cf. Bugiardini's portrait with Cardinal Cibo substituted for Cardinal de' Rossi (Rome, Galleria Nazionale; Vasari, VI, pp. 206-7). Bugiardini's lost double portraits with the seated Clement as the central figure may also have reflected Raphael's composition (see n. 39 above).

Cosimo's wedding (pl. 164).[45] The arrangement of the figures in Vasari's picture reflects Raphael's composition (in reverse), and two of the sitters are those of Battista's lost work: Clement, who is seated, like Leo, in a chair decorated with a golden *palla*; and Alessandro, who stands behind Clement's chair, his profile repeating Vasari's own earlier likeness of him.

The centerpiece of the loggia display—between the two papal portraits and with the subject facing *Leo X with the Cardinals*—can only have been Pontormo's portrait of Cosimo Pater Patriae, borrowed by the duke from Ottaviano de' Medici. As the account cited above indicates, it had previously been exhibited there with many other Medici portraits at Duke Alessandro's wedding. However, at Cosimo's banquet the special significance of the subject dictated that it occupy the place of honor, and an elaborate *quadratura* (framing) of garlands and *tondi* enlarged it to dimensions comparable to those of the papal portraits flanking it. The three pictures of red-robed Medici *illustri*—for we must assume that Pope Clement and Cardinal Ippolito were in red like Cosimo, Leo, and Cardinal Giulio—would have made a splendid display against the crimson, gold-fringed satin backdrop that Giambullari describes. Under these portraits of *antenati* with whom Cosimo wished to be identified was: "la tavola degli sposi . . . dove sederono oltre a cento delle prime Gentil' Donne di tutta la Nobilta" (the table of the bride and groom . . . where were seated more than a hundred of the first gentlewomen of the entire nobility).[46] Cosimo and Eleonora, at its center, would thus have been seated directly under Pontormo's portrait of the first Cosimo, didactically embellished with the "two anchors: DVABVS" *impresa* which announced the exalted legitimacy of his namesake, the new duke.

The dynastic imagery of the wedding *apparato* was echoed in the entertainment at the banquet, which opened with a song by Cosimo's court poet, Giambattista Gelli.[47] The imagery of Medici dynasty, which originated in the time of Lorenzo il Magnifico and was elaborated by Leo X, achieves a kind of apotheosis in this song, as the flourishing Medici *lauro*, the return of the Golden Age, and the notion of the Two Cosimos are all brought together by the singer, Apollo. The god has descended from the heavens to tell the story of his sacred laurel, which is an extended metaphor for the flourishing, dying, and then revived Medici dynasty—from Cosimo Pater Patriae to the new beginning represented by the marriage of Duke Cosimo and Eleonora. This narrative begins with the birth of the deified Cosimo Pater Patriae from Flora-Fiorenza:

> Dentro al bel sen' di Flora origine hebbe
>   La Regia stirpe donde, nato sei,
>   Da un'altro COSMO, a cui non poco debbe
>   Che l'arricchi di mille alti Trofei.

[45] Bologna, Pinacoteca; signed and dated 1540. See Vasari, VII, p. 655, who identifies the portraits of Clement and Alessandro. The bearded man to the right of Alessandro is Ottaviano de' Medici, and the group thus portrays Vasari's chief Florentine patrons.

[46] Giambullari, p. 30.

[47] Giambullari, pp. 38-39. The last four stanzas of the poem (not quoted here) express hopes for the continuation of the dynasty in the descendants of Cosimo and Eleonora and faith in the alliance of Florence with Charles V. For this text and commentary on the poem, see Minor-Mitchell, pp. 142-44.

> Questi lei tanto et sè per fama accrebbe
> Che ascritto fu fra i maggior semidei:
> Et si fur l'opre sue chiare & leggiadre,
> Che morto lo chiamo la Patria padre.

Inside the beautiful breast of Flora, the kingly stock of which you were born had its origin from another COSIMO, to whom she owes not a little because he enriched her with a thousand exalted trophies. This man increased her and himself so much through fame that he was inscribed among the major demigods. And his works were so shining and so pleasing that when he was dead his homeland called him father.

The poet continues (skipping over Piero di Cosimo, as was usual in dynastic imagery of this period), lauding the Golden Age of the "santo Alloro," Lorenzo il Magnifico:

> Di costui nacque poi quel santo Alloro,
>   Premio delle alte et valorose imprese,
>   Sotto 'l qual vide Flora il secol' d'oro,
>   Che'nsino al Ciel le frondi sue distese.
>   Questi co'l suo saver' dall'Indo al Moro
>   Cotal' dell'amor' suo le menti accese,
>   Che in sin' donde i miei raggi son piu ardenti
>   Devote al nome suo venner' le genti.

From him was born then that holy laurel, prize of high and valorous enterprises, under whom Flora saw the Golden Age and that raised its unfolded leaves up to Heaven. This man, with his knowledge from India to Africa, so fired minds with love of him that peoples as far as the places where my rays are most burning became devoted to his name.

Gelli then evokes the Medici popes Leo and Clement as new branches of the flourishing laurel, and then, in imagery familiar from the poetry and art of the last years of Leo's pontificate, he describes the intervention of fate and the deaths of Giuliano and Lorenzo the younger, which left the plant bare:

> Nacquero poi di questa sacra pianta
>   Molti altri rami, et sì crebbero à gara;
>   Che l'alma Roma la sua sede santa
>   N'ornò come di cosa illustre et chiara.
>   Ma perche il Suol' terrestre non si vanta
>   Di cosa alcuna eterna, benche rara;
>   Quando la Parca il fil troncar' ne volse,
>   Ogni alto ramo a questa pianta tolse.

There were then born from this sacred plant many other branches, and they grew one faster than the other, so that beneficient Rome adorned its Holy

Seat with them as with an illustrious and shining thing. But because the terrestrial ground boasts nothing eternal, however rare, when the Fate decided to break her thread, she took every high branch from this plant.

The narrative ends in the present with the New Cosimo, in whom the laurel will be revived with even greater vigor than before:

> Ma hor (vostra Mercè) coppia si bella
>> Risorge à tanta stirpe un nuovo Germe,
>> Che le perdute frondi rinnovella;
>> Et rende vive le sue parte inferme:
>> Et COSMO per principio ha come quella;
>> Ma con radici assai più salde et ferme:
>> Et crescerà con tanto più valore,
>> Quanto è quello il COSMO suo maggiore.

But now, thanks to you, beautiful couple, there arises from such a great stock a new sprout that renews the lost leaves and gives life to the infirm parts. It, like the other one, has COSIMO as beginning, but with rather more solid and firm roots, and it will grow with all more energy because its COSIMO is greater than the other.

*   *   *

The myth of the Two Cosimos, thus crystallized early in Cosimo's rule, was a leitmotif of his imagery. He revived a conceit of older Medicean religious painting in which the head of the family was portrayed as Saint Cosmas, often with another family member as Saint Damian. This iconography, which alludes to the notion of the Medici (= *medici*) as healers, first appeared in Fra Angelico's San Marco altarpiece (pl. 39), where the halos of the saints are inscribed with their names and Cosimo il Vecchio as Saint Cosmas kneels to the left, interceding for the observer. This formula was followed by Botticelli in a *sacra conversazione* of ca. 1470; only this time it is Lorenzo il Magnifico who communicates with the observer as Saint Cosmas, while Saint Damian may be a portrait of his brother Giuliano.[48] This conceit first occurs in Duke Cosimo's art in Allori's *Risen Christ with Saints Cosmas and Damian* of ca. 1559-1560 (pl. 166).[49] Here, Cosimo-Saint Cosmas holds a book, which has an anatomical drawing appropriate to the doctor-saint prominently displayed. (The picture is also of interest because of Allori's revival of the theme of the Medici patron saints with the Resurrection, which had been planned by Michelangelo for the New Sacristy; cf. pl. 35.) In another work, painted a few years later by Vasari, the conceit of the Two Cosimos is conflated with that of the Medici saints. This work is in Cosimo's private chapel in the Palazzo, which

[48] Uffizi 8657; see Lightbown, II, cat. B13. The saints' names are inscribed on the floor beneath the figures.

[49] Brussels, Musées Royaux. Formerly ascribed to Salviati, this work is attributed to Allori by Heikamp (cited in Lecchini Giovannoni, p. 76).

was decorated by Vasari in 1561 and dedicated to Saints Cosmas and Damian.[50] The wings that flank Raphael's *Madonna dell'Impannata* (now replaced by a copy) are portraits of the Pater Patriae and the duke as Saints Cosmas and Damian (pl. 167). The head of the Pater Patriae is based on Pontormo's portrait, which Vasari has turned into a full-length standing figure, with a halo added to transform the revered ancestor into a saint.[51] The duke's portrait is based on a recent likeness of him by Bronzino.[52] But which Cosimo is which saint? There are no attributes or inscriptions to tell us; however, Duke Cosimo's position on the left and his gesture of intercession make it clear that Vasari followed the traditional Medici iconography of portraying the living Medici ruler as Saint Cosmas on the left of the altar (to the Virgin's right). In the tradition of Cosimo Pater Patriae and Lorenzo il Magnifico, who were portrayed as Saint Cosmas, Duke Cosimo now becomes the saint, and his ancestor takes the secondary role. Gelli's wedding song of two decades earlier had declared the New Cosimo greater than his ancestor; now, in the boldest visual statement of the parallel with the Pater Patriae that was so essential to the duke's presentation of himself as legitimate ruler of Florence, the New Cosimo has truly superseded his exemplar.

The myth of the Two Cosimos endured even after the duke's death in 1574. His funeral *apparato* in San Lorenzo included reference to this *topos*: Cosimo's catafalque, surmounted by a baldachin designed by Buontalenti, was placed in front of the high altar directly over the slab marking the tombsite of Cosimo Pater Patriae. Among its mottos were OPTIMO PRINCIPI (to the best prince) and PATRI PATRIAE (to the father of his country).[53] And, in one of the orations for the occasion, the myth merged with the reality: Duke Cosimo himself was awarded the title "Padre della Patria," and it was declared that this honor was bestowed "à imitazione di quel COSIMO di cui meritissimamente egli haveva il nome" (in imitation of that Cosimo whose name he so deservedly held).[54]

Cosimo also continued to be represented as Saint Cosmas, as in a Bronzinesque *sacra conversazione* of 1575, in which all the characters are portraits of members of the Medici family with Cosimo's son, Ferdinando, as Saint Damian.[55] But the apotheosis of the theme

[50] Vasari's *ricordo* no. 269 of 3 January 1561 (Vasari-Del Vita, p. 85) refers to the completion of the chapel, and he mentions the dedication to Saints Cosmas and Damian in his own *vita* (VII, p. 699). Although called the Chapel of Leo X after the main room of the suite of which it is a part in the Palazzo, the chapel is marked as Cosimo's by his *impresa* of the Capricorn on the pavement. See Allegri-Cecchi, pp. 162-65.

[51] Vasari's was not the first copy of Pontormo's *Cosimo* made for Duke Cosimo. See the portrait of Cosimo Pater Patriae in the Bronzino workshop series of ca. 1553 (Vasari, VII, p. 603; Baccheschi, fig. 135), which is inscribed COSMVS MEDICES P P P. There are also a number of later derivations, such as the one by Alessandro Pieroni of 1585 from

the series made for the gallery of the Uffizi (now Uffizi 2217; see Berti, 1979, pp. 700-701, no. Ic 634).

[52] Vasari, VII, p. 601, mentions a portrait of Cosimo at age forty. Various replicas of this picture of ca. 1559-1560, such as the one at Turin, Galleria Sabauda, suggest that it was the model for Vasari's portrait (cf. Baccheschi, figs. 113 a-f), as Langedijk, p. 66, has noted.

[53] For a description of this work, see Borsook, pp. 41-44.

[54] *Orazione funerale di Benedetto Betti . . .* , Florence, 1574, f. 6v.

[55] For this painting (Uffizi 3402), dated A.D. MDLXXV on Saint Catherine's book, see Pieraccini, II, pp. 165-69; Berti, 1967, pp. 185-86;

occurred in the *apparato* for the wedding of Ferdinando and Cristina di Lorena in 1589. For this state occasion, the Ponte alla Carraia was decorated with colossal statues by Giovanni Caccini, lost works which are described by Raffaello Gualterotti in an extended account of the decorations illustrated with engravings by Orazio Scarabelli.[56] According to Gualterotti, the statue of Cosimo, with grand-ducal crown and scepter, was inscribed COSMO MEDICI MAGNI DVCATVS ETRVRIAE CONDITORI (To Cosimo de' Medici, founder of the great dukedom of Etruria), and was accompanied by three of his *imprese*: the "two anchors: DVABVS"; the "tortoise with a sail: FESTINA LENTE"; and the "Capricorn: FIDVCIA FATI (pl. 168).[57] The statue of Cosimo Pater Patriae was inscribed COSMO MEDICI P. P. ET PVB. TRANQVILLITATIS AVCTORI (To Cosimo de' Medici Pater Patriae and creator of public peace), and it depicted him, without attributes, in the same simple robe he wears in Pontormo's portrait (pl. 169). On the base was portrayed one of the most durable of Medici *imprese*—the "laurel tree: VNO AVVLSO"—together with the ever appropriate reminder of the popular origins of Medici rule in Florence:

> E vi si vede dalla parte, che va sopra il ponte una pianta d'allori, che ha tronco il suo fusto, e ne rimette uno da piè più bello; il motto da lui portata, e dalla parte, che guarda sopra la sponda v'è scritto DECRE. PVBL. PAT. P.

> One can see on the side that faces the bridge a laurel plant whose trunk is split and which is sprouting another more beautiful [branch] from its roots. The motto it carries on the side that overlooks the banks reads: Pater Patriae by public decree.

---

and Langedijk, pp. 86, 147. The likeness of Cosimo derives from Bronzino's portrait of ca. 1559-1560.

[56] Gualterotti, II, pp. 77-79. On the engravings see V. Daddi Giovannozzi, "Di alcune incisioni dell'apparato per le nozze di Ferdinando de' Medici e Cristina di Lorena," *Rivista d'Arte*, 22, 1940, pp. 85-100.

[57] For the latter two devices, see chap. 11, "Capricorn and the Crown of Ariadne."

 *Fiducia*
Fati

COSIMO AND LEONINE IMAGERY

Themes of earlier Medici art, especially that of Pope Leo X, were programmatically developed by Duke Cosimo's iconographers in the major commissions of the late 1530s and 1540s—the *apparato* for his marriage, the loggia and gardens of Villa Castello, the first public rooms of the duke's new residence in the former Palazzo della Signoria, and countless individual works of art. Later—after 1555 and the ascendency of Vasari, Cosimo Bartoli, Vincenzo Borghini, and others of the *équipe* in charge of the further decoration of the Palazzo—the Leonine themes and poetic conceits that had been revived by the young duke to shore up his claim to rule Florence and to sustain the myth of the Medici were subsumed into the cult of Cosimo's person and *virtù*—which, in turn, became the subject and substance of his later art.

Familiar imagery of Leonine art reappears in the wedding *apparato* of 1539, which was the first public demonstration of Cosimo's personal iconography. The first court-yard of the Palazzo Medici was largely devoted to a display of *imprese*: there were devices alluding to Cosimo's political alliance with Charles V and Spain through his marriage; there were his own personal devices, such as the "two anchors: DVABVS" (pl. 160); and there was an array of old Medici *imprese* from Leo's time, such as the "laurel tree: VNO AVVLSO" (pl. 162), the "laurel tree: ITA ET VIRTVS" (pl. 8), and the "yoke: SVAVE" (pl. 32).[1] This display of Cosimo's political loyalty and his legitimacy was followed in the second courtyard with *istorie* which paralleled events from the life of the new duke with events from Medici history (fig. 19). The scheme of these *istorie* recalls that of Leo's Salone at Poggio a Caiano (fig. 3): the *Return from Exile of Cosimo Pater Patriae* and the *Visit to Naples of Lorenzo il Magnifico* (both by Bacchiacca) repeat two of the themes from Giovio's program for the earlier work. However, Medici *illustri* are now presented quite differently. In the Salone, the Medici were portrayed in the guise of Roman exemplars

[1] For the imagery of the first courtyard, see Minor-Mitchell, pp. 124-27; and Kaufmann, pp. 54-57.

(pl. 68), but here (and later in Vasari's cycle in the Quartiere of Leo X in the Palazzo) they are portrayed without benefit of historical disguise.

As in Leo's Salone, the theme of the Golden Age underlay these decorations. The rule of the Medici was presented in terms of a running commentary of Virgilian inscriptions, including quotations from *Eclogue* IV, which read like captions to the scene of Duke Cosimo's birth.[2] And the entertainment which accompanied this display reiterated the same themes. Besides Apollo's song (quoted in chapter 10), there was a Virgilian *canzonetta* by Giovambattista Strozzi, "O begli Anni del Oro." In lines recalling the quotation from the *Georgics* in Pontormo's *Vertumnus and Pomona*, it invokes Apollo to bring back the Golden Age:[3]

> O begli anni del Or', vedrovvi io mai?
> Tornagli ò nuovo Sol, tornagli homai.
>
> O beautiful golden years, shall I ever see you?
> Bring them back, O new Sun, bring them back now.

Leonine dynastic imagery recalling that of the Poggio a Caiano Salone was also prominent in Cosimo's projects in the Palazzo in the early 1540s. Bandinelli's *Udienza* was planned to demonstrate Medicean continuity, particularly Cosimo's dual descent from both branches of the family and his relation to the two Medici popes. Thus, as Leo planned a Salone in which the Medici could receive envoys against a background of scenes alluding to their illustrious ancestors, so, in his audience hall, Cosimo (who had sat beneath portraits of his forebears at his wedding banquet) could be set against statues of his ancestors and implicitly elevated to their level.

Salviati's frescos in the Sala delle Udienze, which were commissioned in October 1543, shortly after the final consolidation of Cosimo's power with the return of the Florentine fortresses to his control, also seek to justify Cosimo's rule.[4] The Sala, which was the Hall of Justice in the old Palazzo della Signoria, was redecorated by Cosimo in a way that recalls the great Leonine rooms of 1520—the Salone at Poggio a Caiano and the Sala di Costantino. The scheme of Salviati's decoration (pl. 78), with its *istorie*, framing Corinthian columns, *sopraporte*, and putti on garlands, is reminiscent of that of the Salone; and the program, combining Bacchiacca's *Grotesques* tapestries with the painted decoration, is dependent on the Sala di Costantino.[5] Like that of the Salone, in particular, the program of the Sala juxtaposes Roman histories, Virtues, and cosmological imagery to celebrate the Golden Age of the Medici. In commissioning this updated version of the Salone, Cosimo implicitly placed himself in the line of Lorenzo il Magnifico and Leo X, the great Medicean art patrons of the past; only now, it was not the

[2] Giambullari, p. 27 (quoted in chap. 10, n. 30).

[3] Minor-Mitchell, p. 298. On the music for the wedding, see H. W. Kaufmann, "Music for a Noble Florentine Wedding (1539), "*Words and Music: The Scholar's View (A Medley of Problems and Solutions compiled in Honor of A. Tillman Merritt by Sundry Hands)*, ed. L. Berman, Cambridge, 1972, pp. 161-82.

[4] For the documentation on the cycle and discussion of its program, see Cheney, I, pp. 162-87; II, pp. 359-74; and Allegri-Cecchi, pp. 40-48.

[5] Adelson, 1980, pp. 144-66. I am grateful to Candace Adelson for allowing me to consult her fundamental study prior to its publication.

dynastic and political continuity of the family which was emphasized so much as his own absolute rule. In the Salone, Cosimo's ancestors were allegorized as Cicero and Augustus (pls. 71-72); but here, as Camillus, Cosimo himself takes center stage. He is the sole subject of the room, and the sprouting Medici laurel in the background of the *Triumph of Camillus* refers to his triumphal Medici "return" (pl. 89).

It is at Villa Castello, however, with its ambitious program for a frescoed loggia and garden sculpture celebrating the new Golden Age of Cosimo, that the most extensive reprise of earlier Medici imagery in Cosimo's art is found (or would have been, had the sculptures been completed). The dependence of this decorative program on the unfinished Poggio a Caiano Salone, in particular, is not surprising, since several of those who had participated in the earlier decoration—Giovio, Ottaviano de' Medici, and Pontormo—were still active in Medici affairs, and Pontormo was actually working at the villa. However, the author of the Castello program is not known.[6]

The focal points of the garden were to be two elaborate fountains, both commissioned from Tribolo in 1537: *Hercules and Antaeus*, the statue executed in 1559-1560 by Ammannati (pl. 170), and *Venus-Fiorenza*, the statue executed by Giambologna in 1570-1571 and the fountain installed at Villa Petraia.[7] These were to be surrounded by emblematic foliage in a setting calculated to evoke the mythical Garden of the Hesperides: its golden fruits were sacred to Venus and were obtained by Hercules after he killed Antaeus. This scheme was clearly intended to recall earlier Medici art. Hercules and Venus-Fiorenza were both Laurentian themes: Hercules and Antaeus goes back to Pollaiuolo's painting of the subject owned by Lorenzo; Tribolo's *Venus* (characterized as Venus Anadyomene and set in a grove of laurels and other foliage) seems to conflate themes from the *Birth of Venus* and the *Primavera*, the Botticelli paintings which were installed at Villa Castello by Cosimo himself.[8] The imagery of the fountains also contains echoes of the subjects of the Poggio a Caiano Salone frescos: Venus in her laurel grove recalls Pontormo's gods (one of which is Venus) in their Medicean laurel garden (color pl. 2), and Hercules in the garden recalls the subject of the unexecuted pendant lunette of *Hercules and Fortuna in the Garden of the Hesperides*, later to be painted by Allori (pl. 118). Moreover, the fountains are explicitly related to the themes of the frescos of *Hercules and Antaeus* and *Venus and Adonis* which Cosimo's predecessor, Alessandro, had commissioned Pontormo to paint in the Salone in 1531, and for which Pontormo did cartoons described by Vasari.[9]

The *Hercules and Antaeus* fountain is a monumental statement of the important theme of Hercules in the early art of Cosimo, who followed Alessandro in adopting the ancient

[6] As Wright, I, pp. 354-55, has noted, Varchi cannot have been responsible for the Castello program, since he was in exile and not reconciled with Cosimo's regime until March 1543 (U. Pirotti, *Benedetto Varchi e la cultura del suo Tempo*, Florence, 1971, p. 23). Wright, I, pp. 351-52, suggests that the author of the program may have been Cosimo's major-domo, Pierfrancesco Riccio. It is also possible that Tribolo himself may have been involved: see n. 14 below; also Tribolo's sketch for the *Hercules* fountain with the facade of Poggio a Caiano on the verso (see chap. 3, n. 10).

[7] For the *Hercules* fountain, see Aschoff, pp. 72-96; Adelson, 1975, pp. 66-81; and Wright, I, pp. 303-24. For the *Venus* fountain, see Aschoff, pp. 97-107; Adelson, 1975, pp. 24-47; and Wright, I, pp. 286-302.

[8] Adelson, 1975, pp. 43-44; and Wright, I, pp. 343-47.

[9] Wright, I, pp. 349-50.

Florentine exemplar of justice and *virtù* in his art.[10] One of his earliest medals, in which Domenico di Polo depicts the beardless duke as he appeared in late 1537-1538, shows Hercules and Antaeus with the inscription HERCVLEE VIRTVTIS VLTIMVS CONATVS—the last attempt of Herculean virtue (pl. 171).[11] We are to read this medal, and the fountain, on several levels. They surely allude to Cosimo's Herculean *fortezza*, demonstrated in the victory over his enemies, the *fuorusciti* (exiles), at the Battle of Montemurlo (1 August 1537), the event which definitively established his power in Florence. The fountain, in addition, may refer to the link between Hercules' defeat of Antaeus and his last ("ultimate") labor in the Garden of the Hesperides.[12] Moreover, both works allude to the theme of Cosimo as protector of Florence: the fountain is paired in the "garden of Florence" with the *Venus* fountain, and the medal recalls the old Hercules seal of the commune and of Lorenzo il Magnifico, which Cosimo had adopted as his own by encircling the image with his name and placing the ducal arms on its handle (pl. 121).

Like *Hercules and Fortuna in the Garden of the Hesperides*, which was presumably projected for Leo's Salone, Cosimo's *Hercules* (in his actual Hesperidian garden at Castello) symbolized the virtue of the patron and was to be complemented by representations of Medici *illustri* and their virtues. However, instead of the *istorie* and the Virtue *sopraporte* of the Salone, the garden was to display portrait busts of the Medici and sculptures of the Virtues and the Arts which flourished in Cosimo's Florence. Cosimo was to be paired with Giustizia (Justice is also the symbolic meaning of *Hercules and Antaeus*), and, as at Poggio a Caiano, Liberality was associated with Leo X.[13] Also as in the Salone, this scheme included the Seasons; but, rather than being portrayed together as in Pontormo's *Vertumnus and Pomona*, they were deployed spatially in the four corners of the garden.[14] The renewal of nature, a metaphor of Medici regeneration and a central theme of Pontormo's fresco, was thus brought to life in the scheme for the Castello sculptures, set amidst the actual foliage of the changing seasons.

[10] Alessandro not only commissioned the *Hercules and Antaeus* from Pontormo, but his medal of this subject (Armand, I, pls. 145-46) was the model for Cosimo's *Hercules and Antaeus* medal. For general consideration of Cosimo's Hercules imagery, see Forster, 1971, pp. 72-81; Ettlinger, 1972, pp. 139-42; Adelson, 1975, pp. 66-81; and Richelson, pp. 79-92. Since the sitter wears a Hercules and Antaeus medal (and since the picture was identified in an inventory of 1612 as Cosimo), the so-called *Halberdier* by Pontormo (New York, Stillman Collection) is now widely accepted as a portrait of the duke (see Forster, above, and others). Because of the lack of a convincing resemblance to Cosimo as he appeared after 1537, I have doubted this identification; however, Malcolm Campbell has made the convincing suggestion to me that the portrait might represent the adolescent Cosimo

wearing the Hercules medal as a badge of allegiance to Alessandro's regime. A date in the early 1530s would, I believe, be more acceptable in relation to Pontormo's style as well.

[11] Supino, no. 263.

[12] On the connection of these subjects, see chap. 6; and for this interpretation of the *Hercules* fountain, see Adelson, 1975, pp. 77-79.

[13] Vasari, VI, pp. 83-84. The other pairs were to be *Pietà* (Giuliano il Vecchio), *Valore* (Giovanni delle Bande Nere), *Nobiltà* (Lorenzo il Magnifico), and *Sapienza* (Cosimo il Vecchio or Clement VII). Opposite them were to be "Leggi, Pace, Arme, Scienze, Lingue, e Arti."

[14] See Vasari, VI, p. 83, who asserts incorrectly that the *Seasons* were suggested by Varchi (who was not responsible for the program; see n. 6 above). Niccolò Martelli (p. 23) states in a letter of

The cosmic and astrological themes present in the Salone lunettes were also elaborated at Castello and in other works commissioned by Cosimo in the late 1530s. Cosimo not only presented his rule as a new Golden Age; he carefully fostered the notion of its inevitability, of his special destiny as duke of Florence, and of the forces of fate that had brought him to power. An *Eclogue* by Gelli, written on an anniversary of Cosimo's election, dutifully proclaimed this theme:[15]

> . . . oggi è il più felice e chiaro giorno
> Che a Flora e ad Arno mai recasse il sole:
> Oggi è quel dì che gli alti Dei propizi
> Dieder per Duce il suo buon Cosmo a Flora.

> Today is the happiest and clearest day that the sun ever brought to Flora and to the Arno. Today is the day in which the high and benign gods gave to Flora her good Cosimo as Duke.

And, when Cosimo came to power in January 1537, the ambiance was heavy with carefully contrived rumors of fate and destiny. As we have seen, Cardinal Cibo's speech recommending Cosimo to the electors used Virgil's lines, "Primo avulso non deficit alter / Aureus, et simili frondescit virga metallo" to point up the inevitability of Cosimo's succession to the murdered Alessandro.[16] (It was this same phrase, of course, that had been combined with the flourishing laurel in Pontormo's portrait of Cosimo Pater Patriae and was to be used by Cosimo in his *impresa* of the "laurel tree: VNO AVVLSO" after he became duke; pl. 162.) Cosmological and meteorological portents of Cosimo's rule were also noted by his commentators. Varchi set the stage for his *Storia fiorentina* (commissioned by Cosimo in 1547) by pointing out that each time the Medici returned to power it was "come avvevano i cieli destinato" (as if the heavens had fated it).[17] And he joined this image to the myth of the Florentine spring, noting that at the time of Cosimo's election the weather was "come quasi di primavera" (almost like spring), an omen elaborated by the duke's later biographers.[18]

Many of the inscriptions and emblems in Cosimo's wedding *apparato* reflect these preoccupations and assert that the events which brought him to power were determined by fate. Cibo's metaphor of Cosimo as the new "golden branch" of the Medici was transformed into the conceit of Cosimo as a New Aeneas, and the parallel was presented

1 March 1543 that the sculptures in the "tabernacoli" were to be executed "nella idea di Tribolo," suggesting his possible involvement in the scheme of the work.

[15] G. B. Gelli, *Le Opere*, Florence, 1855, p. 463.

[16] Varchi, III, p. 276.

[17] Varchi, I, p. 55.

[18] Varchi, III, p. 305: ". . . in tutta quella vernata andarono tempi bellissimi, di maniera che i prati fiorirono come quasi di primavera; il che diede occasione di dire a' fuorusciti, che ciò avveniva per la molta festa che faveva il cielo e la terra della morte d'Alessandro, ed agli altri, questi esser felicissimi segni ed auguri che ne dava la terra e 'l cielo per la creazione del signor Cosimo." Among later commentators on this phenomenon, see Matasilani, p. 28: "Per segno dell'imperio, che dovea conseguire, il suo giardino nella villa di Castello solo fra tutti gl'altri, essendo del mese di gennaio, era tutto fiorito con miracolosa abbondanza d'ogni sorte fiori, quando le piante de i poderi vicini pareva che fossero ancora tutte intirizzate d'un continovato freddo."

in such a way that Virgil's prophecy that Aeneas would found a new Golden Age in Italy seemed to refer to the destiny of the Medici as well.[19] In the inscription to Salviati's *Elevation of Cosimo as Duke*, Aeneas addresses Mercury, who brings the message that he is destined to rule Italy: SEQVIMVR TE SANCTE DEORVM (we follow you, holy among the gods).[20] The *impresa* of the scene was Mercury's caduceus, a familiar symbol of fate. The theme of Cosimo's special destiny was also presented in Battista Franco's *Duke Cosimo Invested by Charles V*, which had as its emblem a magpie with the Medici laurel in its mouth. This device was explained by Giambullari as a symbol from Horapollo referring to "him who follows the orders of the oracle."[21] Even the all-powerful emperor, the wedding guests were told, was but an instrument in Fate's plan for Duke Cosimo. Finally, as we have seen, the picture of Cosimo's birth—described by Giambullari as "la ben fortunata Natività dello Illustrissimo Duca Cosimo"—was accompanied by the phoenix, which had long been a symbol of renewal in Medici art (cf. pl. 16). This picture had inscriptions taken from *Eclogue* IV which styled Cosimo as a New Saturn, the last line of the inscription, REDEVNT SATVRNIA REGNA, being shared with the scene of the *Elevation of Cosimo as Duke*.[22]

The forces of destiny or fate which had brought Cosimo to power were also suggested by overtly astrological images referring to auspicious features of his natal horoscope which were introduced into his art with a frequency unprecedented among Renaissance princes. Like his Medici predecessor Leo X, Cosimo made astrology an important part of the life of his court.[23] He employed astrologers, the most important of whom was the Carmelite Giuliano Ristori;[24] he followed the custom of having horoscopes, accom-

[19] See Giambullari, pp. 19, 21, 25-27 (and the commentary in Minor-Mitchell, pp. 130-35), for the lines from *Aeneid* alluding to Aeneas and his descendants which accompanied two lunettes in the first courtyard of the Palazzo Medici and all six of the *istorie* of Cosimo's ancestors in the second courtyard.

[20] *Aeneid*, IV, 576-77; see Giambullari, pp. 27-28.

[21] Giambullari, p. 29. For the emblem, see *The Hieroglyphics of Horapollo*, tr. G. Boas, New York, 1950, II, no. 46.

[22] Giambullari, p. 27. See also Vasari, VI, p. 444, who calls the picture "il felicissimo natale del duca Cosimo" but does give its author. We cannot know whether astrological imagery was included in this "natività" (also the term for a horoscope); however, in Doceno's astrological scheme of 1554 on the facade of the house of Cosimo's intimate, Sforza Almeni, there was a scene in which "molti filosofi ed astrologhi misurano il cielo e mostrano di fare la natività [horoscope] del duca" (Vasari, VI, p. 237). For other references to this astrological decoration, see Thiem, cat. 76.

[23] Cosimo knew astrology, having learned it from his cartographer, Egnatio Danti, as is testified by

Vasari. Discussing the Sala delle Carte geografiche in the Palazzo, which was decorated under Danti's direction and included a celestial globe, he notes (VII, pp. 635-36): "Questo capriccio ed invenzione è nata dal duca Cosimo, per mettere insieme una volta queste cose del cielo e della terra giustissime e senza errori, e da poterle misurare e vedere, ed a parte e tutte insieme, come piacerà a chi si diletta e studia questa bellissima professione: del che m'è parso debito mio, come cosa degna di esser nominata, farne in questo luogo, per la virtù di frate Ignazio, memoria, e per la grandezza di questo principe, che ci fa degni di godere si onorate fatiche, e si sappia per tutto il mondo." For Danti and Cosimo, see M. L. Righini Bonelli and T. B. Settle, "Egnatio Danti's Great Astronomical Quadrant," *Annali dell'Istituto e Museo di Storia della Scienza di Firenze*, 4, 1979, pp. 3-13.

[24] See D. Mellini, *Ricordi intorno ai costumi, azioni, e governo del Sereniss. Gran Duca, Cosimo I*, ed. D. Moreni, Florence, 1820, p. 134, n. 65, in which Moreni notes that Ristori was appointed by Cosimo to the chair of astrology at the Studio in Pisa: ". . . e nell' Astrologia, Cattedra pur da esso eretta, Fra Giuliano Ristori da Prato, Carmelitano, accreditato molto in quest' arte, perchè avea avuto la

panied by lengthy prognostications, drawn up on each birthday; and his astrologers commented on the positions of the planets and the stars at other important junctures of his life, such as the day of his election as duke of Florence.[25]

The fundamental source for astrological imagery in Cosimo's art was, of course, his natal horoscope (figs. 14, 15). And by far the most auspicious feature of this horoscope was the Capricorn ascendant which it shared with the horoscopes of Augustus and, most significantly for Cosimo's political situation as a vassal of the emperor, Charles V (fig. 16). This coincidence was the subject of much commentary by the ducal apologists. Giovio, for example, notes that Cosimo has as his ascendant "il Capricorno, che hebbe anche Augusto Cesare (come dice Suetonio) . . . [et] hebbe anchor egli [Charles V] il medesimo ascendente" (the Capricorn which Caesar Augustus also had, as Suetonius says, . . . and Charles V also had the same ascendant).[26] Later, in the *Ragionamenti*, Vasari explains to Francesco how the Capricorn was named and how its imperial associations indicate Duke Cosimo's destiny as ruler:[27]

> . . . gli hanno dato nome di capricorno, segno appropriato dagli astrologi alla grandezza de'principi illustri, ed ascendente loro; come fu di Augusto, così è ancora del duca Cosimo nostro, con le medesime sette stelle; e così, come egli operò che Augusto fussi monarca di tutto il mondo, cosi giornalmente si vede operare in Sua Eccellenza, che lo ingrandisce e lo accresce, che poco gli manca a esser re di Toscana.

> They called it Capricorn, a sign appropriated by the astrologers for the greatness of illustrious princes, and as their ascendant. As it was that of Augustus, so it is still that of our Duke Cosimo, with the same seven stars. And thus, as it made Augustus a monarch of the whole world, one sees it daily working in the same way for his Excellency, making him always greater, so that he is almost king of Tuscany.

Much favorable propaganda could be made in support of a ruler with such impressive imperial precedents in his stars, but this was not all: like Augustus, and also at an early age, Cosimo had come to power in January; and his victory at the Battle of Montemurlo in 1537 fell on the same day, 1 August, as Augustus' victory at Actium. As Giovio puts it,[28]

> Et parve cosa fatale, che 'l Duca Cosimo, quel medesimo dì, di Calendi d'Agosto, nel qual giorno Augusto conseguì la vittoria contra Marc'antonio et Cleopatra sopra Attiaco promontorio, et quel giorno anch'egli sconfisse et prese i suoi nemici Fiorentini à Monte Murlo.

sagacità di presagire la morte violenta del Duca Alessandro, e di palesare alcune insidie preparate all' istesso Cosimo."

[25] See below, nn. 50-51, for Ristori's comments about the positions of the stars on Cosimo's election day. A number of the yearly prognostications made for Cosimo have survived. See BNF, MS

Magl. XX, 10 ("Pronostico di Sua Ex.ᵗⁱᵃ fatto per Giovanni di Savoia MDXXXVII nella vigilia di San Cosmo e Damiano"); and Laur. MS Plut. 89, 36 (1554 and 1555), etc.

[26] Giovio, 1556, p. 32.
[27] Vasari, *Rag.*, p. 66.
[28] Giovio, 1556, p. 33.

And it seemed fated that Duke Cosimo, on that same day of the Calends of August on which Augustus defeated Mark Anthony and Cleopatra on the Actium promontory, and that day he too should defeat and take over his Florentine enemies at Montemurlo.

This coincidence of dates, which seemed to Cosimo's contemporaries to confirm the promise of the Augustan horoscope itself, became the basis for some of Cosimo's most effective propaganda. He took immediate advantage of his lucky days by making his birthday (11 June), the anniversary of his election day (9 January), and the anniversary of the Battle of Montemurlo (1 August) into public holidays.[29] The last, in particular, was regarded as an "Augustan" day, as in Sebastiano Sanleolini's poem "De Victoria Murliana," the refrain of which echoes:[30]

Clara dies salve: Augustae salvete Calende.

O illustrious day, hail! Hail O Calends of August!

Moreover, following the example of Leo X, model for so much of his myth-making, Cosimo scheduled important ceremonial events relating to his dynastic ambitions to "fall" on one or another of these days, as if they too had been predestined by divine plan. Thus, Cosimo's bride Eleonora made her Florentine *entrata* on Cosimo's birthday, and the baptism of Cosimo's first son, Francesco, was celebrated on the anniversary of the Battle of Montemurlo.[31]

PONTORMO'S DECORATION OF THE LOGGIA AT VILLA CASTELLO

Cosimo's first major commission, after the victory at Montemurlo had demonstrated the truth of his Augustan destiny, was the fresco (no longer extant) in a loggia at Villa Castello which depicted the configuration of the stars believed to have brought him to power.[32] Perhaps not coincidentally, this work was by Pontormo, the same artist who—twenty years earlier—had painted the lunette at Poggio a Caiano which alludes to the horoscope of the young Cosimo. Now, however, this same Cosimo had become duke of Florence, and the form which astrological imagery based on his horoscope could assume was significantly different. In contrast to *Vertumnus and Pomona*, in which the astrological destiny of the new Medici child was hidden by rustic imagery recollective

[29] For Cosimo's Augustan days, see Forster, 1971, pp. 85-86. For the *festa* of 9 January, in particular, see Settimani, *Diario* (ASF, MS 126, f. 133); and Giamboni, pp. 17-18, where the "festa solennissima" in commemoration of Cosimo's election day is described in detail.

[30] S. Sanleolini, *Serenissimi Cosmi Medicis primi Hetruriae Magniducis actiones*, Florence, 1578, bk. I, f. 2r-2v. On the 1 August holiday, see also Giam-

boni, pp. 156-57: "Questo giorno è feriato solenne in memoria delle felicissime vittorie ottenute in detto di l'anno 1537 dal Serenissimo Cosimo primo contro i suoi patente Inimici fuorusciti. . . ."

[31] For these and other such occasions, see Appendix I.

[32] For the loggia see Cox-Rearick, 1964, I, pp. 302-8, where certain details of the interpretation differ from those given here (and where Cosimo's

of Laurentian art, the cosmic imagery of the Castello vault was overt, and it referred explicitly to Cosimo's astrologically predestined rise to power in Florence.

Vasari's description of the Castello loggia fresco links it with the very inception of Cosimo's rule and with the victory at Montemurlo. He relates that Pontormo had been working on the decoration of a loggia for Duke Alessandro at Villa Careggi, a project that was abandoned after Alessandro's murder, and after the Battle of Montemurlo he was commisioned to paint a loggia at Villa Castello to please Cosimo's mother, Maria Salviati, whose portrait he painted there together with one of Cosimo himself.[33] Vasari then goes on to describe the astrological part of the decoration:[34]

> Vi fece dunque nel mezzo della volta un Saturno col segno del Capricorno, e Marte ermafrodito nel segno del Leone e della Vergine, ed alcuni putti in aria che volano come quei di Careggi. Vi fece poi, in certe femminone grandi e quasi tutte ignude, la Filosofia, l'Astrologia, la Geometria, la Musica, l'Aris-metica, ed una Cerere, ed alcune medaglie di storiette fatte con varie tinte di colori ed appropriate alle figure.

> In the center of the vaulting, then, he painted a Saturn with the sign of Capricorn, and a hermaphrodite Mars in the sign of Leo and of Virgo, and some little angels who are flying through the air, like those of Careggi. He then painted, as gigantic women almost entirely nude, Philosophy, Astrology, Geometry, Music, Arithmetic, and a Ceres; with some little scenes in medallions, executed with various tints of color and appropriate to the figures.

Referring to a diagram of the decoration (fig. 20), we may place the allegories of the Liberal Arts and the Ceres which Vasari mentions in the six lunettes of the loggia. Their related *storiette* would have been on the pendentives of the vault, and the portraits of Cosimo and Maria were most likely in similar medallions at either end of the loggia.[35] Pontormo's drawing of the beardless Cosimo (Uffizi 6528Fv), which is identical to the "Augustan" profiles of the 1537-1538 medals (cf. pls. 160, 162, 171), may have been a study for a medallion *all'antica* of the young duke, which would have been in chiaroscuro

---

zodiacal sun sign is listed as Cancer rather than correctly, as Gemini). The program of the loggia is discussed by Adelson, 1975, pp. 61-63, 88-90, who follows my 1964 reading but suggests that Mercury was shown in its domicile of Virgo, the sign associated with Astraea and the Golden Age. It is also discussed by Wright, I, pp. 260-85, essentially in agreement with my 1964 reading.

[33] Vasari, VI, pp. 281-82. That the commission was given in late 1537 would seem to be confirmed by Vasari's subsequent remark that Pontormo kept the loggia closed for five years until Maria Salviati (who lived at the villa until her death in December 1543) ordered it opened. For the Careggi loggia (also lost), which should be regarded as the pro-

totype for the Castello loggia, see Vasari, VI, p. 281, who describes spandrel figures of Fortuna, Giustizia, Vittoria, Pace, Fama, and Amore, with putti holding animals in the vault. For the drawings for these, see Cox-Rearick, 1964, I, cat. 312-20.

[34] Vasari, VI, p. 283.

[35] As suggested by Adelson, 1975, pp. 13-14. Although Vasari's notice is ambiguous as to the location of Pontormo's portraits and R. Borghini's notice (p. 484) is not much more informative (although he does say "vi [in the loggia] ritrasse"), I am now inclined to believe that portrait medallions were an integral part of the decoration.

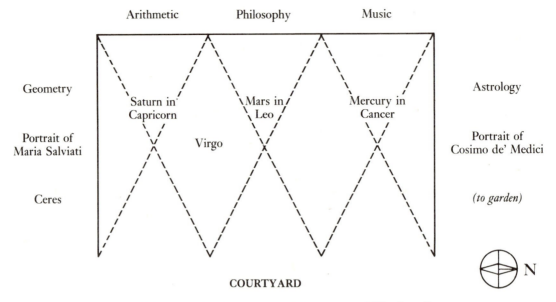

20. Scheme of the decorations of the loggia at Villa Castello

like the *storiette*, and Pontormo's earlier portrait of Maria (pl. 158) or his drawing of her (Uffizi 6680F) served as the model for its pendant.[36] The putti, which Vasari describes as being like those of the Careggi loggia,[37] were on the periphery of the vault, leaving the center free for the astrological images.

Vasari's description of the planetary deities and zodiac signs of the vault is confused and incomplete. This is not surprising, since he himself says that the proportions of the figures were "molto difforme, e certi stravolgimenti ed attitudini che vi sono, pare che siano senza misura e molto strane" (very deformed, and certain torsions and positions which they have make them seem to be lacking in measure and very strange).[38] Vasari also notes that the work was deteriorating from exposure; and when Borghini wrote about the loggia decoration twenty years later, he was able to perceive only "historie degli Dei antiche" (histories of the ancient gods).[39]

In spite of the loss of the frescos and Vasari's incomplete description of the vault, the program of the loggia can be reconstructed. In contrast to works like Peruzzi's ceiling

[36] See Cox-Rearick, 1964, I, cat. 334-35. The Castello portraits, in turn, served as models for Vasari's likenesses of Maria and of the youthful Cosimo in the Palazzo apartments. The medallion of Maria in the Sala di Giovanni delle Bande Nere and her portrait in the *Marriage of Catherine de' Medici* in the Sala di Clement VII are clearly based on Pontormo's portraits of her, and the *istorie* in the Sala di Cosimo representing events of 1537 and the allegories of the eternally youthful Cosimo with the cities of Tuscany are based on Pontormo's 1537 profile portrait of him.

[37] Vasari, VI, p. 33 (quoted in text). For Pon-

tormo's drawing for the Careggi putti, see Cox-Rearick, 1964, I, cat. 319, II, fig. 301.

[38] Vasari, VI, pp. 282-83. For all his disparagement of Pontormo's astrological figures, Vasari was not averse to imitating Pontormo's formula when he was called upon to depict planetary deities in their signs. See the drawings in Brno, Museum, reproduced by L. R. Collobi, "Disegni Vasariani," *Critica d'Arte*, 22, pp. 60-68, especially fig. 6, showing "Saturn in Capricorn."

[39] R. Borghini, p. 484. See Cox-Rearick, 1964, I, p. 302, n. 29, on the subsequent disappearance of the frescos.

decoration for Agostino Chigi (fig. 13), Pontormo's frescos did not show Cosimo's entire horoscope, with all of its planetary positions indicated, but rather it depicted certain favorable aspects of his natal stars (and one feature of the sky at the time of his election), which indicated how the new duke wished his astrological destiny to be interpreted. In this sense, although it is more modest and domestically scaled, the decoration is akin to Perino's astrological decoration for Leo X in the Sala dei Pontefici (pl. 145), where features of Leo's horoscope relating to the theme of rulership are highlighted. However, in the Roman scheme these features are depicted within a traditional encyclopedic scheme in which all the zodiac signs and planets are shown. In the Castello loggia decoration this same theme was presented with a new selectivity and degree of explicitness, for the astrological images in the loggia were only four in number and each depicted a specific aspect of Cosimo's chart.

The first of these images, as noted by Vasari, was "Saturn in Capricorn," which refers to the position of Saturn in the ascendant Capricorn in Cosimo's horoscope (figs. 14-15). Pontormo's sketch for the group (which is on a sheet devoted mainly to studies of the flying putti) shows the traditional bearded old Saturn seated astride the Capricorn (pl. 174).[40] This mode of showing a planet in a zodiac sign recalls that of Peruzzi, in which similar pairs of figures indicate the planetary positions of Chigi's horoscope (pl. 149). However, unlike Peruzzi's simple juxtapositions of the planetary gods and the zodiacal animals, Pontormo's Saturn and Capricorn are intertwined into a serpentine integer typical of the Maniera, and the Saturn (like the planetary gods of the other drawings for the vault) is a paraphrase of Michelangelo's allegories of the *Times of Day* (pl. 34).

The remaining astrological images of the vault present certain problems. Vasari mentions only one further planet, but there must have been more. Moreover, his notice of a "Marte ermafrodito nel segno del Leone e della Vergine" is confused, for Mars is not hermaphrodite, nor can a planet be in two zodiac signs at once. The hermaphrodite Vasari saw can only have been Mercury, who is often shown as a hermaphrodite, especially when in conjunction with Venus, as is the planet in Cosimo's horoscope.[41] The position of Mars noted by Vasari (in Leo) accords with its placement in Cosimo's horoscope, but an explanation must be sought for the presence of the sign of Virgo, in which no planets are located in the chart.

Two drawings by Pontormo can be connected with these features of the vault. One depicts "Mars in Leo" (pl. 172); the other shows "Mercury in Gemini" (pl. 173).[42] The drawing of Mars reclining over a lion presents no problems, but Mercury with Gemini is puzzling, for Mercury is not in its domicile of Gemini in Cosimo's chart but in the sign of Cancer. However, even considering this discrepancy, this sketch still may be Pontormo's idea for the Castello "Mercury in Cancer," with Mercury's own sign in the background, the sign of Cancer to be added later when the group was painted.

40 Uffizi 6510F; see Cox-Rearick, 1964, I, cat. 336. Another drawing shows Saturn alone (Cambridge, Fogg Art Museum 1932.144; Cox-Rearick, cat. 340).

41 See chap. 9, n. 45.

42 Uffizi 6760F and 17405F; see Cox-Rearick, 1964, I, cat. 341-42.

In order to determine why the "Mars in Leo" and "Mercury in Cancer" of Cosimo's horoscope were represented on the Castello vault with his ascendant "Saturn in Capricorn," and in order to determine why "Virgo" was there at all, we must turn to contemporary interpretations of the duke's horoscope. Of particular interest in this connection is Ristori's chart for Cosimo (fig. 15), which is accompanied by a long prognostication addressed to him dated 28 June 1537, only a few months before the Castello commission was given to Pontormo.[43] Not only is Ristori's commentary thus contemporaneous with the horoscope images of the loggia, but its date is significant for other reasons: it was written only two weeks after Cosimo's eighteenth birthday (his first as ruler) and only five days after his title as legitimate successor to Alessandro had been confirmed.[44] Thus, as we shall see, Ristori deals at length with the aspects of Cosimo's horoscope to which he attributes his rise to power.

The first of these is "Saturn in Capricorn," the role of which Ristori considered crucial: ". . . Saturno in Capricorno, benché dopo molte calimatà et fatiche, finalmente dà le attioni grandissime et felicissimi accrescimenti di prosperità" (Saturn in Capricorn, even after many toils and troubles, finally gives great actions and most felicitous increases in prosperity).[45] Ristori also emphasizes the good placement of Saturn and Mars, the two planets traditionally considered to be malefic: "Ancora parlando generalmente d'ogni altro dominio Vostro, essendo per la maggior parte causata [*sic*] le felicità Vostre da stelle per natura maligne, come da Marte e da Saturno, et poi da stelle fisse . . ." (And then, still speaking generally of every other power of yours, since your happiness is caused in the greatest part by planets which are malefic by nature, like Mars and Saturn, and then by fixed stars).[46] Saturn (in domicile in the ascendant Capricorn) is the lord of the ascendant in Cosimo's chart, and Mars (at 21° Leo) is lord of the mid-heaven because it rules Scorpio, the sign at the mid-heaven. Ristori notes Mars' role as "signore del mezo cielo" (lord of the mid-heaven), and he also considers the planet to be well placed "sotto alla regale stella del Leone" (under the royal star of Leo).[47] Finally, Ristori remarks several times on the favorable placement of Mercury, considering the planet to

[43] Ristori, f. 135v-186r. The horoscope is mentioned by Thorndike, V, p. 326; and in Zambelli, no. 3.4.8. I am grateful to Gino Corti for transcribing Ristori's unpublished prognostication for me in 1976.

[44] It should be recalled that on 9 January the Florentine Senate elected Cosimo "Capo e Primario del Governo e della città di Firenze," not duke of Florence. It was only on 21 June that he was recognized by the count of Cifuentes (representing Charles V) as the legitimate successor to Duke Alessandro, an action which was ratified by the Senate on 23 June. For these events see Ridolfi, pp. 548-49; A. Rossi, "L'Elezione di Cosimo I de' Medici," *Atti dell'Istituto Veneto di Scienze, Lettere et Arti*, ser. VII, 1, 1889-1890, pp. 369-435; and G. Spini, *Cosimo de' Medici e la Indipendenza del Principato Mediceo*, Florence, 1945, pp. 27-44.

[45] Ristori, f. 168v; see also n. 48 below. For Capricorn in Cosimo's chart, see chap. 9, "Medici Horoscopes and the Medici Golden Age."

[46] Ristori, f. 168r. On other good aspects of Saturn mentioned by Ristori, see chap. 9, nn. 28-30.

[47] Ristori, f. 154r and 166v. See also f. 166r: ". . . et Marte ancora signore della Xᵃ casa, come dicemmo, è ben posato . . ."; and f. 169r: "Marte ancora per la stabilità del segno et per la parte del cielo, che Vostra Ecc.ᵃ debba conservarsi lo stato dimostra, perciochè il Leone è segno regale et fisso." The "royal star" which Ristori mentions is Regulus (known as the Cor Leonis), traditionally thought to bring honor, fame, strong character, public prominence, and military command when in conjunction with Mars (see V. E. Robson, *The Fixed Stars and Constellations in Astrology*, London, 1923, p. 197).

be a "principe della genitura" (prince of the horoscope) and the "stella principante" (principal star).[48]

There is little question, then, that the Saturn, Mars, and Mercury of the Castello vault were represented by Pontormo in the signs they occupied at Cosimo's birth. However, the placement of these planets in Cosimo's natal chart does not entirely explain their presence here. The particular planets and signs on the vault also relate to the positions of the stars and planets on other dates which were considered significant for Cosimo's rulership: the legendary birth (and rebirth) of Florence, the day of Cosimo's election (9 January 1537), and his eighteenth birthday (11 June 1537).

In his remarks addressed to Cosimo regarding his rulership of Florence, Ristori alludes to the myth of the predestined connection of the Medici with the city. He points out that Florence had never been able to remain long under a government because in the horoscope of the rebirth of the city (fig. 7) the ascendant is in Aries, the most inconstant of all the signs. These and other factors, he tells Cosimo, make it difficult for a ruler to maintain his power in Florence, ". . . se già uno non havessi una felicissima et straordinaria genitura . . ." (unless he already had a most felicitous and extraordinary horoscope).[49] The prospects for Cosimo's long rule are best seen, Ristori continues, in the horoscope for the time of his election, which is extraordinarily close to the horoscope of Florence, having the ascendant in Aries and the mid-heaven in Capricorn. Moreover, the Capricorn mid-heaven of the horoscopes of the city and of Cosimo's election is the very sign in which the ascendant of Cosimo's own natal horoscope is located.[50] Finally, Ristori notes another auspicious portent: at the time of Cosimo's election, both the sun and Mars were at the mid-heaven in Capricorn.[51]

Cosimo's election occurred in the morning of 9 January 1537.[52] Following Ristori's

---

[48] Ristori, f. 166v. See also Ristori's opening remarks on the horoscope (f. 135v): "Mercurio è quella stella che ha più potentia dell'altre sopra la genitura Vostra, havendo più autorità di loro ne' luoghi detti. Saturno a questa dipoi si fa compagno, sì per le molte prerogative ch'egli ha ancor egli (*sic*) ne' luoghi detti et per l'aspetto di detto Mercurio, sì ancora perché appresso di Materno sarebbe il Signor principale. . . . Per la qual cosa diciamo l'ascendente di Vostra Ecc.ᵗⁱᵃ essere il Capricorno et la stella principante Mercurio. . . ." For other commentary on the importance of Saturn, Mars, and Mercury in Cosimo's horoscope, see Gaurico, bk. II, f. 16r (quoted in chap. 9, n. 28); Giuntini, 1573, f. 238v-239r; and Giuntini, 1581, I, p. 127 (quoted in chap. 9, n. 19).

[49] Ristori, f. 167v-168r: "Oltra questo ha la città di Fiorenza, la quale per il principio che s'ha della sua rehedificatione, non può star molto con un governo, come per tanti anni et tanti gli effetti han dimonstrato, havendo per ascendente il più mobil segno di tutti i mobili. Et ancora importa più questo, che chi la rifondò infortunò in tal modo la

casa regale [the tenth house], che è del principe significatrice, ponendo il signore di quella [Saturn] in luogo abiectissimo et retrogrado [10° Virgo], et mettendo il signore della esaltatione di quello in segno opposito alla sua casa, in modo che facile non è stato né fia a' principi di quella tenerne lungamente lo stato, se già uno non havessi una felicissima et straordinaria genitura parlando philosophicamente."

[50] Ristori, ff. 168r-168v: "Dall'altra parte tengo che Vostra Ecc.ᵗⁱᵃ habbia a conservarsi lo stato predetto ancor per quell'hora della elettione, essendo lei simile al principio della città . . . et massime perché l'ascendente della genitura Vostra [Capricorn] è il mezo cielo della città. . . ."

[51] Ristori, f. 168v: "Oltre di questo nella detta elettione il Sole e Marte significatori principali sono nel mezo cielo: il primo è signore della esaltatione dell'ascendente [Aries], cioè il Sole, et Marte poi signor del segno di quello [Aries] et della exaltatione del mezo cielo [Capricorn]."

[52] Ridolfi, pp. 548-49: "El martedì mattina, che fummo a dì 9 di detto mese [January], si ragu-

indication of the sun "nel mezo cielo" and the ascendant in Aries, a chart may be erected for the late morning of that day, the time rounded off to 11:00, at which time the ascendant was at 24° Aries 12' and the sun (☉) and Mars (♂) were in conjunction in Capricorn (♑) near the mid-heaven (fig. 21).

These cheering coincidences between the horoscope of the new duke's election and that of the city he planned to rule would have been sufficient reason for the selection of his natal "Mars in Leo" for representation at Villa Castello along with "Saturn in Capricorn." But Ristori's discussion of the horoscope of Cosimo's recent birthday gives yet another indication of Mars' importance at this critical juncture in Cosimo's life. It also suggests why the sign of Virgo was included among the astrological images of the vault. In a concluding section of his prognostication, "Della Spetie della Grandeza," Ristori analyzes the horoscope of Cosimo's eighteenth birthday for portents of his successful rule. As is customary in astrological practice, he records the planetary aspects of this chart, comparing them with Cosimo's natal horoscope and noting the aspects made by the progressed planets. One of his major conclusions from this complex analysis involves Mars and Virgo. He notes that in 1537 Mars (the ruler of the mid-heaven of Cosimo's natal chart) is in trine to Saturn (ruler of the ascendant in Cosimo's natal chart) in the sign of Virgo, and that this trine is one of the aspects responsible for Cosimo's "grandeza."[53] A chart erected for 11 June 1537 (with the sun at 29° Gemini 03' as in Cosimo's natal chart) shows that, indeed, Mars (in Taurus) is in trine to Saturn (in Virgo); moreover, this Mars (in Taurus) is *also* in trine to Cosimo's natal Saturn (at 20° Capricorn).[54]

This harmonious trine between the potentially malign Mars and Saturn (in Virgo) was indicated by the astrological images on the Castello vault, where "Saturn in Capricorn" and "Mars in Leo" were depicted. Virgo, the sign which Saturn occupied in trine to Mars on Cosimo's birthday in 1537, was shown between them. This configuration, then, is what Vasari's "Saturn in Capricorn . . . and Mars in Leo and Virgo" must mean, and the only error in his description of the vault is his calling Mars a hermaphrodite.

The last image on the vault was Mercury, one of the lords of Cosimo's chart, which also played an important role in the horoscope for his birthday in June 1537. In dis-

norno insieme e' Quarantotto, cioè tutti quelli che si trovavano in Firenze, in nel palazzo de' Medici, presente detto reverendo Cibo; et pensando di modi da ricorreggere il disordine seguito, fuvvi infiniti ragionamenti: che proponeva il rilevare su il figliuolo di detto Duca, e chi istato d'ottimati e chi gonfaloniere a vita e chi altri modi; e all'ultimo, circa ore 18, levorno il romore e feciano capo Cosimo di Giovanni di Giovanni de' Medici, con grida grandissime de' popoli."

[53] Ristori, f. 167r-167v: "Il principio di tal reggimento et grandezza è venuto l'anno XVIII di Vostra vita, mediante la progressione di Marte, signore del mezo cielo, al trino di Saturno, signore dell'ascendente, nel XXI [*recte*: II] grado della Ver-

gine, dove si ritruovano ancora la parte del Re et la duodenaria di Saturno, stante Giove signor de' termini di tal luogo, oltre che Venere vi manda i suoi sestili razi. . . . Et tanto basti circa le spetie della grandezza di Vostra Eccellentia."

[54] The chart for 11 June 1537, 5:45 a.m., calculated for the solar return at 29° Gemini 03', has the ascendant at 13° Cancer 59' and the planets located as follows: Jupiter (11° Taurus 50'), Mars (23° Taurus 50'), Mercury (5° Cancer 32'), moon (9° Leo 28'), Venus (12° Leo 21'), and Saturn (1° Virgo 46'). The commentary by Ristori quoted in n. 53 above is based on the aspects of this chart and a comparison of the aspects of this chart and that for Cosimo's birth.

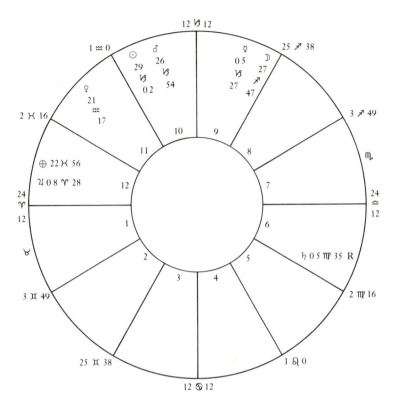

21. Horoscope of the election of Duke Cosimo de' Medici, 9 January 1537, 11:00 a.m.

cussing the birthday chart, Ristori notes that Mercury is rising with the ascendant in Cancer, the same sign it occupied at Cosimo's birth, and that in Cosimo's nineteenth year Mercury would move into conjunction with Mars, an aspect which he says "le confermerà lo stato hauto o le donerà nuove dignitadi" (will confirm its state or confer upon it a new dignity).[55] It seems clear, then, that the "Saturn in Capricorn," "Virgo," "Mars in Leo," and "Mercury in Cancer" of the Castello vault alluded not only to powerful aspects of Cosimo's natal horoscope but to the auspicious configuration of the heavens at his recent election and birthday in 1537.

Certain of these images of the vault had additional symbolic meaning in a decoration which was concerned with Cosimo's astrologically predestined rule of Florence. Capricorn is, of course, the imperial ascendant which Cosimo shared with Augustus, and both the Capricorn ascendant and Mars as ruler of the mid-heaven were shared with the horoscope of Charles V, whose protection Cosimo enjoyed and whom he wished to emulate. The Mars of the decoration also suggests a reprise of the theme of the peaceful Mars as patron of Florence, which goes back to the Poggio a Caiano frieze (pl. 56), and the notion of Cosimo as a peace-giving Mars seen elsewhere in his art, as in Bronzino's portrait of 1544 (pl. 161). Saturn is, of course, the ruler of the Golden Age, and needs no further comment in this context. But Virgo also plays a role in this Virgilian *topos*: the zodiac sign was traditionally identified with Astraea, Virgil's harbinger of the Golden Age of Saturn; and the theme of the justice-giving Astraea and Cosimo-Mars as bringer

[55] Ristori, f. 169v.

of peace was current in poetry related to Bronzino's *Cosimo in Armor*, in which Astraea returns and the "figlio di Marte" closes the gates of war.[56] Cosimo's rule was thus presented in the Castello loggia as a new Golden Age of peace, heralded by the return of Astraea-Giustizia; it was also a new *Saturnia regna* and a new age of Augustus, predicted by Cosimo's "Augustan" horoscope.

It remains to place the images on the vault. Vasari's account provides a clue, for he mentions Saturn first, and if he read the composition in the usual manner from left to right, Saturn would have been in the left bay of the vault, followed by Mars and Virgo (and Mercury, not mentioned by Vasari). Such an arrangement seems correct, since it results in the conventional counterclockwise sequence of the zodiac signs (cf. fig. 6) which occurs in other works alluding to the sequence of the signs, such as Botticelli's *Primavera* (pl. 60) and Pontormo's own *Vertumnus and Pomona* (fig. 18). Reading from the *right*, then, "Mercury in Cancer" was in the first bay and "Mars in Leo" was in the central bay. The placement of Mars in the center of the vault refers to the planet as ruler of Cosimo's "mid-heaven in Scorpio" *and* to the auspicious mid-heaven position of Mars itself in Capricorn (the sign of its exaltation) at the time of Cosimo's election. To the left of "Mars in Leo" was "Virgo," in allusion to the trine of Mars to Saturn in Virgo in Cosimo's election year. Finally, in the left bay, was Cosimo's ascendant "Saturn in Capricorn."

In looking at this right-to-left sequence of signs, it is evident that they are placed in the correct order—Cancer, Leo, Virgo, Capricorn—and that they are "framed" by the ascendant and descendant signs of Cosimo's horoscope. This same arrangement occurs in Pontormo's lunette at Poggio a Caiano, where the crypto-astrological images of "Venus in Cancer" and "Saturn in Capricorn" mark the right and left of the lunette-cum-zodiac. Here, as in the earlier work, the "entrance" to the composition in Cancer and the "exit" in Capricorn may have been intended to allude to the Macrobian notion of the *porta hominem* and the *porta deorum*, in which the soul of the individual descends to earth and ascends to heaven through the solar gates of the summer and winter solstices.[57] Because of the fortuitous coincidence of his horoscope, then, Cosimo (like Augustus, with whose Capricorn ascendant this Macrobian imagery was associated) ascends through Capricorn to immortality.

The astrological images of the Castello vault were accompanied by other images which expanded on the theme of Cosimo's predestined rule of Florence. The portrait medallions personalized the loggia, relating it to Cosimo (just as Vasari's portrait medallions in the Palazzo apartments identify the subjects of the *istorie* painted there). The medal-

---

[56] For the poem by Antonfrancesco Rinieri, which follows Giovio's *elogium* on Cosimo, see Giovio, 1554, pp. 437-38. The first stanza invokes Astraea:

> Astraea per voi, c'havendo il mondo a sdegno
> Lasciatol solo, in cielo era salita,
> Torna, o gran Cosmo, a far lieta & gradita
> Thoscana, & fortunato il nostro regno.

The last presents Cosimo as the peaceful Mars:

> Per voi figlio di Marte anchor le porte
> Del l'empio Giano homai rinchiuse sono;
> Ch'è de la cose al mondo uniche & rade.

Adelson, 1975, pp. 62-63, mentions the symbolic significance of Virgo on the vault. For Virgo and Astraea, see chap. 9, nn. 51-57.

[57] For this theme see chap. 9, n. 33.

lion of Cosimo, which was probably placed at the end of the loggia toward the garden, where it would lead to the "Cosimo" imagery in the garden statuary, depicted the subject of the horoscope imagery of the vault; and the medallion of Maria Salviati referred to Cosimo's lineal descent through his mother from Cosimo Pater Patriae and Lorenzo il Magnifico. The allegories in the lunettes represented the conflation of two familiar themes—that of the "Children of the Planets," in which the various activities of man are seen to be ruled by the different planets,[58] and that of peace and prosperity under a new Golden Age of Medici rule. The latter theme, of course, is the familiar *topos* of peaceful Florence under Medici protection. We have seen it in Laurentian poetry, in Laurentian art—as in the *Seasons and the Months* of the Poggio a Caiano frieze (pl. 54)—and in Leonine art (as in *Vertumnus and Pomona*). In Cosimo's art, however, the theme of a Pax Medicea was not the generalized Golden Age theme of earlier Medici art; it was personalized and it referred to Cosimo's maintenance of peace through power, including the putting down of rebellion if necessary (as at Montemurlo). Moreover, this theme came to be seen as a function of the ducal horoscope, especially its ascendant in Capricorn. In the 1539 wedding *apparato*, for example, an *impresa* showed *alcioni* (kingfishers) nesting in the waters, with the motto VENTOS CVSTODIT ET ARCET AEOLVS (Aeolus guards and keeps the winds).[59] The line is taken from Ovid's story of Neptune's calming the storm, which was a traditional metaphor of the ruler's putting down of civil strife. That it alluded to peace under Capricorn was not specified in 1539, but in the *apparato* for Francesco de' Medici's wedding in 1565, the *alcioni* make their nest under Capricorn, and, like Florence under Cosimo, the sea becomes tranquil and the arts flourish.[60]

It is not possible to determine with certainty the placement in the lunettes of the Liberal Arts which flourish under the peace-giving Capricorn of Cosimo. However, some suggestions can be made. *Ceres* may be placed in the first lunette on the south wall

[58] Wright, I, pp. 282-85. For the theme see F. Saxl, "The Literary Sources of the Finiguerra Planets," *JWCI*, 2, 1938, pp. 72-74.

[59] Giambullari, p. 19: "L'altra lunetta . . . mostrava nel mare un artificioso nidio di alcionii, con un motto d'intorno. . . . " (The motto is taken from Ovid, *Metamorphoses*, XI, 748.)

[60] See Cini, p. 530, for an account of the *impresa* of the *alcioni* on the arch celebrating the flourishing of the arts in Florence: ". . . fu una principalissima impresa sopra tutti gli scudi posta ed a proposito della città messa, che era composta di due alcioni faccenti in mare il lor nido al principio del verno: il che si dimostrava con quella parte del Zodiaco, che dipinto vi era; in cui si vedeva il sole entrare a punto nel segno del Capricorno, con la sua anima, che diceva: *Hoc fidvnt*; volendo significare che sì come gli alcioni per privilegio della natura nel tempo che il sole entra nel predetto segno di Capricorno, che rende tranquillissimo il mare, possono farvi sicuramente i lor nidi, onde sono quei giorni alcionii chiamati; così anche Fiorenza sotto il Capricorno ascendente, e per ciò antica ed ornatissima impresa del suo ottimo duca, può in qualunque stagione il mondo ne apporti, felicissimamente, come ben fa, riposarsi e fiorire." This *impresa* is one of those drawn in Borghini's *Libretto* for the *apparato* (BNF, MS Magl. II, X, 100, f. 57v), where the *alcioni* are shown in their nest in the calm waters with a segment of the zodiac band in the sky showing Sagittarius, Capricorn with the sun, and Aquarius. See also the letter from Borghini to Vasari (in Bottari-Tricozzi, I, pp. 248-50) about the invention of an *impresa* for a member of Cosimo's entourage: "Questo uccello [alcione] fa il nido in mare e nel cuore del verno, in quel tempo appunto che il Sole entra nel Capricorno, felicissimo ascendente del sig. Duca nostro; e sotto questo segno . . . pare che in questi giorni però chiamati Alcioni, il mare si quieti e diventi sicuro per tutti i naviganti." Thus, he concludes, "così sua signoria sotto la felice protezione del sig. Duca sia sicuro e contento."

below Saturn. The harvest goddess personifies the art of Agriculture, traditionally Saturn's domain, and she is also connected with Virgo, the zodiac sign ruling her summer month of August—as in Cossa's *Virgo and the Triumph of Ceres* (pl. 132). Moreover, on the south wall, the earth goddess would not only be near Saturn and Virgo but next to the portrait of Cosimo's mother. *Geometry* and *Arithmetic*, the former under Saturn's patronage, would occupy the next two lunettes, and *Philosophy*, which is associated with Mars in another astrological program connected with Cosimo,[61] may be placed below Mars at the center of the west wall. *Music* and *Astrology*, both connected with the patronage of Mercury, would occupy the remaining lunettes, with *Astrology* probably alone on the north wall with the portrait of Cosimo.

The Castello horoscope loggia served as an introduction to the garden. The realm of the cosmos in the loggia, alluding to Cosimo's horoscope, is complemented in the garden by the realm of nature, alluding to his domain.[62] For example, in addition to symbolizing Cosimo-Hercules and Fiorenza, the two fountains stand for the elements of water (Venus Anadyomene wringing water from her hair) and earth (Hercules' defeat of the earth-given power of Antaeus). Moreover, imagery of water and earth on their bases, in turn, makes reference to the descendant Cancer and the ascendant Capricorn of Cosimo's horoscope. (Each of the four elements is traditionally associated with three of the zodiac signs, which relate to one another in a trine, 120°; thus, the signs of the earth triplicity are Taurus, Virgo, and Capricorn, those of water are Cancer, Scorpio, and Pisces, etc.; cf. fig. 6.) Both fountain bases are decorated with Capricorn heads, which Niccolò Martelli (speaking of the *Venus*) identified as "il felice ascendente del mio signore" (the lucky ascendant of my lord).[63] Those of the *Hercules* are large and prominently displayed on the upper basin, where they suggest the source of the *fortezza* of Hercules-Cosimo in his earth sign of Capricorn. Those of the *Venus*, on the other hand, are inconspicuous; most of the base is decorated with marine creatures, which include reliefs of crabs on the upper part of the shaft. These may be interpreted as alluding to the water sign of Cancer in which the planet Venus appears in Cosimo's horoscope.[64]

The *Venus* fountain was enclosed in a labyrinth of evergreens, but the *Hercules* was to be complemented by sculptures of the Arts, the Virtues, Medici *illustri*, and the Seasons. A glance at this list confirms that the scheme was a rearrangement of the familiar components of the Poggio a Caiano Salone. These were adjusted to suit the possibilities of an actual garden and, of course, updated to suit the requirements of Cosimo's propaganda. For example, in contrast to the Salone, the conceit of the ruler as the virtuous Hercules was expressed spatially, with *Hercules and Antaeus* literally being surrounded by twelve allegories of Virtues and Arts alluding to his twelve labors. (Implicit here may also be the zodiacal theme of Hercules-Sol, later the subject of Vincenzo de' Rossi's

---

[61] Thiem, cat. 76.

[62] For the rich symbolism of the garden, on which I can only touch briefly here, see Adelson, 1975, passim; and Wright, I, pp. 286-342.

[63] Martelli, p. 22. There were also two large Capricorns on the base of the statue of *Fiesole* (Vasari, VI, p. 81).

[64] Vasari, VI, p. 79, notes "cose marine" on the base of the Venus. The "Venus in Cancer" of Cosimo's horoscope may also be the subject of a Pontormesque study for a wall decoration which includes a Venus with the Crab (Uffizi 700S; see Cox-Rearick, 1964, I, cat. A185).

fountain design for Cosimo; pl. 143.) Here too the Medici are linked with the Seasons and the Virtues, as in the Salone. To take the most important configuration as an example: at the foot of the garden nearest to the loggia frescos depicting his astrological destiny was the bust of Cosimo, with statues of *Justice* and *Winter*. A more programmatic combination cannot be imagined: *Justice* carries out the Virgo-Astraea theme of the loggia and the theme of Cosimo's justice represented by the *Hercules* fountain (in which the hero kills the tyrant); *Winter* represents the season in which Cosimo, like Augustus, assumed power, as well as the season of Capricorn, his auspicious Augustan ascendant.

Imagery alluding to Duke Cosimo's Capricorn at the foot of the garden near the horoscope fresco of the loggia was to be repeated in a different form in a Grotto of Pan at the upper end of the central axis of the garden.[65] Tribolo's drawing for one of the fountains of the grotto, which was not executed in this form, shows Pan seated on the crossed *bronconi* (pl. 66). To the left and right are alternate ideas for the side panels, one of which shows Pan's flute crossed with a club, in a possible allusion to the Hercules of the fountain in the garden below.[66] Below the statue of Pan is a large relief of the fishtailed goat into which, according to the legend, Pan transformed himself while fleeing the monster Typhon and then became the constellation of Capricorn.[67] In the imagery of this grotto, Cosimo revived the venerable theme of Pan Medicus, which had its origins in Laurentian poetry and Signorelli's allegory of the peaceful rule of Lorenzo il Magnifico in the *Realm of Pan* (pl. 67). He also (if my earlier conclusion is correct) revived the notion of symbolizing the ascendant Capricorn of a Medici ruler by the god Pan. With a subtlety characteristic of Laurentian art, Signorelli's Pan, who bears the stars of Capricorn on his cloak, alludes to the ascendant of Lorenzo's horoscope.[68] Tribolo's Pan, with Capricorn actually pictured below him, spells out the reference explicitly. In the rustic imagery of this grotto, where the mountain waters first flow through the Castello garden fountains, the theme of peace in the garden thus had its beginning as the music of Pan Medicus brings harmony to Cosimo's city, and under Capricorn, the sign which calms the waters, the arts flourish in Florence.

CAPRICORN AND THE CROWN OF ARIADNE

Duke Cosimo not only commisioned Pontormo to paint his Augustan horoscope at Castello early in his rule but he chose its Capricorn ascendant as a personal device. It first appears on a medal by Domenico di Polo, the imagery of which suggests that it was struck in commemoration of Cosimo's "Augustan" victory at Montemurlo. The obverse shows the beardless young duke, portrayed for the first time *all'antica*, with the Capri-

[65] Vasari, VI, pp. 75-76, mentions the grotto but not the Pan subject. For the grotto, see Aschoff, pp. 115-17; L. Châtlet-Lange, "The Grotto of the Unicorn and the Garden of the Villa di Castello," *Art Bull.*, 50, 1968, pp. 51-58 (on its later execution); and Wright, I, pp. 292-299.

[66] As suggested by Wright, I, p. 297, in allusion to Hercules' use of the club to keep peace. For the drawing see chap. 3, n. 88.

[67] For the legend of the origin of Capricorn, see chap. 7, nn. 59-60.

[68] See chap. 7.

corn decorating his breastplate; and the reverse, inscribed SALVS PVBLICA / FLOREN[TIA], depicts Florentia with a Victory (pl. 175).[69] Two years later Cosimo's Capricorn appears again, this time not as an Augustan emblem associated with Montemurlo and the public well-being of Florence but as a full-fledged astrological *impresa* signifying Cosimo's Augustan destiny. According to Giambullari, in the first courtyard of the Palazzo Medici, which was decorated with old and new *imprese* for Cosimo's wedding, was depicted "il celeste Capricorno, con le VIII stelle della corona di Ariadna, et era il suo motto, FIDVCIA FATI (the heavenly Capricorn, with the eight stars of the crown of Ariadne, and there was his motto, Faith in Fate).[70] Shortly thereafter, the duke's new *impresa* was displayed on Domenico di Polo's medal with the expanded motto ANIMI CONSCIENTIA ET FIDVCIA FATI (Conscience and trust in Fate; pl. 176).[71]

Cosimo's adoption of a zodiac sign for his *impresa* reveals his imperial pretentions. For, although Giovio mentions stars as one of the recommended *corpi* for *imprese*, there had been few astrological medals in the Renaissance. (Isabella d'Este's medal showing Astrology with her ascendant Sagittarius is one of these; pl. 135.) In thus displaying his zodiac sign, Cosimo was directly emulating Roman emperors who used astrological motifs on their coinage. The specific model for Cosimo's Capricorn medal was, of course, the Augustan denarius showing the Capricorn with the globe, rudder, and cornucopia—symbols of Fortuna and Imperium (pl. 134); and the motto FIDVCIA FATI was adopted from the account by Suetonius of Augustus' faith in his stars ("Tantam mox fiduciam fati Augustus habuit . . .").[72] In taking the Capricorn that he shared with Augustus as his *impresa*, Cosimo, in turn, expressed faith in *his* Augustan stars. However, it is significant that at this early date the young duke omitted the Augustan attributes of power, presenting the Capricorn as a purely astrological image alluding to his personal destiny.

In Cosimo's medal (as in the Augustan coin) the "celeste Capricorno" floats against a neutral background signifying the heavens. However, in the illustration to Giovio's *Dialogo dell'imprese*, the Capricorn is depicted in the sky over a view of Florence (pl. 177). This image, of course, expresses the idea of Cosimo's rulership of the city through his imperial Capricorn. It also indicates that the Capricorn is his ascendant, for the view of the city is toward the east and the Capricorn is poised on the eastern horizon, as if rising. Moreover, since Capricorn marks the mid-heaven of the horoscope of the rebirth of Florence (fig. 7) and since Ristori makes much of the coincidence between this place-

---

[69] Supino, no. 264. The motto appears on two other medals of the beardless Cosimo by Domenico. See Supino, no. 255 (SALVS PVBLICA with a female personification) and Supino, no. 256 (PVBLICAE SALVTI within the Augustan Oak Wreath). The motto, frequent on Roman coins, would of course also have echoed the motto of the famous medal of the Pazzi conspiracy (See chap. 1, n. 17). As in the case of the *Hercules and Antaeus* medal, Domenico reused for Cosimo a *rovescio* which he had designed for Alessandro (Vasari, V, p. 384). Barocchi, cat. 279, suggests that Cosimo's medal was later used with Giovanni Antonio de' Rossi's

cameo of Duke Cosimo with his family (Bargello), which is described by Vasari, V, p. 387, as including a tondo of Fiorenza.

[70] Giambullari, p. 20.

[71] Supino, no. 262; Hill-Pollard, no. 315. Vasari, V, p. 384, states that the medal was made "il primo anno che [Cosimo] fu eletto al governo," but Cosimo's beard indicates the date 1539. Since Giambullari, p. 39, does not mention this medal as a source for the Capricorn *impresa* in the wedding *apparato* (as he does in the case of the medal with the laurel), it may even date after June 1539.

[72] See chap. 7, n. 47.

ment and the sign of Cosimo's ascendant, the Capricorn in the sky over Florence of Cosimo's *impresa* suggests the city's own astrological fortune and the predestined connection of her duke with it.

The image of Capricorn over Florence may also allude to broader themes of rulership and immortality. I have mentioned the concept of Cancer and Capricorn as the zodiacal gates of the sun and the soul in connection with Pontormo's *Vertumnus and Pomona* and his Castello loggia fresco, the zodiacal schemes of which are both based on the elevated signs of Cosimo's horoscope, from Cancer to Capricorn. In the Quattrocento this same idea had been used to indicate the astrological destiny of another ruler in whose horoscope Cancer figured prominently. Among Agostino di Duccio's astrological reliefs for Sigismondo Malatesta is one showing Cancer, sign of Sigismondo's sun, hovering over a view of his city of Rimini (pl. 178).[73] As this relief suggests that Sigismondo has descended from heaven to rule through Cancer (the *porta hominem*), so Giovio's illustration implies that Cosimo ascends to immortality through Capricorn (the *porta deorum*) as glorified ruler of Florence.

The horoscopic nature of Cosimo's Capricorn *impresa* is made more emphatic by the addition to the Capricorn of another constellation. These stars do not appear in Giovio's illustration, but in Cosimo's medal and in numerous subsequent representations of the *impresa* there is a group of eight stars above the Capricorn. These are identified by Giambullari (quoted above), the earliest commentator on Cosimo's *impresa*, as the Crown of Ariadne. It has not been recognized in modern accounts of Cosimo's imagery (nor indeed by his later sixteenth-century apologists) that these stars are a diagrammatically accurate representation of the constellation otherwise known as the Wreath and today called the Corona Borealis, or Northern Crown.[74]

The Crown of Ariadne was included in Cosimo's *impresa* because it is the extrazodiacal constellation which is in conjunction with the mid-heaven of his horoscope. We recall that Cosimo's mid-heaven at 19° Scorpio 51′ was considered auspicious because it corresponded with the sign and degree of the great conjunction of Jupiter and Saturn in 20° Scorpio in 1484, a conjunction which was thought to portend the beginning of a new age.[75] We also recall the importance in Renaissance astrology of the *paranatellonta*—the extrazodical constellations which were regarded as important indicators in a horoscope, especially those which corresponded with the angles of the ascendant and the mid-heaven.[76] Now, in his discussion of Cosimo's horoscope, Ristori devotes a long section to these "stelle fisse" in relation to Cosimo's destiny as ruler. The Crown of

[73] See chap. 9, n. 33.

[74] According to the myth of Bacchus and Ariadne, the crown was her bridal wreath, which was placed in the stars by Jupiter. In Renaissance art Ariadne is often shown with the crown of stars over her head (cf. Titian's *Bacchus and Ariadne* or Caraglio's engraving after Rosso). For the names and traditions of the constellation, see R. H. Allen, pp. 174-75. I am indebted to Claudia Rousseau for sharing with me her discovery of the meaning of the stars in Cosimo's *impresa* and for

pointing out the reference made to the *impresa* in Sangallo's medal and Vasari's *Apotheosis of Cosimo*, discussed below (see pls. 190 and 192).

[75] See chap. 9, n. 49. Ristori also remarks on the coincidence between Cosimo's mid-heaven and the famous conjunction (f. 164v): "Hassi non di-meno a considerare che a grandi honori et degnità rileva l'huomo qualunche coniunctione di Giove et di Saturno, venendo negli angoli dell'ascendente o mezo cielo. . . ."

[76] See chap. 8, nn. 47-50.

Ariadne is in conjunction with the auspicious mid-heaven in Scorpio, and "tutta nella casa regale, regale grandeza le indovina" (totally in the royal house [the tenth], endows it with royal grandeur).[77]

But this was not all: since Cosimo's horoscope has the same Capricorn ascendant as that of Charles V (fig. 16), his chart also shares with the emperor's the mid-heaven in Scorpio and the Crown of Ariadne. Thus, when Giuntini compares the horoscopes of Cosimo and Charles, he notes that the conjunction of the mid-heaven in 20° Scorpio with the "Coronam septemtrionalem" brought the emperor to power and that this conjunction was also present in Cosimo's chart.[78]

Cosimo's *impresa* of "Capricorn and the Crown of Ariadne: FIDVCIA FATI" thus signifies not only his Augustan ascendant, on which he would base his cult of Augustus, but it refers most precisely to the auspicious features which his horoscope shared with that of Charles V, under whose protection he enjoyed his rule. And its motto, FIDVCIA FATI, expressed not only the duke's faith in his Augustan destiny but in his fate with regard to the immediate political realities.

✳   ✳   ✳

Its meaning early established, Cosimo's Capricorn was free to appear as an identifying device in his art, its significance sure to be understood. The *impresa* (without motto) was sometimes quoted from Cosimo's medal, as in tapestry borders by Salviati; but generally, as on the bases of the Villa Castello fountains (pl. 170), the Capricorn, or the head alone, stood for the *impresa*.[79]

The device of Capricorn and the Crown of Ariadne also played a role in the first major decorations in the Palazzo, where imagery of Cosimo's astrological destiny is conflated with the familiar Medici symbolism of return, renewal, and rule. One of the earliest of these is Salviati's Camillus cycle in the Sala delle Udienze, which celebrates Cosimo's virtue, seeks to justify his rule by analogy with Camillus, and suggests through astrological imagery that his advent was divinely predestined and sustained.

The triumphs of Camillus-Cosimo are accompanied by allegories of Justice and Peace. The original decorative theme of the room as a Hall of Justice is reasserted by the incorporation into the new decorations of Benedetto da Maiano's late Quattrocento doorway with a statue of Justice; and this theme is related to Cosimo's Pax Medicea by a fresco of *Peace Burning Arms* above it (pl. 78). Opposite, over the central window of the west wall is the *Arno with a View of Florence*, which signifies the peace and prosperity of Cosimo's new Golden Age.[80] The *istorie* are also complemented by allegories of Virtue,

---

[77] Ristori, f. 167r, in a chapter entitled "Quali costellationi faccin grande Vostra Ecc.ª."

[78] Giuntini, 1573, bk, V, f. 238v. For the quotation, see chap. 9, n. 41.

[79] For example, Salviati's *Ecce Homo* tapestry (1549; Uffizi) shows the whole *impresa* (Adelson, in Barocchi, cat. 105). For Capricorn heads on the bases of sculptures which are allegories of Cosimo

and his power, see, for example, Cellini's *Perseus* (Loggia dei Lanzi; commissioned in 1545). Capricorn heads also decorate "Augustan" images of the duke like Bandinelli's marble bust (1544; Bargello).

[80] The significance of this scene was noted by Vasari, VII, p. 24: ". . . dirimpetto alla Pace che arde l'arme è il fiume Arno, che avendo un corno

Time, and Destiny. At either end of the east wall are vertical panels of *Time-Prudence Seizing Occasion by the Hair* (pl. 179).[81] Like the vertical borders of Raphael's *Acts of the Apostles* tapestries (pls. 21, 22, 42), these "borders" comment on the adjoining *istorie*, suggesting that the events represented in the narratives were predestined by an alliance between the ruler's Virtù and Occasion. Moreover, as the celestial globe in the *Hercules* border (pl. 120) suggests the role of the stars in Leo's destiny, the inclusion of Cosimo's astrological *impresa* of Capricorn and the Crown of Ariadne in these panels asserts that his stars aided him in his prudent and timely seizure of power. Such a notion would seem to be carried out in the figure of Camillus-Cosimo (pl. 89), which is immediately adjacent to one of these border panels, for the two elements of the *impresa* are also present here in a less emblematic form: the Capricorn is displayed below him on his chariot and the Crown of Ariadne (or Wreath) is above him—as the laurel wreath held over his head by Fame.

The west and north of the Sala delle Udienze are entirely devoted to cosmological images: reading from the left of the west wall, *Time with the Scales, Mars Triumphant over a Gaul, Diana Huntress, Time with the attributes of Prudence and Temperance*; and, on the north wall (pl. 78), *Hecate-Moon, Favor*, and *Phanes-Sun*.[82] The Medicean theme of Time is central to this cycle; and it is also evident that it alludes in some way to the idea of the cosmic forces which determined and supported Cosimo's rule. Just as Time-Prudence on the east wall is marked as referring to Cosimo by his *impresa*, so *Mars* and *Diana* are signaled as alluding to the duke by the Capricorn heads below them. These figures surely refer, in addition, to Cosimo's military exploits (allegorized in the Camillus *istorie*), and the choice of a Gaul as Mars' victim is a pointed reference to Cosimo's alliance with Charles V against the French. These gods, moreover, form a compositional and thematic unit with the vignette of Cosimo's Golden Age over the window between them. However, it is difficult to see how the whole cycle of gods relates to Cosimo. In

---

di dovizia abbondantissimo, scuopre (alzando con una mano un panno) una Fiorenza, e la grandezza de'suoi pontefici e gli eroi di casa Medici." The juxtaposition of Peace burning arms, Florence with the Arno, and references to abundance recalls Alessandro's imagery, as in Vasari's portrait of 1534 (pl. 155); see also Salviati's *Portrait of a Florentine Nobleman* (St. Louis, City Art Museum), identified by Cheney, II, pp. 425-26, as a possible posthumous likeness of Alessandro.

[81] Vasari, VII, p. 23, notes only the panel on the right, misnaming it "Occasione che ha preso la Fortuna per lo crine." See Cheney, I, pp. 368-69, for the suggestion that the other panel may orginally have been intended to show Prudence, for which drawings exist. It should be noted that the figure who seizes Occasion's forelock has the attributes of both Prudence (the double head) and Time (the snakes around her waist).

[82] Vasari, VII, p. 24, identifies these figures as

follows: "Nell'altra faccia che è vôlta a ponente, fece nel mezzo e ne'maggior vani, in una nicchia, Marte armato; e sotto quello, una figura ignuda, finta per un Gallo con la cresta in capo, simile a quella de' galli naturali: ed in un'altra nicchia Diana succinta di pelle, che si cava una freccia del turcasso, e con un cane. Ne'due canti di verso l'altre due facciate sono due Tempi; uno che aggiusta i pesi con le bilance; e l'altro che tempra, versando l'acqua di due vasi l'uno nell'altro. Nell'ultima facciata, dirimpetto alla capella, la quale volta a tramontana, è da un canto a man ritta il Sole, figurato nel modo che gli . . . [blank] Egizi il mostrano: e dall'altro la Luna, nel medesimo modo: nel mezzo e il Favore, finto in un giovane ignudo in cima della ruota, ed in mezzo da un lato all'Invidia, all'Odio ed alla Maldicenza, e dall'altro agli Onori, al Diletto ed a tutte l'altre cose descritte da Luciano."

spite of the presence of the planetary deities sun, moon, and Mars (and the probable presence of Jupiter, Mercury, and Saturn) and in spite of the fact that these figures correspond with the seven planets (if Diana is substituted for Venus), this scheme alludes neither to Cosimo's horoscope nor to any archetypal zodiac scheme such as the planetary rulerships or exaltations.[83] Rather, as has recently been suggested, it may relate to the alchemical themes which are so prominent in the later decorations of the Palazzo such as the Sala degli Elementi or the Studiolo.[84]

Cosmic imagery also enhances themes of Medici Return and Renewal in the *Story of Joseph* tapestries, designed in 1545-1553 by Bronzino, Pontormo, and Salviati for the Sala de' Dugento.[85] Capricorn heads marking the cycle as alluding to Cosimo are in the centers of the upper borders of the twelve wide tapestries of the series. Moreover, in some of the episodes telling the story of the youthful Joseph, such as *Joseph Fleeing Potiphar's Wife*—a scene celebrating the hero's virtue (pl. 181)—there is a marked resemblance between Joseph and the young Cosimo of his earliest medals (pls. 160, 162). The tapestries draw a parallel between Joseph, chosen by God to rule his people, a second founder of his family, who led them to Egypt; and the duke, a second Cosimo and a second Medici founder under whose protection Florence is led into a new Golden Age. The later scenes deal with these themes of reconciliation and renewal, but the whole cycle is set in motion by two tapestries emphasizing themes of Divine Providence and inevitability. These are devoted to the dreams which predicted Joseph-Cosimo's future greatness, and they contain familiar symbolic motifs alluding to his destiny. In *Joseph's Dream of the Sheaves of Wheat*, not only does the sheaf alluding to Joseph's future rule stand up, but the tree behind him, with one dead branch and the rest sprouting green leaves, clearly refers to Cosimo's *impresa* of the "laurel tree: VNO AVVLSO." In *Joseph Recounting his Dream of the Sun, Moon, and Stars* (pl. 182), astrological imagery points up the same theme of Joseph-Cosimo's predestined rule. Joseph's account of his dream: ". . . behold, the sun, the moon, and the eleven stars bowing down to me" (Genesis; 27:9-10) is taken as a text for a cosmological scene acted out in the sky. Sol-Apollo and Luna-Diana, enclosed in interlinked cosmic spheres, make obeisance to Joseph-Cosimo, while the stars held up by the putti are arranged in the triangular shape of the constellation of Capricorn. The astrological emphasis is even stronger in Bronzino's drawing for this section of the tapestry, which shows the luminaries accompanied by the signs they rule: a large lion's head is at Sol-Apollo's back, and Luna-Diana kneels astride the crab signifying Cancer (Uffizi 6357F).

[83] Reading from the left of the west wall, the figures may be identified as Saturn (god of time, exalted in Libra—the scales), Mars, Diana (substituting for Venus), Mercury (as Prudence), Luna, Jupiter (associated with the Wheel of Fortune on which "Favore" stands, as well as being the ruler of the Pars Fortunae in a horoscope), and Sol (surrounded by a zodiac wheel with the sign of Leo at the top).

[84] An alchemical interpretation of the Sala has been proposed by Lensi Orlandi, pp. 188-215, a work which unfortunately is not documented. For the author, the images read (from the left of the west wall): "L'antro di Mercurio, Marte e Ferro, La Diana nuda, La Dualità e L'Unità, Il Fanciullo è Nato, L'Androgine di Foco."

[85] For the cycle, see Adelson, in Barocchi, cat. 80-99.

In Cosimo's art after 1555 there is an insistent repetition of the theme of his astrological destiny, the iconography of which had been determined by the early 1540s. As a decorative device signifying Cosimo and his Augustan stars, the Capricorn with the Crown of Ariadne (or simply the Capricorn) was ubiquitous. Together with the other ducal devices, it appears throughout Vasari's apartments in the Palazzo and in numerous other locations. By this time, however, Cosimo's astrological *impresa* was being interpreted with a different emphasis. It continued to carry its original horoscopic meaning, but as early as 1540 notions of ducal *virtù* began to accrue to it. Giovio, who had been present at Cosimo's wedding the year before and had seen the *impresa* among its decorations, gave it a new motto in which ideas of destiny and *virtù* are combined: FIDEM FATI VIRTVTE SEQVEMVR (We shall follow with virtue faith in our destiny).[86] And, in explaining the *impresa* in his *Dialogo*, Giovio states that its motto means "io faro con propria virtù forza di conseguire quel che mi promette l'oroscopo" (By my virtue I will have the strength to follow what my horoscope promises).[87] Thus, when the *Dialogo* appeared in illustrated editions in the later 1550s, Cosimo's Capricorn was accompanied by Giovio's new variation on the old Medici theme of Virtù and Fortuna.

Giovio's interpretation of Cosimo's astrological *impresa* was taken up by others, and the Crown of Ariadne came to be regarded as a symbol of *virtù*. In the early 1540s there is already a hint of this reading in Salviati's juxtaposition of the *impresa* with *Time-Prudence Seizing Occasion by the Hair*. And in a number of works of the next decade the *impresa* signifies both astrological destiny and virtue. For example, in Domenico Poggini's *Duke Cosimo de' Medici as Apollo* of 1559 (pl. 180),[88] the god wears a band inscribed with the zodiac signs, with Cosimo's Capricorn ascendant "rising" at his waistline. Apollo is accompanied by a live Capricorn wearing a crown, which is to be read both as the ducal coronet, symbol of Cosimo's *virtù*, and as the Crown of Ariadne, emblazoned with stars. The theme of Virtù is even more clearly spelled out in Poggini's medal derived from this statue, which is inscribed with a line from Horace, INTEGER VITE SCELERISQ[VE] PVRUS (Upright of life and free of evil stain).[89] Moreover, a sonnet, also by Poggini, specifies that Apollo-Cosimo's Capricorn crowned with stars refers to both ducal destiny and Virtù:[90]

[86] In a letter written to Cosimo in March 1540, Giovio states that, in his museum, "risplende el stellato Capricorno col motto al collo: Fidem fati virtute sequemur" (*Lettere*, I, no. 113, pp. 240-41). See also no. 160, pp. 306-7, for another letter, dated 10 March 1543, in which Giovio refers again to the "stanza del Onore" in his museum and the representation of the *impresa*.

[87] Giovio, 1556, p. 33: "Ma à questo Capricorno che porta Sua Eccellenza, non avendo motto, acciò che l'impresa sia compita, io ho aggiunta l'anima d'un motto latino: FIDEM FATI VIRTVTE SEQVEMVR, quasi che voglia dire: io farò con propria virtù forza di conseguire quel che mi promette l'horoscopo. Et così l'ho fatto dipingere figurando le stelle che entrano nel segno del Capricorno nella camera de-

dicata all'Honore, laqual vedeste al Museo, dove è ancora l'Aquila, che significa Giove e l'Imperatore, che porge col becco una Corona Trionfale col motto che dice: IVPPITER MERENTIBVS OFFERT [Jupiter confers on those deserving], pronosticando che Sua Eccellenza merita ogni glorioso premio per la sua virtù."

[88] Barocchi, cat. 682.

[89] Horace, *Ode* XXII, 1. For the medal see Supino, no. 444.

[90] "Ben fu grande e pregiato il tuo valore." For the whole poem, see Ruscelli, f. 114v. See also Poggini's design for the seal of the Accademia del Disegno, in which Pallas-Minerva leans on a Capricorn, "come virtù di S. E. Ill" (Bottari-Ticozzi, I, p. 265).

> Or hai per terza Impresa altera, e nova
>   Coronato il celeste Capricorno
>   D'Oro, e di gemme, e di virtù fregiato.

> Now, for a third proud and new *impresa*, you have crowned the celestial Capricorn with gold and gems, and have decked it with virtue.

Later, the stars of the Crown of Ariadne in Cosimo's *impresa* underwent a significant reinterpretation. Their original meaning seems to have been lost to some interpreters; to others, such as Vasari, their significance was expanded. Discussing the symbolism of Cosimo's Capricorn in the Sala di Jove, he explains in the *Ragionamenti* that the goat was put into the zodiac,[91]

> fra i dodici segni di quello, con la benignità di sette stelle sopra le corna, le quali denotano i sette spiriti di Dio, che hanno cura del duca, e per le tre virtù teologiche, e le quattro morali, . . . ed a queste stelle ancora inclinano i sette pianeti, così sono fautrici alle sette art liberali, delle quale si diletta tanto Sua Eccellenza.

> among the twelve signs of the zodiac, with the benignity of the seven stars above its horns, which stand for the seven spirits of God which look after the duke, and for the three theological and four moral virtues, . . . and then the seven planets incline toward these stars, and they are protectors of the seven liberal arts, which Your Excellency likes so well.

Vasari thus reduced the number of stars to seven, in order to equate them neatly with the Virtues, the Planets, and the Liberal Arts in his schematization of Cosimo's iconography in the decoration of the Palazzo.

COSIMO, SATURN, AND AUGUSTUS

The conceit of Cosimo as Saturn, ruler of the Capricorn ascendant of his natal horoscope, was also explored in Vasari's decorations in the Palazzo. The Sala degli Elementi is the first of the rooms and the only one in the Quartiere degli Elementi which is marked as referring personally to Cosimo, whose *imprese* are on the ceiling beams and whose name, COSMVS MEDI FLORE DVX II, is inscribed on two of the walls.[92] The theme of the room is Cosimo's dominion, which is expressed primarily through an alchemical scheme based on the Four Elements.[93] The element of Air is represented on the ceiling

[91] Vasari, *Rag.*, p. 65. Other late sixteenth-century interpreters also lost sight of the meaning of the stars. V. Borghini, writing to Francesco about the invention of a medal (p. 78), says that on Cosimo's Capricorn medal "veggo alcune stelle separate, che penso voglano significare alcuna cosa specialmente. . . ." And, in his biography of Cosimo, Baldini, p. 59, interprets the stars as symbols of

Divine Providence: "Nella quale impresa egli per le stelle intende la grazia e la potenzia di Dio."

[92] See Vasari, VI, pp. 239-41, and *ricordo* no. 226, giving the dates 15 December 1555 to late May 1556 for Doceno's execution of the decoration. See also Allegri-Cecchi, pp. 63-73.

[93] For Cosimo Bartoli's alchemical program for the room, see Vasari, *Rag.*, pp. 16-35, especially

in a number of panels combining images of time and the cosmos (*Sun, Moon, Night, Day*), with images of virtue (*Truth, Justice*) and its rewards (*Peace, Fame*, which are familiar from earlier Medici cycles such as that of the Poggio a Caiano Salone. This ceiling decoration also includes allusions to Cosimo's astrological destiny. Luna-Diana carries a crescent moon, which according to Vasari shows "quella parte di grandezza in che era quando nacque Sua Eccellenza" (the size it was when His Excellency was born).[94] The central panel (pl. 183) is a scene of primal creation—according to Vasari, "la castrazione del Cielo fatto da Saturno" (Saturn castrating Heaven).[95] This work is the very first painting described by Vasari in the *Ragionamenti*, and its imagery of the cosmos alludes to Cosimo and his rule:[96]

> Quello . . . è un corpo cosmo, che così è nominato dalli astrologi il mondo, che è dritto il nome del duca nostro signore, che è fatto patrone di questo Stato; e Saturno, suo pianeta, tocca il Capricorno ascendente suo, e mediante i loro aspetti fanno luce benigna alla palla della terra, e particolarmente alla Toscana e, come capo della Toscana, a Firenze, oggi per Sua Eccellenza con tanta iustizia e governo retta.

> That is a cosmic body, which is called the world by astrologers, and which is precisely the name of our lord, the duke, who had been made master of this state; and Saturn, his planet, touches his Capricorn ascendant, and by their aspects they cast a benign light on the globe of the earth and, in particular, Tuscany, and, as capital of Tuscany, Florence, which is ruled today with such justice and such good government by His Excellency.

Here, an old wordplay on the name Cosimo—which had earlier been used cautiously, and always in nonvisual imagery, in reference to Cosimo Pater Patriae[97]—is made explicit. As we shall see, it became a metaphor of Duke Cosimo's rule.

There may also be a covert allusion to Cosimo's *impresa* of Capricorn and the Crown of Ariadne (such as I have noted in Salviati's *Camillus*) in this work. As Vasari remarks, Cosimo's planet, Saturn, touches his Capricorn ascendant on the armillary sphere. Above the sphere is a crown: Vasari interprets it rather vaguely as alluding to the power of God, but it may have been so placed above the Capricorn in allusion to the Crown of Ariadne of Cosimo's horoscope.

The allegories of the remaining three elements are on the walls below, where, as in the Villa Castello fountains of *Hercules and Antaeus* and *Venus*, Earth and Water are placed opposite one another. Water, as at Castello, is represented by the birth of Venus from the sea, and may signify the "Venus in Cancer" (a water sign) of Cosimo's horoscope. Earth is astrologically explicit: it is represented by Saturn with the Capricorn (an

---

p. 33; and his letter in Vasari-Frey, I, pp. 410-12. For remarks about this aspect of the room, see Lensi Orlandi, pp. 52-55.

[94] Vasari, *Rag.*, p. 23. The new moon is mentioned by Giuntini, 1581, I, p. 127.

[95] Vasari, *Rag.*, p. 19.

[96] Vasari, *Rag.*, p. 22. Vasari also connects the scepter in the center of the sphere with Cosimo's rule: "Quello è fatto per il Regno . . . e lo scetro è l'imperio del comandar a tutti i viventi: e questo è quanto alla storia del quadro di mezzo."

[97] On this theme, see Chastel, 1961, p. 227.

earth sign), signifying "Saturn in Capricorn," which, in Cosimo's horoscope, is in opposition to "Venus in Cancer." The scene is a tableau of the Golden Age of Saturn-Cosimo, who receives the tributes of Earth (pl. 184). Saturn holds the serpent biting its tail, the familiar emblem of eternal Medici rule (cf. pl. 48). To the right is Cosimo's device of the tortoise; it is held by Fortuna, who presents it to Saturn, "pianeta suo,"[98] and at Cosimo-Saturn's feet is the Capricorn holding a red *palla*, the meaning of which Vasari explains:[99]

> Mostrai qui sotto Saturno il capricorno, segno ed ascendente suo, con la benignità delle stelle, quali sono tanto fortunate in Sua Eccellenza, tenendo sotto una palla rossa dell'arme di casa vostra, che si fa per mostrare il corpo del mondo, che è la palla, tenuto, e retto, e governato da quelle sette stelle, le quali a suo luogo dichiareremo.

> Beneath Saturn here I depicted the Capricorn, his sign and ascendant, with the benignity of the stars, which are so lucky in his Excellency's [horoscope], holding below a red *palla* of the arms of your house, which symbolizes the body of the world, which is the globe, held and governed by those seven stars, which in their turn we will name.

Vasari's Saturn with Capricorn marks a significant turning point in Cosimo's manipulation of his astrological imagery, for it is the first time that the duke actually becomes Saturn in his art (although, of course, the old man is not a true portrait). It is also the first time that Cosimo's Capricorn is combined with the globe (the "corpo del mondo" held by Capricorn) and the cornucopia (held by the goddess of earth)—the emblems of Fortuna (also personified here) and Imperium which accompany the Capricorn of Augustan coins (pl. 134).

✳   ✳   ✳

After 1555, the date of Vasari's allegory of Earth with its Augustan emblems, Cosimo's iconographers emphasized the Augustan parallel ever more emphatically.[100] The Cosimo-Capricorn-Augustus chain of associations that had been a catalyst for the Augustan imagery of Cosimo's early art was kept alive by the coincidence of yet another military victory over the *fuorusciti* in the first days of August—the Battle of Marciano (2 August 1554), which led to Cosimo's annexing of Siena. As Bernardo Davanzati was to claim in his funeral oration for Cosimo, this victory once again confirmed Cosimo's

---

[98] Vasari, *Rag.*, p. 32: "E' la fortuna di Sua Eccellenza, quale, per obbedire a Saturno, pianeta suo, gli presenta la vela e la testuggine, impresa di Sua Eccellenza, dimostrando che con la natura e tardità del cammino di questo animale, e la velocità che fa andare i legni nelle acque, la vela, nel mare delle difficultà, e l'essere Sua Eccellenza temperato sempre riuscire con buona fortuna in tutte le imprese del suo governo." For Augustus' *impresa* of the "crab and the butterfly: FESTINA LENTE," see

Deonna, pp. 47-48, 64-66. When Cosimo used the tortoise with the sail, representing the same principle of moderation, it was usually without the motto, which betrays its Augustan origin.

[99] Vasari, *Rag.*, p. 32.

[100] The Augustan theme in Cosimo's propaganda and art has been discussed in particular by Forster, 1971, pp. 72-90; Adelson, 1975, pp. 60-65; and Richelson, pp. 25-45.

astrological destiny as a New Augustus. His horoscope had been portentous: "Nel suo nascere si viddero molti segni, ed auguro del suo Principato" (At his birth one saw many signs and prophecies of his principate); moreover, he had the same stars as Augustus, and it was on his Augustan days in January and August that the decisive turns of his fortune had occurred: "Il sesto di Gennaio fu l'asce, e il primo e il secondo d'Agosto furono le martella" (The sixth of January was the ax and the first and second of August were the hammer).[101]

The second of August was added to the Florentine holidays celebrating Cosimo's Augustan destiny.[102] However, it was not until the French troops had left Siena in 1559 that peace was achieved and Cosimo was recognized as duke of Florence and Siena. And it was only then that the parallel with Augustus which had been implicit in his art was expressed overtly and in a public context. (The death in 1558 of Charles V, who had styled himself a New Augustus, may also have contributed to the sudden manifestation of Augustan imagery in Cosimo's art around 1560, for the way was now clear for the emperor's Florentine emulator.) Thus, after 1559, Cosimo's *impresa* routinely included the Augustan emblems of Fortuna and Imperium. For example, in an illustration to Ludovico Dolce's sonnet "Sotto questo ascendente il grande Augusto / E Carlo Quinto per mirabile cose," the Capricorn is shown with the globe, rudder, and cornucopia (pl. 185).[103]

Cosimo was identified with Augustus, and his Augustan stars were celebrated, in a number of works of about 1560. His *entrata* into Siena (the city that had been won on his lucky Augustan day) on 28 November 1560 was the occasion for an elaborate *apparato* that presented him as a New Augustus with his Capricorn and his globe. According to Cirni's description of the affair, a page accompanying Cosimo and Eleonora carried a standard triumphantly displaying the Capricorn, and among the decorations was an imitation bronze statue of Augustus "co'l Capricorno suo ascendente à piedi, e co'l mondo d'oro in mano con iscrizione *Aurea condet secula*, significando che il Duca con la pace rinovara l'età dell'oro."[104] This is, of course, the familiar Medici wordplay of the *mondo-palla*, and it was underlined by a Greek inscription on the globe ΚΟΣΜΟΣ ΚΟΣΜΟΥ ΚΟΣΜΟΣ (Cosmos, the world of Cosimo), which Cirni interpreted as meaning "il duca Cosimo honora il mondo, e 'l mondo lui, o vero, che 'l mondo è di Cosimo e egli è di lui" (Duke Cosimo honors the world and the world him, or rather, the world is Cosimo's and he is the world's).[105] A conflation of the wordplay Cosimo-cosmos and the *mondo-palla* was thus introduced into Duke Cosimo's imagery. We see it frequently in his later art, as in an *impresa* illustrating Egnatio Danti's treatise on the astrolabe, dedicated to the duke in 1569 (pl. 186).[106] Here, the *palle* are superimposed on the *mondo*, which is

[101] B. Davanzati, "Orazione in Morte del Gran Duca Cosimo I," *Operette del Signor Bernardo Davanzati Bostichi*, Livorno, 1779, pp. 41-45.

[102] Lapini, pp. 112-13; and Giamboni, p. 158.

[103] Pittoni, pl. XIII.

[104] Cirni, f. 4r-4v. Ammannati, who was responsible for some of the sculptural decorations of the *apparato*, describes the Augustus with Capricorn and globe in a letter of 3 November 1559

(A. Venturi, *Storia dell'arte italiana*, Milan, 1936, X/2, pp. 348-49).

[105] Cirni, f. 5v.

[106] Danti, f. 1v. Below the *impresa* is Giovambattista Strozzi's sonnet, which expands on the conceit:

Non pur la bella Flora
   Sua dolce figlia di bei cerchi adorna,

crowned with the ducal coronet and surrounded by the Order of the Golden Fleece. Below, sprigs of laurel frame a cartouche containing the same Cosimo-cosmos wordplay that was featured in the Sienese *entrata*.

The Augustan imagery of the *entrata* occurs in three contemporaneous works in which Cosimo's Capricorn is combined with other Augustan symbols. In the so-called *Genio mediceo* attributed to the circle of Tribolo (pl. 188),[107] a "live" Capricorn accompanies a youth—much as the animal sits at the feet of Poggini's Apollo-Cosimo and Vasari's Saturn-Cosimo. He holds aloft a *palla-mondo* as a symbol of dominion. In Stoldo Lorenzi's *Tribute of the Cities of Tuscany to Duke Cosimo de' Medici and Eleonora da Toledo* (pl. 187), the ducal couple, both crowned with laurel, receive the tribute of the cities of a newly united Tuscany.[108] Cosimo, who sits directly in front of a great circular temple, wears armor *all'antica* decorated with two Capricorns in imitation of an Augustan coin showing two Capricorns with the Oak Wreath.[109] The third work depicting the Augustan Cosimo with his astrological *impresa* is Vasari's full-length portrait of *Duke Cosimo de' Medici as Augustus* (pl. 189), which is strategically placed in the Sala di Leo X, the largest and most important of the rooms in Cosimo's suite in the Palazzo.[110] Cosimo-Augustus, sword of victory in one hand, baton of dominion in the other, is accompanied by shields bearing his *imprese*: to the left is the tortoise with the sail, the Augustan motto of which (FESTINA LENTE, Make haste slowly) alludes to Cosimo's ideals of rulership; to the right, under Cosimo's sword, is the familiar Capricorn and Crown of Ariadne. Significantly, Vasari associates this portrait with the "Augustan" event of the victory over Siena, explaining that the chiaroscuro below it represents the building of "la fortezza di Siena."[111]

Shortly after the painting of this Augustan image of the duke, Vasari began the decoration of the Salone dei Cinquecento in the Palazzo (1563-1565). This room, which

---

Ma come il Sol che in ogni lido aggiorna,
Mentre di gemme il terren Tosco infiora
Questo; e quello altro Polo,
E tutto il Mondo illustra un COSMO sole.

[107] Heikamp, in Barocchi, cat. 655. Richelson, p. 40, attributes the work to Stoldo Lorenzi.

[108] R. Borghini, p. 608, states that Stoldo made for Luca Martini (d. January 1561) "una historia in marmo di basso rilievo, in mezo à cui si vede il Gran Duca Cosimo, e da una parte il fiume Arno, e dall'altra Arbia con tutte le città d'ambidue gli stati, con vasi in mano, portando il tributo al lor Principe." H. Utz, "Pierino da Vinci e Stoldo Lorenzi," *Paragone*, 111, 1967, pp. 54-55, 61, dates it early in the period 1554/55-1561 as a pendant to Pierino's *Duke Cosimo de' Medici as Patron of Pisa* (1549; Vatican), and identifies Cosimo's companion as Eleonora. It should be noted that all the cities of the newly united province participate in the tribute: in addition to Florence (the Arno, the vase with the *giglio* of Florence behind him) and Siena (the Arbia, the vase with the wolf of Siena

above her), we can recognize Pisa (vase with the cross of Santo Stefano to the left of Eleonora), Volterra (vase with the griffin of Volterra at the upper left), etc. This theme of the Tuscan cities was repeated in Vasari's Sala di Cosimo and Salone dei Cinquecento, as well as in Cosimo's funeral *apparato* (Borsook, p. 44).

[109] Inscribed OB CIVES SER[VATOS]. H. Mattingly, *The Roman Imperial Coinage*, London, 1923-1951, I, pp. 135-36, nos. 109-112. It is possible that the crown held over Cosimo's head directly above the Capricorns on his breastplate alludes to the Crown of Ariadne of his *impresa*. This radiated crown (unlike any other in Cosimo's art) is not the ducal coronet, which is being carried in at the right.

[110] Vasari, *Rag.*, p. 163, where Vasari calls the portrait simply "Duca Cosimo . . . armato."

[111] Vasari, *Rag.*, p. 163. Below the pendant *Alessandro* portrait is the scene of the building of the Florentine Fortezza da Basso, for which Alessandro had been responsible.

sums up Cosimo's accomplishments against a background of the history of Florence from Republic to Principato, contains a number of references to the cult of the New Augustus, including the Augustan configuration of the stars at Cosimo's birth. In *The Foundation of Florence as a Roman Colony* (pl. 62), Augustus is the foremost of the founding triumvirate, and the helmet at his feet carries significant emblems: Hercules Florentinus, copied from the old seal of the commune (pl. 121), and the Capricorn, alluding to the idea of Cosimo as the second founder of Florence. But it is in the great central tondo, *The Apotheosis of Duke Cosimo de' Medici* (pl. 190), which Vasari describes as "la chiave e la conclusione delle storie . . . in questa sala" (the key and the conclusion of the histories in this room),[112] that Cosimo's Augustan imagery reaches its climax. Cosimo, "trionfante e glorioso," achieves immortality in the heavens as Divus Augustus, surrounded by emblems of his rule (the ducal crown, the Cross of Santo Stefano, the Order of the Golden Fleece), ringed by the insignia of the Florentine guilds. The tondo is set into a square with the inscription: SPQF OPTIMO PRINCIPE. CONSTITVTA CIVITATE. AVCTO IMPERIO. PACATA ETRVRIA. (The Senate and the People of Florence. The Best Prince. The State Established. The Realm Enlarged. Etruria Pacified.)

The image is richly allusive, making reference both to traditional Medici imagery of Florence and to the *topos* of Cosimo's astrological destiny. The early plans for the tondo called for a "Fiorenza in gloria coi suoi segni" (Florence in glory with its symbols), as Vasari's compositional study is inscribed.[113] A tondo with Florence at the center of the ceiling would have recalled the Florentia medals of earlier Medici art, such as those made for Lorenzo il Magnifico and Pope Leo's brother Giuliano (pls. 3, 11); it would also have provided a natural climax for the paintings of the military victories of Florence over Siena and Pisa and the statues of *Victory* and *Florence Victorious over Pisa* by Michelangelo and Giovanni da Bologna on the lateral walls of the room.[114] However, instead of Fiorenza, Vasari painted an Augustan Cosimo, who thus quite literally replaces the city he rules. And, in an ultimate accolade, it is Fiorenza herself who crowns her duke with the Oak Wreath of Augustus.

Cosimo's costume *all'antica* and his seated pose echo Stoldo's recent relief figure of the duke, but, more significantly (as has often been noted), Cosimo recalls the so-called *Giuliano de' Medici* of the New Sacristy (pl. 156). Now, there would be little point in Vasari's alluding to a representation of Giuliano, who never ruled Florence. However, if (as I have argued) this statue portrays Lorenzo—the last Medici ruler during the years of the Florentine Republic and the last descendant of Cosimo Pater Patriae to rule the city—then Vasari's derivative image would make a strong propagandistic statement: it would reassert Cosimo's familiar claim that he, too, was just such a legitimate ruler.

Vasari's image of Cosimo in the heavens also makes cosmic references. It brings to mind the Greek motto ΚΟΣΜΟΣ ΚΟΣΜΟΥ ΚΟΣΜΟΣ, which puns on the wordplay Cosimo-

---

[112] Vasari, *Rag.*, p. 220.

[113] Uffizi 7979A. In Vasari's letter of 3 March 1563 he states: "Farei La felicità di Fiorenza in una gloria celeste" (Vasari-Frey, I, p. 724). For the chronology of the program, see Rubinstein, 1967, pp. 64-66.

[114] M. Campbell, "Giambologna, Michelangelo, and Giorgio Vasari's Programme in the Sala Grande of the Palazzo Vecchio," *Congress on Giambologna*, British Arts Council, Edinburgh, 1978. I am grateful to Malcolm Campbell for making the text of his paper available to me.

cosmos (pl. 186). Moreover, this apotheosis of Cosimo in a tondo alludes to the image of the cosmos (*clipeus caelestis*) of ancient art, in which the living emperor in apotheosis becomes the cosmocrator or sun emperor.[115] Indeed, an allusion to the *clipeus*, or shield, would seem to be indicated in Vasari's design by the shields of the guilds, which substitute for the zodiac border which traditionally signified the cosmic character of the *clipeus*.[116]

Other imagery in the tondo carries out this cosmic theme. The Oak Wreath, which emphasizes Cosimo's status as a New Augustus through his accomplishments on behalf of Florence, also alludes to his Augustan horoscope. As in Vasari's allegory of Air, where a crown surmounts the sign of Capricorn, or in Salviati's *Camillus*, where the Capricorn is on Cosimo's chariot and a wreath is held over his head, this wreath alludes to the Crown of Ariadne, which marks the mid-heaven of his horoscope. The Capricorn ascendant of the horoscope (without which the celestial crown has no meaning) is also indicated in the tondo: it is the goat (symbol of the guild of the Beccai), which is placed among the shields to the left about ninety degrees below the wreath, in a position which exactly reproduces the aspect of the ascendant to the mid-heaven in Cosimo's horoscope (figs. 15-16). Cosimo in the cosmos is thus literally surrounded by the Augustan horoscope to which the mythology of his rule attributed his destiny as duke of Florence.

Cosimo's Augustan imagery reached its final stage of elaboration after he became grand duke in 1569, when for the first time he was portrayed in his Augustan guise in a public monument. In a statue which was planned for the cross-arm of the loggia of the Uffizi courtyard—itself conceived as an Augustan forum—Vincenzo Danti paraphrased Vasari's portrait *Duke Cosimo de' Medici as Augustus* (pl. 191).[117] Vasari's relatively realistic likeness of Cosimo (based, as usual, on Bronzino's portraits of him) has been replaced here by an unrecognizably idealized ruler, who is now but a symbol of his own Augustan destiny. This destiny is signaled by the *impresa* of Capricorn and the Crown of Ariadne, which, as in Vasari's painting, is depicted on Cosimo's shield. Now, however, in keeping with the stylization of the whole image, the constellation of the Crown is no longer recognizable but has been reduced to a simple arc of stars above the equally emblematic Capricorn.

[115] For this tradition in ancient art, see L'Orange, pp. 90-109.

[116] See L'Orange, p. 90, who gives as an example the *Four Seasons* sarcophagus (my pl. 152.) For the shields of the guilds, see Vasari, *Rag.*, p. 221.

[117] For Danti's statue of 1571-1573, see Forster, 1971, pp. 86-88; and Barocchi, cat. 668. Uffizi 2128A shows Danti's plan for a different statue—one with Cosimo seated and flanked by allegories of Severe and Just Government. For the courtyard as a forum of Augustus, which expresses in permanent form the Medicean penchant for the evocation of Roman monuments in Florence, see Kauffmann, pp. 37-43. Contemporary with this work, Matasilani, pp. 17-18, published the first of many literary elaborations of the *paragone* that was

to become a permanent part of Cosimo's mythology. As Danti's Cosimo-Augustus rules over his pseudo-Roman forum, so Cosimo brings a Pax Augustae to Florence: ". . . mi ha molto a far comparatione della felicità di Roma a quella di Firenze, e di quella d'Ottaviano a quella di Gran Cosimo. . . . Per disposition de cieli, e per ordin fatale li fu mandato il grand'Ottaviano Augusto che la governò, e ampliò con tanta felicità che così il S. Dio, habbia concesso à punto alla Città di Firenze, il Gran Cosimo de Medici, acciò con l'istessa fortuna, e felicità di Ottaviano ponesse fine alle discordie, si mantenesse, aumentasse, e stabilisse una perpetua felicità alla Città di Firenze, e popoli di Toscana, e apportasse la pace di Ottaviano al Mondo."

Cosimo's new status was also celebrated by the issue of a medal by Francesco da Sangallo (pl. 192).[118] This medal followed a tradition in Cosimo's art of marking each important juncture in his rule by pairing him with the first duke of Florence. An early medal of the beardless Cosimo by Domenico di Polo, inscribed COSMVS MED[ICES] FLOREN-TIAE DVX II, pairs him with the first duke, inscribed ALEXANDER MED[ICES] FLORENTIAE DVX P[RIMVS], and commemorates his succession to Alessandro;[119] Vasari's portraits of the two dukes in the Sala di Leo X commemorate Cosimo's new title as duke of Florence and Siena; and Sangallo's medal, inscribed COSMVS MEDICES ETRVRIAE MAGNVS ATQ INVIT-TISSIMVS DVX MDLXX (Cosimo de' Medici, great and most invincible Duke of Etruria, 1570), with Alessandro on the reverse (identified as in the first medal), announces his grand-ducal title. In this last medal, Alessandro is shown bareheaded and without em-blems of rule, but Cosimo wears his new grand-ducal crown and the Order of the Golden Fleece, and he carries the baton of rule. Both dukes, moreover, are marked by astrological imagery: above Alessandro's head is the comet which appeared at the begin-ning of his rule;[120] to the right of Cosimo's crowned head are the eight stars of the celestial crown of his horoscope, which destined him for Florentine rulership.

The theme of Cosimo's astrological destiny continued to be alluded to even after his death. The Augustan *topos* was prominent in the elaborate funeral *apparato* of 1574 at San Lorenzo, where, in one of the twenty medallions which decorated the nave, was an *impresa* which appears for the first time in Cosimo's art.[121] It showed a Capricorn with an Oak Wreath, in imitation of Augustan imagery. This device thus conflates the theme of Cosimo's destiny—the Capricorn and Crown of Ariadne of his horoscope— and his *virtù*, signified by the Oak Wreath. And, as is explained in a description of the *apparato*, the device signified "la magnanimità, et clementia da lui usata verso molti Rebelli" (the magnanimity and clemency he showed toward many rebels),[122] an inter-pretation that harks back to the very first appearance of Cosimo's astrological *impresa*, when it commemorated his Augustan victory in 1537 over the *fuorusciti* at Montemurlo.

EPILOGUE: FRANCESCO DE' MEDICI AND ARIES

In 1541 the possibilities of an astrological imagery alluding to the destiny of the Medici as rulers of Florence were suddenly expanded, and another zodiacal animal joined Co-simo's Capricorn. By an extraordinary coincidence that was immediately exploited by Cosimo, his first son, Francesco, was born on 25 March, the first day of the Florentine year. Moreover, the horoscope of the Medici heir seemed to announce an even more portentous connection with the city. As can be seen in the chart cast by the court

[118] Supino, no. 274.

[119] Hill-Pollard, no. 316.

[120] F. Giuntini, *Discorso sopra la cometa apparsa nell' mese di novembre 1572 . . . con dichiaratione di tutte le comete apparse da l'anno 1301 fino al 1572*, Venice, 1573, f. 10v. I owe this reference to Claudia Rous-seau.

[121] For this *apparato*, see Borsook, pp. 31-54.

[122] *Descritione della Pompa Funerale fatte nelle Es-sequie del Ser.ᵐᵒ Sig. Cosimo de' Medici*, Florence, 1574, f. 13v.

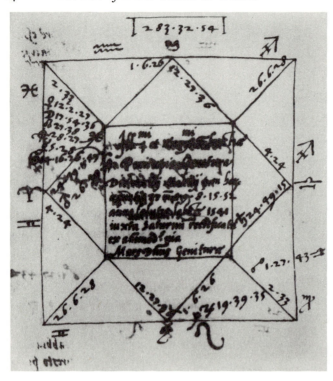

22. Horoscope of
Francesco de' Medici,
25 March 1541, by
G. B. Guidi (BNF, MS
Magl. XX, 19, f. 111v)

astrologer Giovanni Battista Guidi in 1561 (fig. 22)[123] and in a diagram of this horoscope in circular format (fig. 23), Francesco's sun and ascendant are both in Aries, exactly as in the horoscope of the rebirth of Florence (fig. 7), and Mars is in domicile in Aries.

Francesco's fortunate stars, which suggested his destiny as future ruler of the city with which he shared a horoscope, were the subject of much discussion at the time of Cosimo's abdication in 1564 and Francesco's marriage in 1565, when decorations and medals referring to the future duke were being planned. For example, writing to Francesco about the design of a medal with his Aries ascendant, Vincenzo Borghini points out: "Dal caso si puo dire, che il medesimo sia stato ascendente di V. A. et della patria sua insieme" (It is chance, one may say, that Your Highness and the fatherland [Florence] both have the same ascendant).[124] Borghini also recommends that, as in Cosimo's medal of the Capricorn and Crown of Ariadne, Francesco's Aries *impresa* should be accompanied by stars, "come Marte di cui è casa" (like Mars, whose house it is). And, in Vasari's *Foundation of Florence as a Roman Colony* (pl. 62), which is based on a program

---

[123] BNF, MS Magl. XX, 19, f. 111v. This horoscope is cited in Zambelli, p. 380, who cites yearly prognostications for Francesco by Guidi for 1567 and 1583 (BNF, Magl. MS XX, 38; Laur. MS Plut. 89 sup., 36). A time of birth for Francesco which is in agreement with Guidi's is given by Giuntini, 1581, I, p. 158, and by Cosimo's astrologer, Danti,

1569, p. 119: "Adi 25 di Marzo l'anno 1541 a ho. 11 e m. 14 di Horiolo che sono ho. 17 e mi. 37 dopò il mezzo del precedente giorno di Lunedì nel hora del Sole che appunto ascendeva il 14 gr. dell'Ariete, essendo il Sole in esso Ariete à gr. 14. m. 15. 33. secondi."

[124] V. Borghini, pp. 78-79.

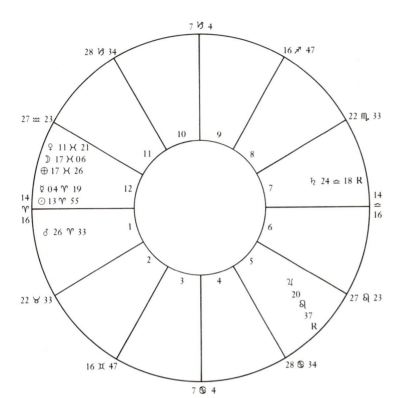

23. Horoscope of
Francesco de' Medici,
25 March 1541, 5:47 a.m.

by Borghini of the same date, the presence in the sky of the zodiac sign of Florence and of Francesco alike reminds the viewer of the happy coincidence of the birth of Cosimo's heir under the very sign of the foundation of the city.[125]

Cosimo's Capricorn was joined by the Aries ascendant of his heir in the art of the mid-1540s. The Ram appears as a decorative motif, as in one of the tapestries designed by Bacchiacca to hang below Salviati's frescos in the Sala delle Udienze, where it is paired with the Capricorn.[126] The same pairing occurs in a Pontormo drawing (for a tapestry?) of *Venus and Cupid with Capricorn and Aries*, datable to the early 1540s (pl. 193).[127] But the most complex work featuring the Aries which Francesco shared with Florence is Bronzino's *Primavera* tapestry of 1545 (pl. 61). With its pendant, *Justice Liberating Innocence*, this work is an allegory of renewal—of Time's Return and the new

[125] Rubinstein, 1967, p. 71.

[126] Adelson, in Barocchi, cat. 73; and Adelson, 1980, pp. 174-75. The theme of Capricorn and Aries also appears in Salviati's *Camillus before Brennus*, where Capricorn heads are used in the metopes of the temple in the background and Ram's heads in the column capital. The Ram, alluding to both Florence and Francesco, is also featured in the *finto*-tapestry on the south wall of the *Sacrifice of Isaac*, a subject that had long been associated

with the myth of Florence (cf. the competition panels of 1401 for the Baptistery doors).

[127] Paris, Louvre 10396. See Cox-Rearick, 1971, pp. 371-72, cat. 344a, for the suggestion that this drawing might have been connected with Cosimo's wedding *apparato* of 1539; however, if the animal to the right is the Ram (it seems to have curved horns), then the study probably dates after Francesco's birth.

286

Golden Age of Cosimo's Florence.[128] In the *Justice*, Giustizia-Astraea (Cosimo) liberates Innocence (Florence) in a setting which symbolizes Time (Saturn; the snake; the *tricipitium* of the wolf. lion, and dog).[129] In the *Primavera*, the old Medici conceits of Flora-Fiorenza and the Return of Time in spring recall Botticelli's *Primavera* (pl. 60), which Cosimo himself had installed at Villa Castello. In a composition not unlike that of Pontormo's contemporaneous *Venus and Cupid with Capricorn and Aries*, Bronzino's Flora-Fiorenza scatters Medici roses and Florentine lilies over a verdant spring landscape. She is accompanied by the three zodiac signs of spring—with the Aries of Francesco, the heir to Cosimo's rule of justice, most prominently displayed.[130]

Late in Cosimo's lifetime, the notion of his astrologically predestined rule of Florence was transferred to Francesco's personal imagery. As Vasari says to Francesco in a lecture on the theme of rulership and the stars in the *Ragionamenti*, the actions of men are guided by heavenly bodies, "secondo il temperamento loro e secondo la malignità e benignità d'essi pianeti guidati da chi governa il tutto; questi lo fanno essere per il suo felice augurio un grandissimo duca" (according to their temperament and according to the malignity and benignity of those planets guided by the ruler of all; they make him [Francesco], as it were, by virtue of his happy auguries, a most great duke).[131] Just as Cosimo's rule was predestined by his lucky stars, so too was Francesco's.

The transfer of power from Cosimo to his son (which took place at Cosimo's abdication on his birthday, 11 June 1564) was symbolized in Cosimo's art by the pairing of their ascendant signs of Capricorn and Aries. This motif appears several times in Francesco's wedding *apparato* of 1565—as, for example, in Ammannati's *Neptune* fountain, which was set up temporarily for the occasion. Neptune's chariot wheels were decorated (according to a contemporary description) with "dua ascendenti, capricorno del duca, ed ariete del principe" (two ascendants—the duke's Capricorn and the prince's Aries).[132]

---

[128] Berti, 1980, cat. 121-22. For the usual interpretation of these tapestries as thematically unrelated, see E. Panofsky, "Father Time," in *Studies in Iconology*, New York, 1962, pp. 84-91.

[129] I am grateful to Lynette Bosch for the suggestion that the animals might signify the theme of past, present, and future time (on which theme see E. Panofsky, *Problems in Titian, Mostly Iconographic*, New York, 1969, pp. 105-6). See her "Time, Truth, and Destiny: Some Iconographic Themes in Bronzino's *Primavera* and the *Vindication of Innocence*," *Mitt.KHIF* (forthcoming).

[130] The imagery of Flora and spring in reference to Francesco continued in later years. See, for example, V. Borghini's notes to Vasari in connection with a design of a medal for Francesco (pp. 80-81): "E il medesimo concetto che della prima, ma un poco più aperto, che vi è Flora à sedere e il cielo che sparge copiosamente fiori et la Terra che ne produce infiniti onde ella ne va scegliendo per farsi nuova ghirlanda: Accennando copertamente alla Corona ottenuta da S. A. dall'Imperio il che ha,

finalmente, chiuso la boccha à tante repliche et difficultà che si son fatte; et con isperanza sempre di nuovi honori. Le parole sono cavate da Lucretio. *Iuvat novos decerpere Flores Atque meo capiti contexere inde Coronam* [It is a pleasure to pick fresh flowers and to weave them into a crown for my head] etc. Quell' altre da Virgilio: *Tibi libia plenis / Ecce ferunt Nymphae Calathis* [Look! the nymphs carry baskets overflowing with lilies for you] etc. quasi che il ciel tutto benigno, et favorevole sia per porger sempre nuove gratie etc. et i Fiori et i Gigli, specialmente, molto convengono col nome di Fiorenza et con la natura del segno."

[131] Vasari, *Rag.*, p. 50.

[132] Cini, p. 565. In the final installation of the fountain, the two signs decorate the cartouches on its base, while the chariot wheels each show six signs of the zodiac. On the left wheel, Francesco's Aries is rising above the water, but on the right wheel Cosimo's Capricorn is one of the signs under the water! The Capricorn and Aries also appeared in the medallions of the first lunette of the

This imagery also occurs in Vasari's *Pallas-Minerva in the Forge of Vulcan* of 1565-1567.[133] In a genial *invenzione*, Vincenzo Borghini changed the story of Thetis, who sees the astral portent of the early death of Achilles in Vulcan's shield, so that Pallas-Minerva replaces Thetis and (as Borghini instructs Vasari) the shield should show "qualche impresa che v'havessi fatte nel mezzo che fusse ingegnosa di qualche bel significato et a proposito et—v.g.—un montone ed un capricorno che l'un di qua et l'altro di là reggessino una palla e assimigliasse il mondo" (some *impresa* which would have deeds in the center which would have some beautiful meaning and purpose and, for example, a ram and a capricorn, which, each on his own side, would hold a *palla*, which would represent the world).[134] Thus, the patroness of Florence (we recall that Pallas is the Manilian ruler of the Florentine sign of Aries) sees in Vulcan's shield the astral signs of Medici dominion, as the zodiacal animals of Cosimo and Francesco hold between them the *mondo-palla* (pl. 194).

After Cosimo's death, Francesco emulated his father's astrological medals. One of these, dated 1577, is based on an *invenzione* by Borghini (pl. 195).[135] In a long letter to Francesco, Borghini explains that he has chosen the duke's ascendant, "l'Ariete celeste," for the medal in imitation of Augustus and of Cosimo, who had used their astrological signs on their medals.[136] And, in a memo to Vasari, Borghini explains further about the medal: it will show "il segno dell'Ariete nella linea ecliptica" (the sign of Aries on the ecliptic), and there are several possible mottos for it, including the Virgilian MAJOR AGIT DEVS (a greater God acts), which means that "la Sicurtà della Felicita di S.A. ha più alta ragione, ne dal favor delle stelle procede, ma del Fattore istesso delle Stelle, dal quale veramente viene ogni bene" (the security of the happiness of Your Highness has a deeper reason, nor does it proceed from the favor of the stars, but from the Creator of the stars, from whom indeed all good comes).[137] Another medal, dated 1576, is even more interesting in relation to Cosimo's astrological imagery (pl. 196).[138] It shows the imperial eagle hovering over Francesco's Aries and three stars. In imitation of Cosimo's Capricorn and Crown of Ariadne, Francesco's Aries is also crowned. However, the crown is not a constellation like Cosimo's; it is the crown of the grand duke of Tuscany, which has come to him through Divine Providence, as the inscription SIC DEO PLACVIT declares.

The last astrological imagery to be painted in the Palazzo in Cosimo's lifetime relates to both Cosimo and Francesco. It is in Francesco's Studiolo, which was decorated under

Palazzo Vecchio courtyard, where they were inscribed ANIMA E CONSCIENTIA and OMNIA FLORENT.

[133] Uffizi; see Monbeig-Goguel, cat. 223; and Berti, 1979, p. 581.

[134] Quoted in Scoti-Bertinelli, pp. 95-96.

[135] Supino, no. 581.

[136] V. Borghini, pp. 75-79.

[137] V. Borghini, p. 82. The ecliptic has been fashioned to resemble the chain of the Order of the Golden Fleece, suggesting that the Aries has both a celestial and a temporal meaning for Francesco.

[138] Supino, no. 528 (incorrectly described as showing Cosimo's Capricorn).

Vasari's direction in 1570-1575 on a program by Vincenzo Borghini.[139] This small room adjacent to the Salone dei Cinquecento is marked as Francesco's domain by *imprese* of his on the ceiling—the Aries of his horoscope (without motto) and the "weasel with the laurel: AMAT VICTORIA CVRAM (Victory loves the task)." Created for Francesco, who was a devotee of alchemy, the decoration of the room is a complex alchemical scheme, involving both paintings and sculptures, which is based on the assignment of each of the walls to one of the Four Elements.[140]

The astrological imagery of the Studiolo contrasts with that of the other rooms in the Palazzo, which depict a "public" imagery of Cosimo as an Augustan ruler. The imagery of this room is instead domestic. Its subject is Francesco and his parents, Cosimo and Eleonora, who are represented in tondo portraits on slate (attributed to Bronzino but probably by Allori) in lunettes at either end of the room.[141] In the initial scheme of 1570, the Seasons were to be depicted in these lunettes;[142] however, by February 1573 (the date of a payment for the frames of the tondi) it had been decided to insert the portraits into frescoed frames with zodiac signs and to flank them with putti representing the Seasons (pls. 197-198).[143]

It has been observed that the portraits of Cosimo and Eleonora are placed so as to carry out a male-female, active-passive polarity which ties in with the alchemical themes of the room, and that there is also a public-private contrast, with Cosimo on the wall adjoining the Salone dei Cinquecento and Eleonora on the wall next to Francesco's bedroom and surrounded by Spring and Summer as indicators of her fertility.[144] These themes are certainly important, but the essential meaning of the portraits depends on the way in which they present Francesco's parents as exemplars. The tondo format of course alludes to the Medici *diamante*, symbol of eternity, as well as to the familiar *palla-mondo* and Cosimo-cosmos wordplays; and the zodiac signs of the frames make the allusion to the cosmos all the more pointed. Within these frames, the likenesses of the ducal couple are presented in an idealized fashion, as they had appeared earlier. Cosimo is portrayed as he looked in Bronzino's state portrait of 1560, but with an up-to-date suit of armor he actually wore in his later years;[145] and Eleonora is shown as in Bronzino's portrait of her of 1545 with her son Giovanni, but in a costume with a high collar

[139] See Borghini's letters of 1570 to Vasari on the details of the program (Vasari-Frey, II, pp. 522-36, 888-91). For the Studiolo in general, see Berti, 1967, pp. 61-84; and Schaffer, passim.

[140] For the alchemical program, see Lensi Orlandi, pp. 109-87; and Schaffer, I, pp. 202-46.

[141] For these portraits see Baccheschi, pp. 94-96, nos. 54e and 54h (as school of Bronzino); and Schaffer, I, pp. 290-91 (as Bronzino; with lit.). Since Bronzino died in 1572, the portraits cannot be by his hand; however, their high quality suggests that they are by his pupil Allori, who also contributed two mythological pictures to the Studiolo ensemble.

[142] As is demonstrated by the drawing by Vasari in Dijon, Musée des Beaux-Arts 774, which shows the east (Earth) wall with Winter and Autumn (Rinehart, pp. 74-76).

[143] See ASF, *Mediceo* 5, f. 31v (28 February 1573), a payment for frames for the Studiolo, including "2 tondi di noce intagliate per 2 ritrati del grande ducha e della duchessa Lionora" (cited by Rinehart, p. 75, n. 6).

[144] Berti, 1967, pp. 61-84; and Lenzi Orlandi, pp. 119-20. Rinehart, p. 75, states that the "choice of the ducal portraits for these spaces was probably fortuitous," while Schaffer, I, p. 70, considers the zodiac bands to be merely "symbolic of the cosmological scheme of the universe."

[145] The suit of armor survives (Barocchi, cat. 237).

which accords with the style of the early 1570s. Now, in the winter of 1572-1573 Eleonora had been dead exactly ten years (she died 17 December 1562), and Cosimo had suffered a series of massive strokes and was not expected to live much longer.[146] These portraits, then, commemorate Francesco's parents, presenting them as the ever youthful rulers of Florence. Moreover, even the slate support on which they are painted contributes to this impression, for, as Langedijk has shown, the popularity of hard materials such as porphyry and *pietre dure* in Medici portraiture of these years is due to an equation that was made between the hardness of the substance and the eternal worth of the subjects depicted.[147]

The setting in which these tondi are placed carries out the commemorative theme, for it is strongly evocative of funerary apotheosis. The tondo with a zodiac frame accompanied by the Seasons is a funerary formula deriving from antique sarcophagi (pl. 152).[148] And, perhaps because of this association with the theme of eternal life, the image of the figure encircled by the zodiac had come to signify Perfection.[149] In the *Four Seasons* sarcophagus, the dead couple is placed within a zodiac wheel, flanked by two Seasons on each side; in the Studiolo, the portrait tondi, each with six zodiac signs and two Seasons, face one another. The familiar Medicean imagery of the Cycles of Time, which suggests their eternal renewal, was thus adapted to proclaim the "perfection" and apotheosis of Francesco's parents, founders of a new Medici dynasty.

But the zodiac signs around Cosimo and Eleonora are more than general symbols of Time and the Cosmos; they are arranged so as to commemorate the linked astrological destinies of the ducal couple. Cosimo's portrait is on the Earth wall, the theme of which is carried out in paintings such as *Gold Mining* by Jacopo Zucchi and in bronzes by Poggini and Ammannati of the earth gods Pluto and Opi. Cosimo is associated with Earth (as he was in the Sala degli Elementi) because of his ascendant in Capricorn, an earth sign. Thus, Cosimo is surrounded by the last six signs of the zodiac, which include Capricorn, and his image is flanked by Autumn (on the right) and Winter (on the left), the seasons corresponding to these signs. Moreover, these signs from Libra to Pisces are depicted in such a way that the signs of the ascendant, moon, and mid-heaven of Cosimo's horoscope are highlighted: the signs are arranged counterclockwise so that the ascendant Capricorn appears to the left of Cosimo's head; Sagittarius, the sign of the auspicious new moon of his birth, is to the right of his head; and the sign indicated by his pointing finger is Scorpio, the mid-heaven of his horoscope, which was generally understood to have predestined his rulership.[150]

Eleonora is placed oppposite on the Air wall, the theme of which is carried out in paintings such as Maso da San Friano's *Fall of Icarus* and in statues by Giovanni Bandini and Elia Candido of the air gods Juno and Borea. Eleonora is flanked by Spring and

---

[146] For the rapid decline in Cosimo's health, precipitated by a cerebral hemorrhage in February 1568, and its turn for the worse in the winter 1572-1573 with another stroke which left him paralyzed, see Pieraccini, II, pp. 40-46.

[147] Langedijk, pp. 67, 81.

[148] Kauffmann, p. 43.

[149] C. Ripa, *Iconologia*, 1603, pp. 391-92 (as quoted in Langedijk, p. 67).

[150] See chap. 9, "Medici Horoscopes and the Medici Golden Age."

Summer and surrounded by the first six signs of the zodiac, which are arranged in clockwise order. The mirror-image relationship of Eleonora's to Cosimo's signs suggests that the astrological destinies of the ducal couple were viewed as balancing and complementary—as another aspect of their exemplary perfection. However, due to a lack of data on Eleonora's horoscope, it is not possible to pursue in detail the way in which this theme was worked out. Eleonora was born exactly six months before Cosimo, on 11 January 1519.[151] Since we do not know the hour of her birth, no horoscope can be erected for her; however a solar horoscope for the *day* of her birth shows the sun at 0° Aquarius 40′, the moon in Gemini, and the outer planets (Jupiter and Saturn) in the same signs of Libra and Capricorn that they occupy in Cosimo's chart. Lacking the all-important ascendant sign, we cannot be certain that the arrangement of the signs around Eleonora relates to her horoscope; however, it may be noted that just as Cosimo is associated with the Earth wall through his ascendant in an earth sign, so Eleonora may have been placed on the Air wall because of some feature or features of her horoscope. Her sun and moon are both in air signs (Aquarius and Gemini), and her ascendant may also have been in an air sign—certainly the placement of Gemini to the left of her head, corresponding to the position of Cosimo's Capricorn, is suggestive. Moreover, the connection between Eleonora and Air in the Studiolo is by no means a novelty, for the duchess had long been associated with air-related imagery. Most important was Eleonora's identification with Juno, goddess of air and the Manilian ruler of her sun sign of Aquarius. The Studiolo Air wall, with its statue of Juno and her peacock and its seasons of Spring and Summer, reflects the imagery of Eleonora's medal by Poggini, which shows Juno's peacock with its young as a symbol of her fertility.[152] Eleonora is characterized as "Giunone, dea dell'Aria" (Juno, goddess of air) in Vasari's description of the Loggia of Juno in the Palazzo, and in a poem by Bronzino she is "la casta Giunon" (the chaste Juno).[153] Moreover, Eleonora is Juno and represents the element of Air in Ammannati's *Fountain of Juno*, which was designed in 1555 for the adjacent Salone dei Cinquecento.[154]

The Studiolo tondi, symbolizing the astrologically auspicious and fruitful union of Cosimo and Eleonora, which started the new branch of the Medici dynasty to which Francesco was now heir, thus close the circle of astrological images in Medici art which allude to Cosimo. The first of these had been quite different in character: Pontormo's *Vertumnus and Pomona* at Poggio a Caiano, painted some fifty years earlier in a poetic mode recalling Laurentian art, asserted the role of the heavens in the destiny of the Medici, hinting at the portentous birth of the new Cosimo under the sign of Capricorn and the planet Saturn. Later, during the rule of Cosimo as duke of Florence, astrological imagery became overt, specific, personalized, and political, as Cosimo identified through his Capricorn ascendant with Saturn and Augustus, proclaiming his rule to be a new

---

[151] Naples, Archivio di Stato, *Manoscritti nobiliari del march. Livio serra di Gerace*, VI, f. 1506: "Eleonora Alvarez di Toledo, n. 11 gennaio 1519."

[152] Supino, no. 440; Hill-Pollard, no. 342. The medal is inscribed CVM PVDORE LAETA FOECVNDITAS

(Joyful fertility with modesty).

[153] Vasari, *Rag.*, p. 73; *Sonetti di Angiolo Allori detto il Bronzino ed altre rime . . .* ed. D. Moreni, Florence, 1823, p. 41.

[154] Heikamp, pp. 120-30.

Golden Age. Here, in this last image of that rule, the tondo of Cosimo surrounded by the Seasons and the Zodiac evokes the theme of the complementary Cycles of Time in the heavens and on earth, as well as the venerable Medici motto LE TEMPS REVIENT. This theme of the Return of Time had been implicit in the seasonal imagery of Laurentian art; it was a metaphor of Medici renewal in Leonine works such as *Vertumnus and Pomona* and the New Sacristy; and, in Duke Cosimo's art, it seems to have become a function of the ducal personage himself: Cosimo is the cosmos, and the seasons of the earth and the stars of the heavens are mere attributes of him as absolute ruler of Florence.

Appendices

APPENDIX I

The Birth and Horoscope of Duke Cosimo de' Medici

Cosimo de' Medici's birthdate is given both as 11 June and as 12 June. However, the seemingly contradictory evidence for the date can probably be reconciled and a birth time of 11 June 1519 at about 9:18 p.m. established.

There are three contemporary documents: one is a letter dated 11 June, written while Cosimo's mother was in labor; another is Cosimo's baptismal record, dated 20 June, which gives the day of birth as 12 June; and the third is an account by Giovanni Batista Tedaldi, secretary to Giovanni delle Bande Nere from 1522 to 1526.

Tedaldi's account contains much useful information about Pope Leo's interest in the Medici child, but gives an inaccurate birthdate and time which appears in no other source (10 June at sunrise):[1]

> Et in questo mentre essendo Madonna Maria sua consorte gravida, partorì un figliuolo maschio: Laonde per commissione di lei si spacciò subito in diligentia il Toso Servitore di Sua Signoria, dando avviso al Sig. Giovanni come addì x di Giugno 1519 al levar del sole gli era nato detto figliuolo: Onde subito letta la lettera sen'andò da Papa Leone, et li disse: Padre Santo, io fo un presente alla Santità Vostra del mio primogenito, del quale pur' hor' hora ho havuto la nuova che mi è nato; et S. Santità rispose che lo accettava per suo proprio figliuolo, ma che voleva, et così comandava, che per rifare il più savio, il più prudente, et il più valoroso huomo che sino alhora havessi havuto la Casa de' Medici, se gli ponesse nome Cosimo, et così per medesimo servitore che tal nuova aveva portata, commesse che se gli facesse porre tal nome, et che i Compari fussino il Reverentissimo Cardinale de Rossi, et il Sig. Malatesta

[1] S. Ciampi, ed., "Discorso sopra Giovanni de' Medici scritto da Gio. Batista Tedaldi a riquisizione di Mess. Benedetto Varchi," *Notizie dei secoli XV & XVI sull'Italia, Polonia e Russia*, Florence, 1833, p. 90 (transcribed from "Orationi et Rime di diversi fatte del Ser^{mo} Cosimo de' Medici," BNF, MS Magl. XXVII, 104, f. 57-75r; passage quoted, f. 58r-59r).

Baglioni, et espressamente Sua Signoria commesse che si remunerasse in quel modo si conveniva quello che tal buona nuova portato gli haveva.

The other two documents are closer in date to the birth, but they contradict one another. The letter was written by Francesco Fortunati on behalf of Maria Salviati to Cosimo's father, Giovanni delle Bande Nere, who was in Rome.[2] In it, the hour and date of birth were left blank and the courier Toso was instructed to fill in these. The relevant passages are as follows:

> In questo punto, che siamo ad hore . . . [blank] a di . . . [blank] del presente, Madonna Maria Vostra consorte ha partorito uno bello figlio masc[h]io. . . . Et ordini quello habbiamo ad seguire, et chi ha ad compagniarlo alle fonte, et essere suo compare; che, come per l'altra le dissi, se essa togliessi bene per compare la Santita di Nostro Signore con tutto el collegio de' Cardinali, non ci dispiacerà punto: haspectereno lo avviso di V. S. et come ce ne habbiamo ad ghovernare. Et perchè Madonna Maria desidera verdolo, non gli fia grave advisarci quando ci sarà, et di gratia speciale domandarne licentia alla Santità di Nostro Signore. . . . In fretto, e perchè el Tosi farà l'officio del tutto ad bocca, non le dirò altro. Et perchè el parto non viene ancora fora, io sig[illo] la presente et rimecterommi in tutto al dì e alla hora che lei partutirà, secondo che li referirà el Toso.
>
> In Firenze, a dì XI di giugno 1519

The baptismal record reads as follows:[3]

> Lunedì adì detto [20 June] Cosimo giuliano et Romolo del Signor Giovanni de' Medici pop. di S.° Lorenzo. Nato adì 12 detto ho[re] 1⅔.

In interpreting these documents it is important to bear in mind that the hours of the day were reckoned from sunset.[4] Hence, "hore 1⅔" indicates that Cosimo was born one hour and forty minutes after sunset. The mean astronomical sunset in Florence on 11 June 1519 may be determined by computer as 7:38 p.m. (and the sunset time for 12 June would be almost the same). Cosimo's birth thus took place at about 9:18 p.m. However, it is less easy to determine the day. If it was the eleventh, common usage would indicate a citation such as "adì 11 hore 1⅔" or "hore 1⅔ di notte," leaving no

---

[2] ASF, *MAP* 112, no. 244. The transcription was corrected by Gino Corti from that published by G. Milanesi, "Lettere inedite e testamento di Giovanni de' Medici detto delle Bande Nere," *ASI*, N.S., 7, no. 2, 1858, pp. 6-7.

[3] Archivio dell' Opera del Duomo, *Libri dei battezzati in Firenze, Maschi dal 1512 al 1522*, f. 140v. My transcription of the entry was corrected from that published by C. Guasti, "Alcuni fatti della giovinezza di Cosimo I de' Medici, illustrati con i documenti contemporanei," *Giornale Storico degli Archivi toscani*, 2, 1858, p. 22, n. 1.

[4] In the Renaissance, the time of sunset was de-termined from astronomical tables, astrolabes, or by the use of *horologii nocturni*, which indicate both Florentine and conventional time by a dial showing the number of hours before sunrise and after sunrise for any given day to which it outer dial is turned. See M. L. Righini Bonelli, *Il Museo di Storia della Scienza, Firenze*, Florence, 1968, pp. 173-74. For a sixteenth-century clock showing the hours beginning at 6 p.m. modern time (the time of sunset at the spring and fall equinoxes), see my pl. 136. I am grateful to Nicolai Rubinstein for clarification on the Florentine custom of reckoning time.

doubt that the eleventh was intended. On the other hand, the baptismal record may be in error, since it seems unlikely that Maria would have been in labor on 11 June (when Fortunati wrote his letter) and not have delivered the baby until after sunset the following day. I would therefore incline toward the 11 June date.

Probable confirmation of this date comes from an authoritative source close to Cosimo. In 1569 Cosimo's cartographer, Egnatio Danti, gives the duke's time of birth as 11 June at 9:16 p.m.[5]

> Per esempio della presente prepositione, piglisi la figura celeste calculata nel punto che nacque nella inclita Città di Fiorenza lo Invittissimo COSMO Medici Duca II. di Fiorenza et di Siena, che fu' nel 1519 à dì undici di Giugno à hore 2 di notte, che sono hore 9 et minuti 16 dopo il mezzo del medesimo dì.

In addition to this evidence that Cosimo was born on 11 June, there is copious documentation indicating that Cosimo celebrated his birthday on that day.[6] After he became duke in 1537, 11 June was declared a public holiday in Florence. A letter from the duke's major-domo, Pierfrancesco Riccio, to a ducal secretary, Lorenzo Pagni, dated 9 June 1541, is explicit:[7]

> Riverentemente ricordo che sabbato è Sco Barnaba, natale felicissimo di S. Ex.[tia] che viene appunto in sabbato, et lo dico perchè S. Ex.[tia] in quel dì nacque.

Saturday, 11 June 1519, was the feast of Saint Barnabas. In a second letter, written on the duke's birthday, Riccio tells Pagni that "la festa del natale feliciss. di S. Ex. s'è ordinato," and recounts plans for a solemn mass, a *palio*, and fireworks that evening.[8]

Not only was Duke Cosimo's birthday observed on 11 June, but, like Leo X before him, he scheduled important ceremonies of his reign to take place on his fortunate day. Eleonora da Toledo left Naples to make her *entrata* into Florence as Cosimo's bride on 11 June 1539, which Giambullari notes in his account of the events was "il bene avventuroso Natale del nostro Eccellentissimo Signor Duca."[9] Many years later Cosimo invested his son Francesco as ruler of Florence on the same date, making a symbolic parallel with his own birth. According to the diarist, Agostino Lapini, the investiture took place "a dì 11 di giugno 1564, in domenica, che fu il dì proprio della natività del duca Cosimo de' Medici."[10]

Having established the time and place of Cosimo's birth on 11 June 1519, in Florence, we can erect his natal horoscope, either by manual calculation or by computer. As calculated by computer, the positions in degrees and minutes of the house cusps and planets for Cosimo's birth (using 9:18 p.m.) are as follows:

[5] Danti, p. 118. I owe this reference to Thomas B. Settle.

[6] In spite of the evidence given in the text that Cosimo regarded his birthday as 11 June, two of his biographers give the date of 12 June. See Baldini, p. 7 ("i dodici giorni di giugno circa à un'hora e duo terzi di notte"); and Mannucci, p. 32 ("à XII del Mese di Giugno, intorno ad un'hora, e due terzi di notte"); and Gaurico's horoscope for him is based on 12 June (see below, n. 13).

[7] ASF, *Mediceo* 352, f. 169. Quoted by C. O. Tosi, "Il Giorno natalizio di Cosimo I," *L'Illustratore fiorentino*, 1907, p. 81.

[8] ASF, *Mediceo* 352, f. 174. Also quoted by Tosi, but mistakenly with the date 9 June.

[9] Giambullari, p. 3.

[10] Lapini, p. 141. Lapini also gives the date 11 June on p. 93.

ascendant	24 ♑ 33, conjunct ♄ 20 ♑ 17R
2nd cusp	10 ♓ 26
3rd cusp	24 ♈ 53
4th cusp	20 ♉ 49
5th cusp	9 ♊
6th cusp	27 ♊ 28, 6th house ⊙ 29 ♊ 03, ♀ 21 ♋ 37
7th cusp	24 ♋ 33, 7th house ☿ 24 ♋ 37, ♂ 21 ♌ 35
8th cusp	10 ♍ 26, 8th house ♃ 12 ♎ 08
9th cusp	24 ♎ 53
10th cusp	20 ♏ 49
11th cusp	9 ♐, 11th house ☽ 15 ♐ 08
12th cusp	27 ♐ 28

Several natal horoscopes for Cosimo dating from the sixteenth century have survived. The earliest known to me was erected by Duke Cosimo's astrologer, Giuliano Ristori, on 28 June 1537, shortly after Cosimo's assumption of power in Florence (fig. 15).[11] This is a rectified chart, which falsifies Cosimo's birthtime by one half hour, with a consequent "improvement" in planetary positions and aspects.[12] This chart, while not corresponding precisely to Cosimo's natal horoscope, is however useful in relation to astrological imagery in art commissioned by Duke Cosimo (see chapter 11). Some years later, in 1552, a chart for Cosimo was published by Luca Gaurico in his *Tractatus astrologicus*, a collection of horoscopes with brief commentaries.[13] This chart uses a correct time of birth, but it is based on the 12 June date. The last of the horoscopes for Cosimo is Francesco Giuntini's chart of 1581 (fig. 14).[14] It is based on a birthtime only five minutes earlier than the time of 9:18 p.m. on 11 June, which can be determined from Cosimo's baptismal citation. The positions of the house cusps and the planets in this chart are as follows:

ascendant	24 ♑ 16, conjunct ♄ 20 ♑ 25R
2nd cusp	9 ♓
3rd cusp	23 ♈
4th cusp	19 ♉ 51
5th cusp	8 ♊
6th cusp	27 ♊, 6th house ⊙ 29 ♊ 04, ♀ 21 ♋ 47
7th cusp	24 ♋ 16, 7th house ☿ 24 ♋ 16, ♂ 20 ♌ 19
8th cusp	9 ♍, 8th house ♃ 10 ♎ 37
9th cusp	23 ♎
10th cusp	19 ♏ 51
11th cusp	8 ♐, 11th house ☽ 15 ♐ 45
12th cusp	27 ♐

[11] Ristori, f. 135r.

[12] This chart is based on a birthtime of 11 June at 8h, 44m, 32s. Rectification, or verification, of the reported birthtime by the astrologer in the light of subsequent events, and the consequent adjustment of the angles and house cusps of the horoscope, was standard practice among Renaissance astrologers (see Giuntini, 1573, f. 12v-13v, on rectification).

[13] Gaurico, bk. II, f. 16r. Gaurico's citation of the time of birth is "1519 Iunio die 12. hora 2. noctis sequentis (diducto quadrante unius horae)," which he also gives as 9:16 p.m.

[14] Giuntini, 1581, I, p. 127. The time citation is as follows: "1519. Die 11. Iunii hora 9.m.13.2.56 post meridiem."

By comparing these figures it can be seen that the horoscope erected on the basis of modern computerized tables (including those used for the determination of mean astronomical sunset) based on a time of birth deduced from contemporary documents (9:18 p.m.) is virtually identical to the chart calculated according to Renaissance manual methods by Guintini on the basis of a reported birthtime of 9:13 p.m. Clearly, charts based on Gaurico's and Danti's time of 9:16 p.m. would be similar. For simplicity (since I reproduce Guintini's chart, fig. 14), I have referred to his planetary positions in the text, as well as using them in fig. 17, in which Cosimo's horoscope is erected according to the equal-house system of domification (see chapter 9, nn. 25-26).

APPENDIX II
Texts related to Pontormo's
Vertumnus and Pomona

Ovid, *Metamorphoses* XIV, lines 623-97, 765-71 (tr. F. J. Miller, London, 1916, II, pp. 344-55).

Rege sub hoc Pomona fuit, qua nulla Latinas
inter hamadryadas coluit sollertius hortos
nec fuit arborei studiosior altera fetus;
unde tenet nomen: non silvas illa nec amnes,
rus amat et ramos felicia poma ferentes;
nec iaculo gravis est, sed adunca dextera falce,
qua modo luxuriem premit et spatiantia passim
bracchia conpescit, fisso modo cortice lignum
inserit et sucos alieno praestat alumno;
nec sentire sitim patitur bibulaeque recurvas
radicis fibras labentibus inrigat undis.
hic amor, hoc studium, Veneris quoque nulla cupido est;
vim tamen agrestum metuens pomaria claudit
intus et accessus prohibet refugitque viriles.
quid non et Satyri, saltatibus apta iuventus,
fecere et pinu praecincti cornua Panes
Silenusque, suis semper iuvenilior annis,
quique deus fures vel falce vel inguine terret,
ut poterentur ea? sed enim superabat amando
hos quoque Vertumnus neque erat felicior illis.
o quotiens habitu duri messoris aristas
corbe tulit verique fuit messoris imago!
tempora saepe gerens faeno religata recenti
desectum poterat gramen versasse videri;

saepe manu stimulos rigida portabat, ut illum
iurares fessos modo disiunxisse iuvencos.
falce data frondator erat vitisque putator;
induerat scalas: lecturum poma putares;
miles erat gladio, piscator harundine sumpta;
denique per multas aditum sibi saepe figuras
repperit, ut caperet spectatae gaudia formae.
ille etiam picta redimitus tempora mitra,
innitens baculo, positis per tempora canis,
adsimulavit anum cultosque intravit in hortos
pomaque mirata est "tanto" que "potentior!" inquit
paucaque laudatae dedit oscula, qualia numquam
vera dedisset anus, glaebaque incurva resedit
suspiciens pandos autumni pondere ramos.
ulmus erat contra speciosa nitentibus uvis:
quam socia postquam pariter cum vite probavit,
"at si staret" ait "caelebs sine palmite truncus,
nil praeter frondes, quare peteretur, haberet;
haec quoque, quae iuncta est, vitis requiescit in ulmo:
si non nupta foret, terrae acclinata iaceret;
tu tamen exemplo non tangeris arboris huius
concubitusque fugis nec te coniungere curas.
atque utinam velles! Helene non pluribus esset
sollicitata procis nec quae Lapitheia movit
proelia nec coniunx timidi, haud audacis Ulixis.
nunc quoque, cum fugias averserisque petentes,
mille viri cupiunt et semideique deique
et quaecumque tenent Albanos numina montes.
sed tu si sapies, si te bene iungere anumque
hanc audire voles, quae te plus omnibus illis,
plus, quam credis, amo: vulgares reice taedas
Vertumnumque tori socium tibi selige! pro quo
me quoque pignus habes: neque enim sibi notior ille est,
quam mihi; nec passim toto vagus errat in orbe,
haec loca magna colit; nec, uti pars magna procorum,
quam modo vidit, amat: tu primus et ultimus illi
ardor eris, solique suos tibi devovet annos.
adde, quod est iuvenis, quod naturale decoris
munus habet formasque apte fingetur in omnes,
et quod erit iussus, iubeas licet omnia, fiet.
quid, quod amatis idem, quod, quae tibi poma coluntur,
primus habet laetaque tenet tua munera dextra!

sed neque iam fetus desiderat arbore demptos
nec, quas hortus alit, cum sucis mitibus herbas
nec quicquam nisi te: miserere ardentis et ipsum,
quod petit, ore meo praesentum crede precari.
ultoresque deos et pectora dura perosam
Idalien memoremque time Rhamnusidis iram!
quoque magis timeas, (etenim mihi multa vetustas
scire dedit) referam tota notissima Cypro
facta, quibus flecti facile et mitescere possis.

. . .

Haec ubi nequiquam formae deus aptus anili
edidit, in iuvenem rediit et anilia demit
instrumenta sibi talisque apparuit illi,
qualis ubi oppositas nitidissima solis imago
evicit nubes nullaque obstante reluxit,
vimque parat: sed vi non est opus, inque figura
capta dei nympha est et mutua vulnera sensit.

Pomona flourished under this king, than whom there was no other Latian wood-nymph more skilled in garden-culture nor more zealous in the care of fruitful trees. Hence was her name. She cared nothing for woods and rivers, but only for the fields and branches laden with delicious fruits. She carried no javelin in her hand, but the curved pruning-hook with which now she repressed the too luxuriant growth and cut back the branches spreading out on every side, and now, making an incision in the bark, would engraft a twig and give juices to an adopted bough. Nor would she permit them to suffer thirst, but watered the twisted fibres of the thirsty roots with her trickling streams. This was her love; this was her chief desire; nor did she have any care for Venus; yet, fearing some clownish violence, she shut herself up within her orchard and so guarded herself against all approach of man. What did not the Satyrs, a young dancing band, do to win her, and the Pans, their horns encircled with wreaths of pine, and Silvanus, always more youthful than his years, and that god who warns off evil doers with his sickle or his ugly shape? But, indeed, Vertumnus surpassed them all in love; yet he was no more fortunate than they. Oh, how often in the garb of a rough reaper did he bring her a basket of barley-ears! And he was the perfect image of a reaper, too. Often he would come with his temples wreathed with fresh hay, and could easily seem to have been turning the new-mown grass. Again he would appear carrying an ox-goad in his clumsy hand, so that you would swear that he had but now unyoked his weary cattle. He would be a leaf-gatherer and vine-pruner with hook in hand; he would come along with a ladder on his shoulder and you would think him about to gather apples. He would be a soldier with a sword, or a fisherman with a rod. In fact, by means of his many disguises, he obtained frequent admission to her presence and had much joy in looking on her beauty. He also put on a wig of grey hair, bound his temples with a gaudy head-cloth, and, leaning on a staff, came in the disguise of an old woman, entered the well-kept garden and, after admiring the fruit, said: "But you are far more beautiful," and he kissed her several times as no real old woman ever would have done. The bent old creature sat down on the grass, gazing at the branches bending beneath the weight of autumn fruits. There was a shapely elm-tree opposite, covered with gleaming bunches of grapes. After he had looked approvingly at this awhile, together with its vine companion, he said: "But if that tree stood there unmated to the vine, it would have no value save for its leaves alone; and this vine, which clings to and rests safely on the elm, if it were not thus wedded, it would lie languishing, flat upon the ground. But you are not touched by the vine's example and you shun wedlock and do not desire to be joined to another. And I would that you did desire it! Then would you have more suitors than ever Helen had, or she for whom the Lapithae took arms, or the wife of the timid, not the bold, Ulysses. And even as it is, though you shun them and turn in contempt from their wooing, a thousand men desire you, and half-gods and gods and all the divinities that haunt the Alban hills. But if you will be wise, and consent to a good match and will listen to an old woman like me, who love you more than all the rest, yes, more than you would believe, reject all common offers and choose Vertumnus as the consort of your couch. You have me also as guaranty for him; for he is not better known to himself than he is to me. He does not wander idly throughout the world, but he dwells in the wide spaces here at hand; nor, as most of your suitors do, does he fall in love at sight with every girl he meets. You will be his first love and his last, and to you alone he will devote his life. Consider also that he is young, blest with a native charm, can readily assume whatever form he will, and what you bid him, though without stint you bid, he will perform. Moreover your tastes are similar, and the fruit which you so cherish he is the first to have and with joyful hands he lays hold upon your gifts. But neither the fruit of your trees, nor the sweet, succulent herbs which your garden bears, nor anything at all does he desire save you alone. Pity him who loves you so, and believe that he himself in very presence through my lips is begging for what he wants. And have a thought for the avenging gods and the Idalian goddess [Venus] who detests the hard of heart, and the unforgetting wrath of Nemesis! And that you may the more fear these (for my long life has brought me knowledge of many things), I will tell you a story that is well known all over Cyprus, by which you may learn to be easily persuaded and to be soft of heart.

. . .

When the god in the form of age had thus pleaded his cause in vain, he returned to his youthful form, put off the old woman's trappings, and stood revealed to the maiden as when the sun's most beaming face has conquered the opposing clouds and shines out with nothing to dim his radiance. He was all ready to force her will, but no force was necessary; and the nymph, smitten by the beauty of the god, felt an answering passion.

Virgil, *Georgics* I, lines 1-42 (tr. H. R. Fairclough, London, 1916, pp. 80-83).

> Quid faciat laetas segetes, quo sidere terram
> vertere, Maecenas, ulmisque adiungere vites

conveniat, quae cura boum, qui cultus habendo
sit pecori, apibus quanta experientia parcis,
hinc canere incipiam. vos, o clarissima mundi
lumina, labentem caelo quae ducitis annum,
Liber et alma Ceres, vestro si munere tellus
Chaoniam pingui glandem mutavit arista,
poculaque inventis Acheloia miscuit uvis;
et vos, agrestum praesentia numina, Fauni,
(ferte simul Faunique pedem Dryadesque puellae!)
munera vestra cano. tuque o, cui prima frementem
fudit equum magno tellus percussa tridenti,
Neptune; et cultor nemorum, cui pinguia Ceae
ter centum nivei tondent dumeta iuvenci;
ipse, nemus linquens patrium saltusque Lycaei,
Pan, ovium custos, tua si tibi Maenala curae,
adsis, o Tegeaee, favens, oleaeque Minerva
inventrix, uncique puer monstrator aratri,
et teneram ab radice ferens, Silvane, cupressum;
dique deaeque omnes, studium quibus arva tueri,
quique novas alitis non ullo semine fruges,
quique satis largum caelo demittitis imbrem;
tuque adeo, quem mox quae sint habitura deorum
concilia, incertum est, urbisne invisere, Caesar,
terrarumque velis curam et te maximus orbis
auctorem frugum tempestatumque potentem
accipiat, cingens materna tempora myrto,
an deus immensi venias maris ac tua nautae
numina sola colant, tibi serviat ultima Thule,
teque sibi generum Tethys emat omnibus undis,
anne novum tardis sidus te mensibus addas,
qua locus Erigonen inter Chelasque sequentis
panditur (ipse tibi iam bracchia contrahit ardens
Scorpios et caeli iusta plus parte reliquit):
quidquid eris (name te nec sperant Tartara regem
nec tibi regnandi veniat tam dira cupido,
quamvis Elysios miretur Graecia campos
nec repetita sequi curet Proserpina matrem),
da facilem cursum, atque audacibus adnue coeptis,
ignarosque viae mecum miseratus agrestis
ingredere et votis iam nunc adsuesce vocari.

What makes the crops joyous, beneath what star, Maecenas, it is well to turn the soil,
and wed vines to elms, what tending the kine need, what care the herd in breeding,

what skill the thrifty bees—hence shall I begin my song. O ye most radiant lights of the firmament, that guide through heaven the gliding year, O Liber and bounteous Ceres, if by your grace Earth changed Chaonia's acorn for the rich corn-ear, and blended draughts of Achelous with the new-found grapes, and ye, O Fauns the rustics' ever-present gods (come trip it, Fauns, and Dryad maids withal!), 'tis of your bounties I sing. And thou, O Neptune, for whom Earth, smitten by thy mighty trident, first sent forth the neighing steed; thou, too, O spirit of the groves, for whom thrice an hundred snowy steers crop Cea's rich thickets; thyself, too, O Pan, guardian of the sheep, leaving thy native woods and glades of Lycaeus, as thou lovest thine own Maenalus, come to thy grace, O Tegean lord! Come thou, O Minerva, inventress of the olive; thou, too, O youth, who didst disclose the crooked plough; and thou, O Silvanus, with a young uprooted cypress in thy hand; and ye, O gods and goddesses all, whose love guards our fields—both ye who nurse the young fruits, springing up unsown, and ye who on the seedlings send down from heaven plenteous rain!

Yea, and thou, O Caesar, whom we know not what company of the gods shall claim ere long; whether thou choose to watch over cities and care for our lands, that so the mighty world may receive thee as the giver of increase and lord of the seasons, wreathing thy brows with thy mother's myrtle; whether thou come as god of the boundless sea and sailors worship thy deity alone, while farthest Thule owns thy lordship and Tethys with the dower of all her waves buys thee to wed her daughter; or whether thou add thyself as a new star to the lingering months, where, between the Virgin and the grasping Claws, a space is opening (lo! for thee even now the blazing Scorpion draws in his arms, and has left more than a due share of the heaven!)—whate'er thou art to be (for Tartarus hopes not for thee as king, and may such monstrous lust of empire ne'er seize thee, albeit Greece is enchanted by the Elysian fields, and Proserpine reclaimed cares not to follow her mother), do thou grant me a smooth course, give assent to my bold emprise, and pitying with me the rustics who know not their way, enter on thy worship, and learn even now to hearken to our prayers!

Virgil, *Georgics* II, lines 458-74; 532-40 (tr. H. R. Fairclough, London, 1916, pp. 148-49, 152-53).

> O fortunatos nimium, sua si bona norint,
> agricolas! quibus ipsa, procul discordibus armis
> fundit humo facilem victum iustissima tellus.
> si non ingentem foribus domus alta superbis
> mane salutantum totis vomit aedibus undam,
> nec varios inhiant pulchra testudine postis
> inlusasque auro vestis Ephyreiaque aera,
> alba neque Assyrio fucatur lana veneno,
> nec casia liquidi corrumpitur usus olivi:
> at secura quies et nescia fallere vita,
> dives opum variarum, at latis otia fundis

> (speluncae vivique lacus et frigida Tempe
> mugitusque boum mollesque sub arbore somni)
> non absunt; illic saltus ac lustra ferarum,
> et patiens operum exiguoque adsueta iuventus,
> sacra deum sanctique patres: extrema per illos
> Iustitia excedens terris vestigia fecit.

O happy husbandmen! too happy, should they come to know their blessings! for whom, far from the clash of arms, most righteous Earth, unbidden, pours forth from her soil an easy sustenance. What though no stately mansion with proud portals disgorges at dawn from all its halls a tide of vistors, though they never gaze at doors inlaid with lovely tortoise-shell or at raiment tricked with gold or at bronzes of Ephyra, though their white wool be not stained with Assyrian dye, or their clear oil's service spoiled by cassia? Yet theirs is repose without care, and a life that knows no fraud, but is rich in treasures manifold. Yea, the ease of broad domains, caverns, and living lakes, and cool vales, the lowing of the kine, and soft slumbers beneath the trees—all are theirs. They have woodland glades and the haunts of game; a youth hardened to toil and inured to scanty fare; worship of gods and reverence for age; among them, as she quitted the earth, Justice planted her latest steps.

> hanc olim veteres vitam coluere Sabini,
> hanc Remus et frater, sic fortis Etruria crevit
> scilicet et rerum facta est pulcherrima Roma,
> septemque una sibi muro circumdedit acres.
> ante etiam sceptrum Dictaei regis et ante
> impia quam caesis gens est epulata iuvencis,
> aureus hanc vitam in terris Saturnus agebat;
> necdum etiam audierant inflari classica, necdum
> impositos duris crepitare incudibus ensis.

Such a life the old Sabines once lived, such Remus and his brother. Thus, surely, Etruria waxed strong, thus Rome became of all things the fairest, and with a single city's wall enclosed her seven hills. Nay, before the Cretan king held sceptre, and before a godless race banqueted on slaughtered bullocks, such was the life golden Saturn lived on earth, while yet none had heard the clarion blare, none the sword-blades ring, as they were laid on the stubborn anvil.

Ariosto, *Capitoli*, III (in L. Ariosto, *Opere minori*, ed. C. Segre, Milan-Naples, 1954, pp. 171-73).

> Ne la stagion che 'l bel tempo rimena,
> di mia man posi un ramuscel di Lauro
> a mezo colle, in una piaggia amena,
>   che di bianco, d'azur, vermiglio e d'auro
> fioriva sempre, e sempre il sol scolpriva,

o fusse all'Indo o fusse al lito mauro
   Quivi traendo or per erbosa riva,
or rorando con man la tepida onda,
or rimovendo la gleba nativa,
   or riponendo più lieta e feconda,
fei sì con studio e con assidua cura,
che 'l Lauro ebbe radice e nuova fronda.
   Fu sì benigna a' miei desir Natura,
che la tenera verga crescer vidi,
e divenir solida pianta e dura.
   Dolci ricetti, solitari e fidi,
mi fur queste ombre, ove sfogar potei
sicura il cor con amorosi gridi.
   Vener, lasciando i templi citerei
e li altari e le vittime e li odori
di Gnido e di Amatunte e de' Sabei,
   sovente con le Grazie in lieti cori
vi danzò intorno; e per li rami in tanto
salian scherzando i pargoletti Amori.
   Spesso Diana con le ninfe a canto
l'arbuscel suavissimo prepose
alle selve d'Eurota e d'Eriamanto.
   E queste ed altre dèe sotto l'ombrose
frondi, mentre in piacer stavano e in festa,
benediron tra lor chi il ramo pose.
   Lassa! onde uscì la boreal tempesta?
onde la bruma? onde il rigor e il gelo?
onde la neve, a' danni miei sì presta?
   Come gli ha tolto il suo favore il Cielo?
Langue il mio Lauro, e de la bella spoglia
nudo gli resta e senza onor il stelo.
   Verdeggia un ramo sol con poca foglia,
e fra tema e speranza sto suspesa,
se mi lo lasci il verno o mi lo toglia.
   Ma più che la speranza il timor pesa
che contra il giaccio rio, ch'ancor non cessa,
il debil ramo avrà poca difesa.
   Deh! perché, inanzi che sia in tutto oppressa
l'egra radice, non è chi m'insegni
com'esser possa al suo vigor rimessa?
   Febo, rettor de li superni segni,
aiuta 'l sacro Lauro, onde corona
più volte avesti nei tessali regni;

concedi, Bacco, Vertunno e Pomona,
satiri, fauno, driade e napee,
che nuova fronde il Lauro mio ripona;
    soccorran tutti i dèi, tutte le dèe
che de li arbori han cura, l'arbor mio;
però che gli è fatal: se viver dee,
    vivo io, se dee morir, seco moro io.

SELECTED BIBLIOGRAPHY

This bibliography includes all works cited more than once in the notes, where they are referred to by the abbreviations given in the left-hand column below. Works which are cited only once are not included here; full bibliographical data for them are given in the notes.

PRIMARY SOURCES

Allori	"I ricordi di Alessandro Allori," ed. I. B. Supino, *Biblioteca della Rivista d'Arte*, Florence, 1908.
Altieri	M. Altieri, "Avviso intorno alla Civiltà donata alla casa de Medici," in F. Cruciani, *Il teatro del Campidoglio e le feste romane del 1513*, Milan, 1968, pp. 3-20.
Aratus, *Phaenomena*	Aratus, *The Phaenomena*, tr. G. R. Mair, London and New York, 1921.
Ariosto	L. Ariosto, *Opere minori*, ed. C. Segre, Milan-Naples, 1954.
Baldini	B. Baldini, *Vita di Cosimo de' Medici Primo Gran Duca di Toscana*, Florence, 1578.
Bellincioni	"Le Rime di Bernardo Bellincioni riscontrate sui manoscritti," ed. P. Fanfani, *Scelta di Curiosità letterarie inedite o rare dal secolo XIII al XVII*, vol. 160, Bologna, 1878.
Boccaccio	*Della Genealogia de gli Dei di M. Giovanni Boccaccio*, Venice, 1581.
R. Borghini	R. Borghini, *Il Riposo*, Florence, 1584.
V. Borghini	*Carteggio artistico inedito di Don Vincenzo Borghini*, ed. A. Lorenzoni, Florence, 1912.
Bottari-Ticozzi	*Raccolta di lettere sulla pittura, scultura ed architettura scritte da' più celebri personaggi dei secoli XV, XVI, e XVII*, ed. G. S. Bottari and S. Ticozzi, 8 vols., Milan, 1822-1825.
Cambi	G. Cambi, "Istorie (1458-1534)," III, ed. Fr. I. di San Luigi, *Delizie degli eruditi toscani*, vol. 22, Florence, 1785-1786.

Canzone   *Canzone pallesca*, Florence: Zanobi di Barba, 1512.

Cardano   G. Cardano, *Libello Duo: Unus De supplemento almanach, Alter De restitutione temporum et motum coelestium; Item Geniturae LXVII insignes, casibus et fortuna cum espositione*, Nuremberg, 1543.

Carmina   *Carmina illustrium poetarum italorum*, ed. G. Bottari, 11 vols., Florence, 1719-1726.

Cartari   V. Cartari, *Le imagini de i dei degli antichi . . .* , Venice, 1571, 1581, 1674.

Cini   G. B. Cini, "Descrizione dell'apparato fatto in Firenze per le nozze dell'Illustrissimo ed Eccellentissimo Don Francesco de' Medici Principe di Firenze e di Siena e della Serenissima Regina Giovanna d'Austria," in Vasari, VIII, pp. 521-622.

Cirni   A. F. Cirni, *La Reale Entrata dell. Ecc.mo Sig.nor Duca e Duchessa di Fiorenza in Siena con la significatione delle Latine inscrittioni e con alcuni Sonetti*, Rome, 1560.

Claudian,   Claudian, *De Consulatu Stilichonis*, tr. M. Platnauer, London
   De Consulatu   and New York, 1922.
   Stilichonis

Columella,   Columella, *De re rustica*, tr. H. B. Ash, E. S. Forster, and
   De re rustica   E. H. Heffner, 3 vols., London and Cambridge, 1955.

Conti   C. Conti, *La prima Reggia di Cosimo de' Medici nel Palazzo già della Signoria di Firenze, coll'appoggio di un inventario inedito del 1553*, Florence, 1893.

Dante   Dante Alighieri, *La Divina Commedia*, tr. J. D. Sinclair as *The Divine Comedy of Dante Alighieri*, 3 vols., London, 1939-1946.

Danti   E. Danti, *Trattato dell'uso et della fabbrica dell'astrolabio di F. Egnatio Danti*, Florence, 1569.

Dati   L. Dati, *La Sfera*, Florence, Biblioteca Medicea-Laurenziana, MS conv. soppr. 444.

De Ruberti   B. De Ruberti, *Osservatione da Astrologia, et altre appartenze circa alla medicina et mutazione de tempi*, Florence, 1567.

Fanfani   "Ricordo d'una giostra fatta a Firenze a dì 7 di Febbraio 1468 [1469] sulla Piazza Santa Croce," ed. P. Fanfani, *Il Borghini: Giornale di Filologia e di Lettere italiane*, 2, 1864, pp. 475-83, 530-42.

Fanti   S. Fanti, *Triompho di Fortuna*, Venice, 1526.

Ferreri   Z. Ferreri, "Lugdunense somnium de divi leonis decimi pontificis maximi ad summum pontificatum divina promotione," ed. G. Bottari, *Carmina illustrium poetarum italorum*, Florence, 1719-1726, vol. 4, pp. 270-97.

Ficino, *De Amore*   M. Ficino, *De Amore*, in *Marsilio Ficino's Commentary on Plato's "Symposium,"* tr. S. R. Jayne, Columbia, Mo., 1944.

Ficino, *Opera*   M. Ficino, *Opera omnia* (Basel, 1576), facs. ed. with introduction by P. O. Kristeller, 2 vols., Turin, 1962.

Fulvio   *Illustrium imagines. Imperatorum et illustrium virorum ac mulierum vultus ex antiquis nomismatibus expressi . . . per Andream Fulvium,* Rome, 1518.

Gaurico   L. Gaurico, *Tractatus astrologicus in quo agitur de preteritis multorum hominum accidentibus per proprias locum genituras ad unguem examanitis,* Venice, 1552.

Giambullari   P. F. Giambullari, *Apparato et feste nelle noze dello Illustrissimo Signor Duca di Firenze, et della Duchessa sua consorte, con le sue stanze, madriali, comedia, et intermedii, in quella recitati,* Florence, 1539 (for a translation, see Minor-Mitchell).

Giannotti   "Lettere inedite di Donato Giannotti," ed. L. A. Ferrai, *Atti del Reale Istituto Veneto di Scienze, Lettere, ed Arti,* ser. 6, III, 1884-1885, pp. 1567-96.

Giovio, 1551   P. Giovio, *Le vite di Leon X et d'Adriano VI sommi Pontefici, et del Cardinale Pompeo Colonna,* tr. L. Domenichi, Florence, 1551.

Giovio, 1554   ———, *Elogi,* tr. L. Domenichi, Florence, 1554.

Giovio, 1556   ———, *Dialogo dell'imprese militari e amorose,* Rome, 1556.

Giovio, 1557   ———, *Elogia Virorum literis illustrium . . . ,* Basel, 1577.

Giovio, *Lettere*   *Lettere di Paolo Giovio,* ed. G. G. Ferrero, 2 vols., Rome, 1956-1958.

Giraldi   L. G. Giraldi, *Herculis vita,* Basel, 1539.

Giuntini, 1573   F. Giuntini, *Speculum astrologiae,* Lyon, 1573.

Giuntini, 1581   ———, *Speculum astrologiae,* 2 vols., Lyon, 1581.

Grazzini   *Tutti i Trionfi . . . del tempo del Magnifico Lorenzo de' Medici fino all'anno 1559,* ed. A. F. Grazzini, 2 vols., Florence, 1750.

Gualterotti   R. Gualterotti, *Descrizione del Regale apparato per le nozze della Ser.ma Madama Cristina di Lorena moglie del Ser.mo Don Ferdinando Medici III Granduca di Toscana,* 2 vols., Florence, 1589.

Guicciardini   F. Guicciardini, *Opere,* ed. R. Palmarocchi, 2 vols., Milan, 1941-1942.

Hyginus, *Poetica astronomica*   Hyginus, *Poetica Astronomica,* tr. M. Grant, as *The Myths of Hyginus,* Lawrence, Kans., 1960.

Landino   *Christophori Landini Commentaria in Bucolica, Georgica, et Aeneida Virgilii ad Petrum Medicem Magni Laurentii filium . . . ,* Florence, Biblioteca Medicea-Laurenziana, MS Plut. 53, 37.

Landucci   *Diario fiorentino dal 1450 al 1516 di Luca Landucci continuato da un anonimo fino al 1542,* ed. I. del Badia, Florence, 1883.

Lapini	*Diario fiorentino di Agostino Lapini dal 252 al 1596*, ed. G. O. Corazzini, Florence, 1900.
Lauretum	*Lauretum, sive carmina in laudem Laurentii Medicis*, ed. D. Moreni, Florence, 1820.
Leopold of Austria	Leopold of Austria, *De Astrorum scientia*, Augsburg, 1489.
Livy, *History of Rome*	Livy, *History of Rome*, tr. F. G. Moore, E. T. Sage, et al., 14 vols., Cambridge, 1949-1958.
Lorenzo, *Opere*	Lorenzo de' Medici il Magnifico, *Opere*, ed. A. Simioni, 2 vols., Bari, 1914.
Machiavelli	N. Machiavelli, *Istorie fiorentine*, ed. P. Carli, 2 vols., Florence, 1927.
Macrobius, *Saturnalia*	Macrobius, *The Saturnalia*, tr. P. V. Davies, New York, 1969.
Macrobius, *Somnium Scipionis*	———, *Commentary on the Dream of Scipio*, tr. W. H. Stahl, New York, 1952.
Manilius, *Astronomica*	M. Manilius, *Astronomica*, tr. G. P. Goold, Cambridge and London, 1977.
Mannucci	A. Mannucci, *Vita di Cosimo de' Medici primo Granduca di Toscana*, Bologna, 1586.
Martelli	*Dal primo e dal secondo libro delle Lettere di Niccolò Martelli*, ed. C. Marconcini, Lanciano, 1916.
Matasilani	M. Matasilani, *La felicità del Ser. Cosimo de' Medici Granduca di Toscana*, Florence, 1572.
Maternus, *Mathesis*	*Maternus, Mathesis*, tr. J. R. Bram, as *Ancient Astrology, Theory and Practice: Matheseos Libri VIII by Firmicus Maternus*, Park Ridge, N.J., 1975.
Naldi, *Bucolica*	*Bucolica, Volaterrais, Hastiludium, Carmina varia Naldi Naldii florentini*, ed. W. L. Grant, Florence, 1974.
Naldi, *Elegiarum*	Naldo Naldi, *Elegiarum libri III ad Laurentium Medicem*, ed. L. Juhász, Leipzig, 1934.
Ovid, *Fasti*	Ovid, *Fasti*, tr. J. G. Frazer, London and New York, 1931.
Ovid, *Metamorphoses*	———, *Metamorphoses*, tr. F. J. Miller, 2 vols., London and New York, 1916.
Palliolo	P. Palliolo, "Narratione delli spectacoli celebrati in Campidoglio," in F. Cruciani, *Il teatro del Campidoglio e le feste romane del 1513*, Milan, 1968, pp. 21-67.
Penni	G. G. Penni, "Cronicha delle magnifiche et honorate pompe fatte in Roma per la creatione et incoronatione di Papa Leone X. Pont. Max.," in G. Roscoe, *Vita e pontificato di Leone X, con annotazioni e documenti inediti di L. Bossi*, Milan, 1816-1817, vol. 5, pp. 189-231.
Petrarch	Petrarch, *De viris illustribus vitae*, ed. L. Razzolini, 2 vols., Bologna, 1874.
Pittoni	B. Pittoni, *Imprese di diversi Principi, Duchi, Signori, e d'altri*

Personaggi, et Huomini illustri: Nuovamente ristampata con alcune stanze, sonetti di M. Lodovico Dolce, Venice, 1602.

Poliziano, *Le Selve*
A. Poliziano, *Le Selve e la strega: prolusioni nello studio fiorentino (1482-1492)*, ed. I. Del Lungo, Florence, 1925.

Poliziano, *Le Stanze*
Le Stanze, l'Orfeo, e le Rime di Messer Angelo Poliziano, ed. G. Carducci, Florence, 1863 (tr. D. Quint as *The "Stanze" of Angelo Poliziano*, Amherst, Mass., 1979).

Pontano
Gli Orti delle Esperidi di Giangioviano Pontano, tr. J. A. Deluca, Venice, 1761.

Ptolemy, *Tetrabiblos*
Ptolemy, *Tetrabiblos*, tr. F. E. Robbins, Cambridge and London, 1956.

Pulci
L. Pulci, *La Giostra di Lorenzo de Medici messa in rima da Luigi Pulci l'anno MCCCCLXVIIII*, Florence, 1518.

Ridolfi
R. Ridolfi, "Diario fiorentino di anonimo delle cose occorse l'anno 1537," *Archivio storico italiano*, 116, 1958, pp. 544-76.

Ristori
G. Ristori, *Della stella di Vostra Ecc.tia*, Florence, Biblioteca Medicea-Laurenziana, MS Plut. 89 sup., 34.

Ruscelli
G. Ruscelli, *Le Imprese illustri*, Venice, 1572.

Salutati
Colucii Salutati, De Laboribus Herculis, ed. B. L. Ullman, 2 vols., Zurich, 1951.

Sanuto
I Diarii di Marino Sanuto (1496-1533), 59 vols., Venice, 1879-1903.

Schöner
J. Schöner, *I Tre Libri della Natività*, tr. G. B. Carello, Venice, 1554.

Sereno
A. Sereno, "Theatrum Capitolinum Magnifico Juliano institutum . . . ," in F. Cruciani, *Il teatro del Campidoglio e le feste romane del 1513*, Milan, 1968, pp. 95-123.

Servius
Servii grammatici in Vergilii carmina commentarii, ed. G. Thilo and H. Hagen, 3 vols., Leipzig, 1878-1902; repr. Hildesheim, 1961.

Sonetti
Sonetti capitoli in laude della inclita casa de Medici nuovamente composti, Florence: Zanobi di Barba, 1512.

Suetonius, *Lives*
Seutonius, *The Lives of the Caesars*, tr. G. C. Rolfs, 2 vols., London and New York, 1914.

Valeriano
P. Valeriano, *I Ieroglifici*, Venice, 1602, 1625.

Varchi
B. Varchi, *Storia fiorentina*, ed. L. Arbib, 3 vols., Florence, 1843-1844.

Vasari
G. Vasari, *Le vite de' più eccellenti pittori scultori ed architettori scritte da Giorgio Vasari pittore aretino*, in *Opere*, ed. G. Milanesi, 9 vols., Florence, 1878-1885 (tr. G. Du C. de Vere as *Lives of the most eminent painters, sculptors and architects*, 3 vols., New York, 1979).

Vasari, *Rag.*
———, "Ragionamenti: Dialoghi intorno alle pitture fatte nelle

	nuove stanze del Palazzo Vecchio," in *Opere*, ed. G. Milanesi, Florence, 1878-1885, vol. 8, pp. 9-225.
Vasari-Del Vita	*Il libro delle ricordanze di Giorgio Vasari*, ed. A. Del Vita, Arezzo, 1927.
Vasari-Frey	*Der literarische Nachlass Giorgio Vasaris*, ed. K. Frey, 3 vols., Munich, 1923-1940.
Versi	*Versi posti a Pasquillo ne lanno MD. xxiij*, Rome, 1513.
Villani	*Cronica di Giovanni Villani*, ed. F. G. Dragomanni, 4 vols., Florence, 1844.
Virgil, *Aeneid*	Virgil, *Aeneid*, tr. H. R. Fairclough, 2 vols., London and New York, 1916 and 1918.
Virgil, *Eclogues*	———, *Eclogues*, tr. H. R. Fairclough, London and New York, 1916.
Virgil, *Georgics*	———, *Georgics*, tr. H. R. Fairclough, London and New York, 1916.
Virgil, *Opera*	*P. Virgilii maioris opera*, Strassburg: Brant, 1502.

SECONDARY SOURCES

Adelson, 1975	C. Adelson, *"Fiorenza lieta": Benedetto Varchi's Program for the Villa and Gardens of Castello*, M.A. thesis, New York University, 1975.
Adelson, 1980	———, "Bachiacca, Salviati and the Decoration of the Sala dell' Udienza in Palazzo Vecchio," in *Le Arti del Principato*, Florence, 1980, pp. 141-200.
Albertini	R. von Albertini, *Firenze dalla repubblica al principato: Storia e coscienza politica*, tr. C. Christolini, Turin, 1970.
Allegri-Cecchi	E. Allegri and A. Cecchi, *Palazzo Vecchio e i Medici, Guida Storica*, Florence, 1980.
D. C. Allen	D. C. Allen, *The Star-Crossed Renaissance: The Quarrel About Astrology and its Influence in England*, New York, 1966.
R. H. Allen	R. H. Allen, *Star Names: Their Lore and Meaning*, London, 1899; repr. New York, 1963.
Ames-Lewis	F. Ames-Lewis, "Early Medicean Devices," *Journal of the Warburg and Courtauld Institutes*, 42, 1979, pp. 122-43.
Armand	A. Armand, *Les médailleurs italiens des quinzième et seizième siècles*, 3 vols., Paris, 1883-1887.
Aschoff	W. Aschoff, *Studien zu Niccolò Tribolo*, diss., Frankfurt, 1966; Berlin, 1967.
Baccheschi	E. Baccheschi, *L'opera completa del Bronzino*, Milan, 1973.
Barocchi	P. Barocchi et al., *Palazzo Vecchio: committenza e collezionismo*

medici, Firenze e la Toscana dei Medici nell'Europa del Cinquecento, Florence, 1980.

Baron   H. Baron, *The Crisis of the Early Italian Renaissance: Civic Humanism and Republican Liberty in an age of Classicism and Tyranny*, Princeton, 1966.

Bartsch   A. Bartsch, *Le Peintre Graveur*, 21 vols., Leipzig, 1854-1876.

Beer   A. Beer, "Astronomical Dating of Works of Art," *Vistas in Astronomy*, 9, 1967, pp. 177-223.

Berti, 1967   L. Berti, *Il Principe dello Studiolo: Francesco I dei Medici e la fine del Rinascimento fiorentino*, Florence, 1967.

Berti, 1979   ———, *Gli Uffizi: Catalogo generale*, Florence, 1979.

Berti, 1980   ———, *Il Primato del disegno, Firenze e la Toscana dei Medici nell'Europa del Cinquecento*, Florence, Palazzo Strozzi, 1980.

Borsook   E. Borsook, "Art and Politics at the Medici Court I: The Funeral of Cosimo I de' Medici," *Mitteilungen des Kunsthistorischen Institutes in Florenz*, 12, 1965, pp. 31-54.

Brummer, 1964   H. H. Brummer, "Pan Platonicus," *Konsthistorisk Tidskrift*, 33, 1964, pp. 55-67.

Brummer, 1970   ———, *The Statue Court in the Vatican Belvedere*, Stockholm, 1970.

Bruschi   A. Bruschi, "Il teatro capitolino del 1513," *Bollettino del centro internazionale di studi di architettura Andrea Palladio*, 16, 1974, pp. 189-218.

Chastel, 1945   A. Chastel, "Melancholia in the Sonnets of Lorenzo de' Medici," *Journal of the Warburg and Courtauld Institutes*, 8, 1945, pp. 61-67.

Chastel, 1961   ———, *Art et Humanisme à Florence au temps de Laurent le Magnifique: Etudes sur la Renaissance et l'humanisme Platonicien*, Paris, 1961.

Chastel, 1975   ———, *Marsile Ficin et l'art*, Geneva, 1975.

Cheney   I. H. Cheney, *Francesco Salviati (1510-1563)*, diss., New York University, 1963; Ann Arbor, 1963.

Clapp   F. M. Clapp, *Jacopo Carucci da Pontormo, His Life and Work*, New Haven, 1916.

Costa   G. Costa, *La leggenda dei secoli d'oro nella letteratura italiana*, Bari, 1972.

Cox-Rearick, 1964   J. Cox-Rearick, *The Drawings of Pontormo*, 2 vols., Cambridge, Mass., 1964; revised ed. New York, 1981.

Cox-Rearick, 1971   ———, "The Drawings of Pontormo: Addenda," *Master Drawings*, 8, 1971, pp. 363-78.

Cox-Rearick, 1982   ———, "Themes of Time and Rule at Poggio a Caiano: The Portico Frieze of Lorenzo il Magnifico," *Mitteilungen des Kunsthistorischen Institutes in Florenz*, 26, 1982, pp. 42-68.

Cruciani	F. Cruciani, *Il teatro del Campidoglio e le feste romane del 1513 con la ricostruzione architettonica del teatro di Arnaldo Bruschi*, Milan, 1968.
D'Ancona	P. D'Ancona, *La miniatura fiorentina*, 2 vols., Florence, 1914.
Dempsey	C. Dempsey, "Mercurius Ver: the Sources of Botticelli's *Primavera*," *Journal of the Warburg and Courtauld Institutes*, 33, 1968, pp. 251-73.
Deonna	W. Deonna, "The Crab and the Butterfly: a Study in Animal Symbolism," *Journal of the Warburg and Courtauld Institutes*, 17, 1954, pp. 47-86.
Devonshire Jones	R. Devonshire Jones, *Francesco Vettori: Florentine Citizen and Medici Servant*, London, 1972.
Dezzi Bardeschi	M. Dezzi Bardeschi, "Sole in Leone. Leon Battista Alberti: astrologia, cosmologia e tradizione ermetica nella facciata di Santa Maria Novella," *Psicon*, 1, 1974, pp. 33-68.
Dotson	E. G. Dotson, "An Augustinian Interpretation of Michelangelo's Sistine Ceiling," *Art Bulletin*, 61, 1979, pp. 223-56, 405-29.
Dwyer	E. J. Dwyer, "Augustus and the Capricorn," *Deutschen Archaeologischen Instituts Roemische Abteilung. Mitteilungen*, 80, 1973, pp. 59-67.
Ettlinger, 1972	L. D. Ettlinger, "Hercules Florentinus," *Mitteilungen des Kunsthistorischen Institutes in Florenz*, 16, 1972, pp. 119-42.
Ettlinger, 1978	———, "The Liturgical Function of Michelangelo's Medici Chapel," *Mitteilungen des Kunsthistorischen Institutes in Florenz*, 22, 1978, pp. 287-304.
Fanelli	G. Fanelli, *Firenze, architettura e città*, 2 vols., Florence, 1973.
Forster, 1966	K. W. Forster, *Pontormo: Monographie mit kritischem Katalog*, Munich, 1966.
Forster, 1971	———, "Metaphors of Rule: Political Ideology and History in the Portraits of Cosimo I de' Medici," *Mitteilungen des Kunsthistorischen Institutes in Florenz*, 15, 1971, pp. 65-104.
Foster	P. E. Foster, *A Study of Lorenzo de' Medici's Villa at Poggio a Caiano*, diss., Yale University, 1974; New York, 1978.
Freedberg, 1961	S. J. Freedberg, *Painting of the High Renaissance in Rome and Florence*, 2 vols., Cambridge, Mass., 1961.
Freedberg, 1963	———, *Andrea del Sarto*, 2 vols., Cambridge, Mass., 1963.
Frommel	C. L. Frommel, *Baldassare Peruzzi als Maler und Zeichner*, Rome, Biblioteca Hertziana, 1967-1968.
Garin	E. Garin, *Lo Zodiaco della vita: la polemica sull'astrologia dal Trecento al Cinquecento*, Bari, 1976.
Giamatti	A. B. Giamatti, *The Earthly Paradise and the Renaissance Epic*, Princeton, 1966.

Giamboni	L. A. Giamboni, *Diario Sacro e guida perpetua per visitare le Chiese della Città di Firenze*, Florence, 1700.
Gilbert	C. Gilbert, "Texts and Contexts of the Medici Chapel," *Art Quarterly*, 34, 1971, pp. 391-408.
Gnoli	D. Gnoli, *La Roma di Leone X: quadri e studi originali annotati e pubblicati a cura di Aldo Gnoli*, Milan, 1938.
Gombrich, 1966	E. H. Gombrich, "Renaissance and Golden Age," in *Norm and Form: Studies in the Art of the Renaissance*, London, 1966, pp. 29-34 (first published 1961).
Gombrich, 1972	———, "The Sala dei Venti in the Palazzo del Te," in *Symbolic Images: Studies in the Art of the Renaissance*, London, 1972, pp. 109-18 (first published 1950).
Gombrich, 1972, "Botticelli"	———, "Botticelli's Mythologies: A Study in the Neo-Platonic Symbolism of his Circle," in *Symbolic Images: Studies in the Art of the Renaissance*, London, 1972, pp. 31-81 (first published 1945).
Haarlov	B. Haarlov, *The Half-Open Door: A Common Symbolic Motif within Roman Sepulchral Sculpture*, Odense, 1977.
Hamberg	P. G. Hamberg, "The Villa of Lorenzo il Magnifico at Poggio a Caiano and the Origin of Palladianism," in *Idea and Form. Studies in the History of Art*, 1, 1959, pp. 76-87.
Hankey	T. Hankey, "Salutati's Epigrams in the Palazzo Vecchio at Florence," *Journal of the Warburg and Courtauld Institutes*, 22, 1959, pp. 363-65.
Hatfield, 1970	R. Hatfield, "The Compagnia de' Magi," *Journal of the Warburg and Courtauld Institutes*, 33, 1970, pp. 107-61.
Hatfield, 1976	———, *Botticelli's Uffizi "Adoration": A Study in Pictorial Content*, Princeton, 1976.
Heikamp	D. Heikamp, "Ammannati's Fountain for the Sala Grande of the Palazzo Vecchio in Florence," in *Fons sapientiae: Renaissance Garden Fountains*, ed. E. B. MacDougall, Washington, D.C., 1978, pp. 117-73.
Hersey	G. L. Hersey, *Pythagorean Palaces: Magic and Architecture in the Italian Renaissance*, Ithaca, N.Y., 1976.
Hill	G. F. Hill, *A Corpus of Italian Renaissance Medals before Cellini*, 2 vols., London, 1930.
Hill-Pollard	———, rev. G. Pollard, *Renaissance Medals from the Samuel H. Kress Collection at the National Gallery of Art*, London, 1967.
Hind	A. M. Hind, *Early Italian Engravings*, 7 vols., New York and London, 1938-1948.
Hopper	V. F. Hopper, *Medieval Number Symbolism: Its Sources, Meaning, and Influence on Thought and Expression*, New York, 1969.
Kauffmann	G. Kauffmann, "Das Forum von Florenz," *Studies in Renais-*

	sance and Baroque Art Presented to Anthony Blunt on his 60th birthday, London and New York, 1967, pp. 37-43.
Kaufmann	H. W. Kaufmann, "Art for the Wedding of Cosimo de' Medici and Eleonora of Toledo (1539)," *Paragone*, 22, no. 243, 1970, pp. 52-67.
Klibansky et al.	R. Klibansky, E. Panofsky, and F. Saxl, *Saturn and Melancholy: Studies in the History of Natural Philosophy, Religion, and Art*, New York, 1964.
Kliemann, 1972	J. Kliemann, "Vertumnus und Pomona: Zum Programm von Pontormos Fresko in Poggio a Caiano," *Mitteilungen des Kunsthistorischen Institutes in Florenz*, 16, 1972, pp. 293-328.
Kliemann, 1976	———, *Politische und humanistiche Ideen der Medici in der Villa Poggio a Caiano: Untersuchungen zu den Fresken der Sala grande*, diss., Heidelberg, 1974; Bamberg, 1976.
Ladner	G. B. Ladner, "Vegetation Symbolism and the Concept of Renaissance," *De artibus opuscula XL: Essays in Honor of Erwin Panofsky*, ed. M. Meiss, New York, 1961, vol. I, pp. 303-22.
Langedijk	K. Langedijk, *De Portretten van de Medici tot omstreeks 1600*, diss., Amsterdam, 1968; Assen, 1968.
Lecchini Giovannoni	S. Lecchini Giovannoni, *Mostra di Disegni di Alessandro Allori*, Gabinetto disegni e stampe degli Uffizi, Florence, 1970.
Lechner	G. S. Lechner, "Tommaso Campanella and Andrea Sacchi's Fresco of *Divina Sapienza* in the Palazzo Barberini," *Art Bulletin*, 58, 1976, pp. 97-108.
Lehmann	P. W. Lehmann, "The Sources and Meaning of Mantegna's *Parnassus*," in *Samothracian Reflections: Aspects of the Revival of the Antique*, Princeton, 1973, pp. 57-178.
Lensi Orlandi	G. Lensi Orlandi, *Cosimo e Francesco de' Medici alchimisti*, Florence, 1978.
Letrouilly	P. Letrouilly, *Le Vatican et la Basilique de Saint-Pierre de Rome*, ed. A. Simil, 2 vols., Paris, 1882.
Levi	D. Levi, "The Allegories of the Months in Classical Art," *Art Bulletin*, 23, 1941, pp. 251-91.
Lightbown	R. W. Lightbown, *Sandro Botticelli*, 2 vols., London, 1978.
L'Orange	H. P. L'Orange, *Studies on the Iconography of Cosmic Kingship in the Ancient World*, Oslo, 1953.
Ludovici	S. S. Ludovici, *Il "De Sphaera" estense e l'iconografia astrologica*, Milan, n.d.
Marchini	G. Marchini, *Giuliano da Sangallo*, Florence, 1942.
McKillop, 1970	S. R. McKillop, "The Meaning of Pontormo's Lunette at Poggio a Caiano," paper read at the College Art Association, Washington, D.C., 1970.

McKillop, 1974 ——, *Franciabigio*, Berkeley, 1974.

McKillop, 1980 ——, "Fra Angelico's San Marco Altarpiece—the first Medici Political Painting?" paper read at the College Art Association, New Orleans, 1980.

Minor-Mitchell A. C. Minor and B. Mitchell, *A Renaissance Entertainment: Festivities for the Marriage of Cosimo I, Duke of Florence, in 1539*, Columbia, Mo., 1968.

Mitchell B. Mitchell, *Italian Civic Pageantry in the High Renaissance: A Descriptive Bibliography of Triumphal Entries and Selected Other Festivals for State Occasions*, Florence, 1979.

Mommsen T. E. Mommsen, "Petrarch and the Decoration of the Sala Virorum Illustrium in Padua," *Art Bulletin*, 34, 1952, pp. 95-116.

Monbeig-Goguel C. Monbeig-Goguel, *Musée du Louvre, Cabinet des Dessins, Inventaire général des dessins italiens: I, Maîtres toscans nés après 1500, morts avant 1600: Vasari et son temps*, Paris, 1972.

Moroni G. Moroni, *Dizionario di erudizione storico-ecclesiastica da S. Pietro sino a i nostri giorni*, 53 vols., Venice, 1840-1861.

O'Malley J. W. O'Malley, *Giles of Viterbo on Church and Reform: A Study in Renaissance Thought*, Leiden, 1968.

Panofsky E. Panofsky, "The Neoplatonic Movement and Michelangelo," in *Studies in Iconology: Humanistic Themes in the Art of the Renaissance*, New York, 1962, pp. 171-230.

Panofsky-Saxl E. Panofsky and F. Saxl, "Classical Mythology in Mediaeval Art," *Metropolitan Museum Studies*, 4, 1932-1933, pp. 228-80.

Parronchi A. Parronchi, "La prima rappresentazione della Mandragola," *La Bibliofilia*, 64, 1962, pp. 37-86.

Partridge-Starn L. Partridge and R. Starn, *A Renaissance Likeness: Art and Culture in Raphael's* Julius II, Berkeley, 1980.

Passavant G. Passavant, *Verrocchio: Sculptures, Paintings, and Drawings*, London, 1969.

Pastor L. Pastor, *The History of the Popes*, 40 vols., Nendeln, 1969.

Pieraccini G. Pieraccini, *La stirpe de' Medici di Cafaggiolo*, 3 vols., Florence, 1924-1925.

Pope-Hennessy J. Pope-Hennessy, *Catalogue of Italian Sculpture in the Victoria and Albert Museum*, 3 vols., London, 1964.

Popham-Wilde A. E. Popham and J. Wilde, *The Italian Drawings of the XVth and XVIth Centuries in the Collection of His Majesty the King at Windsor Castle*, London, 1949.

Popp A. E. Popp, *Die Medici-Kapelle Michelangelos*, Munich, 1922.

Rash-Fabbri N. Rash-Fabbri, "A Note on the Stanza della Segnatura," *Gazette des Beaux-Arts*, 94, 1979, pp. 97-104.

Richelson	P. W. Richelson, *Studies in the Personal Imagery of Cosimo I de' Medici, Duke of Florence*, diss., Princeton University, 1974; New York, 1975.
Ridolfi	R. Ridolfi, "Stampe populari per il ritorno de' Medici in Firenze l'anno 1512," *La Bibliofilia*, 51, 1949, pp. 28-36.
Rinehart	M. Rinehart, "A Drawing by Vasari for the Studiolo of Francesco I," *Burlington Magazine*, 106, 1964, pp. 74-76.
Roscoe	W. Roscoe, *Vita di Lorenzo de' Medici detto il Magnifico*, 4 vols., Pisa, 1799.
Roscoe-Bossi	G. Roscoe, *Vita e Pontificato di Leone X, con annotazioni e documenti inediti di L. Bossi*, 12 vols., Milan, 1816-1817.
Rubinstein, 1942	N. Rubinstein, "The Beginnings of Political Thought in Florence: A Study in Mediaeval Historiography," *Journal of the Warburg and Courtauld Institutes*, 5, 1942, pp. 198-227.
Rubinstein, 1958	———, "Political Ideas in Sienese Art: the Frescoes by Ambrogio Lorenzetti and Taddeo di Bartolo in the Palazzo Pubblico," *Journal of the Warburg and Courtauld Institutes*, 21, 1958, pp. 179-207.
Rubinstein, 1967	———, "Vasari's Painting of the 'Foundation of Florence' in the Palazzo Vecchio," in *Essays in the History of Architecture Presented to Rudolf Wittkower*, ed. D. Fraser, H. Hibbard, M. Lewine, London, 1967, pp. 64-73.
Saxl	F. Saxl, *La fede astrologica di Agostino Chigi: Interpretazione dei dipinti di Baldassare Peruzzi nella Sala di Galatea della Farnesina*, Rome, 1934.
Schaefer	S. J. Schaefer, *The Studiolo of Francesco I de' Medici in the Palazzo Vecchio in Florence*, diss., Bryn Mawr College, 1976; Ann Arbor, 1980.
Scoti-Bertinelli	U. Scoti-Bertinelli, *Giorgio Vasari scrittore*, Pisa, 1905.
Scullard	H. H. Scullard, *Festivals and Ceremonies of the Roman Republic*, Ithaca, N.Y., 1981.
Seznec	J. Seznec, *The Survival of the Pagan Gods: the Mythological Tradition and Its Place in Renaissance Humanism and Art*, New York, 1961 (tr. from the French publication of 1940).
Shearman, 1962	J. Shearman, "Pontormo and Andrea del Sarto, 1513," *Burlington Magazine*, 104, 1962, pp. 478-83.
Shearman, 1965	———, *Andrea del Sarto*, 2 vols., Oxford, 1965.
Shearman, 1971	———, "The Vatican Stanze: Functions and Decoration," *The Proceedings of the British Academy*, 57, 1971, pp. 369-424.
Shearman, 1972	———, *Raphael's Cartoons in the Collection of Her Majesty the Queen and the Tapestries for the Sistine Chapel*, London, 1972.
Shearman, 1975	———, "The Florentine Entrata of Leo X, 1515," *Journal of the Warburg and Courtauld Institutes*, 38, 1975, pp. 136-54.

Shearman, 1975, "Collections"   ———, "The Collections of the Younger Branch of the Medici," *Burlington Magazine*, 117, 1975, pp. 12-27.

Soldati   B. Soldati, *La Poesia Astrologica nel quattrocento*, Florence, 1906.

Sparrow   J. Sparrow, "Pontormo's Cosimo il Vecchio: A New Dating," *Journal of the Warburg and Courtauld Institutes*, 30, 1967, pp. 163-75.

Supino   I. B. Supino, *Il Medagliere Mediceo nel R. Museo Nazionale di Firenze*, 2 vols., Florence, 1899.

Tanner   M. C. Tanner, *Titian: The Poesie for Philip II*, diss., New York University, 1976; Ann Arbor, 1977.

Tervarent, 1958   G. de Tervarent, *Attributs et symbols dans l'art profane, 1450-1600: Dictionnaire d'un langage perdu*, Geneva, 1958-1964.

Tervarent, 1960   ———, "Sur deux frises d'inspiration antique," *Gazette des Beaux-Arts*, 55, 1960, pp. 307-16.

Theim   G. and C. Theim, *Toskanische Fassaden-Dekoration in Sgraffito und Fresco: 14. bis 17. Jahrhundert*, Munich, 1964.

Thorndike   L. Thorndike, *A History of Magic and Experimental Science*, 8 vols., New York, 1923-1958.

Tolkowsky   S. Tolkowsky, *Hesperides: A History of the Culture and Use of Citrus Fruits*, London, 1938.

Tolnay   C. de Tolnay, *Michelangelo*, 5 vols., Princeton, 1943-1960.

Trexler-Lewis   R. C. Trexler and M. E. Lewis, "Two Captains and Three Kings: New Light on the Medici Chapel," *Studies in Medieval and Renaissance History*, N.S. 4, 1981, pp. 93-177.

Vasoli   C. Vasoli, "Temi mistici e profetici alla fine del Quattrocento," in *Studi sulla cultura del Rinascimento*, Manduria, 1968, pp. 180-240.

Warburg, "Botticelli"   A. Warburg, "La *Nascita di Venere* e la *Primavera* di Sandro Botticelli: Ricerche sull'immagine dell'antichità nel primo rinascimento italiano," in *La rinascita del paganesimo antico*, Florence, 1966, pp. 3-58 (tr. from the German publication of 1893).

Warburg, "Schifanoia"   ———, "Arte italiana e astrologia internazionale nel Palazzo Schifanoia di Ferrara," in *La rinascita del paganesimo antico*, Florence, 1966, pp. 242-72 (tr. from the German publication of 1912).

Webster   J. C. Webster, *The Labors and the Months in Antique and Medieval Art to the end of the Twelfth Century*, Chicago, 1938.

Weil-Garris Posner   K. Weil-Garris Posner, "Comments on the Medici Chapel and Pontormo's Lunette at Poggio a Caiano," *Burlington Magazine*, 115, 1973, pp. 641-49.

Welliver, 1957   W. Welliver, *L'Impero Fiorentino*, Florence, 1957.

Welliver, 1961   ———, "Signorelli's *Court of Pan*," *Art Quarterly*, 24, 1961, pp. 334-45.

White-Shearman   J. White and J. Shearman, "Raphael's Tapestries and their Cartoons," *Art Bulletin*, 40, 1958, pp. 193-221, 299-323.

Wind, 1958   E. Wind, *Pagan Mysteries in the Renaissance*, New Haven, 1958.

Winner, 1963-1964   M. Winner, "Pontormo und die Medici in Poggio a Caiano," *Sitzungsberichte Kunstgeschichtliche Gesellschaft zu Berlin*, N.F. 12, 1963-1964, pp. 9-11.

Winner, 1964   ———, "Raffael malt einen Elefanten," *Mitteilungen des Kunsthistorischen Institutes in Florenz*, 11, 1964, pp. 71-109.

Winner, 1970   ———, "Cosimo il Vecchio als Cicero: Humanistisches in Franciabigios Fresko zu Poggio a Caiano," *Zeitschrift für Kunstgeschichte*, 33, 1970, pp. 261-97.

Winner, 1972   ———, "Pontormos Fresko in Poggio a Caiano: Hinweise zu seiner Deutung," *Zeitschrift für Kunstgeschichte*, 35, 1972, pp. 153-97.

Winner, 1974   ———, "Zum Nachleben des Laokoon in der Renaissance," *Jahrbuch der Berliner Museen*, 16, 1974, pp. 83-121.

Wittkower   R. Wittkower, "Chance, Time, and Virtue," in *Allegory and the Migration of Symbols*, London, 1977, pp. 98-106.

Wright   D. R. Wright, *The Medici Villa at Olmo a Castello: its History and Iconography*, diss., Princeton University, 1976; Ann Arbor, 1976.

Zambelli   P. Zambelli, *Astrologia, magia e alchimia nel Rinascimento fiorentino ed europeo, Firenze e la Toscana dei Medici nell'Europa del Cinquecento*, Istituto e Museo di Storia della Scienza, Florence, 1980.

Zimmerman   T.C.P. Zimmermann, "Paolo Giovio and the Evolution of Renaissance Art Criticism," *Cultural Aspects of the Italian Renaissance: Essays in Honour of Paul Oskar Kristeller*, ed. C. H. Clough, Manchester and New York, 1976, pp. 406-24.

INDEX

Fortuna-Occasio, pl. 84;
103, 148
    medal of Cosimo de'
    Medici Pater Patriae (Hill
    909), pl. 23
    medal of Cosimo de'
    Medici Pater Patriae (Hill
    910), pl. 24; 31, 36, 44, 54,
    57, 58
    medal of Cosimo de'
    Medici Pater Patriae (Hill
    910bis), 57n
Weil-Garris Posner, Kathleen,
91, 192n
Wheel of Fortune (Fortune's
    Wheel), 17, 40, 50, 51, 52,

120n, 129, 148, 178, 183,
202, 274
Windsor Castle, copy after Michelangelo's *Jonah*, pl. 115;
141
Winner, Matthias, 124, 127,
128
Winter (personified), 74, 126,
127, 130, 202, 203, 269,
288n, 289

Year (theme), 70, 71, 72, 73,
80, 221

Zacharias, 224n

Zephyr, 78, 171
zodiac (signs of the zodiac), 70,
75, 118, 127, 159, 161-63,
166, 170, 171, 175, 201,
202-204, 209, 218, 221,
266, 282, 286, 288, 289
    archetypal, fig. 6; 163, 171-
    73, 268
    Manilian guardianships, 169,
    190, 195-96, 219, 287, 290
    planetary rulers of, *see* planets
    as rulers of geographical loca-
    tions, 163, 183, 185, 190,
    197
Zucchi, Jacopo, *Gold Mining*,
289

LIBRARY OF CONGRESS CATALOGING IN PUBLICATION DATA

Cox-Rearick, Janet.
    Dynasty and destiny in Medici art.

    Bibliography: p.
    Includes index.
    1. Medici, House of—Portraits, caricatures, etc.
2. Art, Italian—Italy—Florence. 3. Art, Renaissance—
Italy—Florence. 4. Cosmology in art. 5. Allegories.
6. Horoscopes in art. 7. Medici, House of—Art patronage.
I. Title.
N7606.C69 1984   709'.45   83-13738
ISBN 0-691-04023-0

PLATES

1. Pontormo, *Portrait of Cosimo de' Medici Pater Patriae*, Uffizi

2. Pontormo, *Vertumnus and Pomona*, Poggio a Caiano, Salone

1. *Impresa* of the Medici,
"diamante and three feathers: SEMPER"
(after Giovio, *Dialogo dell'imprese*)

2. Sperandio, medal of Tito Vespasiano Strozzi,
Oxford, Ashmolean Museum

3. Niccolò Fiorentino, medal of Lorenzo de' Medici with Florentia, Bargello

4. Benozzo Gozzoli, *Procession of the Magi*, Chapel, Palazzo Medici-Ricardi

5. Botticelli, *Adoration of the Magi*, Uffizi

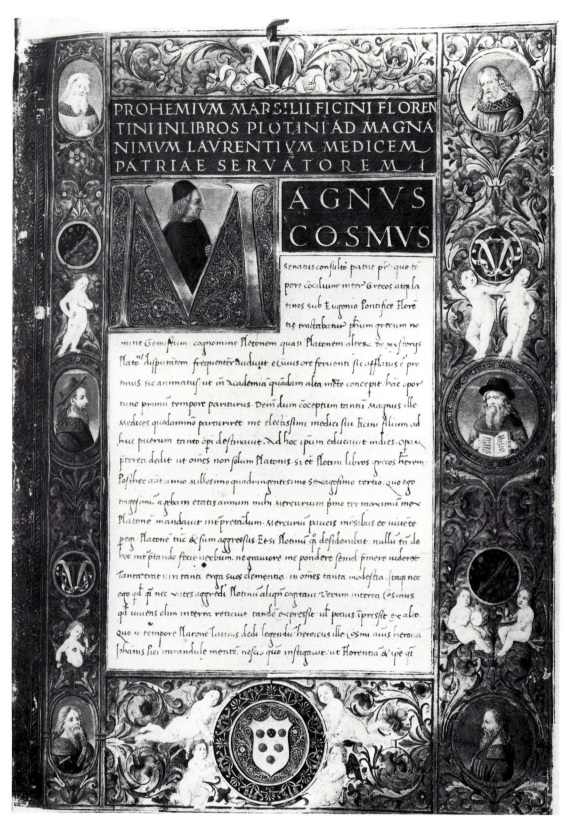

6. Manuscript of Lorenzo de' Medici. Laur. MS Plut. 82, 10, f. 3r

8. *Impresa* of Lorenzo de' Medici the younger,
"laurel tree: ITA ET VIRTUS"
(after Giovio, *Dialogo dell'imprese*)

9. Manuscript of Lorenzo de' Medici. Laur. MS Plut. 82, 10, f. 3r,
detail of the *impresa* "broncone and roses: LE TEMPS REVIENT"

7. Manuscript of Piero di Lorenzo de' Medici. Laur. MS Plut. 18, 2,
f. 9r, detail of the *impresa* "broncone: PER LE FUE REVERDIRA"

10. Manuscript of Piero di Lorenzo de' Medici.
Laur. MS Plut. 18, 2, f. 9r, detail of Fiorenza with the *palle* and the flaming *broncone*

11. Medal of Giuliano de' Medici with Florentia, Washington, National Gallery of Art,
Samuel H. Kress Collection

12. Piero di Cosimo, *Perseus Liberating Andromeda*, Uffizi

13. Andrea del Sarto, *Two Men with Bronconi*, Uffizi, Gabinetto Disegni e Stampe 91614

15. Manuscript of Leo X. Attavante, Chantilly, Musée Condé, MS lat. 1419, f. 2r

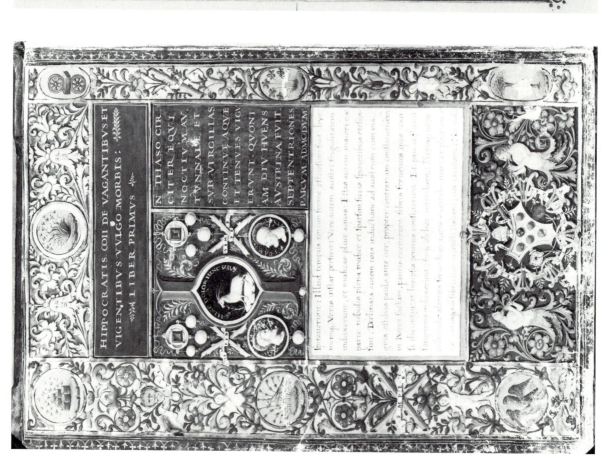

14. Manuscript of Leo X. Laur. MS Plut. 73, 12, f. 2r

17. Attavante, *Monte della Scienze*, from Tommaso Sardi, *L'Anima Pellegrina*, Rome, Biblioteca Corsiniana 55· K· I

16. Apollo and the Muses (frontispiece of *Lauretum, sive carmina in laudem Laurentii Medicis*)

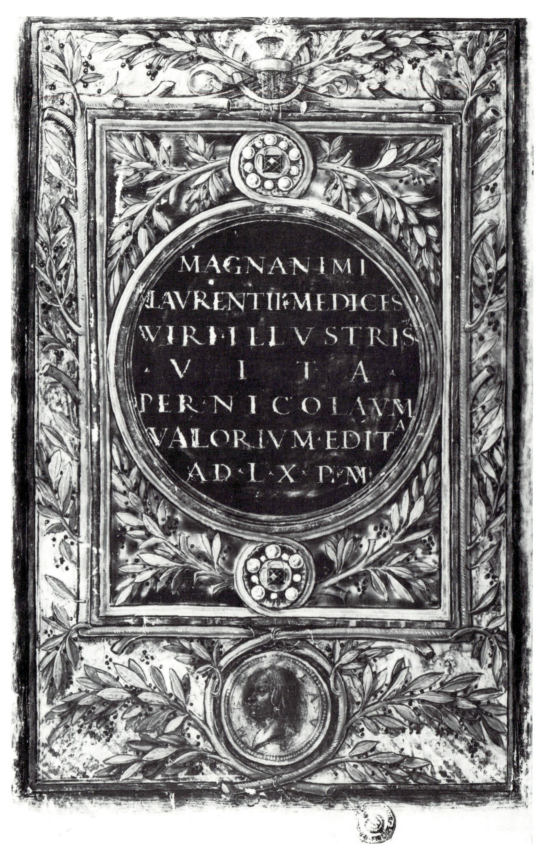

18. Manuscript of Leo X. Monte di Giovanni, title page to Niccolò Valori, *Vita Laurentii Medicis*, Laur. MS Plut. 61, 3, f. 2r

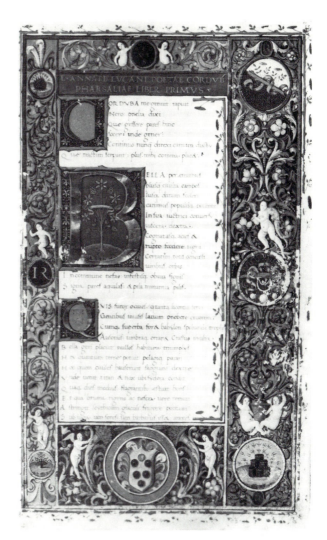

19. Cover of *L'Anima Pellegrina* with a medallion of
Cosimo de' Medici Pater Patriae,
Rome, Biblioteca Corsiniana 55. K. I

20. Manuscript of Lorenzo de' Medici.
Laur. MS Plut. 35, 2, f. 2r

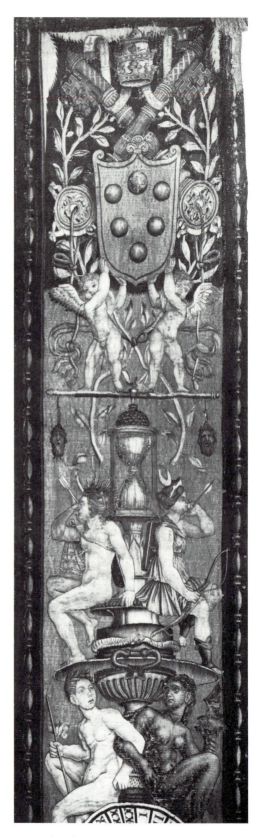

21. After Raphael, *The Times of Day*, tapestry border, Vatican, Pinacoteca

22. After Raphael, *The Seasons*, tapestry border, Vatican, Pinacoteca

23. Posthumous medal of Cosimo de' Medici Pater Patriae (Hill, no. 909), Washington, National Gallery of Art, Samuel H. Kress Collection

24. Posthumous medal of Cosimo de' Medici Pater Patriae (Hill, no. 910), Washington, National Gallery of Art, Samuel H. Kress Collection

25. Coin of Julius Caesar with Aeneas and
Anchises, London, British Museum

26. Raphael, *Fire in the Borgo*, detail,
Vatican, Stanza dell'Incendio

27. Manuscript of Lorenzo de' Medici. Laur. MS Plut. 53, 21, f. 3v

28. Manuscript of Leo X. *The Medici Codex*, Laur. MS Acq. e doni, f. 3r

29. Giulio Romano, *Leo X as Clement I with Moderatio and Comitas*, Vatican, Sala di Costantino

30. Bandinelli, *Orpheus*, Palazzo Medici-Riccardi

31. After Raphael, *impresa* of Leo X and scenes of the Medici restoration, tapestry border, Vatican, Pinacoteca

32. Pontormo and Andrea di Cosimo Feltrini, vault, S. Maria Novella, Cappella del Papa

33. Pontormo, *St. Veronica with the Sudarium*, S. Maria Novella, Cappella del Papa

34. Michelangelo, New Sacristy,
San Lorenzo

35. Reconstruction of Michelangelo's
scheme for the *sepoltura di testa* of the
New Sacristy (after Popp)

36. Salone, Poggio a Caiano, view toward *Vertumnus and Pomona* and *Pietas, Virtus, and Iustizia*

37. Michelangelo, New Sacristy, *sepoltura di testa*, San Lorenzo

38. Maffeo Olivieri, medal of Francesco di Pier Antonio Roseti, Oxford, Ashmolean Museum

39. Fra Angelico, *Madonna and Saints*, San Marco, Museum

40. Medals of Piero di Cosimo and Giovanni di Cosimo de' Medici (after Hill)

41. Manuscript of Lorenzo de' Medici. Laur. MS Plut. 71, 7, f. 1

42. After Raphael, *The Three Fates*, tapestry border, Vatican, Pinacoteca

43. Bacchiacca, *Saints Cosmas and Damian in a Landscape*, in Laur. MS Palat. 225, f. 5v

44. Manuscript of Leo X. Genealogical tree of the Medici, Laur. MS Palat. 225, f. 3v-4r

45. Justus van Ghent, *Portrait of Vittorino da Feltre*, Paris, Louvre

46. Coin of Cicero
(after Fulvio, *Illustrium imagines*)

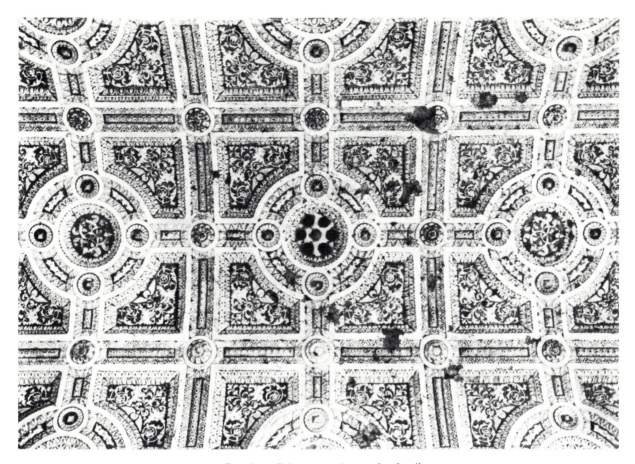

47. Poggio a Caiano, portico vault, detail

48. Medal of Lorenzo di Pierfrancesco de' Medici
with the snake, Bargello

49. Poggio a Caiano, portico

50. *The Cavern of Eternity, Apollo, and Nature* (after Cartari, *Imagini*)

51. *Eternity*, Poggio a Caiano, portico frieze

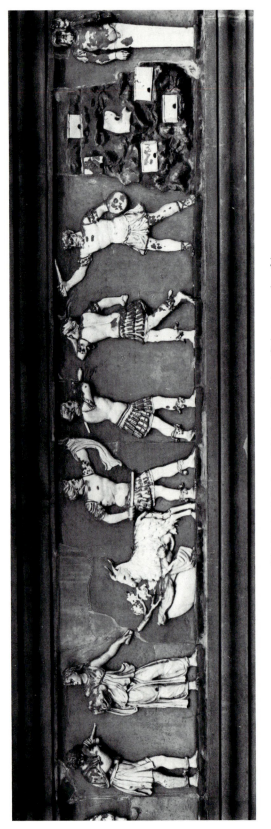

52. *The Birth of the Age of Jupiter*, Poggio a Caiano, portico frieze

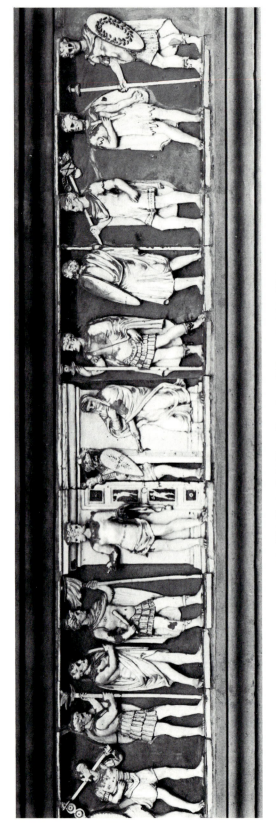

53. *The Birth of the Year*, Poggio a Caiano, portico frieze

54. *The Seasons and the Months*, Poggio a Caiano, portico frieze

55. *The Birth of the Day*, Poggio a Caiano, portico frieze

56. *The Birth of the Year*, detail of Janus, Mars, and the temple priest, Poggio a Caiano, portico frieze

57. Roman sarcophagus with Mercury Psychopompos, detail, Museo dell' Opera del Duomo

58. Marco da Faenza, *Mars-March*, study for the Sala di Opi, Uffizi 15872F

59. Luca della Robbia, *June*, London, Victoria and Albert Museum

60. Botticelli, *Primavera*, Uffizi

61. After Bronzino, *Primavera*, tapestry, Gallerie

62. Vasari, *The Foundation of Florence as a Roman Colony*, Palazzo Vecchio, Salone dei Cinquecento

63. *The Seasons and the Months*, detail of Spring, Poggio a Caiano, portico frieze

64. Roman *Flora*, Uffizi

65. Ammannati, *Flora-Fiorenza*, Bargello

66. Tribolo, Study for a grotto with Pan, satyrs, and Capricorn, London, Sir John Soane's Museum

67. Signorelli, *The Realm of Pan*, formerly Berlin (destroyed)

68. Salone, Poggio a Caiano, view toward *Hercules and Fortuna in the Garden of the Hesperides*
and *Fama, Gloria, and Honor*

69. Salone, Poggio a Caiano, vault with Medici *imprese*, detail

70. Shutters of the Stanza d' Eliodoro, detail of the *imprese* of Leo X
(after Letarouilly)

71. Andrea del Sarto, *Tribute to Caesar*, Poggio a Caiano, Salone

72. Franciabigio, *Triumph of Cicero*, Poggio a Caiano, Salone

73. Michelangelo, study for the New Sacristy tomb with Day and Night, Paris, Louvre 838

74. Michelangelo, study for the New Sacristy, *sepoltura di testa*, Paris, Louvre 837

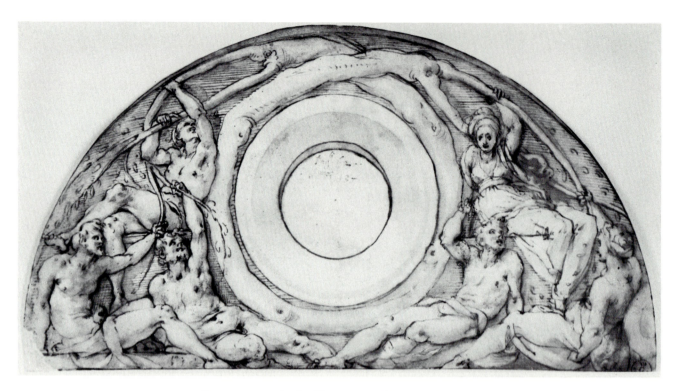

75. Pontormo, study for *Vertumnus and Pomona*, Uffizi 454F

76. Pontormo, study for *Vertumnus and Pomona*, Uffizi 6600Fv

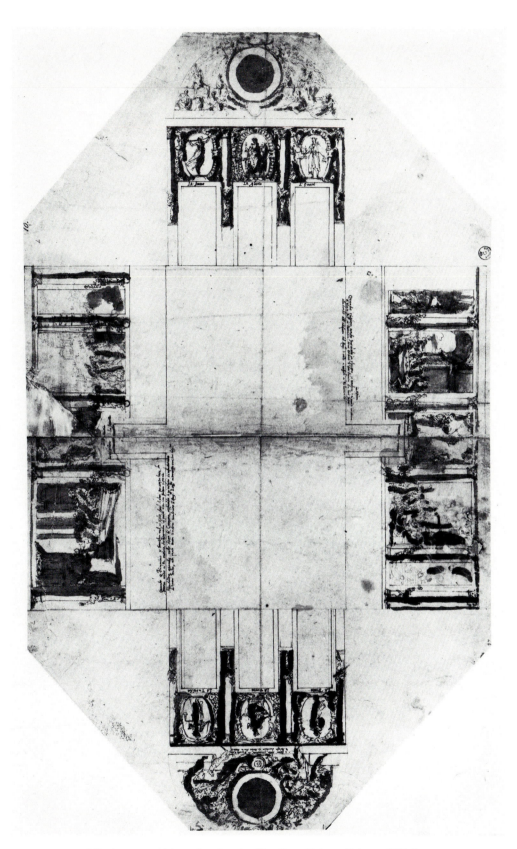

77. Allori, composition plan for the Poggio a Caiano Salone, Uffizi 10 *orn*.

78. Salviati, north and east walls of the Sala delle Udienze, Palazzo Vecchio

8o. Allori, *Titus Flaminius at the Council of the Achaeans,* Poggio a Caiano, Salone

79. Allori, *Scipio Africanus meeting Hasdrubal at the Court of Syphax,* Poggio a Caiano, Salone

81. Allori, *Magnanimitas, Magnificentia, and Liberalitas*,
Poggio a Caiano, Salone

82. Master of the Die after Giovanni da Udine, *Giuochi di putti*,
Rome, Gabinetto Nazionale delle Stampe

83. Franciabigio, *Triumph of Cicero*, detail of Cicero, Poggio a Caiano, Salone

84. Medal of Giuliano de' Medici with Virtù and Fortuna-Occasio, Washington, National Gallery of Art, Samuel H. Kress Collection

85. Medal of Leo X with Liberalitas, London, British Museum

87. Aurelian *Liberalitas Augusti* relief, Rome, Arch of Constantine

86. Andrea del Sarto, *Tribute to Caesar*, detail of Caesar and his entourage, Poggio a Caiano, Salone

89. Salviati, *The Triumph of Camillus*, detail of Camillus and his entourage, Palazzo Vecchio, Sala delle Udienze

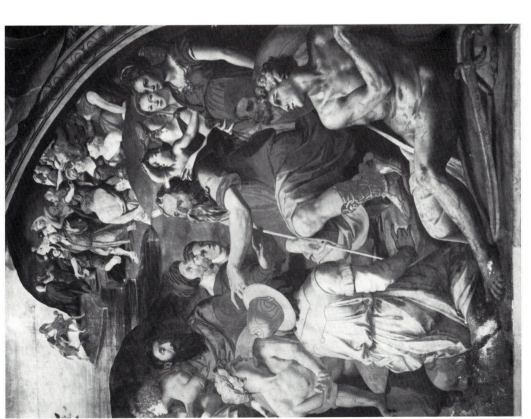

88. Bronzino, *The Crossing of the Red Sea*, detail of Moses and his entourage, Palazzo Vecchio, Cappella di Eleonora

90. Vasari, *Tribute to Paul III*, Rome, Palazzo della Cancelleria, Sala dei Cento Giorni

91. Pontormo, study for a portrait of Piero de' Medici, Rome, Gabinetto Nazionale delle Stampe F. C. 137r

92. Vasari, study for the ceiling of the Sala di Cosimo il Vecchio, Paris, Louvre 2176

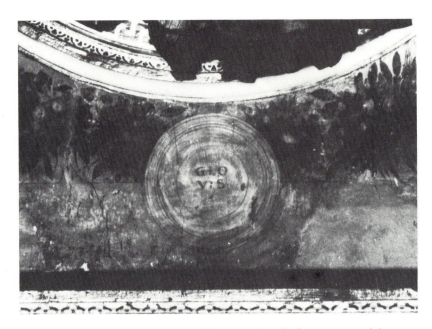

93. Pontormo, *Vertumnus and Pomona*, detail of GLOVIS roundel

94. Brunelleschi, Old Sacristy, San Lorenzo

95. Florentine late 15th century, mirror with Venus and Mars in a
diamante frame, London, Victoria and Albert Museum

96. Medici manuscript. Laur. MS Plut. 63, 33, f. 45r, detail of *imprese*

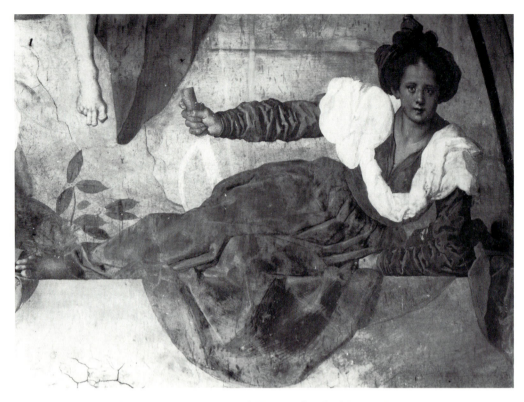

97. Pontormo, *Vertumnus and Pomona*, detail of Spring-Pomona

98. Pontormo, study for *Vertumnus and Pomona*, Uffizi 6673Fv

99. Pontormo, *Vertumnus and Pomona*, detail of Winter-Vertumnus and the dog

100. *The Triumph of Vertumnus and Pomona* (after Colonna, *Hypnerotomachia Poliphili*)

101. Virgil, *Georgics*, Edinburgh,
University Library MS D.b.VI.8, f. 19r

102. *Georgics*, frontispiece (after Virgil, *Opera*)

103. Pontormo, *Vertumnus and Pomona*, detail of Sol-Apollo

104. Pontormo, *Vertumnus and Pomona*,
detail of Luna-Diana-Ceres

105. Virgil Solis, *Summer*, detail of Ceres

106. Pontormo, *Vertumnus and Pomona*, detail of
the putto with a banner inscribed IVP P

107. Pontormo, *Vertumnus and Pomona*, detail of the standard inscribed VTINAT

108. Pontormo, *Vertumnus and Pomona*, detail of Summer-Venus

109. Pontormo, *Vertumnus and Pomona*, detail of Autumn-Saturn

110. *Georgics*, "Saturn and the Cosmos" (after Virgil, *Opera*)

111. Vasari and Doceno, *Winter*, Palazzo Vecchio, Sala di Opi

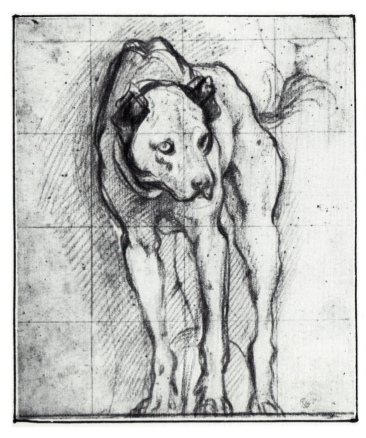

112. Pontormo, study for *Vertumnus and Pomona*,
Cambridge, Fogg Art Museum 1932.342r

113. Pontormo, study for *Vertumnus and Pomona*,
Stockholm, Nationalmuseum 931/1863r

114. Franciabigio, *Portrait of a Medici Steward*,
Hampton Court, Collection of Her Majesty the Queen

115. After Michelangelo, *Jonah with the Stemma of Julius II*, Windsor Castle, Collection of Her Majesty the Queen 10363

116. Gambello, medal of Leo X with Apollo, the sun, and a lion (after Hill)

117. *Apollo* (after *Versi posti a Pasquillo*)

118. Allori, *Hercules and Fortuna in the Garden of the Hesperides*, Poggio a Caiano, Salone

119. Pontormo, study for a Fortuna, Rome,
Gabinetto Nazionale delle Stampe F. C. 121r

120. After Raphael, *Hercules Holding the Celestial Globe with Fame*, tapestry border, Vatican, Pinacoteca

121. Hercules seal of the Medici, Museo degli Argenti

122. Vasari, *Entrata of Leo X into Florence*, detail of Bandinelli's *Hercules* and Michelangelo's *David*, Palazzo Vecchio, Sala di Leo X

123. After Raphael, *God the Father and the Celestial Universe*, Rome, S. Maria del Popolo, Chigi Chapel

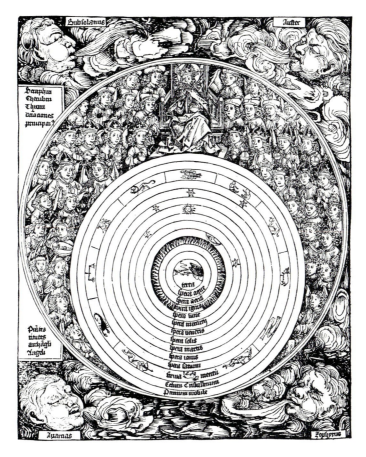

124. *The Cosmos* (after the *Nuremberg Chronicle*)

125. Zodiac wheel with solar disk, Baptistery

126. *Jupiter with Pisces and Sagittarius*, from *De Sphaera*, Modena,
Biblioteca Estense, MS Est. lat. 209, α.X.2.14, f. 5v

127. Domenico di Michelino, *Dante and Florence*, Duomo

128. Celestial cupola, Old Sacristy, San Lorenzo

129. Fra Angelico, *Adoration of the Magi*, detail of
an astrologer (Cosimo de' Medici), San Marco

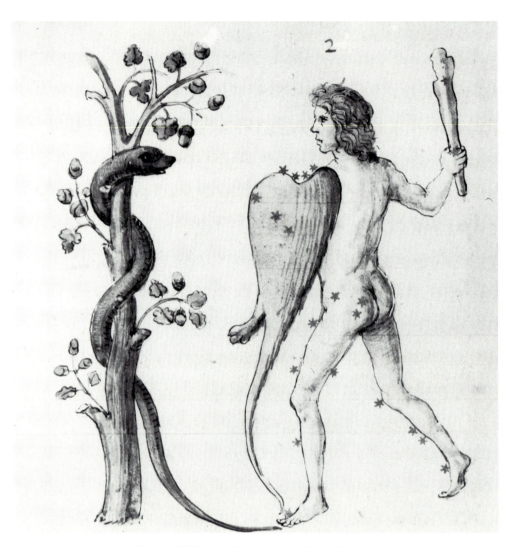

130. *Hercules Killing the Dragon of the Hesperides*,
from the *Medici Aratus*, Laur. MS Plut. 89 sup., 43, f. 11r

131. Botticelli, *Venus and Mars*, London, National Gallery

132. Francesco Cossa, *Virgo and the Triumph of Ceres*, Ferrara, Palazzo Schifanoia

133. *The Gemma Augustea*, detail, Vienna, Kunsthistorisches Museum

134. Coin of Augustus with Capricorn, London, British Museum

135. Gian Cristoforo Romano, medal of Isabella d'Este with Astrology and Sagittarius, London, British Museum

136. After Peruzzi, frontispiece of Fanti, *Triompho di Fortuna*

137. Perino del Vaga, zodiacal lunette with Aquarius, Vatican, Logge

139. *Giustizia* (after De Ruberti, *Osservatione di Astrologia*)

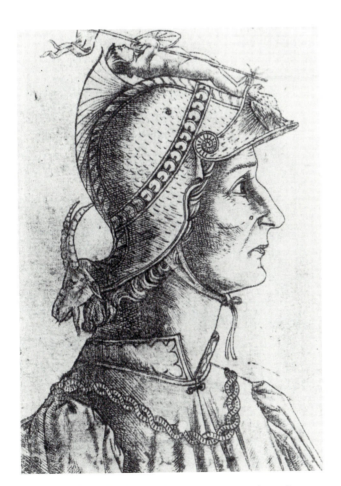

138. Florentine late 15th century, engraving of
a helmet with Mars, an eagle, and Capricorn head,
London, British Museum

140. Raphael, *Astronomy with the Celestial Globe*,
Vatican, Stanza della Segnatura

141. Posthumous medal of Leo X with Peace, Justice, and Abundance (after Hill)

142. After Raphael, *Hercules*, tapestry border,
detail of the celestial globe, Vatican, Pinacoteca

143. Vincenzo de' Rossi, study for a fountain of
The Labors of Hercules-Sol,
New York, Cooper-Hewitt Museum 1942-36-1

144. After Raphael, *Hercules Killing the
Centaur*, detail of tapestry border,
Mantua, Palazzo Ducale

145. Perino del Vaga, Vatican, Sala dei Pontefici

146. Perino del Vaga, ceiling, detail, Vatican, Sala dei Pontefici

148. Perino del Vaga, *Stemma of Leo X with Pallas-Minerva*, Vatican, Sala dei Pontefici

147. Perino del Vaga, *Victories with the Emblems of Leo X*, Vatican, Sala dei Pontefici

150. Pontormo, study for *Vertumnus and Pomona*, Uffizi 6509Fv

149. Peruzzi, Sala di Galatea, Rome, Villa Farnesina

151. Pontormo, study for *Vertumnus and Pomona*, Uffizi 6531F

152. *Four Seasons* sarcophagus, Washington, Dumbarton Oaks

153. *Virgo* (after Leopold of Austria,
De Astrorum scientia)

154. Francesco Poppi, *The Golden Age*, Edinburgh, National Gallery

156. Michelangelo, so-called *Giuliano de' Medici* (here identified as Lorenzo de' Medici the younger), New Sacristy, San Lorenzo

155. Vasari, *Portrait of Duke Alessandro de' Medici*, Gallerie

158. Pontormo, *Portrait of Maria Salviati with Her Son Cosimo,* Baltimore, Walters Art Gallery

157. Vasari, *Portrait of Lorenzo il Magnifico,* Uffizi

159. Ridolfo Ghirlandaio, *Portrait of Cosimo de' Medici at Age Twelve*, Gallerie

160. Domenico di Polo, medal of Duke Cosimo de' Medici with the two anchors, Bargello

161. Bronzino, *Portrait of Duke Cosimo de' Medici in Armor*,
Kassel, Staatliche Kunstsammlungen

162. Domenico di Polo, medal of Duke Cosimo de' Medici with the laurel tree, Bargello

163. After Bronzino, *The Arms of Duke Cosimo de' Medici and Eleonora da Toledo with Apollo and Minerva*, tapestry, Pitti

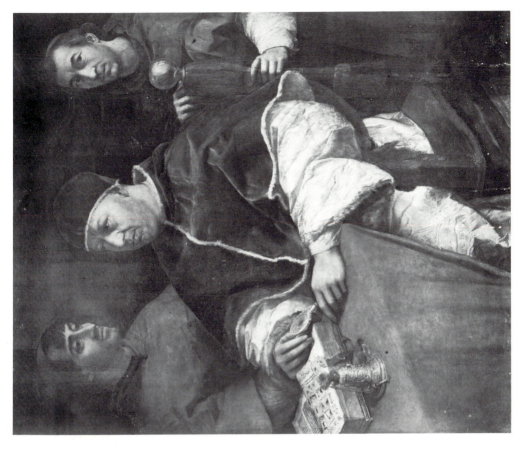

165. Raphael, *Portrait of Leo X with Cardinals Giulio de' Medici and Luigi de' Rossi*, Uffizi

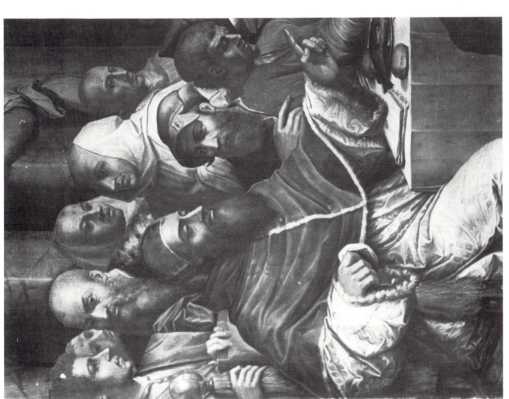

164. Vasari, *Supper of St. Gregory*, detail of Clement VII, Alessandro de' Medici, and others, Bologna, Pinacoteca

166. Allori, *The Risen Christ with Saints Cosmas and Damian*, Brussels, Musées Royaux

167. Vasari, *Cosimo de' Medici il Vecchio and Duke Cosimo de' Medici as Saints Cosmas and Damian*, Palazzo Vecchio, Chapel of Duke Cosimo

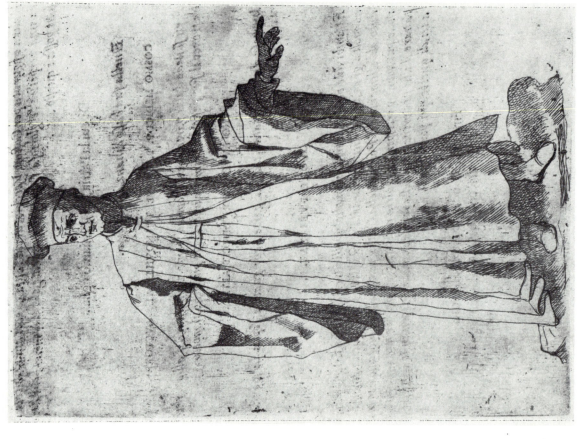

169. Scarabelli, after Giovanni Caccini, *Cosimo il Vecchio*
(after Gualterotti, *Descrizione del Regale apparato . . .*)

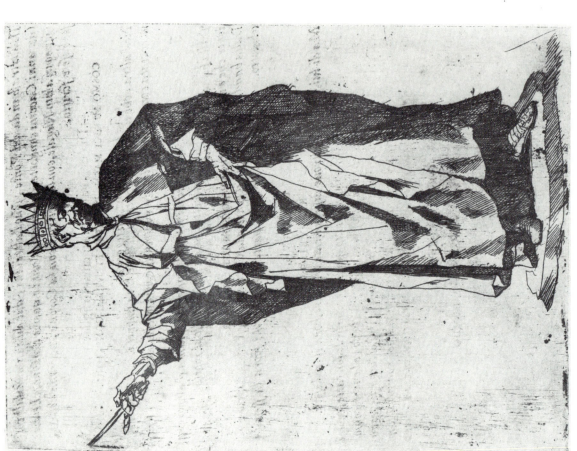

168. Scarabelli, after Giovanni Caccini, *Duke Cosimo de' Medici*
(after Gualterotti, *Descrizione del Regale apparato . . .*)

171. Domenico di Polo, medal of Duke Cosimo de' Medici with Hercules and Antaeus, Bargello

170. Tribolo and Ammannati, fountain of *Hercules and Antaeus*, Villa Castello

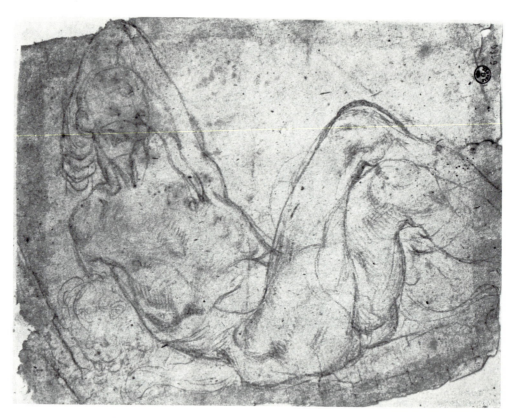

172. Pontormo, study for the Villa Castello loggia, Uffizi 6760F

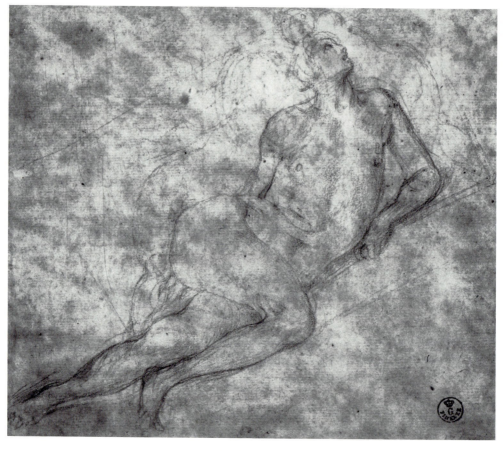

173. Pontormo, study for the Villa Castello loggia, Uffizi 17405F

174. Pontormo, study for the Villa Castello loggia, detail, Uffizi 6510F

175. Domenico di Polo, medal of Duke Cosimo de' Medici with Florentia and a Victory, London, British Museum

176. Domenico di Polo, medal of Duke Cosimo de' Medici with Capricorn and the Crown of Ariadne, Bargello

177. *Impresa* of Duke Cosimo de' Medici. Capricorn and the Crown of Ariadne (after Giovio, *Dialogo dell'imprese*)

178. Agostino di Duccio, *The Sign of Cancer and the City of Rimini*, Rimini, Tempio Malatestiano

179. Salviati, *Time-Prudence Seizing Occasion by the Hair*, Palazzo Vecchio, Sala delle Udienze

180. Poggini, *Duke Cosimo de' Medici as Apollo*, Boboli Gardens

181. After Bronzino, *Joseph Fleeing Potiphar's Wife*, detail of Joseph, Palazzo Vecchio, Sala dei Dugento

182. After Bronzino, *Joseph Recounting his Dream of the Sun, Moon and Stars*, detail, upper section, Palazzo Vecchio, Sala dei Dugento

183. Vasari and Doceno, *Saturn Castrating Heaven*, Palazzo Vecchio, Sala degli Elementi

184. Vasari and Doceno, *Saturn Receiving the Tributes of the Earth*, detail of Saturn with Capricorn, Palazzo Vecchio, Sala degli Elementi

185. Capricorn, *impresa* of Duke Cosimo de' Medici (after Pittoni, *Imprese di diversi Principi*)

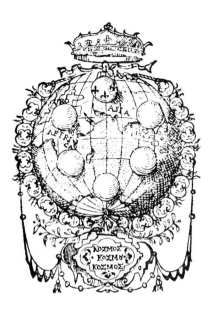

186. *Impresa* of Duke Cosimo de' Medici
with the *palla-mondo* (after Danti, *Trattato*)

187. Stoldo Lorenzi, *Tribute of the Cities of Tuscany to Duke Cosimo de' Medici and Eleonora da Toledo*,
Norfolk, Holkham Hall

188. Circle of Tribolo, *Genio mediceo*, Pitti

189. Vasari, *Duke Cosimo de' Medici as Augustus*, Palazzo Vecchio, Sala di Leo X

190. Vasari, *The Apotheosis of Duke Cosimo de' Medici*, Palazzo Vecchio, Salone dei Cinquecento

191. Vincenzo Danti, *Grand Duke Cosimo de' Medici as Augustus*, Bargello

192. Francesco da Sangallo, medal of Grand Duke Cosimo de' Medici and
Duke Alessandro de' Medici, Bargello

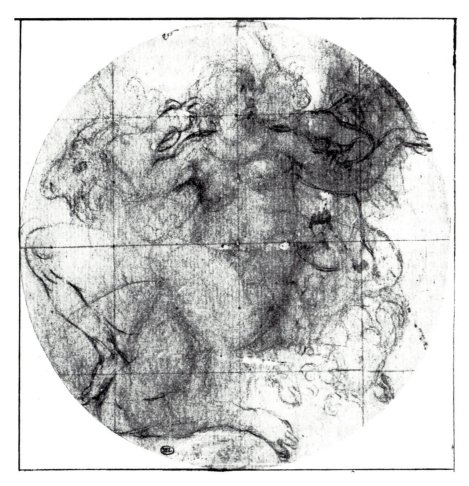

193. Pontormo, study for *Venus and Cupid with Capricorn and Aries*,
Paris, Louvre 10396

195. *Medal of Grand Duke Francesco de' Medici with Aries,* London, British Museum

196. *Medal of Grand Duke Francesco de' Medici with Aries, the grand-ducal crown, and the imperial eagle,* London, British Museum

194. Vasari, *Pallas-Minerva in the Forge of Vulcan,* detail of the shield, Uffizi

197. Allori and Poppi, *Grand Duke Cosimo de' Medici with Autumn and Winter*, Palazzo Vecchio, Studiolo

198. Allori and Poppi, *Eleonora da Toledo with Spring and Summer*, Palazzo Vecchio, Studiolo

134 **Cox-Rearick**, Janet. Dynasty and Destiny in Medici Art: Pontormo, Leo X, and the Two Cosimos. Dynastic continuity (1490-1582), appendices, a genealogical tree; text, notes, bibliography; index; 23 and dynastic continuity (1490-1582), appendices, a genealogical tree; text, etc; 199 illus. on plates (from text illus. of horoscopes; tispiece in color). 4to. Cloth, illus. d.j. Princeton (Princeton Univ. Press) 1984. $85.00